PastMasters

The Best of
History

■■■ TODAY ■■■

EDITED BY DANIEL SNOWMAN

SUTTON PUBLISHING
HISTORY TODAY

First published in 2001 by
Sutton Publishing Limited · Phoenix Mill
Thrupp · Stroud · Gloucestershire · GL5 2BU

Published in association with History Today Ltd
20 Old Compton St · London W1V 4TW

Reprinted in 2001 (twice), 2003

Pages 163–171 reprinted by permission of David Higham Associates

The editor of *History Today* would like to thank the contributors or,
where appropriate, their estates for their support in preparing this
volume. All articles in this anthology are reproduced as far as possible as
they first appeared (except for occasional cuts for comprehensibility).

British Library Cataloguing in Publication Data
A catalogue record for this book is available from the British Library

ISBN 0 7509 2717 8

Typeset in 10/12pt New Baskerville.
Typesetting and origination by
Sutton Publishing Limited.
Printed and bound in England by
J.H. Haynes & Co. Ltd, Sparkford.

Contents

Contents

Preface

In May 1995, on the fiftieth anniversary of the ending of the war in Europe, Vladimir Dolmatov, editor of the Moscow-based history magazine *Rodina*, wrote that the time had come to look again at the myths of recent European history. Soviet historiography had taught his country that the West had done little practical to help the USSR in its heroic battle with Nazism, but now 'it is time to put everything in its place and to say to our allies honestly, "thank you!".'

The occasion was a remarkable joint publication between Dolmatov's magazine, its German equivalent *Damals* and *History Today*, in which the events of May 1945 were viewed from the perspectives of three countries. The issue helped, in its own way, to bury some ghosts of the past – for as Dolmatov said: 'when the soldiers are buried and a funeral has been held for them, they will no longer call for vengeance and our genetic memory will be cleansed of the spirit of bloody wars'.

The burial of those ghosts has been a task close to the heart of *History Today*, right from its first appearance in January 1951. The magazine was in many ways a fruit of the Second World War, and its early years in particular are suffused with the imperative for educated people to understand the strange new world that that conflict had spawned. Inspired by Churchill, founded by his friend and assistant Brendan Bracken and named in the Palace of Westminster, it was co-edited by Churchill's historical research assistant Alan Hodge and launched in the year of the Festival of Britain. *History Today* was one limb of the great postwar effort to re-interpret the place of Britain in a confusing age of optimistic internationalism and menacing bipolarity. In the first issue, the editors wrote: 'We have witnessed gigantic changes. Our class structure has been remodelled, our social institutions have been re-built, and our imperial prospects revolutionised. . . . The map of the world we admired in our schoolroom wore an imposing belt of British red. It is a very different map we examine in the present day.' The historian's perspective, they knew, was needed to help people to understand this unfamiliar new world.

The early years are marked by efforts to look again at the classic works of history, to explore the deep roots of the mistrust between East and West, and to revisit the centres of European civilisation that had been so bruised in recent conflicts.

It was an impressive effort, with its joint editors – Hodge and the biographer Peter Quennell – well-placed in London literary society to attract a staggering array of talented writers to its pages, by no means only 'proper' historians as the appearance of writers such as Quentin Bell, Naomi Mitchison or Freya Stark makes clear. The support of Lord Drogheda brought the marketing might of the *Financial Times* and the Pearson Group to bear on behalf of the fledgling journal, and attracted a powerful range of corporate advertisers. Beyond this, it was a truly innovative notion to publish an *illustrated* history magazine, with the images selected and captioned in as scholarly (yet accessible) manner as the text itself. It was fifteen years before the rest of the publishing industry began to catch up, and illustrated history books became two-a-penny.

Also from the word go, *History Today* performed the remarkable trick of bridging the gap between scholars, teachers and 'general readers'. History is a compulsory subject – taught sometimes dutifully, sometimes inspirationally – in schools, yet one for which many people retain a passion throughout life, their understanding and appreciation growing even as scholars beaver away to undermine (or at least improve upon) the very notions their audience may have acquired years before. *History Today* has always given its readers the opportunity to read – without being talked down to or lectured at – what the top scholars have had to say, while it allows those scholars to test their notions in a serious manner but concisely and without too much solemnity.

To read the early issues of *History Today* from the vantage point of our new century is to enter a historical archive of its own, to hear the mostly-departed voices of civilised Englishmen and women wrestling with the ideas of Toynbee and Spengler about the largest patterns of history, and to read the memoirs of elderly men and women intimately involved in their own youth in the great events of the Victorian era. History was both a scholarly and a literary art, focused on courts and parliament, diplomacy and battlefields, with not much about our current fascination with gender, minorities or cultural perceptions; yet it was arguably more ambitious in its moral depth than the less flamboyant productions of some of our over-assessed academics today. Style mattered, and history offered a key to unlock some of the secrets of the *condition humaine*. Many of the early contributors were at pains to combat their 'dry-as-dust' image, to insist they were not grey men ferreting in archives; they presented themselves as convivial partners in an enquiry as to the nature of the 'good life', adding colour and vitality to their strange new world. And, to judge from their readers' comments, they succeeded with flying colours.

There was a great chronological and geographical span in those days. 'History' began with the Sumerians and ended yesterday: in only 1953 the magazine carried a detailed description of the Stauffenberg plot, and a few years later included a historical assessment of de Valera, written while he was still in office. While much of what they wrote about was courts and high culture, the magazine never shirked from Lenin or Stalin, and there was always a peppering of what would become *History Today*'s trademark – the feature on a quirky topic that you had never considered until the moment you picked up the magazine. In explaining how, for example, the head cook in a great eighteenth-century house planned for a banquet, or how Venice suffered aerial bombing in the mid-nineteenth century, the magazine offered both the fascination of an odd story engagingly told, and new and surprising insights into more familiar topics.

Yet 'those days' were not so very long ago: several of the very first contributors (not to mention readers) are still with us and many others were the teachers, supervisors and friends of today's generation of historians. And the controversies they engaged in on our pages – such as the famous 'decline of the gentry' debate that whirled around Hugh Trevor-Roper in the 1950s – have moulded the interests of modern scholars, and come to the attention of countless A-level students.

The phrase 'continuity and change' is an old standby of those who set examinations and write the less imaginative kind of history book. But it has its place. Continuity served the magazine well: every editor remained faithful to the ideal outlined in the very first issue, where Quennell and Hodge proclaimed the intention of producing a magazine written by experts to interest the general reader, and like 'open-cast miners, but more gently and more beneficently, we hope to bring a wealth of historical treasure into the twentieth-century daylight'. The academic advisors and the readers both remained remarkably loyal; and so too did the staff – the pictures, for example, so often praised as miraculously apposite to the text, were magically rustled up by the redoubtable Jackie Guy every month for over thirty years.

But the world has changed over the last fifty years, and the magazine eventually changed with it. Hodge and Quennell remained in their posts for a remarkable 28 and 29 years respectively, and their magazine was a haven of calm through the turbulent 1960s and 1970s. By the late 1970s, editorial, publishing and commercial change came in the form of a new editor – the distinguished Africanist Michael Crowder – a new format with colour printing and contemporary graphics (to the dismay of one or two of the older readers) – and, in 1981, a change of ownership. Life in the corporate world (as part of Longmans within the Pearson Group) had eventually proved uncomfortable for a small, idiosyncratic magazine, and to prevent closure it was sold for a song to a group of private investors. They saw their purchase as an act of cultural conservation, and they have cherished their property ever since, nurturing its unique identity, ensuring its continuity and defending its independence, now protected by the foundation of the History Today Trust for the Advancement of Education.

And history was changing. New universities brought new jobs, and the number of professional historians grew. New dimensions of the study of the past were clamouring for attention – women's history, popular cultural history, oral history, history of crime, of medicine and much more. A new generation of historian appeared, to whom the 1930s and 1940s were themselves part of history and not of personal experience.

So the editors, particularly Juliet Gardiner in the early 1980s and then Gordon Marsden, broadened and deepened the magazine, until it provided a unique showcase for the talents of professional historians. Maintaining a blend of the old history and the new, they gave many readers their first taste of the intellectual debates over the nature of history that were raging in the universities, and gave some younger historians their first opportunities to reach a wider public. They turned *History Today* into an umbrella for all those involved in the study of the past, however disparate their interests. And, realising that North America had nothing to match *History Today*'s remit, they developed transatlantic links and opened a whole new market for the magazine.

Meanwhile, the world itself changed. Suggestions were made in some quarters that the end of the Cold War meant the 'end of history': but it did not mean the end of history-writing. Quite the reverse. Just as Quennell and Hodge had felt that the 'bewilderingly swift' changes of the 1940s 'sharpened our sense of historical perspective', so the same thing happened in the 1990s. Access to new documents in previously closed archives; the redrawing of the map of much of Europe; the reinvigoration of nationalisms that had been all but suppressed – all these changes and more galvanised history and caused an outpouring of imaginative, challenging and important new writing, much of it lapped up by an eager public. And as the tide of globalisation threatened to wash us into a world where distinctions of place and culture were meaningless, so the study of history, intrinsically rooted in the particulars of place, time and personality, offered a crucial lifeline to those who seek to keep their feet on firm ground. Today, history flourishes on television and on the internet, historical debates are regularly heard on news broadcasts. It has become big business for the media, a thriving dimension of education at all levels, a treasure-house of intellectual and imaginative enquiry, and an enjoyable leisure activity for people of all sorts, whether as tourists, genealogists, re-enactors, or whatever. The sometimes lonely furrow that *History Today* has ploughed has borne a fruitful harvest.

History can never be just a leisure activity, or even an intellectual one: its moral dimension is inescapable. In the South Africa of the 1990s it was used as an agent of truth and reconciliation; likewise in May 1995, Marsden, Dolmatov and the *Damals* editor, Brigitte Rothlein, sought together to transcend the hostilities and mistrust of a tortured century. As Dolmatov rhetorically asked his German readers, 'Do we not grasp that you cannot build a bright future on discord, and that blood only gives birth to blood?'

History Today has always tried to serve the needs of the present just as much as to enliven the past. Every one of our articles seeks to throw new light on familiar topics; and this book will, I hope, throw a little unfamiliar light on the last fifty years as well as on the wider vistas of the past. And help make the future bright.

Peter Furtado
Editor
History Today
2001

Introduction

In the inaugural edition of *History Today* in 1951, the editors, Peter Quennell and Alan Hodge, compared themselves to open-cast miners, hoping to bring into daylight some of the historical riches that lay all around. 'History, to-day, has a very large popular audience,' noted G.M. Trevelyan, the grand old man of English history, in his introductory message. Like Quennell and Hodge, he was committed to what a later editor called 'the marriage of elegant prose with incisive scholarship'.

Quennell and Hodge were appointed to their task by Brendan Bracken, factotum to Churchill and chairman of the magazine's parent company *The Financial Times*. Gentlemen of a certain vintage with cultivated literary tastes, Q & H bridged the Great War and Cold War, harnessing a faintly Edwardian aesthetic to the new world of NATO and the bomb and the benevolent cultural *dirigisme* of the Welfare State, Arts Council, BBC Third Programme and Festival of Britain. Part time warp, part Time Team, Q & H embraced a degree of old-world insouciance – while also providing a platform for the pungent pronouncements of the latest generation of historical diggers and toilers. On the one hand, the gentle elegance of Nancy Mitford on Mme de Pompadour (**no. 5**) or of Quennell's own occasional contributions (**21**); on the other, the combative brilliance of Hugh Trevor-Roper or Geoffrey Elton (**12, 13**), each of them fearlessly asserting a thesis radically at odds with the received wisdom of their peers and predecessors.

The roll call of contributors to the magazine in its early years was formidable. Every prominent historian of the day seems to have been enlisted, among them Bullock (**1**), Brogan (**3**), Namier (**7**), Rowse (**8**), Hill (**19**), Taylor (**23**) and Wedgwood (**24**). The editors encouraged (and occasionally penned) informed speculation about the nature of history itself and the role of the historian (**1, 2, 6, 14**). Thus, the appearance of a new book by Asa Briggs gave rise to a stimulating editorial (**20**) and subsequent correspondence (**20a**) about the nature of periodisation in history. And in an era just becoming familiar with the interview and what would later be called oral history, Quennell and Hodge were pioneers in the publication of the evocative personal memoir. From this distance it is almost uncanny to come across a detailed account of conversations with the exiled Kaiser (**10**) – not to mention being present, at a single remove, at the farce of King Louis-Philippe in 1830 being told to hurry up and abdicate and the pear-faced monarch replying tetchily that it takes a little time to vacate a throne (**26**). History, surely, is rarely more vivid!

From the outset, the subject-matter covered in *History Today* was impressively wide-ranging. English history predominated. This, however, could in those pre-post-imperial days provide the hub of a wheel with spokes leading into remote parts of Africa or Asia widely regarded as exotic but which serious scholars were beginning to demystify (**18, 22**). In those early years, the magazine contained a lot more about art, literature and music than latterly, more military history – and regular contributions from historians like Michael Grant (**9**) about the classical and medieval worlds. Religious history, too, was a frequent presence, Professor Brandon often managing to ruffle the starched susceptibilities of readers unaccustomed to considering the Old or New Testaments as history (**28**). Britain's postwar sense of solidarity with America and the western alliance found historical echoes in the pages of *History Today* (**14, 15**), as did the characteristic 'French 'flu' of the English intellectual (**5, 32**) and the anxious ambivalence towards Germany and the nature of war (**6, 9, 10, 23**). Germany predictably aroused the strongest passions: see Elizabeth Wiskemann's excoriating review of A.J.P. Taylor (**27**). Most writers were men, though it is noticeable that arts-related features were often by women (as here, in **5, 24** and **32**), while the first historical article by Antonia Fraser to be published appeared in *History Today* (**30**). Book reviews (*pace* Wiskemann) were often anodyne and letters to the editor(s) unfailingly polite, sometimes obsessional – and occasionally downright eccentric (**16**).

The joint editorship of Quennell and Hodge lasted over 28 years until Hodge's death in 1979 and the retirement of Quennell shortly afterwards. It was an astonishing achievement though, reading through their later volumes, one gets the impression that the magazine began to lose something of its earlier *élan*. The 1960s and 1970s had seen a radicalisation of both the subject-matter and methodology of history. While some of the pioneers of the 'new history' (Christopher Hill, George Rudé, Eric Hobsbawm) had occasionally written for *History Today*, the magazine developed a rather clubby, leather armchair feel, inappropriate for an era increasingly concerned with issues of race, gender, popular and regional cultures, Third World history and the global environment.

From about 1980, under the editorship of Michael Crowder, Michael Trend and then Juliet Gardiner, *History Today* (by now independently owned) took on new vitality. Crowder, whose expertise lay in African history, noted in the magazine's thirtieth anniversary edition (January 1981) that the 'Euro-centric perception of the world' had given way to 'a search for an understanding of the past of the non-European peoples so recently emerged from imperial domination'. He went on to welcome the new willingness of historians 'to embrace the methods and techniques' of other disciplines such as anthropology, sociology and ('even') mathematics.

Produced to a larger format, the magazine sought a new, up-to-date readership through the introduction of colour photography, more adventurous articles, coverage of history in schools and in the media and a history of food column. Historians such as John Brewer (**35**), Conrad Russell (**42**), David Starkey (**43**) and Douglas Johnson (**47**) began to appear regularly, some contributing not only key scholarly features but also the shorter, pithier pieces that came to be commissioned for the opening pages of the paper (**40, 43**). Running series were introduced and, for a while, a regular forum which asked practitioners to define 'What Is?' their particular kind of history: political history, economic history, the history of science or women's history (**44**). On occasion, an issue would be devoted in large part to a single topic. In September 1981, for example, no less than seven articles were on the featured topic of 'The History of Blacks in Britain' (**38**). In its attempt to regain the high ground, *History Today* was done no harm, I suspect, by the occasional controversy spilling over into the national press – such as that resulting from the article by Jacob Boas (**36**) chronicling the extraordinary visit of a Nazi to Palestine.

Formats and formulators continued to change, but the fundamental purpose did not. Churchill, who would have known of *History Today* from its birth, is said to have noted admiringly that it was a magazine 'written by young historians for serious people', a comment quoted with relish forty years later by Gordon Marsden (editor, 1985–97). Sir Peter Quennell, happily, was present to cut the cake at *History Today*'s fortieth anniversary party. It seems he approved of the new directions his creation was taking.

No doubt Churchill (and Brendan Bracken) would have been bewildered by the glossy ads, quizzes and competitions and the deals with publishing houses and tour companies that, in the coldly commercial '90s, guaranteed the magazine's continued survival. They may have wondered at the widespread interest in regional (and 'counter-factual') history (**55**), and I am not sure they would altogether have approved of articles on subjects like Bestiality (**62**). But I hope they would have liked new regular features such as 'Cross Current', 'Mediawatch' (**49**) and Richard Cavendish's series on some of Britain's smaller museums (**50**). The forcefulness and intelligence of historians like Felipe Fernández-Armesto (**48**), Jeremy Black (**55**), Nigel Saul (**56**), Roy Porter (**58**) and

David Cannadine (**60a**), too, would have left them in no doubt as to the magazine's continuing seriousness of purpose. And one development would surely have caused them to rub their eyes with gleeful incredulity: the sight of joint issues of *History Today* co-edited with its counterpart magazines in post-Communist Russia and re-united, democratic Germany (**53**).

There are of course many pasts – as many histories, perhaps, as historians – and a rich variety of approaches has always been reflected in the pages of *History Today* and is included in the selections below. Do 'Great Men' make history (**7, 13, 15, 24, 25, 42**) or is it properly the story of ordinary people (**12, 18, 19, 29, 34, 35, 57**)? We include absorbing studies of intellectual and ideological interpretations of the past (**6, 8, 14, 31, 51**) as well as glimpses of the bizarre, the eccentric and the controversial (**19, 54**). What early experiences led historians to their profession in the first place (**59, 59a and 61**) and what is history's proper domain (**1, 44**)? If you use proper care and discrimination, it seems, almost anything can teach you something of the past – including the reading of imaginative literature (**39**) or wondering what would have happened if things had worked out differently (**55**). But don't read *too* much: it could damage your health (**58**)!

History Today may deal with the past. But the fluctuating fortunes of the magazine over half a century have closely reflected the ever-changing present. From the optimism (tinged by a touch of triumphalism) of the early 1950s, through the heady doubts and divisions of the 1960s and '70s, to the multicultural, multivalent world of the '80s and '90s, *History Today* has necessarily responded to the environment in which it has been produced. Like the world at large, there were even moments when it was not obvious that it would survive. The magazine – and, I hope, this anthology of some of its finest writing – can act as a bellwether of some of the shifting intellectual concerns and preoccupations of the past half century.

The seeds of the future, it has been said, lie in the way we regard the past. If so, the pages that follow, a collection of writings about the past as viewed from the second half of the twentieth century, should provide essential reading as we embark upon the twenty-first.

Daniel Snowman
January 2001

1

The Historian's Purpose

ALAN BULLOCK

(February 1951)

In the second-ever issue of the magazine, Alan Bullock (doubtless deep in his study of Hitler) argued that the job of the historian was not so much to embrace grand, metaphysical theories but to find out – and if possible to explain – what actually happened.

Since Hegel delivered his lectures on the Philosophy of History in Berlin, he has had many imitators. Not that Hegel was the first to make the attempt at reading the meaning of history, but since his time historical prophecy has established its own apostolic succession from Hegel himself and Marx to Spengler and Wells, Croce and Toynbee. These interpretations are various and contradictory, but they have this in common: they are all attempts to discover in history patterns, regularities and similarities on whose recurrence is built a philosophical explanation of human existence, or at the very least a panoramic view of the stages of its development. It is this sort of *Weltanschauung* – metahistory, to borrow a phrase of Mr Isaiah Berlin's – which is the fascination and justification of historical study to many people.

Equally obviously, it is not what most historians themselves mean by history. On the contrary, this is a kind of speculative activity which many professional historians eye with distrust and dislike. When G.N. Clark delivered his Inaugural Lecture as Regius Professor at Cambridge, he said: 'To me it seems that no historical investigation can provide either a philosophy, or a religion, or a substitute for religion. . . . I think I should have a general consensus of the working historians with me, if I confined myself to the simpler conclusion that we work with limited aims. We try to find the truth about this or that, not about things in general. Our work is not to see life steadily and see it whole, but to see one particular portion of life right side up and in true perspective.' Professor Butterfield, though prepared to assume the rôle of a prophet, was careful to dissociate his speculations from his work as a professional historian. 'Those are gravely wrong who regard history as the queen of the sciences' (he wrote in *Christianity and History*), 'or think of it as a substitute for religion. . . . Those who complain that technical history does not provide people with the meaning of life are asking from an academic science more than it can give. . . . When we have reconstructed the whole of mundane history it does not form a self-explanatory system, and our attitude to it is a matter not of scholarship, but of religion.'

The commonest explanation for the hostility of many professional historians towards philosophical history in the grand style is to put it down to what Carlyle called 'the poor, peddling dilettantism of Dryasdust', the contrast between the bold speculations of the philoso-pher of history and the narrow-mindedness of bloodless academic minds. But not all historians have been pedants or lacking in imagination. Is it true that the historian is confronted with a simple choice between metahistory on the model of Spengler or Toynbee and the desolate wastes of an arid historical erudition? Some historians at any rate – men like Halévy, Pirenne, Mathiez, Marc Bloch – seem to have found a way between these two extremes.

The historian, of course, does not live on a desert island. He is sensitive to the interests and problems of the society in which he lives. It is often the preoccupations and experiences of his own time which suggest to an historian the particular subject or period which he takes up. But once he begins work, the question he is trying to answer is: What happened? His interest is in the past, not in the present or the future.

The historian finds his satisfaction in three things. First, in searching for and discovering new material to use as evidence. Second, in handling his material when he has found it, trying to discover whether it is authentic or a forgery – if so, why it was forged; whether the man who wrote this document is telling the truth or lies – if so, why he lied; trying to make it yield unexpected evidence. The third and supreme satisfaction is to put the evidence together, to produce not only an account of what happened, but a connected account, illuminating the motives and ideas of the actors, the influence of circumstances, the play of chance and the unforeseen. What the historian finds fascinating is to come as close as he can to the concrete and the individual, to try and get inside the skin of *this* man or group of men, Napoleon, Cromwell, the Jacobins, or the Bosheviks; to trace the causes, the connections and consequences of this particular revolution of 1848, or a particular series of events like the famines and plagues of the Middle Ages, or the rise of the English cotton industry.

This is not to identify history with historical research: that makes as little sense as to confuse literature with textual criticism. To borrow a quotation from Pirenne: 'Historical criticism, or historical erudition, is not the whole of history. It does not exist for its own sake. . . . Its sole purpose is the discovery of facts. . . . Criticism provides materials for what is properly called history. . . . Important and indeed essential though it be, its rôle remains subordinate. Once the authenticity of texts has been established, the sources criticized, the chronology of events fixed, there still remains the task of making history. . . . Without hypothesis or synthesis, history remains a pastime for antiquarians; just as without criticism and erudition it loses itself in the realm of fantasy.'

Still less am I putting forward an argument in favour of reducing history to chronology, a bare recital of facts. History is always an attempt to explain the sequence and connection of events, to explain why, after the events of 1789, there followed the Revolutionary Wars, the execution of the King, the Jacobin dictatorship, the Terror and the Thermidorian Reaction. Not why they *had* to follow – this is prediction is reverse, and the historian has no business with prediction – but why *in fact* they followed.

Now, the moment the historian begins to explain, he is bound to make use of general propositions of all kinds – about human behaviour, about the effect of economic factors and the influence of ideas and a hundred other things. It is impossible for the historian to banish such general propositions; they are smuggled in by the back door; even when he refuses to admit it. He cannot begin to think or explain events without the help of the preconceptions, the assumptions, the generalization of experience which he brings with him – and is bound to bring with him – to his work. When Mathiez for example began to work on the history of the French Revolution, his mind was not a blank, it was full of views and prejudices about revolutions and their causes, about the way people behave in times of revolution, about how much importance to attach to economic, how much to intellectual factors. The historian gives a false account of his activity if he tries to deny the part that general ideas and assumptions play in his work.

There is, however, a difference between the historian on the one hand and the metahistorian, seeking for patterns of historical evolution, or the sociologist, seeking for general laws governing human development, on the other. This difference lies in their purpose and in the use which they make of such generalizations. What the metahistorian and the sociologist are trying to do is to clear away the confusion of facts and reveal the pattern, or establish the law, which lies beneath. But this is not the historian's purpose: what he wants to know is what happened. For him general propositions are both necessary and illuminating, but they are not the essential purpose of his work. When Marx says 'The history of all hitherto existing society is the history of class struggles', Marxism as a system stands or falls by the truth of such a generalization. Its only interest in history is to produce such general propositions. But when Professor Namier says, 'The relations of groups of men to plots of land form the basic content of political history', it does not matter whether this is only partially true. It does not invalidate his investigation and interpretation of English politics in the later eighteenth century, and it is this which represents his main purpose, the epigram is thrown off as an aside. For the historian such generalizations are hypotheses which he can use to open up a subject and suggest lines of approach, discarding, adapting, or continuing with them, as they prove fruitful. Few historians today, for instance, would fail to make use of the economic interpretation of history as one of the most valuable instruments of historical analysis – but only as one. As an experimental hypothesis, to be dropped or taken up as it fits, it is indispensable; as a dogmatic belief it cramps the mind and forces the historian to distort the evidence. It is in this way, as hypotheses, as the expression of probabilities, of what to look out for, that the historian treats his general propositions; not as the basis of something that can be built up into a general law. His purpose is not to form general propositions about revolutions or civilizations as such, but to give an account of the French or the Russian Revolution, to trace the rise and fall of the Hellenic or Chinese Civilizations.

In such work it is obvious that the first rule of the historian must be to keep a critical eye on his own assumptions and pre-conceptions, lest these should lead him to miss the importance of some piece of evidence, the existence of some connection. His whole training teaches him to break down rather than build up generalizations, to bring the general always to the touchstone of particular, concrete instances. His experience of this discipline and its results makes him cautious and sceptical about the possibility of establishing uniformities and regularities of sufficient generality to bear the weight of the conclusions then built up on them. Probabilities, yes – rules of thumb, the sort of thing you can expect to happen – but not more than this.

When I first came across the bold generalizations of the metahistorian in Spengler's *Decline of the West*, I was bowled over by them. But I have become more wary since, not least because I have encountered many other equally bold but frequently contradictory generalizations. The suspicion has grown that this is to treat history as a rag-bag in which every man will find what he wants to find, and what he expects to find. There is indeed no limit to the lessons of history, or to their contradictions.

In short, the historian does not believe that you can annex history to a metaphysical system or turn it into a science on that out-of-date nineteenth century model on which the original expectations of the social sciences were founded. Perhaps, as Marc Bloch suggests in his *Métier de l'Historien*, the temper and attitude of the twentieth century scientist is a good deal closer to that of the historian than the dogmatic assertions of those who have constituted themselves the prophets of science in the past.

There is another objection to be met, however. Professor Butterfield, for instance, might well agree with a good deal of what has been said so far. 'Nothing' (he wrote in *Christianity and History*) 'can exceed the feeling of satisfaction that many people have when they meet some system which helps them through the jungle of historical happenings, and gives them an interpretation of the story seen as a whole. In such cases, however, our interpretation is a thing which we bring to history and superimpose upon it. We cannot say that we obtained it as technical historians by inescapable inferences, from the purely historical evidence. Therefore the Liberal, the Jesuit, the Fascist, the Communist, and all the rest may sail away with their militant versions of history, howling at one another across the interstellar spaces, all claiming that theirs is the absolute version. . . .'

But Professor Butterfield seems to feel that, deprived of these broad sweeps and metaphysical perspectives, the historian's work must be very limited in scope and interest. The historian emerges from Professor Butterfield's pages as a poor creature, blinkered and earthbound, labouring to produce the fragments which the metahistorian combines into the glittering pattern of his mosaic.

I find it hard to believe, however, that if history cannot be made to bear the weight of the systems of moral absolutism after which so many people hanker, that it must therefore be regarded as a study which is either dull or meaningless. It is too easily assumed that the only approach to knowledge and understanding of human life and behaviour is by the search for general factors, regularities and uniformities, which can be reduced to formulas and general propositions. This is not a popular objection to raise. I can still remember the look of horror on the face of a young sociologist when I suggested there was more to be learned from Dostoievski's novels or Shakespeare's plays, with their series of individual portraits, than from the abstract and meagre generalizations of his own study. In that preference for the concrete and the particular, that distrust of the abstract and general which is the characteristic of many historians, there may be something akin to the approach of the painter and the novelist – think of Proust, for instance, and his incomparable re-creation of the past.

Probably it is a question of temperament, of the way your mind works. But behind the historian's distrust of the metahistorians and the dogmatists there often lies an instinctive feeling that, alongside the approach to knowledge of human nature and human behaviour represented by the attempt to frame general laws and trace broad general patterns of historical development, there is another approach, equally legitimate and to some people's way of thinking more fruitful. That is, by studying and trying to penetrate in all its individuality and uniqueness the development of one society, or one civilization, the behaviour not of men and women in general, but of one particular group in a given period of time. And it is a fair question to ask – who sees the more – the airman who flies continually across several countries five thousand feet up, from where he can see the land for miles and miles, or the countryman who has lived in one place all his life but knows the valleys, the woods and lanes of his own countryside like the back of his hand?

*　　*　　*

Alan Bullock was born in Wiltshire in 1914 and educated at Bradford Grammar School before going up to Wadham College, Oxford. He has been Fellow, Dean and Tutor in Modern History at New College, and Founding Master of St Catherine's College as well as serving for a period as the University's first full-time Vice-Chancellor. Bullock's internationally renowned biography of Adolf Hitler, *Hitler: A Study in Tyranny* (1952) paved the way for the authoritative *Hitler and Stalin: Parallel Lives* (1991). His critically acclaimed biographies also include a three-volume life of the mid-twentieth century Labour statesman Ernest Bevin. He was awarded a life peerage in 1976.

2

When Did It Become Impossible to Know Everything?

ALAN HODGE AND PETER QUENNELL

(April 1952)

A typically teasing editorial from Alan Hodge and Peter Quennell.

When did it become impossible for an educated man to grasp, at least in its broader and more general outlines, the entire extent of European learning? During the sixteenth and early seventeenth centuries he might have accomplished the feat, mastering not only the literature and philosophic writings of the ancient and modern worlds, but astronomy, mathematics and physics as they had so far developed. Bacon, evidently, was such an 'all-round man'; and Milton no doubt could claim to have conquered most of the branches of contemporary learning. The Age of Specialization (we hazard a guess) began about the middle of the seventeenth century with the rapid and brilliant development of the Natural Sciences; and from that period the artist and the scientist, the philosopher and the politician, each embarked on a separate course, gradually losing sight of the splendid ideals of the great Renaissance humanists. One of the chief tragedies of twentieth-century life is the lack of any form of coordination between intelligent men of goodwill, who, if they are engaged in different fields of research, inevitably speak in different languages and are almost incapable of associating for any common purpose. Can our readers re-trace this tragedy to its historical origins? When, precisely, did the divorce occur? How long could the ambitious and industrious scholar still feel that he was himself a well-balanced microcosm of the civilization he represented? To these loosely framed rhetorical queries we hope that we may receive some satisfactorily concrete answers for publication in our columns.

* * *

Alan Hodge (1915–79) was joint editor of *History Today* from 1951 to 1979. As an undergraduate at Oriel College, Oxford, he wrote avant-garde verse and later collaborated with Robert Graves in two works of literary and social criticism, *The Long Weekend: A Social History of Great Britain 1918–1939* (1940) and *The Reader Over Your Shoulder* (1943). In the 1940s he was personal assistant to Brendan Bracken and helped him write a weekly column entitled 'Men and Matters' for the *Financial Times*. In the 1950s he worked for Winston Churchill as a research assistant on his *History of the English-Speaking Peoples.*

* * *

Poet, historian, biographer and editor, Peter Quennell (1905–93) was educated at Berkhamsted Grammar School and Balliol College, Oxford. He was editor of the *Cornhill Magazine* (1944–51) and joint editor of *History Today* (1951–79). His first publication, *Poems* (1926), was followed by numerous works including *Byron: The Years of Fame* (1932); *Byron in Italy* (1941); *Caroline of England* (1939); *Four Portraits* (1945) and *John Ruskin* (1949). He also edited, amongst others, *The Private Letters of Princess Lieven to Prince Metternich, 1820–1826* (1948) and wrote two autobiographies: *The Marble Foot* (1976) and *The Wanton Chase* (1980).

3

London 1900–1951

D.W. BROGAN

(July 1952)

Denis Brogan, expert on French and American history and politics and a lot else besides, wrote a series of city portraits for History Today.

Perhaps 1897 would be a better date for beginning a sketch of the history of modern London. In 1897 was celebrated the Diamond Jubilee of Queen Victoria, the last, great untroubled pageant of English history. All the nations of the earth came to celebrate her reign; all the splendour of the greatest empire, the wealth and pride of the world's greatest city were on display. Few took seriously Kipling's warning that this pomp might go the way 'of Nineveh and Tyre'. Then, in January, 1901, the Queen died. A new era opened, if not in fact, at least in feeling. But between the two dates there had been a crack in Victorian complacency. The South African war had begun, and with a series of disasters the more agonizing because they were humiliating.

Peace came and the novelty of a King and a coronation followed the Queen's funeral. The brief glowing period, to be known later as 'pre-war', began. And the privileged classes, at least, looking back at that golden sunset, could say what Talleyrand said of the *ancien régime*, that those who had not known it had never known the *douceur de vivre*. There were still the great houses; the balls and dinners and parties; all the glory of 'the Season'. Income tax and death duties were low; American money, money from the Rand and from Kimberley, poured in; Victorian rigours were over. And Edward VII seemed like a new if elderly Charles II after the virtuous boredom of the previous reign.

It was not like that for everybody. London still struck the foreigner as the city where the contrast between rich and poor was greatest. There was the London of Berkeley Square and the London of Richard Whiting's *Number Five John Street*, of Jack London's *People of the Abyss*. It was a London that had just begun to be modernized. True, the great Victorian monuments were there; the Houses of Parliament, the Law Courts, the Embankment, the Albert Hall. But unlike Paris, New York or Berlin, London impressed more by its size than by its appearance. It was still a city of houses and gardens, where most of the splendid things were the work of private individuals or corporations; the city companies; the Inns of Court; the great private mansions, Devonshire House, Stafford House, Norfolk House; the great squares laid out by Cavendishes, Russells, Grosvenors. It was still a city of gaslight, of steam trains, of horse buses, of four-wheelers and hansoms. If not the London of Dickens, it was the London of Sherlock Holmes.

All that was to change. A veteran French diplomat, coming back to London just before the Second World War, said no city had changed so much in the fifty years he had known it. In 1900 it had been brick and stucco; by 1939 it was largely stone in the central regions. Not all Londoners thought this an improvement. Mr Osbert Lancaster, contemplating the results of finding London brick and leaving it marble or at any rate freestone, had doubts about the beneficial effects of Augustus on Rome. Most Londoners had something to regret and not many rejoiced at the new additions to the skyline. Some deplored the passing of Nash's Regent Street, some the intrusion of a paint company's offices into the façade of Carlton House Terrace. Others, while not regretting overmuch what had been pulled down, regretted what had been put up. Thus the view of Trafalgar Square, got by demolishing the Golden Cross, was soon hidden by the erection of South Africa House. The threatened destruction of city churches, to provide funds for church extension in the outer suburbs, aroused protests before the *Luftwaffe* did the job for the Ecclesiastical Commissioners. But, in the main, the Londoner did not care. It was not for its looks that he loved his city – at any rate, not for the looks of its buildings.

Parks were another matter. They were vigilantly protected, but the old, royal and aristocratic conception of the Mall and Hyde Park broke down after the First War. Taxis used the sacred processional way, and quite ordinary people rode in the Row. Perhaps the greatest change was the turning of the Serpentine into a 'Lido' and the name of that great Londoner, George Lansbury, ought forever to be remembered for that, if for nothing else. Though the Londoner may not have noticed what was going on, the face of his city was altering. The driving of the new avenue through the slums of St Clements to which the name of 'Kingsway' was given, marked one achievement of the new reign. There were numerous street-widening schemes, none of them very impressive in detail but, in the mass, making many important changes. But far more decisive for the future of London was the vast extension of the underground system. London had been the pioneer in underground transportation; the new electric trains, however, were very different from the old smoky carriages of the Metropolitan, celebrated in *Iolanthe*. With their appearance, the territorial expansion of London became much easier, although the great days of expansion were still to come after the First War. The replacing of the horse-bus by the motor-bus, combined with the new undergrounds to make London less an agglomeration of towns and more of a community. All the railway lines began to profit by the sprawl of London across the Home Counties; though, again, not until after the First War and the electrification of many of the lines was completed that curious amalgam of London, its suburbs and the new boroughs sprung from villages, which some inspired publicist was to call 'Metroland'.

While outer London sprawled, inner London climbed. Already this upward trend had been seen in the erection of what, for London, were sky-scraper blocks of flats like Queen Anne Mansions. There were to be more of them, especially after the First War, when taxation, servant-trouble and a new view of life made fewer people ready or able to bear the expense of the great houses, or even of the less great houses in the terraces and squares. Some great houses began to come down, and many 'good' houses were converted into flats. New buildings now were mainly official or commercial. Thus, there was the new Waterloo Station, the County Hall, the new block of the British Museum and the new government offices in Whitehall, carrying on the tradition of Palmerston and Gilbert Scott. Large commercial blocks were rising in the City, though the great era of bank building came between the wars. There were ostentatious department-stores like Selfridges; new hotels; new theatres like the ill-fated opera house in Kingsway, now demolished. Perhaps the only public monument of the old kind was Westminster Cathedral, and that was not designed in the old style, for its Byzantine form and decoration were unprecedented in the architectural history of London. In 1888, with the establishment of the London County Council, London for the first time in its history had a unified government. And, in 1903, the L.C.C. replaced the famous London School Board and, at the same time, acquired new powers for the provision of secondary education. The rulers of the L.C.C. were energetic and hopeful. These 'Municipal Reformers' put passenger steamers on the river and electric trams wherever they could. They did not control water, gas, electricity as did the rulers of Birmingham and Glasgow; but they pushed 'gas and water socialism' in every direction. In 1907 the electorate turned against them, but by then the tradition was established.

By 1914, London was well on the way to being the London we know today. It was a capital that delighted in shows, in State visits like that of the French President in 1903; ceremonials like royal marriages, funerals and coronations. Few who saw the State funeral of Edward VII, with its cluster of royal mourners and (if they saw him in one of the last carriages) the ex-President of the United States, Theodore Roosevelt, could have guessed that never again would they witness such a spectacle; that the royal mourners in a few years would be, for the most part, dethroned and, in some cases, murdered. By the time of the coronation of George V in 1911, the shadows of war were visible to some, and a general air of crisis was felt by all. Two general elections had been held within a year; the assault on the House of Lords had succeeded; and there had been the 'Battle of Sidney Street', where a few mysterious foreign bandits were attacked by the Guards under the eye of the energetic, if flamboyant, Home Secretary, Mr Winston Churchill. Soon the apparently endless Irish crisis was to break out. In 1913 a peace conference for the warring Balkan states took place in Downing Street. There were railway and dock strikes. It was a long way from 1897.

There had been other innovations, of course. Astonishing and outrageous paintings were introduced from Paris and the Russian ballet invaded Covent Garden. Caruso sang and so did Chaliapin; and the first season of plays by Bernard Shaw filled the Court Theatre. One day, in 1909, there had come the momentous news that a Frenchman had flown the Channel. Soon aeroplanes were a common sight and there were stories of the German airships, the 'Zeppelins'. Then came August 1914, and the old world went.

Round the bright new façade of Buckingham Palace the crowds gathered, cheering the King. They saw the orderly mobilization of the British Expeditionary Force; they heard that civil war in Ireland was postponed. Only gradually did people begin to understand that this was not a new Boer War. The young men, who had poured into the recruiting stations in their tens of thousands to join Kitchener's army, had no need to fear that the war would be over before they got to France. As hostilities developed, London became the great leave town. Shows like 'Chu Chin Chow' and 'The Bing Boys' were part of the war effort and London, in a special sense, was 'Blighty', that magical country so near to Flanders and yet so remote, only linked to 'the Front' by the nightly leave trains from Victoria Station. On still days, in the outskirts of London, you could hear the mutter of the guns; but the Londoners in 1914–18 never knew the war at first hand. There were a few air raids, taken very seriously; there was exultation when a Zeppelin was shot down over Potters Bar, but the threat of the war in the air came to little. Paris suffered more from Big Bertha than London from Zeppelins or planes. Yet war-weariness grew; and one symptom was the premature exultation at the 'victory' of

Cambrai in 1917. 1918, which brought more disasters, was marked with signs of strain like the police strike; but victory was at hand. On November 11th London was given over to rejoicing, rowdy but far more serious than the mere animal high spirits of Mafeking Night.

1919 saw high pageantry; the victory parade; the visit of President Wilson; but it saw, too, the beginning of the time of troubles, the slow recognition that the old world was dead. A gallant attempt was made to revive 'society'. But the losses in blood and treasure were too great. The pace of change was accelerating. There were the new, smart, cheap restaurants, so unlike the old eating-houses. New sports arrived: ice hockey; dog racing; the dirt track; and there was the '*palais de danse*'. In dress and habit, egalitarianism was growing. The picture palace was now a great social phenomenon; the film star received an adulation never lavished, at any rate by so many, on the matinée idol. What were the clubs of girls, 'mad about Waller', to the hysterical 'fans' who adored the men and imitated the women of the screen? Other signs appeared of a loosening of the old social rules. Women smoked in public everywhere and went to boxing matches to see how the home of the noble art was faring in international competition. It was faring badly; but the shift from the limited National Sporting Club (or from Hoxton Baths) to the vastness of the Albert Hall was significant. In 1924 came the Empire Exhibition at Wembley, a financial failure that left a permanent memorial in the Stadium that housed the Cup Final, now a great national rite, presided over by Royalty. According to moralists, London was dance-mad, sport-mad.

There were other phenomena to alarm the timid. The first Labour government was returned, and in County Council and borough elections London was moving away from its predominantly Tory traditions. The Labour Government fell, and the General Strike of 1926 failed; but the tide was creeping in. In 1929, there was another Labour government, one of its ministers being a Cockney of Cockneys, Herbert Morrison, who put in hand the unification of all London Transport, which became the 'London Passenger Transport Board'. The making and remaking of London went on. New university buildings arose in Bloomsbury; and another great monument, the Power Station, was erected at Battersea. The Embankment was now fringed, from Blackfriars to beyond Westminster Bridge, by gigantic office buildings where Somerset House had once lorded it alone. There were great new L.C.C. housing estates and more and more new hotels, flats, cinemas. Such London landmarks as the Empire, the Alhambra, Daly's became cinemas. The most famous of all, the Gaiety, was simply closed down and left empty. In the City, Sir Herbert Baker built a vast structure inside the old screen of the Bank of

England soon to be hemmed in by buildings that were a cross between modern Wall Street and medieval Florence. Only Sir Edward Lutyens' Cenotaph in Whitehall escaped the wrath of the critics.

London's economic life was also changing. It suffered less from permanent unemployment than did the northern cities tied to heavy industry, or the Lancashire cotton towns whose export markets were vanishing. There was a shift to light industry, helped by the adoption of a protective tariff. Soon the arterial roads round London were lined with new factories; some indigenous; some branches of American or French firms erected to get round the duties. London was fast becoming the industrial centre of Britain; its population was less exclusively composed of clerks, dockers and minor tradesmen. On the outskirts, the new boroughs came to look much alike, with their branch banks, new town halls, giant cinemas; they were cleaner, better planned, less cramped than the old industrial towns of the North and Midlands. The drift to the North that had begun in the late eighteenth century was now reversed; and the groups of Welsh miners singing in the London streets had some of the effect of men coming from the front in the war. As seen from Oxford Street, South Wales was a remote, unhappy, neglected place.

The war of 1939 found Londoners in a very different mood from that of August, 1914. No curious and excited crowds gathered outside Buckingham Palace; and, if there was no panic, there was apprehension. The reasons for the change were clear enough. In 1914, war was romantic, and unknown. In 1939, people knew that the war might be long, that its issue was doubtful (as far as any British war could have a doubtful issue). Too many remembered the casualty lists of 1914–1918 for any easy exultation. In 1914 war had come as a surprise to most people; only a few days separated the news of crisis from the news of war. But by 1939 the crisis had for years been mounting in intensity, and London had had the Munich rehearsal of 1938, with its frenzied and inadequate last minute preparations. Those memories had had a year to sink in. As early as August 10th, 1939, a trial 'black-out' had been ordered; and, on September 1st, at sunset, London went dark. The formal war was a few days ahead, but for Londoners it had then begun.

Londoners were facing the unknown. No one knew what the Germans would do and it was generally expected that they would begin by a mass air attack on London that would, in a few hours, kill thousands. As it turned out, the most dramatic sights of London were the gas masks issued to the civilians and the evacuation of women and children. That done, London settled down to what the Americans were soon to call the 'phoney war', so phoney that some papers began to complain that the black-out was an unnecessary nuisance and bad for business. And, as the months dragged on, the women and children drifted back. In the first year of war it seemed that boredom would be the chief enemy of London life; but with the late spring, a new tension, a new seriousness appeared; Mr Churchill's elevation to supreme authority symbolized a new phase in the nation's life. Then came Dunkirk, the French armistice, the beginnings of raids on the coast, and the German assault, the Battle of Britain, whose final stages were fought in the London sky. London had not known a real military threat since the Civil War; and no great country, or great capital, had ever had its fate decided in so spectacular a fashion. Few knew how close-run the battle was, how near exhaustion the defenders; till on September 15th, the last German day assault was beaten off.

A week earlier, on the night of September 7th, London had entered on the third stage of her war experiences. For seventy-two nights – except for one, when the *Luftwaffe* descended on Coventry – the bombers came over a minute or two after dusk and left a minute or two before dawn; siege had succeeded assault. It was a test of endurance – and of organization. At first the organization seemed to break down, everywhere to some extent, and completely in some regions like the East End. For the true problems created by the raids had not been foreseen. There were far fewer casualties than had been expected – more civilian sick were turned out of hospital beds than wounded were found to fill them. What had not been foreseen was the extent of damage from blast, the numbers of citizens thrown out into the streets, homeless, half naked, dirty. Conditions were so bad that they produced a reaction far more violent than any caused by death and wounds. Faced by the anger of the victims, the Government, in spite of the protests of the service chiefs, was obliged to rank the London problem among those to which it gave highest priority. Stores were drawn on, Treasury control dropped; soldiers were drafted from the army to repair the damage. Civilians, not soldiers, were now in the front line. But gradually London adjusted herself to the conditions of total warfare; and she was proud of the rôle she played in the winter of 1940–1. Proud and also a little amused by the position she assumed as a capital for other nations. Her streets filled with exotic figures as the European exiles poured in – Poles and Dutch, Norwegians and Free French, including, for a time, some of the Foreign Legion. One day you might see the King of Norway, on another the King of Greece or the Queen of the Netherlands, or the tall figure of General de Gaulle; for, by a curious inversion of history, it was from London, on June 18th, that he launched his famous appeal and started the movement that was to culminate, four years later, in the Cathedral of Notre Dame.

Then, in thousands and in tens of thousands, came the Americans. They arrived with a great deal of money and a plentiful stock of self-assurance, some of it slightly false; for many were seeing a big city for the first time in their lives. The usual camp-followers of war, crooks and prostitutes, descended on their prey. 'Piccadilly commandos' shocked some soldiers who at home were not accustomed to open prostitution. Between white and Negro troops there were quarrels and fights; and Londoners grew accustomed to the admirable American military police, 'Eisenhower's "snowdrops"', with their white helmets, gloves and gaiters, who patrolled Soho and other amusement quarters in pairs, one white and one coloured. Yet most of the fears of friction proved groundless; and, as D-day drew nearer, the realities of war helped to ease the social tension. On June 7th, 1944, came the news: the invasion had at last begun. The reply followed on June 12th; the long-rumoured secret weapon, the flying-bomb, struck London and the second 'Blitz' got under way. As the victorious armies mopped up the bomb sites, flying bombs were followed by rockets, and there was a brief return to the conditions of 1940. March saw the end of the bombardment, and May the end of the war. But the London of 1945 was more tired, more battered than the London of 1918. There was less exultation, more sheer relief.

London suffered less loss of life than had been feared; thirty thousand deaths in all – half of what Hamburg lost in a week, a third of what Hiroshima lost in a minute. The damage to the great monuments was also less than had been expected. The House of Commons was burned out; but the Houses of Parliament were not destroyed. City churches and the halls of the city companies suffered badly; so did the Inns of Court, St Thomas's Hospital and University College. Holland House was perhaps the greatest loss among the private buildings. But St Paul's, Westminster Abbey, Westminster Cathedral, hardly suffered at all; and the damage to the British Museum was not disastrous. But there was no region of London without its scars, and some parts like Stepney, Bethnal Green and a large area of the City had now the appearance of Pompeii. As Mr John Rayner, an acute student of the iconography of London, had once foretold, it was in 1945 as in 1666; erect among expanses of ruin the church spires were the landmarks of the blasted areas.

In 1945 London had never looked so drab. The end of the black-out and the cessation of bombing seemed the only change that victory made. Wild flowers grew in the ruins; wild birds nested in the City; but, quite apart from damage, London, still mostly brick and stucco, needed a thorough spring-clean. Old social habits were slow to return; theatres still opened early; while, even for the prosperous, rationing and sumptuary legislation made London a far less attractive city than Paris or New York. Not only was the burden of reconstruction heavy, but disillusionment with the 'peace' came more quickly than after 1919. When the new

United Nations met in the Central Hall, the fine hopes with which the organization had been launched were already cooling. There was bad luck, too. The months of January and February, 1947, were the most severe in recent London history. Coal gave out; the black-out returned, and in many ways conditions were worse than during the war. Yet certain improvements did take place. Clothing and some foods became more plentiful, though bread was rationed for a time; some of the uglier scars began to vanish. Characteristically, the great London festival was not the Victory Parade, but the marriage of the heiress to the throne to the Duke of Edinburgh. Preparations for the 'Festival of Britain' went on across from the new Waterloo Bridge that had been finished during the war. A vast new government building took shape off Whitehall, and, highly significant, a huge stone temple was erected in the City to house the Commissioners of the National Debt. The Festival itself, though it received a somewhat tepid welcome, marked a real resurgence. Where its gay and ambitious buildings rose along the South Bank, a year earlier Londoners had seen only a gigantic heap of war rubble. In spirit, if not in its material possessions, London was coming to life again.

*   *   *

Denis Brogan was born in 1900 and educated at Glasgow University and Balliol College, Oxford. A year at Harvard University then ignited his passion for American history and politics. While lecturer at the London School of Economics, he wrote his best-known work, *The American Political System* (1933). The following year he gained a fellowship at Corpus Christi College, Oxford, where he expanded his interests to France. *The Development of Modern France, 1870–1939* (1940) was the first detailed examination of modern French politics. A renowned polymath and raconteur and a frequent broadcaster, Brogan was for many years a Fellow of Peterhouse College, Cambridge. Knighted in 1963, Sir Denis Brogan died in 1974.

4

British Prime Ministers

DUFF COOPER

(December 1952)

Duff Cooper, equally famous as biographer, politician and husband of Lady Diana (and father of John Julius Norwich), had served Churchill during the war, known several other recent British PMs and was intrigued by their predecessors. Here are the final paragraphs of an article that was, itself, the summing up of a series by various authors on British PMs that History Today *had run over previous months.*

In the course of two centuries, the type of British Prime Minister has been remarkably consistent. They have all been intelligent, well-meaning gentlemen, who have received very much the same kind of education and have intended to do very much the same sort of things. There has not been a bad man among them. They have wished to uphold the strength of Great Britain, to maintain the peace of Europe and to improve the condition of the people. It might be questioned whether the list includes a really great statesman. Among them there is certainly no Richelieu, no Cavour, no Bismarck. Perhaps there is hardly a Mazarin, a Metternich or a Masaryk.

But, if no figures of world importance have appeared on the British political stage during these two centuries, it may have been because there was no need for them. There were none of those prodigious tasks to be performed which we associate with the names mentioned in the previous paragraph. The United Kingdom was firmly united before the period begins; the Monarchy was securely established; religious controversy, despite remnants of intolerance, had ceased to present a political problem. The foundations of the Empire had been already laid by private enterprise, and its astounding growth and development occurred not thanks to our statesmen but in spite of them. The one problem that called for the exercise of high statesmanship was the settlement of relations between Great Britain and Ireland. Unhappily the statesman who shall settle that problem has yet to be found. It is possible that Pitt might have succeeded, if the conscience of King George III and the ambition of Napoleon had not prevented him. The former rendered abortive the measures of Catholic emancipation on which Pitt's policy was based, and the latter diverted his attention, and that of his colleagues, to the more important task of winning the war.

It is difficult to accomplish great things in politics without exercising great powers. Such powers have never been at the disposal of British Prime Ministers. The duration of their office is short and uncertain. Its continuance depends upon the goodwill of the House of Commons; and, although the House of Lords is sadly shorn of its powers, it can still prove a thorn in the flesh of a Prime Minister who does not please it. Opinion outside Parliament, rendered raucously vocal by the Press, has also to be taken into consideration and carefully studied between every move. The Prime Minister is only *primus inter pares*. He has, therefore, to carry his colleagues with him, and attempt to obtain unanimity in every decision. 'It doesn't matter much what we say,' Lord Melbourne observed in the days before Cabinet minutes were recorded, 'so long as we all say the same thing.' A divided Cabinet cannot long survive and may involve the whole Party in its ruin. Prime Ministers are usually well past middle age when they reach what Lord Beaconsfield irreverently called 'the top of the greasy pole,' and unlikely to embark upon any vast scheme the completion of which will require many years of toil. Nor does the age of leading politicians tend to diminish. Democratic institutions may open the road to talent; but it is a long, straight road, with none of those short cuts by which the aristocratic system of privilege used to enable youthful talent to find its way rapidly to the front. Perhaps experience and caution are more valuable ingredients in leadership than are energy, courage and vision.

When they come to review the two score men or so who have held this high office since it came into being, the people of Great Britain will have little cause for complaint. If genius is rare, talent is common; and the high level of mediocrity has been illuminated now and then by the personality of a Chatham, the eloquence of a Pitt, the wit of a Canning, the glitter of a Disraeli, the grand manner of a Gladstone, and the transcendent effulgence of a Winston Churchill. As for the rest, how fortunate are we to have been governed by these benevolent mediocrities, honest men doing their best for their fellows according to their lights, and to have been spared the experience of those so-called supermen, the Alexanders, the Caesars, the Genghis Khans, the Bonapartes, the Hitlers, the Stalins, who have done only evil on a gigantic scale and left the world more miserable than they found it!

*   *   *

Duff Cooper, 1st Viscount Norwich of Aldwick (1890–1954), was elected to Parliament as a Conservative (Unionist) in 1924 and served as Secretary of State for War, 1935–7 in the coalition cabinet. He was First Lord of the Admiralty 1937–8, resigning from the latter post in protest at the Munich Pact. After the outbreak of the Second World War he re-entered government serving as Minister of Information, 1940–1; Chancellor of the Duchy of Lancaster 1941–3; representative to the French Committee of National Liberation 1943–4 and Ambassador to France 1944–7. He was raised to the peerage in 1952. He was the author of several books including *Talleyrand* (1932), *Haig* (1935) and an autobiography *Old Men Forget* (1953).

5

Mme de Pompadour's Theatre

NANCY MITFORD

(August 1953)

Nancy Mitford, the popular and successful author of Love in a Cold Climate, *was researching a book about Mme de Pompadour when this charming article appeared.*

Versailles, in the eighteenth century, presented the cheerful spectacle of several thousand people living for pleasure and very much enjoying themselves. Pleasure, indeed, had an almost political significance, since the nobles, removed from their estates and drugged with useless privilege, had to be kept contented and amused.

The four main pastimes were love, gambling, hunting and the official entertainments. Love was played like a game, or like a comedy by Marivaux; it had, of course, nothing to do with marriage. Children, in those days, were married off in their teens, and these little husbands and wives usually grew up to be very fond of each other, sharing the same interests, absorbed in the family and its fortunes. Even if they did not like each other, which was rare, they could generally manage to get on, since good manners demanded that they should; it was quite unusual for a women to go back to her father or into a convent because she could not bear to live with her husband. She had a lover, he had a mistress; everything was most friendly. 'I allow you every latitude,' the courtiers used to say to their wives, 'except footmen and Princes of the Blood.' A husband, finding his wife in the arms of her lover: 'Madame! Is this prudent? Supposing somebody else had seen you!' Mademoiselle de Richelieu and the Comte de Gisors played together when they were very small and fell in love. When they were of marriageable age they so desperately wanted to marry each other that various sentimental relations tried to help them. It was a perfectly suitable match. But Gisors, though one of the paragons of that age, enormously rich and son of the powerful

Maréchal de Belle Ile, had bourgeois blood; he was the grandson of Fouquet. The Duc de Richelieu would not hear of such a connexion; he absolutely refused his consent to the marriage, saying coldly: 'If they are in love, they will find each other in society.'

The bourgeoisie of Paris did not see things with the same eye. The financier la Popeliniere discovered a revolving fireplace in his wife's bedroom by which the Duc de Richelieu used to come from the next door house and visit her. He turned her into the street there and then. The pretty creature went straight off to a race meeting which was going on near Paris, found Maréchals de Saxe and de Lowendal and persuaded them to take her home and use their influence with her husband. It was just after Fontenoy, and they were at the very height of their glory. But la Popeliniere was adamant, his door remained shut. Richelieu gave her a house and an income but she very soon died of cancer. At Versailles such tragic dramas were unheard of. Good manners – *bon ton* – prevailed in love as in everything else; the game must be played according to the rules. Gambling was a more savage pursuit; enormous fortunes were won and lost at the tables and, as in eighteenth-century England, everything was the subject of a bet. At the Queen's table, where they played the dowdy cavagnole with dice, it was possible to lose 200 louis (guineas) in an evening; at the King's table, where piquet and whist were played, 1,000 louis and more quite often changed hands, a huge sum in those days. As for the hunting, this existence would hardly have been possible without it. The men were properly exercised and properly fed; since man is, after all, an animal, he can rather easily be happy under these circumstances. It is the fashion now, among those who have never hunted, to regard it as a dull and cruel sport. Dull it is not; and for cruelty it cannot compare with the long awful journey to the gruesome slaughterhouse, against which no voice is ever raised. A day on horseback in the immeasurable forest, with its rides starring out, each ending in a blue distance, and its varying carpet of leaves and flowers: the smell of earth and horses, the cold rain on a warm face, the distant horn when the hunt seemed lost, the kill by a lake with wild swans circling overhead, the tunes, unchanged in those woods since Charlemagne, which the hunters play over the dead beast: the gathering cold and darkness of the ride home, the lighted warmth of the arrival, the relaxed nerves and physical well-being – these things once felt can never be forgotten. Louis XV, so delicate as a child that they hardly expected to rear him, grew up with iron health; he never felt tired. During the thirty years of his prime he killed the enormous average of 210 stags a year, without counting wolves and wild boar. His huntsman, Lasmartre, was a privileged being who could say what he liked to the King. 'The King treats me well,' said the Maréchal de Saxe, 'but he doesn't talk more to me than to Lasmartre.' After killing two stags one day the King said:

'Lasmartre, are the horses tired?'

'Yes, Sire, they're just about finished.'

'And the hounds?'

'Tired? I should say they were.'

'All right, Lasmartre. I'll be hunting again the day after tomorrow.' Silence. 'Did you hear me, Lasmartre? The day after tomorrow.'

'Yes, Sire, I heard you the first time.' Loud aside: 'It's always the same thing, he asks if the animals are tired, he never thinks of the men.'

One of his keepers calculated that in one year Louis XV covered 8,100 miles on horseback, on foot, or in a calèche. If the hunting had to be put off because of hard frost, he would go for a three-hour gallop, regardless of the horse's legs. He was also fond of partridge shooting, and an excellent shot.

The palace entertainments were organized by the Duc de Richelieu who, as First Gentleman of the Bedchamber, had *Les Menus Plaisirs* under his direct control; they were always the same and had hardly varied for fifty years. Twice a week theatre, the *Comédie Italienne* and the *Comédie Française*; and on special occasions, such as a royal wedding or birth or the celebration of a victory, there were ballets, balls and fireworks. They were all well done, but there was no originality and no surprise; except for the balls, they did not much amuse the King. He was a restless man who loved change and novelty.

Soon after her arrival at Versailles Madame de Pompadour, always thinking how best to amuse and interest him and keep off the yellow colour which meant that he was bored, decided to get up private theatricals among their little set of close friends. She herself, having been taught to sing by Jeliothe of the Comédie Française, and to speak alexandrines by Crébillon, the old dramatist, was well known to be one of the best amateur actresses in France; and she was certainly not averse from showing off her talent to the King. All her friends received the idea with enthusiasm. Everybody enjoys private theatricals. Choosing the play, distributing the parts, the rehearsals, the dressing up, the gossip, the jokes and even the quarrels involved, give rise to all sorts of diversions; the whole thing is fun. Though they had never been held at Court before, they were a favourite amusement of the age; when people were exiled from Versailles, or ruined, or for some other sad reason obliged to go and live on their estates, the first thing they always did, even before adding a modicum of comfort to some old, semi-ruined château which had not been lived in for years, was to build a theatre. King Stanislas had a famous theatre at Lunéville; so had Maréchal de Saxe at Chambord; and so, later on, after his disgrace, had the Duc de Choiseul at Chanteloup. Almost every educated person could act, or play a musical instrument; even in the depth of the provinces enough neighbours could usually be found to form an orchestra capable of playing light opera. When Madame de Pompadour began looking for talent among courtiers of the King's set, she found that they could nearly all act or dance, some could also sing and play some instrument and many of them had musical servants.

A tiny theatre, holding an audience of fourteen, was now built, under the supervision of the Marquise, in a gallery which led to the Cabinet des Médailles, and decorated by Pérot and Boucher. Perronet designed the costumes and Notrelle the wigs. Rehearsals took place at Choisy, in deep secret, even the King not being allowed to attend; and in a remarkably short time the curtain went up on the first of the many plays to be produced in the Théâtre des Petits Cabinets: *Tartuffe*, on January 17th, 1747. The King was so excited for it that he came home from hunting before he had killed his stag; its foot arrived in the middle of the entr'acte.

Madame de Pompadour issued a set of rules for her troupe, which she and the King drew up together:

1. Nobody may join the Society who is not an experienced actor. Beginners are not admitted.
2. It is forbidden to change parts without the consent of all the other members of the Society.
3. Each person will state in what capacity he or she is joining.
4. In case of absence the absentee may not choose a substitute, this to be done by the other members of the Society.
5. The absentee goes back to his original job on his return.
6. Nobody may refuse a part because it is unflattering or tiring.

These six rules apply to actors and actresses alike.

7. Works to be acted will be chosen by the actresses.
8. They will fix the date of the performance, as well as the number, the day and the hour of the rehearsals.
9. The actors will arrive punctually at the rehearsals, subject to a fine for lateness to be imposed by the actresses.
10. The actresses will be allowed half an hour's grace; if later than that they will be subject to a fine which they themselves will fix.

Madame de Pompadour also laid it down that an author could go to the rehearsals only if his play was being given for the first time. The author of an established play was, however, always invited to the performance.

On January 24th two more plays were given, *Le Préjugé à la Mode* by la Chaussée and *l'Esprit de Contradiction* by Dufresny. After that there was a new play every other week until the 'season' ended on April 17th. In all these plays Madame de Pompadour took the chief woman's part; she was acknowledged to be far better than the other women, though some of the men were up to professional standards. While nearly every inhabitant of Versailles was passionately anxious to get somehow, by hook or by crook, an invitation to Madame de Pompadour's theatre, the Marquise herself was longing for the presence of the one person who would not spring forward when she lifted her little finger: the Queen, the dowdy, sleepy Queen, impervious to fashion and charm. She knew all about the theatre because Moncrif was always showing her little odds and ends he wrote for it. 'Very nice to be sure,' she said at last, 'and now, Moncrif, that's enough.' She was very kind and polite to Madame de Pompadour, who continued to pay her court most punctiliously, although it must often have bored and tired her to do so. The outward appearances were thus perfectly maintained; but the Marquise wanted more than that; she really seems to have wanted, in her affectionate bourgeois way, to be looked upon as one of the family. In the end, it must be said that she succeeded, but these were early days, and tactful and clever as she generally was, she started off by making a curious mistake. She saw that the Queen's happiness, interest and occupation was in her religion, and she thought a good way to approach her would be by showing an interest in the life of the Chapel.

Now Madame de Pompadour was totally irreligious; that is to say, she was not one of those who, believing in God, and understanding the protocol with which He is surrounded, are kept away by some weakness of the flesh; she simply did not understand the meaning of religion. All her life she behaved with an extraordinary denseness where anything to do with the Church was concerned. The first step she took towards a greater intimacy with the Queen was to ask if she could assist at the ceremony, on Maundy Thursday, when the Queen and fifteen ladies of the Court washed the feet of poor little girls. How could she have expected the Queen to allow this? The answer was kind but firm: there were enough ladies already to wash the feet: the Marquise would have the merit of her wish without the inconvenience of its fulfilment. Nothing daunted, Madame de Pompadour had another idea. Why should she not take round the plate on Easter Sunday? (This was a function reserved for particularly holy Duchesses.) She set about it rather differently. 'Everybody tells me,' she said to the Duchesse de Luynes, the Queen's lady-in-waiting, 'that I am expected to take round the plate on Sunday.' Madame de Luynes went with this news to her mistress, who said that she supposed even the King would hardly think Madame de Pompadour a very suitable choice, and quickly named Madame de Castries. Madame de Luynes, a thoroughly nice person, was always smoothing out matters between Madame de Pompadour and the Queen. When the Court was about to leave for Fontainebleau, Madame de Pompadour asked if she could travel in the Queen's coach, a suggestion that was ill received. It was an enormous honour at Versailles to travel with the King or the Queen. Madame de Luynes, instead of inflaming the Queen against her, as so many people would have done, pointed out that Madame de Pompadour would not ask for such a thing unless the King wanted it. She said, privately, to her husband that it must be remembered how nice the Marquise always was to the Queen. Finally, she almost forced her mistress to say that the coaches were quite full, but that, if one of the ladies were to drop out, Madame de Pompadour would be given her place. Eventually this very thing happened; the Queen accepted her company with a good grace and even invited her to dinner before starting.

The Queen was not at all ill disposed towards Madame de Pompadour, quite the contrary; she could not, of course, allow her to take part in the religious life at Versailles, but the theatre was a different affair.

The enthusiastic players went from strength to strength; soon they began to long for a bigger stage and more numerous audience. In 1748, while the Court was away at Fontainebleau, a theatre was constructed in the well of the Ambassador's Staircase which led to the state rooms in the north wing. As this staircase had to be used twice a year for certain diplomatic functions, as well as for a procession of the *Cordons Bleu* (knights of the *Saint Esprit*), the theatre was made in movable sections; it could be taken down in fourteen hours and put up again in twelve. There is a gouache by Cochin of this little blue and silver theatre; Madame de Pompadour and the Vicomte de Rohan hold the stage; they are singing in the opera *Acis et Galatée*, the Marquise in a huge skirt of white taffeta embroidered with reeds, shells and fountains, a bodice of palest pink and green gauzy draperies. The King and his friends in the auditorium are all holding copies of the libretto; in the orchestra the Prince de Dombes can be seen, the *Saint Esprit* on his bosom, puffing into a big bassoon. Many ambitious works were given there during the next year, with great success where comedy was concerned, though the King was apt to yawn rather at tragedy. After a play called *Le Prince de Noisy* in which Madame de Pompadour, dressed as Prince Charming – but very decently, not showing more leg than in a riding habit – had played the title rôle, the King, least demonstrative of men, kissed her in front of everybody and said 'you are the most delicious woman in France.'

Things were not always so rosy, however. During a performance of *Tancrède* the King received the news that, on his orders most reluctantly given, Prince Charles Edward had been arrested outside the Opera in Paris and taken to Vincennes. Charles Stewart was a hero to the French, as well as an honoured guest, and that evening was spoilt for everybody. Then there was the dreadful day when the Prince de Dombes downed his big bassoon and killed M. de Coigny, one of their very best actors, in a duel. Coigny was the King's greatest friend. He was told the news at his *lever*, immediately cancelled the hunt and went straight to the Marquise; when he came away, his eyes were red with weeping. The Prince de Dombes was really not to blame; Coigny had lost a lot of money to him, lost his temper and said 'only a bastard could be so lucky.' This was a bit too near the knuckle, as Dombes was a grandson of Louis XIV and Madame de Montespan. He said nothing at the time; but, when the party broke up, he whispered to Coigny that he would be by the river below Passy at the *point du jour*. The place where they met has been called that ever since. Forthcoming performances in the little theatre were cancelled, and Madame de Pompadour had migraine for a week.

Soon after this a strong smell of musk in the King's rooms indicated that Son Excellence (Richelieu) was back from the wars, with a *baton* in his hand, Marshal of France. He was in particularly high favour with the King because he had succeeded in conquering Parma, an establishment that would do very well for Madame Infante, until something better should turn up. She had really wanted a throne; but anything was better than being the wife of a younger son at the Spanish court. While he was away, the Marquise had been writing very friendly little notes to Richelieu: 'I look forward so much to your return, do let it be as soon as possible,' and so on; perhaps she thought he would now feel better disposed towards her. She was soon to be undeceived. Richelieu was First Gentleman of the Bedchamber; and, by all the rights of Court usage, the *Théâtre des Petits Cabinets* should have been directly under his control, first of all because he was responsible for the palace entertainments and the department of '*Les Menus*,' and secondly, because the Ambassador's Staircase was part of the state rooms, which were also his department. The Duc d'Aumont, who had been First Gentleman during his absence, had always been perfectly agreeable when furniture, carriages, costumes, chandeliers, stage jewellery, and a thousand and one other properties were borrowed from the warehouse of *Les Menus* by the Marquise and her producer, the Duc de la Vallière. On one occasion, he did query a bill. Madame de Pompadour went to the King, who sanctioned it at once, but remarked, 'Just you wait until Son Excellence gets back; things will be very different then.' He was perfectly right. Richelieu had not been in the palace twenty-four hours before he wrote a strong letter to the King, protesting against the abuses which M. de la Vallière had introduced while his back was turned. The King did not reply.

Richelieu then struck. He gave orders that no properties were to be taken from *Les Menus,* that none of their workmen, or musicians, were to be employed, by anybody whomsoever, without a chit signed by himself. The musicians, who received this warning on their way to a rehearsal, rushed to his office to ask for further instructions; they were plainly told that they must work no more for Madame de Pompadour. M. de la Vallière then went round to protest; the terrible Duke merely made a gesture which indicated that, as indeed everybody knew already, he was very friendly with Madame de la Vallière. The Marquise now entered the fray. What she said to the King is not known; but that evening, while his hunting boots were being pulled off by Son Excellence, the King asked him how many times he had been to the Bastille? 'Three times, Sire.' That was all, but it was enough. The Duke was obliged to take the hint and to reverse the orders he had given. He said to the Duc de Luynes, who was always so much occupied with questions of Court usage, that, of course, the offices of state would lose all their meaning if abuses like this were allowed to creep in – it had been his duty to protest – he had protested – Madame de Pompadour was the mistress – no more to be said. Meanwhile this accomplished courtier had been all the time in the company of Madame de Pompadour and her troupe, at his most delightful, covering them with compliments, laughing, joking, and telling stories of his campaign. He had been particularly cordial with M. de la Vallière. His manner never changed in defeat, and nobody unaware of the truth could have guessed that anything was going on behind the scenes. The King, however, thinking that the Duc de la Vallière had been rather badly treated, consoled him with the *Cordon Bleu* at Candlemas.

The Théâtre des Petits Cabinets went on for five years, after which it became too much for Madame de Pompadour and she gave it up. During this time, 122 performances, in all, were given of sixty-one different plays, operas and ballets. They were rehearsed until they could not be improved: even the most acid critics of the Marquise were obliged to admit that never did any performance fall below first-class professional standards, and that she herself was perfection in all of them. This venture had two important consequences for her. It consolidated her position at Court; even so mighty a nobleman as the Duc de Richelieu was forced to agree that he had met his match, while the other courtiers had to go on their knees to her if they wanted invitations to the plays. People became almost hysterical in their efforts to be given the smallest walk-on part, to be allowed to play in the orchestra or to see the performances; they even bribed Madame du Hausset, her maid, who thus obtained a very good job for her nephew, with the knowledge and amused consent of the Marquise.

On the other hand, the great unpopularity with the Parisians, from which she suffered for the rest of her life, began at this time. Hated by the crowd at Versailles because she was a bourgeoise, Madame de Pompadour was soon hated by the bourgeoisie because of her association with the government, in other words the tax collectors. The theatre was merely a convenient peg on which to hang their grievances. It was said to be an unjustified extravagance; taxes were high; there was a good deal of misery; and ridiculously inflated stories of expenditure were bandied about the capital. The temporary theatre in the staircase was supposed to have cost thousands. It must be remembered, too, that in those days plays and players were considered slightly immoral. The great Molière himself had almost been refused Christian burial because he had once been an actor; many priests would not give them the sacrament – the *Comédie Italienne* had special dispensation which made the *Comédie Française* very angry – and the pious Dauphin signed himself with the Cross whenever he passed a theatre. D'Angerville says that, in imitation of the Marquise, 'the whole of France now took a taste for the stage, princes and bourgeois alike; it penetrated even into the convents and finished by poisoning the morals of quantities of children who were brought up to this profession. In short, it carried corruption to its extreme limits.' It was not true, the taste had existed already, but it was convenient to blame Madame de Pompadour for it. From now on she could not do right in the eyes of the general public.

* * *

Nancy Mitford (1904–73), sister of Unity and Jessica, came from a remarkable family – the granddaughter of Gibson Bowles, creator of *Vanity Fair* and the first Baron Redesdale, an intimate friend of Edward VII. She was educated in her father's inherited library, he having refused to send her to boarding school, deeming the formal education of his daughters unnecessary. Leaving home at the age of twenty-four, Mitford stayed in the London flat of Evelyn Waugh and took to writing for *Vogue* and *Harper's Magazine*. Her first novel, *Highland Fling*, was published in 1934. Her fifth, *The Pursuit of Love* (1945), sold over a million copies and made her fortune, but she became even more famous for *Love in a Cold Climate* (and the invention of 'U' and 'Non-U' speech). *Madame de Pompadour*, of which this article is a precursor, was her first and liveliest biography.

6

The Course of German History

JAMES JOLL

(September 1953)

James Joll explains the radically differing preconceptions that British and German historians bring to their study of German history – a valuable corrective at a time when it was all too easy for the British to generalise about 'the Germans' and feel superior to their recent enemy.

The study of foreign history presents particular problems, and nowhere more than in the case of Germany. Yet German history has a curious attraction: the more so because of its impact on our lives. The spectacle of the physical and moral collapse of a highly organized society in 1945 was an unforgettable one, and must have drawn many people, as it did the present writer, into an attempt at historical explanation. It was not only the Third Reich which had collapsed; many of the foundations of the Bismarckian Empire had crumbled. The industrial centres of Germany were at a standstill. The territorial divisions between the traditional states of Germany were being replaced by the boundaries between the lines of advance of the victorious Allied armies; vast areas in the East were being cut off and their populations expelled. If anything could be called the end of an epoch, it seemed to be this.

Yet in fact more survived the collapse than at the time one thought possible. The course of German history continues with one more catastrophe added to a long list. To understand contemporary Western Germany one has to go back beyond 1945, beyond Hitler and even beyond Bismarck, and to understand political events one has also to understand traditional psychological attitudes. One has, to take an example again from 1945, to reconcile the picture of a nation capable of the concentration camps and the destruction of the Jewish people with that of a number of simple and industrious individuals piecing together with amazing patience and skill some kind of life amid the ruins of their cities and the destruction of their homes. Here is a challenge to the historian's psychological insight as well as to his specifically historical skill.

One of the main difficulties that any historian has in writing about the history of another country is that he has to assess what parts of past history live on as emotive forces in the lives of later generations. As Heinrich von Treitschke put it: 'He who wishes to count the age of a people should not count the years of its history: the profounder question will lead him more surely to his goal – which part of the past is still living as history in the soul of the people?' Many of the actions of the citizens of any nation are governed by beliefs about that nation's past. One of the problems of writing history, therefore, is to see what these 'living parts' of history are at any given moment. It is not the considered judgments of historians that are important in this connection but the hazy recollections of history as taught at school or commemorated in popular literature. Out of these pictures – Hermann in the Teutoburgerwald, Henry IV at Canossa, or, in England, the landing of the Normans at Hastings or the Barons forcing King John to sign the Magna Carta at Runnymede – the general picture of the past that influences political action is formed. One of the problems for a foreign historian, therefore, even if he is only concerned with a modern period, is to understand what the rudimentary, often half-formed beliefs about the past are that influence the conduct of the ordinary man. How does a nation look at its own history?

The point can perhaps be illustrated by considering some of the differences between the way the ordinary English man-in-the-street looks at his own national history and the way the ordinary German seems to look at his. Two points stand out immediately. First, the Englishman necessarily has a far greater feeling for the continuity of his history than the German. There is in England the sense of a continuous political development 'broadening down from precedent to precedent,' and embodied in the English Common Law or in the unwritten usages of the British Constitution. There are few cataclysms in English history. Even the Civil War in the seventeenth century left scars that were quickly healed. There are only a few periods (the fifteenth century is one of them) where the ordinary man tends to lose the thread of a continuous constitutional and political development. The great tradition of English historical writing from Macaulay to G.M. Trevelyan has done much to foster this way of looking at things. Views about the goal of this historical development will, of course, vary with the political convictions of the individual writer or reader; the important thing for our purpose is that English history can be, and often is, represented as a continuous story of development leading to – whatever you like, universal suffrage, the British Commonwealth of Nations, or the victory of the Labour Party in 1945.

German history is regarded by Germans very differently. Instead of a continuous steady development culminating, say, in Bismarck or Hitler, there is, from the period of the Ottonian Emperors onwards, a series of catastrophes, of political failures, where a great achievement was snatched from the German people by a cruel fate (like the early death of Henry VI in 1197), or by the ill will of the French, or the Catholic church, or of conspirators inside Germany itself. Again and again, from Frederick Barbarossa in the twelfth century until Freiherr vom Stein in the nineteenth, the German people on the verge of a great historical achievement have fallen back into anarchy, confusion and reaction. Inevitably these disasters tend to be attributed to outside influences, such as the secular hostility of the French, or to a recurrent bunch of traitors who give a stab in the back – a *Dolchstoss* – to the German nation on the eve of triumph. There is room for differing interpretations of these events, but the pattern of rise and fall, growth and decay, is more striking and more cataclysmic than that presented by the history of any other European people.

This, then, is the first point that strikes an English student of Germany. While the Englishman can admire the continuity of his own history, the German looks back over centuries of hopes disappointed and achievements unfulfilled, ascents towards dizzy peaks of political power and falls back into abysses of confusion and barbarity like the Interregnum at the beginning of the thirteenth century or the Thirty Years War in the seventeenth century. I am not, of course, saying that these ways of looking at the respective courses of English and German history are correct, but I want to suggest that these are perhaps the ways in which his nation's past appears to the ordinary man in each country.

But there is another difficulty which confronts an Englishman trying to understand the way in which a German looks at his own national history. Geographically, England has been a unit since the early Middle Ages; the commitments of the medieval English kings in Normandy, Aquitaine or Gascony, the gradual union first with Wales then with Scotland, even the perennial unresolved Irish Question, do not stop one looking at English history as the history of an island with recognizable frontiers and a continuous geographical existence. Here again German history lacks a continuity which English history has. Again and again Germans complain that theirs is a land with no natural frontiers. In the East are the Slav lands and the interminable plains of Poland and Russia. Many times, from the Teutonic Knights to Hitler's armies, the Germans have tried by force to extend their boundaries in the East and on each occasion the lack of natural frontiers, the boundless nature of the task have proved too much for them. In the West, too, the boundaries have changed; once the old Middle Kingdom of Lorraine and Burgundy had disappeared, the valley of the Rhine became an object of struggle between Germany and France. In the period of the French revolution for instance, France was to claim the Rhine as her 'natural frontier,' while in the romantic enthusiasm for the German national cause that was born during the Napoleonic wars, the Rhine was to be '*Deutchlands Strom nicht Deutchlands Grenze.*' (Germany's river, not Germany's frontier – a famous phrase of E.M. Arndt's.) Even in the south, the Alps, in appearance the most solid of natural barriers, have not sufficed. The Italian policy of the Hohenstaufen Emperors, the dynastic ambitions of the Habsburgs, the Rome-Berlin axis have constantly involved German incursions into Lombardy. And this lack of natural boundaries makes German history in many of its periods hard to define and hard to supply with any geographical continuity; you start to write the history of Germany and before you know where you are you are writing the history of south-east Europe or of Italy.

It is not only the lack of external geographical boundaries, however, that makes German history confusing to an outsider. There is also the fact that for a great part of the time 'Germany' was only a loose geographical expression with little political meaning, while from 1648 until the nineteenth century the history of Germany is the history of '*Kleinstaaterei*' where the historian is dealing with a very large number of individual states with little or no coherence. During the eighteenth century German history seems to become the story of the decline of one great power, Austria, and the rise of another, Prussia. With the emergence of this dualism in Germany and the beginning of a struggle for supremacy, we enter on the last and most exciting phase of German history. The point I want to make here is that, in addition to the lack of firm frontiers, the lack of any internal political cohesion makes the course of German history liable to different interpretations. While in England we have, with some exceptions, tended to regard our political history as developing continuously right up to the present time in what we can call a liberal, Protestant, and secular direction, it is possible to see in Germany two rival traditions, the one north German and Protestant, the other Austrian or south German and Catholic.

There is also another and perhaps more important difficulty that confronts the foreign student of German history. This is the whole question of the standpoint from which history is written, of the basic presuppositions of the philosophy of history on which a History of Germany is to be founded. There are very roughly two ways of looking at history: the one to attempt to collect what is known about the past quite dispassionately into a connected narrative that will give an account '*wie es eigentlich gewesen ist*', to quote a celebrated phrase of Ranke (as it actually happened). The other sees history as a vast but predictable process – an '*ewiges Werden*' (perpetual development) – whose course it is important to understand so as to be sure of being carried along on its main stream and not being borne aside by an eddy into a back-water. German historiography can show plenty of examples of the first sort of historical writing. Ranke himself is a splendid example, though even he admitted in 1870 'it would be impossible to have no opinion in the decisive struggles of power and ideas, yet the essence of impartiality can be preserved.' But it seems to me that the other trend is dominant in much of German historical writing, a trend that began with Hegel.

According to Hegel and his followers, including, of course, Karl Marx, the future course of history, or at least the way things are going, can be ascertained, and the important task for the historian is to point out what the prevailing trends are, just as the important task for the statesman is to see that he is going in the right direction in accordance with the laws governing historical development. The worst crime a statesman can commit, on this view, is to fail, for such failure is what is called 'flying in the face of history' – a futile attempt to evade the inexorable laws of history seen as a dialectical process. The causes that finally emerge triumphant are the ones that it was right to support; they are justified by history whatever incidental human suffering and distress they may have caused. This doctrine has had a particular influence on the Germans' view of their own history, and this is perhaps due to some of the factors already mentioned, especially to the idea of recurrent collapse and catastrophe that seems to haunt the earlier, and now, I suppose one must also say, the later epochs of German history.

During the latter half of the eighteenth century the great flowering of the German genius began. In philosophy, poetry and science the Germans occupied a place in European culture that had been theirs at no previous period. And, simultaneously with this, the old political structure of Germany was shattered by the impact of the French revolution and Napoleon. The old Holy Roman Empire vanished in 1806; the territorial arrangements of Germany were much simplified, and many of the smallest states and the ecclesiastical principalities disappeared. Even the Prussia of Frederick the Great was shaken to its foundations at Jena and needed a period of radical reform to recover. It was out of this combination of cultural superiority and political collapse that a new attitude to German development was born. Cultural eminence was not enough: the old decayed political organizations in Germany must be replaced by something new, grander and more powerful. At first many people held that the achievement of a German national state would be accompanied by the growth of liberal institutions. These hopes were largely shattered in 1848; yet another failure of political achievement was added to the list. Many German liberals were now prepared to abandon all the other items in their political creed in order to achieve national political unity.

The place of Bismarck in German historical writing is the best example of the way of looking at German history which I have tried to suggest. Bismarck was the 'world-historical individual' able to master the forces of history and ride along with them to his goal, the statesman who, to use his own phrase, listened to God's footstep resounding through events and then caught the hem of his mantle. The liberals, or most of them were prepared to forgive him for his contempt for the Prussian constitution in the years before the victorious wars of 1864 and 1866, and to forget the unscrupulousness of his political methods and the ruthlessness he showed towards his opponents. He was the one man who had finally achieved German unity, who had met with success where so many had failed. Germany at last seemed destined for a powerful and glorious future. The lack of clear boundaries, from which it had seemed that German development was perpetually to suffer, had at length been remedied. For Bismarck, by a self-imposed renunciation, had decided on a *kleindeutsch* (little German) solution of the German question – a deliberate limitation of Germany's frontiers so as to exclude Bohemia, German Austria and an indeterminate commitment of Germany's resources in south-east Europe. At the same time, it seemed that the particularism that had so often crippled German development was at last overcome. Prussia had not merged in Germany as had been hoped in 1848, but Germany was unified under Prussian leadership. No wonder that Bismarck should have achieved such pre-eminence in subsequent German historiography that a German historian, writing his life during the Second World War, could say in his introduction 'The book, composed in hard times, constitutes my contribution to the national effort during the War.'

But both the manner of Bismarck's success and the way in which it was regarded in German history has had its dangers. To quote Friedrich Meinecke: 'Today we must admit that in the brilliance of the achievement we saw too little the hidden dark points where it was vulnerable and where disease might later set in.' The whole notion of a '*Realpolitik*' which Bismarck embodied, the idea that reasons of state absolved their practitioners from the ordinary demands of traditional personal morality, could lead to terrible disaster. 'It is the lees left by Bismarck that still foul the cup,' Sir Edward Grey remarked of international diplomacy in 1906. The notion that, to quote Bismarck himself, 'Austria and Prussia are states too great to allow themselves to be bound by the text of treaties,' though by no means peculiar to German diplomacy, was to have a poisonous influence on international relations. The idea that basic right could be suspended, and constitutional provisions ignored or circumvented, was to have an even more disastrous effect on German internal development. Ruthlessness began to be condoned because it was successful, treachery, like that recorded in Kleist's *Hermannschlacht*, approved if it served the national cause. The only crime was failure: and the outside observer cannot help feeling that there are still many people in Germany who think that this was the only offence of which Hitler was guilty.

I want to suggest in the above argument that Bismarck's success in solving the German problem – a significant phrase, by the way, that recurs constantly in the title of books about Germany but not in books about England and France: we do not talk about the French problem or the English problem – did three things. First, it encouraged people to overlook the weaknesses, moral and political, of Bismarck's achievement. Second, it could easily be interpreted in terms of the Hegelian theory of history and of the state, and thus at last give a culminating point to the broken and disjointed course of German history. Finally, it seemed to give a firm territorial foundation to the new Germany. The real disaster in what followed was that the first two factors remained, while the latter was lost after Bismarck's departure. *Realpolitik* and the belief in Germany as a dynamic nation with a boundless destiny were joined at the turn of the century, for a variety of reasons, economic, social and psychological, by a refusal to accept the Bismarckian territorial settlement. A spirit of ill-defined but limitless ambition took possession of Germany – desire for '*Weltpolitik*,' desire for a '*Drang nach Osten*,' desire for '*Lebensraum*'; and this time, both before 1914 and before 1939, the most formidable economic and military forces were at the disposal of the German state.

It is thus, in fact, difficult for non-Germans to see German history as Germans see it both because of the differences – geographical and political – that distinguish German history from that of other countries, and because the theories that Germans have held about the nature and course of history have themselves influenced outside observers, but inversely. That is to say that, because the Germans often seem to regard themselves as having a particular world-historical role, a special place in some pre-ordained historical dialectical process, foreigners for their part tend to regard the Germans as a consistently wicked and incorrigible race. There are many writers (sometimes themselves of German origin) who trace a consistent line of development from the Germans of Tacitus through Luther and Frederick the Great to Hitler, showing that, at each stage, the Germans were guilty of the same crimes of cruelty, treachery and aggression. Obviously any *a priori* interpretation of this kind will be as wrong as one based on the assumption that the Germans consistently were right, and all other people wrong, and that, when they did fail, it was not due to their own shortcomings but to the machinations of their enemies – the French, the Jews or the Pope.

The real difficulty that an Englishman has, in writing about Germany, is that he, too, has to divest himself of pre-suppositions and see each situation with fresh eyes. As one looks back over any period of history, it is always too easy to regard what actually happened as the inevitable consequence of what went before. The problem for the historian is to explain the dilemmas that actually confronted men in the past, and not to neglect alternative courses because they were not, in fact, ultimately taken. One must not, for example, condemn from an English liberal standpoint the German liberals of the 1860's until one is really clear what the alternatives before them were – on the one hand, support for Bismarck and a national state, where one day they might perhaps be able to introduce the parliamentary government and the liberal safeguards of human rights in which they believed: on the other hand, the petty dynastic politics of the small states or, in Prussia, a perpetual struggle with the whole machinery of the Prussian state in which the liberals, like the social-democrats of a later generation, would finally be forced to give in to the possessors of armed force. There are many prejudices, too, which an English writer will have to get rid of. If, for example, we condemn Prussian militarism and at the same time criticize the work of Bismarck, we must remember, as Professor Namier has reminded us, that it was members of the Prussian ruling class who in 1871 were the fiercest critics of Bismarck's policy, just as it was members of the Prussian military class who were prepared to undertake, however unsuccessfully, the one overt act of resistance to Hitler – the attempted *putsch* of July 1944. Equally, it is too easy to forget that it is among the Prussians that, from the time of Lassalle onwards, the Left has been strongest in Germany, while it is among the southerners – Bavarians and Austrians – in general noted for good temper and *Gemütlichkeit,* that the most dangerous doctrines of German expansion and racial persecution have often been born.

English misconceptions about the Germans are as numerous as German misconceptions about the English. And the difficulty for an Englishman who wants to study German history lies in the ambivalence of the relations between our two peoples. During the last 150 years there have been English people who have been filled with the warmest uncritical admiration for every aspect of German life, and others who have abhorred it. Germans, too, have wavered between the extremes of Anglophobia and Anglomania – and often felt both at once, as in the case of the Emperor William II.

An English historian writing about Germany, therefore, has to analyse his own prejudices as well as understand the Germans' prejudices about their own past. Perhaps the task is too difficult; but it has to be tried if any serious study of German history is to be undertaken in this country.

*   *   *

James Joll (1918–94) was educated at Winchester, the University of Bordeaux and New College, Oxford. He taught at Oxford, Harvard, Stanford, Tokyo and Princeton and later became Stevenson Professor of International History at the University of London from 1967 to 1981 (thereafter Professor Emeritus). His career as a leading historian of Western Europe since the French Revolution was marked by his rejection of the purely conventional. In the 1960s, he was the first to introduce English-language readers to the work of the German historian, Fritz Fischer, and his revisionist theories about German aims in the First World War. In *The Anarchists* (1964), Joll argued that failure was as legitimate a topic for historical research as success. Joll was one of the few historians of his time to integrate social and cultural insights into an understanding of more traditional fields like political or military history. *Europe Since 1870* (1973), one of his last books, was arguably the most important and widely read.

7

Be Kind to King George III

SIR LEWIS NAMIER

(September 1953)

Sir Lewis Namier has a reputation as a somewhat dry and difficult historian whose expertise and legacy lay in his ant-like devotion to detail. These extracts from his elegant defence of George III reveal a warmer, more human side.

There were three large pictures of George III at the exhibition of Royal Portraits arranged by the Academy of Arts in the Spring of 1953. Looking at the first, by Reynolds, painted when the King was 41, I was struck by the immaturity of expression. The second, by Lawrence, painted in 1792 at the age of 54, depicts him in Garter robes; face and posture seem to attempt in a naïve, ineffective, and almost engaging manner to live up to a grandeur which the sitter feels incumbent on him. The third, by Stroehling, painted in November 1807, at the age of nearly 70, shows a sad old man, looking dimly at a world in which he has no pleasure, and which he soon will not be able to see or comprehend.

A picture in a different medium of the King and his story presents itself to the student when in the Royal Archives at Windsor he surveys the papers of George III. They stand on the shelves in boxes, each marked on a white label with the year or years which it covers. The eye runs over that array, and crucial dates recall events: 1760, '65 and '67, '74 and '75, '82 and '83, 1789, '93, '96, 1802, 1805 – the series breaks off in 1810; and brown-backed volumes follow, unlabelled: they contain the medical reports on a man shut off from time, which means the world and its life.

Fate had made George III ruler when kings were still expected to govern; and his active reign covered half a century during which the American conflict posed the problem of Imperial relations, while at home political practice constantly ran up against the contradiction inherent in the then much belauded 'mixed form of government': personal monarchy served by Ministers whose tenure of office was contested in Parliament.

Neither the Imperial nor the constitutional problem could have been solved in the terms in which the overwhelming majority of the politically-minded public in this country considered them at the time; but George III has been blamed ever since for not having thought of Dominion status and parliamentary government when constitutional theory and the facts of the situation as yet admitted of neither.

In the catalogue, *Kings and Queens,* on sale at the exhibition, the introduction dealing with the reign of George III gave the traditional view of his reign:

> Conscientious and ambitious, he tried to restore the political influ-ence of the Crown, but his intervention ended with the humiliating American War of Independence.

Conscientious he certainly was, painstakingly, almost painfully, conscien-tious. But was he ambitious? Did he try to exercise powers which his pre-decessors had relinquished, or claim an influence which was not universally conceded to him? And was it the assertion of Royal, and not of Parliamentary, authority over America which brought on the conflict and disrupted the First British Empire?

Let us place ourselves in March 1782. Dismal, humiliating failure has turned public opinion, and the House of Commons is resolved to cut losses and abandon the struggle; it is all over; Lord North's government has fallen; and the King is contemplating abdication. He has drafted a message to Parliament (which was never sent); here are its first two paragraphs:

> His Majesty during the twenty-one years he has sate on the throne of Great Britain, has had no object so much at heart as the maintain-ance of the British Constitution, of which the difficulties he has at times met with from his scrupulous attachment to the rights of Parliament are sufficient proofs.
>
> His Majesty is convinced that the sudden change of sentiments of one branch of the legislature has totally incapacitated him from either conducting the war with effect, or from obtaining any peace but on conditions which would prove destructive to the commerce as well as essential rights of the British nation.

In the first paragraph the King declares his unswerving devotion to the British Constitution, and shows himself conscious of his difficulties in America having arisen through 'his scrupulous attachment to the rights of Parliament'; the second paragraph pointedly refers to the Commons as 'one branch of the legislature,' and gives the King's view of the American war: he is defending there the vital interests and essential rights of the British nation.

A year later, in March 1783, when faced by the necessity of accepting a Government formed by the Fox-North coalition, George III once more contemplated abdication; and in a letter (which again was never sent) he wrote to the Prince of Wales:

> The situation of the times are such that I must, if I attempt to carry on the business of the nation, give up every political principle on which I have acted, which I should think very unjustifiable, as I have always attempted to act agreable to my duty; and must form a Ministry from among men who know I cannot trust them and therefore who will not accept office without making me a kind of slave; this undoubtedly is a cruel dilemma, and leaves me but one step to take without the destruction of my principles and honour; the resigning my Crown, my dear Son to you, quitting this my native country for ever and returning to the dominions of my forefathers.
>
> Your difficulties will not be the same. You have never been in a situation to form any political system, therefore, are open to adopt what the times may make necessary; and no set of men can ever have offended you or made it impossible for you to employ them.

Alongside this consider the following passage from a letter which George III wrote on December 29th, 1783, after having dismissed the Coalition and while he was trying to rally support for the newly-formed Administration of the younger Pitt:

> The times are of the most serious nature, the political struggle is not as formerly between two factions for power; but it is no less than whether a desperate faction shall not reduce the Sovereign to a mere tool in its hands: though I have too much principle ever to infringe the rights of others, yet that must ever equally prevent my submitting to the Executive power being in any other hands, than where the Constitution has placed it. I therefore must call on the assistance of every honest man . . . to support Government on the present most critical occasion.

Note in these two passages the King's honest conviction that he has always attempted to do his duty; that he has been mindful not to infringe the rights of others; but that it would be equally wrong in him to submit 'to the Executive power being in any other hands, than where the Constitution has placed it.' And while I do not for a moment suggest that these things could not have been done in a happier manner, I contend that the King's statements quoted above are substantially correct.

In the eighteenth century, a proper balance between King, Lords, and Commons, that is, the monarchical, aristocratic, and representative elements of the Constitution acting as checks on each other, was supposed to safeguard the property and privileges, the lives and liberty of the subjects. Single-Chamber government would have been no less abhorrent to that century than Royal autocracy. The Executive was the King's as truly as it is now of the President in the United States; he, too, had to choose his Ministers: but from among Parliamentary leaders. And while aspirants to office swore by the 'independency' of the Crown and disclaimed all wish to force themselves on the King, if left out they did their level best to embarrass and upset their successful rivals. The technique of Parliamentary opposition was fully established long before its most essential aim, which is to force a change of government, was recognized as legitimate; and because that aim could not be avowed in its innocent purity, deadly dangers threatening the Constitution, nay the life of the country, had to be alleged for justification. Robert Walpole as 'sole Minister' was accused of arrogating to himself the powers of both King and Parliament; the very tame Pelhams, of keeping George II 'in fetters'; Bute, who bore the name of Stuart, of 'raising the standard of Royal prerogative'; and George III of ruling not through the Ministers of his own choice whom he avowed in public, but through a hidden gang of obscure and sinister 'King's friends.' In reality the constitutional practice of George III differed little from that of George I and George II. William Wyndham was proscribed by the first two Georges as a dangerous Jacobite, and C.J. Fox by the third as a dangerous Jacobin; while the elder Pitt was long kept out by both George II and George III on personal grounds.

I go one step further: in the eighteenth century the King had to intervene in politics and was bound to exercise his political influence, for the party system, which is the basis of Parliamentary government, did not exist. Of the House of Commons itself probably less than half thought and acted in party terms. About one-third of the House consisted of Members who looked to the King for guidance and for permanency of employment: epigoni of earlier Courts or forerunners of the modern Civil Service; and if they thus pursued their own interest, there is no reason to treat them as more corrupt than if they had done so by attaching themselves to a group of politicians. Another one-fifth of the House consisted of independent country gentlemen, ready to support the King's Government so long as this was compatible with their conscience, but averse to tying themselves up with political groups: they did not desire office, honours, or profits, but prided themselves on the disinterested and independent line they were pursuing; and they rightly claimed to be the authentic voice of the nation. In the centre of the arena stood the politicians, their orators and leaders fighting for the highest prizes of Parliamentary life. They alone could supply the façade of governments: the front benches in parliament. But to achieve stability a Government required the active support of the Crown and the good opinion of the country. On matters about which public opinion felt strongly, its will would prevail; but with the House constituted as it was, with the electoral structure of the unreformed Parliament, and an electorate which neither thought nor voted on party lines, it is idle to assume that modern Parliamentary government was possible.

I pass to the next point: was George III correct in saying that it was 'his scrupulous attachment to the rights of Parliament' which caused him the difficulties in America? Undoubtedly yes. It was not Royal claims that the Americans objected to, but the claims of 'subjects in one part of the King's dominions to be sovereigns over their fellow-subjects in another part of his dominions.'[1] 'the sovereignty of the Crown I understand, wrote Benjamin Franklin; 'the sovereignty of Britain I do not understand. . . . We have the same King, but not the same legislature.' Had George III aspired to independent Royal power nothing could have suited him better than to be Sovereign in America, the West Indies, and possibly in Ireland, independent of the British Parliament; and the foremost champions of the rights of Parliament, recalling the way in which the Stuarts had played off Ireland and Scotland against England, would have been the first to protest. But in fact, it would be difficult to imagine a King simultaneously exercising in several independent countries executive powers in conjunction with Parliamentary leaders. Of the measures which brought on the American conflict none was of the King's making: neither George Grenville's Stamp Act, nor the Declaratory Act of the Rockinghams, nor the Townshend Duties. All that can be said against him is that once the struggle had started he, completely identifying himself with this country, obstinately persevered in it. He wrote on November 14th, 1778:

> If Lord North can see with the same degree of enthusiasm I do, the beauty, excellence, and perfection of the British Constitution as by law established, and consider that if any one branch of the Empire is alowed to cast off its dependency, that the others will infalably follow the example . . . he . . . will resolve with vigour to meet every obstacle . . . or the State will be ruined.

---

[1] Benjamin Franklin to the Rev. Samuel Cooper of Boston, June 8th, 1770.

And again on June 11th, 1779, expecting that the West Indies and Ireland would follow:

> Then this island would be reduced to itself, and soon would be a poor island indeed.

On March 7th, 1780:

> I can never suppose this country so far lost to all ideas of self importance as to be wiling to grant America independence, if that could ever be universally adopted, I shall despair of this country being ever preserved from a state of inferiority and consequently falling into a very low class among the European States . . .

And on September 26th, 1780:

> . . . giving up the game would be total ruin, a small State may certainly subsist, but a great one mouldering cannot get into an inferior situation but must be annihilated.

When all was over, Lord North wrote to the King on March 18th, 1782:

> Your Majesty is well apprized that, in this country, the Prince on the Throne, cannot, with prudence, oppose the deliberate resolution of the House of Commons: . . . Your Majesty has graciously and steadily supported the servants you approve, as long as they could be supported: Your Majesty has firmly and resolutely maintained what appeared to you essential to the welfare and dignity of this country, as long as this country itself thought proper to maintain it. The Parliament have alerted their sentiments, and as their sentiments whether just or erroneous, must ultimately prevail, Your Majesty . . . can lose no honour if you yield at length . . .
>
> Your Majesty's goodness encourages me . . . to submit whether it will not be for Your Majesty's welfare, and even glory, to sacrifice, at this moment, former opinions, displeasures and apprehensions (though never so well-founded) to . . . the public safety.

The King replied:

> I could not but be hurt at your letter of last night. Every man must be the sole judge of his feelings, therefore whatever you or any man can say on that subject has no avail with me.

What George III had never learnt was to give in with grace: but this was at the most a defect of character.

I have never been able to find the man arrogating power to himself, the ambitious schemer out to dominate, the intriguer dealing in an underhand fashion with his Ministers; in short, any evidence for the stories circulated about him by very clever and eloquent contemporaries. He had a high, indeed an exaggerated, notion of royalty but in terms of mission and duties rather than of power; and trying to live up to this idealized concept, he made unreasonable demands on himself. Setting himself unattainable standards, he could never truly come to grips with reality: which condemned him to remain immature, permanency of inner conflict precluding growth. Aware of his own inadequacy, he turned to others and expected them to enable him to realize his visionary program; and he bitterly reproached them in his own mind, and blamed the age in which he lived, for his own inevitable failure. The tension between his notions and reality, and the resulting frustration, account to a high degree for his irritability, his deep-seated resentments, and his suppressed anger – for situations intolerable and disastrous for himself and others; and it may have been a contributory factor in his mental breakdowns. The desire to escape from that unbearable conflict repeatedly shows itself in thoughts of abdication which must not be deemed insincere because never acted upon (men of his type cannot renounce their treadmill). He himself did not understand the nature and depth of his tragedy; still less could others. There was therefore room for the growth of an injurious legend which made that heavy-burdened man a much maligned ruler; and which has long been accepted as history.

*   *   *

Sir Lewis Namier (1888–1960), Professor of History at Manchester University 1931–53, was one of the most influential historians of the mid-twentieth century. Born in Poland, he came to England to study at the London School of Economics and Balliol College, Oxford. He took British nationality and changed his name by deed poll in 1913. The same year, he began research into eighteenth-century English parliamentary history, the subject which would occupy him throughout much of his professional life. *The Structure of Politics at the Accession of George III* (1929) and *England in the Age of the American Revolution* (1930) established him at the forefront of British historical study. Namier was knighted in 1952.

8

Queen Elizabeth and the Historians

A.L. ROWSE

(September 1953)

A.L. Rowse, Elizabethan historian and controversialist renowned inter alia for his views on the authorship of Shakespeare's plays, was a frequent contributor to History Today *for over thirty years.*

Queen Elizabeth I has this in common with the Duke of Wellington – besides a hawk-nose – that she has been much exposed to authors. The most celebrated and the most brilliant figure among our sovereigns, how could it not be so? Though we can hardly say of her, as it has been said of the circulation of Macaulay's *History*, that it went up and down with the figures for the annual production of coal in the nineteenth century, still her reputation has waxed and waned with movements of political feeling, varied with party bias. It may be of interest, and possibly instructive, to watch the ebb and flow of opinion about her, especially with the historians: it may tell us something about them as well as about her.

In the fifty years or so after her death we can already observe people's opinions forming according to their prejudices. We can hardly expect James I to have had anything but an awkward attitude towards the disagreeable aunt who had given him so many scoldings in her time and kept him on tenterhooks about her inheritance. The correspondence of Elizabeth I and James VI makes a comic chapter in the relations of monarchs; in any case, sovereigns – and not they alone – are apt to be sensitive on the subject of their immediate predecessors. But after some grudging expressions at the beginning, James recovered himself in time to pay tribute in his first Parliament to 'one who in wisdom and felicity of government surpassed all the princes since the days of Augustus.' There speaks the don in him; but it was a generous tribute, and it was as well. It set the standard for such a reference as that familiar to us from the Preface to the Authorized Version – 'upon the setting of that bright Occidental star, Queen Elizabeth of most happy memory.' Cromwell himself, in the days of the Republic, did not hesitate to cite Elizabeth's name before Parliament, 'Queen Elizabeth of famous memory – we need not be ashamed to call her so'; and he went on to refer in terms almost of gallantry, for a Puritan, to the 'assassinations designed upon that lady, that great Queen.'

But the horrid, the detestable, Civil War divided England, and we find a different view suggested by Clarendon. He quotes an axiom of hers with a wry, dry comment:

the popular axiom of Queen Elizabeth that as her greatest treasure was in the hearts of her people so she had rather her money should be in their purses than in her own Exchequer (which she never said but at the closing of some Parliament when she had gotten all she could from them).

And against the glories of the age, he sets:

the charge, trouble and anxiety of a long continued war (how prosperous and successful soever) even during the Queen's whole reign; and (besides some domestic ruptures into rebellion, frequently into treason, and besides the blemish of an unparalleled act of blood upon the life of a crowned neighbour, queen and ally) the fear and apprehension of what was to come (which is one of the most unpleasant kinds of melancholy) from an unknown, at least an unacknowledged successor to the crown: clouded much of that prosperity then which now shines with so much splendour before our eyes in chronicle.

There you have a pretty disingenuous picture of the reign from the pen of a Stuart partisan, who happens to be the first of our great historians. Prejudice speaks in the insinuations of the Lord Chancellor's majestic parentheses. Prejudice betrays itself in the historical error as to the duration of the war: which occupied not the whole reign, but the last twenty years of its forty-five. And within the country people had reason to remember the reign as a long period of internal peace: that is the theme of the famous speech Shakespeare put into the mouth of Cranmer in

Henry VIII: like Shakespeare's whole attitude on such matters it was representative, not exceptional. Note, too, the partisan statement of Mary Stuart's case, whom Elizabeth protected for years against the indignation of Parliament. Then there is the quite unjust innuendo as to Elizabeth's attitude towards taxation. As an historian I know how genuine her concern was to protect the pocket of the citizen. She thought the subject's money was best in his own purse and most profitably employed by himself.

It is interesting to see in this – in Cromwell's admiration and Clarendon's dislike – the formation of the tradition: Queen Elizabeth as the heroine of Parliament, the Protestant, the Whig Queen; Mary Stuart, the martyr in the eyes of the Tories and Jacobites, the heroine of the long Stuart romance. Actually how ironical it is! Elizabeth conducted a life-long struggle with her Parliaments, on one issue after another. Her 'affection to govern princely' was disapproved by her own Archbishop; in other words, her views of her prerogative might be described as very much anti-Whig and high Tory.

In the middle of the eighteenth century the issue is brought into the open with the controversy aroused by Hume's *History of England* and Robertson's *History of Scotland*. For a Scot who professed not to care very much for England and the English, Hume did us proud in his remarkable *History*. He discovers a real enthusiasm for the English Queen, unwonted in one who prided himself on the cool and even temper of his judgments:

> Her vigour, her constancy, her magnanimity, her penetration, vigilance, address are allowed to merit the highest praises and appear not to have been surpassed by any person who ever filled a throne. . . . By the force of her mind, she controlled all her more active and stronger qualities and prevented them from running into excess. . . . Her singular talents for government were founded equally on her temper and on her capacity. Endowed with a great command over herself, she soon obtained an uncontrolled ascendant over her people; and while she merited all their esteem by her real virtues, she also engaged their affections by her pretended ones. Few sovereigns of England succeeded to the throne in more difficult circumstances; and none ever conducted the government with such uniform success and felicity. Though unacquainted with the practice of toleration, the true secret for managing religious factions, she preserved her people, by her superior prudence, from those confusions in which theological controversy had involved all the neighbouring nations.

Perhaps this is the core of her achievement: at a time when other nations were divided from top to bottom by ideological conflict and civil war – France, the Netherlands, Scotland, Germany – she kept her country united so that it could forge ahead, where other countries were held back for decades or even centuries. No conception of this among her critics. I suppose that is because most people are capable of appreciating only the private and family virtues, not those essential in public and political life. But a Tudor queen has to be estimated as a statesman, not as a cosy helpmate in the stress of suburban life. Elizabeth I was certainly not a cosy character. What won her Hume's intellectual sympathy was that she was a Laodicean, a moderate, a trimmer: all that made the odious Knox call her 'neither good Protestant nor yet resolute Papist.' Like the most intelligent people of her time – or of any time – she was a *politique*, not a fanatic engaged in making life intolerable for sensible people.

Then, too, Hume as a Scot, and a very frugal one, understood the wisdom of her financial prudence. 'The natural frugality of her temper, so far from disqualifying her for . . . great enterprises, only enabled her to execute them with greater certainty and success; and all the world saw in her conduct the happy effects of a vigorous perseverance in judicious and well conducted projects.' In truth, finance was the clue to the success of her rule: when other powers – including her greatest adversary, who had all the treasure of America at his disposal – went bankrupt, she was not held up in the course thought best in the interests of the country, her policies never thus frustrated. We in our time are in all too favourable a position for appreciating how economic circumstances set limits to what we can do in the world.

Hume, who understood everything, understood this very well; where 'middling historians,' as he calls them, are apt not to. Robertson, who – in spite of the fact that he was a best-seller – was more than a middling historian, appreciated this too. (It was left to the Victorians – perhaps they were too well off – to attack Elizabeth on the grounds of parsimony.) Robertson has a strong tribute to Elizabeth as a great queen. But he was writing the history of Scotland; and 'whosoever undertakes to write the history of Scotland finds himself obliged, frequently, to view her in a very different and in a less amiable light.' He concludes that the hand Elizabeth took in the contending Scots factions of the time effected 'what the valour of her ancestors could not accomplish' the reduction of 'that Kingdom to a state of dependence on England.' But must an Englishman regret that she was successful in this? From an English point of view, she was engaged in rendering Scotland – so often dangerous – innocuous. From a wider point of view, she was engaged in preparing the eventual union of the island. Who can say that she was wrong to do so? She was pursuing an obviously right and sensible policy from both points of view.

But it is when he touches Mary Stuart that the Presbyterian reveals himself a gallant. 'No apology can be offered for her [Elizabeth's] behaviour to Queen Mary; a scene of dissimulation, without necessity, and of severity beyond example. In almost all her other actions Elizabeth is the object of our highest admiration: in this we must allow that she not only laid aside the magnanimity which became a queen, but the feelings natural to a woman.' Feelings natural to a man, perhaps – a better knowledge of psychology would suggest. For Mary certainly had a way of appealing to the soft side of menfolk. The utmost that the Doctor can bring himself to utter against her is – 'To say that she was always unfortunate will not account for that long and uninterrupted succession of calamities which befel her; we must likewise add that she was often imprudent.' As for her passion for Bothwell and the murder of her husband, 'Humanity will draw a veil over this part of her character which it cannot approve and may, perhaps, prompt some to impute some of her actions to her situation more than to her dispositions,' etc.

This was not enough for William Tytler, Writer to the Signet, who in 1760 produced '*An historical and critical Enquiry into the evidence produced by the Earls of Murray and Morton against Mary, Queen of Scots; with an Examination of the Rev. Dr. Robertson's Dissertation and Mr. Hume's History with respect to that evidence.*' I fear the lawyer proved himself neither historical or critical. I have read his work and it is worthless – though it made a stir in its day. Nothing would suit him but the assertion of Mary's purity and innocence. There is nothing more boring than such *parti-pris*. One studies history to discover what the truth is; this lawyer to make a case. It is a poor one. Nothing is said of Mary's aggressive step in laying claim to the English succession when Dauphiness in France or the danger she constituted – and meant to be – to Elizabeth, or of her long run of follies, mistakes, crimes, conspiracies. As for Elizabeth's attitude, it was temporizing; she did not want to have to let down the common front of crowned and anointed heads; she would have given Mary support at various critical junctures if Mary had genuinely wished to cooperate. What was fatal about Mary was that with very weak cards she insisted on gambling. She would have come through perfectly all right if she had played the game by, and with, her royal cousin. Elizabeth was under constant pressure from Parliament to execute Mary after her plots. Not unnaturally she wished to be rid of such a torment, going on year after year, and in the end, she certainly wished Mary made away with. Mary not only wished as much for Elizabeth, but attempted it – ineffectively as usual. Such became the mutual feelings of these two ladies for each other.

Tytler allows that Elizabeth was a 'great Queen (for such, according to the ordinary sense of the word, she was).' But 'the hand of time has now pulled off the mask from this imperious and arbitrary Queen. . . . The humane will drop a tear to the memory of an unfortunate princess, the most amiable and accomplished of her sex who, by the unrelenting cruelty of a jealous rival, though a series of bitter persecutions, was at last brought to the grave!' One recognizes the *clichés* of the eighteenth-century epitaph in this third-rater. But he succeeded in impressing Dr Johnson, who was already convinced, and in annoying Hume, which was not so easy.

Johnson, who was brought up a Jacobite, wrote: 'It has now been fashionable, for near half a century, to defame and vilify the house of Stuart, and to exalt and magnify the reign of Elizabeth: the Stuarts have found few apologists, for the dead cannot pay for praise; and who will, without reward, oppose the tide of popularity?' In fact, the Stuarts will never want defenders: one half of the English aristocracy are descended from them. Wherever you go in great English houses – such as have not put up the shutters for good and all – you will find romantic and dazzling defenders of Mary Stuart. Among them it is Elizabeth, who left no progeny, who wants defenders and has little sympathy. Perhaps her personality is apt to alienate it, since she was one of those persons very capable of looking after themselves – and people somehow find that unattractive. Yet ought that fact to prevent people from yielding their sympathy on her? For behind the brave face she put on the world, there was an essential loneliness, a deeper pathos, than those of the romantic prisoner. There was an essential heroism about the woman who for forty-five long years of strain and stress bore the supreme responsibility for the well-being of her people; and in the end, was always and utterly alone. She once said, 'To be a king and wear a crown is more glorious to them that see it, than it is pleasure to them that bear it.' And it is said that when she came to the end of her journey and felt life ebbing from her, she took off the ring that was placed on her finger at her Coronation and that was her only wedding-ring to lay it by at last.

But Hume, who was Tytler's real target, was very much annoyed. He did not reply, since he had made a sensible resolution at the beginning of his literary life not to reply to anybody. But he wrote round to mutual friends protesting at being misrepresented. 'That trick is so frequently practised by thieves, pickpockets and controversial writers (gentlemen whose morality are pretty much upon a footing) that all the world has ceased to wonder and wise men are tired of complaining at it.' Wise man that he was, he did complain: his correspondence has some very unphilosophical expressions about Tytler: from which we see that the great philosopher was just as touchy as the rest of us at being attacked. We may wonder why *le bon David*, who was hardly ever annoyed by anything, should have been so vexed by this insignificant lawyer. I think it may be that nothing infuriates a clever man like being misrepresented by a stupid one: there is somehow an indignity about it.

Walter Scott, whom we must regard as an historian as well as historical novelist and everything else, has, in spite of his Stuart sympathies, a just portrait of Elizabeth in *Kenilworth*. 'Elizabeth united the occasional caprice of her sex with that sense and sound policy in which neither man nor woman ever excelled her.' And there comes that memorable image: 'the mind of England's Elizabeth . . . was of that firm and decided character which soon recovers its natural tone. It was like one of those ancient druidical monuments called rocking stones. The finger of Cupid, boy as he is painted, could put her feelings in motion, but the power of Hercules could not have destroyed their equilibrium.' (It is interesting to note that this and other things in the book, like the character Tresillian, come from Scott's reading of Cornish lore at this time.)

The nineteenth century presents us with a continuation of these themes, with a much wider spread and greater variety. There is Queen Victoria's well-known dislike of her predecessor – 'so unkind to my ancestress, the Queen of Scots.' It is with something of a shock that we realize that Queen Victoria was a descendant of Mary Stuart – whose domestic life was so very unlike that of the dear Queen. We are apt to think of her much more as a successor of – and in some sense a parallel to – Elizabeth. Her disapprobation was part of her romantic *schwärmerei* for the Stuarts; but might there not also be in it a little feminine jealousy of so famous a precursor? It went back very early: at her accession a motion was proposed in Parliament that she should take the title of Elizabeth II. The young woman of nineteen was determined that she would do no such thing: she would stick to her own name Victoria and make something of that.

We open up with the heavy howitzers of the Whig historians. Hallam has a just appreciation of Elizabeth. 'Her own remarkable talents, her masculine intrepidity, her readiness of wit and royal deportment, which the bravest men unaffectedly dreaded, her temper of mind, above all, at once fiery and inscrutably dissembling, would in any circumstances have ensured her more real sovereignty than weak monarchs, however nominally absolute, can ever enjoy or retain.' This, if a trifle wooden – like everything about that estimable man – is at any rate sensible. What dogs him is a rather silly moralism, which leads him, oddly enough, to praise Essex – he cannot have known what sort of man Essex really was; and to condemn Leicester, as everyone does – much too easily, in my opinion: 'that bold, bad man, whose favour is the great reproach of Elizabeth's reign.' Whatever Leicester was, he was not a bold man; and though he was not a nice man, he was not exactly a bad one. He was a sly customer, out for his own ends, like everybody else. But Elizabeth made of him a life-long servant of hers and of the State, in difficult and sometimes humiliating circumstances.

When we come to the young Macaulay, to the famous essay on Burghley in which he trounced the unfortunate Dr Nares with such terrific spirits, all the flags are out, all the drums beating. We are first given a very sombre picture of an England without the delights of a free press. The Queen 'often spoke to her parliaments in language as haughty and imperious as that which the Great Turk would use to his divan. She punished with great severity members of the House of Commons who, in her opinion, carried the freedom of debate too far. She assumed the power of legislating by means of proclamations. She imprisoned her subjects without bringing them to a legal trial.' And so on. Then comes the other pan of the scales, bumping down heavily with a celebrated tribute. 'Such was this government. Yet we know that it was loved by the great body of those who lived under it. We know that during the fierce contests of the sixteenth century, both the hostile parties spoke of the time of Elizabeth as of a golden age. That great queen has now been lying two hundred and thirty years in Henry VII's chapel. Yet her memory is still dear to the hearts of a free people.'

The saxophone note of Victorian moralizing is now heard:

We are far from saying that the English of that generation were irreligious. [Would it not have been better if they had been – or, at least, less religious? They would have had the less excuse for killing each other.] That which is the great stain on the character of Burghley is also the great stain on the character of Elizabeth. Being herself an Adiaphorist, having no scruple about conforming to the Romish church when conformity was necessary to her own safety, retaining to the last moment of her life a fondness for much of the doctrine and much of the ceremonial of that church, she yet subjected that church to a persecution even more odious than the persecution with which her sister had harassed the Protestants. We say more odious. For Mary had at least the plea of fanaticism. She did nothing for her religion which she was not prepared to suffer for it. If she burned the bodies of her subjects, it was in order to rescue their souls. Elizabeth had no such pretext.

You perceive what nonsense all this is, besides the inaccuracy of its conception of Burghley and Elizabeth's attitudes towards religion. Both may justly be described as Anglican, Burghley more Protestant, Elizabeth less so; in fact, as with Palmerston's choice for bishops, one Low Church, one High Church. The fact that Mary believed the nonsense for which she burned is no plea to my mind. Elizabeth at least had the plea of self-defence, a course regrettably forced upon her by necessity. The young Macaulay has the brashness to reproach Elizabeth with the ease with which she 'might have united all conflicting sects under the shelter of the same impartial laws and the same paternal throne, and thus have placed the nation in the same situation, as far as the rights of conscience are concerned, in which we at last stand, after all the heart-burnings, the persecutions, the conspiracies, the seditions, the revolutions, the judicial murders, the civil wars of ten generations.'

'After'! – the twentieth century has had something to say to all that. What incomprehension it reveals of the illimitable depths of human folly! Intelligent people in the sixteenth century, like Burghley and Elizabeth, Erasmus and Montaigne, had a pretty good understanding of them. They realized that a moderate middle way was the only chance of any peace, and that external conformity was the necessary condition for the maximum freedom of which humans were capable. 'I desire to open a window into no man's conscience,' said Elizabeth; and that was saying a lot in the sixteenth century. Moreover, she meant it.

'This is the dark side of her character,' says Macaulay. 'Yet she surely was a great woman. Of all the sovereigns who exercised a power which was seemingly absolute, but which in fact depended for support on the love and confidence of their subjects, she was by far the most illustrious.' I hate the antithetical rhetoric of the Victorians – so unsubtle, and so untrue. If the Queen were so great a woman, is it likely that she was so wrong about the matter of the preceding paragraph, that she could have achieved a toleration at all, let alone with any ease? Catherine de Médicis, who tried it by bringing the two sides together into conference at Poissy, found that it only gave them the excuse to get at each others' throats; France lapsed into civil war over religious doctrine; society was split from top to bottom. No: Elizabeth, with the spectacle of the world around her, was right: in the circumstances of the sixteenth century, it could not be done.

Let us leave Macaulay: he had not the advantage of our melancholy experience of the twentieth century. The leading Catholic historian of England, Lingard, expresses a more balanced view – even if he states it somewhat equivocally as that generally held, rather than necessarily held by him.

'In the judgment of her contempories,' he wrote, '– and that judgment has been ratified by the consent of posterity – Elizabeth was numbered among the greatest and most fortunate of princes. The tranquillity which, during a reign of nearly half a century, she maintained within her dominions, while the neighbouring nations were convulsed with intestine dissensions, was taken as a proof of the wisdom or the vigour of her government; and her successful resistance against the Spanish monarch, the severe injuries which she inflicted on that lord of so many kingdoms, and the spirit displayed by her fleets and armies . . . served to give to the world an exalted notion of her military and naval power. When she came to the throne, England ranked only among the secondary kingdoms; before her death, it had risen to a level with the first nations of Europe.'

This stately pronouncement by the distinguished historian who was a cardinal *in petto* – even if uttered with a personal caveat – puts in its proper place the nonsense written about Elizabeth by some of his co-religionists in our time. But when the priest can say a derogatory word for himself as to Elizabeth's private character, he does. 'The woman who despises the safeguards, must be content to forfeit the reputation of chastity.' He proceeds to insinuate that Leicester and others were her lovers. There is no evidence whatsoever that this was so; and a knowledge of psychology would suggest the contrary: Elizabeth had all the symptoms of the disappointed spinster: she displayed an unattractive, if understandable, jealousy of the young couples around her who were free to enjoy each other, when she was not. The very archness and freedom of her behaviour in public to Leicester and so many others is in itself an indication of the sad truth, of what the situation was with her.

The most interesting case is that of Froude, and the most important; for the second half of his *History* – a work of brilliance, imagination and literary power, the one possible rival in the century to Macaulay – is devoted to Elizabeth's reign up to the Armada with which he ended. He started with a prejudice in her favour, as the daughter of Henry VIII – the hero of the first half of his *History* – and as the continuer of Henry's policy. In Volume I we read, 'In her vital convictions she represented the free proud spirit of the educated laity, who would endure no dictation from priests of either persuasion, and so far as lay in them, would permit no clergy any more to fetter the thoughts and paralyse the energies of England.' Perhaps we see here Froude getting his own back on those clergymen, his father, his brother and the Oxford Movement. But of Elizabeth, it is true. In Volume III his judgment is: 'A middle course was therefore chosen – a course which at the time pleased no one but the Queen and the half-dozen or dozen intelligent persons who surrounded her; but it was the same which her father had marked out before her, and its eventual success may be allowed to prove that it was wise.' He could even state her sensible Laodiceanism justly: the Queen told the Huguenot leader, Cardinal Châtillon, that 'whatever he and his party might think of the abomination of going to mass, she would herself sooner have heard a thousand than have caused the least of the million villainies (*méchancetés*) which had been committed on account of it.'

As the years went on and his successive volumes came out, Froude grew more and more out of sympathy, until in the end he became incapable of doing her justice. In the concluding pages of his *History*, in his summing up of her character, we read: 'To Elizabeth the speculations of so-called divines were but as ropes of sand and sea-slime leading to the moon, and the doctrines for which they were rending each other to pieces a dream of fools or enthusiasts.' (Well, weren't they, very largely?) 'Unfortunately her keenness of insight was not combined with any profound concern for serious things.' (Her profoundest concern as Queen of England was the well-being of her country and peace at home and abroad. What more could any one want or expect of her?) 'She saw through the emptiness of the forms in which religion presented itself to the world. She had none the more any larger or deeper conviction of her own.' (Suppose there is none?) 'She was without the intellectual emotions which give human character its consistency and power.' (I should have thought that consistency and power were precisely what her character showed, and her intellectual emotions were sufficient to provide the driving force for them. Indeed, unflagging energy of mind was her most marked characteristic.)

We are told that 'her entire nature was saturated with artifice. Except when speaking some round untruth Elizabeth never could be simple. She was unnatural even in prayers, and she carried her affectations into the presence of the Almighty. . . . Obligations of honour were not only occasionally forgotten by her, but she did not seem to understand what honour meant.' Well, she was a woman, and honour is a masculine concept; for a woman, Elizabeth was exceptionally responsive to considerations of honour, more particularly of her honour as a queen. Froude concludes: 'Vain as she was of her own sagacity, she never modified a course recommended to her by Burghley without injury both to the realm and herself. . . . The great results of her reign were the fruits of a policy which was not her own, and which she starved and mutilated when energy and completeness were most needed.'

This is wholly unjust and quite untrue. Yet it is a charge that has often been repeated: we owe its reverberations, especially among naval historians, mainly to the impression made by Froude's *History*, read – like Macaulay – by thousands. The charge that Elizabeth starved her navy of resources has been completely disproved in our time by historians who today understand better the difficulties that condition the action of all government. In fact, the Queen struggled all her life to keep the government of her country financially sound; when her hand was removed we see the difficulties the Stuarts got into at once. I do not propose to say any more on the subject: it has been dealt with once and for all in the work of Professor Neale, and I have dealt with it myself in *The England of Elizabeth.*

But Froude is a fascinating case. To some extent his repugnance may be due to the growing distaste of the researcher living for too many years with his subject. He wrote of Burghley to a friend: 'He, it is more and more clear to me, was the solitary author of Elizabeth's and England's greatness. . . . The private letters which passed between him and Walsingham about Elizabeth have destroyed finally the prejudice that still clung to me that, notwithstanding her many faults, she was a woman of ability. Evidently in their opinion she had no ability at all worth calling by the name.' That does not at all represent the opinion of this very exclusive men's club. Both Burghley and Walsingham had much to put up with: above all the Queen's determination that they, not she, should bear the responsibility of necessarily unpopular measures. But that was all in the game: the popularity and prestige of the Crown must be preserved at all costs. Unfair, but quite right: they understood the terms of the game, and – bemoaning their lot to each other when it became too intolerable – accepted it. Burghley in fact never ceased to admire, and came to stand in awe of her: there is his political testament to his clever son and successor Robert to witness: always to present the true facts of the case to the Queen, but never to press her beyond her better judgment, her knowledge of men and her experience were such and so great.

Froude's judgments are emotional and go back to an element of instability in his personality. There was an ambivalence in his make-up, which gives him an uncertainty of focus – by contrast with the too great clarity of Macaulay. The child of the Oxford Movement who had lost his faith had been rescued by Carlyle and given a harsh injection of Calvinism of a kind; the boy who had been bullied by his brother, the inquisitorial Hurrell, and beaten so badly at school as to have been ruptured, grew out of his early weakness to admire force and understand, better than any other Victorian, the rôle of violence in history. Froude was all his life under attack for what he understood about human beings; to my mind he is more vulnerable where he conformed to the nonsense they thought. The muscular Victorianism that was indoctrinated upon him, as with the cult of the manly virtues that was inculcated by his brother-in-law, Charles Kingsley – both were over-compensations for something they felt lacking in themselves, for both bore the stigmata of genius.

Hence Froude's harping on Elizabeth's feminine tortuousness, her unfathomable guile, her lack of candour, the insincerities of her pro-longed marriage negotiations. All this was politics and well understood by others in the game. Froude's Victorian manliness was disgusted. Things were too simple for him. The only time he made an incursion into politics himself – in South African affairs – he put his foot in it, and, though right on the main issue, made a frightful hash by his candour. We may not be able to accept the necessary disingenuousnesses of politics in practice; but as historians we should at least understand them. That practical politician, Catherine the Great, well understood the foolish superiority of the armchair doctrinaire, who supposes that in great affairs things happen *'comme sur le papier, qui souffre tout.'* So did Elizabeth: her tortuousness served England well: she never slipped up.

This was what Creighton appreciated better than anyone: he was a bishop, and no mean *politique* himself. Of Elizabeth's personal character he writes: 'Self-mastery and self-restraint had been forced upon her. Bitter experience had taught her how little she could satisfy her own desires, how little she could confide in the wisdom or discretion of others.' But, of course, self-control is the indispensable condition to control of others; and that was her magnificent, lonely, sad job. She had this advantage – unthinkable for either Mary Tudor or Mary Stuart – that 'she was both intellectually and emotionally cold. In politics and in private life alike she cared little for decorum, because she knew that she could stop short whenever prudence made it needful.'

It is the great virtue of Creighton's biography that he understood completely the inner significance of Elizabeth's political rôle; that in a world torn in two, like ours, by ideological conflict, she could not afford to be too clear: she must wait and go on waiting with complete self-restraint – in a way that no man could have done, except possibly her grandfather, Henry VII – until the success of her rule over the years vindicated her and showed others what fools they had been. 'The one thing she strove to avoid was an outburst of strong feeling, or aught that would divide England into opposite camps.' The identification of the Queen with her country and her country's long-term interests was Creighton's theme; to appreciate that one has to have a long-term perspective. 'She represented England as no other ruler ever did. . . . By avoiding risky undertakings, by keeping down public expense, she was not merely indulging her tendency to parsimony; she was warding off from her people demands which they were unequal at that time to sustain. . . . But when it came to decisive action she fell back upon her instinctive perception of what England wanted. As she could not explain this, she was driven to all sorts of devices to gain time. She could not, on the other hand, fully take her people into her confidence. It was the unconscious tendency of their capacities which she interpreted, not their actual demands' – in other words, their long-term interests, of which the people themselves are not always the best judges. In short, 'Elizabeth's imperishable claim to greatness lies in her instinctive sympathy with her people.' They have rewarded her, and time – always her friend – has vindicated her: the best-remembered of all the figures in the long pageant of those who have occupied the English throne.

It is nice to think that the man who would have been Archbishop of Canterbury, if he had lived, understood her best. His is by far the most perceptive and true judgment of Elizabeth there has ever been by any historian. Creighton was by nature a statesman; his special bent as an historian was for high politics and statesmanship. Not for nothing had he served his apprenticeship and trained his eye on the Popes of the Renaissance. His short biography came out at the end of the nineteenth century; his judgment stands unlikely ever to be reversed.

So that we do not have to bother with the captiousness of lesser Victorians – the puerile antitheses of the egregious Freeman, for example, who made himself the life-long enemy of Froude. Gardiner, though an Irvingite, was more just, and in his own way may be taken to answer Macaulay on the question of the religious settlement. 'In taking her stand, as she did, against the abolition of Episcopacy, Elizabeth was on the whole acting on behalf of the liberty of her subjects.' But, perhaps, we may think, in spite of Gardiner's Parliamentarian sympathies, to be an Irvingite is to be in a sense High Church.

It is curious to note what a fuss the Victorians made about the adulation, the language of devotion in which Elizabeth was addressed in her own time: Macaulay, Froude, Freeman, Dean Church – they all were shocked and protested at what they called gross flattery. 'The gross, shameless, lying flattery paid to the Queen,' writes mild Dean Church; 'there is really nothing like it in history. . . . It was no worship of a secluded and distant object of loyalty: the men who thus flattered knew perfectly well, often by painful experience, what Elizabeth was: able, indeed, high-spirited, successful, but ungrateful to her servants, unjust, and in her old age, ugly.' Ungallant Dean! Inaccurate Dean! We may well apply to him the words she used to a tactless bishop who referred to her advancing years in preaching before her – 'I see that the greatest clerks are not the wisest men.' It is surely anachronistic to condemn the language in which the sixteenth century thought it proper to address such a lady, such a queen. I find it has a charm – so revealing of the fantasy, the romantic mirror of the Renaissance world in which they lived. And was it so unexampled with the Victorians? What about the language in which Tennyson addressed his Queen? Or the demonstration Disraeli was making of how effective such language could be in sweetening the relations between a Victorian sovereign and her Prime Minister?

The besetting sin of the Victorians, in regard to Elizabeth, as in so much else, was their moralism. It made it almost impossible for them to do a Renaissance woman justice. Even Creighton, according to the dragon, Mrs Creighton, regarded the age as 'more and more demoralized the better he understood it; those whom Froude had called 'wanderers on the Spanish main' or 'pioneers in the tangled path of discovery' he saw to have been [!] men who deserved no better name than buccaneer or pirate; while with an increasing appreciation of the extraordinary ability of Elizabeth, he had a constantly diminishing opinion of her morals.'

Morals! There you have the incessant grinding concern of the Victorians. It is as if everything – politics, literature, philosophy, economics, but especially aesthetics – had to be translated into morals before it could be understood or discussed. And the high censoriousness! – what gluttons they were, how they indulged themselves: the greatest pleasure, it would seem, of the high-minded.

We live in a world, like the sixteenth century, too sad, too distracted, too dangerous, for such cheap and facile condemnations. We know how difficult it is even to keep society together, how easy to plunge it into the abyss, how thin is the ice of civilized conduct covering what black waters beneath. The standards of the Victorians were the product of an epoch of exceptional security in human history: never, never, never again shall we see such another. We are back in the recognizable main stream of history once more. On the threshold of the twentieth century, with the irreversible verdict of Creighton, we may take leave of a woman who in her time did what she could to hold up the avalanche and strove, with greater success than is given to most, to build some fabric of sense and sanity, of moderation and internal peace, within this fortunate island amid the storms outside.

*   *   *

A.L. Rowse (1903–97), the son of a labourer, won a scholarship to Christ Church, Oxford, was elected to a fellowship at All Souls College, Oxford, and became one of the twentieth century's foremost authorities on

Elizabethan England. His most important work was the historical trilogy *The Elizabethan Age* (1950–72). Rowse also turned his attention to biography, including a two-volume study of the Churchill family (1956 and 1958) and a controversial life of Shakespeare (1963). The latter was supplemented by a work published in 1976 which dared to reveal the identity of Shakespeare's 'Dark Lady'. Rowse's last book, *Historians I Have Known*, was published in 1995, and he died two years later.

9

Attila the Hun

MICHAEL GRANT

(January 1954)

Michael Grant wrote for History Today *on classical Greece and Rome – and, here, on one of the most notorious figures from the early Dark Ages.*

I was sitting in a little public garden of a town in central Anatolia, and on the next bench sat a young Turkish mother, watching her plump baby as it tottered about on the path. then, to my surprise, she addressed the angelic infant by a name which to us carries memories of horror, of the Scourge of God: 'Attila,' she said, 'Attila darling, come here and let me wipe your face.'

I made enquiries and discovered that Turks call their children Attila because some of them are disposed to defend the Hun conqueror's reputation. They protest that western Europeans do not like him since instinctively we take the side of the Romans and Byzantines whose lands he ravaged in that fearful series of raids 1500 years ago; but, they maintain, he was not without merits, and, in any case, a tremendous conqueror. In some accounts of Turkish history, he figures as an ancestor, as the first of the Turkish monarchs. Likewise, on patriotic Hungarian medals, we find him placed in the same seat of honour, as the first Magyar king. The Bulgarians, too, have some reason to count the Huns among their ancestors. And the Germans also have staked a claim to this curious distinction: for Attila, as Etzel, is an important figure in the Nibelungen saga; 'let us be like the Huns,' exclaimed Wilhelm II in one of his wilder outpourings.

From the disappearance of the Huns from history, soon after Attila's death, to the emergence of any of the nations we know today, the historian must take a 'mortal leap'. But I confess that to me the German theory looks wrong and that, if Hun survivals have to be sought, the Balkans and Anatolia seem to be the places to search for them. It would help if we knew whence the Huns came. But we do not. They appeared near the Sea of Azov in the fourth century AD. Where had they been before? They have been identified with nomads who had plagued China two centuries earlier, the Hsiung-nu. Possibly this is right; but modern scholarship will not commit itself.

So the Huns are a mystery. They were already a mystery when they first struck the northern frontiers of the two Roman empires, the one based on Italy and the second on Constantinople – for the potential dangers from the north had been so pressing that one supreme commander did not seem enough to oversee the whole long frontier. Then in the year AD 376, the intelligence officers of the Lower Danube garrisons – which depended on Constantinople – received strange and unwelcome information. They learnt that new and unusually large movements had begun among the northern barbarians. It was said that all the peoples between Hungary and the Black Sea were in commotion.

> A savage people of great ferocity had struck the nations with terror and sent them fleeing from their homes. The officers received the news with indifference. They rarely heard of barbarian wars beyond the great river until the fighting had completely died down, or had, at least, come to a temporary close. Their experience told them that no exceptional events could be expected. But the rumours persisted; and then the first refugees appeared on the northern bank, begging to be taken into the safety of the Empire. The first fugitives were joined by others and yet others, until an immense multitude crowded on the bank of the river. The officers had been mistaken.

What had happened was that a vast, recently formed kingdom of Germans – which covered the Ukraine and separated the Romans from the unknown dangers farther east – had been attacked by the Huns, and blotted out of existence; it was already, when the Romans heard of these events, almost as if it had never been, and its collapse brought down too a second German kingdom in Rumania; and from these two kingdoms and elsewhere came a horde of panic-stricken refugees who, in a year or two, nearly brought down the empire of Constantinople.

I have here been drawing on a recent book, *Attila and the Huns* by E.A. Thompson of Nottingham University, who is, in turn, translating a Roman historian on whom he is an expert – the last great Roman historian, Ammianus, and perhaps the best of all, though spared service as an educational textbook since his Latinity not unnaturally deviated from the norm established four centuries earlier. Ammianus also described how the Huns lived:

This people, but little known from ancient records, exceed every degree of savagery . . . they are so hardy in their mode of life that they have no need of fire nor of savoury food, but eat the roots of wild plants and the half-raw flesh of any kind of animal whatever. They are never protected by any buildings – not even a hut thatched with reed can be found among them. But, roaming at large amid the mountains and woods, they learn from the cradle to endure cold, hunger and thirst . . . They dress in linen cloth or in the skins of marmots sewn together . . . and do not take off or change their clothing until by long wear and tear it has been reduced to rags and fallen from them bit by bit . . . Their shoes are formed upon no lasts, and so prevent their walking with free step. For this reason they are not at all adapted to battles on foot, but they are almost glued to their hardy, ugly horses . . . From their horses every one of them buys and sells, eats and drinks, and bowed over the narrow necks of these animals by night they sleep.

These horses were what counted. The wandering Huns were utterly primitive, and lacking in every conceivable sort of civilization or productivity. But they were fantastically good 'natural horsemen,' of portentous speed, endurance and dexterity – far too good for the professional cavalry of the Romans. So both Roman empires suffered appallingly destructive invasions. The provincials were terrified; and so were the Roman armies. To say that the Huns looked unattractive is an understatement. Even the Hun babies, says one writer casting around for superlatives, have faces of a quite peculiar gruesomeness. As for the adults, they were very short, bull-necked and seemed scarcely human; they were so monstrously ugly and misshapen, with faces – if that word could be used – like formless, perforated lumps.

The Romans claimed that the Hun armies were immensely numerous. But this was to make excuses. The Huns had subjects without number; but their mounted archers with their lassos, though they were dangerous beyond measure, may have been surprisingly few. Perhaps they normally operated in commandos hardly more than 1000 strong, each under one of numerous independent chieftains. Sometimes Rome itself employed these Hun squadrons as mercenaries. Their first really frightening appearance was in AD 395, when they penetrated the Caucasus, traversed the frozen Danube and moved into the Balkans – and this span of hundreds of miles shows that their range was already formidably large. 'The wolves of the North,' said Saint Jerome, 'they filled the whole earth with slaughter and panic alike, as they flitted hither and thither on their swift horses. May Jesus avert such beasts from the Roman world in the future!'

But they came again. Ten years later, Italy received advance notice of them in the familiar shape of masses of panic-stricken German refugees, while similar hordes burst across the Rhine and obliterated its frontier for ever. Then, in 408, it was the turn of the Balkans again. This is the occasion on which we meet the first Hun whom we know by name: he was called Uldis. Soon others are mentioned, Uptar or Oxtar, who ate so much dinner that he burst, and Rua, who finally amalgamated all the separate Hun realms into a great confederacy stretching from far into Russia almost to France. In 434 Rua died, thus vindicating, according to the Church, a text of Ezekiel; and he was succeeded by his two nephews, Bleda and Attila.

On Bleda, let me quote Thompson's version of a contemporary account.

We find him in possession of a Moorish dwarf called Zerco. Bleda was amused beyond all measure, not merely by Zerco's stammering talk, but particularly by his twisted and painful gait. He kept him by his side both at his banquets and on his campaigns; he even made him a little suit of armour to increase the grotesqueness of his figure. Once Zerco escaped with a number of other Roman prisoners. Bleda cared nothing for the others, but he was wild with rage at the loss of Zerco. Horsemen scoured the countryside until the dwarf was found, and Bleda roared with laughter when he saw him brought back in chains. He asked him why he had tried to escape. Zerco, in his strange, halting speech, said that it was because Bleda had never given him a wife. The Hun laughed more loudly than ever. He swore that he would give him one of the ladies-in-waiting from the Empress's palace in Constantinople.

Attila was entirely different from his brother Bleda, whom he wasted little time in murdering. Attila did not find Zerco in the least funny. Attila was sullen and grim. Though there were still Huns outside his rule, he extended Rua's already vast confederacy over enormous new territories in Northern Europe – we now have reason to believe that he even controlled islands in the Baltic, such as Bornholm and Gotland. And somehow – this was perhaps his great talent – he held his extraordinary string of possessions together. The swarthy, large-headed little man with his pig eyes, flattened nose and wispy chin – faun-like features which fascinated the medallists of the Italian Renaissance – knew he was not as other men; and, by concocting a story of the sword of the war-god discovered in the earth, he got the pagan Huns to believe that his authority should be accepted by divine right.

The position of the governments at Rome and especially Constantinople was now extremely uncomfortable. Their relations with Attila hinged upon money, and his series of appalling invasions were punctuated by financial talks. It was a matter of prestige for him to extort as much as he could from the wealthy eastern empire; it was a barbarian custom to hoard vast quantities of gold; and some, or much, of it was needed to keep his chiefs loyal, and his army in food and weapons, since the Huns were totally unproductive, and a large Hun state could scarcely hang together without external plunder. Besides, Attila's chief advisers had learnt to live lavishly; and he like to send them in relays to negotiate in Constantinople, where the government would give them expensive personal presents, of which Attila insisted on receiving full details.

In any case, it was the policy of the Eastern Emperor Theodosius II to buy the Huns off. On a single occasion alone he sent Attila 6000 lb. of gold; and that was only one of many consignments. Divergent views are nowadays taken of this policy. Either it was feeble, shameful appeasement, only leading to further demands – and further demands continued unceasingly – or Theodosius was only doing what emperors habitually did in dealing with barbarians, a far cheaper and less self-destructive method than facing Attila in the field, and one to which in any case there was no alternative: the Byzantine army could not stand up against Attila's cavalry, or – worse – would not, for we cannot say how far the Roman armies and provinces were reliable. National frontiers, it has been pointed out, were not then the last word; landowners and churchmen no doubt hated Attila – and hated appeasing him, because they had to foot the bill – but many subjects led such oppressed and miserable lives during the later Roman empires that a possible change could not much alarm them. Business men and trades people, moreover, according to this view, may have thought it profitable to conciliate a firm power across the frontiers; and we hear of at least one trader who preferred life with Attila to an existence in the hideously over-taxed empire, where a poor man had no chance in a court of law. But, as it happens, we cannot pronounce on the merits of the appeasement policy, because of an historical accident. The successor of Theodosius, Marcian, decided to adopt a 'tough' policy. He was never to try it. For Attila died; and whether it would have worked remains a matter for imaginative speculation.

One delegation to Attila's distant camp, from the imperial court at Constantinople, included a certain Priscus – he is the man who met the renegrade trader. Priscus has left us a strange account of his mission. It was not made any easier by the fact that, at a dinner party with Huns on the way, at Sofia, the delegation's interpreter made an unfortunate reference to Attila, which was only glossed over by cornering the Huns after dinner and pressing rich gifts upon them. A greater complication was the fact that the same interpreter had actually been commissioned by a statesman to arrange Attila's murder, and Attila discovered this. Nevertheless, he received the delegates, though it is true that at the meeting he himself talked, rudely, all the time. Then, following him back to his remote headquarters, somewhere (it is suggested in Wallachia) they attended royal banquets, and heard Attila's two bards – important stimulators of loyal emotion among his subjects, and of an epic tradition for the future. Incidentally, they met the dwarf Zerco – still without his wife – and Priscus called on Attila's wife. Another experience was a visit to the only Hun bathroom. On their return to Constantinople, they had many alarming experiences to report; but they had at least survived, and later even the interpreter was rescued.

But Attila soon decided to strike again, this time not at the Balkans but the west, into Gaul. Caesar's conquests in Gaul were at last breaking apart; for instance, there was now a German Gothic kingdom based on Toulouse. In AD 451 that kingdom was Attila's first objective. At this moment, however, his unwelcome attention was diverted towards the western Roman emperor in Italy, Valentinian III. This was the result of a strange episode involving the emperor's sister, Honoria. That lady had disgraced herself, and was about to be married off to a dull senator. To avoid this fate, she formed the enterprising plan of becoming the wife, or rather one of the wives, of Attila. She offered, as Gibbon puts it, 'to deliver her person into the arms of a barbarian, of whose language she was ignorant, whose figure was scarcely human, and whose religion and manners she abhorred. By the ministry of a faithful eunuch, she transmitted to Attila a ring, the pledge of her affection; and earnestly conjured him to claim her as a lawful spouse to whom he had been secretly betrothed. These advances were received, however, with coldness and disdain; and the king of the Huns continued to multiply the number of his wives, till his love was awakened by the more forcible passions of ambition and avarice.' And then, Gibbon imaginatively assures us, 'almost in the spirit of romantic chivalry, the savage monarch professed himself the lover and the champion of the princess Honoria.' This intrigue now came to the western emperor's notice, and his sister disappeared from view. But Attila had his pretext. He sent Valentinian an ambassador, who declared: 'Attila, my master and your master, has ordered you through me to make your palace ready for him'; and the Huns forthwith moved into panic-stricken Gaul. The Romans, joined by the German immigrants, somehow stopped him south-east of Paris in one of the decisive engagements of history, known as 'the battle of Chalons' – though perhaps it was really fought near Troyes. But in the next year

Attila drove far into Italy itself, only retiring – after being met by a delegation including Pope Leo I (whose companions were shown by Raphael as Saints Peter and Paul themselves) – because the country, very short of food, failed to support his troops.

The threat to both Roman empires was now intense; it seemed as if either or both of them might at any moment receive a fearful blow. At this juncture, in AD 453, Attila had yet another wedding night – this time with a girl whose name is said to signify 'little Hilda', identified with Siegfried's widow Kriemhild, and, in the earlier Norse sagas, with Guthrun, the sister of a king of Burgundy whom Attila had worsted. His wedding night with this complicated personage was his last night on earth. What actually happened is faithfully recorded by Chaucer's reference to his *Bledying at the nose in drunkenesse – a capitayn should live in sobrenesse*. But 'poetical imagination,' as Sir Maurice Bowra points out in his book *Heroic Poetry*, 'was inflamed by his death, and told how he was killed by his wife in revenge for his treacherous murder of her brothers in his halls. This is not what history relates . . . but a great king who dies on his wedding night is a fit victim for legend . . . the dire tale told in the *Elder Edda* provides a more than fitting end for the Scourge of God.'

Attila's death meant that the danger from the Huns was over.

As the dead man's successors tore each other's throats, hordes of quite different nomads swept west and swamped their disintegrating forces. The empire of the Huns was gone as quickly as it had come. They disappeared from history. They had shaken the Roman empires to their foundations. They had also, more obligingly, removed potential German dangers from the Roman borders. The western empire in any case was on its last legs; but the eastern empire recovered itself and had exactly one thousand years more to live. The Huns themselves had given the world nothing whatever except panic and destruction. To have lived as a conquered subject of the Huns provided the *reductio ad absurdum* of a desire for 'peace at any price.'

But how great a man was Attila? Here there is a divergence between J.B. Bury and E.A. Thompson. For Bury, 'Attila's genius alone had sustained the huge and disjointed fabric.' For Thompson, Attila was not in the first class either as soldier or as a diplomat. True, he extended and strengthened the Hun empire and knew well how to exploit its subjects; but his uncle Rua and others had laid the foundations of his power. That sort of interpretation, denying that general trends of history are changed by 'great men,' is in tune with the theories of thinkers like Plekhanov, whose followers describe even Stalin as 'the vehicle of anonymous forces at work in the background.' But, even at the lowest estimate – assuming that Stalin and Attila knew only how to use their times and chances –

both of them, in their different ways, gave a remarkable jolt to history. H.A.L. Fisher preferred a marine metaphor. The successive emergencies of history 'follow one another,' he says, 'as wave follows wave.' Many men are overwhelmed by the waves; but a few come into view on top of their crests. In the sense that they are conspicuous, they are 'great,' and on the crest of one such historical wave appeared, briefly, the terrifying, sullen, flatnosed face of Attila.

*   *   *

Michael Grant (b. 1914) was educated at Harrow and Trinity College, Cambridge, where he was Fellow 1938–49. He went on to become Professor of Humanity at Edinburgh University (1948–59) and the first Vice-Chancellor of the University of Khartoum (1956–8). He was also President and Vice-Chancellor of Queen's University, Belfast (1959–66). Grant has written over forty books on all aspects of the ancient world. His autobiography *My First Eighty Years* was published in 1994. Since then he has written *The Antonines* (1994), *Art in the Roman Empire* (1995), *The Severans* (1996), *From Rome to Byzantium* (1998) and *The Collapse and Recovery of the Roman Empire* (1998).

10

The Kaiser in Exile

SIR ROBERT BRUCE LOCKHART

(January 1955)

The historian and diplomat Robert Bruce Lockhart was the first British subject to be received by the Kaiser after the Great War.

As a young student in Berlin in 1905 I had seen the Kaiser riding majestically down Unter den Linden at the head of his Guards. He was then a resplendent figure in white and black with his famous moustache pointing its waxed ends perpendicularly to the heavens. Nothing could then have been further from my mind than the thought that twenty-three years later I should meet him, visit him in exile and maintain with him until the outbreak of the Second World War a more or less regular correspondence.

The manner of our meeting was wholly unexpected. In November 1928, I had just become a journalist and had been sent on a short visit to Berlin as a test of my abilities. I had been sumptuously entertained by my old German friends, but had discovered nothing of particular interest to my newspaper and had already booked by sleeper for the homeward journey when I received an invitation to lunch with Richard Kühlmann, the former German Foreign Minister.

At the luncheon at Kühlmann's house I met Karl Friedrich Nowak, the author of *The Downfall of the Central Powers* and of *Versailles* and at this time the Kaiser's historical adviser. We got on well. He asked me to dine alone with him and took me into his confidence. In that autumn of 1928 there had appeared in England a book entitled *The Letters of the Empress Frederick*. It had a preface by Sir Frederick Ponsonby, then the Keeper of the Privy Purse. The Empress Frederick, daughter of Queen Victoria, was the Kaiser's mother, and the Kaiser, bitterly hurt by the references to himself, wanted to have the book withdrawn. He had placed the handling of this business in Nowak's hands. Could I recommend a British authority on copyright?

I told Nowak that the copyright of these letters belonged without a doubt to the Kaiser and I gave him the name of a well-known English expert. The Kaiser could get an injunction, but would it help? The book, I said, had not attracted much attention. But an action, however successful it might be, might well create a publicity which would embarrass the Kaiser.

'What are we to do?' said Nowak, 'for something must be done.' I suggested that the Kaiser might write a dignified explanation of his relations with his mother and have it published in England and Germany. The idea pleased Nowak, and he improved upon it. 'We could have a German edition of the letters,' he said, 'and the Kaiser could write the preface.'

I went back to England. Nowak followed me. We saw Sir Frederick Macmillan, the publisher of the Empress's letters. There were no difficulties, and on November 24th and 25th, 1928, I went with Nowak to Doorn. The Kaiser agreed to Nowak's plan, and within sixteen days of my luncheon with Kühlmann a difficult and delicate negotiation had been settled amicably.

On this occasion I had no conversation with the Kaiser, because he had taken a vow not to receive any British subject so long as British troops remained on German soil. Hospitality, however, was lavished on me, and, like an actor, the Kaiser showed himself to me on several occasions. The moustache was now grey and no longer *erreicht*. Moreover, it was supplemented by a grey beard. The war lord of 1905 had become an amiable old man. In spite of missing my talk, I went away well pleased, for I had obtained the exclusive right to publish the English translation of the Kaiser's preface in my newspaper and a promise that, as soon as the British troops left the Rhine, I should have the first authentic interview granted by the Kaiser since his abdication.

I received the preface early in 1929, and it was published in the *Evening Standard* in February of the same year. I gave little thought to the promised interview. Journalists of all countries regarded the Kaiser's ban on interviews as inviolable, and the general opinion was that my interview would not take place.

The last British troops left Germany on December 12th, 1929. On December 14th, by the Kaiser's invitation, I was on my way to Doorn. The invitation stated that 'His Imperial Majesty wished to express to me personally his gratitude for my help in relation to the Emperor's preface to the Letters of the Empress Frederick, his august Mother.' Doorn is about fifteen miles south-east of Utrecht and lies in typically flat Dutch country. The Kaiser's house was formerly a Bishop's palace and stands in a small park. It was a dismal day when I set out from Utrecht, but when I reached Doorn the rain had stopped. I found the Kaiser in the drive. He was wearing a soft Homburg hat, knickerbockers and a long, loose

Byronesque cape. He was then seventy and looked ten years younger. Taking me by the arm, he began to ask me about his English relations. He told me that of the British Royal Family only Princess Beatrice had written to condole with him on the Kaiserin's death.

When we went indoors to his study in the upper story [*sic*] of the tower, everything had been prepared for the reception of a British visitor. On the table by his desk were several portraits of the Kaiser as a boy in England: one in a kilt at Balmoral and another in a sailor-suit at Cowes. The portrait which he prized most was of himself as a child of two in skirts. It had been painted by Queen Victoria. I was not surprised when he told me that he had been the favourite grand-child.

His English was excellent. He spoke in quick, animated sentences, his face lighting up with enthusiasm as he warmed to each of the numerous subjects which he discussed. In some respects he was ultra-German. His household was regulated with German punctuality. The discipline of his own life was also German in its thoroughness. He rose at seven, was dressed by eight, and took a vigorous walk before family prayers at which he always read a chapter of the Bible. Breakfast at nine was his chief meal. From 9.30 to 11.30 he worked in his garden. From noon to one he received the reports of his secretaries and attended to his correspondence. Luncheon was a simple meal and was followed by a short rest. After tea he went back to his study to read or write till eight. After dinner, his most frugal meal, the household assembled in the smoking-room and listened while the Kaiser read aloud. At 10.15 he retired to bed. From this routine he never varied.

On the other hand, he could laugh at himself as only an Englishman can. Moreover, although for the part of my interview which was to be published I had to submit written questions to which he wrote written answers, he was amazingly frank in the conversation which we agreed was to be 'off the record.' It was clear that he felt no responsibility whatsoever for the war. He also claimed that during the Boer War he alone had prevented France, Germany and Russia from attacking Britain and giving full aid to the Boers. He left me in no doubt as to whom he liked and disliked. During this first visit Shaw was in high favour because of his play, 'The Apple-Cart,' which the Kaiser knew almost by heart. Those whom he detested ranged from Lloyd George to Lenin, and everyone in this category was dismissed invariably as 'the greatest scoundrel unhung.' In world affairs he still saw himself as the man who had first warned Europe against the dangers of the Yellow Peril. The Russian revolution, which as an intensely religious man he detested, seemed to him to increase the menace and he foresaw very clearly the day when Western Europe must unite against the East or go under.

By all standards he seemed to me a remarkable man. In his exile religion was obviously his greatest solace, and his belief that one day he would face His Maker was, I think, genuine. 'The materialism of the present age will pass,' he said to me. 'Man's spiritual development has not kept pace with his material progress. The great races, especially England and Germany, will experience a religious revival. . . . Religion is for all peoples and is for all mankind God's law-book for eternity. . . . That I have to live far from my dearly-loved country and my people to whom my whole being was dedicated is a trial imposed by God to which obediently and unresistingly I submit.'

It was his faith which made him the least discontented person in the rather dismal household at Doorn. He could be humorous, too, although many of his funny stories were hoary with age. But when one of the gentlemen of the household interrupted us with a staccato 'Quarter to one, majestät,' the Kaiser replied with a smile: 'All right, all right, I haven't committed any indiscretions yet.' There was more bitterness than humour when he told me that on that very morning he had felled his 20,000th tree, and added 'Don't put this in your paper or Theodore Wolff[1] will say: "What are 20,000 trees compared with 2,000,000 German lives?"' there was the same consciousness of all that had been said against him when he gave me a fine portrait of himself with the inscription taken from Abraham Lincoln: 'Nothing is ended finally until it is ended rightly,' and added quickly: 'Put it away in some corner. It may compromise you.'

Most marked was his bitterness in regard to England. After my first day at Doorn I sat up half the night in my hotel writing an account of my visit and submitted it to him the next day. In one place I had written: 'I think that the Kaiser still regards England as his second fatherland, that he did his personal best to keep peace, and that he regrets the English point of view which attributes to him the responsibility for the war.' The Kaiser made several significant alterations. 'Still regards England' was changed to 'regarded England'; 'regrets the English point of view' became 'is deeply wounded by the English point of view.'

His attitude to me remained friendly. When in 1933 he sent Prince Louis Ferdinand, his grandson and today heir to the German throne, to England, he put him more or less under my tutelage. I took the Prince to see our Prince of Wales and to have tea on the terrace of the Houses of Parliament with Mr Lloyd George and Mr Winston Churchill. All three made themselves pleasant to the young prince, who got on famously with the Prince of Wales and heard kind words about his grandfather from Mr Lloyd George and Mr Churchill, both of whom, doubtless, had neither

---

[1]   Editor of the *Berliner Tageblatt*.

the wish nor the bad manners to run down the Kaiser in the presence of his grandson.

On Prince Louis Ferdinand's return to Germany, I received a characteristic letter from the Kaiser. On the whole he was well pleased with the reception given to his grandson. There were compliments to all who had entertained him, gracious words to the address of the Prince of Wales, a slightly mollified attitude towards Mr Churchill, but as regards Mr Lloyd George a sarcastic sentence of surprise that the man who had won an election on a promise to 'hang the Kaiser' had now changed his mind.

Six years passed before I made my third visit to Doorn. During the interval I had carried on an intermittent correspondence with the Kaiser, who from time to time sent me books and monographs which interested him. The books dealt with his two political manias: Communism and the Yellow Peril. Some of the monographs were written by himself, and I remember particularly his booklet on the Chinese monad, the forerunner of the Nazi *hakenkreuz*, and his learned treatise on the influence of climate and soil on racial culture.

My new invitation to Doorn came as a complete surprise. I had told the Kaiser that I was going to the South of France to finish a book. His reaction was to invite me to take in Doorn on my way. I arrived at Utrecht on February 19th, 1936, and spent the next day at Doorn. The Kaiser looked marvellously well. He talked as vigorously as ever, and I noticed how cleverly he still managed his deformed left hand. At that time not more than five feet eight in height, he still had the broad shoulders and figure of a man of fifteen to twenty years younger than himself. Doorn itself had not altered at all since my first visit in 1928, but the Kaiser's mental preoccupations had undergone a change. The Nazis were in power in Germany. Edward VIII had replaced his father on the English throne. The Kaiser had always like the new King. He remembered him as a small boy. He was particularly pleased because King Edward had told Prince Friedrich, another grandson of the Kaiser, that 'all this enmity nonsense between the two families must now cease.'

The Nazis were in a different category, and the Kaiser was outspoken in his dislike. He had no news from Germany because his correspondence was now controlled as it never had been by the Weimar Republic. The Nazis, he said, had made a major mistake in their treatment of the Lutheran Church, which had behaved splendidly and was bound to win in the long run. He was also confident that the Nazis feared the growing sympathy with the monarchy.

During the visit his talk was almost entirely political, and for the first time he seemed to be optimistic about the restoration. If the monarchy were restored, he said, the British must not assume that the new German Parliament would be like the British Parliament. Much of Europe was not yet ripe for universal democracy. The new German Parliament would be vertical and not horizontal and would be based on the old Nuremberg system under which patrician, burgher, and apprentice were members of the same guild. Representatives would be selected from the best men in all professions.

'I am writing something on this subject,' he said, 'but not for your paper.'

He had also a good deal to say to the address of England. The white races, he declared, must stick together and Germany and England must unite to prevent Europe from fighting. Bolshevism was the greatest danger, and Britain's policy was incomprehensible. How could Britain trust Russia or back Russia against Japan! Britain was very foolish to break her alliance with Japan who was a bulwark against Bolshevism. England's allies in Asia should be Japan and the Mohammedans.

He was not at all pro-Italian, but he regarded the sanctions against Italy as madness and the League of Nations as worse than futile. More than once Britain had given quasi-encouragement to Mussolini to go into Abyssinia. And how could the proud English allow second and third grade countries like Paraguay and Colombia to dictate her foreign policy! The trouble in Europe since the war arose from the fact that there were too many politicians and no statesmen. All this was said with vigour, but without ill-will, and, when the Princess Hermine, the second Kaiserin, came to tell him that it was time for his rest, he turned to me with a smile: 'You say that I look so well. Now you see why. All due to Her Majesty.'

As parting gifts, he presented me with a new portrait of himself and a heavy book entitled *The Struggle for the World Control of Cotton*.

Even in the dullness of Doorn he lived a happy family life. Indeed, he seemed to have only one sorrow. Since my second visit Karl Nowak had died, and the Kaiser could find no one else to write his memoirs for which he had already prepared the material for a third and perhaps a fourth volume. Nowak had helped with the earlier volumes.

My last visit to the Kaiser was on August 16th and 17th in 1939 when I went there with John Wheeler-Bennett, the English historian. In 1939 the Kaiser had celebrated his eightieth birthday, but his energy seemed unimpaired, and we spent a day which was as strenuous for us as it was for him. At that time Wheeler-Bennett was planning to write a new biography of the Kaiser, and much of the talk, which went on before, during, and after luncheon, and again before and after dinner, was concerned with historical questions and the merits of various historians, several of whom received again the imperial epithet of 'the greatest scoundrel unhung.'

He was in good spirits and talked much of the greed which had brought many great nations to their doom. He had, he told us, evolved a new theory during his years of trial. No nation should occupy more territory than Providence intended for it. Otherwise, retribution would follow sooner or later. One might have asked who was to interpret Providence's intentions. Instead, I put the question in another form. Did his reference to punishment apply to the British Empire or to the Third Reich of Hitler? He paused for a moment and then replied: 'to all empires and, therefore, to both.' He was still pre-occupied by his religious faith and said to us without fear: 'I may be called next year.' In point of fact, he lived on until June, 1941.

If there was little alteration in him, the household had changed considerably. Loyal and aged members like Count Hamilton and Count Finckelstein had been replaced by younger and sterner men devoted to the Nazis. In the afternoon we had tea with the Empress Hermine, who urged Wheeler-Bennett to finish his book quickly because it would give such pleasure to the Kaiser. She promised him all help, but begged him never to write to Berlin. The Nazis opened all the Kaiser's correspondence. She also warned us to beware of the new members of the Kaiser's household and to reveal no confidences to them. They reported everything to the Nazis.

After tea, as a highly privileged favour the Empress showed us the room in which the Kaiser's first wife had died. It had been left exactly as it was in the Kaiserin's life-time. On the bed lay a sheaf of bronze palm leaves and on the pillow a bronze chaplet. I thought of Queen Victoria and the Prince Consort. The departed were commemorated in Doorn in the same way as at Windsor.

I felt sad and slightly emotional when we said good-bye to the Kaiser soon after ten p.m. We were going back to war, and I knew that I should never see him again. In October of 1953, I re-visited Doorn, which has now been turned into a private museum held in trust for the Hohenzollerns. Little has changed, although most of the smaller treasures, Frederick the Great's snuff-boxes and the Kaiser's cigarette cases, have been put under glass lest they might be stolen by visitors.

The Kaiser's Dutch servants were still there, recognized me at once, and from the archives produced some copies of the Kaiser's letters to me and also a copy of Marlborough with the following inscriptions written in a neat and well-known hand:

To His Imperial Majesty,
The Emperor William II of Germany
from
Winston S. Churchill.

The Dutch attendants spoke highly of the Kaiser's kindness to, and consideration of his staff, said that he had remained anti-Nazi to the last, and told us how General Dommes, Marshal of the Court, refused always to answer the 'Heil Hitler' salute of the high Nazi officials who visited Doorn during the war. They also told me that up to October 1953, 54,000 people had visited Doorn that year and that the vast majority of them consisted of German ex-officers.

*   *   *

Sir Robert Bruce Lockhart was born in Fife, Scotland, in 1887 and took pride in having 'no drop of English blood' in him. Having spent many years abroad – in Berlin and Paris for education, Malaya as a rubber-planter and Moscow as vice-consul – he joined the *Evening Standard* as the editor of the Londoner's Diary in 1928. He performed this job until 1937 and pulled off some impressive scoops, including the first British interview with the exiled Kaiser Wilhelm II in 1929. Bruce Lockhart's books, the first of which was *Memoirs of a British Agent*, were based mainly on his memories of people and events. He died in Hove in 1970.

11

The Great Rebuilding

W.G. HOSKINS

(February 1955)

W.G. Hoskins, advocate of local history, argued that few events in English social history had so escaped the notice of historians as the revolution in popular housing that occurred between the 1570s and the outbreak of the Civil War seventy years later.

The wave of ostentatious building that produced the country houses in the Elizabethan and Jacobean period has been amply recorded; but the remarkable wave of rebuilding and new building among all other social classes, except the poorest, has received little or no attention. This movement was so widespread all over England, except in the four most northerly counties, as to warrant the description of the Great Rebuilding.

Because it involved only minor domestic building, and nowhere called for architects, it was not documented in any direct way. Yet tangible evidence survives abundantly from Cornwall up to Lancashire, and from Shropshire across to Suffolk. If only historians would learn to appreciate the high value of visual evidence, as prehistorians are obliged to do! But as the documents multiply, so we tend to forget the other kinds of evidence of which the prehistorians make such good use. Documents can become an obsession to the exclusion of all else, and their importance can sometimes be overrated.

The Great Rebuilding involved both the towns and the countryside. In the urban areas there has necessarily been much more replacement of buildings, and a great deal of the evidence has been destroyed; but there seems little doubt that many English towns were substantially rebuilt or enlarged in these two generations. At Yarmouth, we have a rare piece of literary evidence to this effect. Henry Manship, writing one of the earliest town histories, about 1610, says: 'Neither was this town so replenished as then it was, in 220 years after [the Black Death]: for within these forty years last past many void grounds be now builded (and the town is more than a fourth part both in the building augmented, and in the number of inhabitants increased), which during that time lay waste and in a manner desolate.' Here we are specifically told that the rebuilding of the vacant sites began about 1570; and the well-known Rows remain as an example of this age of recovery.

The town of Oxford was in a state of decay during the same period of two hundred years or so, and vacant sites abounded. Here, too, the rebuilding began in the late sixteenth century and was especially active in the early seventeenth, when the town was, judging by the surviving houses, largely rebuilt. Shrewsbury retains a good deal of Elizabethan domestic building, reflecting a renewed prosperity, based mainly on the handling of Welsh cloth. In Leicester, much rebuilding took place during the early seventeenth century, as we know from a study of Flower's drawings, made in the 1820's and 1830's, before the Victorian period of industrial expansion obliterated nearly all traces of the past in domestic buildings.

In south-western England, the three generations or so after 1550 were a particularly prosperous time. Here the evidence of rebuilding and new building in the towns is striking, though once again it is derived to a considerable degree from nineteenth-century drawings, for the original buildings have been largely swept away by thoughtless town councils. At Dartmouth, the years between 1580 and 1643 saw the building of a great number of houses in the new style, a new quay, and the reconstruction of one of the churches.

At Plymouth there was a tremendous physical expansion in the late sixteenth century, as might be expected, since it had become the western base in the wars with Spain. The parish register suggest that the population of the town about doubled between 1580 and 1610; and we hear of at least half a dozen new streets in the municipal records in this period.

In the countryside, too, the building activity of the two generations or so after 1570 is very striking. In Devon one finds overwhelming testimony to rebuilding and enlargement from about 1560 onwards in many hundreds of scattered farmhouses; while at Chiddingstone, in Kent, there survives a virtually complete Elizabethan street. Much of the most-photographed minor Cotswold building originates in this period; so, too, does the equally pictorial 'black-and-white' building of the West Midlands and the Welsh Border.

It becomes apparent, as one examines the surviving structures and follows them up through the documentary evidence of probate inventories and manorial surveys, that this great building activity took three main forms. It involved either a 'modernization' of a medieval hall-house, so thorough that its medieval character is almost obliterated until one penetrates to the hall roof; or a complete rebuilding from the ground up on the ancestral site. There was also a good deal of new building on new sites – additional houses to meet the demands of a rising population.

This new building seems to have consisted mainly of cottages, though here and there new farmhouses were put up in regions of late colonization, such as Rossendale Forest in Lancashire, or the upland heaths of mid-Devon. There is a good deal of documentary evidence that large numbers of new cottages were being erected from the last quarter of the sixteenth century onwards, but, so far as one knows, not a single example of this class has survived. The earliest true cottages that we possess today date from the late seventeenth century. All the Elizabethan and Jacobean cottages have fallen down long ago; they were built by farmers and landlords and may have lasted a hundred years or so. What the estate agent today calls 'an olde worlde cottage' was – if it is genuine – the home of a husbandman and not a cottager.

As for farmhouses, thousands were modernized in the years between 1570 and 1640, and thousands more entirely rebuilt. These 'modernized' medieval houses are particularly common in Devon (though fieldwork may reveal numbers of them elsewhere) and they are all stone-built. As a type, they can be described broadly as fifteenth-century hall-houses, modernized about 1600 by the insertion of a ceiling in the hall, so giving a bedroom-floor above, and by the insertion of internal partitions on both floors so as to give smaller and warmer rooms. This fundamental change usually involved the making of a staircase to the upper floor, the putting in of glazed windows, and the provision of fireplaces additional to the original hearth in the medieval hall. Not all these internal changes were necessarily made simultaneously – they may have been spread over a generation or two – but in many instances one can see that the transformation was carried through in one major operation. In Devon, perhaps in the South-West generally, this kind of modernization appears to have been more common than complete rebuilding, possibly because the original house was already built of stone and formed a solid shell.

Where we find a region in which complete rebuilding was the rule, as in the Cotswold limestone and the Northamptonshire ironstone districts, we may suspect that it reflects a fundamental change in building materials. The older tradition of the Stone Belt, before the sixteenth century, seems to have expressed itself in timber buildings like those in the rest of the Midlands. In the sixteenth and seventeenth centuries one finds widespread changeover from timber to stone buildings, not only on the oolitic lime-stone and the ironstone, but also on the millstone grits, and sandstones and limestones, of northern England – Whitaker says this happened in

Lancashire during Elizabeth's reign – and this meant a total rebuilding and a new plan. This new plan was essentially one of a two-floored house, with several more or less small rooms on each floor. But where stone-building was already established at an early date, as over a good deal of Devon (which was rich in local building stones), modernization was the rule.

Who was responsible for this wave of building throughout most of England, and why does it make its appearance with this suddenness? In the towns there is plenty of evidence that the wealthier merchants were enlarging their medieval houses, or building entirely new houses on the old sites. We do not know how far down the social scale this activity went, for we must not forget that the evidence we possess (both documentary and structural) relates only to the main streets of the towns, or the former main streets, and we know little or nothing about the lanes and the suburbs where the labouring population lived. In the country, similarly, the greater part of this building activity can be traced back to freeholders, who were more numerous in all counties than we are perhaps inclined to believe, and to the larger copyholders and life-leaseholders, who were often as secure in their tenure as freeholders.

For both the merchant-class and the big-farmer class, the second half of the sixteenth century was a time of profit-inflation. The price-revolution was well under way by the 1540's, and thereafter selling-prices were rising faster than costs. Money-savings accumulated steadily in town and country coffers. We discover ever larger sums of ready money in Elizabethan and Jacobean inventories; and literary observers, such as Harrison and Carew, remark upon the greater plenty of money. It is one of the symptoms of inflation in any age. Elizabethan farmers certainly had the financial means to rebuild, reconstruct, and enlarge the comfortless and cramped houses of their forefathers. By the 1570's they had enjoyed a generation or more of rising profits; by 1600 they had two generations of savings to draw upon, and we find them able to put down hundreds of pounds if necessary in marriage settlements or for the purchase of leases for three lives. Their houses, too, were infinitely better furnished in all respects than those of their fathers and grandfathers.

But the new abundance of money is not the fundamental explanation for the housing revolution. That must be looked for in the development of a sense of privacy among the middle strata of society. Ever since the fourteenth century the magnates had been acquiring this desire for a private life – Langland complains of their growing habit of withdrawal from the common life around them – and by the middle of the sixteenth century the yeoman and the merchant were copying their betters. It was this sense of privacy, as Lewis Mumford rightly says, that destroyed the form of the medieval dwelling-house. We find in the inventories of the

1570's and 1580's yeomen's houses with eight to ten rooms, each with a specialized use, and husbandmen's houses with three or four rooms, instead of the basic medieval type of hall and bower only. In the wealthier towns like Exeter, merchants' houses might have ten to fifteen rooms, and smaller men (butchers and glaziers, for example) had four or five. One merchant's house in 1578 had no fewer than twenty-two rooms: each floor must have been minutely subdivided.

In this multiplication of small rooms, instead of the two or three large medieval rooms, the coming of cheap window-glass and the marked increase of coal production both played their part: the new rooms could be better lit, and there was no longer any physical need to herd around the common fireplace in the hall. It was not only a revolution in housing, but almost a revolution in human psychology. The merchant in his counting-house and the yeoman in his 'best parlour' could develop a private life. It is no accident that in this period we get the first diaries from the 'middle class,' both in town and country.

There is one important point upon which one cannot be dogmatic: that is the connection between the Great Rebuilding and the remarkable increase of population to be observed during the period. Where new cottage-building is concerned, I think the rise of population was the cause: no landlord was likely to build cottages for tenants in advance of the demand. It may also be, however, that a greater availability of cottages in the Elizabethan countryside encouraged earlier marriages (Carew in Cornwall remarked in the 1580's that people were marrying much earlier in life), and so increased the birth-rate. But some increase of population must have been well under way in the first place.

In regard to farmhouses, on the other hand, there is good reason to believe that the rise of population was primarily an effect of the housing revolution. By Jacobean days it is true that the farmer's or parson's family of six to twelve children (there is ample documentary evidence for this statement) needed a bigger house, and some enlargement would follow; or possibly the need was met by inserting more internal partitions within large, old rooms. One can easily detect these later partitions by rapping on the bedroom walls with the knuckles. But we have to account for the rise of population in the first place, and I suggest that one fundamental cause – besides the earlier marriages already spoken of – was a dramatic fall in infant and maternal mortality in this new type of house. It was larger, lighter, warmer, and better ventilated than the medieval house it had superseded, and easier to keep clean because there were more rooms devoted to specialized uses. There was far less dirt and risk of infection: mother and child were more or less segregated in a clean bedroom instead of lying within a few feet of the dirt of everyday life and work.

The quantities of linen and napery in household inventories testify to this new cleanliness, in farmhouses at least. Domestic life was revolutionized in the Elizabethan period and the early seventeenth century; and among the many consequences of this revolution fewer mothers and infants died. A better standard of diet, more fruit and garden-stuff and medicinal herbs, also helped to increase vitality and resistance to infections; but the simultaneous increase in house-room, cleanliness, and ventilation must have been of major importance in lowering death-rates. By the 1630's this rapid increase of population in town and country produced a new congestion of housing, and these good effects were undone. In the provincial towns the slums begin to appear in the seventeenth century, and in the open-field villages, too, a century of ill-health sets in.

*   *   *

W.G. Hoskins (1908–92), pioneering historian of landscape history, was born and studied in Exeter. He taught economics at University College, Leicester (1931–41, 1946–8), served on the price regulating committee (1941–5), and joined the history department at Leicester (1948), becoming professor in 1965. He is best known for his book *The Making of the English Landscape* (1955), and for his BBC series, *Landscapes of England* (1976–8). He was the first to explain the historical evolution of the landscape, and created a new interest in local history.

12

The Social Origins of the Great Rebellion

HUGH TREVOR-ROPER

(June 1955)

The 'gentry' were not 'rising', 'capitalism' played little part in the Revolution of 1640–60 and the Revolution itself fundamentally failed. Here is Hugh Trevor-Roper, practising the polemical skills for which he was to become feared and famous.

The social interpretation of the Great Rebellion, or Puritan Revolution of 1640–1660, is one of the most controversial subjects among English historians today. Not only conflicting, but entirely opposite and incompatible, views are held about it. But before considering these views, let me remind readers briefly of the course of events to which they apply.

The Great Rebellion began in 1640 with the summoning of the Long Parliament which, having forced Charles I to end his period of 'personal rule,' and having removed the ministers who had governed in his name, enacted a series of constitutional reforms. Unfortunately, the Parliament had just grounds for distrusting the King's good faith, and this distrust, combined with certain political accidents, led, in 1642, to Civil War. In order to win this war the Parliament was obliged, in 1645, to create a new army, and this new army soon became the instrument of a new party in the country. This new party, the party of the Independents, soon showed itself as a revolutionary party which made all previous politics obsolete: it overpowered the Parliament, executed the King, destroyed the monarchy, and set up, under Oliver Cromwell, a military régime which did not founder until after his death.

Now in the social interpretation of these events the crucial question is, who were these Independents? What social forces did they represent?

What did they seek to do? What did they succeed in doing? And this is the question which has elicited the most various answers.

The classic answer, which has been underwritten by some of the most distinguished historians and promptly accepted as the orthodoxy of the Schools, is that of the doyen of English social and economic history, Professor R.H. Tawney. This view rests on three major premises. First, Tawney accepts, at least in some sense, the view of Max Weber that Puritanism was the ideology of capitalism, that 'capitalism was the social counterpart of Calvinist theology.' Secondly, he supposes that the period from 1540–1640 was a period, in England, of continuous economic advance by the 'capitalist' and puritan classes, who, with increasing prosperity, became increasingly resentful of the paternal restrictions imposed by the state. Thirdly, he supposes that the gentry was a force on the side of capitalism. The gentry, he argues, by introducing capitalist principles of land-management, became a rural branch of the bourgeoisie, a continuously 'rising' class, unlike the aristocracy, who, being committed to obsolete methods, were rapidly declining into debt and ruin. On the basis of these premises, Tawney interprets the Great Rebellion as the last, violent episode of the victory of the prosperous, self-confident, impatient bourgeoisie over the old order, impoverished, anachronistic, but tenacious. According to this view, the crown and the aristocracy were a debtor class, the merchants and gentry a creditor class; and the Great Rebellion was a kind of forcible foreclosure of impatient *nouveau-riche* creditors on evasive aristocratic debtors: 'It was discovered, not for the first time, that as a method of foreclosure war was cheaper than litigation.'

Now this view, which of course I have greatly (but, I think, not unfairly) simplified, has recommended itself to a very wide range of historians. Roman Catholics, seeing Protestantism equated with capitalism by scholars, and capitalism turned into a word of abuse by socialists, have been quick to seize their advantage and declare that the Protestant Reformation in England is thus proved to have been 'a rebellion of the rich against the poor,' leading to all the ills that modern socialists complain of. Marxist historians, declaring summarily that the equation of Puritanism with capitalism is one of 'the irresistible conclusions of modern research,' announce that the Puritan Revolution was the crucial victory in the world struggle of capitalism to burst its 'feudal' bonds: it was 'the decisive shift' from a generally feudal to a predominantly capitalist society. . . . 'Had the English revolution failed, as so many other revolutions in the seventeenth century failed, it is entirely possible that economic development might have been long retarded.' As it was (they say) 'the Revolution triumphed, with portentous results': the puritan onslaught broke down the resistance of feudalism and by its success secured the victory of capitalism in the world. The army of Cromwell provided the shock-troops of the bourgeoisie.

Now my interpretation is very different from this view of the Tawney school. It could hardly fail to be, because I disagree fundamentally with all three of its major premises. First, I do not think that there is any exclusive connection between Puritanism and Capitalism: I find that the English Puritans included strong anti-capitalist forces, and that orthodox Calvinism, so far from being the ideology of the merchant classes in the seventeenth century, prevailed largely – in Protestant countries – among backwoods squires, as in Scotland and Gelderland. Secondly, whatever may be said of the period before 1590, I do not think that the years 1590–1640 were a period of growing general prosperity in Europe, or even in England (though certain special trades, centred in London, brought prosperity to certain great London merchants and, of course, government financiers). Thirdly, I do not think that the gentry were 'rising' in that period: on the contrary, I find evidence of general decline among those whose income came solely or largely from land. In fact, I do not think that 'capitalism' played any great part in the Revolution: the City of London was royalist and had to be drastically purged four times in order to keep it in line with the rebels, and the parliamentary boroughs, whose support to the opposition has been claimed as evidence of mercantile feeling, did not represent merchant feeling at all: they were 'rotten boroughs' controlled by great magnates whose opposition was far from mercantile in character. Finally, I do not believe that the Revolution 'triumphed with portentous results.' I believe that it failed.

I shall not use time here in destructive argument. In this essay I propose to consider the social nature of the revolution by asking two questions of fact: first, what was the economic position of the gentry, who, since they dominated both Parliament and local government, were the essential social class in any parliamentary and national movement? and, secondly, what were the most insistent claims of the 'Independents' who provided the revolutionary force in this movement? Fortunately, in the increasing quantity of local and family history, in the parliamentary records and vast pamphlet literature of the period, we have abundant evidence on which to attempt an answer to this question.

First, what was the economic state of the gentry? In my opinion, Tawney has misrepresented this problem by selecting, as instances of a general economic 'rise of the gentry,' only those families whose fortunes, in fact, can be shown to have come not from land but from office. Office-holders naturally owned land; but land was not the source of their wealth: it was not even necessarily an economic investment: it was a social asset –

it may even have been an economic liability. If we wish to learn about the state of the gentry, we must not consider such office-holding gentry but the 'mere gentry,' *'les pauvres gentilhommes,'* as Cardinal Richelieu called them, *'dont le bien ne consiste qu'en fonds de terre.'* If we do this, I think we discover overwhelming evidence that such men, in England as in France, were in economic difficulty.

Wherever we look, it is the same. In North Wales, the gentry were all declaring themselves ruined. In Staffordshire, between 1600 and 1660, half the land was said to have been sold. It was out of the estates of decayed northern gentry that the Countess of Shewsbury and Lord William Howard endowed the noble houses that they founded, and in 1614, when the first Earl of Cork wanted to establish his family in his home county, he was told that he could please himself 'for half of Herefordshire is for sale.' In the same year, 'most of the ancientest gentlemen's houses' in Northamptonshire were declared 'either divided, diminished or decayed.' In the last few years, many good manors had been sold, but 'not a gentleman of the county hath bought any, but strangers and they no inhabitants.' In Nottinghamshire, in 1625, the sheriff reported that the resident gentry had been much diminished, bought out by strangers. The lands in Berkshire were likened to skittish horses which often threw their owners. Modern scholars have shown that the gentry of Devonshire were almost universally in debt in the 1630s, that those of Lincolnshire were almost all declining, and that, in Bedfordshire, Buckinghamshire and Northamptonshire, one family in three among them, between 1600 and 1640, was selling its land. Clearly the decline was not merely local: it was general, throughout England.

And who were the 'strangers' who are named as thus buying up the decaying gentry: The Earl of Cork, the Countess of Shewsbury, her son the Earl of Devonshire, Lord William Howard – officers and grandees of the court; Alderman Soame, Alderman Craven, Alderman Cokayne, Sir Thomas Middleton, Sir Arthur Ingram, Sir Baptist Hicks – great merchants and government financiers from the City of London. It is an oligarchy of metropolitan plutocrats, aldermen of London and courtiers of Whitehall, who are sucking the life out of the 'mere gentry' and 'decayed boroughs' of the provinces. For it is because boroughs are economically 'decayed' that they become politically 'rotten,' and sell their independence to aristocratic patrons. Thriving towns, like Newcastle-upon-Tyne, linked to London by the coal trade, or Bristol, the port of Western trade, continue to elect their own representatives.

What were the gentry to do in such circumstances? In Spain, the impoverished *hidalgo* had a solution: *iglesia o casa real o mar*, office in

Church or Court, or the sea. The English gentleman thought in the same terms. 'It is impossible,' wrote one of them, 'for a mere country gentleman ever to grow rich or raise his house. He must have some other vocation with his inheritance, as to be a courtier, lawyer, merchant or some other vocation. If he hath no other vocation, let him get a ship and judiciously manage her, or buy some auditor's place, or be vice-admiral in his county. By only following the plough he may keep his word and be upright, but will never increase his fortune. Sir John Oglander wrote this with his own blood, June the 25th, 1632.' It was no accident that the first thirty years of the seventeenth century saw an unprecedented scramble for office, an unprecedented and rising market in office, a desire to make office hereditary, as in France; and that, in the 1630s, when the more parsimonious government of Charles I cut down the opportunities at court, there was an unprecedented emigration of the gentry to North America. Nor is it an accident that the gentry, who thus embarked on colonial schemes, were puritans and became the leaders of the Independents. Puritan austerity was often not the religion of rich capitalists, saving to invest: it was the religion of poor gentry, saving to make ends meet, and morally disgusted at the ostentation and extravagance of a court from which they were excluded and which flourished at their expense. It was appropriate that the leader of these gentry, when they became revolutionary, should have been Oliver Cromwell – the representative of a former court family, now reduced to their land and obliged, in his youth, to sell their great house in Huntingdonshire to a new family drawing its income from office and the law.

Thus the Great Rebellion, in my opinion, is not the clear-headed self-assertion of the rising bourgeoisie and gentry, but rather the blind protest of the depressed gentry. In the 1630s, incidental political factors increased this depression, and the radical gentry willingly supported the aristocratic politicians who sought, by parliamentary pressure, to bring the King back into the ancient constitutional ways. Unfortunately, these aristocratic leaders afterwards proved unable to contain their radical followers. Under the pressures of fear and civil war, the aristocratic leadership crumbled; and, in 1645, the Independents stood forth, mobilized, invincible, revolutionary, demanding satisfaction.

What were the demands of the Independents? Socially they are clear enough. They wanted independence from Court and City, the two swollen products of Tudor centralization to which the provinces – the 'mere gentry' and the 'decayed boroughs' – had so long been sacrificed. They wanted decentralization of government – the Cromwellian government would cut down the borough seats in Parliament and treble the county seats; decentralization of religion – toleration instead of a centralized Anglican or Presbyterian Church; decentralization of trade – 'I thought,' protested a West Country gentleman, 'that long ere this we should have trade dispersed all the nation over, but this City, it seems, must have all the trade'; decentralization of law – local county registries, local courts; decentralization of education – local schools, local universities. It was in the reign of the Independents that universities were projected in Wales and Cornwall, at York and Manchester, and a short-lived university founded in Durham. Socially, the Independent revolt was a revolt of the provinces against a century of Tudor centralization: against that enslavement of the country by the Court and City to which the depressed gentry ascribed their present plight.

But what of their political claims? When we ask this question we soon find that they were entirely negative. The Independents knew what they hated. They hated the Court, with its office-holders, its lawyers, its pensioners, its monopolists, its archaic taxes; they hated the Lords, those great courtiers – he hoped, Cromwell once said, to live to see never a nobleman in England; they hated the centralized Church, which had tried, under Archbishop Laud, to rob them of their patronage and their tithes. They hated the all-absorbent City – 'this nation,' they said, 'was falling into the rickets: the head bigger than the body.' And, in their radical mood, they duly destroyed these things. They executed the King, abolished the House of Lords, sold up the Church, purged the City.

But what were their positive alternatives? They were not republicans or whigs or mercantilists. A little 'whig' republican group, which did obtain the leadership in Parliament for a time, was soon eliminated. The Independent gentry had no positive theories: one form of government, they said, was as good as another; they would really prefer to be governed than to govern, to be 'tolerated' by a paternal government, under which they could prosper, than to exercise direct power, which they found too difficult. As to the form of that government – if pressed, they thought that 'a government with something monarchical in it' was probably the best thing. On second thoughts, Lords were a good thing too: 'We would keep up nobility'; and so was an established Church – they had never wanted to separate from the Anglican Church but only to live more comfortably in it than Archbishop Laud had allowed. The only thing that was *not* good was government by or for capitalists. Every aspect of Cromwell's rule aroused squeals of despair from the mercantile classes; but, when they protested, he told them sharply to keep to their counting-houses. A whig champion of the merchant class really answers the theorists of the capitalist revolution, long before they had spoken, when he entitled his diatribe against the economic policy of the Protectorate 'The World's Mistake in Oliver Cromwell.'

In truth, the Independents did not know what they wanted in politics. As Cromwell himself once said: 'None climbs so high as he who knows not whither he is going.' Or rather, what they wanted was so vaguely envisaged that they could not think of any constitutional formula to achieve it. What they wanted was 'a commonwealth.' The conception of 'the commonwealth,' of an organic, almost a collectivist society, had been a commonplace under the Tudors and the great Tudor statesmen, Thomas Cromwell and Lord Burghley, and their social philosophers, 'the Commonwealth men,' had sought, however imperfectly, to realize it. But with the coming of the Stuarts, those feckless Scottish kings, this ideal had been rejected by a government of irresponsible courtiers and favourites and had been inherited instead by the puritan opposition to government: an opposition not only inflamed by gentry grievances but also fired by a just indignation against feeble, bad and irresponsible government, the betrayal by selfish governors of 'the honest part of the nation.' Hence the cult, by the puritans, not of new or mercantile or republican ideas, but of a vague, romanticized English monarchy such as they supposed had existed under the last sovereign of the old dynasty, 'Queen Elizabeth of glorious memory.' When the Independent Army reasserted itself and effortlessly drove out of power the little côterie of 'whig' republicans who had usurped authority in its absence, the essential justification for that act was that the republican government thus over-thrown was not, as it called itself, a 'commonwealth,' but 'an oligarchy, detested by all men that love a commonwealth.' And so Oliver Cromwell and his Independents replaced the policy of *laissez-faire* at home and mercantile aggression abroad against England's trade rivals, the Dutch, by an anachronistic revival of 'Elizabethan' policy: paternal government, enforcement of poor law and tillage laws, leadership of the 'Protestant interest' in Europe, a protectorate over the Netherlands, a piratical war in the West Indies to tap the American treasure of Spain.

The Independent ideal was thus essentially an archaism. Unfortunately, the Independents could think of no institutions in which to crystallize and preserve such an archaism. Their philosopher, James Harrington, the author of *Oceana*, proposed a parliament of gentry holding office by rotation. That would prevent the rise of a privileged bureaucracy. More radical, Thomas Hobbes advocated the preservation of the old Tudor hierarchy and 'degree' – which alone, according to the Tudor philoso-phers, prevented man's natural wickedness from destroying the common-wealth – by an open resort to naked, unsanctified power. Both Harrington and Hobbes conveniently ignored the existence of mercantile classes. But in fact even these disparate philosophies could not recreate that obsolete ideal. After a series of short-lived constitutional experiments, the

Independents threw up the sponge and submitted again to the time-honoured rule of King, Lords, Commons and Established Church. Harrington died and was forgotten. Hobbes survived and was tolerated, in the new age, as a harmless old crank. The whole world of the Independents was rejected and became, in gay Restoration England, something of a joke. It is difficult to describe this as 'success' or 'triumph'. 'Success' by the Independents would have been a kind of decentralized anarchical gentry-republic, a Polish Diet. It is just as well that they failed.

And yet, protest our theorists, whatever the *nature* of the revolution, surely the *result* of it was a capitalist advance? If a new class had not come to political power, may it not nevertheless, behind the appearance of political continuity, have occupied the seats of social power? For, at the Restoration, one great change that had taken place was not reversed: the great transfer of land by enforced private sale. Now of the purchasers of these lands, says the Marxist historian Archangelsky, fifty-one per cent were London merchants; and thus, says another scholar, the Restoration settlement was economically 'a triumph for the "new men" – men who may best be described . . . as business men who had thriven under the Commonwealth.' But alas, even this conclusion cannot now be sustained. Recent research has shown that the 'new men,' of whom Marxist historians have made so much, were, to a very large extent, merely agents, buying back their lands for the old families, and that the land settlement of the Restoration passed through a royalist Parliament so easily because, in fact, the net effect of these sales had been insignificant. Socially, as politically, the Revolution had been a failure, and the history of England after 1660 was a continuation of its history before 1640. The Interregnum was merely an untidy interruption. The only permanent changes were a few changes of detail that could have been, and sometimes had been, achieved by peaceful legislation, and certainly did not require civil war, revolution and military dictatorship.

Thus I conclude that the Great Rebellion was not a 'capitalist' rising, nor did it 'succeed' in any sense, nor in any way directly forward the advance of capitalism in England. It was the blind revolt of the gentry against the Court, of the provinces against the capital: the backwash against a century of administrative and economic centralization. Since they were animated by passion, not by positive political ideas, and since they soon either lost by death, or overpowered and destroyed their political leaders, the radical gentry, when they were in power, found themselves without a policy. Ultimately, after a period of fumbling expedients, they gave up the effort, accepted back the old political system, and sank into political quietism. They might still grumble about

Court and City; but, instead of arming themselves with radical ideas, they consoled themselves with conservative ideas: they became high-flying tories, preachers of non-resistance and divine right.

Thus, in my opinion, whatever results followed from the Great Rebellion followed not from its success but from its failure. The rebellion itself was a blind rebellion, which took place because a failure of political ability coincided with a general economic crisis. There were reformers; there were capitalists; there were political thinkers; and, had there been no rebellion of the gentry, these might well have achieved their aims by peaceful progress. But the rebellion of the gentry, a rebellion of mutinous, impoverished, backward-looking provincial squires, gave them no chance – at least until that rebellion had consumed itself and outlasted some of its causes. Perhaps *indirectly* the rebellion may have forwarded the undoubted change of mentality between the early and the late seventeenth century in England: by burning up both itself and its mental fuel, it may have cleared the way for the progress of new and very unpuritan ideas. But, equally, it may have impeded that progress for a generation. We cannot say. What we can say – or, at least, what I am prepared to say – is that it was not, in itself, a successful stage in the rise of the bourgeoisie. As in most revolutions, much of its momentum was self-generated; but in so far as it can be reduced to simple, fundamental terms, it was a protest, by the victims of a temporary general depression, against a privileged bureaucracy, a capitalist City.

*   *   *

Hugh Trevor-Roper (b. 1914) was educated at Christ Church, Oxford. Since 1940, with the publication of *Archbishop Laud, 1573–1645*, he has covered a wide range of historical topics, from *The Last Days of Hitler* (1947) and *Princes and Artists* (1976) to *From Counter-Reformation to Glorious Revolution* (1992) a study of seventeenth-century England, his principal area of study. Regius Professor of Modern History at Oxford from 1957 to 1980, Trevor-Roper was created a life peer (Lord Dacre) in 1979, and was Master of Peterhouse from 1980 to 1987.

13

Thomas Cromwell

GEOFFREY ELTON

(August 1956)

Geoffrey Elton, by dint of a powerful personality backed by painstaking research, came to dominate Tudor scholarship for a generation, refocusing attention on the great power brokers of the age, notably Thomas Cromwell.

Thomas Cromwell was born about 1485; he died on the scaffold in July 1540. Of the fifty-five years of his life, the first twenty-five are quite obscure, illuminated only by some romantic stories with a thin substratum of fact. His father was a shearman of Putney who seems to have possessed a quarrelsome temper. Thomas, thrown early on his own resources and without the career in the Church that so often rescued low-born ability from oblivion, made his way abroad; he travelled through France and Italy, served as a soldier in the Italian wars, may have seen the Pope, made lasting friends with some eminent Italian merchants, and then set off home again, with the beginnings of a fortune acquired in a thoroughly unconventional fashion. About the year 1510 he appears in the light of accurate, if still very limited, knowledge as a merchant with interests in the Low Countries, and at this time, too, he must have begun that training in the common law which enabled him to secure admission to Gray's Inn in 1524. Whatever else may be thought of this helter-skelter education, it suggests the most lively intelligence and general curiosity. Cromwell knew Latin and spoke French and Italian fluently; he was an experienced trader with an understanding of economic problems; he knew enough law to practise successfully, and especially to win renown as an arbitrator in commercial matters; he had also acquired an interest in the theory of politics and in writing both new and old.

When he was approaching the age of thirty-five, he began to settle down, and in the 1520's he found an outlet for his gifts in the service of Cardinal Wolsey. The cardinal's fall in 1529 brought dangers, but

Cromwell survived them without abandoning his old master. He entered Parliament on the strength of his Wolsey connection, but on the understanding that he would support the king's policy; he worked his way up in the king's council and service, and by late 1532 had taken Wolsey's place as the king's chief minister. Cromwell never aspired to emulate the cardinal by appearing as the king's *alter ego* and sole confidant, but observers throughout the rest of his life had no doubt that he held the strings of power. In these last eight years of a very full life he revealed himself to history, so that at times it almost becomes possible to follow him from day to day, and on the work then done his stature and standing must be judged.

The judgment has usually been severe. Even those who have approved the consequence of his work have had nothing better to say for him than that he was a man of his time who would therefore naturally incline to despotism, and that his crimes, though not to be excused, must be seen in their political context. Such comment, while no doubt true in the abstract, offers more heat than light. Friends and enemies of the Reformation have combined in vilifying the minister who guided its first steps in England as a cold, cruel, subservient man, clever indeed but totally unscrupulous, a servant and promoter of irresponsible absolutism, a man without larger aims or at best with larger aims that no one should approve, venal and sly, a low-born creature, whose ultimate downfall must restore faith in the justice of events. It was not always thus: while English opinion remained fixed in stern Protestantism, Cromwell appeared as God's great instrument in the destruction of Popery. But when that pendulum swung, it swung too far, and today few people avoid some uneasiness at the thought of both Cromwell and the Reformation. Fundamentally, views of Cromwell can be traced back to two sources. John Foxe's *Book of Martyrs* (1563) treated him as a Protestant hero, while in Reginald Pole's *Apology to Charles V* (1538), an account of Henry VIII's proceedings, he played the part of Satan's messenger. Foxe now counts as discredited, though in fact he has only been convicted of modifying the truth for propagandist purposes; Pole, as a cardinal, a humanist, and an attractive personality, earns a credence which his unquestioned interest in the events he describes, his inconsistencies and inaccuracies, and his lack of critical sense, should call in doubt. By and large, it is best to ignore both these early authors until such a picture of Cromwell's character, intentions, and achievements has been constructed as the evidence of the record permits.

Cromwell's private character is the less easy to ascertain because he remained so obscure until he became a leading figure in politics. By then he was turned forty; his wife was dead, though her relatives still beset him; he had a son of no ability and less ambition, for whom he seems to have cared with a methodical rather than an affectionate love. Nevertheless, the scattered evidence permits a few notions. At any rate, before politics came to absorb all his time, he formed the centre of a circle of friends: thus one wrote from Spain to recall with great longing the walks and talks they had had in Cromwell's garden, while others sent friendly and merry greetings to him, to his wife, and to the mother-in-law whom, with some good nature, he accommodated in his house until she died. He was noted for his brilliant conversation, informed both by a flashing irony and a lively humour; there are few more innocently self-revealing pictures than that drawn by Reginald Pole when he described the way in which Cromwell, gently but unavailingly, punctured the younger man's impractical enthusiasm for theorists like Plato with some sound if worldly advice. He enjoyed wealth: like everybody else in his day, he saw nothing wrong in accepting gifts and considerations, and he built up a good body of estates to support the earldom with which he died. But even though he had no objection to owning lands in the provinces, he remained a Londoner: the four houses at which he commonly resided in the 1530's were at the Austin Friars in Throgmorton Street, at the Rolls in Chancery Lane, at Canonbury Manor in Islington, and at Stepney. In these matters of property he could be high-handed, as when he took away some small men's gardens to enlarge his grounds in Throgmorton Street (as John Stowe alleges), or when he kept the Rolls House, after giving up the mastership of the Rolls, and forced his successor to dine at the King's Head Tavern. But he spent the wealth he got: Stowe also tells us of the hundreds of poor people who were fed at his gates. Hated as he became by many, hard and unrelenting as he could be when his judgment endorsed his actions, he never altogether lost a personal attractiveness. Even ambassadors who detested his policy enjoyed their interviews with him. A woman in trouble like Mary Boleyn, who had married without the king's, her brother-in-law's, permission, found him ready to help. As he notoriously never forgot early friends and never acquired the pride and ostentation of the upstart, so he also used his power to put down injustice and humble the arrogant. When the abbot of Rievaulx was removed from his place at the instance of his patron, the earl of Rutland, Cromwell assisted; but when the abbot's successor would not pay him the agreed pension, Cromwell took the dispossessed man's side. Cranmer's secretary, who lost a suspiciously heretical document and heard that the finder wanted to establish himself with the king by denouncing him, had to thank Cromwell's sense of humour rather than his Protestantism for his decisive intervention.

All this only amounts to saying that Cromwell was in fact a human being, and one whose intelligence, brilliance, and genuine affability made his acquaintance widely sought. It would be the less necessary to stress these minor points if popular legend had not turned him into an unpleasant, inhuman, deadly toady. The trouble, of course, was that Cromwell's lifework consisted in the carrying through of a revolution, and that revolutionaries are liable to make more enemies than friends. He was either the author or the chief agent of the policy that destroyed the link binding England to Rome, wiped out the monasteries, killed a number of eminent men, and began to turn the country Protestant. Since I believe it can be shown that he was the moving spirit, the man with the ideas and the ingenuity, while the king retained the ultimate control and the real power of decision, it is important to know what he was about. Was he simply interested in serving Henry VIII's matrimonial and financial needs, in gaining wealth for himself and his like, in carrying on a feud against nobler and better men such as Thomas More? Or did he act upon a plan of principle, and because he believed he was serving his country and her future?

The theory once prevalent that he was an ardent Protestant who, having seen the light, could do no other than wipe out Popery and obscurantism has now been replaced by one which allows him no religion at all. Of these the second probably comes a little nearer the truth. Cromwell was certainly a secular man, concerned with the immediate problems of this world and content to solve them. But the occasional expressions of piety that escaped him were neither hypocrisy nor blasphemy; they marked rather a general acceptance of a divine order and of the truth of the Christian revelation which, together with a willingness to leave the details to the ecclesiastical experts, characterized the age and was replaced by a more inward religion and a greater personal fervour only as the Protestant revolution and the Catholic reaction to it did their work. Cromwell once went so far as to tell some Lutherans that, by and large, he was of their opinion in matters of faith, but would, 'as the world now stood,' believe as his master the king did. He was less attached than most to the formalism of the old religion; being no conservative by instinct, he found it easy to escape the hold of familiarity which was to prove the greatest obstacle to the Protestant advance. But if in logic he saw no reason why all that business of mass and priesthood should not go the way of Rome, he did not feel strongly enough to justify historians in seeing a Protestant zeal behind his actions.

His real inspiration was political. Like others of his day and after, he fell under the spell of a potent ideal – the ideal of the self-contained national state. The practice of strong national kingship was nothing new in England; it rested on the solid foundations laid by the strongest monarchy of medieval Europe, and the work of restoring and developing it had gone forward ever since Edward IV emerged the victor from the dynastic wars of the fifteenth century. Even over their clergy the kings of England exercised quite remarkable powers of control. Nevertheless, the structure lacked completion and definition, largely because England was involved with the international monarchy which the Popes claimed over all Latin Christians. The papalism of Henry VII and the young Henry VIII looked almost naïve by comparison with the attitude of kings such as Ferdinand of Aragon or Francis I of France, who treated the Pope as but another factor in the diplomacy of Italy and Europe. It would appear that Cromwell, too, acquired a – so to say – southern attitude to the papacy from his sojourn in Italy. After all, it is of some significance that Wolsey, who conducted English affairs so as to serve papal interests, derived much of his power and glory from a Rome he never visited, while Cromwell had first-hand experience of the things he was attacking. His chance came with the king's disappointment over the Divorce question, but there is sufficient indication that he saw the problem from the first in the light of wider statesmanlike principles. He was less concerned with freeing Henry VIII for re-marriage than with establishing the 'Empire of England' of which he gave a powerful and lucid definition in the famous preamble to the Act of Restraint of Appeals to Rome (1533). With this document he signalled the revolution. The act cost him much labour, but its preamble was fixed in all its essentials from the start. It describes Cromwell's idea of the true polity of England: a sovereign realm, cut free from all outside authority, an organic body governed by a divinely sanctioned king who must rule through and under the law.

It has been common to see in these elements of political theory no more than the formalities with which a practical statesman ornaments his doings, and it is of course perfectly true that Cromwell was in the first instance concerned with political realities. It is also true, however, that he had an informed and eager interest in theories. In part this rested on an acute perception of the value of propaganda: he employed a group of writers to embody the government's programme in pamphlets for the generality. But the really surprising thing is that this hard-headed practical man had a native predilection for the intricacies of political theory. Friend and enemy combine to testify to this intellectual alertness. Cardinal Pole described a conversation about the nature of government and the office of a councillor in which Cromwell had no hesitation in matching authorities and arguing first principles. He certainly read and approved Marsiglio of Padua and very possibly knew something of Machiavelli. Naturally he was interested in the books and views which bore on the work in hand; he was not – and I must not be taken as suggesting that he was – a disinterested student. But that he greatly valued theory as well as practice tells one a good deal about his mind and disposes of the interpretation which would see in him simply the business man, looking only to the immediate stroke of policy or the satisfaction of Henry VIII's desires.

If the sovereign national state was his political ideal, his practical ideal was efficiency. He himself worked extraordinarily hard at an astonishing variety of things. The very list of his major appointments is impressive when one remembers that he never altogether neglected the routine duties of an office and commonly exploited its practical possibilities in a new manner. Master of the Jewels, Clerk of the Hanaper, Chancellor of the Exchequer, Principal Secretary, Master of the Rolls, Lord Privy Seal, Vicar-General, Vicegerent in spirituals – a striking list of duties for any man of affairs. Even nominal offices involved him in activity: thus, as Chancellor of the University of Cambridge, he found his aid invoked in the University's troubles with the town and wrote frequent letters in their behalf. As a councillor and chief minister he was not only a target for thousands of begging letters and appeals but also wrote many a letter in response to such supplications. He was constantly in demand as an arbitrator in litigation and occasionally sat formally in court, especially in Star Chamber. Every session of Parliament – and there were eight between 1532 and 1540 – meant anxious months of preparation and activity: electioneering influence had to be coordinated, bills prepared, legislation steered through the Houses. Cromwell was the first parliamentary manager of whom we have knowledge. Finance and foreign affairs, each quite sufficient work for any man, were only part of his burden. The dissolution of the monasteries is worth studying from the point of view of administrative method; it certainly increases one's respect for a minister and an organization capable of so much well-considered, thorough, and efficient business.

Cromwell translated his desire for efficiency in two main ways: he carefully overhauled existing institutions and supplemented them by the introduction of new ones if this was necessary, and he codified existing practices and thereby gave them a new and permanently effective twist. His work in central government amounted to a revolution because, once again, he was concerned not only with practical ends but rested his reforms on a general principle. He desired to replace the characteristic administrative principle of the past – action by, from, and in the king's Household – by organized national institutions that were bureaucratically defined and, unlike Household institutions, did not depend on the vigour of the Crown to keep them in being.

In all these matters – the sovereign state, bureaucratic efficiency, the review of the structure of the realm – Cromwell was very much abreast of the times. Other countries in Western Europe were moving along similar lines towards a similar goal, often employing strikingly comparable methods. Cromwell had some advantages, in the ancient strength of the English monarchy, and in the geographical unity of the island – barring Scotland. He also had the inestimable advantage of Henry's quarrel with the Pope, which gave him the chance of tackling the fundamental difficulty, the position of the Church, in an unusually radical manner. Lastly, he served a master who, though unduly given to opportunism and the gratification of his desires, was always formidable, never frivolous or negligible, and highly skilled at exploiting the position of the Crown to obtain willing obedience to his policies. For all these reasons Cromwell's reconstruction of the body politic went quite uncommonly far, achieving more than one might have expected in a mere eight years and enduring, both in general and in particular, far longer than is usually given to revolutionary work.

Even the apparent collapse of the Tudor state in 1640 did not destroy the more fundamental aspects of Thomas Cromwell's polity; indeed, in one important matter the seventeenth-century revolution really carried through an essential part of Cromwell's thinking. For if Cromwell was very much a man of his time in his concentration on the national state, he proved exceptional among statesmen of the day in the views he held of the internal structure of that state. He grasped the meaning of sovereignty: he realized that what mattered was the existence in a body politic of a law-making authority, an agency to express the common will, and he found that agency in the King-in-Parliament. His weapon was statute, not royal decree. He argued that, since statute embodied the will of all the interests of the realm represented in Parliament, its competence was complete and universal so far as the king's dominions extended and not to be tested by reference to any other body of law that might be cited against it – imaginary – the law of nature – or real – the canon law of the Church.

But it follows from this that Cromwell did not wish to set up a despotic monarchy. Like everybody else – more perhaps than some – he flattered the king and used devotional language about monarchy. But when it came to the point, he rested his work on statute and therefore on the fact that in the truly sovereign act, the making of law, the king is limited by his dependence on consent. Perhaps the outstanding thing about Thomas Cromwell is not that he was a successful revolutionary who created the political basis of the Church of England, but that, unlike other men elsewhere who assisted in the building of national states, he was a common lawyer and a parliamentarian. When his views on statute are remembered, when one looks at his labours in and through Parliament, it becomes perfectly reasonable to see in him the first of that great line of parliamentary statesmen who, as both king's ministers and members of the assembly, have given to English government the strength and stability which can only come from consent.

Such was the man and such his work. He did his work without compassion or regret; the native friendliness and kindness, which have been illustrated, were put aside without hesitation when great problems were at issue. At the same time, Cromwell remained cold in his ruthlessness: he never killed to please himself or unless he thought it absolutely necessary. The tally of victims mounted high in the 1530s, though it is not large if we regard the age (as we should) as one of true revolution. For this tally Cromwell has always borne a blame that was almost entirely the king's. He is said to have had spies everywhere and to have condemned men for slight and harmless words. Certainly, the new treason laws were ferocious and could be used cruelly, as they were against Fisher and More (the second of whom Cromwell had hoped to save); but there is no evidence that they were widely applied. Many men were denounced, by local magistrates, by personal enemies, very occasionally by the Lord Privy Seal's private correspondents and personal agents; but few of those denounced got into trouble, fewer still suffered more than temporary imprisonment, and the spy system is a myth perpetuated by hostile historians. Cromwell had his contacts, as was his duty, but they were the usual and open channels of communication between the central government and local authorities. If one excepts those that suffered for the Pilgrimage of Grace (which, after all, was an open rebellion) the victims were nearly all highly placed – those that stood at the turbulent centre of a dynastic and political storm whose circumference grew more and more benign with distance.

In the end Cromwell, too, fell victim to the storm. He had never valued his chances of survival beyond the reasonable, though in the event he was caught a little by surprise, mainly because he had the year before (1539) fought off a very vigorous attack from his enemies and got the king more firmly on his side. A combination of diplomatic and royal matrimonial mistakes undermined his position, and Henry listened to the tales carried by Norfolk and Gardiner that Cromwell was a heretic and aiming to be an 'overmighty subject.' Cromwell never came to trial, being condemned unheard by attainder; his most serious mistake had been that he never poisoned Henry's mind against those who at the last proved to have no such scruples. The king – a notably better Machiavellian than the minister – put upon him and his memory all the odium inseparable from so revolutionary a decade. Not that one would want to whitewash Thomas Cromwell. A man of his strength, wisdom, and sombre power deserves better than that. If his sins were scarlet, his deeds are yet read in the history of the country which he served with such foresight and skill.

*   *   *

G.R. Elton (1921–94) was the most influential Tudor historian of the later twentieth century. *England under the Tudors* (1955) was for three decades the most widely read book on the period at sixth-form and undergraduate level. It was joined in 1977 by *Reform and Reformation.* He was renowned for his powerful advocacy of the revolution in government undertaken by Thomas Cromwell. Elton was an important figure in Cambridge University – a professor in 1967 and Regius Professor of Modern History from 1983 to 1987. He was knighted in 1986.

14

The Relevance of European History

CHRISTOPHER DAWSON

(September 1956)

At a time when early voices were beginning to argue for 'world history',
Christopher Dawson pleaded for the continuing importance of the European
contribution.

World history, as it is understood today, is an entirely new subject. Sixty
years ago, when Acton was planning the Cambridge Modern History, he
conceived it as a universal history which would not be a mere combined
history of modern states, but a study of the development of universal
historical forces. Yet at the same time, he took for granted that this history
would be a European one and that it was only, or primarily, in Europe and
its colonies that the movement of world history was to be found. But the
new conception of World History rejects this conception entirely and
aspires to produce a work which will be ecumenical in treatment and
scope, embracing the whole history of every people from China to Peru
without preference or prejudice.

The old European view of history is now condemned as provincial or
parochial or 'ethnocentric,' and it is generally admitted that if we wish to
study world history we must pay as much attention to China and India
and Islam, not to mention Indonesia and Africa, as to Europe.

At first sight this seems to represent a great advance, but even if this is
so, the advance has still to be made. For the great European historians of
the past, like Ranke and Acton, were members of an international society
of learning and they spoke to a wide audience who knew what they were
talking about. Today world history has no such educated public. General
historical knowledge has not kept pace with the advance of specialized
studies.

And it is inevitable that this should be so, since the linguistic barriers to the study of oriental history are almost insurmountable at the present time, except for a small class of specialists. Thus there is a serious danger that the relative widening of the historical perspective to include the non-European civilization may be accompanied by an absolute decline in the quality and standard of general European history.

Curiously enough it has been left to an Indian writer – 'an unknown Indian,' he calls himself, Nirad Chaudhuri – to point out how grave this danger is. He writes[1] as follows:

> In the last few decades there has certainly been seen in Europe, or at all events in England, a decline in historical knowledge, accompanied by a pronounced recoil from the historical attitude. This is a retrograde phenomenon, for if there is anything that distinguishes man from the other animals, it is memory or consciousness of duration, and I cannot understand how the European man, having attained the high degree of historical consciousness that he did in the nineteenth century, can have stepped back from it to the uncultured man's bondage to the present and, the still more uncultured man's bondage to the eschatology of political dogma. Yet what the European man is displaying more often than not today is an utter lack of the historical sense. I sometimes seek the solution of the puzzle in that Spenglerian vision, the dreadful and tragic *Untergang des Abendlandes*, the untimely decline of the European peoples on their home continent, brought about by an internal strife as insensate, as inescapable and as suicidal as that of the Greek cities. I ask myself: Are we witnessing a whole society's senile decay of memory?

This is a very severe judgment, but it is not altogether lacking in justification. It is borne out for instance by Professor Barraclough's recent volume *History in a Changing World*, which is all the more instructive because it represents the views of a professional historian as offered to a popular audience largely through the medium of the BBC. Now Professor Barraclough starts from the conviction that the Russian victory at Stalingrad makes a total revision of European history necessary, and he even goes on not only to discard the nineteenth-century conception of Europe as the centre of universal history, but to question the very existence of Europe as a cultural unity and of any real continuity

---

[1]   N. Chaudhuri: *The Autobiography of an Unknown Indian*, p. 341.

between classical, medieval and modern history. 'The European inheritance,' he concludes, 'is a tangle of unsolved contradictions, a thicket of dead ends, offering no direct line of advance' for the future. And so instead of the old Western tradition that is centred on Europe and Greece and Rome, he demands a 'history that is truly universal – that looks beyond Europe and the West to humanity in all lands and ages.'

Unfortunately, he does not explain how this new history is to be discovered. He is himself highly qualified in the field of German medieval studies, but when it comes to the non-European world, he is completely at sea. He does not even suggest where we are to begin. He only refers us to Herr Spengler's view of independent culture cycles and suggests that some new culture is going to arise in Russia or elsewhere – which will in time take the place of the defunct civilization of Europe.

But it would be a mistake to kick down the ladder of European historiography before we have found a foothold in the new world. The fact that Western Europe has lost its position of world leadership does not affect the significance of the European historical tradition. So instead of saying Farewell to European History, I would rather advocate a Return to European History, since I believe that it is only by way of Europe and the Western historical tradition that it is possible to approach that universal world history which has so long been the ideal of the philosophers of history.

Throughout the past, down to a century or two ago, the historic world was not an intelligible unity. It was made up of a number of independent civilizations, which were like separate worlds, each of them with its own historical tradition and its own idea of world history. During the last thousand years these great world civilizations have been four in number – China, India, Islam and Europe (or rather Christendom, for the divisions between Western civilization and its great Eastern neighbours was always a religious rather than a geographical one).

It is true that the isolation of these four cultures was never complete. Europe was in contact with Islam, Islam was in contact with India and India was in contact with China. But these contacts did not go very deep. In particular they did not extend to a knowledge of the other historical traditions, so that each civilization tended to ignore one another's pasts. Moreover, these four civilizations were far from being world wide. Altogether they represented an island of higher civilization in an ocean of darkness. And these barbarous outer lands were seen as lying outside the world of time as well as on the frontiers of the world of space. They were lands without history and even without common humanity.

Now the unique significance of Europe for the development of world history is to be found in the part that it has played in breaking down the isolation of the ancient world civilizations and bringing the unknown outer world into the light of civilization and history. This achievement is so momentous that there is nothing to be compared with it in human history since the original creation of higher civilization (which, however, preceded the dawn of history). Whatever is happening to Europe at the present time or may happen in the future cannot affect the significance of this world changing event. It must, however, be admitted that modern European historiography has failed to do justice to it. Professor Barraclough is quite right in criticizing the disproportionate amount of attention that has been devoted to the political and diplomatic history of the Western European and North American States – to the English party system, to Frederick the Great and Bismarck and so on – as compared with the all important question of the relation of Europe to the outer world. Here the nationalist and politicist bias of modern history has distracted attention from the epoch-making changes which have been Europe's real contribution to world history.

It is true that the field is overpoweringly wide and over-runs all the conventional limits of conventional academic history. Economics, politics, religion, science and technology are all involved and all exercise a mutual influence on one another. The first step in this process – the breaking of the oceanic barriers of the Old World by the Portuguese and Spanish navigators – is no doubt familiar enough, and yet even here comparatively little study has been devoted to the social and economic background of the movement and to the problem of the continuity between the new forms of colonialism, and those which had already been developed by the Italian maritime republics in their establishments in the Black Sea and the Levant.

The second stage of the European world movement – the penetration of the closed world of the other old-world civilizations – was a much more gradual process, since it began earlier in the thirteenth century with the first great travels of the Friars and of Marco Polo to Central Asia, India and China and has continued throughout the centuries ever since. Here it was the Christian missionaries who played the leading part, though the name of Marco Polo shows that the economic element was also present from the beginning. It was, however, the great missionaries like St Francis Xavier, Matteo Ricci, Rodolfo Acquaviva, Robert de Nobili and the rest, who alike in India, China and Japan were the first to establish contact between East and West on the higher cultural level. The Jesuit mission to China in the seventeenth and early eighteenth centuries, above all, was unique for its double achievement in convincing Chinese scholars of the scientific values of European culture and in unveiling to Europe the whole extent of Chinese culture – its history, its literature and its institutions. And it is, I think, a legitimate criticism of our current methods of teaching history that for a hundred people who are familiar with the names of the geographical explorers, like Tasman and Dampier and Bougainville, there is hardly one who knows the names of the scholars who discovered Chinese culture – like Ricci, Couplet, de Mailla and du Halde.

The only excuse for this is that the work of the great Jesuit missionaries and scholars belongs to the earlier phase of the European world expansion and did not lead on directly to the triumphant expansion of the third phase. The world hegemony of Western culture was introduced by the three great changes that took place during the eighteenth century – first the Europeanization of Russia – the one province of Christendom that had remained isolated from the West from the Mongol conquest to the age of Alexis and Peter the Great; secondly, the establishment of an autonomous centre of Western culture outside the Europe in North America, and thirdly, the British conquest of India. Owing to these developments the influence of European culture which had hitherto been limited to the coasts and the islands, penetrated to the heart of the Asiatic and American continents and gradually subjected the trade and the resources of the non-European world to the new Western economic and technical organization.

During the great age of Western capitalism in the nineteenth century, the whole world lay open to the enterprise of the Western financier and merchant and to the skill of the Western technician and engineer. All over the world Europeans and Americans were prospecting for new sources of wealth and opening up new markets and new channels of trade. During its central period from the time of Adam Smith to that of Cobden and Bright, this economic movement was cosmopolitan rather than imperialist in spirit, and was inspired by the ideals of the liberal enlightenment. The process which is now regarded as the exploitation of the weaker peoples and classes by Western capitalism, was seen by contemporaries as the great means of world progress and international peace. In the words of J.S. Mill, 'it may be said without exaggeration that the great extent and rapid increase of international trade in being the principal guarantee of the peace of the world is the great permanent security for the uninterrupted progress of the ideas, the institutions and the character of the human race.' In the past 'the patriot wished all countries weak, poor and ill-governed except his own; now he sees in their wealth and progress a direct source of wealth and progress to his own country.'

And these ideas were not so absurd as they appear today. So long as the economists and the politicians accepted the liberal ideology, they were more interested in the expansion of trade than in territorial conquest and the establishment of a world-wide system of communications was regarded as the common interest of all civilized peoples. As the Roman road was at once the organ and the symbol of the Pax Romana, so the steamship, the railway and the telegraph were the organs of the new pacific world unity which was the ideal of the Western Liberal economists.

Nor was this expansion of Western culture purely material. It involved the advance of knowledge and the communication of ideas – and that in both directions. Towards the end of the eighteenth century, Western science took up the work of the Jesuit missionaries and began to reveal an unknown world of oriental religion and philosophy. The discovery of Sanskrit literature by Anquetil-Duperron, Sir William Jones, Sir Charles Wilkins and Henry Colebrooke was one of the most epoch-making events of modern times. In the West, it prepared the way for an oriental renaissance which had a profound effect on European thought especially in Germany and France in the first decades of the nineteenth century. At the same time, in the East, the influence of Western ideas combined with the European interest in Sanskrit studies, produced important changes in Indian culture. The spread of education, the development of the vernacular literatures, above all Bengali, and the influence of personalities like Ram Mohun Rai (1780–1833) and Debindra Nath Tagore prepared the way for the revival of Hindu culture and the growth of a new educated class and a new national spirit. Thus it was the West that created Indian nationalism by giving India a new sense of its cultural values and achievements.

This two-sided process of Western scientific study and Oriental cultural awakening went on all over the East during the nineteenth century and has extended in the present century to the more primitive peoples of Africa and the Pacific. Here Europe achieved something that had never been done before, since neither the Greeks nor the Arabs nor the Persians, in spite of their interest in the manners and customs of strange peoples, ever succeeded in getting inside the minds of the societies that they studied and comprehending their culture as a living whole. Today this has become the normal procedure of the modern social anthropologist, but its origins are much older than scientific anthropology, and are to be found in the new oriental and historical studies. Edward Lane's *Account of the Manners and Customs of the Modern Egyptians* published in 1836, is a classical type of what I mean, though no doubt it is by no means the earliest example. It seems to me to be closely related to the achievements of nineteenth-century historians – to works like de Tocqueville's work on American Democracy, on the one hand, and to Fustel de

Coulanges' book on the Ancient City or Burckhardt's Renaissance, on the other.

But, on the other hand, it may be argued that it was Kipling's 'Sons of Martha,' the engineers and civil servants and sanitary inspectors, who performed the essential task of breaking through the inherited tyranny of prejudice and custom and thrusting the new scientific and technical order on a hundred unwilling peoples. It may be objected that this function might have been performed by the oriental peoples themselves without Western control. But Japan is the only example of a people accepting a radical change in its way of life without being forced to do so by Western economic or political power. The natural reaction of oriental nationalism to Western contact was reactionary in both senses of the word. Those reactionary nationalists or traditionalists who led the resistance to Western imperialism in the nineteenth century were by no means inferior in character to the leaders of the later nationalist movements – some of them like 'Abd al Khadir in Algeria, Shamyl in the Caucasus, the Khalifa 'Abdullah in the Egyptian Sudan, were heroic figures, but they were doomed to inevitable defeat because they did not possess the techniques and the scientific organization of the civilization that they resisted. All the triumphs of modern oriental nationalism have been the work of men of Western education, who were able to use the ideas and knowledge of the West in the service of their own people.

This new class was, however, literary rather than scientific in training. It was composed, especially in India and in the Near East, of lawyers and journalists and schoolmasters, rather than engineers and doctors and economists. It remained for a long time suspended between two worlds – filled with enthusiasm for the material civilization and democratic ideals of the West, but still profoundly attached to the memory of its ancient cultural traditions.

Hence the ambivalence of the modern nationalist movements. The Westernized intelligentsia acted as the spearhead of national mass movements which were animated by anti-Western xenophobia. But the moment that independence had been secured, they took over the rôle of the European administrators and proceeded to modernize oriental society far more drastically than the old colonialism had ever dared to do. And this tendency is most pronounced in Communist states, where the traditional religious foundations of oriental culture are being destroyed just as ruthlessly as the alien power of Western capitalism, which is much less deeply rooted. Thus the movement of world changes that was inaugurated in Western Europe several centuries ago, has now been so fully assimilated by the East that it is being carried forward by the very forces that are most overtly hostile to the West.

The study of the European past is still relevant to modern world history, since Europe was the original course of the movement of change in which the whole world is now involved and it is in European history that we find the key to the understanding of the ideologies which divide the modern world. Modern nationalism would never have become so formidable if it had not been inflated by the genius of the great nineteenth-century national historians, and in the same way the Stalinist parody of socialist history could never have been possible without the work of Karl Marx, a man of genius whose real historical gifts were perverted and poisoned by his genius for hatred.

But there is no reason why history should always be used as the servant of ideological propaganda. It is time that we returned to the tradition of the great European orientalists and historians of whom I wrote earlier – men who were not concerned with political ideologies but with the patient investigation and interpretation of the thought and social institutions of other peoples. What we need is a new historical analysis of the whole process of world change, tracing the movement from West to East and taking account of the new factors which emerge at each stage in the process.

This process is so great that it transcends all the current ideological interpretations. In order to understand it, we shall need, on the one hand, the help of the Western historians who can trace its origins in the European past, and on the other, the work of the orientalists who can appreciate the part of the non-European cultures and understand their reactions to the impact of modern civilization.

* * *

Christopher Dawson, cultural historian and educational theorist, was born in 1889 in Wales and educated at Winchester and Trinity College, Oxford. He became the first Chauncey Stillman Professor of Roman Catholic Studies at Harvard University, where he remained until 1962. Dawson was the author of many works on the history of culture and religion, including *Progress and Religion* (1929), *The Age of the Gods* (1928), *Religion and the Rise of Western Culture* (1950), and *Medieval Essays* (1952). He died in Devon in 1970.

15

Alexander Hamilton

Founding Father

ESMOND WRIGHT

(February 1957)

Esmond Wright epitomised all that was best in the post-war spirit of Anglo-American intellectual co-operation. His attitude towards the founding figures of the American republic was admiring but – as here – not uncritical.

The decade from 1790 to 1800 in American history remains largely *terra incognita*. While other periods, especially the Revolution and the Civil War, have been chronicled abundantly, the first years of the Republic remain clouded and its citizens shadowy beings – unless, in their own lifetimes, they were seen to be 'demi-gods'. Franklin was so seen, to his amusement; Washington, to his embarrassment. But this process of 'amplification', largely the work of Weems and Marshall, Gilbert Stuart and the Peales, was highly selective.

The mythology and hero-worship inseparable from nation-building are of course largely fortuitous. Soldiers are preferred to 'organizers of victory', adventurers to politicians and financiers; simple men of action make better symbols than the complex and the paradoxical. Yet, in any reckoning the indifference shown by American historians to Alexander Hamilton, and to the drama of his career, is astonishing.

A man of effervescent charm, short in stature, but fair and 'uncommonly handsome'; a West Indian immigrant working his way through college, who made the Revolutionary cause his own; for more than four years 'first aid' to the Commander-in-Chief, as the Spanish envoy happily described him, and a fighting soldier with Lafayette at Yorktown; joint author with Madison of the Constitution and of *The Federalist*, the eighty-five essays which, more perhaps than anything else, secured the adoption of the Constitution in New York; 'prime minister' to the first President; Secretary of the Treasury, whose report on credit and whose banking policies established the solvency and set the course of the new state; major contributor to Washington's Farewell Address and thus to the shaping of American foreign policy for the next century; a meteor that swept across the political scene and whose brilliance was so dramatically extinguished: why has Hamilton's personality left so little mark?

Was it that his point of view, often so arrogantly voiced, was distasteful and even alien? – 'your people, Sir, is a great beast'. Was his confidence in himself, so well-justified, nevertheless too extravagant, his capacity for work too overpowering, his long and masterly essays, written almost without pause or need of correction, too persuasive for the man himself to be accepted, much less loved? Was his integrity itself too lofty and too conspicuous, his devotion to the new nation a shade exotic? Or did he merely die too early, cut off before he was fifty by Aaron Burr's pistol shot? Yet his work was done four or even eight years before. And the end was surely in itself material for legend – his life sacrificed in part for the sake of the Union, his devoted wife and large family destitute, his murderer a hunted fugitive with his schemes for secession largely destroyed. His death proved good business for John Trumbull, who was kept profitably employed for years turning out replicas of his Hamilton portraits. Yet the legend never came to birth, hard though his family tried to induce it.

The success of Hamilton's work deepens the mystery of the failure of his reputation. He fought for, and secured, the funding of the national debt, irrespective of the question of its ownership, at a time when the great majority of Congressmen expected it to be scaled down. This led to a split between Hamilton and Madison, and fostered the growth of parties; but it tied the rich and adventurous to the new state. He secured also the assumption by the Federal Government of the debts of the states; and this step, even more bitterly fought over, enabled the Federal Government to dominate the revenue sources of the country and greatly consolidated national authority. He established a Bank in which the government owned stock; and, when Jefferson objected that the Constitution did not permit this, he answered with the famous doctrine of implied powers – that the power to charter private corporations or a bank was a natural outcome of the power to coin money, raise taxes and incur debts. He provided a national revenue by imposing indirect taxes on imported goods and an excise tax on home-produced liquor – two measures of profound significance; for the first demanded a high volume of imports from Britain and so linked the United States with her economically and diplomatically, and the second produced the Whisky

Rebellion of the Pennsylvania farmers in 1794. Hamilton's vehement suppression of this was designed as a display of national strength.

These measures can be criticized, for they divided the country sectionally and politically. But few American historians have criticized the programme of 1791–4: it has been for the most part praised as inspired and percipient; as giving prestige to American currency; as assuring national stability and the supremacy of the propertied classes; as making for close relations with Britain and as providing a base for the steady expansion of the rôle of the Federal Government. It has been assessed less on financial than on political grounds, as Hamilton intended it should. For his intentions were primarily political, even imperial.

At a time when few dared to tackle the economic problems of a bankrupt and agrarian society, a clear direction was given to the new nation and an 'energy to government,' in Hamilton's own phrase, as well as 'Order to the finances.' And they were imposed from above. Hamilton, in 1791 as in 1787, advocated republicanism but not democracy.

All communities divide themselves into the few and the many. The first are rich and well-born, the other the mass of the people. The voice of the people has been said to be the voice of God; and however generally this maxim has been quoted and believed, it is not true in fact. The people are turbulent and changing; they seldom judge or determine right.

The sentiments like the financial policy, proved peculiarly useful to nineteenth-century America. They seemed prophetic when Carnegie and Rockefeller appeared; and Lincoln's Republicanism was soon subverted into Hamiltonianism, although then, as now, the imagery was of Illinois rather than New York: the log-cabin is still preferred to 'The Grange', homespun, even coon-skin, to Hamilton's white waistcoat and black silk small clothes. Although the language was of *laisser-faire*, enterprise was abetted by high tariffs and railway subsidies. The Fourteenth Amendment abolishing slavery was twisted into a defence not of negroes but of big business. Grover Cleveland, the only Democrat in the White House from 1860 to 1912, appealed to businessmen to participate actively in politics. The young Virginian Democrat, Woodrow Wilson, proclaimed in 1889: 'Ever since I have had independent judgements of my own I have been a Federalist.' This was the America with which Joseph Chamberlain had sympathy; F.S. Oliver's essay of 1906, the only English biography of Hamilton, sought in High Federalism the solution to Britain's own Imperial problems.

It is true that Beard, Bryan, Populists and muck-rakers voiced other opinions; but not all Beard's research could impugn Hamilton's own motives and integrity, or deny his achievement as architect of Federalism. In the boom-years of the nineteen-twenties, Hamilton's name, coupled with Andrew Mellon's, was on everyone's lips. In the gloom of the thirties Hamilton's stock was still high, when Mellon's was not, as the assessments of Tugwell and Dorfman reveal. In 1934, when Hamilton's Papers on Public Credit, Commerce and Finance were re-published by the Columbia University Press, they were described by Elihu Root in his foreword as 'the lucid and powerful expositions of controlling principles . . . the guide by which our nation has become great and respected . . . as applicable now as they were then.' In 1947 as radical a critic as Louis Hacker declared that Hamilton's reading of his times and of the future of America 'was that of the wise statesman.' His work as financier and as constitutional draughtsman has received all-but-unanimous praise. But there is still no Hamilton legend. Why?

Behind the rounded and remarkable doctrines was a figure almost as paradoxical as Jefferson himself. For the first of the Federalists and the founder of the nation was born a West Indian; the advocate of aristocracy was born not only in poverty abroad but in shame.

Hamilton was born on January 11th, 1755, on the island of Nevis. He was always – perhaps deliberately – vague about the year, and 1757 has long been thought the year of his birth, since he described himself in 1773 as 'about sixteen.' He was the second son of Rachel Faucitt and James Hamilton. His mother, strikingly beautiful and rumoured to be in part coloured, but in fact of French Huguenot stock, had been married, at the age of sixteen, to a certain John Michael Lavien, a middle-aged merchant of the Danish island of St Croix. There was a son of this marriage; but it was an unhappy affair. The husband won a divorce that, by the stringent law of the time, prevented the wife's re-marriage, and she returned to her native Nevis. There she met James Hamilton, a younger son of an Ayrshire family; he was gentle, scholarly and unsuccessful; yet he gave to his younger son a family pride that offset the poverty and ignominy of his boyhood. His home in New York was to be named after the family house, 'The Grange', in Ayrshire.

The young Hamilton was brought up in Christiansted on St Croix – where his father abandoned his mother, and where, when Alexander was thirteen, his mother died. He worked in Nicholas Cruger's store and showed great talent at business. He never received much affection and grew up gifted, ambitious and self-contained. He sought success and power in a bigger world, as he wrote in his first extant letter to his friend, Ned Stevens, then at King's College in New York (November 11th, 1769) –

. . . to confess my weakness, Ned, my ambition is prevalent, so that I
contemn the grovelling condition of a clerk or the like, to which my
fortune condemns me, and would willingly risk my life, though not
my character to exalt my station . . . I wish there was a war.

The opportunity came in violent form, more devastating than a war, in
the hurricane of August 1772. Hamilton's account of this came to the
notice of Hugh Knox, Presbyterian clergyman in the islands. Knox
persuaded the boy to go to Princeton, and provided him with letters of
introduction to William Livingston and Elias Boudinout in New Jersey,
who became his mentors. At least a year before the Revolution began,
Hamilton was a student at King's College, N.Y., absorbing High Toryism
from Dr Myles Cooper, but also absorbing – and voicing – revolutionary
sentiments in the student clubs and debating societies. The war he
sought came and, with it, an enthusiasm for his new country and a
determination to shine in her service.

The war provided opportunity; the pamphleteer became a captain in
the New York Artillery and, perhaps on Boudinot's recommendation, a
military secretary to Washington in March 1777. From that point
Washington's letters increased in number, in length – and in literary
quality. But, like many another clerk in wartime, Hamilton had dreams of
military prowess and, with an eye on a political career, perhaps thought
them imperative. Passed over in 1781 for the post of Adjutant-General, he
quarrelled with Washington and resigned as aide. In July he got his field
appointment and saw action at the redoubts at Yorktown.

In December 1780, Hamilton had put the war to that other traditional
use of an aide-de-camp; he married General Philip Schuyler's daughter,
Elizabeth, and merged his fortunes with those of the rich patronage of
the Hudson Valley. He was thought to be twenty-three – he was, in fact,
twenty-five – and he had arrived. Already he had drawn up memoranda
on the establishment of a National Bank. After Yorktown he practised as a
lawyer, was receiver of continental taxes for New York and represented
New York at the Annapolis and Philadelphia conventions. He was
appointed Secretary of the Treasury in September 1789, and served until
January 1795. The years after Washington's retirement were years of
disappointment, of partisanship and of anticlimax.

The first obstacle, then, to the growth of a reputation was that
Hamilton rose from nothing and rose fast. Looking, and believed to be,
younger than he was, he was thought of, and described, as precocious and
brilliant; his talents were regarded as mercurial, and the extraordinary
capacity he showed for sustained work during the war was appreciated by
few except Washington. Surrounded by older men, and flattered by them,

his vanity grew. Yet, although no one doubted his patriotism, he was considered an outsider in wartime and was naturally passed over for posts of real responsibility. Adams thought of him in this way to the end, and in 1809 excused his errors on the grounds that he was 'not a native of America,' and that 'he never acquired the feelings and principles of the American people.' Hamilton recognized this himself – 'Every day proves to me more and more that this American world was not made for me.' Moreover, he was backed by men of substance, Boudinot, Schuyler and Washington; he saw himself as a natural *aristo* and became the advocate and apologist of the Right, a Burke to the great Oaks of the Revolution, but with a skill in finance to match his skill in words. Yet like Burke he was never quite accepted, isolated by his abilities, by his foreignness and by his arrogance. In the New World careers were open to talent; but even there a man could be too obviously on the make.

The doubts about the man's background and stability were reinforced by his declared beliefs. For Hamilton has earned misdirected and unmerited approval as a designer of the Constitution. He accepted it and worked for it, but only as a second best; and his doubts about its durability continued until the day he died. He described it in 1802 as 'a frail and worthless fabric which I have been endeavouring to prop up.' What he admired was discipline and authority in government; what he preached was mercantilism. He subsidised those who invested in manufactures and public securities; he taxed the landed interest. He favoured an 'hereditary' chief magistrate, representing the 'permanent will' of society and capable of curbing the 'turbulent and uncontrouling disposition' of democracy. He wanted an upper house chosen for life on a property basis. 'Our real disease,' he wrote on the night before he was shot, 'is democracy.'

His economic-cum-political views were shaped in fact less by America than by his youth in the store in the lush sugar islands, where prosperity depended – hurricanes permitting – on an elaborate trading system, and where society was hierarchical. He had no sympathy with Jefferson's farmer-democrats, but at least the rich, the well-born and the able were given every encouragement, and the fluidity of a free society allowed them to be creative, not destructive.

But in the last analysis it was neither Hamilton's background nor his ideas that lost him sympathy. No society has been more sympathetic than the American to the immigrant and the man on the make, as the Revolutionary catalogue and later years attest. Ideas about the Constitution varied widely; Paine and Jefferson and George Mason had their own doubts about it, of a different kind from Hamilton's. Hamilton's failure was a failure of personality; the creed was bigger than the man. Although his financial doctrines were wise, he could be as inconsistent as Jefferson himself. In *The Federalist* (Nos 12 and 21) he declared that 'the genius of the people' hated excises; but they were an essential part of his revenue system in 1791; and in 1794 he was employing force to crush the resistance to them of the Whisky Rebels in Pennsylvania. The advocate of isolation in *The Federalist* No. 11 became in 1794 the notorious Anglophile of the Jay Treaty; the supporter of free elections and free choice in 1787 tried in 1800 to nullify the popular vote and threatened force in the process. He claimed in 1787, and in 1791–4, to 'think continentally'; yet by 1800 he was the not-fully-avowed leader of the High Federalists, at odds with President Adams and wrecking both Adams' administration and his own party. Increasingly he advocated the use of armies: in 1794 to crush Pennsylvanian farmers; in 1798, when he became Inspector-General, to go to war with France – or perhaps to embark on a great crusade as Libertador in Spanish America; in 1800 to preserve Federalist power in New York. 'In times like these,' he told John Jay, 'it will not do to be over-scrupulous.' He split with Adams because the President kept peace with France. He thought Jefferson ought to go to war to gain Louisiana; but, when Jefferson achieved its purchase in a staggering diplomatic triumph, Hamilton wrote

> the advantage of the acquisition appears too distant and remote to strike the mind of a sober politician with much force. . . . It . . . must hasten the dismemberment of a large portion of our country, or a dissolution of the Government.

The passionate nationalist could become the most bitter and irrational of partisans.

To these contradictions he added a capacity for quarrelling with almost every one of his closest associates. The high integrity and devotion to his country were outmatched by a devotion to his own career that involved him in endless intrigues. He quarrelled with Washington in 1781, when his Commander-in-Chief charged him with tardiness and disrespect. 'I replied, without petulancy, but with decision; "I am not conscious of it, sir, but since you have thought it necessary to tell me so, we part".' He explained to his father-in-law that he 'always disliked the office of an aide-de-camp as having in it a kind of personal dependence.' Washington, he said, was 'neither remarkable for delicacy nor good temper.' Yet Washington sought to apologize within the hour, to be sharply rebuffed, and he continued, in 1781, as in 1789, to harbour no grudge. Though both men were under strain – it was eight months before

Yorktown – the fact remains that the older man emerges with the greater honour.

Washington was fully aware of Hamilton's ambition, but appreciated his talents. Adams was less kind and, like his party, suffered acutely with Hamilton's men; and for four years Hamilton was 'the worm at the root of the peach,' 'the Creole adventurer,' 'the Creole bastard.' Adams' son, John Quincy, thought Hamilton's ambition

> transcendent, and his disposition to intrigue irrepressible . . . he was of that class of characters which cannot bear a rival – haughty, over-powering, jealous, bitter and violent in his personal enmities, and little scrupulous of the means he used against those who stood in the way of his ambition.

If the Adamses cannot be thought impartial, Noah Webster, a staunch Federalist, equally deplored Hamilton's wrecking of the party. In his *Open Letter to General Hamilton,* in 1800, he said 'your ambition, pride and overbearing temper have destined you to be the evil genius of this country.' Abigail Adams saw the trend even more sharply. 'That man,' she said, 'would become a second Bonaparte if he was possessed of equal power!' The charge was valid; Hamilton's hero was Julius Caesar.

The years after 1800 were years of failure. Although devoted to his wife, he was not faithful, and was ready to reveal his liaison with Maria Reynolds rather than allow the blackmailing activities of her husband to be thought attributable to any political immorality. With the Republican victory in 1800, largely due to his own quarrel with Adams, his power had gone. By ensuring Jefferson's election as President he made a mortal enemy of Aaron Burr, who had tied with Jefferson in the Electoral College.

In 1801 Philip, Hamilton's oldest son, was shot in a duel and his daughter, Angelica, became permanently insane with grief; his wife was pregnant with her eighth child at the time. He emerged from his private life in 1804 to oppose Burr's bid for the Governorship of New York, which carried with it the danger of a secession of New York and New England from the Union. The charges ran high; and for some of them, of which he heard at second hand, Burr demanded satisfaction. Trumbull always argued that Hamilton need not have fought and it is not clear from his letters to Burr that Hamilton meant to accept his challenge. He seems in these last years to have been changing and to have been facing religious and ethical problems for the first time. He recognized that some of his criticisms of Burr had been 'extremely severe,' and that, according to the code of honour, he owed Burr the right to shoot at him at twelve paces. He made his plans quietly.

On Tuesday night, July 10th, 1804, as one account has it – even here there are variants – he arranged for his twelve-year-old son, John Church, to sleep with him. The son never forgot how he and his father recited the Lord's Prayer in unison. Before dawn on Wednesday he rose without waking the boy, rode the eight miles from 'The Grange' to New York City and was rowed across the Hudson to the New Jersey Heights of Weehawken.

It was shortly after seven when the two duellists stood to their stations in the wooded clearing high above the river. At the word 'Present' two reports rang out, one shortly behind the other; and the shorter of the antagonists, rising convulsively on tiptoe, staggered a little to the left and fell headlong upon his face. As the surgeon hastily examined the gaping hole in his right side, the wounded man had just strength to gasp before fainting, 'This is a mortal wound, Doctor . . .'

And fast as a spreading bush fire, the news went through New York City that Colonel Burr had shot General Hamilton in a duel – that Hamilton was dying – was already lying dead in Mr. Baynard's house at Greenwich.

The bullet had pierced his liver and lodged in his spine. He lingered on in great pain and died the following afternoon.

Hamilton was a man of great gifts, great achievements and transcendent integrity, perhaps the most creative figure thrown up by the American Revolution. Like some other eminent conservative leaders, he was a social climber, and he cultivated men with power. He had no sympathy for the West, or for notions of local self-government, or for the rights of the States. Although his view of the Union was synoptic, it hardly included its citizens; administration was more important than the ends it served. Like his hero, Caesar, he was obsessed by the love of fame – 'the ruling passion of the noblest minds,' he called it himself. As Adams noted, he was too fond of crises and too ready to use armies to be a good democrat; and he did not hide his scorn for 'the people.' For a democracy his very talents could carry their own danger; love of power and lack of compassion could be as serious a menace to the republican experiment as conspiracy within and without. The death of Hamilton at the hands of Burr ended a double threat to the future of the state.

*   *   *

Esmond Wright (b. 1915) is Emeritus Professor of American History at the University of London. From 1946 to 1967 he taught at Glasgow University, for the last ten years as Professor of Modern History. From 1971 (after a brief spell as an MP) until 1983, he was Director of the Institute of US Studies in London. Among his many works on American history are the biography, *Franklin of Philadelphia* (1986) and a completion of Franklin's own unfinished autobiography, *Franklin: His life as he wrote it* (1989). Esmond Wright has been a regular contributor to *History Today* from the 1950s to the 2000s.

16

Letter: History Today *v. A New Car*

K.B. VON KOEPPEN

(May 1957)

Letters to the Editors in the early years were usually polite, prolix and often a touch trainspotty. Few were as attractively eccentric as this one from an American reader.

History Today v. A New Car

Sir,

I have recently received a letter from you bewailing the fact that I failed to renew my subscription to *History Today*.

In the first place, I did not subscribe to your magazine. My father purchased the subscription for me, as a birthday gift. I believe he was under the impression that *History Today* was a sort of British *Time*, giving monthly reports of world events. I know that I was under the impression that I would get a new car for my birthday.

Secondly, I believe your magazine appeals to two types of people: the general reader who is intrigued by history itself, and is willing to read it in unrelated bits and pieces; and the scholar, who is interested in new work being done, and also in observing the errors and delusions of his colleagues.

Thirdly, you have no idea how hilarious a postman in a small Eastern Oregon town becomes when he sees an address like 'K.B. Koeppen, ESQ.'

I have not the background to criticize, except in a few instances, the accuracy of your articles. I am quite willing to criticize their style. None of the articles which I noticed were thoroughly unreadable; conversely, few were well written. Apparently the dispassionate manner with which an historian is supposed to view his subject often prevents him from writing with ease and colour. Your authors seem to enjoy using what might be termed the genteel bromide.

You might follow the example of that charming American magazine, *The Police Gazette.* I can't say that I have ever read it, but I have noticed that about every six months the cover bears a large banner, 'IS HITLER ALIVE?' You could do something quite similar, but in a more scholarly manner. I might suggest a monthly series, consisting of 'German Sadism, 1933–45; An Evaluation,' 'Eva Peron – Was She Eva Braun's Sister?', and perhaps 'Hitler's Sex Life: A Photographic Supplement.' The possibilities are limitless.

      Your, etc.,
        K.B. VON KOEPPEN,
          Pendleton, Oregon.

*   *   *

17

The Origins of the Popular Press

HAROLD PERKIN

(July 1957)

The social historian Harold Perkin argued that, contrary to the received wisdom, the existence of a sensationalist, popular press long predated the new mass literacy supposedly produced by the 1870 Education Act. This article marked a turning point in Perkin's career which led to pioneering work on social history in Britain.

No historical myth dies harder than the belief that the modern popular press grew up in direct response to the introduction of State education in 1870. In the words of Lord Northcliffe's latest biographer, 'Forster's Education Act had made the acquisition of the hitherto privileged arts of reading and writing universally compulsory, and a Conservative Prime Minister, Lord Salisbury, had made them free of all costs to parents. So, by the time that Harmsworth began his adventures as a popular editor he had, ready and eager to be exploited, a vast reading public of youthful citizens who had learnt to read over the previous twenty years.' 'In 1880,' R.C.K. Ensor writes, 'ten years after Forster's Education Act, a branch manager of a fancy-goods business, named George Newnes, became aware that the new schooling was creating a new class of potential readers – people who had been taught to decipher print without learning much else, and for whom the existing newspapers, with their long articles, long paragraphs, and all-round demands on the intelligence and imagination, were quite unsuited. To give them what they felt they wanted he started in that year a little weekly, well described by its name, *Tit-Bits*.' For the historian of *The Times*, '*Tit-Bits* at a copper fell exactly within the intellectual and financial reach of a generation new to reading.' For Newnes' assistant, Alfred Harmsworth, it was a short step, via *Answers* (1888), to the founding of the *Daily Mail*, and the inauguration of the modern 'yellow press.' The myth is especially dear to the rival 'quality press': the reviews of Richard Hoggart's recent book, *The Uses of Literacy*, all stressed 'the compulsory literacy of 1870.'

However attractive to intellectual *amour-propre* or the perennial nostalgia for an imaginary past before cultural standards were debased, the belief rests on very slender foundations. On the one hand, the origins of the popular press go back far beyond 1870. On the other, it took much longer than a generation for the cheap London dailies to become the staple reading at the levels occupied by the illiterate before 1870. The rise of the mass-circulation dailies was an important phase in the history of journalism; but it was not the complete revolution it is usually supposed. In the dramatic form in which it is traditionally stated, and from which it receives its supposed significance, the belief in a direct causal connection between the 1870 Education Act and the 'Harmsworth revolution' is almost pure myth, without foundation in fact.

The belief implies that the working class, who today form most of the readership of the cheap London dailies, were largely illiterate before 1870. The assumption makes nonsense of the history of the previous hundred years. As Professor Aspinall and Dr R.K. Webb have shown, the fears of English governments from the anti-Jacobin to the Chartist period, from the younger Pitt to Lord John Russell, were grounded in the knowledge that large numbers of working men could read, and had access to inflammatory propaganda. The stamp duty on newspapers was increased between 1789 and 1815 from 1½d. to 4d., making the final price 7d., for the express purpose of discouraging their circulation among the reading poor. The press and the poor found ways of circumventing the purpose. Unstamped journals, ostensibly containing no news, like Cobbett's *Twopenny Trash*, were widely read. Samuel Bamford, the 'weaver-poet,' tells how in 1816 the writings of Cobbett 'were read on nearly every cottage hearth in the manufacturing districts of South Lancashire; in those of Leicester, Derby and Nottingham; also in many Scottish towns.' Artisans clubbed together to buy the *Black Dwarf* and other 'seditious' papers. Newspapers were read aloud in ale-houses and clubs. In 1831, according to the Attorney-General, Cobbett's *Political Register*, at a shilling, was widely read amongst the working classes. After the reduction of the stamp duty to a penny in 1836, the Chartists had their own journals, like Ernest Jones's *People's Paper* (1852).

Working-class Radicals were perhaps educationally superior to their fellows. The same cannot be said of the London street-folk described by Henry Mayhew in the 1850's. Though they had next to no schooling, and few of them could read, 'even costermongers have their taste for books. They are very fond of hearing anyone read aloud to them, and listen very attentively. One man often reads the Sunday paper of the beershop to them, and on a fine summer's evening a costermonger, or any neighbour who has the advantage of being "a schollard," reads aloud to them in the courts they inhabit.' Mayhew found the very prostitutes literate. Three-quarters of the 42,000 'disorderly prostitutes' prosecuted in London in the 1850's could at least read.

Reading, then, if not writing, was by no means a privileged art before 1870. Though the State did not itself provide instruction until then, elementary education was of much older date. Leaving aside older and less formal developments, the hundreds of charity schools founded in the eighteenth century did much to spread the three R's amongst 'the lower orders.' The early nineteenth century saw a great expansion, chiefly through the agency of the rival religious bodies, the Society for the Education of the Poor according to the Principles of the Church of England, and the British and Foreign Schools Society. For those children who could not attend day-schools, Sunday schools expanded rapidly from 1780. With their emphasis on Bible study as the main foundation of moral conduct, they had a considerable influence on literacy. Some of them even taught writing, though against opposition. In 1833 a group of cotton operatives in Glossop, Derbyshire, unable to persuade the existing Sunday schools to teach their children to write, founded their own, and met, for lack of other accommodation, in the largest local public house.

By 1818, it is estimated, there were 675,000 children attending day-schools, and nearly half a million attending Sunday schools in England and Wales, though, of course, they overlapped. By Horace Mann's educational census of 1851 there were over two million and nearly 2½ million respectively – that is, about one child in three under the age of fifteen was attending a day-school. Since few working-class children attended for more than one or two years, a much larger proportion received some instruction. In the twenty years before 1870 the numbers expanded still further as the State increased its financial aid until it bore a larger share of the costs than the voluntary bodies and the parents together. The 1870 Act was not a beginning but a point on a steadily rising scale. If the average attendance at public elementary schools almost quadrupled between 1870 and 1901, only part of the increase represented children not previously educated. Apart from the growth of the child population, most of it was due to the longer school-life of most children – six or seven years instead of two or three.

Those who attended neither day-school nor Sunday school were not always illiterate, for they were not necessarily mentally backward, and in an age of self-help might teach themselves with the help of parents and friends. It is not surprising, then, to find that, as early as 1841, two-thirds of the bridegrooms and more than half the brides could sign the marriage register. By 1871, before the board schools could have affected them, four-fifths of the men and three-quarters of the women could do so, while in Scotland the figures were even better. This is not proof that they could read, but it is circumstantial evidence. It is reinforced by con- temporary surveys, like that of the Manchester and Salford Educational Aid Society in 1865 in New Cross and St Michael's wards: 'half the youthful population were unable to write, and about one-quarter unable to read' – in other words, three-quarters were literate. It is clear that in the mid-nineteenth century, a generation before the school boards appeared, there was a reading public large enough to have supported a popular press of considerable size.

The myth that a generation of new readers called forth the popular press thus reduces itself to the improbable claim that the early halfpenny London dailies were chiefly supported by the third or less of the population which became literate between 1870 and 1900. It is reasonable to assume that most of these belonged to the lower strata of the working class. It is just these levels that Charles Booth and Seebohm Rowntree found living in poverty. In Booth's London in the early eighties over thirty per cent of the population belonged to the poor and the very poor. In Rowntree's York, in 1899, very nearly the same proportion were in primary or secondary poverty. It is extremely improbable that the purchasers of the Edwardian halfpenny dailies came mainly from among those who could not afford enough food to keep them in health, and had nothing to spare for inessentials. If they read them in ale-houses or at second hand, they could hardly have had much effect on the character and circulations of the new papers.

Again, if the new dailies were already reaching so low for their subscribers, whence came the huge subsequent increases in newspaper circulations? Earlier estimates of total circulations are unreliable, but since 1920 the national dailies have increased in circulation from less than 5½ to over 16 million. At the earlier date less than two families in three purchased a national morning paper. It was not until the Second World War that the sales of national dailies overtook the number of households in the country. Sunday circulations, significantly, did so by the First World War; but theirs is an older story to which we must return. It took up to half a century for the popular daily press as created – or remodelled – by Harmsworth to absorb the new readers produced by State education.

Without universal education, of course, the mass-circulation press could not exist. To that extent a causal thread, beginning long before 1870 and ending long after 1896, runs through both Forster's Act and the founding of the *Daily Mail*. Reduced to these terms, the connection between the two becomes a truism of egregious triviality. For all the significance left in it, the myth collapses under the weight of the evidence.

Its collapse, however, leaves us with two further problems. Where, if not in 'the Harmsworth revolution,' are the origins of the popular press to be found? Secondly, allowing that the rise of the mass-circulation dailies was an important stage in the history of the press, to what causes must it be attributed?

The origins of the popular press go back long before Northcliffe. They are to be found, in part at least, where the most casual reader of nineteenth-century newspapers would expect to find them – in the press itself. The belief that all or even most newspapers before the *Daily Mail* were uniformly high-toned, serious and unbiased will not survive even a cursory reading of them. Long articles, long paragraphs, few headlines and fewer illustrations they may have had; but their demands on the intelligence and the imagination are easy to exaggerate. The *Report of the Royal Commission on the Press* (1949), the most considered critique of the modern popular press, has two major criticisms to make of its perform-ance: that devotion to truth and absence of political bias were not maintained by most papers at the highest possible standards, and that they contained too much triviality and sensationalism, resulting from the desire to provide excitement and to 'minister to the imaginative gratifi-cation of the reader.' The same criticisms were, with justice, made of the nineteenth-century press.

The historian W.E.H. Lecky, writing in 1882 before 'the Harmsworth revolution,' saw a very few men in control of the press acquiring a greater influence than most responsible statesmen. 'They constitute themselves the mouthpiece and representative of the nation, and they are often accepted as such throughout Europe. They make it their task to select, classify and colour the information, and to supply the opinions of their readers, and as comparatively few men have the wish or the power or the time to compare evidence and weigh arguments, they dictate absolutely the conclusions of thousands. If they cannot altogether make opinion, they can at least exaggerate, bias, and influence it.' Their success came from writing down to the level of their readers: 'A knack of clever writing, great enterprise in bringing together the kind of information which amuses or interests the public, tact in catching and following the first symptoms of change of opinions, a skilful pandering to popular preju-dice, malevolent gossip, sensational falsehood, coarse descriptions, vin-dictive attacks on individuals, nations, or classes, are the elements of which many great newspaper ascendancies have been mainly built.'

These strictures, with their familiar ring for modern ears, are fully borne out by the evidence. Lack of political bias was rare, even in the most reputable papers. Comment on political opponents was frankly partisan. 'Mr. Babbletongue Macaulay,' said *The Times* of the early forties, was 'hardly fit to fill up one of the vacancies that have occurred by the lamentable death of Her Majesty's two favourite monkeys.' In a Corn Law debate in 1842, according to the *Manchester Chronicle and Salford Standard*, 'Lord John Russell, whether from mere presumptuous imbecillity [*sic*] or from *treachery*, ignominiously broke down in the midst of his argument.' For the *Manchester Courier and Lancashire General Advertizer*, Mr Gladstone, 'stumping it at Chester' in support of his son's candidature on Derby Day, 1865, when every gentlemanly statesman was at Epsom, was 'the prince of humbugs of the present day; and . . . we never knew a time in which humbug was so rampant as it is at present.'

Headlines, though restricted to a single column, could wring every drop of sensation out of the news. A random sample from the local press around mid-century reads as follows: 'HORRIBLE MATRICIDE NEAR BIRKENHEAD', 'RAPE BY AN EX-LOVER', 'FRIGHTFUL BOILER EXPLOSION; MELANCHOLY LOSS OF LIFE'; 'THE MYSTERIOUS FRUITS OF SECRET LOVE', AND 'MELANCHOLY DESTRUCTION OF A CHILD BY ITS MOTHER, WHILE FRANTIC WITH PAIN.'

The verbatim reports of sensational legal cases, which today form the Sunday reading of a large part of the population, were a Victorian staple at a higher level of society. In an attack on the 'attractive and lucrative indecency of *The Times*' in 1864, the *Saturday Review* remarked, 'We want a Moral Sewers Commission. To purify the Thames is something, but to purify *The Times* would be a greater boon to society. . . . The unsavoury reports of the Divorce Courts, the disgusting details of harlotry and vice, the filthy and nauseous annals of the brothel, the prurient letters of adulterers and adulteresses, the modes in which intrigues may be carried out, the diaries and meditations of married sinners, these are now part of our domestic life.'

Working men rarely read *The Times*. What did they read? Local papers were more in touch with what they knew. Published usually once or twice a week, they could be read and passed on before they were out of date. When penny morning papers appeared about the time of the repeal of the stamp duty in 1855, most working men had neither the time nor the money for them. In some areas, an attempt was made to reach them with the halfpenny evening paper, the first being *The Events*, 'a Daily Newspaper for the MILLION,' which appeared in Liverpool in 1855. It was not a success; but others in Liverpool, Manchester, South Shields and elsewhere did succeed; and in many places a halfpenny press was available to the working class long before the *Daily Mail.*

Without doubt, the preferred reading of the Victorian working classes was the Sunday press. Published once a week at a moment when, if at all, the working man had both leisure and money, the Sunday paper was the true progenitor of the popular press. In 1828, when newspapers were at 7d., Toby Tims, the barber, quoted in *Blackwood's Magazine*, got *Bell's Weekly Messenger* 'from a neighbour, who has it from his cousin in the Borough, who, I believe, is the last reader of a club of fourteen.' The Royal Commission found that the events which had the greatest news-value for the modern popular press were 'those concerning sport, followed by news about people, news of strange or amusing adventures, tragedies, accidents, and crimes, news, that is, whose sentiment or excitement brings some colour to life.' *Bell's Weekly Messenger*, according to Toby Tims, was 'a most entertaining paper, and beats all for news. In fact, it is full of everything, sir – every, every thing – accidents – charity sermons – markets – boxing – Bible societies – horse racing – child murders – the theatres – foreign wars – Bow-street reports – and Day-and-Martin's blacking.'

By 1854, before they brought their price down to a penny at the repeal of the stamp duty, *Lloyd's Weekly News* (1842) and the *News of the World* (1843) had achieved circulations of 100,000, and *Reynolds' News* (1850) was not far behind. Over the next half-century *Lloyd's*, the prototype of the modern popular newspaper, outclassed all the rest, rising to 900,000 in 1890, when *Reynolds'* had little more than a third the circulation and the *News of the World* had sunk to 30,000. In 1896, when the *Daily Mail* began to appear, *Lloyd's* reached a million, the first newspaper to do so. In popular appeal the Sunday press always led the way. In 1920 the total circulation was 13½ million – more than one for every family in the country. The new readers created by State education, like most working-class readers before them, turned first to the Sunday press.

Even the Sunday press does not exhaust the favourite reading of the Victorian working-class, or the origins of the popular press. Until surprisingly late in the nineteenth century there was, at the lowest levels of society, a thriving indigenous literature of street-ballads, broadsheets and chapbooks. Sold in the countryside by pedlars or chapmen and in the towns by itinerant street-singers, they were the natural vehicle for the information and entertainment of a lively, inquisitive people for whom the sung or spoken word meant more than the written. They were a complete literature in themselves: 'cock-crows' or romances, nursery rhymes, songs sentimental like the often-printed 'Drink to me Only,' or humorous like 'Pretty Polly Perkins of Paddington Green.' In 1856 Jenny Catnach's successor at the Seven Dials Press stocked more than four thousand different titles. The most popular were the gallow-sheets, which had been known to sell 40,000 copies at an execution: execrable, moralizing verses on the murderer – Palmer the Rugeley poisoner, Mrs Maybrick, Burke and Hare, and others whose fame still lives. Sporting events, especially prize-fights, were favourite topics. News of any kind was a bestseller. Every notable event produced its crop of ballads: the Nore mutiny, the battles of Trafalgar, Waterloo, Navarino, Inkerman, and the rest, the various coronations, the 'Happy Reform' of 1832, Queen Victoria's marriage and the birth of every royal baby, Corn Law Repeal, the Great Exhibition, and so on. Peel's Income Tax in 1842 provoked a ballad of Gilbertian measure:

Oh! poor old Johnny Bull has his Cup of Sorrow full,
And what with underfeeding him, and leaching him, and bleeding him,
Though overdrained before, he must lose a little more,
He'll now be bled again by the Income Tax.

The standard of comment was hard-hitting and uninhibited. The rhymers thought nothing of advising the Queen in the interests of the Exchequer to 'do it no more'; of accusing 'little Al, the royal pal,' thought to oppose the Crimean War, of being a Russian; or of spreading malicious gossip about 'Margaret Slack and the Prince of Wales.' The 'human angle' was the basic approach; 'And my love fell with Nelson upon that very day' is a fair example. Sex, violence and crime were the most favoured ingredients and the moral tone grew shriller as the prurience increased. But what gives the street-ballad an even stronger claim to the ancestry of the popular press is the eye-catching, sensational lay-out. Black headlines and garish illustration begin with the ballads. A villainous woodcut is captioned by 'SHOCKING RAPE AND MURDER.' Another has 'SELF DESTRUCTION OF FEMALE BY THROWING HERSELF OFF THE MONUMENT.' 'THE IRISH NEW POLICEMEN' shows a prisoner being bludgeoned in a Dublin police station, while 'PENAL SERVITUDE FOR MRS. MAYBRICK: She Will Not Have To Climb Golden Stairs' needs no illustration. The street-ballad beats the modern 'yellow press' in vulgarity, sensationalism, moral indignation, outspokenness and, above all, robustness.

Apart from the similarity of interests, style and audience, it is possible to show something like a continuity of readership from the street-literature to the Sunday paper, and so to the modern popular press. The link is provided by the penny serial novels. Romantic or heroic, lush or violent, and garnished with a woodcut, the serial novel showed that the market could be more continuously exploited. Illiterate costermongers, Mayhew was told, would go mad if they could not learn 'about the picture.' 'What they love best to listen to – and, indeed, what they are most eager for – are Reynolds' periodicals, especially the "Mysteries of the Court",' he was told by the men who read to them; 'They've got tired of Lloyd's bloodstained stories, and I'm satisfied that, of all London, Reynolds is the most popular man among them.' Edward Lloyd and G.W.M. Reynolds are a personal link between the street-literature and the popular press. Having learnt their trade and their audience with the serial novel, they developed the Sunday papers named after them.

The line runs back, then, from the modern popular press, through *Lloyd's Weekly* and *Reynolds' News* and the penny novels to the street-ballads. And the street-ballads themselves have an ancestry almost as old as printing. Before newspapers existed, the sixteenth-century ballads, full of monstrous births, lewd romances, popish plots, famine, war and pestilence, and the accessions and deaths of princes, were an established tradition. News-ballads threw up news-pamphlets, and they in their turn, by publishing under a continuing name and date-line, the *corantos* of the 1620's. The ballads were thus the progenitors not only of the popular but of all the newspaper press. When in the mid-nineteenth century they finally threw up the popular Sunday paper to cater for the last and lowest layers of society, they cut off their own blood-supply. By the seventies they had withered, by the eighties almost disappeared – but *Lloyd's* and *Reynolds'* were selling by the hundred thousand.

There still remains the problem of 'the Harmsworth revolution.' If a flourishing popular press existed before the advent of Harmsworth, to what can we attribute his achievement, the inauguration of the mass-circulation daily? For it was an achievement, marking a major turning-point in newspaper history. It has been flagrantly misrepresented. Neither the *Daily Mail* nor the *Daily Mirror* – nor, for that matter, even *Tit-Bits* – lowered the standards of popular journalism. If anything, they raised them. *Tit-Bits* and *Answers* may have been put together with scissors and paste; but they were putting together snippets of wholesome, edifying information. Newnes, Pearson and Harmsworth were working for a public as restless and self-improving as themselves. Samuel Smiles is their godfather. The *Mail*, the *Express* and the *Mirror*, in their early days at least, were purveyors of daily news and comment of a scope and quality hitherto unavailable at less than twice the price. Superficial, biased, trivial, sensational perhaps, they were none the less paragons by the side of the street-literature and many earlier news-sheets – not to mention some of the newsless newspapers of today.

The achievement of Harmsworth is that he did for the newspaper what Leverhulme did for soap, or Ford for the motorcar. He found a product ripe for exploitation by mass-production methods. The Sunday press had shown its possibilities. He raised its quality to a uniform level, cheapened it, and sold it by the million. In the process he built himself, like them, a great commercial empire, to be imitated by others. He could only do so because of the enormous economic opportunities created by the social changes going on around him. For half a century before 1896, and with increasing speed in the great price-fall of the last twenty years, real incomes had been rising for the lower middle and working classes. For many of them, though not yet for the poorest, that meant a larger surplus after meeting necessities. This was an opportunity for the supplier of mass-consumer goods – soap, groceries, haberdashery, and the like – which made more than one millionaire's fortune. Part of the surplus was spent on a daily newspaper, as well as the Sunday and the local press. The early readers of the *Daily Mail* were the lower middle and the 'respectable' working classes. As layer after social layer rose out of poverty in the twentieth century, so the London morning press expanded to meet it, and adjusted its appeal.

The modern popular press is a phenomenon grounded in social and economic fact. It was not so much State education as the expansion and redistribution of the national income, which at every stage has fed and nourished it. If the morals, taste and truthfulness of this wayward mistress of the public are no better than they should be, that is not because they have declined. Rather is it because, since the days of the broadsheet ballads, the penny novels and the Victorian Sunday press, they have not progressed enough.

*   *   *

Harold Perkin is Emeritus Professor of History and Higher Education at Northwestern University, Chicago, and Honorary Professor at Cardiff and Lancaster Universities. He was educated at Jesus College, Cambridge. In 1967 he became Britain's first Professor of Social History at Lancaster University before moving to Chicago in 1985. In 1976, Perkin founded the Social History Society of the UK. His publications include *The Origins of Modern English Society, 1780–1880* (1990) and *The Rise of Professional Society: England since 1880* (1990).

18

The Tents of Kedar

BASIL DAVIDSON

(October 1957)

Basil Davidson was one of the earliest British scholars to devote himself to serious understanding of African (as opposed to colonial) history.

'I am black but comely,' sang the maiden in the Song of Solomon: black 'as the tents of Kedar, as the curtains of Solomon.'

> Look not upon me, because I am black
> Because the sun hath looked upon me:
> My mother's children were angry with me;
> They made me the keeper of the vineyards;
> But mine own vineyard have I not kept.

Discovering the African slave trade at about the same time as the Bible, a newly mercantile Europe firmly replied that this black but comely maiden ought to have laboured in her own vineyard: far from deserving sympathy, she was much to be censured for idleness and dismal error. If Africa was the 'dark continent,' it was not because Africa was obscure, but because Africa was perverse. Surely these African peoples were unreasonably childlike and immature: no doubt incapable, from some inner lack, of the same social and individual growth as the peoples of Europe? There evolved, across the years, a rich mythology that explained how right and proper it really was to enslave Africans, and afterwards to take their countries from them, since they were manifestly so little capable either of saving themselves or of managing their own affairs. It is part of the contemporary emancipation of Africa that scholarship – and largely, so far, European scholarship – should now displace this mythology of enslavement and conquest by the facts of pre-European African history.

Yet the notion that negro Africa has a history of its own – and moreover a history of civilization – is new enough to be controversial. Not many years have passed since it was generally accepted, at any rate in Europe, that Africans had lived in a land of man-eating solitude and mental darkness. Against those who now deny this it is still argued, often enough with heat and passion, that peoples who had never known the wheel, the plough, or the use of writing, and whose societies had become so far removed in growth and sentiment from the societies of Europe – and perhaps of Asia – could not be said to have a history of their own, much less a history of civilization. But we are still living in an age of discovery. Within the past few years a growing number of historians, archaeologists and anthropologists have gone far on journeys of historical exploration, in Africa, that challenge comparison with the great geographical marches of the nineteenth century. Just as Europe learned a century ago that the Niger river flowed from west to east – and not from east to west, as maps of Africa had showed since Antiquity – so now we find that the course of pre-European negro history passed through many cultures and politics that were neither primitive nor savage.

Even fifty years ago, in the haste of conquering an Africa whose inhabitants were generally regarded as something less than human, there were thoughtful men who saw these long-isolated peoples under a different and more generous light. Pushing through dense rain forest into the old Bushongo kingdom of the Central Congo in 1904, Frobenius 'could still find villages whose approaches were bordered on either side, for several miles, by four rows of palms, and whose houses were decorated with charm and were works of art': their silks and skins, their tools, their spoons, he thought, were of an artistry 'comparable to the creations of the Roman style in Europe.'

Of these same people of Bushongo another witness, Emil Torday, wrote at much the same time that 'if they were, as we have good reason to believe, a good picture of the Bushongo (of long ago), then we must admit that the natives of this part of the world were in the sixteenth century a very happy people.' And it is true that the facts about Bushongo, so far as they are now known, suggest relatively peaceful and well ordered government over several hundred years. Life in Bushongo, for much of that time, was possibly a good deal less disagreeable for most of the people than it was in Europe. As to the antiquity of this kingdom – there in the core and centre of Africa's 'heart of darkness' – enough was said in 1904 when its last king, Kwete Peshanga Kena, went down before the Belgian invaders: he was mourned as the hundred and twentieth monarch in the line of oral tradition.

But how reliable is oral tradition? Early investigators were inclined to dismiss it as of small historical value. This view, as the brilliant work of a contemporary Belgian ethnologist in the Congo, Monsieur J. Vansina, has lately emphasized, is in course of serious revision; and Torday's dating of the 'great king' of Bushongo, Shamba Bolongongo, was perhaps the beginning of this revision, although it was made some fifty years ago. It is worth recalling in Torday's own words:

> As the elders were talking of the great events of various reigns, and we came to the 98th chief, Bo Kama Bomanchala, they said that nothing remarkable happened during the reign, except that one day at noon the sun went out, and there was absolute darkness for a short time.
>
> When I heard this I lost all self-control: I jumped up and wanted to do something desperate. The elders thought I had been stung by a scorpion. It was only months later that the date of the eclipse became known to me . . . the 30th of March, 1680, when there was a total eclipse of the sun, passing exactly over Bushongo. . . . There was no possibility of confusion with another eclipse, because this was the only one visible in the region during the 17th and 18th centuries.
>
> As there were three reigns between that of Shamba Bolongongo and of Bo Kama Bomanchala, and the great king's as well as that of his two successors had been of more than usual length, we cannot be far from the truth if we put the beginning of Shamba's reign as 1600 or thereabouts.

It was an important revelation of the *possibility* of African history; but, as well as that, it threw a new and unfamiliar light on the stability and dignity of African social tradition. 'A central African king,' comments Torday, 'of the early days of the seventeenth century, not a warrior but a man of peace' – he is said to have disbanded the standing army of Bushongo and abolished the use of the bow and throwing knife – 'whose only conquests were on the field of thought, public prosperity, and social progress, and who is still remembered in our day by every person in his country . . . must have been a remarkable man indeed.'

Later judgments on negro polities of the pre-European period have tended to strengthen, rather than deny, this view. Many advances in knowledge have followed the pioneering of Torday's time. Within the past ten years the study of African history has become a subject in its own right. A 'first conference on African history and archaeology' was held in London in 1953, under the aegis of the School of Oriental and African Studies. A second conference, held in July this year, was attended by more than a hundred scholars of several nationalities and many fields of research: it declared itself to be 'primarily concerned with the possibility of establishing outlines for the history of Africa since the Stone Age.'

The study of African history has therefore come of age. But the age is still a young one. 'No such history,' said Dr Mathew at this year's conference, 'could dream of being definitive in the twentieth century. We are still finding new things every six months.' The broad outlines none the less appear. Where did the negro peoples grow and develop? What factors, whether of environment or of cultural drift, governed their development? Why was this development different from that of peoples elsewhere? Was it really stagnant through recent centuries? Some tentative answers become possible.

'When the descendants of Noah spread across the earth, the sons of Cush, son of Canaan, travelled towards the west and crossed the Nile. There they separated: some of them, the Nubians and the Beja and the Zanj, turned to the rightward, between the east and the west: the others, very numerous, marched toward the setting sun . . .'

Thus El Mas'udi, who was the greatest of the medieval Arab geographers, in his *Meadows of Gold and Mines of Gems*, written shortly before AD 950. Basing himself on contemporary tradition and such knowledge as there was, as well as on travels half across the world, El Mas'udi has much to say of Africa; and, at any rate in essence, this legend of the sons of Cush certainly contains an element of truth. The peopling of Africa has been a long and complex story of migrations.

Some of the oldest human bones come from Africa. 'It seems more and more likely,' wrote the Abbé Breuil not long ago, 'that, even from times that are hundreds of thousands of years distant . . . Africa not only knew stages of primitive civilization that are comparable with those of Europe and Asia Minor, but is also perhaps the origin of these civilizations in the classical countries of the north.' In that remote time before the last Ice Age, it is possible, even probable, that migration moved northward out of Africa: there is in any case a near coincidence of style and method between the Bushman rock paintings of Africa and rock paintings in southern Europe. But the migrations of the New Stone Age, and since, were migrations *into* Africa, southward and south-westward. These were the migrations – comparable, perhaps, with those of the Indo-Europeans who filled Europe with our own ancestors – that peopled Africa in times beyond memory but not, it may now emerge, beyond definition.

What became of these small pioneering groups, moving westward and southward into the desert and the rain forest, can as yet be little more than guessed at here and there. Two great factors seem to have worked upon them. The cultures and civilizations that were gradually evolved by

Bantu-speaking and other African groups were the fruit both of their own native genius, reacting and readjusting in conditions that were often severely hostile, and of cultural borrowing from peoples and lands they had left behind them. They evolved, that is, both by skilful invention and by the application of ideas that reached them from outside; but the product of this union was specifically their own.

No clear or regular pattern can be traced of this long-enduring process of readjustment and invention. But, when measuring the capacity of these peoples both to survive and multiply in new and difficult conditions, one needs to bear in mind two further circumstances that governed their existence. The first is that they advanced, as it were, into the past. They collided with no cultures superior to their own. Where the Dorian Greek barbarians migrated towards the splendour of Mycenae, and transformed themselves, the migrant peoples of Africa encountered only the remnants of people who had yet to make the agricultural revolution out of the Old Stone Age. Where the Indo-European invaders of northern India clashed with the civilization of Mohenjo-daro, and changed their nature in the process, negroes, moving south and west across unknown centuries into Africa, could find nothing and no one to show them superior forms of social life.

The second circumstance that must have worked for conservatism was the very greatness of the land they knew. At least in central and southern Africa there could be no question of those creative conflicts which derived, elsewhere, from sheer surplus of population. Unlike the relatively crowded populations of the Fertile Crescent – of Mesopotamia and the delta of the Nile – these African peoples were never confronted with an absolute need for more efficient ways of production. Whenever the number of people at any one place exceeded the local food supply, some of them could always depart for new land and new supplies of game. Tribes would hive off sub-tribes, who would forage further on and settle elsewhere. They were doing this right into our own times: only European 'law and order,' and latterly the beginnings of industrialism and the growth of cities, have prevented them from continuing to do it.

This process of continual migration was fruitful over the centuries; for it enabled these peoples to sustain themselves and multiply under severely adverse conditions. Across this often inhospitable continent the Bantu and their fellow peoples spread themselves thinly, and survived. Yet the very thinness of their occupation set close limits on their chances of evolution. It meant that their economy generally continued to be one of subsistence: and this, in turn, meant that there could only be a slow progress towards the division of labour, systematic growth of trade, production of trading surpluses, which elsewhere fathered the growth of cities, the invention and the use of writing, the discovery of mechanical technique, and, little by little, the paraphernalia of urban civilization. The real progress that occurred may have been much hampered by these two great governing circumstances: first, by the absence of any stimulatingly superior cultures in their path of migration; secondly, by the plenitude of land which let them solve their social problems simply by migration, instead of forcing them into new paths of development. Against this background, the civilizations which Africans did evolve reveal a high talent for adaptation, great vigour in survival, and unusual flexibility of social attitude and organization.

Those sons of Cush, 'very numerous,' who 'marched toward the setting sun' in the legend recorded by El Mas'udi a thousand years ago, would have found well-trodden paths leading through equatorial Africa to the savannahs and the forests of the west. Whatever real migrations lie hidden within that legend, there is little doubt that the civilizations of medieval West Africa owed much to the earlier civilizations of the Nile Valley, and perhaps especially much to the civilizations of Meroe, that notable African kingdom which flourished above the Nile cataracts between 700 BC and the fourth century AD. To this line of influence may ultimately be traced something of the stimulus that evolved the ancient kingdom of Ghana, whose probable capital was partially excavated by French investigators not long ago at Kumbi Saleh in southern Mauritania, some hundreds of miles west of Timbuktoo.

The early Arab writers knew of Ghana. El Fazari first mentions it, shortly after 800, as 'the land of gold'; and some time before 833 El Kwarizmi placed it on a map. Yakoubi, in 872, speaks of 'the king of Ghana, a great king; in his territory are gold mines, and he has under his domination a great number of kingdoms.' But the most famous of these Arab descriptions of Ghana is that of El Bekri, writing of 1067, who says that 'the king of Ghana can raise 200,000 warriors, 40,000 of them being armed with bows and arrows': by this time, moreover, the Arabs knew Ghana from the Almoravid conquest which had lately destroyed that kingdom. 'When he gives audience to his people,' recalls El Bekri of the king whom Ibn Yacin the Almoravid had conquered, 'to listen to their complaints and set them to rights, he sits in a pavilion around which stand his horses caparisoned in cloth of gold: behind him stand ten pages holding shields and gold-mounted swords: on his right hand are the sons of the princes of his empire, splendidly clad and with gold plaited into their hair . . .' a barbaric king and a barbaric empire? But were they more barbaric or less civilized than the king and people whom William of Normandy conquered at almost exactly the same time?

The Arab-Berber armies of the Almoravids 'spread their dominion over the negroes (of Ghana), devastated their territory and plundered their property,' as Ibn Khaldoun was to write two hundred years later; but they in turn were absorbed by these negroes. After the fall of Ghana there followed in West Africa, through five hundred years and more, a succession of semi-feudal empires and kingdoms that spread across the wide savannah belt between the desert and the rain forest, proving once again how mistaken was the later European view that Africans had no history of state-building and ordered government. If their ruling groups were Muslim by faith, the origins and dominant culture of Mali, Songhay, and other medieval kingdoms of the Western Sudan were specifically African. Arab records speak respectfully of them. 'A traveller may proceed alone amongst them,' wrote Ibn Battuta in the mid-fourteenth century, 'without the least fear of brigands or robbers or ravages.' Even in their waning after-glory the cities of the Western Sudan could still show dignity and greatness. On the threshold of the nineteenth century, after more than three hundred years of the oversea slave trade and its appallingly destructive consequences, Mungo Park could say of Segu on the Niger that 'the view of this extensive city; the numerous canoes upon the river; the crowded population, and the cultivated state of the surrounding country, formed altogether a prospect of civilization and magnificence which I little expected to find in the bosom of Africa.'

These pastoral empires looked northward: their kings and princes travelled to Mecca when they could. They failed to penetrate the rain forest to the south of them, although they certainly tried. There, meanwhile, other African peoples were evolving radically different but no less solid or advanced cultures. The terra-cotta heads of Ifé and the bronzes of Benin – their earliest dating is perhaps tenth to twelfth century – reveal a high order of sensitivity and social consciousness. Was the stimulus West African, or was it also Meroitic – from the valley of the Upper Nile? Once again, the likely answer is that both were present. Dr Dike and his colleagues, Nigerian and British, may be able to throw new light on this when their researches into the history of Benin are complete.

But the peoples who 'turned rightward, between the east and the west,' and penetrated into the southern lands of Africa, met with other destinies. In this direction, too, modern scholarship has new and interesting things to say. Those who peopled the equatorial forests and the southern plateau – in times beyond memory or tradition but conceivably within the last three thousand years – had, in any case, achieved much for themselves. They evolved agriculture under rain-forest conditions: they discovered iron and copper and other metals, and began to mine and smelt and use them: they developed efficient forms of tribal organization, not very different from those that were surviving, here and there, even yesterday, and whose degenerate remains may still be seen today. They grew from primitive origins into barbarism; and from barbarism they moved far towards those same kinds of feudal centralism which held good in Europe. 'Their legal institutions,' Dr H.J. Simons has pointed out, 'had progressed beyond the primitive stage and showed many resemblances to the archaic laws of the Anglo-Saxon, German and Frankish peoples before the rise of feudal society. Indeed, in some respects, such as the absence of self-help or the judicial duel, the existence of centralized courts with a defined jurisdiction, the compulsory submission of cases such as treason, homicide, and sorcery to the courts, the African legal system had advanced to the stage reached in Europe during the early medieval period.'

In short, despite its isolation from the main stream of human development, African society before the coming of the Europeans was neither savage nor stagnant. The difficulty of evaluating its achievement lies partly in the fact that the rediscovery of Africa during the nineteenth century took place long after the oversea slave trade and European conquest – in southern Africa, mainly by the Portuguese – had done their destructive work; partly in the deficiency of written vernacular records; and partly because archaeology is still at the beginning of its task. We are still faced by more questions than answers.

Yet there were, it would seem, two main currents of cultural drift into east and southern Africa in pre-European times: from Meroe and medieval Axum, southward up the course of the White Nile into what is now Uganda and onward into the rain forest and the southern plateau, as well as southward along the coast; and across the sea from Arabia, Persia, India, Indonesia, China. For at least fifteen hundred years before the Portuguese rounded the Cape of Good Hope and discovered the Indian Ocean, these coastal lands of East Africa had formed the western terminal of a great trading circuit that encompassed much of the Eastern world. Vasco da Gama, cruising up this coast in 1498, found the harbours of what are now Tanganyika, Zanzibar, Kenya, busy with shipping from Arabia and India; and it was with an Indian pilot that he sailed for Calicut. Eighty years before him, although he could not have known it, Chinese ships had anchored off Melinde, the (Kenyan) harbour from which he sailed.

In this great trading circuit, the Arabs followed Greco-Roman and Indian forerunners; but they probably enlarged it. By the eighth century they had established trading stations in southern China, and by the tenth century they were similarly established as far south in Africa as Sofala, in modern Mozambique: they joined the ends of the Eastern world together. For China and India, the gold and ivory of eastern and southern Africa were certainly important by the eleventh century, and possibly much earlier. Demand for these commodities must certainly have played a big part in developing the civilizations of the East African coast – Islamized but African – as well as the civilizations of the African interior. El Mas'udi, who seems to have travelled as far as Sofala some time before the middle of the tenth century, could write of the people of that region that the Zanj, as he calls them, 'have a king called the Waqlimi, which means Supreme Lord: they call him thus because they choose him to govern them with equity. From the moment he begins to tyrannize over them or depart from the established laws, they kill him and exclude his posterity from succession to the throne, for they say that in behaving thus he has ceased to be the son of the Master, that is, the king of heaven and earth . . .' And he goes on to provide us with a detailed description of a partly pastoral, partly agricultural society, animist in religion, tolerant in manners, and evidently well fed, 'whose country produces gold in abundance and other marvels.'

Was this the mining civilization of Zimbabwe, the culture that erected the stone walls of what would later become the completely historical kingdom of the Monomotapa, and which the Portuguese, over six hundred years after El Mas'udi's report, would invade and finally destroy? It seems likely. Radiocarbon tests of timber fragments from Zimbabwe suggest a foundation date in the eighth century or perhaps earlier; and beads from the same locality – mainly of Indian provenance – point to the same order of antiquity.

Many complex problems must be solved before the history of these coastal and hinterland civilizations can emerge in more than vague and tentative outline and the myth of 'savage Africa' gives way to history: to the history of African civilization.

*   *   *

Basil Davidson's (b. 1914) name is, to many, synonymous with African history. A journalist and historian, Davidson served in the Balkans, North Africa and Italy during the Second World War. He began writing about Africa in the early 1950s and became familiar with a number of African leaders in the anti-colonial struggles of the 1950s and 1960s. Central to his many books on the continent is Davidson's desire to communicate to Africans as well as to those in the West. His publications include *Old Africa Rediscovered* (1959), *Black Mother* (1961), *The Black Man's Burden* (1992) and *The Search for Africa* (1994). He has received academic honours in countries across the world.

19

The Mad Hatter

CHRISTOPHER HILL

(October 1957)

'Go and sell that thou hast, and give to the poor.' Christopher Hill contributed this portrait of Roger Crab, a mid-seventeenth century hatter from Chesham, who took the biblical injunction literally. But was Crab the original mad hatter?

Sober as a judge, drunk as a lord, black as a sweep: all these proverbial expressions are self-explanatory, since they describe a condition that is naturally incident to the occupation in question. But why mad as a hatter? No obvious reason suggests itself why this trade should render men especially liable to insanity. The answer appears to be that the proverbial madness of hatters derives from one particularly notorious example, Roger Crab, hatter at Chesham in the mid-seventeenth century. Crab studied his New Testament carefully, and came across the words 'If thou wilt be perfect, go and sell that thou hast, and give to the poor.' Crab was not a rich young man, but he wanted to be perfect. So he sold all he had, and gave it to the poor. Naturally, all good Christians thought him mad. If the text extended to us, Crab pictured the rich saying, 'it would make the poor richer than ourselves.' They would rather deny Scripture than part from their riches.

Roger Crab was an interesting character in many ways. He was born somewhere in Buckinghamshire in 1621. He tells us that his mother had £20 a year, or his father would never have married her: they were not the poorest of the poor. About 1641 the young Crab, already seeking perfection, vowed to restrict himself to a diet of vegetables and water, avoiding butter, cheese, eggs and milk. He also decided to remain celibate, perhaps in despair of finding a lady who would accept his vegetarian régime. Next year war broke out between King and Parliament, and Crab joined the Parliamentary army. He served in it for seven years. On one occasion he was 'cloven through the skull to the brain,' and once he was condemned to death by his Commander-in-Chief, Oliver Cromwell, and imprisoned for two years by Parliament. Punishments of such severity can only have been for political offences, and it may be suspected that Crab was involved in the Leveller agitation of 1647–9.

On demobilization he set up as a 'haberdasher of hats' at Chesham. He can never have been very successful during the three years he carried on the business, since he held it a sin to make a profit even before he finally demonstrated his madness by giving away all his property to his poorer neighbours. He retained only enough to lease a rood of land at Ickenham, near Uxbridge, for 50s. a year. Here he built himself a house, and settled down to lead the life of a hermit. He quickly won a reputation as a herbal doctor, probably because he gave his patients the sensible advice to abstain from flesh and strong beer. He had often over a hundred patients at a time, he tells us, and was much sought after by women. He also indulged in prophecy, and was denounced as a witch by a local clergyman. He made his own clothes, of sackcloth, and wore no band, the seventeenth-century equivalent of a neck-tie. He thought it wrong to have a suit of Sunday best, since that was to observe times and seasons. As the years passed he dropped luxuries like potatoes and carrots from his diet: he subsisted on bran broth and a pudding of turnip leaves and bran boiled together. Finally he got down to dock leaves and grass. On this diet he claimed to be able to live at a cost of ¾d. a week. He made one convert to his régime, a Captain Norwood, who possibly had Leveller connections. But the Captain soon died of it, and there were no other disciples. In 1657 Crab moved to Bethnal Green, where he joined the Philadelphians, a religious sect founded by John Pordage, himself a man with a radical political past. In his old age Crab allowed himself the delicacy of parsnips. He died in 1680, aged 59, and was buried in Stepney parish.

Crab wrote several pamphlets, including an autobiography, *The English Hermit, or The Wonder of the Age*, published in 1655. He had an interesting theology. Soul and body, he thought, are separate entities, which can be divided in life as they will be after death. The soul in natural (that is, sinful) man is subject to the body, is indeed enslaved to the flesh. The only way to win true happiness is to make the body subject to the soul. This was the object of Crab's ascetic practices, his vegetarianism and celibacy. Here is his description of how he reduced his body to obedience: 'The old man (meaning my body), being moved, would know what he had done that I used him so hardly. Then I showed him his transgressions . . .: so the wars began. The law of the old man in my fleshly members rebelled against the law of my mind, and had a shrewd skirmish; but the mind, being well enlightened, held it, so that the old man grew sick and weak with the flux, like to fall to the dust. But the wonderful love of God, well pleased with the battle, raised him up again, and filled him full of love, peace and content in mind. And [he] is now become more humble; for he will eat dock leaves, mallows or grass, and yields that he ought to give God more thanks for it than formerly for roast flesh and wines.' We are reminded of St Francis of Assisi by this combination of extreme asceticism with a friendly attitude towards the body, seen as an alien entity.

Crab continued to hold many traditional Leveller views. Here is his account of the civil war and its aftermath. God 'hath tried almost every sort of men and every sort of sects' in the government. First 'the King and bishops were exalted.' Then 'the Parliament, who found fault with them, not pulling the beam of covetousness out of their own eyes, and their sects depending, were all exalted instead of the other.' Thirdly, 'the Army, with their trades and sects depending upon the same account, became exalted. So the gentlemen and farmers have had their turn in offices, . . . and now they will try inferior trades, as journeymen and day-labourers . . . even to the orphan and almsman. . . . It will be a hard matter for a low capacity to judge which of all these parties hath been most just. But I, being of the lowest sort and unlearned, being amongst day-labourers and journeymen, have judged myself with them the worst of all these parties.' Bad as all the others had been, Crab thought, there was not much to be said for 'labouring poor men, which in times of scarcity pine and murmur for want of bread, cursing the rich behind his back; and before his face, cap and knee and a whining countenance.'

So he concluded that all the social groups that had tried their hands at government during the Interregnum were equally unfitted for the task. The moral he drew was that fighting solved nothing. Like many an ex-Leveller Quaker, he became a pacifist, and washed his hands of responsibility for civil government. For all our fighting 'in pretence of liberty and peace,' for all 'our fighting to regulate government in the old man, we see it still as bad [as], if not worse than it was before.' But – again like the early Quakers – Crab retained much of the fierce radical criticism of the existing social order, government and church. The church was 'the old jade.' To keep Sunday was 'to observe her market day.' The Sabbath was 'an abominable idol,' he told the Justices of Clerkenwell. He had no mercy for those enemies of Milton, the Levellers and Quakers – 'hireling priests,' 'tithemongers,' all ministers who did not depend on the voluntary offerings of their congregations. Crab made many offers to meet any minister in public disputation of the kind beloved by the early Quakers; but these offers, he tells us, were never accepted.

Crab's vegetarianism and teetotalism were part of a political and social programme. Drink and gluttony, he thought, raised the price of corn, and so led to high prices, high rents and oppression of the poor. Teetotalism was by no means typical of the early Puritans; we remember Oliver Cromwell telling the Governor of Edinburgh Castle that 'Your pretended fear lest error should slip in is like the man that would keep all wine out [of] the country lest men should be drunk.' Crab was one of the earliest preachers of the sort of teetotalism that was to have a long history in English non-conformity. It is interesting to find that for him it was associated with political radicalism, just as it was for such advocates of total abstention as some of the Chartists, Keir Hardie and Tom Mann. At one time Crab had accepted the conventional view that 'if we should not wear superfluous things, thousands of people would starve for want of trading.' But, by considering the birds and coming 'to know God in nature,' he learnt better. (Gerrard Winstanley the Digger also found God in nature.) The problem of poverty, Crab felt, could be solved by the poor for themselves if they freed themselves from that dependence on the things of the flesh by which the rich enslaved them.

Crab was very scathing about rich 'Christians.' 'If John the Baptist should come forth again, and call himself Leveller, and take such food as the wilderness yielded, and such clothing, and preach up his former doctrine, "He that hath two coats should give away one of them, and he that hath food should do likewise," how scornfully would our proud gentlemen and gallants look on him, that hath gotten three or four coats with great gold and silver buttons, and half a score dainty dishes at his table, besides his gallant house and his furniture therein. Therefore this Scripture must be interpreted some other way or else denied.' That is what men do 'if the Scripture will not serve our own ends to fulfil selfish desire, to uphold the old man is his fleshly honour.' 'Thus we see for the love of this world people are destroyed.' (With John the Baptist calling himself Leveller we may compare Winstanley's statement in 1650 that 'Jesus Christ . . . is the head Leveller.') Crab ended, as Winstanley did in some of his pamphlets, with some lines of verse:

> Such are our lusts and covetousness,
> The belly and back to please,
> With selling and buying, dissembling and lying,
> Yet we cannot live at ease;
> But still in discontent abide,
> Desiring after more . . .
> If pride should banished be away,
> Then tradesmen out would cry:-

'Come let us kill, eat and slay,
Or else for want we die.'
Then would the gentry mourn,
Without pride they cannot live,
And slaves to get them corn,
Whilst they themselves deceive.
Thus pride becomes our God,
And dear to us as life;
Whose absence makes us sad,
And cannot please our wife.
If the poor labouring man
Lives of his own increase,
Where are the gentry then
But gone among the beasts?

But, with the resignation common in the sixteen-fifties among former members of the defeated radical groups, Crab had no hope of immediate and rapid improvement. The conservative forces in society were too strong. The Fifth Monarchists hoped for the direct political intervention of Christ to bring about a change: Crab dreamed of a scarcely less miraculous inner revolution, without which political reform would not achieve its purpose. 'Let not the rich men mistake me and think that I would have them sell their goods before God hath enlightened their understandings and let them see the danger of keeping it, for then they would play the hypocrites, and do as bad to themselves as if they had kept it, although good to others.' There was not much danger of social revolution here. And Crab's conclusion was:

If men and angels do prove silent, then
Why should not I, an inferior man?
Now am I silent and indite no more:
Pray use no violence then against the poor.

Crab thus marks a curious transition. He looks back to St Francis of Assisi and those medieval ascetics who strove to overcome the world by contracting out of it. But he also looks forward to those nonconformist radicals who believed that man's life here on earth could be made better, and that the way to control the blind forces that rule our competitive society was through individual self-mastery. It was no doubt this belief in the possibility of human perfectibility that made Crab oppose the death penalty.

We may conclude by quoting Crab's epitaph, since it not unfairly stakes his claim to the sympathetic remembrance of posterity:

> Tread gently, reader, near the dust
> Committed to this tombstone's trust;
> For while 'twas flesh it held a guest
> With universal love possessed;
> A soul that stemmed opinion's tide,
> Did over sects in triumph ride.
> Yet, separate from the giddy crowd,
> And paths tradition had allowed,
> Through good and ill report he passed,
> Oft censured, yet approved at last.
> Wouldst thou his religion know?
> In brief, 'twas this, to all to do
> Just as he would be done unto.
> So in kind Nature's laws he stood,
> A temple undefiled with blood,
> A friend to everything that's good.
>
> The rest angels alone can fitly tell.
> Haste thee to them and him. And so farewell.

*   *   *

Christopher Hill (b. 1912) is one of the leading historians of seventeenth-century England. He was educated at St Peter's School, York and Balliol College, Oxford. After a spell at the University of Cardiff, he returned to Oxford in 1938 as Fellow and Tutor in Modern History and later became Master of Balliol College (1965–78). A pioneer of grass-roots history, Hill sees the Civil Wars of the mid-seventeenth century as bourgeois revolutions and as instrumental in shaping England's development and heritage. During his student days in the 1930s, Hill became a confirmed Marxist. He went on to become a member of the Communist Party Historians Group, and in 1952 co-founded *Past and Present* as an outlet for innovative scholarship. Hill was one of the first historians to acknowledge the presence, and importance, of ordinary people, a revolution in thought that subsequently touched work across the historical spectrum. His publications include *Puritanism and Revolution* (1968) and *Intellectual Origins of the English Revolution* (1965).

19a

Letter: Why are Hatters Mad?

DR JOHN L. MCDONALD

(April 1958)

Enlightenment from Dr John L. McDonald.

Sir,

In reference to 'The Mad Hatter' by Christopher Hill in the October 1957 issue there is indeed an obvious reason why 'this trade should render men especially liable to insanity.'

Until recently mercury was used in the making of felt hats. Chronic mercury poisoning causes an interesting and curious type of eccentricity culminating in a very serious and disabling disease of the nervous system. It must certainly have been common knowledge that felt-makers or hatters were quite frequently 'mad.'

The origin of the use of mercury in this industry is not known but we do know that it was employed by French Huguenot hatters in the seventeenth century. When the Huguenots were driven out of France by the revocation of the Edict of Nantes they carried the secret to England and for a period thereafter the French depended on the English for their felt.

The source of my information is the book *Exploring the Dangerous Trades* by Alice Hamilton, MD, published by Atlantic-Little Brown and Company, 1943, page 285 *et seq.*

Yours etc.,

John L. McDonald, MD
Colorado Springs, Colorado.

*   *   *

20

No Terminus at Waterloo

Alan Hodge and Peter Quennell

(April 1959)

Many historians (including Churchill) thought of 1815 and the Battle of Waterloo as the end of an age; a new book by Asa Briggs covered the period 1780–1867. When, and why, readers were asked by the editors of History Today, *do historical periods begin and end?*

A jovial critic of the third volume of Sir Winston Churchill's *History of the English-Speaking Peoples* remarked that the great man had taken 'a hussar's gallop' through the eighteenth century. By this he meant that a large proportion of the book was concerned with the waging of war. It is hardly surprising that this should have been so, when one recalls that war is a subject on which Sir Winston is expert, and that there were a great many wars between 1688 and 1815.

Many volumes have been published under the convention that the year of Waterloo marked the end of an age. Professor Asa Briggs has swept this convention away. His study of England deals with the years between 1780 and 1867 and is aptly entitled *The Age of Improvement* – a term that embraces all forms of social, technological and political advance. 'No single interpretation of these years may be regarded as definitive,' writes Professor Briggs, 'but in the scope of "improvement" and the reactions to it we have a clear-cut theme.' It is a theme that he handles with mastery. His choice of period nevertheless gives rise to speculation upon what is a 'period'. In our own century, for instance, do the two decades between the Great Wars form a 'period'? or is the Great Slump of 1929 a sharper turning point in the perspective of history? On this, and allied questions, we invite readers' views.

20a

Letters: No Terminus at Waterloo

(May 1959)

Periodisation in history; the debate continues.

Gentlemen,

I was born in '84, and still preserve a mind unclouded by the dust and confusion of two world wars; and memories of the last decade of the Victorian Age, and sixty years of the twentieth century come crowding in.

In my humble opinion the 'great slump of 1929,' as you describe it, is very small beer indeed. In fact, 1929 was the year chosen to usher in that great piece of modern legislation 'The Local Government Act 1929,' and 1930 saw the change over from the old Poor Law Administration to County and County Borough Administration which subsequently (1948) culminated in the Welfare State.

The two decades between the two world wars I view with repugnance. Politically uninspiring.

Remember *one* vast revolution in National aspirations. The women of this country became warriors in both world wars. They fought side by side with their menfolk in all the Civil and fighting Services, and proved their mettle. Manumitted, they still keep the flag flying.

Lastly, forgetting all our old ideas of glorious Empire, we now, though economically handicapped by the astronomical cost of those two world wars, tag along in the wake of what Arthur Balfour once, in an inspired moment, described (circa 1910) in a Tariff Reform Speech in the House of Commons, as 'the greatest commercial empire that this world has ever known.'

To the past there is, in the old Poor-Law jargon, no *Animus revertendi.*

Yours, etc.,

G.E. Chapman,

Teddington, Middx.

Gentlemen,

I am a technician by occupation and have therefore no professional historical axe to grind, but having read history as a hobby, with great interest for over thirty years, perhaps my observations might be less prejudiced than most.

It happens that I am just reading, with great enjoyment, Asa Briggs's *The Age of Improvement* and cannot acclaim too heartily the disposition (which he supports) to be done with the nonsense of arbitrary 'periods.' Surely the matter is deep and psychological. It takes a generation to get new ideas spread about, and another to decide to translate them into action. So that (vide M. Jaeger: *Before Victoria*) a lot of what appears in active history was generated even as long as a hundred years before. You have, moreover, individuals and groups who lag behind and some, like Ruskin, who are far ahead of their contemporaries. Although no Marxist (I am an active socialist, however, being a city Councillor and candidate for Parliament), I fancy there is much in the theory that fundamental changes in the technique of living usually precede, and indeed often necessarily stimulate the evolution of, new ethics designed the better to cope with new conditions.

If you must, then, divide a fluid thing like human life at all, divide it as Professor Briggs does into the Age of Development, or the Age of Steam or the Age of the Horse or (as young people say nowadays Bang On) the Age of Nuclear-Automation.

I am Sirs, etc.,
Hugh W. Peck,
Nottingham.

* * *

21

Excavations at Sperlonga

PETER QUENNELL

(October 1959)

A characteristic contribution from the pen of Peter Quennell, a versatile belletrist and aesthete with a classical training, as well as joint editor of History Today *from its foundation to 1979.*

About two hours' drive from Rome on the modern motor-road that leads to Naples, the traveller reaches Terracina, an agreeable little seaside town, with gimcrack modern restaurants facing the sea and the ruins of an ancient city climbing the hill behind. To the west rises Monte Circeo, legendary home of Homer's sorceress: to the south stretch a gently curving bay closed by the village known as Sperlonga and, past the village, a second and smaller bay which concludes in a tall and rocky headland. Here the modern highway plunges into a tunnel; and, if one looks down to the right through a steeply terraced olive-yard, full of vetch and wild lupin and a multitude of other spring flowers, one notices a group of sheds and a pumping engine, amid miscellaneous cranes and tackle. This is the site of the so-called 'Cave of Tiberius,' where since 1957 excavations have been carried on under the direction of Professor Giulio Jacopi, *Soprintendente alle Antichità di Roma I*, whose workmen have now almost cleared the site, unearthing in the process more than five thousand separate fragments of sculpture.

Many statues, though not the sculptural groups of which they were intended to form a part, have now been patiently reconstructed by Professor Jacopi; and the huge grotto that opens above the shore presents an extraordinarily romantic scene. A great circular pool has been excavated from the mass of fallen rubble; and it has re-filled, nearly to the brim, with a sheet of pellucid fresh water, which spreads out into the big quadrangular pool that adjoins it on the seaward side. Around the circumference of the inner pool runs a fairly narrow walk; and the path and a couple of subsidiary grottos are littered with bulky fragments of marble, carved in expressive human shapes – prodigious trunks, gigantic muscular legs, immense feet and enormous severed hands. Some statues, more or less reassembled, have been provisionally roped together. They recline on the floor of the cavern or – with surprising effect – stand suspended beneath primitive wooden cranes, thick cords binding the trunk or looped beneath marmoreal thighs. It makes a subject worthy of Pannini, which might also have been treated by Salvator Rosa or Magnasco – the rugged background of the cavern, suffused with a soft subaqueous light: pale statues, in various stages of decrepitude, propped against the rocky walls: pulleys and tackle: blue-clad workmen: a troop of strangely picturesque dogs: piles of rubbish not yet sorted, which included small heaps of brilliant blue mosaic: and an occasional luminous drop of water, falling from the roof into the pool below.

A further accumulation of broken statuary is housed in the adjacent sheds – a Ganymede: tragic and comic masks: a head of Athena: the lovely reproduction of an archaic statue, believed to represent the Palladium of Troy, grasped by a powerful masculine hand considerably larger than the face of the statue itself. How did this astonishing hoard of sculpture come to be discovered in a seaside cavern? When was the cavern-gallery abandoned? What story did the groups of statues tell? Who were the sculptors chiefly responsible for the conception and the execution of the work?

Only the last question can yet be answered with any degree of archaeological certainty. As early as the autumn months of 1957, four slabs were discovered that bore the following fragmentary inscription: 'Athanodoros [son] of Agesander, Age[sa]nder [son] of [Pha]nia, and [Poli]doros [son] of [Poli]doros.' Now these are the names of the three Rhodian sculptors who, according to Pliny, created the sculptured group of Laocoön and his sons, originally set up in the House of Titus, unearthed on that site during the lifetime of Michelangelo and today exhibited in the Vatican Museum. Pliny describes the group as monolithic – carved *ex uno lapide* – which is not true of the Vatican group: and the inscription is cut in 'Lartos stone,' the type of stone that the Rhodian School employed. Hence the attractive conclusion has been drawn by Professor Jacopi that the prototype of the existing Laocoön may have stood in the Sperlonga cave, upon the square base, built of cement, that still rises from the centre of the circular pool. The fragments unearthed seem to confirm his opinion: they consist of the remains of figures, slightly larger than ordinary human bodies and apparently convulsed in the agonies of death: parts of a gigantic central figure: together with vestiges of two fantastic monsters, presumably the two 'dragons' mentioned by Virgil in the *Aeneid*.

But, if the Laocoön dominated the pool, what were the subjects of the other groups? The cavern appears to have been crowded with sculpture; and not all the five thousand fragments unearthed can be fitted into the framework of the same legend. It is believed that a group, portraying Menelaus with the corpse of Patroclus, of which a replica is preserved in a Florentine museum, also found a home there; while on the right hand of the cavern's entrance – from the point of view of a spectator who is looking outwards from the grotto – an even more ambitious composition was built to cover a projecting spur of stone.

Here the virgin rock has been remodelled in the semblance of a vessel's beaked prow; the stony basis was sheathed with mosaic, yellow and red, green and dark blue; and a series of life-size marble statues were erected along the level of the ship's deck. Again they are violently convulsed and contorted; and vulpine or canine heads are shown fastening their teeth into the flesh of struggling human bodies. It is thought that they must be the companions of Ulysses, attacked by the fearful monster Scylla, when he attempted to run the gauntlet between Scylla and Carybdis. Scylla, Dr Jacopi concludes, occupied a small niche in the cliff above, from which she was stooping to grasp and devour her prey; while the Palladium statue was the tutelary protectress of the vessel, held up with an imploring gesture by a desperate sailor as he faced extinction. One extended figure clutches the stem: a head, assumed to be that of Ulysses, registers an expression of the wildest dismay and fear. What other legendary subject then could the Hellenistic artist have had in mind? But this explanation has not yet been established; for a scrap of mosaic lettering has come to light that unmistakably reads '*Navis Argo.*'

Perhaps the craftsman who affixed it was a little weak in his knowledge of Greek mythology. Perhaps his employer was an ignorant parvenu, a local Trimalchio who collected Rhodian statues. Perhaps, as Professor Jacopi believes, the name 'Argo' may have been attached to any adventurous seagoing vessel, and here designates Ulysses' craft, not that of the equally daring Argonauts, although they too, in some versions of the story, are said to have fallen foul of the many-headed Scylla. At all events, our picture of the seaside sculpture-gallery, once installed in the cavern at Sperlonga, is now becoming more and more vivid. A further inscription, in Latin hexameters, makes fragmentary reference to a certain Faustinus, who has been identified with a prosperous landowner who lived near Terracina and was a patron of the poet Martial, a literary amateur, himself the author of verses that Martial urges him to have published.

This Faustinus, whoever he may have been, claims to have constructed a 'happy piece of work' – for the benefit of the *domini*, or members of the imperial family – refers to the genius of the 'divine' Virgil, and boasts of the splendid realism with which the Homeric legends are here represented. Did Faustinus purchase the Rhodian masterpiece, the creation of Hellenistic sculptors who flourished during the first century before Christ, make it the focus of his natural pleasure-dome, and add the supernumerary embellishments – mosaics, marble plaques, dramatic masks, *sileni*, *putti* and the rest – that accorded with his Roman taste for rather vulgar and expensive magnificence, on the edge of his paternal estate bordering the Tyrrhenian Sea?

If eccentric splendour was his aim, he must have succeeded beyond all expectation. The result may well have been a trifle showy; but, when the tremulous water-light of the translucent pool flickered and undulated across the central group – so that Laocoön and his agonized sons seemed miraculously to come alive – and the sun blazed down on the prow of Ulysses' ship, where the hero and his companions stood fixed in their eternal death-struggle, with Ganymede being snatched away to heaven, poised above the grotto's mouth, it must no doubt have delighted Faustinus as much as it dazzled the appreciative friends he gathered. Yet Faustinus' stately pleasure-dome had also been adapted to serve a practical end. The system of pools that he planned, beneath the roof of the cave and just outside it, were employed, Professor Jacopi thinks, as stewponds for the breeding of edible fish – the delicate fish that Roman epicures loved and used to nourish with special provisions of salt fish, cheese and dried fruit.

Inserted in the flanks of a square platform that juts into the quad-rangular pool are a series of earthenware jars, horizontally arranged, some way below the level of the water, which would have provided its fishy inhabitants with the breeding-grounds they needed; while not far off stand the ruins of a villa built during the period of the late Republic. His slaves would have drawn the fish from the stewpond, hurried them indoors to the owner's kitchen, and thence to his elegant dining-room, frescoed probably in the same cheerful style as the dining-room of the House of Livia now shown upon the Palatine.

After dinner, it is pleasant to imagine, the master and his guests may have liked to take the air, have strolled in twos and threes around the cave over finely laid mosaic paths, marvelled at the groups of white statuary reflected on the surface of the water, and admired the long stretch of the coastline running west towards the Circean Mount. . . . Professor Jacopi's excavations at Sperlonga are still hampered by lack of financial support; and some time may pass before they have been completed, or the statues unearthed have been adequately housed.

Meanwhile, the cave has already yielded, as its excavator points out, 'one of the most singular and surprising' hoards turned up in the course of the present century. Few recent discoveries have thrown more light on the qualities and defects of Graeco-Roman taste. Here the spirit of Hellenistic Baroque was combined with a typically Roman sense of grandeur, to prove an appropriate setting for a rich and extravagant country gentleman.

* * *

22

Portuguese Timor: A Rough Island Story 1515–1960

C.R. BOXER

(May 1960)

Charles Boxer wrote for History Today *on aspects of Portuguese and Dutch colonial and Far Eastern history from the early 1950s to the late 1990s.*

Of all the obscure corners of the world which the Pacific War of 1941–45 dragged temporarily into the headlines, Portuguese Timor is probably even more unfamiliar to the average newspaper-reader than, say, the Kuriles or the Marianas. Joseph Conrad's admirers may recall his description of Timor-Dilli, but the agitated history of this isolated colony is seldom given even the most cursory coverage in the numerous recent books that deal with South-East Asia. Now that Indonesian Ministers have laid claim to Portuguese Timor – as well as to Dutch New Guinea and British North Borneo, a brief outline of the Portuguese past in this island may be useful to some readers.

Timor is the easternmost and largest of the Lesser Sunda Islands, and the one nearest to Australia. It measures some three hundred miles in length and has a mean breadth of about sixty. The island has a much drier climate and a correspondingly poorer vegetation than the other Sunda islands, although during the rainy season the tropical vegetation that covers the hillsides affords scenes of great beauty. The island has no considerable river and only two ports (Dilli and Kupang) worth mentioning. The surface is everywhere extremely rugged and mountainous, the lower ranges of the hills being covered with scrubby eucalyptus that only occasionally grows into lofty forest trees, although the fragrant sandalwood formerly flourished in this region. The mountains are ranged in confused ridges, rising to over 10,000 feet in places, the higher altitudes often swathed in mist and fog. The population is a very varying mixture of Papuan, Malayan, Melanesian and Indonesian elements of a rather primitive type, whose favourite occupation was head-hunting until within living memory. They were divided into numerous more or less mutually hostile tribes speaking many different languages or dialects. The total population is probably little over three-quarters of a million, of which the slightly larger half are in Portuguese territory.

Long before Vasco da Gama rounded the Cape of Good Hope, Timor was known to the Chinese as their best source for the supply of sandalwood. A Chinese chronicle of 1436 remarked that 'the mountains are covered with sandal-trees and the country produces nothing else.' It was sandalwood that attracted the Portuguese to Timor about the same time as they reached the Spice Islands, soon after Albuquerque's conquest of Malacca in 1511. Their first recorded settlement in the Lesser Sunda group dates from 1566, when some Dominican missionary friars built a stone fort on the island of Solor in order to afford protection to the converts they had recently made among the natives of the Flores and Solor groups. Around this fort there grew up a settlement populated by the offspring of Portuguese soldiers, sailors, and traders from Malacca and Macao, who intermarried with the local women. This mixed race, and the natives who were connected with them, were later called the Topasses (from the Dravidian word *Tupassi*, interpreter), and similar communities made their appearance in due course in the eastern half of Flores and Timor.

Although Timor was the main source of sandalwood for the Chinese market, the Portuguese only visited the island annually for collecting the wood, and their mercantile and missionary activities remained based on Solor until after the appearance of the Dutch in these waters. The Dutch attacked and took the fort of Solor in April 1613, and the Portuguese then shifted their base to Larantuka on the eastern tip of Flores, where they founded a settlement that gave the Dutch constant trouble. The fort on Solor changed hands several times in the next sixty years, and although it was eventually abandoned by both sides, the Portuguese maintained a shadowy claim over Solor (or part of it) until the nineteenth century.

The Topasses – or *Larantuqueiros* as they were also called from their new base – received a fresh injection of European blood when the Dutch commandant of Solor, Jan de Hornay, deserted to Larantuka in 1629, turned Roman Catholic, and married a Timorese slave-girl by whom he had two sons. This was the origin of the family of De Hornay or De Ornay, who were later transplanted to Timor and provided some of the most powerful chieftains on that island, alternatively champions and enemies of Portuguese rule. Another Larantuka family, called Da Costa, also provided a line of powerful chiefs, who were at first rivals and later allies of the de Hornays. One of Jan de Hornay's sons, Antonio de Hornay, ruled Larantuka, Solor and Timor virtually as an independent prince in 1673–1693, but he acknowledged the suzerainty of the Portuguese Crown and sent generous contributions of gold-dust to the indigent viceregal treasury at Goa. Larantuka remained the centre of Portuguese influence in the Lesser Sunda islands throughout the seventeenth century, and although the Dutch successively drovethe Portuguese from all their other settlements between the Moluccas and Malabar, they never succeeded in stamping out this particular hornets'-nest.

The missionary efforts made by the Dominican friars in Timor lagged a long way behind their successes in the Solor group and the eastern half of Flores. Not until the sixteen-forties were lasting results obtained in Timor, but in that decade a number of pagan chiefs accepted Christianity and the overlordship of the Portuguese Crown. The friars then began to build a fort at Kupang, which place they rightly selected as the best harbour and the strategic key of the island; but the Dutch seized the unfinished building in 1653, converting it into a stronghold of their own, which, under the name of Fort Concordia, henceforth became their local headquarters. Their attempts to subdue the tribes on the western half of the island, as a preliminary to monopolizing the coveted sandal-trade, were frustrated by the 'Black Portuguese' – as the Dutch called the Topasses from Larantuka – whom the Dominican friars summoned to their aid from Flores and Solor. The Costas and Hornays both took a prominent part in this fighting – Antonio de Hornay killing one of the Dutch commanders in single combat – and their settlement in Timor dates from this period.

Apart from the Dominicans, the white Portuguese still had no fixed establishment on Timor in 1663, when news reached these remote regions of the Luso-Dutch treaty signed at The Hague in 1661, which put an official end to the fifty years of warfare between Portuguese and Dutch on the Sunda Islands. The favourite port of call for the sandalwood-traders from Macao was the little harbour of Lifao (the modern Ocussi) on the North-west coast, but they visited all the villages or *kampongs* on the northern and southern coasts in search of sandalwood cargoes. The island was then, and for long afterwards, divided into two roughly equal districts, the eastern being called Bellos (*Belum*) and the western Servião (*Surviang*). Although the tribes of Servião were the first to accept Portuguese suzerainty, those of Bellos, who did so shortly afterwards, proved more faithful vassals in the long run. This was partly because the tribes in the eastern half of the island were smaller and weaker than those in the western, and partly because the powerful Black Portuguese families who established themselves in Servião soon aspired to the *de facto* overlordship of the whole island, although generally prepared to concede theoretical sovereignty to the Kings of Portugal. The chiefs of the Timorese tribes were known as *Liu-Rais*, but the Portuguese termed them 'kings,' dividing the island into sixty-two petty kingdoms, forty-six of which were in the province of Bellos and sixteen in Servião. Many of the natives accepted Christianity from the Dominicans, but in most cases it was only skin-deep. Their attendance at the mission churches alternated with their participation in animistic sacrifices and orgiastic war-dances.

During the second half of the seventeenth century, the viceroys at Goa made sporadic attempts to enforce their nominal authority over Solor and Timor by appointing governors in the name of the Crown, but the Dominican friars combined with the Hornays and Costas to expel these unwanted intruders. The viceroys constantly complained of the turbulence, intractability and even of the immorality of the Dominican missionaries in Timor, whom they more than once thought of replacing by Jesuits. They had to drop this idea, however, as the Black Portuguese chiefs informed Goa that they would allow only Dominican friars in the island: 'These are they who formerly taught our ancestors and forefathers and who at present teach us. We were brought up by them, and it is not right that we should abandon them and turn to others,' they wrote defiantly to the viceroy in 1677.

It was not until 1702 that a governor appointed from Goa, Antonio Coelho Guerreiro, succeeded in founding a fort and establishing a permanent Portuguese position on the island at Lifao, where he was closely besieged for nearly three years by a rebellious chieftain of the Da Costa family. In an effort to equalise the power of the friendly chiefs, some of whom claimed suzerainty over others, he conferred the rank of colonel on the tribal heads and gave lower commissioned ranks to the *Datus* (nobles) and others. This custom was continued and extended by his successors and has survived down to the present day, the chiefs being inordinately proud of their honorific military ranks. Despite his precarious situation at Lifao, Coelho Guerreiro sent glowing reports to Goa of the alleged natural riches of the island, claiming it contained vast mines of gold, silver and copper, apart from agricultural resources of every description. In point of fact, the island did produce a little alluvial gold, but the only other products of any importance besides sandalwood were beeswax, slaves and a hardy breed of horses.

The history of Timor in the eighteenth century is a monotonous record of inter-tribal warfare, of petty squabbles between the Dutch of Kupang and the Portuguese at Lifao, and of periodic attempts by the more powerful chiefs of Servião to expel the Portuguese altogether from the island. These efforts more than once came very near to succeeding, as the white Portuguese in the island never amounted to as many as a hundred men, apart from the Dominican friars, who were likewise the merest handful and were mostly Goanese. But the hostile tribes could never combine for any length of time, and the governors of Lifao could always count on the assistance of at least some of the tribes of Bellos to uphold the cause of the Crown or *Partido Real.*

In 1719, a number of disgruntled chiefs held a secret assembly at which they swore to expel the white Portuguese and then to turn on the Black Portuguese, whom for the time being they would take as allies. This oath was celebrated by the traditional Timorese blood-pact of sacrificing an animal – in this instance a dog – and mixing its blood with that of the participants, drawn from an incision in the left breast, and a liberal dose of *tua-sabo* or local brandy. Violent quarrels between the Dominican Bishop of Malacca, whose episcopal seat was at Lifao, and the governors of Timor at first facilitated the rebels' progress, but the inevitable dissensions soon appeared in their ranks. In November 1726, two punitive columns of four thousand loyal tribesmen under Portuguese command attacked the rebels in their almost inaccessible headquarters on the precipitous crags of Cailaco. They were driven from one position to another, but were saved at the last moment by torrential rains that forced the attackers to withdraw just when they had cornered the rebels on the summit. This rebellion lasted on and off for over fifty years, punctuated by fitful intervals of uneasy peace. During one such pause in the fighting, the Black Portuguese suddenly turned to attack the Dutch at Kupang in November 1749, only to be defeated with great slaughter and the loss of nearly all their leaders. As a result of this resounding success, the Dutch were able to bring most of the western half of the island under their control.

The Portuguese position, on the other hand, steadily deteriorated. In 1750 there were only seven or eight white Portuguese in the island, apart from a few Dominican friars 'whose fruit was not so much that which they gathered in the vineyard of the Lord, as that which they begat in the freedom and licentiousness in which they lived,' as the viceroy of Goa complained. A previous Dominican vicar-general alleged that the local women were exceedingly lascivious and forced their way into the houses of the younger clergy, 'leaving them with no other remedy but flight from their own homes.' The sandalwood trade also steadily declined during this period, owing to the reckless felling of the trees and the neglect to replace them. The nadir of Portuguese power in the island was reached with the loss of Lifao in 1769, when the governor abandoned that place to the rebels and evacuated the 1,200 inhabitants (over half of whom were women and girls) by sea to Dilli. This unhealthy and malarial site has remained the capital ever since, but a new town is now being built on the healthier foothills a few miles inland.

The English occupation of the Netherlands–Indies during the Napoleonic wars included the Dutch half of Timor, although we were twice repelled at Kupang, which was one of the few Dutch forts to offer more than a token resistance. When HMS *Glatton* left an English flag at Solor as a mark of sovereignty, the governor of Dilli promptly secured its removal by the local chieftainess and obtained a formal acknowledge-ment of Portuguese suzerainty. After the former Dutch possessions had been returned to the kingdom of the Netherlands in 1816, boundary disputes in this region broke out anew, and a delimitation of the disputed frontiers was attempted in 1850. Lopes de Lima, a former governor-general of Goa, was appointed governor of Timor and Portuguese plenipotentiary for the negotiations with the Dutch. Though only empowered to negotiate *ad referendum*, he signed a convention whereby he ceded the district of Larantuka and all Portuguese claims on Solor to the Dutch, in return for the Maubara district in Timor and an indemnity of 200,000 florins, payable in three instalments, after the first of which the Dutch were to take possession of Larantuka, as they promptly did. The Portuguese government repudiated the convention and recalled Lopes de Lima in disgrace; but since they would not, or could not, find the money to repay the sum paid by the Dutch, the latter remained in possession of Larantuka and Solor. Eventually a convention exactly like that of Lopes de Lima was ratified in 1860, but traces of Portuguese influence still remain in the folklore and language of Eastern Flores, apart from the Roman Catholic community at Larantuka. Boundary disputes in Timor recurred throughout the nineteenth century and a final settlement was made at The Hague in 1902, which left Portugal in possession of the enclave of Ocussi (Lifao) and the eastern half of the island, a total of some 7,330 square miles.

Timor was one of the last Portuguese colonies to be completely pacified. As late as 1912, a widespread revolt threatened Dilli itself for a short time, and was only suppressed with the aid of African troops from Mozambique in 1913. The colony subsequently achieved a mild pros-perity, principally from the cultivation of coffee, which was introduced in the nineteenth century and has taken the place of the nowadays very rare sandalwood as the island's principal product. Copra, tea and rubber have also been grown with success; but oil, though known to exist, has not yet been found in paying quantities. The missionaries, who now include the Jesuits, have been very active among the native tribes. It was largely owing to their influence that so many of the chiefs remained loyal to Portugal during the Pacific War, when the short-lived Dutch–Australian occupation of December 1941, was followed by the Japanese invasion and eventual conquest of the island. Timor suffered severely from its forcible inclusion in the 'Greater Asia co-prosperity sphere,' all the towns and villages being destroyed, the plantations devastated, and many people killed. The Portuguese administration protested against both the Allied and the Japanese invasions, but in each case accepted the *fait accompli*, having no other alternative in view of the disparity of strength involved. When news came of the Japanese surrender in August 1945, the governor and such of the officials as had survived internment or collaboration re-established Portuguese control with a speed and thoroughness that afforded a marked contrast to what happened in Java, Indochina and elsewhere.

The withdrawal of the Dutch from Indonesia has left Portuguese Timor, like British Borneo and Dutch New-Guinea, in rather an invidious position. The Indonesian government at first disclaimed any intention of demanding Portuguese Timor, but they have lately changed their attitude. This is not the place to prognosticate future developments, but although thirteen thousand miles separate Timor from Lisbon, Australians may remember the words of the Chinese proverb: 'when the lips are gone, the teeth will feel the cold.'

*   *   *

C.R. Boxer (1904–2000) was one of a small number of historians who have been instrumental in defining the nature and extent of their chosen fields. His prodigious output (more than 300 works by 1984) set the horizons for the study of Portuguese imperial history. He also wrote many substantial works which cover not only Portuguese, but also Spanish and Dutch colonial expansion. Boxer was as influential in the Lusophone world as he was in Britain and the USA.

23

Who Burnt the Reichstag?

A.J.P. Taylor

(August 1960)

This article reads with all the fluency of one of A.J.P. Taylor's legendary television lectures – and concludes with his controversial view that Hitler did not plan his outrages but tended to improvise them.

On the evening of February 27th, 1933, the Reichstag building in Berlin was set on fire and went up in flames. This was a stroke of good fortune for the Nazis. Although Hitler had been appointed Chancellor by President Hindenburg on January 30th, the Nazis did not have a parliamentary majority, even with their Nationalist allies. The Reichstag was dissolved; and the Nazis began a raging electoral campaign. They were still doubtful of success. They badly needed a 'Red' scare. On February 24th the police raided Communist headquarters. It was announced that they had discovered plans for a Communist revolution. Evidently they did not discover much: the alleged subversive documents were never published. Then came the burning of the Reichstag. Here was the Red scare ready-made. On the following day, Hindenburg promulgated an emergency decree 'for the protection of the People and the State.' The constitutional guarantees of individual liberty were suspended. The Nazis were able to establish a legal reign of terror. Thanks largely to this, they and the Nationalist won a bare majority at the general election on March 5th; and, thereafter, first the Communist party, and then all parties other than the National Socialist, were made illegal. The burning of the Reichstag was the vital preliminary to Hitler's dictatorship.

Who then committed the decisive act? Who actually started the Reichstag fire? The Nazis said it was the work of Communists. They tried to establish this verdict at the trial of the supposed incendiaries before the High Court at Leipzig. They failed. Hardly anyone now believes that the Communists had a hand in the Reichstag fire. If not the Communists, then who? People outside Germany, and many inside it, found a simple answer: the Nazis did it themselves. This version has been generally accepted. It appears in most textbooks. The most reputable historians, such as Alan Bullock, repeat it. I myself accepted it unquestioningly, without looking at the evidence. A retired civil servant, Fritz Tobias – an anti-Nazi – recently looked at the evidence. He published his results in an illustrated German weekly, *Der Spiegel*, from which I take them. They are surprising. Here is the story.

Shortly before nine o'clock, on the evening of February 27th, a student of theology called Hans Flöter, now a lecturer in Bremen, was going home after a day in the library. As he crossed the open space in front of the Reichstag, he heard the sound of breaking glass. He looked up, and saw someone climbing into the Reichstag through a window on the first floor. Otherwise, the place was deserted. Flöter ran to the corner, found a policeman. 'Someone is breaking into the Reichstag.' The two men ran back. Through the window they saw not only a shadowy figure but flames. It was three minutes past nine. Flöter had done his duty. He went home to his supper and out of the story. Another passer-by joined the police-man: a young printer called Thaler, who was incidentally a Social Democrat. He died in 1943. Thaler shouted out: 'Shoot, man, shoot.' The policeman raised his revolver, and fired. The shadowy figure disappeared. The policeman ran back to the nearest police-post, and gave the alarm. The time was recorded as 9.15. Within minutes police poured into the Reichstag. At 9.22, a police officer tried to enter the Debating Chamber. He was driven back by the flames. At 9.27, the police dis-covered and arrested a half-naked young man. He was a Dutchman called Marinus van der Lubbe.

Meanwhile, the fire brigade had also been alarmed. The first report reached them at 9.13. The first engine reached the Reichstag at 9.18. There were inevitable delays. Only one side-door was kept unlocked after eight o'clock in the evening. The firemen, who did not know this, went to the wrong door. Then they wasted time putting out small fires in the passages. There was confusion as one alarm crossed another. The full strength of the Berlin fire-brigade – some sixty engines – was mobilized only at 9.42. By then, the whole building was irreparably lost. It still stands, an empty shell.

There was an alarm of a different kind. Just across the road from the Reichstag was the house of its President, the Nazi leader Goering. But Goering had not moved in. The house, or Palace, was unoccupied except for a flat at the top which Goering had lent to Putzi Hanftstaengel, an upper-class hanger-on of the Nazis. Hanftstaengel looked out of his window and saw the Reichstag burning. He knew that Hitler and Goebbels were at a party near by. He telephoned Goebbels. Goebbels thought this was one of

Hanftstaengel's practical jokes and put down the phone. Hanftstaengel rang again. Goebbels checked with the Reichstag and found the report was true. Within a few minutes he and Hitler and a swarm of Nazi attendants were also in the Reichstag. An English journalist, Sefton Delmer, managed to slip in with them. Hitler was beside himself with frenzy: 'This is a Communist plot, the signal for an uprising. Every Communist official must be shot. The Communist M.P.s must be hanged.' Maybe he already saw the advantages. If so, those standing by were all taken in. To them Hitler appeared as a man surprised, outraged, even fearful.

Van der Lubbe was taken to the nearest police station. He was interrogated until three in the morning. Then he slept, was given breakfast, and at 8 a.m. questioned again. He gave clear, coherent answers. He described how he had entered the Reichstag; where he had started fires, first with the aid of four fire-lighters, then by stripping off his garments and setting light to them. The police checked his story by going round the Reichstag according to his statement with a stop-watch. They found that it fitted precisely up to the moment of his arrest. Van der Lubbe was clear about his motive. He had hoped that the entire German people would protest against the Nazi government. When this did not happen, he determined that one individual at any rate should make his protest. Although the burning of the Reichstag was certainly a signal for revolt – a 'beacon' he called it – he had given the signal alone. He denied steadily that he had any associates. He knew no Nazis. He was not a Communist – that is, he was not a member of the Communist party. He was, in fact, a Socialist with vaguely left-wing views. Van der Lubbe also described his movements during the previous weeks, drifting across Germany from one casual ward to another; he even described the shops where he had bought fire-lighters and matches. Here, too, the police checked his story. Every detail was correct. The police officers concluded that he was unbalanced, but more than usually intelligent, with an exceptionally accurate sense of place and direction. His interrogators were experienced men, without political commitment. They were convinced that he was speaking the truth and that he had set fire to the Reichstag all alone. The officers of the fire-brigade were also agreed that, so far as they could tell, the Reichstag had burnt exactly as van der Lubbe said it had.

This did not do for Hitler and the other Nazi leaders. They had committed themselves from the first moment to the view that the burning of the Reichstag was a Communist plot. Whether they believed this, or not, it had to be sustained before the German public. When van der Lubbe came to trial, four others stood in the dock with him: Torgler, leader of the Communist group in the Reichstag, and three Bulgarian Communists who were living in Germany, one of them the famous Dimitrov. The trial before the High Court at Leipzig had little to do with van der Lubbe. He had been found in the Reichstag; he had started fires; the case against him was so clear as to be hardly worth making. The public prosecutor and the Nazi government behind him were concerned to pin the guilt on the four Communists. They failed entirely. Torgler had been in his room in the Reichstag until 8 p.m. Then he left; witnesses saw him go. All was then quiet in the Reichstag. There was no evidence to connect them either with van der Lubbe or with the fire. This was awkward for the High Court judges. They were conscientious lawyers, not Nazis. They would not condemn individuals without evidence. But they were willing to please the Nazi government where no flagrant injustice to individuals seemed to be involved.

The High Court therefore listened complacently while so-called experts demonstrated that the fire could not have been started by one man on his own. Perhaps the High Court even believed the experts, as judges sometimes do. These experts were not fire officers, policemen, or fire assessors. They were professors of chemistry and criminology, who laid down theories about the fire, without even visiting the Reichstag. Van der Lubbe was in despair. He had meant to shake Nazi rule. Instead, he had consolidated their dictatorship and, as well, involved innocent men. For most of the time he remained broken and detached, his head sunk on his chest. Some people attributed this to drugs. Independent psychologists who examined him thought that there nothing wrong with him except despair. Once he came to the surface. For six hours he tried to convince the judges that he had started the fires all alone. He spoke clearly, coherently, accurately. A Dutch observer – himself an experienced criminal judge – was persuaded that van der Lubbe was speaking the truth. The German judges thought otherwise. With unshakable prejudice, they stormed and bullied. How, they asked, could he withstand the evidence of expert witnesses? Van der Lubbe answered: 'I was there, and they were not. I know it can be done because I did it.'

The High Court arrived at a strange verdict. Van der Lubbe was found guilty, and, though arson was not a capital crime when he committed his offence, Hitler made it so by retrospective law. Van der Lubbe was duly sentenced to death and executed by beheading with an axe. The four Communists were acquitted, but the judges recorded that van der Lubbe must have had assistants. The Reichstag therefore was burnt by persons unknown; and the Nazis had to be satisfied with the implication that these mysterious persons, never seen and vanishing without trace, were Communists. Hardly anyone now accepts this verdict. If the Nazis, with all the resources of dishonesty and of the German state, failed to produce any real evidence against the Communists, we may safely conclude that the

Communists had nothing to do with the burning of the Reichstag. But nearly everyone accepts part of the High Court verdict. They agree that van der Lubbe could not have set fire to the Reichstag all on his own. And, since his associates were not Communists, who could they be? Who but those who benefited from the fire – Hitler and the Nazis themselves? Dimitrov already seized on this interpretation while the trial was proceeding. As a good Communist, he was concerned to attack the Nazis, not to save himself. Therefore he hardly bothered to demonstrate his own innocence, which was indeed obvious enough. He grasped at the evidence of the experts, endorsed it, underlined its implications. When Goering was in the box, Dimitrov said to him more or less straight out: 'Van der Lubbe had help. He did not get it from me. Therefore he got it from you.' Goering found it difficult to beat off this charge without repudiating the expert evidence which the Nazis were putting forward. Hence his almost inarticulate rage.

Nor was this all. German Communists in exile, led by the redoubtable Willi Münzenberg, took up the Reichstag fire as a wonderful instrument for anti-Nazi propaganda. They published a Brown Book of alleged evidence about it. They staged a counter-trial in London that duly brought in a verdict of guilty against the Nazis. Münzenberg and his collaborators were a jump ahead of the Nazis. Not only had they the evidence of the experts, demonstrating that van der Lubbe could not have done it alone and therefore implicating the Nazis; they also produced a mass of evidence to show how the Nazis had done it. The vital point here was an underground passage from Goering's house to the Reichstag, which carried electric and telephone cables and pipes for central heating. Through this passage some S.A. men (Brown Shirts) were supposed to have entered the Reichstag. Then they either soaked the curtains and woodwork in some inflammable material, which caught fire when van der Lubbe set to work; or – in an alternative version – they started the fire themselves. At the last minute, when all was ready, van der Lubbe was pushed through the window by some unknown and unseen companion, there to be picked up by the police. The compilers of the Brown Book also showed that van der Lubbe, far from being a Socialist of some intelligence, was a degenerate half-wit, and a homosexual prostitute, kept by the S.A. leader, Roehm.

This is the story that we all believed in 1933 and that most have gone on believing from that day to this. The evidence for it has now been examined by Herr Tobias. The result is very like the Sheep's shop in *Alice Through the Looking-Glass*:

Whenever Alice looked hard at any shelf, to make out exactly what it had on it, that particular shelf was always quite empty, though the others round it were crowded as full as they could hold.

Each piece of evidence dissolves when closely examined; yet all the time you have the impression that the rest of the evidence must be solid. Take, for instance, the allegation that the fire brigades were deliberately delayed. This is disproved by the service-books at brigade headquarters. Again, nearly all the books say that the records of van der Lubbe's interrogations by the police have mysteriously disappeared. Herr Tobias found them at the office where they had always been – in eight copies. The blackening of van der Lubbe's character was peculiarly unscrupulous. After all, he had done something to show his enmity to the Nazis, which is more than the compilers of the Brown Book had done. They obtained a statement from a Dutch friend of his. One sentence read: 'I often spent a night in the same bed with him.' There was the proof of his homosexual character. As a matter of fact, the sentence originally went on: '. . . without observing any homosexual tendencies in him.' All the stories about van der Lubbe's bad upbringing, about his disreputable family, about his lack of friends, were in fact lies, Communist forgeries.

The vital evidence, however, was about the tunnel and its use by the party of Brown Shirts. This evidence was supposed to have been provided by unnamed Brown Shirts who repented and confessed secretly to the Communist exiles in Paris. One Brown Shirt appeared before the counter-trial, muffled to the eyes. This was a wise precaution: he was in fact a well-known Communist, and unmistakably Jewish. The most important confession was not anonymous. It claimed to be the work of Karl Ernst, Brown Shirt leader in Berlin. Very conveniently it only turned up when Ernst was dead – killed by Hitler in the great purge of June 30th, 1934. Even more convenient, Karl Ernst went out of his way to improve on earlier versions, where these had been shown to be inaccurate. For instance, the anonymous Brown Shirt informers had confessed that they were led by Heines, another Berlin Brown Shirt chief. Heines was far away from Berlin, making an election speech in his constituency; and this could be proved from the newspapers. So Ernst kindly named himself as leader. Again, the Brown Shirt men said they came through the tunnel. Evidently they did not know that the tunnel was lined with steel-plates and that anyone going through it in ordinary shoes made a noise like thunder; the night-porter would certainly have heard them. So Ernst added the detail, surprisingly left out of earlier accounts, that they all changed into plimsolls.

There was one thing Karl Ernst got wrong. He agreed with the other confessions that the Brown Shirts entered the Reichstag at 8.40 p.m. This had to be the time if they were to do their work before van der Lubbe was pushed through the window at 9.03. Unfortunately, Ernst – or the

Communist forgers – did not know one little event in the Reichstag routine. At 8.45 p.m. a postman came through the side-door to collect the deputies' mail. On February 27th, he entered as usual; walked through the deserted building; and left at 8.55 p.m. He saw nothing out of the ordinary – no shadowy figures, no smell of petrol or other inflammable liquid. The worthy postman, in fact, demonstrates the falsity of all stories about the Reichstag which assume that there was anyone present before van der Lubbe broke in at 9.03. It seems equally unlikely that the Brown Shirts could have got in at 9 p.m. and have escaped, their work finished, before the police began to search the building at 9.22.

The mysterious tunnel presents some other odd features. Immediately Goering arrived in the Reichstag building, at 9.35 p.m., he exclaimed: 'They [the fire-raisers] must have come through the tunnel.' He went off with policemen – not with Nazis – to examine it. They found the doors at either end securely locked. It was surely risky of Goering to search the tunnel if he was in the plot and knew that the Brown Shirts were on the way out. He and the police might have caught them. On the other hand, it was highly incompetent of the Brown Shirts, if there were any, to lock the doors. They ought to have left some indication of how the supposed Communists came in and went out. The very fact that no serious evidence was ever produced against the Communists really acquits the Nazis also. For if the Nazis had, indeed, set fire to the Reichstag, they would have manufactured evidence against the Communists – as the Communists later tried to manufacture evidence against them. All the evidence of the Brown Book breaks down, in its turn, on close examination. After all, it was not designed to be presented at a real trial. If it achieved a propaganda effect against the Nazis, Münzenberg and his assistants were satisfied. The more we look at the story, the clearer it becomes that, whatever else happened that night, no one came through the tunnel. There was no other way to enter the Reichstag, except past the night-porter; or by breaking a window. No one went past the porter. Only van der Lubbe broke a window.

Those who have tried to defend the 'traditional' version are now inclined to admit that there is no clear or satisfactory explanation of how the Nazis got into the Reichstag. But they still point to the evidence of the experts at the trial that van der Lubbe could not have done it alone. Yet this expert evidence is the shakiest part of the story. The most emphatic expert was a crank distrusted by his colleagues. He claimed to be an authority on a strange 'fluid' which, he said, was necessary for starting fires. He alleged that this 'fluid' had a distinctive smell. No fireman, no policeman, noticed any smell except smoke – no 'fluid,' not even petrol. Against this rigmarole, we can set the solid opinion of the police and of the fire officers that van der Lubbe's story was perfectly consistent with the facts as they knew them. At first sight, it seems astonishing that one man could have set fire to this huge building. As a matter of fact, these gaudy public buildings burn easily. Dusty curtains, wooden panelling, high ceilings, draughts under the door – they were made for fires. In 1834 the Houses of Parliament at Westminster were entirely destroyed by fire, simply from one stove-pipe becoming too hot. Or if this be thought an antiquated story, the Vienna Stock Exchange was burnt out in 1956 as the result of one smouldering cigarette-end in a wastepaper basket. Van der Lubbe had over twenty minutes in which to start fires. This was more than enough.

The conclusion is clear. Van der Lubbe could have set fire to the Reichstag by himself; there is a good deal of evidence that he did so; there is none that he had any assistants. Of course, new evidence may turn up to disturb these conclusions. So far, none has done so. There is one worrying point. The postman left the Reichstag at 8.55. Van der Lubbe broke in almost immediately afterwards, within a matter of minutes. How did he know when it was safe to break in? The only answer can be: he did not know. We have to assume a lucky coincidence, from his point of view. It is a smaller assumption than that demanded by any other story.

There has been an outcry in Germany, and still more in Communist countries, that Herr Tobias, by making this case, has whitewashed the Nazis. Even if this were true, it would be the fault of those who manufactured the Brown Book, not of Herr Tobias. That is the worst of forgeries: ultimately they come home to roost. But the new version does not, in fact, acquit the Nazis. Even if they had nothing to do with the fire, even if they genuinely believed that it was the work of Communists, this does not justify their subsequent illegalities and the reign of terror. They remain the evil men they always were. But the affair should change our estimate of Hitler's methods. He was far from being the far-sighted planner that he is usually made to appear. He had a genius for improvization; and his behaviour over the Reichstag fire was a wonderful example of it. When he became Chancellor, he had no idea how he would transform his constitutional position into a dictatorship. The solution came to him in a flash as he stood among the smouldering ruins of the Reichstag that February evening. It was, in his own words, 'a heaven-sent opportunity'; and we can agree with him that it came to him by chance from outside, though hardly from heaven. That is the way of history. Events happen by chance; and men then mould them into a pattern. Van der Lubbe set fire to the Reichstag; but the legend that the Nazis did it will probably prove indestructible.

*   *   *

A.J.P. Taylor (1906–90) was educated at Oriel College, Oxford, graduating with first class honours in 1927. He became a lecturer at Manchester University in 1930, then moved to Magdalen College, Oxford where he was Fellow and Tutor in Modern History from 1938 to 1976 (and thereafter Honorary Fellow). One of the best-known (and most controversial) historians of the twentieth century, Taylor was one of the earliest academics to appear regularly on television. His books include *The Struggle for the Mastery of Europe* (1954), the first volume of the Oxford History of Europe series, and *The Origins of the Second World War* (1960). *English History 1914–45* (1965) was also influential in shaping perceptions of this period.

24

Rubens and King Charles I: The Story of a Legend

C.V. WEDGWOOD

(December 1960)

As much at home in art and literature as in history, Veronica (C.V.) Wedgwood described a delicate diplomatic mission undertaken by a man better known for his paintings than his politics.

On Whit Monday, 1629, Peter Paul Rubens, the most famous painter in Europe, disembarked at Dover from His Majesty's ship *Adventure* and proceeded immediately towards London. He remained in England until the middle of the following March, a period of nearly ten months, during which he completed the preliminary negotiations for a treaty of peace and friendship between King Charles I and King Philip IV of Spain. He also visited the finest collections of paintings in the country, was lavishly entertained by the courtiers and ministers of King Charles, painted two or three original works and wrote a great number of official despatches and private letters, full of lively comment on the English scene.

The purpose of his visit was diplomatic. The Archduchess Isabella, daughter of Philip II, and ruler of the Spanish Netherlands, had shown her usual tact in selecting her Court-painter and trusted confidant for the delicate mission of approaching King Charles I, whose knowledge and judgment of painting was admitted to be much greater than his knowledge and judgment of foreign affairs. Her choice had caused some eyebrow-raising in Madrid, where her nephew, King Philip IV, felt that a painter was not a sufficiently aristocratic representative for the Crown of Spain. The problem was settled by giving Rubens authority only to smooth out the way for a treaty to be completed by a noble ambassador. He was also given the nominal office of Secretary to King Philip's Privy Council, to invest him with a more official appearance. It was not that King Philip undervalued Rubens: he had a high respect for him, both as a painter and a man, and at an earlier time had given him a grant of arms; but, in the formal relations between European sovereigns, the Spanish King demanded a respect for his emissaries that a painter might not command. King Philip need have had no fears about Rubens. He was at this time fifty-two years old, an experienced, widely travelled and confident man of the world, valued in most of the Courts of Europe as a superb and prolific painter and as an expert on all aesthetic questions: a man who shone in any society and counted among his friends some of the most remarkable men and women of Europe.

The complex negotiations with King Charles by which Rubens secured the neutrality of England in the religious conflicts then raging in Europe, are not in the long perspective of history of outstanding importance: but the character of the two men involved – the greatest painter and the greatest connoisseur of the time – make them unique in the annals of diplomacy. The interest of Rubens in these diplomatic affairs, and especially in establishing peace between England and the Spanish Netherlands, of which he was a citizen, had begun some four years before his arrival in England; and his personal interest in King Charles I some years earlier still. Already as Prince of Wales, Charles had been an ardent collector; he was undoubtedly behind the project, mooted as early as 1621, that Rubens should paint the ceiling of the new Banqueting House at Whitehall. A little later, he had sent the great painter a special request for a self-portrait, which, after a becomingly modest hesitation, Rubens had agreed to gratify. His personal relations with King Charles were then already on a friendly footing. As to the political interest of Rubens in English affairs, this had begun in 1625, when he met the Duke of Buckingham. Early in that year he had received a summons to come to Paris with all speed, bringing with him the series of paintings commissioned by the Queen-mother for the Luxembourg Palace. Her youngest daughter, Madame Henriette, now betrothed to Charles of England, was expecting soon to leave for her new home and wanted very much to see the pictures before she left. Rubens, with long experience of Courts, knew that the journeys of royalty were usually subject to delays and did not hurry unduly; but he was glad to hear that the Princess showed an interest in painting for, he wrote, the King whom she was to marry was the greatest connoisseur in Europe.

He arrived in Paris in good time for the wedding of the Princess, which was solemnized in May, and for which he had a most advantageous seat on a balcony. Unhappily the balcony was overloaded and a section of it collapsed in the midst of the ceremony, though Rubens himself remained safe and sound on the extreme edge of the broken planks.

Chief of those who had come to Paris to fetch home the bride of King Charles was the Duke of Buckingham, his favourite and chief minister. As a patron of the arts and himself a collector, Buckingham did not lose the chance of meeting Rubens, from whom he ordered a superb equestrian portrait. He also discussed with him the extension of his fine collection of works of art. Amid all this interesting professional conversation, Rubens took the opportunity of sliding in some political hints.

He had long been a chief confidant of the Archduchess Isabella; and, as a resident of Antwerp, he knew the ill-effect that the war between England and Spain, that had broken out in 1624, was bound to have on the trade of the southern Netherlands; still more, how hampering it would prove in the contest with the Dutch in the northern part of the Netherlands. The Spanish Netherlands, though their government was independent, were under the Crown of Spain and were associated automatically with Spain in all matters of war and peace. Rubens, a good Catholic and a good Fleming, wanted to see a blessed peace restored to Europe, with Spain in command of the seas, and the rebellious Protestant provinces of the northern Netherlands, who had for the last sixty years asserted their independence under the leadership of the Princes of Orange, brought back into harmony with Catholic Flanders and Brabant.

In 1624, the King of England, James I, who had for twenty years been in peaceful agreement with Spain, had declared war. This change of policy was well known to be the work of Buckingham and Prince Charles, who a few months later became King. But the war, undertaken in a spirit of easy arrogance, had gone badly. Buckingham was not Sir Francis Drake. There had been defeats by sea and land, and in the summer of 1625 Rubens found the Duke favourably disposed to the idea of a negotiated peace.

On his return to the Netherlands, Rubens gained the authority of the Archduchess to carry the exploratory discussions somewhat further. It was done under cover of a different matter – namely, the sale of numerous antiquities and works of art to the Duke. Buckingham sent over Balthasar Gerbier, a minor artist and a knowledgeable intriguer, whom he often employed to put through his purchases. But the sale of the art treasures moved more swiftly than the peace talks. Buckingham, whose foreign policy was almost equally silly and capricious, suddenly involved England in a war with France, without even waiting to bring the war with Spain to an end. Temporarily, Rubens gave up his project of engineering an Anglo-Spanish treaty. His criticisms were, however, confined to the Duke. He felt only sympathy for King Charles. 'When I consider the caprice and arrogance of Buckingham,' he wrote, 'I pity that young King who, through false counsel, is needlessly throwing himself and his kingdom into such an extremity.'

He had never met the King; but the tone of genuine regret and anxiety in his comment is unmistakable, though perhaps more so in the Italian, in which the letter is written, than in the English version. '*Io ho compassione de quel Re giovenetto.*' He could not but like all that he had heard of Charles, since what he had heard – either through Buckingham or through Sir Dudley Carleton, the highly civilized English ambassador at the Hague – was principally about his excellent taste and his enthusiasm as a patron and collector.

In England, another year of unsuccessful and mismanaged warfare, with a restive and critical Parliament refusing the necessary grants of money to wage it, caused Buckingham in the spring of 1627 to re-open the exploratory talks through Rubens. 'The reconcilement of Great Britain and Spain,' said the Duke, now full of ideas about international peace, 'will be the best preparative and most assured means to pacify the Empire.' But the moment was not propitious. Spain and France, whose national enmity was almost a constant of European politics, were both Roman Catholic countries. Their rivalry caused France from time to time to ally with the enemies of the Church – the Turks, the Protestant Germans, or the Dutch. But there was a so-called 'devout' party in France, that deplored these agreements and would have preferred an alliance with Spain, at least until heresy was defeated. King Charles, by declaring war on both of them at the same time, had given them at least one interest in common. There was a brief rapprochement between them, and some talk at Madrid of launching a new Armada, with French cooperation, that would effectively eliminate England from European politics. The danger was perhaps never serious, because neither Spain nor France had the resources to spare for such an undertaking; but, while this kind of plan was in the air, there was no immediate hope for an Anglo-Spanish peace.

Rubens was quietly persistent. In the summer of 1628, he took care to make much of the Earl of Carlisle, when he came through Brussels on his way to represent King Charles at the Court of Savoy. He even persuaded the Archduchess Isabella to receive him, and though she was not very cordial – his master was, after all, at open war with her – the gesture indicated that the renewal of peace talks was still a possibility.

By the late summer of 1628, King Philip of Spain was disheartened by the egoism of his French allies – their policy was being conducted by the subtlest and most ruthless practitioner of *Realpolitik* in Europe, Cardinal Richelieu. He began to think seriously of making peace with England, and Rubens was sent for to Madrid. In the same month, August 1628, the murder of Buckingham removed the most incalculable and the most influential figure in English policy. Things were likely to be easier.

In Madrid, Rubens received his instructions for England, while painting prolifically in the lengthy intervals between official decisions. He met the young Velasquez, who visited with him the great collection of pictures in the Escorial; he painted the King, some of the royal family and a number of subject pieces. He also had time to go in quest of exotic perfumes to satisfy the '*exquise curiosité*' of the Earl of Carlisle, with whom he had kept up friendly relations, and for whom he hoped to find something really unusual in the cargo of a merchant ship from Goa.

In April 1629, he was back in Brussels for a brief final consultation with the Archduchess; and at last, on June 4th, after four years of patient endeavour, he arrived in England charged with the task of making clear the way for a treaty of peace.

He was surprised and delighted with the country. 'This island,' he wrote to a friend, 'seems to me to be a spectacle worthy of the interest of every gentleman, not only for the beauty of the countryside and the charm of the nation; not only for the splendour of its outward culture which seems to be extreme, as of a people rich and happy in the lap of peace, but also for the incredible quantity of excellent pictures, statues and ancient inscriptions which are to be found in this Court.'

In the last generation, the study of antiquities and the collection of works of art had certainly wrought a great change in England. Rubens, who had assumed that this northern isle had relatively little to show him, was excited at the prospect of much pleasure and intellectual profit from his political mission. The two greatest collections of paintings were those of the King himself and of the late Duke of Buckingham, both rich in the works of Italian masters, many of which Rubens would have seen before in the great European collections from which they had recently been bought. There were also the Greek and Roman antiquities collected by the Earl of Arundel, including numerous important inscriptions of which the scholar John Selden had published the text with a valuable commentary. Rubens was distressed to learn that this learned gentleman had recently been involved in politics, had opposed the King in the last Parliament, and was temporarily in prison as a result. He thought it a pity that Mr Selden, with talents that could be so much better employed, had involved himself in an indecorous opposition to his sovereign.

Apart from these three great collections, there was also the library of Sir Robert Cotton, the famous antiquary, full of rarities. England indeed proved to be a land rich in scholars, connoisseurs and collectors, with some other odd and distinguished residents as well. There was Cornelis Drebbel, the Dutch philosopher and inventor, who is credited with having made the first navigable submarine. Rubens was struck by his appearance, when he met him in the street, and wished to see more of him.

During his mission, Rubens stayed at the house of Balthasar Gerbier, which was a centre for all those interested in the arts and sciences, and where he was well entertained. He was also frequently in the houses of the nobility and was surprised, and a little shocked, by the splendid manner in which the English aristocracy thought it essential to live. His old acquaintance, the Earl of Carlisle, was a by-word in Europe for his extravagance, but the Earl of Holland was not far behind him; and all the principal courtiers of King Charles entertained with great sumptuousness. Sir Francis Cottington, the minister with whom Rubens had most of his dealings, lived, he said, like a prince. High living was no novelty to Rubens, who knew the splendid Courts of the Italian princes and whose countrymen had a reputation for lavish entertaining. But the English nobility in 1629 seem to have taken even his breath away. Few of them could afford it: he saw that at once. Most of them were deeply in debt and therefore open to corruption. Several were said to be taking bribes from Richelieu, he reported. He did not trouble to report that several more were taking bribes from Spain, because those to whom he addressed his despatches would be aware of that.

Now and again there were untoward accidents. Early in his visit, he was distressed at the loss of a priest in his suite, who had been given a lift in the barge of the ambassador of Savoy. The boat overturned, while shooting the rapids at London Bridge; the poor priest encumbered by his cassock was drowned, and the ambassador was saved with difficulty, because someone managed to drag him out of the water by one of his spurs.

Meanwhile Rubens had been received by Charles on June 6th, 1629, as soon as possible after his arrival in London. The meeting was successful. His despatches to the Spanish first minister, Olivares, and his private letters alike make it clear than an instant sympathy was established. His stiffness and shyness were more often the subject of comment; he was said always to hold men at a distance. He made no such impression on Rubens; the warmth of the great painter's personality thawed him completely, thawed him indeed into uttering several useful indiscretions as the weeks went by. Gerbier had noticed that Rubens had a gift, most useful in a diplomat, for making people talk without, on his side, committing himself. He certainly showed this in his conversations with the King.

A French treaty was also under discussion at this time; and Rubens had at first considerable apprehensions that the French ambassador would defeat him. There was a strong French party at Court, led by the Queen whose influence Rubens instantly noticed. The arrogant French ambassador also did all in his power to render the mission of Rubens difficult. But the King, in one of those bursts of confidence to which Rubens inspired him, told him that he detested the French, regarded them as wholly untrustworthy, and put no faith in any of their promises. After this, it was clear to Rubens that he had relatively little to fear from this rival negotiation. A treaty of peace would no doubt be signed with France, but it would be a peace and no more: the alliance directed at Spain, for which the French ambassador hoped, would not come into being. Spain, not France, was the monarchy with which King Charles really wished to be on terms of close friendship.

This was the first indiscretion of the King. His second was even more remarkable. The whole supposed purpose of his foreign policy, and more especially of his war with Spain, had been to help his only sister and her husband Frederick, a penniless exile who called himself King of Bohemia. This unfortunate German prince, originally Elector Palatine of the Rhine, had become involved in the revolt of the Protestants of Bohemia against the Habsburg Emperor, who was himself the cousin and ally of the King of Spain. Elected to the Crown of Bohemia in 1619, Frederick had been driven out in less than a year; the Emperor and his Spanish allies had taken the occasion to deprive him of all his lands, those on the Rhine being occupied by Spanish troops. King Charles had entered into war with Spain for the ostensible purpose of restoring his brother-in-law to his original dominions.

Now this precisely was what King Philip in Madrid and the Archduchess in the Netherlands wished to prevent. The Rhenish Palatinate lay right athwart the route by which troops were transported overland from the north Italian recruiting grounds to the battlefront in Flanders. The occupation of that country, either by the Spaniards or by their imperial allies, was vital to the successful prosecution of their war against the rebel Dutch, because it kept this most important line of communication open.

There was, however, another vital line of communication, this time by sea. Spanish ships, bearing bullion, arms and ammunition for the troops of the Archduchess, came up the English Channel and through the Narrow Seas to Antwerp. They would have been at the mercy of the English, if the English had had any effective sea-power at the time. They were actually at the mercy of the Dutch, who were dominant in those waters. But if England became an ally, instead of an enemy, or at least became neutral, Spanish ships would be able to take refuge from the Dutch in English waters, or even in English harbours, and there safely await a favourable moment to dart across to Antwerp. Thus what King Philip IV and the Archduchess wanted was to maintain *both* their life lines, to have peace with Charles *and* to keep the lands of his dispossessed brother-in-law. How could it be done?

Rubens soon found out. The King had begun by emphasizing his devotion to the cause of his dispossessed brother-in-law. Three weeks after the arrival of Rubens, he was asserting that 'neither his faith, conscience, nor honour would permit him to enter into any accord with His Catholic Majesty without the restitution of the Palatinate.' Rubens played his hand cautiously, accepting the King's protestations at their face value but, for his part, indicating that the Palatinate was, after all, a part of Germany and under the ultimate jurisdiction of the Emperor. It was not in the direct power of the King of Spain to take decisions about it.

Six weeks later, the King, increasingly anxious for the Spanish alliance, and feeling every day more at home in the company of the most amiable and sympathetic envoy he was ever likely to encounter, had allowed it to become apparent that he found the whole business of the Palatinate a wearisome and unwelcome obstruction in his way. 'I know for certain,' wrote Rubens to Olivares in August, 'that in his heart he curses the day when the Elector Palatine crossed his path.' As for his alleged unwillingness to treat with Spain unless his brother-in-law were restored, 'the King had protested to me more than once that if he could save his reputation and honour in any other way . . . he would not postpone for an hour the conclusion of peace with Spain.'

What was needed, to buy the neutrality of England, was not any dangerous concession about the occupation of the vital stretch of the Rhineland. All that was needed was a clause that would save the King of England's face. From this moment onwards it was clear that, if the King of Spain promised to intercede with the Emperor for the restoration of the Palatinate, Charles would be quite satisfied. The intercession, if it were ever made, would of course be unsuccessful.

Rubens had noticed other elements in the English situation that were favourable to the friendship of Charles with Spain. The Puritans, who, in his observation, seemed to be the greater part of the population, were critical of the King. The troubles in the last Parliament, of which Rubens heard much, had been largely their work. The Puritans were also in close contact with the Dutch. Rubens conceived it a possibility that, with this fifth column to help them, the Dutch might one day establish control over England. He was not entirely right in this opinion, because he based his ideas of the strength of the Puritans and of their close connections with the Dutch on what he saw of London, and he did not understand the extent to which Puritanism was also a manifestation of the English countryside and was often linked with an Elizabethan and aggressively nationalist outlook. He did not grasp that many English Puritans found it possible to have great religious sympathy with the Dutch, to applaud the strongly Calvinist government in power there, and yet to dislike and distrust them as commercial rivals.

He was, however, perfectly right in perceiving that the spiritual affiliations of the English Puritans to the Dutch made it logical for King Charles, whose crown was endangered by their pretensions, to align himself with Spain, the active enemy of the Dutch Republic, and seek Spanish help to bolster his own prestige.

The French ambassador, whose tactlessness was in sharp contrast to the good judgment of Rubens, stimulated the natural sympathies that were leading Charles towards friendship with Spain. He wanted the King to enter into an offensive alliance with France, and thereby to become one of the Protestant allies who, with French help, were fighting the Spaniards by sea and land. For such an alliance the King would naturally have to swallow his disagreements with his subjects, call a new Parliament and behave to it in such a way as to get a vote of money. Charles was not likely to forgive the French ambassador for uttering the hateful name of Parliament, or for trying to teach him how to govern his country.

In September 1629, the King did, indeed, sign a treaty with France, but it amounted to no more than the re-establishment of peace between the countries. Charles remained firm against all fresh attempts of the French ambassador to enhance its meaning or to gain him as an active ally for French policies in Europe. Indeed, his answer to this continued and distasteful pressure was to give orders that the ambassador he had selected to go to Spain should immediately set forth. His choice was the Chancellor of the Exchequer, whom Rubens – puzzled like all foreigners by English titles – calls 'Sir Cottington.' Sir Francis Cottington had been a warm ally of Rubens throughout, although his advocacy of the Spanish treaty arose from no nobler motive than a very good idea he had for raising money for his King. In effect, when he got to Madrid, he made an agreement by which English shipping was to be put at the disposal of the Spanish government for transporting money to the Spanish Netherlands – later arms and men were also included in the arrangement. These ships, being neutral, could not be attacked by the Dutch on their journey to Antwerp. In return, the royal mint in London got a share of the bullion.

After Cottington had left for Spain, Rubens was ready and anxious to go home; but again he had to abide the interminable delays of the Spanish government. He could not leave until Don Carlos Coloma, the newly appointed ambassador, reached London; and this was not until January 1630. Even then, a few more weeks intervened before he could return to his home in Antwerp and his long-abandoned studio. At least, during the time he had spent in Spain in the previous year, he had been able to paint, but in England he had had little time for it. Much as King Charles may have wished to have his own or his Queen's portrait from the hand of Rubens, etiquette hardly permitted him to sit for his picture to the emissary of a King with whom he was still at war. He did, however, confirm the plan made eight years before for commissioning Rubens to decorate the Banqueting Hall. The pictures could not, of course, be done until the painter was back in his studio in Antwerp. Meanwhile, he had painted a portrait of Madame Gerbier, the wife of his host, with some of her children, and he had presented to the King two subject pieces, the opulent 'War and Peace,' now in the National Gallery, and a charmingly romantic landscape of the Thames valley, in which King Charles, in the person of Saint George, chivalrously rescues Queen Henrietta Maria from a dreadful dragon.

On February 21st, the King knighted him at Whitehall, and shortly afterwards gave him authority to carry the lion of England as an augmentation to his arms. More substantial gifts were also presented – a diamond chain to wear round his hat and a diamond ring. These two costly objects had been supplied by the efficient Gerbier, who was complaining a day or two later that he had been paid neither for these nor for the expenses he had sustained by accommodating Sir Peter Paul Rubens at his house during the whole of his stay in England. For once the money was forthcoming with surprising rapidity, and within a few weeks he received £500 for the jewelry and £128 2s. 11d. for the board and lodging of Rubens and his suite.

Two enormous feasts were given by the extravagant Earl of Carlisle to speed Rubens on his way; and by the middle of March 1630, he was at Dover. Here he met his last diplomatic problem. A party of boys and girls, sons and daughters of Catholic gentry, had been stopped as they tried to leave England, the boys to be educated at Douai, the girls (each with her dowry) to become nuns in the English convents in the Netherlands. This practice, by which English money was carried abroad, was frowned on by authority and forbidden by the penal laws. The young people now sought permission to travel under the diplomatic protection of the departing envoy. He would gladly have taken them, but could not do so without authority from the King. Some days passed, during which he sent to his successor, Don Carlos Coloma, to use his influence. Unhappily at this point a gap occurs in our evidence, and we shall never know if Rubens, when at length he put to sea for his homeward journey, was or was not accompanied by a party of grateful and devout young people.

Admirably as he had fulfilled his task, Rubens received more criticism than praise from Olivares in Madrid. The haughty minister was inclined to suspect, at every step forward that Rubens made with the King, that he was overstepping his instructions, or his authority, or both. Rubens took all this very calmly. He had no resentment of the inferior position allotted to him as a mere forerunner of the more aristocratic Don Carlos Coloma. After the conclusion of the treaty, he received not only praise from King Philip but an urgent suggestion a year later that he should consolidate his work by becoming for a time the resident representative of Spain in England. This he would not do; for he was now fifty-four years old and did not feel like sparing any more time for politics and diplomacy. A flattering offer from King Charles, to pay him an annual salary for regular bulletins of news and comment from the Netherlands, was also rejected.

Although he would not resume his diplomatic activity, Rubens must, as an artist who took pleasure in good craftsmanship, have felt satisfaction at the way in which he had engineered the Anglo-Spanish treaty, largely by patiently talking to the King and discovering where his true inclinations lay. In this he not only showed more perception than many other envoys to the Court of King Charles, but more perception than most later historians of the epoch have done. In his massive history of this period, S.R. Gardiner allowed himself to be deceived by the persistent protests of King Charles that his chief aim was to help his poor sister and her husband to regain their German lands. He builds his analysis of the King's foreign policy on this idea; and his opinion has been constantly repeated. Gardiner used the letters of Rubens, but seems to have missed his comments on this point, or at least to have missed their significance. It is only when we grasp, as Rubens did, that the King's protests about the Palatinate were merely for show that his foreign policy becomes clear: as a simple alignment with the dominating Habsburg power in Europe. The knowledge of this, more general in Europe at that time than it has been among English historians since, explains the contempt that was so often the fate of the envoys whom he sent out from time to time, with the apparent mission of helping his German relations and the Protestant Cause, but with no real power to do so.

In the setting of the European conflict, the policy of King Charles was weak and egotistical. In the setting of the contemporary English politics, it was disastrous, because it offended too many sections of his people in both their religious and their commercial interests. This, of course, was not the fault of Rubens. He had been inspired throughout by a genuine desire for peace between two peoples, the English and his own, who had in the past enjoyed fruitful and friendly relations. He naturally assumed that the ultimate pacification of Europe through the dominance of Spain and her allies was preferable to a pacification that made France, the Dutch and the Protestant states dominant. He had served his patroness, the Archduchess, and his sovereign the King of Spain, with signal and lucid success. No one would have been more distressed than he, had he known that he was contributing, in the long run, to the ruin of the young King whose aesthetic judgment he admired, whose tastes he shared and whose conversation he enjoyed.

*   *   *

C.V. Wedgwood's (1910–97) works on the Stuart period of English history won her a large public. A popularist in the best sense, her books and essays are stylishly written and saturated with facts and primary sources, albeit at the expense of theory. Wedgwood believed that small-scale, detailed studies could achieve much more than wide-ranging, quantitative surveys. Her output was largely biographical, the best-known being the two-volume study of the reign of Charles I, *The Great Rebellion* (1955–8). Her books were reprinted regularly until the 1970s, and many are still available today. Veronica Wedgwood was created a Dame in 1968.

25

The Irish President: The Later Career of Eamon de Valera

EDGAR HOLT

(February 1961)

The grand old man of Irish politics, President of Eire by the time of Edgar Holt's article, de Valera was still something of a bête noire to older English readers.

The Irish Balladmonger's prophecy has not come true. They have never crowned de Valera King of Ireland. Even in the years between 1932 and 1959, for most of which he was chief Minister of what is now the Irish Republic, he never enjoyed the kind of majority in Dail Eireann which might have suggested any near approach to absolute authority. The old and persisting cleavage between pro-Treaty and anti-Treaty parties in Irish politics has made it impossible for him ever to have the whole country behind him – except on particular issues during the Second World War, when there were few in Southern Ireland to oppose his resolute maintenance of neutrality. None the less it is self-evident that he has been the greatest political figure in Southern Ireland since its twenty-six counties were given their own Government in 1922. Yet this is the man who was sentenced to death by the British and clapped into gaol by his own countrymen, both in the Irish Free State and in Northern Ireland. The transformation of the rebel of 1923 into the respected President of 1961 is a remarkable example of how personality and perseverance can win through, even when all the odds have been heavily against them.

The Eamon de Valera whom the Government of the newly-formed Irish Free State interned in Arbour Hill barracks in 1923 had already many proud memories to console him. In spite of his international origin – he was born in New York, the son of a Spanish father and an Irish mother – he had become established as an Irish patriot and had the great prestige of being the only surviving senior commandant who had fought in the Easter Rising. By profession he was a teacher of mathematics; he was also a keen Gaelic student, and his practical abilities had made him an enterprising military commander at Boland's Mills in Dublin. Indeed, it was due to his skilful deployment of small outposts that the British troops suffered their heaviest casualties of the Rising in the battle of Mount Street bridge, where two hundred and thirty-six officers and men of the Sherwood Foresters were killed or wounded in an ambush he had prepared. The defences of Boland's Mills were still intact on the Saturday of Easter Week, when Pearse ordered all the rebel commandants to surrender. After the Rising, de Valera was tried by court-martial and sentenced to death, but the fact that he had been born in the United States saved him from execution with the other leaders. He was thus able, when released from British imprisonment in 1917, to become the political chief in the struggle for Irish freedom.

From 1917 to 1921, although he was absent from Ireland for over two years, owing to a further spell of imprisonment in Britain and his own insistence on paying a long propagandist and fund-raising visit to the United States, his supremacy on the political side of the Irish revolution was never seriously challenged, and it was inevitable that he should become the first President of the southern Irish Parliament – Dail Eireann – when it was set up in 1919. In this capacity he began the discussions that led to the signing (but not by him) of the Anglo-Irish Treaty of 1921; thereafter, although he had often declared that he was not a doctrinaire Republican, he opposed the Treaty settlement because it provided for an Oath of Allegiance to the King of England, separated Ulster from Southern Ireland and did not give the south a Republic. He thus found himself on the side of those dissident officers of the Irish Republican Army who precipitated the Civil War of 1922–23. When the rebellion collapsed in April 1923, de Valera was virtually an outlaw. Yet in the Irish Free State general election of 1923 he stood for his old constituency in Clare and daringly decided to address a meeting at Ennis in August. As he began to speak, he was arrested and he was subsequently imprisoned without charge and without trial. But Clare returned him at the head of the poll, and when he was released from prison in June 1924, he could have sat in the Dail if he had been willing to take the Oath. He declined to do so. For the time being, he thought it better to remain in the political wilderness.

De Valera was then forty-one, rather older than Kevin O'Higgins and the other young men whom William Cosgrave, as chief Minister of the Irish Free State, had taken into his Government. He was known in particular for the obstinacy with which he clung to his views. Michael Collins had once said despairingly, 'You know what it's like to argue with Dev,' and over the years many people were to feel that to argue with de Valera was to run one's head against a brick wall. What made him all the more difficult to argue with was that he was apt to give such baffling and often ambiguous reasons in support of his views. Years later, when he was President of the Dail, he once asked John Dillon if he was sure about a statement supposed to have been made in an earlier speech. 'Oh, I am never sure of anything the President says,' Dillon retorted, 'because if there was a possible method for the President to say anything so that it could be interpreted in six different ways he would certainly choose that way of saying it.'

To all except die-hard Republicans the views that de Valera upheld so tenaciously seemed quite unrealistic when he came out of prison in 1924. He considered that the Irish Republic, established in the Easter Rising of 1916 and confirmed at the first session of Dail Eireann in 1919, was still in existence and that the Cosgrave Government had no legal right to disestablish it. Complete independence of England was now his avowed aim. In a press interview before his arrest he had explained that his policy, if he were returned to power, would be 'to govern the country on Sinn Fein lines as in 1919, refusing to co-operate with England in any way until England was ready to make with us such an arrangement as would make a stable peace possible; that is, an arrangement consistent with the independence and unity of our country and people as a single State.' But such a policy ignored the plain facts that England would not have tolerated such a revival of Irish non-co-operation, that his programme could never have been carried out effectively in view of the acute division in Irish politics and that 'unity,' involving the incorporation of Northern Ireland in an Irish Republic, was an outright impossibility.

By the time that he became President of the Dail, de Valera had discarded the idea of cutting the Free State off from all ties with England and had adopted a more gradual and realistic approach to his goal; but in 1924 both the Presidency of the Dail and the proclamation of an Irish Republic seemed far away from a released prisoner confronting a firmly established Government. It was true that de Valera already held the nominal title of 'President of the Republic and Chief Executive of the State,' which had been conferred on him during the Civil War by the Republican deputies of the Dail. Yet the title was plainly absurd since his Sinn Fein party had been well beaten by Cumann na nGaedheal (League of Gaels), the party of Cosgrave and the Free State Government, in the 1923 general election. Now that de Valera was free again, he resumed his denunciation of the mild Oath of Allegiance that had been embodied in the Free State Constitution and continued to proclaim that the partition of Ireland was an outrage imposed on the Irish people by the British Government. The fact that he stood exactly where he had stood before was illustrated by one of those rare flashes of humour that occasionally shine through his usual solemnity. On returning that autumn to speak at Ennis, where he had been arrested, he began with a smile: 'People of Ireland, as I was saying to you when we were interrupted . . .'

This obstinate clinging to rejected policies might have led an outsider to think that de Valera would soon cease to be an important factor in Irish politics. But in fact the Cosgrave Government already contained the seeds of eventual disintegration. In founding Cumann na nGaedheal, Cosgrave had tried to attract a representative cross-section of the best elements in the country, and the party contained many who had fought in the Anglo-Irish struggle, together with farmers, business men, professional men and others. It was easy for such diverse elements to come together at a time of national crisis, but there was no unbreakable link to keep them together once the immediate crisis was over. De Valera had only to bide his time and he would see Cumann na nGaedheal coming to pieces before his eyes.

De Valera made good use of the years between 1924 and 1927 in which he and his party stayed out of the Dail. Yet it looked as if everything was going wrong for him. His attempts to preach the anti-partition gospel in Northern Ireland brought him a month's imprisonment in Belfast, followed by deportation to the Free State. In November 1925, the IRA – which never had very much use for politicians – withdrew its allegiance from de Valera and his shadow Cabinet and set up its own entirely independent Army Council. A few months later, de Valera asked the Sinn Fein general meeting to agree that there was no fundamental objection to Republican deputies taking their seats in the Dail or the Northern Ireland Parliament if the Oath of Allegiance were removed. It declined to do so, on the grounds that it could not countenance the entry of Sinn Fein deputies 'into any usurping legislature set up by English law in Ireland,' and de Valera resigned from Sinn Fein to form, in May 1926, his new party of Fianna Fail (Warriors of Fal, a poetical name for Ireland).

Rejected by both the IRA and the Sinn Fein extremists, de Valera seemed to be more in the wilderness than ever. Yet in the midst of all his defeats and disappointments this astonishing man was working out an elaborate political programme to be put into action if and when he came into power. The years of apparent frustration left him equipped with practical legislative proposals to be produced when occasion offered.

When a general election was held in June 1927, there were 87 Fianna Fail candidates, of whom 44 were elected, and the disintegration of Cumann na nGaedheal was now becoming evident. Its numbers in the

Dail fell from 63 to 47, though as long as the Fianna Fail deputies declined to sit there was still no challenge to Cosgrave's leadership. De Valera and his followers made a slightly farcical attempt to enter the Dail without taking the Oath, and, when this failed, they resumed their earlier abstention. But not for long. The new Dail was elected on June 9th. On July 10th, Kevin O'Higgins, Minister of Justice, was murdered by three gunmen on his way to Mass at Blackrock, county Dublin.

O'Higgins was the strong man of the Free State Government. He had acted firmly to suppress activities that threatened the State, and if he had lived he would surely have succeeded Cosgrave as leader of Cumann na nGaedheal. It is anyone's guess what would have happened in Ireland if two forceful and inflexible men like O'Higgins and de Valera had faced each other in the Dail as respective leaders of the two chief political parties. It is at least certain that, for better or for worse, the history of Ireland would have been quite different from what it has been.

A savage murder, for which de Valera had not and has never been thought to have any shadow of responsibility, thus removed from his path his most formidable opponent. But the immediate effect of O'Higgins' death was also of great significance. For it gave de Valera and his party their opportunity to enter the Dail.

To Cosgrave the murder was clear warning of the danger of allowing the country to stay in its existing state of unrest, which was at least partly due to the fact that so many Dail deputies still declined to have any share in the government of the Free State. In addition to introducing a stringent Public Safety Bill, which soon became law, he brought in an Electoral Amendment Bill, designed to force Fianna Fail into the Dail by providing that every candidate for election either to the Dail or to the Senate should swear an affidavit that if elected he would take the Oath prescribed by the Constitution. This, too, was quickly passed, and de Valera and his followers saw that they must either agree to take the Oath or submit to the disappearance of their party at the next election. A distinguished historian of the period describes de Valera's position as 'a cruel dilemma.' Yet he was clearly anxious to get into the Dail, and it cannot have been altogether unwelcome to him that he could now make his entrance with the excuse that the Oath had in fact been forced on him. When at last the Fianna Fail deputies took their seats in the Dail on August 11th, 1927, de Valera coolly announced that the Oath – which had been a bone of contention for so long – was now a mere formality. He said to the Dail officer in charge of the Oath Book: 'I am not prepared to take an oath. I am not going to take an oath. I am prepared to put my name down in this book in order to get permission to go into the Dail, but it has no other significance.' The evasiveness was characteristic, but at all events he was in the Dail again. He was not to leave it for thirty-two years, and then only to become the real President of the Republic of Ireland.

The shakiness of Cosgrave's majority caused a second general election to be held later in 1927. It showed that pro-Treaty and anti-Treaty still marked the great dividing-line in Irish politics. Smaller parties lost ground, and the voters returned 62 members of Cumann na nGaedheal and 57 of Fianna Fail, out of a total of 153. An understanding with the small Farmers' Party enabled Cosgrave to command enough votes to carry on the government.

The fruits of de Valera's years in the wilderness now began to be seen, for in the first big debate after the second general election he outlined his new theories of economic nationalism. Yet his four and a half years as leader of the Opposition were more notable for an event that happened outside the Dail than for the harassing tactics he used against the Government inside it. This was the Statute of Westminster of 1931, which made the Irish Free State a completely autonomous nation, with the King as the sole surviving link with Great Britain. The ease with which de Valera was able later to make his constitutional changes was largely due to the great expansion of Irish independence under the Cosgrave regime.

De Valera's turn came at last. Cumann na nGaedheal's hold on the country was gradually diminishing, and in the 1932 general election its numbers fell from 66 to 57 while those of Fianna Fail rose from 56 to 72. This was not a clear majority for de Valera, but the seven Labour deputies sided with him, and when the new Dail met on March 9th he was duly elected President of the Executive Council, the post he had lost during the great Treaty debate of 1922. Old revolutionary colleagues like Sean T. O'Kelly, Sean Lemass and Frank Aiken found posts in his first Ministry, but he kept the Ministry for External Affairs for himself. It was to be he, and no one else, who would conduct whatever negotiations with Britain were necessary in his task of reshaping the Free State nearer to his heart's desire.

As President of the Executive de Valera had two different, though complementary, sets of objectives. The first of these was to remove one by one the features of the Treaty that he found objectionable and then to give the country a new Constitution. The other objectives were economic: the nineteen-thirties was the era of economic nationalism, and it was de Valera's design to change the pattern of Irish agriculture, to foster new industries and gradually make Southern Ireland self-supporting. In his speeches he constantly proclaimed another and very familiar objective – the ending of partition – but he was in no position to take any practical steps to achieve it.

The inflexibility of de Valera's character is clearly revealed in his dogged perseverance in carrying out the programme he had formulated years before. The Oath went first. Though he had once called it a mere formality, he was determined to be rid of it, and he used the Statute of Westminster as his justification for telling the British Government that he proposed to abolish it. In reply to protests that he was breaking the Treaty he insisted that the Free State, like any other Dominion, had full right to manage its own affairs in its own way.

There was a graver clash with Britain over the land annuities, which represented the interest on loans given by previous British Governments to Irish tenants to enable them to buy their farms. These payments, amounting to £3,000,000 a year, had been collected by the Free State Government and passed on to the British Treasury, but de Valera declared that such payments to Britain were unjustified and on July 1st he defaulted on the half-yearly £1,500,000. This was the beginning of the Anglo-Irish economic war, which continued until 1938. After de Valera had refused to submit the issue to Commonwealth arbitration, the British Government announced that it would collect the amounts owing by means of Customs duties on imports from the Free State. De Valera retaliated by imposing duties on imports from Britain, and he may well have congratulated himself on the fact that Britain had played into his hands. He had wanted to make the Free State self-supporting; the virtual disappearance of Anglo-Irish trade made it essential for both the agricultural and the industrial patterns to be reshaped, and the policy of economic nationalism became an immediate – though in some ways a painful – reality.

Next on de Valera's list were the office of Governor-General and the Senate, both of which had been set up in the original Free State Constitution. The status and salary of the Governor-General were reduced; the Senate was abolished after much argument, in the course of which de Valera made an amazing speech quoting all kinds of authorities (some of them wrongly) to prove that two-Chamber government was not necessarily a good thing. The speech was a typical de Valera curtain lecture. He has never been an attractive orator, but he has always been able to impress listeners by his obvious sincerity and to dazzle them with portentous displays of learning.

While all these changes were in progress at home de Valera had the singular good fortune to find a platform in world affairs. The year in which he came to power was the year in which it was the Free State's turn to supply the president of the League of Nations Assembly, and de Valera made a considerable impression on his new international audience, both then and in the years that followed.

The Irish Free State had already shown that it was taking its League membership seriously; under Cosgrave's Government it had signed the Kellogg Pact for the renunciation of war and also the so-called 'Optional Clause,' which made the jurisdiction of the Permanent Court of International Justice compulsory in justiciable disputes between signatory States. De Valera continued and extended this policy. In his very first speech at Geneva, he declared that: 'we in Ireland desire peace – peace at home and peace abroad'; thereafter he used the League as a platform on which a small country could make its voice heard on the side of world peace and collective security. He spoke forcefully in the Assembly, warning the League against inertia and condemning both Fascism and Communism; and he gave practical support both to the abortive League policy of economic sanctions against Italy during the war in Ethiopia and to the later policy of non-intervention in the Spanish Civil War. His attitude in the Spanish war was, indeed, a striking proof of his determination that his country should stick to the League as long as the League had even the slightest chance of being effective. Irish Roman Catholic feeling was so heavily on General Franco's side that it needed all de Valera's pertinacity to maintain that non-intervention was the right policy for his Government to follow.

In Ireland, as well as at Geneva, the first years of de Valera's government dispelled any belief that he was no more than a revolutionary agitator. He soon showed himself a capable President of the Executive, and dealt firmly with a semi-Fascist movement that arose under the leadership of General Eoin O'Duffy, though he was less successful in restraining the IRA, which had become a vigorous underground movement, carrying out many outrages both in Ireland and in England. In 1937 he produced a new Constitution that changed the Free State's name to Eire, abolished the Governor-Generalship and established the new post of President of Ireland, and set up a new Senate that was largely vocational in character. Rather oddly, the Constitution was intended to be valid for Northern Ireland as well as for the south, and the name of Eire was taken to represent the whole country, not merely the twenty-six counties.

In the following year, de Valera scored one of his greatest political triumphs. Finding Neville Chamberlain, the British Prime Minister, in his prevailing mood of appeasement, he agreed with him on terms for ending the economic war and persuaded him to hand back unconditionally to Eire the three Irish naval ports in which Britain had retained the right to fortify and use the harbours under the terms of the Treaty. These were the ports whose loss was to cause Winston Churchill so much heart-searching during the unrestricted submarine warfare of the Second World War. It may be noted that de Valera approved of the Chamberlain appeasement policy towards other countries as well as Eire. He was in Geneva in 1938, when the news came through that Chamberlain was going to Berchtesgaden to see Hitler. At a British Empire dinner, where he was sitting next to Lady Diana Cooper, de Valera solemnly declared: 'This is the greatest thing that has ever been done.'

Successive elections in 1937 and 1938 confirmed him in power, and when the Second World War broke out, he could count on general support for his decision to keep Eire neutral. He did so throughout the war, in spite of all British and American attempts to persuade him to join the alliance against Germany. But the fortunes of Fianna Fail were now beginning to fluctuate; in the election of 1943, de Valera had no clear majority and remained in power only because the opposing parties could not unite under another leader. Yet only a coalition could succeed him, since the principal opposing party, Fine Gael (Tribe of Gaels), which had replaced the old Cumann na nGaedheal, showed no sign of ever becoming strong enough to form a Government on its own.

A break in his long tenure of power came in 1948, when a general election left Fianna Fail with 68 seats out of 147, and his opponents were able to form an inter-party Government under John A. Costello, a member of Fine Gael. It was Costello, and not de Valera, who actually took Eire out of the Commonwealth and made it the Republic of Ireland. He did so in the hope of appeasing the IRA and 'taking the gun out of Irish politics.'

But de Valera was not finished yet. At sixty-five he was full of vigour, and he set out on speech-making tours of the United States, Australia and New Zealand to denounce his old bogy, the partition of Ireland. In 1951 the inter-party Government split over a health service proposal, and de Valera found himself in power again, thanks to the marginal votes of a few Independents.

The last phase had begun. De Valera was out of office again during another spell of inter-party government in 1954–57, but he returned to power in 1957, with many of his old friends of the Civil War once again in important offices. The years had changed him little. He was still an economic nationalist, still a devotee of the Gaelic tongue (though attempts to make it generally spoken in the Republic had had little success), and he was still attacking partition, though he frankly admitted that it was necessary to get the goodwill of Northern Ireland before there could be any Irish unity. But he was now nearly seventy-five, and the time for his retirement from active politics could not be far away.

In the nineteen-thirties, when an applicant for a post on de Valera's newspaper, the *Irish Press*, had apologized for not being politically-minded, de Valera had replied, 'Curiously enough, neither am I.' Perhaps he meant that he had no real enthusiasm for the cut and thrust of parliamentary debate, but he had certainly played his full part in Irish politics. It was amazing, moreover, that he had kept going so long, for eye trouble had more than once threatened to cut short his career. Now at last in 1959, when his old comrade Sean T. O'Kelly came to the end of his second term as President of the Republic, de Valera decided to be a candidate for the Presidency.

Even at this late date, long after the Anglo-Irish Treaty had been discarded, the old pro-Treaty and anti-Treaty division was still to be found in politics, and General Sean MacEoin, a one-time supporter of the first Free State Government, put up as a rival candidate. The issue was never in doubt, and de Valera was duly elected, though MacEoin polled 417,482 votes against de Valera's 538,058. By an ironical twist, de Valera's last political move – an attempt to abolish multiple constituencies and proportional representation – was defeated in the referendum held simultaneously with the Presidential election.

The voting was on June 17th, 1959, almost forty-two years since the excited Dublin crowds had welcomed him home from imprisonment in England. He had gone a long way since then, and in the end he had got most of the things he wanted for Ireland, except her unity. For four decades he had been a man to be reckoned with. He could settle down to the duties of the Presidency with the knowledge that he had always stood up for his principles and that not only Ireland, but Britain and other countries, had learned from long experience what it was like to argue with Dev.

*   *   *

Edgar Holt (b. 1900) was a journalist and historian, who worked as deputy editor of *The Listener*, chief assistant editor of the *Liverpool Daily Post* and assistant editor of the *Daily Dispatch*. In 1961 he was Chief Press Officer of the Church Information Office. Holt was the author of *The World at War, 1939–1945* (1956), *The Boer War* (1958), and *Protest in Arms: The Irish Troubles, 1916–1923* (1960).

26

Recollections of Lord Palmerston

CHARLES GEORGE BARRINGTON

(February 1961)

Charles George Barrington was a grandson of the Prime Minister, Earl Grey, and a descendant of the family that had produced Lord Barrington, Secretary at War, during the early years of the American War of Independence. Through his many connections with the leading political families of the day, Charles Barrington in 1856, at the age of twenty-nine, was appointed Private Secretary to Henry John Temple, third Viscount Palmerston, the Prime Minister. He served Palmerston until the Prime Minister died in office in 1865. In the pages that follow, Barrington's admiration for the humanity, wit and decisiveness of his chief are affectionately apparent. He offers a portrait of the great Whig Prime Minister at the height of his powers, seen from the intimate point of view enjoyed by a confidential assistant at No. 10 Downing Street.

Barrington's Recollections were drawn up towards the close of his life – he died in 1911 – and transmitted to his relation, the third Earl of Durham. In a letter to Lord Durham, conveying his manuscript, Barrington wrote: 'In order to enable one to judge of the merit or demerit of a Man's action, his real character must be taken into account; and, this cannot be done except by those who have known the man as he was at home.' This extract from Barrington's papers offered some penetrating glimpses of Palmerston's 'real character' as it was revealed to his secretary. It was published, with some cuts, but without change of style, by courtesy of the third Lord Durham's great-nephew, Lord Lambton, M.P.

Lord Palmerston's life has been written down to comparatively late days; thus his actions and early opinions are well known. I became his private Secretary in 1856 and, from that year to his death, had opportunities of acquainting myself with his social relations and his character which were afforded to few of his political associates. Further, there were instances in which true versions of what occurred were, and are, still unknown and must remain generally unknown for some time to come, yet the truth ought to be recorded so that one day it may be brought to light. In order to appreciate the conduct of famous people it is well to have in your mind's eye, the men themselves as they appeared in life to those with whom they lived.

Lord P. was to my mind the type of an English gentleman and statesman – his success in life was due greatly to his great common sense, his industry and his love of his country. When we have a Prime Minister or a Cabinet Minister of this type, we may forecast with some certainty what his action will be in difficulties which were faced by Lord P., for the most part, with good results.

At the beginning of Bulwer's life of Lord P. a letter is published from the late Sir Augustus Clifford. It runs thus: 'When I went to Harrow in 1797 (the late) Lord Palmerston was reckoned the best tempered boy in the school, as well as a young man of great promise. We were in the same house which was Dr Bromleys by whom we were often called, when idle, 'young men of wit and pleasure' – the late Lord De Mauley, Poulet and I were fags to Althorp, Duncannon and Temple, who messed together, and the last was by far the most merciful and indulgent. I can well remember Temple's fighting behind School, a great boy called Salisbury twice his size and he would not give in, but was brought home with black eyes and a bloody nose, and Mother Bromley taking care of him.'

This letter corroborates the old saying that the boy is father to the man. Pluck, good temper, mercy, were all his to the day of his death. Added to these qualities, he was of great perseverance and shrank from no amount of work. He had, by nature, fine temper, and was always ready to forgive a friend who might have behaved ill to him.

When our Admiral Sir C. Napier came home after a most unsatisfactory campaign in the Baltic,[1] he was severely attacked by Sir Robert Peel;[2] Sir Charles wrote to Lord Palmerston to defend himself, but Lord P., whose only business fault was that of sometimes neglecting to answer letters at once, had omitted to reply. Sir C. Napier waited for a short time and then called in Downing St. Lord P. happened to be in the House of Commons, so the Admiral was shown in to my room – very sore and angry he was,

---

[1] Sir Charles Napier commanded the Baltic fleet during the Crimean War.
[2] Eldest son of the former Prime Minister; Member of Parliament for Tamworth, 1850–1880.

having got it into his head that Lord P. had put his appeal on one side deliberately. I smoothed him down, saying Lord P. would be sure to see him very shortly and that pressure of business was the only reason for the delay in answering his letter. Now, Lord Palmerston had every reason to be dissatisfied with Sir Charles, but instead of showing any dissatisfaction he received him kindly and went so far as to write to Sir Robert Peel and asked him if he could not say something to soothe the wounded feelings of the old Admiral.

Sir Robert Peel, not long afterwards, took great offence at (as he thought) a want of courtesy on Lord Palmerston's part in not sending an immediate reply to one of his letters, resigned his office and strongly attacked his former chief. Lord Palmerston's comment was 'it is a pity, for I liked the fellow and would have helped him on, but after this speech, that is no longer possible.' Two tolerably fair examples of Lord P.'s generous disposition.

Lord Palmerston was in all respects a thorough gentleman, and by that I do not mean merely a man of good manners, but one who thinks of others and is gentle and considerate in his bearing, yet when he thought it necessary he had no hesitation in writing a strong private reproof to those serving under him, never a public one. Bulwer[3] himself affords a remarkable example of this: I once copied a letter in which Lord P. remonstrated with him upon his extravagance. How, said he, can the Turks, to whom we are constantly preaching economy, pay attention to a man who is himself over head and ears in private debt?

Lord Palmerston once wrote me a lecture, in consequence of a complaint from some one (I believe it was a certain Mr Behan, sub-Editor of *The Observer*) that I was not civil to people who called in Downing Street. It was to this effect. 'In receiving a man, treat him however tiresome, with civility and do not let him perceive that you take him for a bore. Even such persons may often tell you something you may be glad to know, and always offer them a chair. This has a double advantage; it is polite to do so and after the interview has lasted long enough you may push your own chair back, get up, and shake hands with your man, when he will probably do the same and depart.' Mr Behan's grievance against me was that, catching him peeping over my shoulder at a letter of Lord Palmerston's which I was copying, I gave orders that he should not be allowed to come in to my room again, but be kept in the waiting room.

Lord Palmerston's love of his country and his loyalty to his colleagues

---

[3] Sir Henry Bulwer Lytton, elder brother of the novelist; Ambassador in Constantinople, 1858–1856.

were well known, whilst those who served under him knew that if they did their best, even though their efforts might fail, they might rely implicitly upon him to defend them. When suffering from a sharp attack of his old enemy, the gout, it was essential that he should be kept free from annoying or troublesome affairs; and, on such occasions, I, as his Private Secretary, did not hesitate to take the responsibility of answering people in the sense in which I thought he would have replied. On his recovery, and on my reporting anything which had occurred, he would ask with some eagerness, 'Well and what did you say?' It has been a source of great satisfaction to me to be able to record that in no instance did he find fault with what I had done; on the contrary, I well remember his pleasant smile of approval on finding that in a ticklish case some touchy supporter had been judiciously handled.

The consequence of his methods with regard to Ministers abroad and others was that his knowledge of passing events was sound, so that he was well aware of what he was about. As a proof that such was the case, it may be mentioned that one day when walking with him at Broadlands the subject of French politics came up. I remarked that he, Lord Palmerston, was popularly believed to have had a good deal to do with Louis-Philippe's abdication. 'How so?' said he. 'Because when the Turks and Mohamet Ali were at one another's throats, you in defiance of Louis-Philippe's government backed up the Turks.' Lord P. looked at me for a moment or two, smiled and said, 'I had been aware for some time that the French were dissatisfied with the King and that his reign would not last much longer (the straight tip from a clever Ambassador) and' – with one of his pleasant laughs – 'I knew besides that the French were in no condition at the time to go to war.'

Here I will digress for a moment to give a short account of Louis-Philippe's abdication. I had it from the foreign gentleman who, if not present, heard the story from one who was. It may amuse. The King and some members of his family were at luncheon, when the Duc de Montpensier came hurriedly into the room crying out, '*Sire, les troupes sont en accord avec les Rouges, il faut abdiquer tout de suite.*' The old man turned up the tablecloth and proceeded to write his abdication, while Montpensier kept thumping the table saying, '*Dépêchez vous, sire.*' The King finished his proclamation and handing it to his son, remarked '*Il faut un peu de temps même pour abdiquer,*' then calling for his portefeuille which held his money, he put it under one arm, took Queen Amélie under the other, dived his pear-shaped head into his hat and ran out of the room crying out '*J'abdique, j'abdique.*'

After Napoleon I had been got rid of and the Allies were occupying Paris, Lord Palmerston went over to France, as many English gentlemen did, and rode one day with the Duke of Wellington to see the troops reviewed in the Champ de Mars; a Nassau Regiment was on the ground, which attracted Lord Palmerston's attention owing to its smart appearance and he remarked to the Duke how well set up the men seemed to be. 'Ah, yes,' said the Duke, 'they ran away at Waterloo and when I tried to rally them, they fired a volley at me.' This anecdote Lord P. told me. The last remark I heard him make was at Brocket not long before his death. I had a book in my hand by Erckmann-Chatrian called '*Le Conscrit.*' Lord P. inquired what I was reading and I replied that in it was an account of the battle of Waterloo – 'Well,' said he, 'how does the author account for the loss of the battle?' I told him it was put down to the French troops not having had their breakfast in the morning. 'At all events,' was his comment, 'if they did not get their food in the morning, they had a belly-full before night.'

Lord Palmerston's readiness to seize on the humorous view of things and his readiness of expression were remarkable. William Cowper,[4] afterwards Lord Mountemple, was in the habit of bringing to Broadlands lions of a sort, Burton, Ruskin and others, and one of the great travellers was giving an account of his travels, in the course of which he came across an idol worshipped by one of the savage tribes he fell in with. This idol was a statue of a Goddess, her open hand extended with an eye painted in the palm. 'Ah,' said Lord P. 'Liberality tempered with discernment.' On one occasion, when pressed in the House of Commons to find a way to get through business without resorting to constant late sittings, he showed that, with our system the practice would hardly admit of alteration; he finished, a genial smile on his face, with a quotation from Tom Moore: 'the best of all ways to lengthen our days is to steal a few hours from the night.' Coming from a man who probably did more work than anybody, and who was well over seventy, these words settled the question.

That Lord Palmerston was popular is not surprising; perhaps the knowledge that he got through an amazing amount of work useful to the country had something to do with it. An omnibus driver, who worked in Piccadilly, as he passed along would point out to the passengers Lord P.'s grey head, which could be plainly seen at the window where he wrote at his standing-up desk, and say ''e earns 'is wages; I never come by without seeing 'im 'ard at it.' As to those about him, from Lord Shaftesbury to the old stud groom, they were, one and all, much attached to him. Some of

---

4 Son of Emily Lamb, sister of Melbourne the Prime Minister, and wife of the fifth Earl Cowper, who subsequently married Palmerston.

his opponents found fault with his (as they said) unduly jaunty manner in speaking publicly on serious subjects; but he could be as weighty and impressive, when he chose, as most men. If anyone doubts the fact, let him read Lord P.'s speech on the Don Pacifico case.

As a man, he might perhaps have been found fault with for not attending promptly to matters which, though not of vital importance, should have been settled without delay. He was, however, often pressed with affairs of state to an extent that might have overwhelmed an ordinary man, and probably made up his mind that everything which could be put off must wait for an easier time. Indeed, he admitted as much, for one day, coming into my room, he asked for a letter to which he wished to refer. This letter was underneath some of the numerous documents which were being dealt with, and I proceeded to turn them over to get at it; observing this, he said with a good natured smile, 'Every man understands his own chaos best; send the letter after me to the House of Commons.' As it happened, I found what he wanted and gave it him before he left. On the other hand, he carried on work of all sorts on the only sound principle. He left those under him to deal with matters of lesser consequence. Before settling things of greater importance, he read every paper bearing on the case so as to make himself thoroughly acquainted with every particular. As an instance of this, and of the extent of his knowledge of subjects with which he might be supposed to have slight acquaintance, a question of currency (something to do with paying troops or public servants when in India in Rupees, I believe) was referred to him as First Lord of the Treasury. He returned it with his decision written on two sheets of notepaper. The man in charge of the Department which attended to such matters, and who was deservedly held to be the best authority of his time on currency questions, after reading Lord P.'s Memo. said to me, 'this minute of His Lordship's contained in a few words the essence of the currency question.'

Another quality he possessed was of great service to him. It naturally happened in the course of business that sometimes, having carried correspondence up to a certain point, it became necessary to bring the case before him. He would listen to what I had to say with the same patience and attention he would have given to the words of a Cabinet Minister, and then decide the point at issue – the decision clearing away any doubt as to what should be done; and this way of going to work he adopted not only in my case, but invariably.

I never knew him to change his opinion, though in matters of second importance he might not insist on having his own way. One one occasion, some question had arisen on which he and Lord John Russell agreed, but the majority of the Cabinet took a different view. Lord John was much annoyed; but Lord Palmerston took things more easily and wrote to Lord John saying he must bear in mind that they could not always carry on their wishes – that in the time of Fox and Pitt this might have been done, but that their colleagues were men of talent and ability, who would not always submit to having their opinions set aside. It was therefore necessary sometimes to give way on matters which did not affect the welfare of the country.

Enough has been said to assist any fair dealing man in forming his opinion as to Lord Palmerston's character, and what bearing it had upon his career. After a short time spent in his service, I discovered that in addition to great talent he was, so to speak, the essence of common sense; this it was, added to a well-known love of his country, which caused the popularity he enjoyed during the later part of his life. It is time to refer to a few matters of history which are still kept in the dark or of which a version, far from the true one, has been accepted by the public.

First, the circumstances which led to his dismissal from the Foreign Office, for practically acknowledging Louis Napoleon as Emperor of the French. It had become evident to Lord Palmerston for some time that Napoleon would be chosen as their head by the people of France. He did not think that the will of a friendly nation should be interfered with by an Allied power; and, in agreement with this view, he wrote a despatch in December 1851 to our Ambassador in Paris, Lord Normanby, saying he had Her Majesty's commands to express her desire that nothing should be done which could even wear the appearance of an interference of any kind in the internal affairs of France. In addition to this, Lord Palmerston expressed to the French Ambassador, Monsieur Walewski, his approbation of, or, his satisfaction at, the act of the President in dismissing the assembly 'as it was clear that their co-existence could not long have continued, and that it seemed to him better, for the interests of France and of Europe, that the power of the President should prevail, inasmuch as the continuance of his authority might afford a prospect of the maintenance of social order in France; whereas the divisions of opinions and parties in the assembly appeared to betoken that their victory over the President would be the starting point for disastrous civil strife.'

Before the recognition of the President as Emperor, Lord P. had according to constitutional practice sent his official despatch to Lord John Russell and the Queen who returned it with several alterations. Lord Palmerston is said, I believe truly, to have taken no notice of these alterations, and to have sent it off in its original shape. This I am nearly certain is a correct version of what occurred; for long afterwards and when engaged in sorting Lord P.'s papers after his death, I came across a Memorandum in which he states with reference to the events of 1851, that he thought it high time to play a *match off his own bat*. He must have known that, in playing this match, he ran the risk of being caught out; but he had for some time been much thwarted by the Queen and the Prince Consort, and foresaw that Lord John's Ministry, without his aid would not last long (hence his allusion to its being high time, etc.). Moreover, he probably believed that Lord John would not be sorry to get rid of him – here he was mistaken as will appear presently. His dismissal took place a few days after his communication to Lord Normanby.

In 1852 Lord John was defeated on his Militia Bill, Lord Palmerston having carried a proposal to substitute the word 'regular' for 'local,' the effect of which was to maintain the old Militia plan for the new one proposed by Government – the world said Lord Palmerston took his revenge for his dismissal in this way; and he was reported to have remarked that he had had his 'tit for tat' with Johnny.

It is to be noted, however, that Lord P. had strong opinions about the Militia and expressed his view that it was constitutionally the standing army of the country. When he was Prime Minister, schemes were constantly brought before him for the improvement of the National forces; he invariably pushed aside any which interfered with the Militia. It was surmised, probably with reason, that considerable soreness had arisen between the two Chiefs of the Liberal Party; indeed Sir William Hayter, who had been Lord John's Whip, told me that, when the difference between these two Chiefs had been got rid of, the Conservatives would be turned out.

Now for the root of the affair and the truth. For two years before the crisis in France, the Queen and the Prince Consort had constantly done their best to stand in the way of Lord P.'s liberal policy abroad – he was not in the Queen's good books, and the Prince was, as far as foreign affairs were concerned, a Tory (he had been brought up by Baron Stockmar, an able man but a German Tory of the worst type). They went so far as to urge Lord John repeatedly for two years to dismiss him; but he, during those two years, loyally supported him, though I believe Lord P. was ignorant of the fact. When Lord P. took the action described above, Lord John could no longer support him and his dismissal became inevitable. Eventually, mutual friends interfered; and in 1859, Lord Palmerston and Lady P. drove down to Pembroke Lodge, where leaving Lady P. and Lady John to keep one another company, the two statesmen went into the garden to talk matters over; at that meeting the truth came out as to the part played by the Queen and Prince, so that no further differences between the two leaders arose.

When Private Secretary to Lord John, after Lord Palmerston's death, I became aware of the line taken by the Queen. I know she did not much like Lord P. from remarks let drop by Lady Palmerston and my Uncle Charles Grey; but I was not aware to what lengths the Queen had gone, and how loyally Lord John had behaved towards his colleague, until informed of the truth by the Honourable George Eliot. George Eliot, Lord John's brother-in-law, secretary and executor, had in the latter capacity possession of Lord John's papers. One day I met him coming out of Buckingham Palace; 'hallo,' said I, 'have you been having tea with Her Majesty?' 'No,' he replied, 'I have just returned the letters she wrote to Lord John.' 'What, including her notes urging him to dismiss Lord P.?' 'Yes, but I have kept copies of every one of them.'

The Queen's letters recently published show how hostile she and the Prince Consort were to Lord P. I do not think any serious or well-informed man doubts the loyalty of either Lord P. or Lord J. Russell. This I know, that when the late Lord Grey[5] was Secretary for the Colonies, the most violent attacks made upon the government of which he was a member were directed against his Department; and his brother and Private Secretary told me that the only members of the Ministry who loyally defended him were Lord John and Lord Palmerston. This was the more worthy of praise in Lord Palmerston's case because he thought Lord Howick, as he then was, had not always behaved well to his father, to whom he was attached and whom he (Lord P.) much admired. Lord Palmerston told me this and added: 'Old Lord Grey, too, was so kind and so gentle.'

Here is an additional corroboration of Lord Palmerston's loyalty. It is perhaps not needed; but, as it affords rather an amusing example as to how fortuitously legislation is now and then conducted, it is inserted. The story relates to the repeal of the paper duties.[6] When this measure was proposed in the Cabinet, Lord Palmerston opposed it, saying that without going into the merits or demerits of the case, he wished it to be put off for a year, because we could not well afford the loss of revenue at the moment. A majority of the Ministers, however, insisted on immediate repeal. Lord Palmerston then announced that he did not consider the course taken by the majority of his colleagues of sufficient importance to break up the Government, and that it might be brought in as a Government bill; but that, if it were not carried, he should feel himself at liberty to take whatever steps he might think fit.

When the Bill was debated, it seemed likely that it would be thrown out. Just before the division, which was expected to be a hostile one, a

---

[5] Henry George Grey, third Earl; Secretary for the Colonies, 1846–1852.
[6] Duties on newspapers were finally abolished in the Budget of 1861.

great friend of mine, Mr Cayley, M.P. for the N. Riding, an old Whig protectionist, who did not answer the Government whip on account of Free Trade, sent for me to see him at his house in Deans Yard. On my arrival, he addressed me to this effect: 'I consider that in speaking to you in the strictest confidence, I am speaking to Lord Palmerston. I have a strong belief that, in his heart, he is not anxious to repeal the Paper duty; I share that belief with several friends in the House of Commons and I wish you to make the following proposal to him. I and my friends will abstain from voting, in sufficient number to give the Government a small majority, if Lord P. will then say that, in consideration of the strength of the minority, whilst not condemning the measure, he will put it aside for a year. I and my friends desire to avoid his being turned out.' I told him it would be useless to make such a proposal, because Lord Palmerston would vote for the Bill and he had agreed in the Cabinet to do so. 'Nevertheless,' said Cayley, 'I must beg you to lay it before him.'

Accordingly, I drove up to 96 Piccadilly, where I found Lord P. eating his dinner before going to the House of Commons. I gave him Mr Cayley's message and my answer word for word (of which he approved – I mean my answer). He sent me back with this reply: 'Tell him that he is a good fellow, and that I am much obliged to him, but that the Bill is a Government Bill and that I must stick to it.' As I was leaving the room, he called me back and said with a pleasant laugh, 'Ah ha, I begin to think we shall have a majority.' When I got back to Mr Cayley, I found him extended on a sofa, rolled up in wet sheets, blankets, and oil skins, undergoing a cold-water cure. Upon giving him Lord Palmerston's answer, he lifted up his joined hands towards the ceiling and cried with a loud voice – 'I shall pray to God that I may be rightly directed.' It is hardly necessary to add that, whether owing to divine interference or not, he and his friends walked out of the House in sufficient number to give the Government a majority.

Changes of consequence would have taken place had Lord Palmerston's Government then been defeated. Who knows if such changes would have been of advantage to the country? This I do know, that he would have been no party to them, unless it was clear to him that such would be the result.

In writing to the Queen before the formation of his last Ministry, he said, 'Viscount Palmerston would not have taken the part he did in overthrowing Lord Derby's Government, had he not seen his way to a better one; he was ready to serve under Lord John or Lord Granville.' Lord John agreed to serve under Lord Palmerston, but not under Lord Granville. He said with reason that, if Lord G. became Premier he would be only third, as Lord P. would go to the Foreign Office. He was willing to be second but not third.

Lord Palmerston had many admirers and friends amongst whom his memory has been cherished; but, as far as I know, there was no one of these with whom he was on terms of close intimacy, no one to whom he might communicate his inmost feelings, with the exception perhaps of his brother-in-law, Mr Sullivan. Men engaged in public life liked him personally, even when opposing his policy. In the last speech made by Sir Robert Peel, he made use of these words, 'we are all proud of him.' For years after his death, the remark was often made to me, 'Ah! if we could only have Lord Palmerston back again.'

In one instance Lord P. was found fault with, even by some of his own supporters, for not affording active support to the Danes (when the Germans went to war with them), although he had made a speech in which he said, if they were attacked, he thought they would not fight alone. I believe he expected the French would have gone to their assistance and that we should have joined the French. Napoleon, however, stated that, if he went to war, he should claim the right of compensating himself on the Rhine, and this made it impossible for our Government to take any further steps in the matter.

Perhaps Lord Palmerston should not have said what he did; but, after the answer of the French Emperor, it was clear enough that it would not have suited England to fight for the Danes. It was at the time held to be much more advantageous to have a powerful ally like Prussia than that Germany should be split up into numerous petty constellations which would have but little influence in war or in peace. Lord Palmerston pointed this out in a letter to the Queen, which probably caused her some irritation. (Coburg, Gotha, etc!)

I was myself surprised at the conduct of the French Emperor. The French party in Denmark had always been the popular one in that country, and it apparently would have been sound policy on L. Napoleon's part to cement the English alliance even at some cost to himself. It was not till many years after that the true cause of his conduct became known to me; when M. Lavalette was French Ambassador here, an old friend of mine, the Honourable James Howard, in speaking about Louis Napoleon, asked M. Lavalette, with whom he was on intimate terms, how it was that such an opportunity of reducing the power of Germany had been neglected? Lavalette's reply was: 'Do you not know, *mon ami*, that we had not at the time a man or a gun available?' In fact, Louis Napoleon could not give us the real reason; and his talk of compensation on the Rhine was only an excuse meant to throw dust in our eyes.

Fault has been found with Lord Palmerston for the line he took about the Suez Canal. He was opposed to its construction, first, because he thought it would tend to our being forced to occupy Egypt for an indefinite time, if it were made; second, because he had received a letter from the King of the Belgians enclosing a report from three eminent civil engineers, expressing their unanimous opinion that it could not be made. Lord P. wished to warn English people against embarking in a speculation which he had reason to believe would fail.

*   *   *

C.G. Barrington (1827–1911) was Private Secretary to Lord Palmerston and Lord John Russell and subsequently Assistant Secretary at the Treasury.

27

Review of A.J.P. Taylor's The Origins of the Second World War

ELIZABETH WISKEMANN

(June 1961)

Elizabeth Wiskemann was a frequent contributor to History Today. *Alan Taylor knew that his book on the origins of the Second World War would be controversial, but he probably did not expect reviews as authoritatively damning as this!*

HITLER'S REPUTATION

It seems a pity that someone who writes as well as Mr A.J.P. Taylor should have made so many unwarrantable statements. Germany was the central inter-war problem – this is true enough – but, according to Mr Taylor, the German problem dissolved into smoke during the second world war. This seems a curious reaction to the conflict of the two Germanies and the situation in Berlin since 1945.

Apart from putting Germany into the centre of things, there is little else in the inter-war period about which Mr Taylor is not misleading. He states blandly that 'Hitler was appointed Chancellor by President Hindenburg in a strictly constitutional way and for solidly democratic reasons.' This is a travesty of the facts. In January 1933 the democratic parties, whom the Nazis had sworn to annihilate, still had a majority in the Reichstag, the Nazis themselves having lost some two million votes at the last general election two months earlier (November 1932). They were the biggest single party, but this was not the reason why Papen and Oscar von Hindenburg urged the President to accept Hitler as Chancellor: the reason was that the Nazis had fomented so much disorder by defying the law that Papen and his friends, who had no popular support but wished to rule Germany, believed that their only course was to enrol the Nazis as their allies. Thanks to the judicious use of terrorism by the S.A. or Storm Troopers, who had been trained for this very purpose, Hitler could pose as a popular tribune; he could stick to the principle he had adopted after his abortive coup in 1923, the principle never to use force openly until he had gained as much power as was possible without it. He accepted the Chancellorship on condition that the Reichstag should be dissolved and a fresh election held under S.A. control; in spite of unprecedented intimidation, the Nazi party still failed to obtain an absolute majority. On being appointed Chancellor, Hitler took an oath to the Weimar constitution which was soon after – by banning the Communists, suppressing freedom of expression and passing the Enabling Act – suspended for the rest of Hitler's days. So much for the 'solidly democratic reasons.'

Mr Taylor seems singularly ill-informed about Czech-German relations before 1938. In the Weimar period, no responsible German thought of 'revising' the Czech-German frontier which was the traditional boundary between Bavaria and Saxony on the one hand and Bohemia on the other. But when Mr Taylor says that in 1936 'The Germans of Czechoslovakia were hardly aware as yet that they were an oppressed minority,' he has strayed a long way in the opposite direction. For anyone with any knowledge of the campaign carried on by Konrad Henlein's *Sudetendeutsche Heimatfront* (which then changed into the *Sudetendeutsche Partei*) before the Czechoslovak elections of May 19th, 1935, knows that its striking success was an expression of the grievances of the Germans in the Czechoslovak Republic.

About the Saar plebiscite of January 1935, again, Mr Taylor makes astonishing statements. 'The inhabitants were mostly industrial workers – Social Democrats or Roman Catholics. They knew what awaited them in Germany: dictatorship, destruction of trade unions, persecution of the Christian churches. Yet, in an unquestionably free election, 90 per cent voted for return to Germany.' It would be a good deal more accurate to say that those who knew what awaited them voted for the League of Nations or France; the vast majority believed what the Nazi *Deutsche Front* told them, that the new Germany was heaven on earth. The propagandist bribes and ugly threats distributed by the *Deutsche Front* incidentally, make it difficult to regard the Saar plebiscite as 'unquestionably free.'

This, then, is Mr Taylor's way in his latest book – to make any assertion he chooses in order to come to the rescue of Hitler's reputation. 'Besides,' he writes, 'it was never Hitler's method to take the initiative. He liked others to do his work for him; and he waited for the inner weakening of the European system, just as he had waited for the peace settlement to crumble of itself.' The reader quite expects to hear that he waited until the Russians attacked him, but the book fortunately ends in 1939, not in 1941.

Had he simply complained of the monotony with which all the evidence, whether of documents or freshly unearthed speeches, stacks up to confirm Hitler's long-term programme for the extermination of the races the *Führer* despised, one might have sympathized with Mr Taylor. Adolf Eichmann's trial tells the story once more. To plan destruction on this scale was to plan war and court disaster. Mr Taylor, being understandably bored by repetition, discards the evidence.

*   *   *

Elizabeth Wiskemann was Montagu Burton Professor of International Relations, University of Edinburgh, 1958–61 and Tutor in Modern History, University of Sussex, 1961–4. She was a regular contributor to *History Today* in the 1950s and 1960s, and the author of several titles including *Europe of the Dictators, 1919–1945* (1966) and *Czechs and Germans* (1967). She died in 1971.

28

The Jesus of History

S.G.F. BRANDON

(January 1962)

Samuel George Frederick Brandon was Professor of Comparative Religion at Manchester University and a prolific author who wrote regularly for History Today *until his death. Brandon often stirred the theological dovecotes – as here. The idea that it was the Jews rather than Pontius Pilate who had wanted Jesus condemned to death, argued Brandon, was a falsification added a generation later by Mark in his gospel in order not to incite further persecution by the Roman authorities.*

Each day, for some fifteen centuries, in its liturgical services the Christian Church has made a formal declaration of its faith. Its creeds, in which this faith is defined, embody many metaphysical statements such as those concerning the doctrine of the Trinity; but they make also reference to an historical event that is basic to the whole structure of the faith – it is the statement that Jesus Christ 'suffered under Pontius Pilate, was crucified, dead and buried'.[1]

This reference imparts to Christianity its distinctive character among the religions of mankind. For, whereas the other religions attach no essential significance to the historical careers of their respective founders, Christianity owes its very *raison d'être* to certain events in the life of Jesus of Nazareth. The credal reference to his crucifixion by Pontius Pilate attests this essential anchoring of Christianity to a specific historical situation; for Pontius Pilate was the Roman procurator who governed Judaea between the years AD 26 to 36.

---

[1] The practice of reciting the (Nicene) Creed at the Eucharist started in the fifth century. Before that time various forms of credal statement were used in Baptism.

In earlier centuries the fact of the historical career of Jesus was taken for granted, and attention was concentrated upon the transcendental significance of the events of his life; in other words, emphasis was laid rather upon the divine Christ, the saviour of mankind, than upon the historical Jesus of Nazareth who had lived and died in first-century Palestine. Christian art provides eloquent witness of this attitude. Thus, the favourite representation of Christ in the catacombs and on the early sarcophagi (4th cent.) is as the Good Shepherd, in which rôle he is depicted as a beardless youth in Greek attire. Where incidents of the Passion are represented at this period, both Christ and the other actors are shown in contemporary Roman dress, no attempt being made to depict the original Judaean setting of the drama. This apparent indifference to the actual historical event manifests itself in turn in Byzantine art; and its traits are well known in mediaeval and renaissance religious painting in that, for example, the Roman soldiers attendant at the Crucifixion are presented in the arms and armour contemporary to the time of the artist.

The change that began to show itself early in the nineteenth century in the appreciation of historical evidence and the ideal of historical accuracy soon affected the study of Christian origins. If the historian's essential duty in his exploration of the past was to discover and state the relevant facts, 'how it actually happened' according to Ranke's famous dictum, then the beginnings of Christianity must be investigated as objectively as any other historical phenomenon. The task was soon taken in hand. The writings of the New Testament now began to be interrogated as historical documents to evaluate their evidence for the events that they purport to describe, or as witnesses to the situation that produced them – as in the case of St Paul's Epistles. This new attitude naturally provoked vigorous and sometimes bitter controversy. In particular, since the Gospels were now approached with a critical mind and not in the spirit of the traditional piety, interest was concentrated on the many obvious discrepancies in their record: instead of the former effort to harmonise their witness concerning the life of Jesus, significance was seen in the variations of their traditions. This research has continued to the present day, and it still goes on as vigorously as ever. As has happened in many other fields of scientific investigation, the problems involved here have generally been found more complicated and harder of definitive solution as more has been learned about them. For example, it has come to be recognised that the emergence of Christianity cannot be treated as an isolated phenomenon: it can only be understood in the context of its historical environment. This has meant an increasingly detailed investigation of the political, economic, and cultural situation of both Jewish and Graeco-Roman society during the period 100 BC to AD 200. And the materials for such investigation have been steadily increased by archaeological research, most notably in recent years by the discovery of the Dead Sea Scrolls and the Coptic documents found at Nag Hammadi. However, despite the increasing complexity of the quest and the many unsolved problems that remain, it is possible to draw certain conclusions about our knowledge of Jesus of Nazareth as an historical person.

II

First, it may be said, as being beyond dispute in all serious scholarship, that Jesus of Nazareth did actually live. It is necessary to say this, since the view was put forward at the beginning of this century, with considerable ingenuity and apparent learning, that Jesus was a creation of mythical thought – a view that is sometimes repeated today in semi-learned publications. The historicity of Jesus is clearly attested by the Roman historian Tacitus, who was a pagan and obviously hostile to Christianity. Writing in the early years of the second century about the persecution of the Christians by Nero (AD 64), he says: 'Christus, the founder of the name (i.e. Christians), had undergone the death penalty in the reign of Tiberius, by sentence of the procurator Pontius Pilate, and the pernicious superstition was checked for a moment, only to break out once more, not merely in Judaea, the home of the disease, but in the capital itself (i.e. Rome).' The unequivocal, though hostile, nature of this testimony was undoubtedly matched by the record of the first-century Jewish historian, Josephus – unfortunately in the extant Greek text of his *Antiquities of the Jews* the account given there of Jesus has evidently been amended by later Christian censorship. But the most convincing evidence of all to the historicity of Jesus is surely provided unconsciously by the Christian Gospels. It lies in the admission that the founder of the movement had been crucified as a revolutionary by the Roman governor of Judaea, Pontius Pilate. In view of the incriminating character of this fact, which, as we shall see, was a cause of extreme embarrassment to the first Christians, it is incredible that it could ever have been invented by them.

But, if the fact of the historical existence of Jesus is beyond reasonable doubt, it does not necessarily follow that the records that we have of him can be accepted as reliable historical accounts. It is here that we begin to encounter the complexities of research into the origins of Christianity.

The earliest non-Christian references to Jesus, as we have just seen, attest the fact of his execution in Judaea at the hands of the Romans; but beyond that they tell us nothing more than that a Roman and a Jewish historian writing some seventy or eighty years after the event viewed Jesus, and the movement that stemmed from him with cynical hostility. We are, therefore, left with the Christian records, preserved in the New Testament, as our only source of detailed information about the person and career of Jesus. These writings, however, were all composed by men who were profoundly convinced that Jesus of Nazareth was the incarnated Son of God, and that by his death he had saved mankind from eternal perdition; moreover, they believed also that he had risen to a new super-natural form of life and that he would soon return again in power and glory to judge mankind. Accordingly, we have here to do with theology and not with history: however, the issue is not quite as simple as that; for the theology is essentially theological interpretation put upon historical fact. Can we, then, reach back to the fact behind the interpretation? Here is the peculiar task of the historian of primitive Christianity.

It is demonstrably a task of the most baffling complexity; but it is also one that demands the most delicate handling on other grounds. For the subject of investigation is not just an ancient historical situation of merely academic interest – it concerns the very origins of one of the world's great religions that still commands the allegiance of millions of persons.

III

The earliest Christian writings that have been preserved to us are the letters of the Apostle Paul. They afford us an insight into Christian thought and activity within some twenty years of the Crucifixion. The evidence of these writings is very puzzling. They show that Jesus was already regarded as the divine saviour of mankind; but they exhibit very little concern with the earthly career of Jesus as an historical person. Moreover, Paul's letters reveal the existence of a serious difference between his interpretation of the person and mission of Jesus and that taught by the original community of Jewish disciples at Jerusalem.

When we turn to the Gospels, our first impression is that here we certainly have straightforward narratives about Jesus. The impression, however, cannot be sustained on closer scrutiny. For not only is the presentation of Jesus in the *Gospel of John* markedly different from that in the other three Gospels, but these latter in turn differ among themselves on some fundamental points. For example, the *Gospel of Matthew* locates the appearance of the Risen Christ to the disciples in Galilee, whither they are divinely commanded to go – a tradition that appears to be confirmed by the *Gospel of Mark*. On the other hand, the *Gospel of Luke* and the *Acts of the Apostles*, writings having a common authorship, both locate the post-Resurrection appearances in Jerusalem and its immediate environs, and in *Acts* i. 4 it is expressly stated that the disciples were forbidden to leave the city. That such a discrepancy about so important a matter could exist surely indicates that the writings concerned embody traditions that must have grown up among different, and possibly rival, groups of believers.

Discrepancies such as this have long since caused scholars to recognize that each of the Gospels contains its own cycle of tradition about Jesus, which in turn reflects its own peculiar outlook and interests. Moreover, it is also agreed that these traditions, before reaching their present literary form, had been shaped to meet the needs of the various Christian communities, some of them located outside Palestine, to which they severally belonged. This is a factor of great importance in any assessment of the historical significance of these traditions. But it is particularly important in connection with the *Gospel of Mark*, since authoritative opinion is agreed that the *Gospels of Matthew* and *Luke* have generally followed the narrative framework of *Mark* – a fact which means that *Mark* is the earliest written account that we have of Jesus.

This priority of the Markan Gospel accordingly invests it with a peculiar significance. As the first narrative record of Jesus, its composition must surely mark a new departure in Christian practice – what event, it may reasonably be asked, had brought about this change? We have no evidence to enable us to give a categorical answer; there is, however, a strong case for believing that the cause was the series of events, beginning in Palestine in AD 66, that culminated in the destruction of Jerusalem by the Romans four years later. During that bitter struggle of the Jewish people to throw off the yoke of Rome, leading to its awful *dénouement* in the utter ruin of their holy city and Temple, the original Christian community in Jerusalem disappeared. Since this community, which included the disciples and 'eye-witnesses' of Jesus, had hitherto been the source of tradition and authority to the infant Christian movement, the catastrophe of AD 70 left Christians elsewhere facing a difficult and a dangerous situation. For, not only had they lost the guidance of the mother church of Jerusalem; they were in danger, through the Jewish origins of their faith, of being suspect to the Roman government as implicated with Jewish nationalism – had not their founder himself been executed as a revolutionary against Rome?

It is generally accepted that the *Gospel of Mark* was written in Rome. Hence it was written for the Christian community dwelling in the very metropolis of the Empire, whose rule had been repudiated by the Jewish rebels – it was a community too that, a few years before, had suffered terribly under the Emperor Nero as convenient scapegoats to be blamed for a fire that had devastated the city. It was in this perplexing and dangerous situation, therefore, that a member of the church in Rome undertook to provide for his fellow Christians an account of the life of their Master that would give them guidance about recent events and a defence against the charge of subversive sympathies.

Obviously the most embarrassing fact for these Roman Christians was the crucifixion of Jesus by Pontius Pilate on a charge of sedition. The fact was clearly so well known that it could not be denied. *Mark* is, accordingly, faced with the task of explaining away its implicit offence. He does this by transferring the responsibility for the condemnation of Jesus from the Roman governor to the Jewish authorities. Thus, he represents Pilate as convinced of the innocence of Jesus but forced by the evil machinations of the Jewish leaders to crucify him as a rebel. In handling his case *Mark* was not very adroit, and the discrepancies in his account of the two trials of Jesus and the episode of Barabbas are so obvious on analysis that his intention can be clearly discerned.

The conclusion to be drawn from this attempt of *Mark* to transfer the responsibility for the Crucifixion from the Romans to the Jews is of fundamental importance for our knowledge of the historical Jesus. It puts beyond doubt the fact of the execution of Jesus as a revolutionary by the Romans – a fact so significantly inconvenient to the Christians of Rome at the time of the Jewish war. But was Jesus really guilty of such a charge? According to *Mark*, our earliest Gospel, Jesus was not guilty; and, as we have seen, he tries, not very successfully, to represent the condemnation as due to the false accusations of the Jewish authorities, who sought the death of Jesus for other reasons. However, *Mark* unwittingly provides evidence that there may have been other grounds for the Roman condemnation. Most notably, in his list of the twelve disciples of Jesus (iii. 14–19), he names one as 'Simon, the Cananaean'. The word 'Cananaean' comes from an Aramaic expression meaning 'Zealot'. Now, the Zealots were the extreme nationalist party among the Jews and played the leading rôle in the revolt against Rome. If *Mark* had followed his usual practice of explaining Aramaic terms to his readers, he would have been obliged to have recorded here that one of the disciples of Jesus had been a Zealot. The fact that he leaves the word 'Cananaean' unexplained is, accordingly, indicative of his embarrassment about the matter: it may be noted that, when *Luke* wrote some twenty years later, the Jewish war was a thing of the past and he could safely describe Simon as 'the Zealot' (vi. 15; *cf. Acts* i. 13).

This tacit Markan admission of the existence of compromising evidence relative to Jesus' condemnation by Pilate illuminates and confirms other information. For example, not only do all the Gospels record that armed resistance was offered by the disciples in Gethsemane when Jesus was arrested, but *Luke* relates that Jesus actually gave instructions to the disciples to arm themselves before going there – instructions that were, significantly, unnecessary since they were already armed (xxii. 36–38). Then, it is also recorded that, when he made his triumphal entry into Jerusalem, Jesus had been acclaimed in terms of political Messianism as 'Blessed is the King that cometh in the name of the Lord' (*Lk.* xix. 38).

In our quest for the historical Jesus it would seem, therefore, that behind the apologetic of the Gospel record there lies the memory of certain facts that provide at least a *prima facie* explanation for the execution of Jesus by the Romans. Now, as is well known, at this period the Jews expected that God would save them from their heathen bondage by sending His Anointed One, i.e. the Messiah, to effect their liberation. It is also equally well known, and the fact is attested by the very use of the title 'Christ', that from the beginning Christians had identified Jesus with this expected Messiah or Christ. But how this identification arose is obscure, and on its elucidation our understanding of the historical Jesus vitally depends.

Once more we must turn to *Mark* for our earliest information. On analysis it is found that the apologetical theme that runs throughout this Gospel is concerned not only with explaining that Jesus was innocent; it seeks also to show that the divine nature of Jesus was not recognized by any Jew during his lifetime – the first person to perceive his divinity was, according to *Mark*, the Roman centurion at his crucifixion (xv. 39). The theological intention operative here has, of course, to take account of the attitude of the original Jewish disciples of Jesus. This is done most notably by *Mark* in the episode at Caesarea Philippi recorded in viii. 27–33. Here he relates that when Jesus had asked his original disciples who they believed him to be, Peter, as their spokesman, acknowledged him as the Messiah. But that was not enough; and *Mark* goes on to explain that, when Jesus next told them that he must suffer and die, Peter would not accept this rôle for his Master and was in consequence terribly rebuked. Thus, according to *Mark*'s presentation, Jesus' own disciples could only accept him as the Messiah of Israel; it was left to the Gentiles, guided undoubtedly by Paul, to perceive his true character as the divine saviour of mankind who redeems by his own death – a truth symbolized in the recognition by the Roman centurion of the dying Jesus as the son of God.

It may be reasonably concluded, therefore, that the actions and teaching of Jesus had been such as to cause his original disciples to recognize him as the Messiah. But this conclusion raises the vital question: how far did Jesus conform to the expected rôle of the Messiah? Attempts to answer this question have long been confused by the instinctive Christian belief that the divine saviour of mankind could not have involved himself in contemporary Jewish politics. This conviction, as we have seen, first found expression in *Mark*'s attempt to explain the Roman execution of Jesus as due to Jewish malice. However, not only have we noted evidence that might suggest that there was a political aspect to the activity of Jesus, we must recognize also that Jesus himself would have been obliged to have made his position clear concerning the Roman rule in Judaea. It would seem that three courses of action would have been open to Jesus in this connection. He could conceivably have refused to commit himself either way on the issue. But it is difficult to believe that any Jew could have abstracted himself so completely from the life and interests of his countrymen at this time; moreover, it would not be credible that one who had adopted such a non-committal attitude could have won so great a measure of popular support as Jesus had evidently done. Alternatively, he could have maintained that it was better to accept the Roman rule as a *fait accompli* than risk the perils of rebellion – a view that was taken by the Sadducean priestly aristocracy. But, if he had thus counselled submission to Rome, how could he have stirred any of his fellow Jews to recognize him as the Messiah? – and would such a pacific attitude have brought him ultimately to death at the hands of the Romans? There remains, therefore, but the third possibility: that, as a patriotic Jew, Jesus acknowledged the Roman rule as contrary to the divine will and identified himself with his people's aspiration for freedom.

But, if it is likely that Jesus accepted the justice of his people's cause against Rome, to what extent did he identify himself with an active policy to secure their political freedom? To this question no certain, or even probable, answer can be returned. The extant evidence is equivocal. On the one hand, there are indications, which we have noticed, that the Roman condemnation might have had at least some appearance of justification. Against this are a number of points that suggest that Jesus refused to accept fully the rôle of the militant Messiah. The Gospel tradition clearly reflects Jesus' concern with the profounder spiritual issues of man's relationship to God; the Temptation stories seem to pre-serve a recollection that Jesus had turned from the easier path of worldly success; and the betrayal by Judas Iscariot may have been due to that disciple's disillusionment because of Jesus' pacifism or to an attempt to force his Master's hand to violent action against his enemies.

IV

Whatever may have been Pilate's reasons for condemning Jesus, it is certain that the Crucifixion had demoralized his disciples and overthrown their faith in his Messiahship. For there was no expectation that the Messiah should be killed: still less that he should die the accursed death of the Law, which was crucifixion. The death on the cross should, therefore, on all human reckoning, have been the dismal end of the movement that Jesus had initiated. There had been before, and there were to be later, other Messianic claimants in Israel, but the influence of none long survived their overthrow. Consequently, the fact that from the crucified Jesus stemmed one of the world's great religions is explicable only in terms of the strength of his disciples' subsequent conviction that God had raised him from death and that they had communion with him.

The process of the disciples' mental adjustment after this tremendous experience can still be traced in the Gospel tradition. As Jews, they instinctively sought in their sacred scriptures for some foretelling of the death of the Messiah. They found it in *Isaiah*'s mysterious prophecy of the Suffering Servant of Yahweh. Their identification of Jesus with this tragic figure is vividly presented in narrative form in *Luke* xxiv. 13–27 and *Acts* viii. 26–35.

Having thus found a satisfactory explanation for the Crucifixion, the original disciples naturally continued to think of Jesus as the Messiah, to whose glorious return in power to 'restore the kingdom to Israel' they now eagerly looked forward. In the meantime, in presenting him as such to their fellow-countrymen, they used incidents from his life and reminiscences of his teaching as proof of his Messianic character and in justification of their own faith. Hence, an oral tradition about Jesus, in anecdotal form, was formulated which was in time to form the basis of the written Gospels. But it was a tradition that was essentially shaped by the catechetical and apologetical needs of these primitive Christian communities in Palestine: there was, of course, among them no intention to preserve an accurate historical record of Jesus for posterity. The events leading up to the Crucifixion naturally constituted the chief topic of concern and were dealt with at greater length than the rest of the career of Jesus: but, having found scriptural warranty for the death of the Messiah, his execution by the Romans was no problem for the Jewish disciples such as it became later for Gentile believers – indeed, among Jews it would rather have redounded to the credit of Jesus as being a martyr's death for Israel.

Such, then, appears to have been the formation of the tradition about Jesus among the Jewish Christians of Palestine prior to the catastrophe of AD 70. It is consistent, too, with the fact that those original followers of Jesus continued to live as zealous orthodox Jews, worshipping regularly in the Temple at Jerusalem – obviously there was nothing in their faith in Jesus that they felt to be incompatible with their continuing allegiance to Judaism. It is, accordingly, difficult to see how Christianity, thus interpreted, could ever have become a world religion but for the genius of Paul. It was Paul's inspired interpretation of the Crucifixion as the essential nexus in a divine plan for mankind's salvation and his exaltation of Jesus as the divine saviour that provided the definitive pattern of subsequent Gentile Christianity.

But the moulding of the tradition of the historical Jesus to this transcendental pattern was not the work of Paul. It was the supreme achievement of *Mark*. Faced, as we have seen, with the perilous situation confronting the Christians in Rome about the year 70, *Mark* fashioned that oral tradition of Jesus as the Messiah of Israel into the superb narrative that unfolded his true character of the divine saviour of mankind.

*   *   *

Samuel George Frederick Brandon (1907–71) was Professor of Comparative Religion in the University of Manchester. He did more than any other postwar British academic to defend the case that comparative religion should be a necessary fixture in any university's curriculum. Brandon was the author or editor of numerous titles including *A Dictionary of Comparative Religion* (1970).

29

British Life and Leisure and the First World War

ARTHUR MARWICK

(June 1965)

Arthur Marwick, best known for his work on the history of popular culture since 1945, wrote this early article on life in Britain during the First World War.

'No cricket, no boat race, no racing,' R.D. Blumenfeld, editor of the *Daily Express*, sadly confided to his diary after twelve months of war. Eighteen months later a working man in Lancashire, harassed by the Government's new licensing regulations, was heard to murmur grimly as news filtered in from Russia, that: 'Russia was never troubled by revolution till she went teetotal.' By the end of the war, Evelyn Wrench noted, the country had become so 'accustomed to restrictions of every sort . . . that we found it difficult to jump back in our minds to the pre-war world in which we lived in July 1914.'

Restrictions and austerity in all walks of life are an obvious influence of the war on society, but other more complicated, and sometimes contradictory, influences must be examined if the deeper changes wrought in the patterns of British life and leisure during the war period are to be understood. The daily round was dull, and made more so by the long hours worked in the national interest; long hours meant less time for such leisure activities as had not been interfered with, but they also meant more money to spend. The war was horrible – private bereavement and the implacable daily lists of casualties (4,000 on average), and even the air raids (over 5,000 casualties in all) made that clear; yet it was also exciting, when one contemporary could exclaim, 'all the world is topsy-turvy'; another, 'we are living at a time when days and weeks have the fulness and significance of years and decades,' and when young women and youths could escape from parental control into the personal freedom and economic independence of well-paid employment in the national interest. The war showed the dreadful destructive power of modern science, but it also involved the exploitation of discoveries that could be used for social purposes.

Austerity did not become severe in Britain until 1917, when shortages of sugar, potatoes, margarine and coal were serious enough to bring a new phenomenon upon the civic scene, the queue. Government attempts at voluntary rationing, local authority and cooperative society rationing schemes, and compulsory rationing for London led eventually in April and May 1918 to a nation-wide rationing system. At its lowest point, the weekly meat ration was fixed at three-quarters of a pound. All through the war recipes for such revolutionary delicacies as haricot-bean fritters, savoury oatmeal pudding and barley rissoles, were much publicized; but it seems clear that they were aimed at middle- and upper-class households in which pre-war protein consumption had been high. Bread, after December 1916, was 'Government Bread'; in its later forms it contained various combinations of extraneous matter, such as potato flour or bean flour, some of which went 'ropey' in warm weather. Upon this bread the civilian, from late 1917 onwards, spread margarine manufactured under the direction of the Ministry of Food, and with it he drank the anonymous mixture, Government Control Tea. Yet there was certainly at no time widespread privation in Britain, and the effect of shortages and rationing was rather to spread standards of nutrition as between social classes than to diminish them: with Government control of purchase and distribution of meat, for instance, prime joints would frequently find their way to East End shops, while poor and scraggy cuts, equally, could make a first appearance on the shelves of high-class West End butchers.

In the first months of upper-middle-class enthusiasm for a war in which, as it seemed to one who spoke for all, 'Honour has come back, as a King, to earth,' it was, naturally, the leisure pursuits of the upper segment of society, as Blumenfeld lamented, that suffered interruption. Professional football, which since the 1890s had been at the very centre of working-class and lower middle-class leisure, continued in the first winter of war in front of crowds, bigger, if anything, than ever before. Prodded from the top, however, by David Lloyd George, then Chancellor of the Exchequer, and bullied from below by patriotic press Lords, such as Lord Northcliffe of the *Daily Mail*, and religious busy-bodies, such as Frederick Charrington, Evangelical zealot and leader of the campaign against football, society as a whole was made to feel that professional football was twice-cursed: it kept the man who played from the trenches, it kept the man who watched from the factory. Sandwich men who had once proclaimed, 'Repent for the time is at hand,' now carried such messages as: 'Be ready to defend your home and women from the German Huns' down to the gates of the football grounds. The Football League capitulated in the spring of 1915, and from the following season football ceased for the duration of the war. Yet there was no lasting effect here: when war ended, football, along with cricket, horse racing and the rest, started up again very much as before.

Where wartime restrictions had a much deeper and more enduring effect was in their impingement upon the sale of alcoholic liquor, regarded by many an Edwardian working man as both a solace in leisure and a support to manual labour. Public houses in London were open from five in the morning till half past midnight; in other English towns, from 6 a.m. to 11 p.m.; in country areas, from 6 a.m. to 10 p.m.; and in Scotland, from 10 a.m. to as early as 9 p.m. in some areas, 11 p.m. in others. The undesirability of recruits coming on duty in a state of intoxication was at once perceived by War Office and Admiralty; the threat to domestic war production was not revealed in its full dimensions until Lloyd George's dramatic declaration in March 1915 that of the three foes facing the country, 'Germany, Austria and Drink,' the deadliest was 'Drink.' First moves were made under the Defence of the Realm Act and gave the authorities in certain militarily sensitive areas power to impose restricted opening hours. But the major acts, which within four years effected a revolution in British drinking habits, were the Intoxicating Liquor (Temporary Restriction) Act of August 31st, 1914, and the Defence of the Realm (Amendment No. 3) Act of May 19th, 1915. Under the provisions of the latter a Central Control Board was established for the purpose of controlling liquor licensing in all areas where excessive drinking could be held, in some way or another, to be impeding the war effort. By the end of the war, control extended to all the main centres of population, covering thirty-eight million people out of a total of forty-one million. It was still possible in rustic parts to drink from dawn to dusk without let or hindrance.

In the controlled areas two main measures prevailed. The first limited hours of sale to two-and-a-half in the middle of the day and to three (or, in some cases, two) in the evening. The second followed up an early appeal by the Secretary for War, Lord Kitchener, asking the public to refrain from 'treating the men to drink' and to give them 'every assistance in resisting the temptations which are often placed before them': it prohibited 'treating,' thus, in the words of the Bootle Chief of Police, wiping out the 'public-house bummer.' Special restrictions were placed upon spirits, including a maximum potency of 70 degrees proof, and a total prohibition on sales at weekends. In some areas publicans were instructed not to permit the simultaneous purchase of a 'nip' of spirits and a 'chaser' of beer.

A pint of beer, or a glass of spirits, in 1914, cost 3*d*, contributing one farthing to the Imperial Exchequer. Heavily discriminatory taxation during the war took spirits by 1920 into the luxury class at four or five times the pre-war price. Beer, drastically reduced in gravity and known derisively as 'Government Ale,' rose to 7d. a pint, of which half went in taxation. The innovations of the war period were regularized and applied to the whole country by the Licensing Act of 1921, by which time there can be no doubt that regulation and reduced supply had brought about a salutary change in one of the most important of British social habits. From the enormous figures of pre-war years, convictions for drunkenness dropped to manageable proportions: 'frequent drunkenness,' reported the *New Survey of London Life and Labour*, once 'half admired as a sign of virility' was now regarded as 'rather squalid and ridiculous.'

That alcoholism involved a squandering of the community's physical and moral resources had been a commonplace for over a century; that every summer British families squandered the early morning hours of valuable daylight was a point forcefully made in 1908 by William Willett, F.R.A.S., who succeeded in having a bill proposing that all clocks in summer should be put forward by an hour introduced into Parliament, where it made no further progress. The manifest necessity in war-time to maximize the country's productive resources ensured that when Willett's idea was revived in May 1916 by Sir Henry Norman, it was enthusiastically adopted. From May 21st to September 30th, 1916, all British clocks ran one hour in advance of Greenwich mean time, giving longer and lighter evenings. A Government committee, appointed to investigate the effects, reported enthusiastically upon increased efficiency and greater opportunity for healthful recreation; children, it was true, were causing their parents some trouble by refusing to go to bed, but the committee was clear that Summer Time should remain as a 'Permanent Institution,' as indeed it did.

The reality behind press stories of the working classes 'warming themselves in the sun of affluence' is not always easy to deduce from the official statistics. A much-quoted passage from the report of a Board of Trade Committee on Prices, published in 1916, which remarked that there 'was less total distress in the country than in an ordinary year of peace,' also pointed out – this part was less-quoted – that families where a principal wage-earner was in the Army, or where there were several children below school-leaving age, were 'hard pressed by the rise in prices.' None the less, because of the enhanced bargaining power of labour at a time when its willing cooperation was essential to the country's survival, wage rates, by the end of the war period, had roughly doubled, keeping just ahead of price rises; families with several supplemental earners found themselves for the first time with a surplus that could be spent on items other than essentials. Sales among the working classes of pianos – 'that coveted proof of respectability' – fur coats, gramophones and motor-bicycles boomed. Most important of all, women, and to a lesser extent juveniles, began, from the autumn of 1915, to earn good money in occupations opened to them by the departure of men to the front. The working classes were not alone in their affluence. Gilded upper-class life, reinforced by the advent of the war profiteer, continued in a giddy whirl of hedonism, apparently unmoved by the appalling slaughter across the Channel.

The type of entertainment for which there was highest demand, both from civilians with money in their pockets and soldiers with time on their hands, was that which provided speediest release from present reality. In pre-war days suburban and provincial music-halls had derived much of their support from the lower classes, though for the poor only very infrequent visits were possible. The theatre as a whole was very much a middle-class preserve and, true to the pattern already described, it suffered very severe disruption at the beginning of the war; for a time London theatres, a contemporary said, were 'desolate and dreary wastes.' But from the winter of 1914–1915 theatres entered upon a period of boom that outlasted the war. A visitor to Edinburgh in the summer of 1918 noted in his diary:

> Thursday, August 15th: Start for King's Theatre. Full up. On to Empire Theatre. Full up. On to some more pictures. Friday August 16th: . . . Theatre . . . succeeded in getting a seat at last. Seymour Hicks in 'Sleeping Partners'. Quite amusing.

Everywhere melodrama, sentimentality, or, more usually, scantily-dressed revues, often with elaborate patriotic trimmings, predominated.

For the future of the theatre there were two more serious developments. War-time casting difficulties and war-time inflation, together with the popular rejection of serious theatrical productions, hit many suburban and provincial theatres before they had any opportunity to profit by the boom. Another medium, well-adapted to prevailing appetites, standardized in cost, and unhampered by casting difficulties, the cinema, was ready to take over. There were over three thousand cinemas in pre-war Britain, but it was now that there came a first burst of conversions of theatres and music halls into cinemas. The West End theatres which were able to benefit from the inflated war-time demand soon fell under the acquisitive eyes of the property dealers. There followed a revolution in

British theatrical management, paralleled elsewhere in the economy by the sudden blossoming of large-scale banking and industrial concerns. Before the war an important position was still held by actor-managers, such as Norman Marshall, who ran their own theatres according to their own well-defined policies. During the war, as Mr Marshall remarked:

> theatres became just another asset on the list of assets held by business magnates, regarded as impersonally as the factories, the hotels, the chains of shops, the blocks of flats which also figured on the list. With the individual managers no longer in control, a frightful sameness descended upon the English theatre. The public was given what they wanted, as theatres were packed, but they were given no chance of proving whether they wanted anything else.

The picture, however, was not unrelievedly gloomy; although the majority undoubtedly wanted frivolity and spectacle, the emotional impact of war also elicited from the few in all social classes some signs of serious aesthetic appreciation. The plays of Ibsen, in their gloomy irony matching well the world tragedy of civilization in crisis, enjoyed a sudden popularity; and the Old Vic, drawing some at least of its audience from the proletarian environs of Waterloo Road, was packed out night after night for its Shakespearian productions.

The new and converted cinemas of the war period began to attract the patronage of the middle classes. This development was fostered by the new respectability the film derived through being used, after initial resistance from the War Office and Admiralty, for propagandist purposes. A significant turning point is the first showing on December 27th, 1915, of the pioneer British propaganda film, *Britain Prepared*, at the Empire Theatre, Leicester Square, once the focal point of the theatrical world in the Nineties. Before the war, as the chairman of the London branch of the Cinematograph Exhibitors' Association pointed out, 'the vast majority of picture house patrons were not in the habit of attending any other places of amusement': the picture house, he emphasized, was 'the poor man's theatre.' To meet the fears of the prudish, a Board of Film Censors had been established at the end of 1912, and pre-war cinemas employed specially trained supervisors to guard against the dangers implicit in an entertainment, freely attended by members of both sexes, that took place in the dark. In fact, the mass female invasion of the cinema audience, a by-product of women's new independence and earning power, came only in the middle years of the war – coinciding exactly with the withdrawal, on account of the labour shortage, of the moral supervisors. The new audience created a vogue for the society drama and, above all, for the star system.

Ninety per cent of the films shown in British cinemas on the outbreak of war were American. The British film industry was handicapped by technical backwardness and, at a time when films were made out of doors, by the British climate: the grip of Hollywood tightened as the demand for escapist entertainment mounted, and, simultaneously, scarce British resources were directed away from commercial film-making towards the requirements of war. Hollywood was only too well qualified to meet the demand for spectacular or sensual films, though there were many protests in Britain over films in which scenes of rape were only faded at the last instant. Magistrates and newspapers readily blamed the rise of juvenile delinquency, clearly a consequence of the upheavals of war, on the cinema. Yet intelligent critics recognized the intellectual and aesthetic potential of the film, and Chaplin and Griffith, in their different ways, were already demonstrating what could be done with the medium. The Chaplin films shown on the Western Front received an enthusiastic response from British troops, a response upon which could be built his subsequent massive popularity in Britain.

Ragtime and jazz had reached Britain shortly before the war. During the dancing craze which affected fevered society in the middle years of the war, they were used as the basis for such sophisticated and complicated new dances as the foxtrot. Because of the difficult nature of the steps, so a dancing master declared, couples began to spend entire evenings together rather than risk dancing with a clumsy outsider. A more potent reason, however, for flouting the older convention that one should never dance twice successively with the same partner was the shadow of the Western Front, constantly demanding the parting of sweethearts. Out of war-time hedonism, war-time darkness and dullness, war-time liquor restrictions, and the war-time presence of young officers on leave, there sprang up a much-discussed new growth, the night club, whose two main functions were the provision of liquor, sold, at fantastic prices, as 'ginger ale' or 'tea,' and of facilities for gambling. In its many denunciations of these clubs, the press printed harrowing stories of young officers ruined through being tempted into uttering cheques they could not honour.

Night-clubs were patronized only by a small segment of society; gambling affected all classes. From such evidence as there is, it seems clear that while drinking, and, in the long term, prostitution, declined during the war, gambling, as a leisure pursuit of the British people, increased in importance. The reasons are to be found partly in the enforced shortage of the alternative opiate, drink, but mainly in the strange war environment in which the greyness of immediate domestic existence was combined with the false excitement of living through one of history's turning points, and when the horror of war's reality was combined with a high level of ready spending money. The suspension of normal spectator sports only diverted, did not suppress, the need; in the immediate post-war years there came the poor man's racecourse, the greyhound track.

The war fostered unhealthy emotions and encouraged the growth of debased entertainment designed to satisfy them, but it also created what the musicologist, Ernest Newman, called a 'keener psychosis.' 'The temper of a selection of the people,' in the words of Sir Thomas Beecham, became 'graver, simpler, and more concentrated': 'the thoughtful intelligence,' the great conductor explained, 'craves and seeks these antidotes to the troubled conscience of which great music is perhaps the most potent.' Clearly the musical renaissance, which has been a significant feature of Britain's twentieth-century history, would have come even had there been no war; but equally there is no doubt that during the war audiences for serious classical music increased significantly in size. On the whole, pressures for the total banning of all German music were successfully resisted, but excess of patriotism did provide Beecham with the opportunity to play the music of unfashionable French, Russian, Italian, and, above all, British composers.

The visual arts were not at first so fortunate. Attendances at the principal art collections declined during 1914 and 1915. In 1916 the Government took the obscurantist decision to close them to the public, though strong protests ensured that the decision was never fully implemented. Later in the war there came the same sort of upsurge as had affected the world of music; so great were the crowds at the National Gallery that on some days the turnstiles had to be put out of commission. While the Asquith Government had proposed closing the art galleries, the Lloyd George Government, spurred on by C.F.G. Masterman and Arnold Bennett, who had the powerful support of Lords Beaverbrook and Rothermere, had the vision to commission a great cycle of war paintings, to be executed without hindrance or instruction by the best young painters then in uniform. The Government, in thus rising, in the words of the art critic, P.G. Konody, 'to art patronage on an unprecedented scale,' did immeasurable service to the future of British painting.

The war paintings, like British war poetry, showed that the community's creative workers had taken a decisive turn towards the aesthetic of modernism: the older techniques simply could not deal adequately with modern war. As Paul Nash put it in a letter to his wife, 'I am no longer an artist interested and curious, I am a messenger who will bring back word from the men who are fighting to those who want the war to go on for ever. Feeble, inarticulate will be my message, but it will have a bitter

truth, and may it burn their lousy souls.' The art and poetry of dis-
enchantment of the last months of the war led on to some of the greatest
creative work of the 1920s. But the despairing vision of the artist, the
disillusionment of the literary soldier, were not, of course, necessarily
representative of society as a whole, or even of all returning soldiers.

In fact, the two most relevant characteristics exhibited by society were,
first, low standards of literacy, yet, second, among a minority of working
men, an optimistic, rather than disenchanted, desire for self-improvement. The main staple of the working classes was the Sunday press, such
dailies as Northcliffe's *Mail* and Beaverbrook's *Express* being obviously
aimed at middle- and lower-middle-class readership. The shortage of hard
news caused by the censorship put a premium upon pictorial features,
and the steady trend in this direction during the war was exemplified by
the launching of the *Sunday Pictorial* in March 1915. To convey the
excitement of war – the official releases scarcely did this – there were
experiments in the use of banner headlines and cross headings. But most
newspapers continued to print advertisements on the front page.
Opportunity for self-improvement was fostered by the educational work
carried out in the army, while the drama of world events, according to a
Government Report on Adult Education, was stimulating the desire for
instruction on contemporary politics. Immediately after the war there was
a rapid expansion of working-men's institutes, extension centres (halved
in number during the war) and adult education classes, all providing for
what the *New Survey of London Life and Labour* called 'cultural pursuits.'

The upheavals of war reacted most directly upon social attitudes and
social *mores*. The famous 'War Babies' episode of 1915 proved to be a
gross exaggeration, for in that year there was actually a very low illegitimate birth rate and an extremely high marriage rate, 19.5 per thousand
inhabitants. But it was clear that the war was bringing an intensification
of emotional activity and responses. A sharp rise in the illegitimate birth
rate did take place in 1916 and subsequent years: in explanation of the
1916 figures, the Registrar General referred to 'the exceptional circumstances of the year, including the freedom from home restraints of large
numbers of young persons of both sexes.' He might have added that at a
time when life itself appeared so cheap, old standards, for many, also
seemed scarcely worth preserving. Before the war, the upper and middle
classes, in public at least, maintained the old standards, though, within
the family unit, contraception was already being practised. The lower
orders had never been so trammelled by these standards, but they did not
have easy access to contraceptives. What happened during the war was
that promiscuity spread up the social scale, and contraceptives, made
available in war for prophylactic purposes, spread down it.

In war the market for prostitution was good, some of its higher-class practitioners attaching themselves to the new night clubs which were displacing the luxurious brothels of Edwardian days. On the wider view, however, the social and economic changes associated with the war – the moral climate that accepted extra-marital relationships of an emotional rather than a commercial nature, and the improved economic circumstances of women of the lowest classes, in particular – brought a permanent diminution in the number of professional prostitutes in Britain (to around 3,000 in the case of London during the inter-war years).

In the early stages of the war chaperons disappeared: they shrank from the hazards of travel in war conditions; they had other work to do, canteening, knitting and so on; and hosts, in times of scarcity, were reluctant to cater for them. Men, too, were scarce. Young women, therefore, had to appear in public on their own feet, ordering meals in restaurants, smoking cigarettes, often travelling long distances to their various arduous patriotic tasks: they began to rely, to an extent that older contemporaries found appalling, upon the heavy use of cosmetics – in his diary Arnold Bennett noted the prevalence of 'painted women.' Their skirts at the same time grew shorter. Altogether, the changes in appearance were symbolic of a new-found pride and self-confidence among women, above all among those who before the war had been the ill-kempt industrial drudges of society. Men's wear also changed, it may be noted: the older badges of class, top hats, wing collars, dropped from sight; there was a common level of discreet shabbiness.

'From the trenches, the prisoner's camp, the hospital, and the home the question has been put in the stark brevity of mortal anguish: is there now a God?' So said a tract written in 1918. While the war lasted the churches were crowded; on Armistice day, Birmingham Cathedral, to choose one example, held three separate services, so strong was religious feeling. But the 'moral anguish' provoked by the hideous irony of war, and, more critically, the reaction against the blatant war-time jingoism of the churches soon brought a sharp acceleration in the decline (apparent before 1914) in church-going as a Sunday pastime. The working classes had never been great church-goers – now they were increasingly joined in non-attendance by their social superiors.

However powerful the attack on established canons, however real the bitterness between soldier and civilian, however wide the gulf separating the older generation from the younger, the fundamental point emerging from a study of the war experience is that in leisure pursuits British society was becoming increasingly homogeneous, both as between men and women and as between social classes. The technological basis of this was not immediately apparent while the war was in progress; but as radio valves and motor vehicles were developed for military purposes, so there was ultimately a stimulus to their use for civilian purposes; broadcasting and motor transport in the Twenties and Thirties were to draw society still more closely together. That apart, the greater wealth available to working men during the war gave them a taste for the amenities characteristic of a modern technological society. Admittedly, the upper-class high life of the 'gay Twenties,' so often seen as a reaction against the war, had its origins, too, in the frenetic activities of the war years; but even those whose lives were lived far outside this much-discussed social set could dance in the public ballrooms established in the aftermath of war.

*　　*　　*

Arthur Marwick (b. 1936) was appointed founding Professor of History at the Open University in 1969 and established the Sixties Research Group there. He has held visiting professorships at the State University of New York, Stanford University, l'Ecole des Hautes Etudes en Sciences Sociales in Paris, Rhodes College in Memphis and the University of Perugia. His publications include *The Sixties: Cultural Revolution in Britain, France, Italy, and the United States, c.1958 – c.1974* (1998), *A History of the Modern British Isles, 1914–1999: Circumstances, Events, Outcomes* (2000) and *The New Nature of History: Knowledge, Evidence, Language* (2001).

30

The Murder of David Riccio

ANTONIA FRASER

(April 1966)

This was the first historical essay by Antonia Fraser ever to be published. She was writing her biography of Mary Queen of Scots at the time.

On March 9th, 1566, Mary Queen of Scots, six months pregnant with the future James VI, witnessed the murder of her secretary David Riccio at the instigation of her husband Henry Lord Darnley and was then left to spend the night alone in the rooms still stained by Riccio's blood. For a parallel, one turns to Jacobean melodramas, such as Webster's *Duchess of Malfi*, rather than to episodes of actual history. Yet this explosion of feeling into action, violent and public though it was, had complicated and subterranean causes: and the chief actors were animated by many very different motives.

Queen Mary had married her cousin Henry Stewart, Lord Darnley, son of the Earl and Countess of Lennox, on July 29th, 1565, only eight months before the night of the murder. She had done so against the wishes of her cousin Elizabeth of England, and those of her half-brother James Stewart, Earl of Moray, who headed the party of the reformed religion in Scotland, and who resented the fact that Darnley, like Mary herself, was a Catholic. Mary's motives for making this contentious match were at least partly political. Darnley, being a grandson of Margaret Tudor, stood in the line of succession to the English throne; and the marriage thus helped to consolidate Mary's own claim. He was also in the line of succession to the Scottish throne and, in certain circumstances, could have been his wife's next heir to both thrones.

But, besides being strategically placed in the royal genealogical trees, Darnley, we are told, was 'the lustiest best-looking long lad' that ever the Queen did see. In Eworth's portrait painted two years before the marriage, his handsome face gazes blandly forth with the complacent and self-confident regard that had fascinated the twenty-two-year-old Queen during the first months of their acquaintance. Unfortunately, to royal blood and a personable appearance Darnley joined a weak pleasure-loving character, tortured by vanity – a combination that was to prove disastrous. At the time, in the first flush of love, Mary readily agreed that her husband should henceforth be known as King Henry, and promised that his signature should lie next to hers on every document with the result that bands and charters thereafter show the signatures MARIE R. and HENRY R., while the preambles refer to 'our sovereign lord and lady'. But Darnley, having been granted the shadow of power, soon began to covet the substance. In particular, he coveted the Crown Matrimonial, which would have made his power co-equal with that of his wife during her lifetime, and if she predeceased him would have ensured its continuance after her death.

The rebellion of the Protestant faction had been crushed in August; and, that autumn, with Moray and the other rebel lords safely in exile at Newcastle, Mary felt able to turn once more to the business of personal government. But Darnley's personal defects, which made it inconvenient, if not dangerous, to give him power, seemed to grow at the same pace as his demands. He alternately claimed increased privileges and idled his time away, either on the field of sport or in what John Knox termed 'Venus' Chamber'. His frequent absences made the double signature an administrative problem; and eventually business was so often delayed that an iron seal, bearing his signature, was cast. This seal was entrusted to the Queen's secretary, David Riccio.

Riccio had come to Scotland in 1561, in the train of the Ambassador of Savoy; and Mary Stuart's defenders have sometimes found it necessary to assert that he was an old man, as well as a remarkably ugly one. In fact, Riccio was about thirty-five when he died – that is to say, twelve years older than the Queen, but of an age with Moray and Arran, and, by the standards of the age, still in the prime of life. Of his ugliness, however, there appears to be no doubt: every contemporary record refers to his 'ill-favouredness' in some form or other; while even Mary's harsh critic Buchanan declared 'his face spoiled his ornaments and rich dress'.

Although he had originally come into her service when she needed a bass singer to make up a quartet with the valets of her household, it was Riccio's intelligence and political skill that attracted the Queen. He was appointed her French secretary, when the post fell vacant. In theory he was responsible only for her French correspondence; but the bulk and importance of that correspondence made his office one of unusual responsibility. Like Mary a Catholic, and like her an exile who remembered the distant enchantment of the world beyond the sea, Riccio was an agreeable companion for a sovereign who had never learned to love her Scottish subjects. Riccio was a loyal servant of the Crown because he owed all his advancement to the Queen he served. Here he was in marked contrast to the grasping Scottish nobles.

Mary's predilection for Riccio was understandable. It was none the less unwise. The very circumstances that had caused her to select him as her trusty agent were bound to provoke furious resentment among the nobles whom she thereby slighted. Her blend of innocence and indiscretion also provided valuable ammunition for those who wished to manufacture a scandal, although the stories they spread about the Queen and Riccio suggest a woman careless of appearances rather than a *grande amoureuse.* So far the most evil-tongued gossips had not managed to impugn her reputation; and her reaction to Châtelard's advances, we know, had been positively hysterical. Her feelings for Darnley seem to have been the romantic infatuation of an inexperienced woman for a handsome man. To satisfy the scandal-mongers, this same woman must simultaneously have embarked on a clandestine love-affair with her secretary, a man of unattractive appearance and low birth, and must, finally, have conceived an illegitimate child by him, only two months after her marriage.

It was not long before the Scottish nobility saw a serious threat to their position – both in the influence of Riccio and in the behaviour of the Queen herself. As the winter of 1565 drew on, Mary felt a growing sense of personal power, despite her pregnancy, her chronic gastric ailments and Darnley's mounting excesses. Now was the moment to summon a Parliament in March, at which Moray and his fellow rebels were to be attainted and more important perhaps, their property forfeited. Catholicism was no longer to be merely tolerated in Scotland; but positive efforts should be made to help on its cause. Furthermore, according to Sir James Melville, it was feared that the Queen planned to reclaim, as was her statutory right, property disposed of during her minority.

Darnley was the weapon with which the nobles decided to hack their way out of the hedge of thorns that was growing up round them. By December 25th, 1565, Randolph the English Ambassador at the Scottish Court, reported back to London: 'A while ago there was nothing but King and Queen; now the Queen's husband is the common word. He was wont in all writings to be first named; now he is placed in the second.' When Darnley was invested in February with the Order of St. Michael by an emissary from the French King, Mary turned a deaf ear to pleas that he should bear the royal arms on his shield, which would have indicated that she was about to grant him the Crown Matrimonial. Darnley retaliated by deliberately making the young men in the train of the French Ambassador drunk; and for the affront he blamed David Riccio.

Prominent among the disaffected nobility was the house of Douglas, including its head, the Earl of Morton, later Regent after Moray's death, George Douglas the illegitimate son of the 6th Earl of Angus, and the Lords Lindsay and Ruthven, both of whom had married Douglas wives. Not only were the Douglases kin to Darnley, whose mother had been a Douglas – so that any rise or fall in the King's status affected their own – but Morton may also have had an additional reason for detesting Riccio; if the rumour it be true, that the Queen was proposing to take away the Chancellorship, his prerogative, and to give it to Riccio, on the grounds the Morton was 'unlettered and unskilful'. Another noble who had no reason to love Riccio was Maitland of Lethington, since the Italian superseded him as the Queen's Secretary. On June 2nd, 1565, Randolph had written that Riccio 'now worketh all' and that Maitland had 'both leave and time enough to make court to his mistress.' And then Maitland, like Morton, was an adherent of the reformed religion, a member of the pro-English party who worked for the return of Moray.

On February 6th, Maitland wrote to Cecil in England that Mary was completely set against the pardon of Moray, and that, in view of this and her newly determined Catholic policy, there was nothing for it but to 'chop at the very root'. On February 13th, matters were at such a pitch that Randolph wrote to Leicester:

I know now for certain that this queen repenteth her marriage, that she hateth (Darnley) and all his kin . . . I know there are practices in hand contrived between father and son to come by the crown against her will. I know that if that take effect which is intended, David, with the consent of the King, shall have his throat cut within these ten days. Many things grievouser and worse than these are brought to my ears, yea of things intended against her own person. . . .

But the band signed by the conspirators made no mention of any sort of violence; and the compact struck between Darnley and the nobles – in which Moray joined from Newcastle – was that they should obtain the Crown Matrimonial for him, in return for his support for their religion and for the return and pardon of Moray. From the events that followed, it is clear that the murder of Riccio, although not specified, was precisely envisaged. Much less clear, in spite of Randolph's words to Leicester, is exactly what, if anything, was intended against the Queen herself.

The date of the murder was determined by the fact that Tuesday, March 12th, had been appointed for Moray's attainder before Parliament. Riccio and Mary seem to have had little inkling of their peril, and Riccio dismissed all warnings of the dangers of his position, including one from the astrologer Damiot, who told him to beware of 'The Bastard'. He replied confidently that he had seen to it that Moray would never set foot in Scotland again – ignoring the fact that a good many other Scottish nobles at that period also qualified for the description.

On the fateful evening of March 9th, the Queen was holding a small supper party in her own apartments. These rooms, in the north-west corner of the ancient palace of Holyrood, were few in number – a spacious presence chamber at the head of the main staircase, a large bedroom leading from the main staircase, a large bedroom leading from the presence chamber, with two smaller rooms lying off it, one a dressing-room, and one, in the far corner, not more than twelve feet square, which Mary used as a supper room. Perhaps the warmth of the small room in a cold age and a cold climate make up for what would now seem remarkably cramped quarters. One other feature of the royal apartments deserves note, because it was essential to the murderer's plan – a tiny circular staircase led into the Queen's bedroom, its door at the far end of the bedroom from the presence chamber.

Thus, the Queen's supper room was completely cut off from the outside world by a series of large outer rooms, except for a staircase that was intended only to connect husband and wife. The question immediately arises as to why the conspirators should have singled out the supper room as the scene of the assassination – a room in the very heart of the Queen's own chambers. Though it was easy to enter by surprise, to escape might well be difficult. Secondly, the murder would have to be carried out under the Queen's very eyes, with the possibility that she might be shocked and injured – unless, of course, these were exactly the effects that the conspirators intended to produce.

In his subsequent account of the crime, Lord Ruthven blamed Darnley for choosing the place, and asserted that the lords themselves had wished to take Riccio in his own rooms, or somewhere less public in the purlieus of Holyrood, but Darnley had been determined to avenge his honour in the presence of the Queen. By this time Ruthven was anxious to exonerate the lords and to put the blame on Darnley. His account, however, is scarcely convincing. Darnley was a man notoriously easy to persuade, as the conspirators themselves were to discover the day after the murder. The choice of Mary's private room for the crime suggests that the lords had some sinister intention.

The supper party that night was an agreeably intimate one, probably typical of many that had taken place during the winter and spring of the Queen's pregnancy. In candlelight and firelight the Queen, her half-brother and sister, Lady Argyll and Lord Robert Stewart, Arthur Erskine her equerry, and Riccio himself supped, with pages and servants attending. To their surprise, the king suddenly appeared, an unexpected figure; for Darnley was more given to roistering in the town than dancing attendance on his wife. But the unexpected guest was greeted with the conventional respect due to the Queen's husband. Not so the next apparition in the doorway – Patrick Lord Ruthven, who was widely suspected by his contemporaries of being a warlock or, in Knox's phrase, of 'using enchantment', at all events a man of a most unsavoury reputation. Mary knew, or thought she knew, that Ruthven was lying sick in a house close to Holyrood; and so astonished was she by his appearance, burning-eyed and deathly pale, wearing a steel cap, armour showing through his gown, that she first thought he must be delirious, pursued perhaps by the spectre of one of his victims.

Ill though Ruthven was – he died three months after the murder – his opening words left Mary in no doubt as to his intentions: 'Let it please your Majesty that yonder man David come forth of your privy-chamber where he hath been overlong.' At which Mary turned quickly and angrily to her husband, and asked if this was of his doing. Darnley gave a muttered embarrassed reply; and now Ruthven's followers had come pressing up behind him, up the narrow staircase and into the little room where the Queen was still holding Ruthven at bay with words. Then words gave place to blows; in the general confusion, tables and candles were overturned; and, had not Lady Argyll snatched up one light as it fell, only the light of the fire would have lit the scene. As it was, the chamber was filled with a mêlée of struggling men and women, some intent on attacking Riccio, who cowered for protection at the Queen's feet, others attempting to defend him. Riccio was finally dragged forth from the room, his fingers having been mercilessly wrenched from Mary's skirts, '*Giustizia, Giustizia!*' he cried, as he was hauled across the bedroom and presence chamber, to be done to death at the head of the main staircase. Whether the first blow was actually struck over Mary's shoulder, as she later stated in a letter to the Archbishop of Glasgow, her Ambassador in Paris, or with the others at the head of the stairs, it was dealt by George Douglas, Morton's illegitimate kinsman; and the astrologer's warning was thus fulfilled.

The disturbance now spread through Holyrood, as shouts of 'A Douglas, a Douglas' resounded from the main staircase. Here Morton's men, preparing to seize the palace, encountered Mary's butlers and scullions, who, ignorant of what was going on in the inner rooms, but aware that their Queen was in danger, rallied to her defence with spits and staves. All the conspirators were heavily armed; and, as Mary valiantly did her best to protect her servant, until her husband, at Ruthven's direction, held her down, pistols may well have been pointed at her.

Towards the end of his life, one of her pages, then living in Rome, stated that he had parried a blow aimed at her with a torch that he had been holding up to light the royal music. Mary herself certainly believed that Ker of Fawdonside had aimed his pistol at her, and that the intention of the conspirators had been to cause her death and the death of her unborn child.

Although her removal would have left Darnley *de facto* King, with a claim to be also sovereign *de jure*, it still seems doubtful if the conspirators had any very definite plan to kill the Queen; for, had any such plan been discussed in detail, it is difficult to understand why it was not carried out, when the conspirators had her at their mercy. Meanwhile the apartments presented an appalling scene; estimates of the number of wounds Riccio received vary between fifty-three and sixty. Outside, the sounds of conflict in the Palace had disturbed the people of Edinburgh; and the alarm bell of the city tolled. To quiet the citizens, Darnley went to the window, and reassured them with his familiar voice. But when Mary strained to make her own voice heard, Lindsay brutally threatened to 'cut her in collops' should she attempt another move. Now that Holyrood was in the hands of the Douglases, and Edinburgh passive, the power of Darnley and the lords seemed assured. The only hitch in their plans had been the escape of Bothwell and Huntley, lords known to be friendly with the Queen, who had jumped out of the windows of the Palace when they discovered what was afoot. As for Riccio's lacerated corpse, it was dragged down the winding stairs to be stripped of its possessions by a porter, a personage who might have come straight from a Shakespearian tragedy, since, as he did so, he moralised at length on the Italian's fate.

Mary was abandoned in a room that now contained only her husband and Ruthven, who felt himself too weak to proceed until, seated in the Queen's presence, he had drunk a draught of wine. A series of terrible exchanges took place between husband and wife, before Mary was left to spend the night alone, without company or medical attention. But the episode that had revealed Darnley in all his viciousness brought out Mary Stuart's finest qualities – her immense physical courage and endurance, her indomitable spirit, and her gift of thinking quickly and coolly in a moment of crisis. She did not collapse or indulge in self-pity. 'No more tears, I will now think on revenge', she is said to have exclaimed. Whether or not she spoke these words, the determination was unquestionably there.

At some point, she analysed her situation with sufficient clarity to see that Darnley was the chink in the conspirators' armour, just as he had been the chink in hers. Headed by Darnley, they might succeed in imprisoning her for life or killing her, since they had a ready made figurehead to hand. But, without Darnley, faced by a united King and Queen, they would be powerless. Thus, next morning, she was able to greet him with astonishing composure; and, during the course of that vital Sunday, she managed to wean him away from the conspirators. We shall never know what words she used: it is enough that they were effective.

That Monday morning, knowing that she had secured her husband's support, Mary met the lords with the utmost calm and dignity, and assured them that she was prepared to let past feuds rest in peace. When her brother Moray arrived, she flung herself into his arms in a flood of tears and, still unaware of his complicity, cried: 'Oh my brother, if you had been here, they had not used me thus'. But her emotion did not prevent her from planning a daring escape from the bounds of Holyrood that very night. At eight in the evening, she sent for Stewart of Traquair, captain of the Royal Guard, Erskine, her equerry, and Standen, one of her gentlemen, and appealed to them in the name of chivalry to help her, describing herself as not only a defenceless woman but the future mother of the race of Scottish Kings. Her appeal did not fall on deaf ears. Midnight found Mary and Darnley crawling down an underground passage that led through the charnel house of her ancestors, to keep a rendezvous by the old Abbey of Holyrood with these gallant gentlemen and their horses. They then set off on a desperate ride to Dunbar, Mary mounted on a crupper behind Erskine, the King riding alone, and Standen and Traquair in attendance. They reached Dunbar at daybreak. For a woman in Mary's condition the journey must have been gruelling. Yet even now her energies did not fail; and she is said to have sent immediately for fresh eggs; and herself overseen their preparation. In the days that followed, far from resting, she wrote letters, describing her plight and begging for help, to her relations across the Channel, and even to her cousin Elizabeth.

Help was indeed forthcoming – but from Scotland itself; within four days there were eight thousand men at Dunbar, summoned by Bothwell and Huntley since their own escape. Mary's fortunes appeared to have taken a dramatic turn for the better, not least because Darnley's fellow plotters, on hearing the news of his defection, had not dared to linger in Edinburgh but had fled in different directions from their sovereign's wrath. Mary, with a subdued Darnley at her side, was soon marching back to Edinburgh in triumph. The body of Riccio was recovered from the churchyard of the Canongate, where it had been interred without any religious ceremony, and reburied in the Chapel Royal at Holyrood, the only place in Scotland where it could receive Catholic rites of burial. It was not interred, however, in the royal vault, as was falsely asserted by Buchanan, who declared that the final proof of Mary's adultery with

Riccio was that she should have laid his body between that of her father and his first wife Queen Magdalene. Riccio was buried in the main body of the Chapel.

Morton, Lindsay, Ruthven and Ker of Fawdonside now fled to England, Maitland to Dunkeld, and Argyll to the West; and Mary was apparently more secure on the throne than ever. It is true that she was shown the proofs of Darnley's guilt – the conspirators naturally took care that she should see the bands he had signed – and was obliged, on March 21, to issue a humiliating proclamation of his innocence at the Market Cross of Edinburgh. But she had wisely pardoned the rebels of August in order to pursue the assassins of March; and, with Moray at her side, she was not bereft of counsellors.

Very far from forgiving Darnley, it is clear that Mary now detested him, and that her seeming forgiveness was a matter of expediency. Already on the return journey from Dunbar to Edinburgh, she was railing to Melville about his folly and ingratitude. In a scene of some bitterness after the birth of their son, according to the memoirs of Lord Herries, she burst out furiously: 'I have forgiven, but never will forget! What if Fawdonside's pistol had shot, what would have become of him and me, both? Or what estate would you have been? God only knew, but we may suspect!'

Side by side with Mary's hatred of Darnley grew her liking for Bothwell. Every contemporary account agrees that, from this moment, the Queen turned to Bothwell and began increasingly to lean on him – not yet with love but with a sense of gratitude. Was it not Bothwell who had resourcefully made his escape from Holyrood on the night of the murder? And was it not he who had helped gather the forces that had brought her back in triumph to Edinburgh? How different from the weak disloyal Darnley was this strong and loyal supporter! Darnley wandered around the countryside, a man of no account, while the power of Bothwell waxed.

By now Mary had witnessed the ruin of her short-lived Catholic policy, which the Protestant lords were obviously too powerful to tolerate. Moray, who had reached the nadir of his fortunes at Newcastle, found himself in a position of rapidly growing importance as head of the Protestant nobility – a position that he would strengthen still further as Mary's own fortunes declined. These long-term effects were not immediately apparent; but the rise of Bothwell and the decline of Darnley were soon obvious to all eyes. As Hume Godscroft wrote in the *Lives of the Douglases*: 'Thus were the dice changed . . . the Earl Bothwell was now become the Queen's favourite, all Men followed him, all Preferment came by him. His thoughts were High, his Ambition no less than to enjoy the Queen if she were free from a husband.' The stage was now set for a second murder, a bare eleven months after the murder of Riccio – at Kirk o'Field, where Darnley, like the Italian, was to meet a violent death.

*   *   *

Lady Antonia Fraser (b. 1932), biographer, broadcaster and member of the 'Literary Longfords', an aristocratic family that boasts eight writers in three generations, was educated at Lady Margaret Hall, Oxford. Among her most highly acclaimed historical works are her biographies *Mary, Queen of Scots* (1969), *Cromwell: Our Chief of Men* (1973) and *King Charles II* (1979). Her other books include *The Gunpowder Plot* (1996) and four which address the role of women in history: *The Weaker Vessel: Woman's Lot in Seventeenth Century England* (1984); *Boadicea's Chariot* (1988, later republished as *The Warrior Queens*); *The Six Wives of Henry VIII* (1992); and a forthcoming biography of Marie Antoinette. She has also produced a series of detective novels and two books of short stories featuring TV presenter Jemima Shore.

31

Houston Stewart Chamberlain: Prophet of Teutonism

Michael D. Biddiss

(January 1969)

It is easy to dismiss as absurd the racial theories that fed Nazism. But in the decades before Hitler, many intellectuals were drawn to such philosophies, among them Houston Stewart Chamberlain, an Englishman who became besotted by Wagner and married the Master's daughter. As Michael Biddiss showed, Chamberlain based an entire interpretation of history on theories which he and others found alluring but which were later to lead to Auschwitz.

In the history of European racism, the year 1855 is particularly notable for two events. In Paris there appeared the final two volumes of Count Arthur de Gobineau's *Essay on the Inequality of the Human Races*, the work that, more than any other, represents the culmination of the first half-century in the history of the great delusion of Aryan supremacy. In the same year, in humbler Southsea, there was born Houston Stewart Chamberlain who, nearly fifty years later, was to publish *The Foundations of the Nineteenth Century*, the study that not only summarized the work of racist philosophy in the intervening period, but also provided one of the most famous bases for its regrettable twentieth-century career.

Chamberlain, as the son of an English Rear-Admiral and the nephew of a Field-Marshal, seemed destined for entry into one of the services, but his continual ill-health and neurotic disposition dictated otherwise. Early studies at Cheltenham College were followed by instruction at the Lycée Impérial at Versailles where, after his mother's death, Chamberlain resided with his grandmother. In 1870, at the time of the Franco-Prussian War, he was sent to a private tutor, Otto Kuntze, who for four years instilled into his youthful pupil the virtues of Prussianism. In 1874 he became infatuated with a Prussian girl and fellow neurotic, Anna Horst, whom he married in 1878. The following year he began studies in Geneva upon natural history, chemistry, physics and medicine; but the formal pursuit of these was halted by a major nervous breakdown which he suffered in 1884.

By that time Chamberlain had, in any case, became even more attracted by subjects of directly aesthetic interest. In particular, he had been captivated by the Wagnerian conception of art and drama. In 1882, the year preceding the composer's death, Chamberlain visited Bayreuth and came away from his meeting with the Master duly impressed. Wagner, already in 1850 the author of an infamous polemical antisemitic diatribe *Judaism in Music*, had in his last years taken up the friendship of Count Gobineau and had used his own immense prestige and popularity to improve the Frenchman's then limited fame. Thus, when Chamberlain fell beneath the Wagnerian spell, Bayreuth was already the centre for the propagation of a version of Gobineau's doctrines of racial inequality.

During the late 1880's, while living in Dresden, Chamberlain became still more completely absorbed by the Wagner cult and his full acceptance into the charmed circle of Bayreuth can be dated from his first meeting in 1888 with the widowed Cosima Wagner who devoted herself, as well as the Festival Theatre and Wahnfried the family home, to the posthumous glorification of the Master. But the Bayreuth circle also devoted a share of its energy and much of its journal, the *Bayreuther Blätter*, to the posthumous adulation of Gobineau, who had died in 1882, and it was therefore scarcely surprising that in 1894 its members should have been prominent among those who founded the Gobineau Society in order to give further publicity to the idea of Aryan supremacy.

Chamberlain's first writings were obviously and directly the product of this atmosphere and of the will – no doubt fostered by Kuntze, Anna Horst and the Wagners – to be more German than the Germans. In 1892 he published both an essay on *Lohengrin* and a fuller study entitled *The Wagnerian Drama* which had, however, no immediate commercial success. Four years later, he produced a large biography of Wagner which was soon translated from German into a lavishly illustrated English edition. With these works already to his credit, Chamberlain was invited by his publisher, Bruckmann of Munich, to undertake a major study of nineteenth-century civilization. The author was at first reluctant; but, once having consented, he set to work and between April 1897 and October 1898, in a truly remarkable burst of physical and intellectual energy, he completed at Vienna two volumes, running to a total of more than a thousand pages in the eventual English translation.

This work, *The Foundations of the Nineteenth Century*, G.P. Gooch has called 'a glittering vision of mind and muscle, of large-scale organization, of intoxicating self-confidence, of metallic brilliancy, such as Europe has never seen'. It was intended merely as a preparatory study, covering mainly European history before 1800, and it was Chamberlain's desire, never fulfilled, that it should be followed by the more substantive account of the nineteenth century itself. Though it makes few and generally unsympathetic references to Gobineau, it can be interpreted fairly as in part an adaptation of racist historical philosophy to some of the new conditions that had arisen since the Frenchman's major work of the 1850s. The full development of 'anthroposociology', the attempted application of physical measurements to social investigation, and the cult of social Darwinism clearly postdated Gobineau's work. Chamberlain also felt the necessity for a more explicitly Christian gloss to racism. There was, moreover, from his point of view, a pressing need to replace the fundamentally pessimistic note of Gobineau – the failed and oppressed self-styled aristocrat, howling in vain against the inexorable march of nineteenth-century 'progress' – with a more positive and optimistic prognosis for the Aryan peoples, and especially for the modern Germans of whom the Count had been so critical. Only thus could racist theory be properly and usefully harnessed to the new juggernaut of continental and inter-continental Pan-Germanic imperialism.

When the two volumes first appeared in 1899, Chamberlain stated explicitly that they were written not for professional historians but for the educated general reader. Following yet again in the steps of Gobineau, he made no apologies for adopting 'dilettantism' as a historical method. Thus he confidently plundered works, not on history alone, but also on ethnology, anthropology, psychology, natural science, art and philosophy. From his vast collection of sources he endeavoured to substantiate two basic racist arguments: first, that the races of man are not merely different from one another, but are also arranged according to a hierarchy of talent and value, wherein the Aryan peoples are supreme; secondly, that the interplay of these unequal races is the fundamental key for the explanation of social and political phenomena in all their complexity.

He suggested that there were five fundamental influences upon nineteenth-century civilization which he enumerated as follows: the art, literature and philosophy of Greece; the law and state-craft of Rome; the world-redeeming revelation of Christ; the alien and destructive influence of the Jews; and the regenerative power of *der Germane*, the hero of the Aryan-Teutonic races. These last, which are at first said to include the Celts and Slavs, become in Chamberlain's work increasingly equated almost exclusively with their most illustrious branch, the Germans. And it is with the destiny of these above all others that he is concerned as the prophet of Teutonism.

Chamberlain regarded the birth of Christ as the most significant single event in world-history. With his appearance the legacy of Greece and Rome began to be changed into a form upon which the Teutons could draw. Because Chamberlain himself wished to endow his book with such a strongly Christian theme, not surprisingly he chose to contest the Jewishness of Christ. Using, for instance, Christ's alleged inability to pronounce the Aramaic gutturals, which the Jews so easily managed, he argued that there was no positive evidence for his Jewish ancestry and that, on the contrary, there was every reason to suppose that a Galilean would have some element at least of Aryan blood. Chamberlain was perhaps less than fully satisfied with his own convoluted argument; and, as a second line of defence, he propounded the view that, whatever Christ's origin, his teaching and attitudes were certainly fully represent- ative of the Aryan spirit. The Christ depicted in *The Foundations* is proud, aggressive and self-indulgent – perhaps more like a Prussian Junker than the paragon of humility found in more conventional descriptions. In this new form, he becomes the God of the young and vigorous Indo- Europeans, among whom the Teutons are the most suited to hearing and answering his call. It is suggested that Christ had chosen to live in the midst of the Jews, for the very reason that it was there that his particular qualities would stand out in contradistinction to those about him. To Chamberlain the crucifixion was the complete justification for this argument.

The history of civilization from the time of Christ until 1800, which provides the subject-matter for most of the work, is essentially the tale of the struggle between Teuton and Jew over the heritage of the ancient world, over the survival or destruction of Christianity and, not least, over the very existence of the two races. A number of earlier racists, though they had vividly depicted the qualities and achievements of their master- race, had failed to appreciate the dramatic necessity of matching it with a particular countervailing racial enemy against whom hate could be mobilized. Chamberlain, however, was aware of this need and, though he points also to what he calls the 'Chaos of Peoples' of greatly mixed blood, his thesis centres upon the explicit polarization of Teuton and Jew – rivals who, strengthened by their comparative purity, struggle to decide the issues of racial redemption and damnation. We cannot but be reminded of the more ancient doctrine of the Manichees, who maintained that all the joy and sorrow of the universe flowed from two basic and irreducible principles of Good and Evil locked in eternal combat. In a similar sense,

Chamberlain presented his readers with a more secularized version of the Christian eschatological myth of Michael and Satan.

By the time that Chamberlain wrote, antisemitism was already a political force of some consequence, particularly in German-speaking Europe; and it was perhaps understandable that he should devote the longest chapter in his work to describing the destructive influence of the Jews. Although, with the forensic skill of an orator, he pleads against crude antisemitism and the invention of general scapegoats, and though he talks occasionally of the 'completely humanized Jew', the dominant tone of his reflections is bitter. He writes this, for instance: 'Materialism in philosophy . . . the limitation of imagination, the forbidding of freedom of thought, deep-rooted intolerance towards other religions, red-hot fanaticism – these are things that we must expect to meet everywhere to a greater or less extent where Semitic blood or Semitic ideas have gained a footing.'

It is these evils that the Teutons are pledged to combat. His depiction of the race conforms to the standard Aryan typology that had been conjured up time and again in the nineteenth century: blond long-heads, combining idealism and practicality, lovers of loyalty and freedom, but of honour above all else. Until the end of the twelfth century, they had been fully engaged in fighting for the very survival of a rejuvenated Christian culture. Only since that time, in 'The Rise of a New World', have they been able to give more positive indications of their regenerative power in the fields of science, industry, economics, politics, religion, philosophy and art.

Chamberlain naturally regarded the Protestant Reformation as a laudable achievement, a decisive political act that restored the freedom of the Teutonic nations. Accompanying his text with a line-drawing of the supposedly typical Germanic features of Martin Luther, Chamberlain strove to envisage the great reformer at one with his heroic ancestors: 'One can picture to oneself this man fifteen hundred years ago, on horseback, swinging his battle-axe to protect his beloved northern home, and then again at his own fireside with his children crowding round him, or at the banquet of the men, draining the horn of mead to the last drop and singing heroic songs in praise of his ancestors.' Yet it is not only the Reformation, but also the Renaissance, that Chamberlain desires to portray as an efflorescence of Teutonic genius. Thus, by the same intuitive method, the achievements of such men as Leonardo and Michaelangelo are brought within the fold of the great race. Even Dante, who could scarcely look less like Luther, is included with the devastating argument that it is in the very contrasts of their particular features that their intimate racial relationship is revealed.

The account of recent centuries is one of progress – yet of progress achieved in the face of the unrelenting Semitic enmity which must be actively combated. Here Chamberlain, unlike Gobineau, offers the possibility of meaningful political action against a known enemy and thus provides not merely a racial diagnosis of the remaining ills of civilization but also an actively racist cure. There are in *The Foundations* marked messianic and dynamic elements, urging the Teutons to greater efforts. Evading the contentious issue of whether there had ever been a pure Aryan race in the distant past, he emphasized that the really important point was its creation for the future: 'Though it be proved that there never was an Aryan race in the past, yet we desire that in the future there be one. That is the decisive stand for men of action.' For the achievement of this desirable racial creation it was necessary that one should begin with a nation composed of ethnic elements that had in the past suffered only limited blood-mixture and that subsequently the strain should be improved by rigid programmes of inbreeding and artificial selection. This emphasis upon future fulfilment is that which Hitler himself was to adopt in the later stages of the evolution of Nazi race-doctrine, when the Führer stressed that the Germans were not *yet* properly a race and that they could only become one by devoting themselves totally to his messianic programme of racial redemption.

In his methods Chamberlain is also a notable forerunner of the Nazi pseudo-philosophers. They share an oscillation between the pole of intricate 'scientific' justification of racial tenets and that of reliance upon intuition and subjectivism. Chamberlain includes paragraph upon paragraph of specious pleas for objectivity, impartiality and scientific exactitude. Yet, as we have seen exemplified in his treatment of the Aryan past and of the racial characters of such figures as Christ and Dante, he does not hesitate to indulge in the play of intuition whenever facts fail. *The Foundations* is concerned above all with Race – which may uplift or condemn man, which dominates his emotions and his subconscious and which is here the mould of his existence. Yet Chamberlain's concept of Race is nowhere clearly defined, and the reader might be forgiven for doubting whether, in his work, it has much to do with biology or heredity at all. The allegedly fundamental link between physical structure and mental characteristics is maintained in the case of a Luther – but it seems that a Christ could be possessed of an Aryan vision even if his racial origins were quite different.

When facts refuse to yield to his racist illusions, Chamberlain is capable of evading the difficulty with such astonishing remarks as this: 'Whoever behaves as a Teuton is a Teuton whatever his racial origin.' Conversely, concerning the anti-race he can argue: 'One does not need to have the authentic Hittite nose to be a Jew; the term Jew rather denotes a special way of thinking and feeling. A man can very soon become a Jew without being an Israelite; often he needs only to have frequent intercourse with Jews, to read Jewish newspapers, to accustom himself to Jewish philosophy, literature and art.' It is this kind of double-talk that allows the antisemite to stigmatize all enemies, regardless of ancestry, as 'inner Jews', and encourages a nation to accept the sort of declaration best epitomized in Hermann Goering's remark, 'I determine who is a Jew.' In its sheer immunity from empirical examination and refutation, and in its reliance upon the subjective romanticist vision, such an attitude to history and society reminds us forcefully also of Hitler's declaration that his doctrines and actions were developed 'with the security of the sleep-walker'.

Chamberlain did of necessity fall into many of the other errors of race-thinking. His monism reduced the complexity of society and history to a single order of causation. Like Gobineau before, and Hitler afterwards, he claimed that all the greatest triumphs of civilization and culture were the product of Race – and of a single race, at that. By race everything was explained – and therefore, in reality, nothing. Chamberlain's alleged proofs often depended upon tautology and circular argument, though through his persuasive style and by sheer force of repetition he was capable of enchanting superficial readers with their plausibility. Like many commentators of his time, and encouraged especially by his own early studies in natural history, he was addicted to the fashion of picturing society as an organism. Eventually he came to regard as real the mere metaphors of growth and disease that he applied to it. The chaos of his approach can be best summarized by his own unconsciously self-condemnatory assertion that his conclusions resulted from 'intuition born of ceaseless observation'.

The whole tendency of his arguments went contrary to any meaningful idea of a common humanity equal in rights and dignity, and worked against such associated political ideas as liberalism and democracy. Chamberlain wrote: 'The notion of "humanity" is nothing more than a linguistic makeshift, a *collectivum*, by which the characteristic feature of man, his personality, is blurred, and the guiding thread of history – the different individualities of peoples and nations – is rendered indivisible. I admit that the notion humanity can acquire a positive purport, but only on condition that the concrete facts of the separated race-individualities are taken as the foundation on which to build.' Thus the emphasis throughout was upon the racial divisions among men, and upon the categorical imperative of war and struggle for racial survival. Intention-ally or otherwise, it was a tract that perfectly fitted its times. The nations of Europe, aggravated by rivalries upon their own continent and in regard to their new colonies, were moving towards that Great War which Chamberlain not only predicted but welcomed as a vital stage in the fulfilment of the Teutonic destiny of world-domination.

Chamberlain's remarkable synthesis so ably epitomized the aspirations of German racism at the turn of the century that, unlike Gobineau fifty years before, he saw his *magnum opus* credited with immediate success. His study quickly won him the friendship of the Kaiser, who declared, 'It was God who sent your book to the German people.' Wilhelm not only treated the royal family to readings from the prophet, but also arranged for the circulation of his inspired writings to be subsidized. A popularly-priced edition appeared in 1906; and by 1914 over 100,000 copies of the work had been sold. In 1911 an English translation was issued with what now reads as a tragi-comic introduction by Lord Redesdale. Meanwhile Chamberlain, having divorced Anna Horst, had married Wagner's daughter Eva in 1908, and had come to settle in Bayreuth – 'the home of my soul'. There he continued with his philosophical investigations; and, now recognized as something of an oracle, he produced in due course works on Goethe (1912) and Kant (1915), as well as an intellectual autobiography *The Life-History of My Thinking* (1919).

With the outbreak of the Great War, Chamberlain turned his polemical talents to promoting the German war-effort and, in particular, to deriding his native England. His war-essays were soon translated and published in London under a title, *The Ravings of a Renegade*, which indicates that someone appreciated that their exaggerations and stupidities were self-condemnatory, and that they were sufficiently preposterous to discredit without much further comment the Germans who purveyed them. With regard to England, Chamberlain attacked her Parliamentary system and her stupidity in allowing herself to become the tool of the Jews. As for Germany, he stressed her love of peace, declared that she possessed a higher conception of the meaning of freedom, and descanted upon the allegedly irrefutable superiority of the German language.

A sample passage, on Sir Edward Grey, epitomizing the tone and content of these essays, runs: 'For years gone by he has presided at peace conferences, so that the intended war should by no means fail to be brought about. For years he has sought "rapprochement" to Germany, so that the honest German statesmen and diplomatists should not perceive the firm intention of the war of annihilation. In the last moment the German Emperor nearly warded off the danger of the war. Grey, the canting apostle of peace, finds means to shuffle the cards in such a manner that it is impossible.' Though treated contemptuously in England, such passages were no doubt better appreciated by those who read them in the special German 'Trench Edition'. For this work and for his participation in the War Aims Movement – especially upon the editorial board of its monthly *The Renewal of Germany* – Chamberlain was in 1915 awarded the Iron Cross, with the white ribbon of the non-combatant. In April 1916 he took the final, and by now natural, step of becoming a German citizen.

Even after the German defeat, Chamberlain continued his correspondence with the Kaiser in exile at Doorn. But, though he had been a prophet of the Wilhelmian age that was past, he could also serve as an oracle of the Nazi era that was beginning to dawn. In 1923, immediately after their first meeting, Chamberlain wrote to Hitler: 'That in the hour of her deepest need Germany gives birth to a Hitler proves her vitality.' While the Führer languished in Landsberg prison composing *Mein Kampf*, Chamberlain wrote a lengthy article in his praise; and he became one of the earliest members of the Nazi Party. Its official organ, the *Völkischer Beobachter*, returned the praises when Chamberlain, now ailing and partially paralysed, reached his seventieth birthday in January 1925. In September it referred to *The Foundations* as 'the Gospel of the Volkish movement'; and during the next month Hitler, himself an admirer of Wagner, came to a party meeting in Bayreuth to pay public homage to Chamberlain.

Though *Mein Kampf* had given Chamberlain but passing mention and though it is unlikely that anyone of Hitler's temperament would have read the renegade Englishman's works in detail, he was evidently, during that most formative period in the evolution of Nazi racial doctrine, one of the major influences on such writers as Alfred Rosenberg, the chief tame philosopher of the party.

In January 1927, when Chamberlain died without issue, Hitler was the sole public figure to attend his funeral. In that year Rosenberg produced a volume on Chamberlain, sub-titled *The Pioneer and Founder of a German Future*. Yet others saw him purely as a figure of the past. For instance, *The Times* in its obituary commented thus of *The Foundations*: 'Its vogue was indeed one of the measures of the demoralization of German intelligence by the religion of *Macht*.' Looking at the Weimar Republic in that year, the writer was no doubt wishfully thinking that his sentence could remain a judgment merely upon what had been. The *Völkischer Beobachter* was more perceptive in looking to the future, for its obituary referred to Chamberlain as 'one of the great blacksmiths whose weapons have not yet found in our day their fullest use'. The years immediately following did indeed bear out this self-fulfilling prophecy, as the influence of Chamberlain and of his work upon the religion of Power and its cult of Race came to enjoy its greatest and most terrible triumph.

*   *   *

Michael Biddiss was a Fellow of Downing College, Cambridge from 1966 to 1973 and has been Professor of History at the University of Reading since 1979. Biddiss' books include *Father of Racist Ideology: The Social and Political Thought of Count Gobineau* (1970), *Images of Race* (ed, 1979); *Thatcherism: Personality and Politics* (co-ed, 1987) and *The Nuremberg Trial and the Third Reich* (1992). In 2001 he was working on a co-authored study of the European nation-state in the nineteenth and the twentieth centuries. His work for the Historical Association (of which he was President between 1991 and 1994) has aimed – very much in the spirit of *History Today* itself – to promote the widest possible public understanding of the past.

32

Offenbach

Joanna Richardson

(May 1969)

Joanna Richardson wrote many popular articles for History Today *on the great artistic and cultural figures of nineteenth century France.*

On June 20th, 1819, a son was born to the wife of Isaac Juda Eberst, a cantor at the synagogue in Cologne. Eberst was a native of the town of Offenbach-am-Main, and he was generally known as Der Offenbacher, the man from Offenbach. His son was to make the name his own, and to make it celebrated ever after. Even when he was a child, Jacques Offenbach showed exceptional skill on the cello; but there was already strong anti-semitism in what would one day be Germany, and Eberst felt that only in Paris would his son be given his chance. In 1833, when the boy was fourteen, he boldly took him to Paris. Cherubini, the director of the Conservatoire, recognized him as a prodigy, and accepted him as a pupil.

Young Offenbach spent only a year at the Conservatoire, before he embarked on his career; he was bitterly poor, but he believed in his abilities, and he showed an indomitable love of work. He established himself as a virtuoso on the cello, and played in various theatre orchestras – an experience he found intensely frustrating. He also imposed himself on his public by force of personality; his hawk-like nose, his flowing hair, his remarkable thinness, made him a figure not to be forgotten. When he played his cello, he seemed to fuse with the instrument, and he played like one possessed. There was a wild glitter in his glance which gave rise to the legend that he had the evil eye.

It was this formidable, gifted young man who fell in love with a girl by the name of Herminie d'Alcain. Her mother insisted that Offenbach should prove himself by earning acclaim in London as well as in Paris. In the summer of 1844, Offenbach went to London, where he played triumphantly before Queen Victoria and a constellation of royalty. On August 14th, when he had embraced Catholicism, he duly married Herminie d'Alcain, and the marriage seems to have been ideally happy.

It is sometimes said that Offenbach's triumph lasted exactly as long as the Second Empire. It was, in fact, in 1850, when Louis-Napoleon was President of the French Republic, that Arsène Houssaye, the director of the Théâtre-Français, asked Offenbach to conduct the orchestra. He offered him the modest salary of 6,000 francs a year. It was in Houssaye's office that Offenbach met Alfred de Musset, and, at his request, set his *Chanson de Fortunio* to music. But if the first theatre of France gave Offenbach a certain security, it did not give him what he most wanted: the chance to write his own music for the stage. Not until 1855 did he have his opportunity. It was the year of the International Exhibition in Paris; and, just before the Exhibition opened, someone mentioned to him that a tiny theatre was vacant, near the Palais de l'Industrie. It was sure to be well attended by the crowds of visitors, especially on a rainy day. Offenbach immediately applied for the licence of the little wooden building, hidden among the trees on the Champs-Élysées. The opening of the Bouffes Parisiens, as the tiny theatre was now called, was announced for July 5th.

There was little time to arrange a programme, and Offenbach was forced to turn to an unknown young man of twenty-two for his libretti. But luck was with him: the young man happened to be Ludovic Halévy, whose words matched Offenbach's music to perfection. The theatre opened with *Les Deux Aveugles*, a sketch about two supposedly blind beggars; it was so successful that, when Mme. Offenbach came to see it, she could only find a seat on the stairs. As if this was not enough good fortune, Offenbach discovered his principal interpreter. In the summer of 1855, a young girl arrived in Paris to seek her fortune; she was Hortense Schneider, the daughter of a German master-tailor who had married a French wife and settled in Bordeaux. At the age of three, Hortense had been singing; at the age of twelve she had threatened to commit suicide unless she was allowed to go on the stage. She had finally had her own way, taken singing lessons, and joined a provincial troupe. Now, at the age of twenty-two, she arrived in Paris, and she was advised to see Offenbach, who engaged her at once.

She made her début in a sentimental piece, *Le Violoneux*; she was acclaimed in *Le Figaro* for her grace and polish, and Offenbach's music was highly praised for its wit and feeling. But though Offenbach's operettas played to full houses, his theatre did not prosper, because he was a bad businessman. He had lavish tastes, and it never occurred to him to economize, or to save for the future. It was soon clear that only a resounding triumph would save him, and in 1858 he set all his hopes on the new operetta, *Orphée aux Enfers*, which he was composing. Such were his straits that he even worked at his operetta in the hotel bedrooms where he had to stay to escape his creditors.

The first performance of *Orphée aux Enfers* took place on October 21st, 1858. It was not the success that he needed; but a few weeks later Jules Janin, the Jupiter of criticism, condemned it roundly in the *Journal des Débats* as a profanation of 'holy and glorious antiquity.' Adverse criticism – as so often happens – proved to be the making of the work. All Paris became convinced that mighty issues were at stake, and every self-respecting Parisian felt obliged to see *Orphée aux Enfers* and to judge for himself. After about the eightieth performance, the crowds flocked to it in an endless stream.

Offenbach's life was full of unexpected incidents, and *Orphée* brought him one of the strangest episodes of all. One of the principal performers, wrote the Hon. Denis Bingham, in his *Recollections of Paris*,

> was an actor called Bache, who, off stage, had more the appearance of a Methodist parson than a comedian. Now when *Orphée aux Enfers* was in full swing, and sending away crowds every night, poor Bache became immersed in a sea of trouble. He was summarily arrested, tried, condemned, and packed off to Sainte-Pélagie, to be there incarcerated for the space of one month. The manager of the *Bouffes* was in despair . . . You might as well have attempted to play *Orphée aux Enfers* without Bache as *Hamlet* without the Prince of Denmark. In his despair, the manager of the Bouffes appealed to the Duc de Morny – why should many suffer for the fault of one? The Duc, with his usual tact and good-nature, soon arranged matters to the satisfaction of all parties. It was settled that Bache, while continuing to be a prisoner, should be taken to the Bouffes every evening, under good escort, to play his part, and, the performance over, be reintegrated in his cell.

Thanks to Janin and the Duc de Morny, half-brother of Napoleon III and President of the Corps Législatif – and, of course, to his own musical brilliance – Offenbach was saved; he enjoyed the glory of the man who gives a whole generation what it needs. As a Parisian critic wrote: 'When everyone finds what they want in a work, the general public and the connoisseurs, there is no longer any doubt of its value. Jacques Offenbach is modern. His music is *daemonic*, like the century we live in – the century which rushes on, full steam ahead.' The music of *Orphée aux Enfers* set all Paris dancing, from the Tuileries to the smallest suburban taverns. After the 228th performance, the players were so exhausted that the operetta had to be taken off. In 1860, it was staged again at a gala evening at the Théâtre des Italiens. The Emperor had consented to be present on condition that it was on the programme.

Offenbach had found his first librettist in Ludovic Halévy, and in 1860 Halévy happened to come across an old school-friend, Henry Meilhac, who was a boulevardier with an eye for situations and a limitless ability to turn them into plays. From now on, he and Halévy were inseparable collaborators.

The profits from *Orphée* had enabled Offenbach to build himself a summer house at Étretat, which was then in fashion. The Villa d'Orphée, as it was called, became a meeting-place for all his friends. The operetta also brought him official recognition of all kinds. In 1860 he became a naturalized Frenchman and in the following year he was awarded the Legion of Honour. Yet Offenbach was far from content. He wanted to write an even more successful operetta than *Orphée*. Halévy suggested writing about Greek mythology again, this time in collaboration with Meilhac, and the three of them agreed on the subject of Helen of Troy. Hortense Schneider was engaged to play Hélène, and the first night of *La Belle Hélène* took place at the Théâtre des Variétés on December 17th, 1864.

In *La Belle Hélène* Offenbach once again held up the mirror to the Second Empire. Indeed, he showed it up so pitilessly that he made its early end look inevitable. *Orphée* had contained no hint of the future; but the revels in *La Belle Hélène* are accompanied by a foreboding of doom. Once again Offenbach caught the mood of the moment. *La Belle Hélène* became the rage. In 1865 the whole of France was singing, with Helen of Troy:

> *Dis-moi, Vénus, quel plaisir trouves-tu*
> *A faire ainsi cascader, cascader la vertu?*

On February 6th, 1866 came the first performance of *Barbe-Bleue*, in which Hortense Schneider delighted the audience as a peasant girl. On October 31st came the première of *La Vie Parisienne*. 'We have sold the score for 10,000 francs,' Halévy reported in his diary, 'we have sold the libretto for 1,500 francs, the takings are more than 4,000 francs an evening, and the theatre is booked up for the next ten or twelve nights. It will probably be our longest run; and many people think that the theatre will keep it on all the winter.' As one dramatic critic wrote: 'Offenbach's music is known throughout the world; and even the cannibals, when they come to dessert, are probably singing *Tout tourne*, from *La Vie Parisienne*.'

Offenbach gave the age what it wanted. He understood its feverish tempo, its reckless love of pleasure, its brilliance and its immorality. He satirized the peacock Court of Napoleon III, the vulgar love of money that was typical of the Second Empire. He was perfectly in tune with Second-Empire Paris, and, so long as the Empire lasted, his triumph was assured.

Sometimes, it must be admitted, his work received unorthodox publicity. Early in 1867, Cora Pearl, the celebrated courtesan, appeared at the Bouffes as Cupid in *Orphée aux Enfers*. The *Daily Telegraph* correspondent recorded the occasion:

> The scene at the *Bouffes* – Offenbach's temple – was peculiar, striking, 'a caution.' The stalls filled like magic, the boxes were as crowded as first-class carriages on the Great Northern of France, and the pit was a sea of heads, belonging to those, too, who do not usually 'go down to the pit.' It was 'How goes it, Prince?' 'How is this dear little Duc tonight?' . . . and so on. Then there were Duchesses and diamonds by the dozens. I am certain of the diamonds. All the *gandins* were there, nobody was left at any club; private society was a desert. A great run seems probable for the new cast of *Orphée aux Enfers*.'

But Cora Pearl, whatever her renown as a *grande cocotte*, was an indifferent actress; she appeared a mere three times on stage.

Whatever the failure of Cora Pearl, the year brought Offenbach yet another triumph. On April 1st, 1867, in the midst of a political crisis over Luxemburg, Napoleon III opened the new International Exhibition in Paris. Most of the sovereigns of Europe, their heirs and ministers, would come to visit it. On April 12th, the curtain rose at the Variétés on the first act of *La Grande-Duchesse de Gérolstein*. Halévy predicted that it would be 'the longest and the most resounding of our successes. For this is where luck comes in, and politics come to our aid, and M. de Bismarck is working to double our takings. This time we are laughing at war, and war is at our gates, and the Luxemburg crisis comes just in time to give the spice of topically to our play.' *La Grande-Duchess de Gérolstein*, as an English observer pointed out, 'was also a satire on the petty German states which Prussia had been annexing or mediatizing since her victory over Austria at Sadowa. There is a story that Bismarck, who was in Paris for the Exhibition, remarked to a high French personage: "We are getting rid of the Gerolsteins, there will soon be none left. I am much indebted to your Parisian artistes for showing the world how ridiculous they were." I have always understood,' continued the English memoir-writer, 'that the book, by Meilhac and Halévy, was Offenbach's own idea. He used to tell amusing stories about life in petty German duchies and principalities; how, for instance, railway trains would suddenly stop in the open country, and how the engine-driver, on being asked the reason for this unexpected break in the journey, would reply complacently: "I am waiting for the washing of His Serene Highness the Grand Duke" – at the same time pointing to a portly, perspiring, basket-laden female who was trying to hurry across some ploughed fields.'

Once again, Offenbach reflected the mood and interests of Second-Empire Paris, and, night after night, Hortense Schneider played la Grande-Duchesse de Gérolstein 'to an audience of crowned heads, princelings, and tourists from all parts of the world. La Schneider was credited with having fascinated all the potentates who visited Paris during the Exhibition, from the Tsar downwards. Her most conspicuous admirer, however, was the Viceroy of Egypt (Ismail Pasha), who during the half-dozen weeks he spent in Paris patronized the Variétés' performances almost forty times.' The Prince of Wales, the future Edward VII, went home with a pocketful of photographs of la Grande-Duchesse.

After *La Grande-Duchesse de Gérolstein*, the form and content of Offenbach's operattas changed. He started dropping contemporary satire, and tried to approach the comic opera form. In *La Princesse de Trébizonde*, produced at Baden in 1869, he plunged into a world of fantasy. In 1870, the world of Offenbach really ended. The Franco-Prussian War broke out, France was soon defeated, and the Second Empire fell. If France had accepted Offenbach as one of her sons, it was clear that all his own sympathies were with France: 'Alas!' he wrote, 'what terrible people these Prussians are, and what despair I felt at the thought that I myself was born on the Rhine! Alas! my poor France, how warmly do I thank her for accepting me among her children!'

After the War, he was more active than he had ever been. His friend, the journalist Henri de Villemessant, recorded: 'Offenbach's activity is prodigious. Few copyists have written more than this man, who has done nothing but compose for twenty years. Even his gout has never been able to stop him.' Offenbach was a dauntless worker, and a ruthless perfectionist; he never allowed himself a moment's rest. Those who happened to look through his carriage window as he drove from theatre to theatre would see him, wrapped in his fur coat, bending over a specially constructed desk, writing away incessantly.

From 1872 to 1876 he directed the Théâtre de la Gaiété. But the venture was a financial failure, and in 1876 he made a tour of the United States. As his ship drew into New York harbour, a boat approached with musicians on board, playing selections from his operettas. When he reached his hotel in Fifth Avenue, there was an even more spectacular welcome. 'Over the balcony of the hotel, in huge letters, were the words "WELCOME OFFENBACH!" An orchestra of some sixty musicians,' he remembered, 'gave me a serenade. They played *Orphée* and *La Grande-Duchesse.* I don't dare tell you about the clapping and the cries of "Long live Offenbach!" I was obliged to appear on the balcony, and shout a formidable "Thank you, sir!"'

On July 8th he sailed for home; but he was greatly changed. Henceforward he was haunted by a thought that had never troubled him before: the thought of his own inevitable death. Financial worries compelled him to continue producing operettas, but he longed to write an opera. Suddenly he remembered *Les Contes Fantastiqe d'Hoffmann.* It had been produced as a play at the Odéon in 1851. Offenbach now knew that it belonged to him, and to him alone. He discovered that he shared the fate of Hoffmann: indeed, that he was Hoffmann's double. Like Hoffmann, who had failed to conquer any of his three loves, he had never attained the object of his love, grand opera. Now he put his whole being into the music. In a race against time – for his health was failing – he wrote, re-wrote, and again re-wrote the music of *Les Contes d'Hoffmann,* as if he had been conscious that the opera would be the apotheosis of his career. He did not live to hear the première. On the afternoon of October 4th, 1880, he attended a reading for the Variétés. 'In the evening, on returning home, he felt unwell. The gout from which he had long been suffering ascended to the heart, and,' said *The Annual Register,* 'he died a few hours afterwards. Light opera has sustained an irreparable loss.'

His funeral service, held at the Madeleine, was like a final march-past of the Second Empire. Famous singers took part in it, and even the most indifferent wept when *La Chanson de Fortunio* was sung. The procession did not make straight for the Cimetière Montmartre. It made a détour along the Boulevards, to allow Offenbach to take a final farewell of his theatres. The rain thinned out the mourners, but Hortense Schneider followed the cortège to the end.

A few weeks later, a desperate dramatist at the Nouveautés tried to persuade her to star in *Les Parfums de Paris,* a theatrical review of the year. Hortense Schneider was adamant: she would not appear on stage again. After half-an-hour's fruitless pleading, the dramatist expressed his regret: he had hoped that she might sing a selection from 'poor Offenbach, whom you loved so well . . . I thought,' he said, 'you would like to pay him tribute.' 'And so it was [wrote the critic Arnold Mortier] that the author overcame Hortense Schneider's resistance. It was to remind us of the brilliant age of the operetta, the great triumphs of Jacques Offenbach, a whole *boulevardier* and Parisian past, that the Grande-

Duchesse made her return to the stage. It was not only the history of Offenbach's repertoire, it was her own history that Hortense Schneider sang to us that night.'

*　　*　　*

Joanna Richardson was educated at The Downs School, Seaford and studied Modern Languages at St Anne's College, Oxford. A Fellow and Member of the Council of the Royal Society of Literature from 1961 to 1983, she has translated plays for the BBC and written numerous features for Radios 3 and 4. She has written widely on leading literary figures of nineteenth-century France and England including *Theophile Gautier: his Life and Times* (1958), *The Pre-Eminent Victorian: a study of Tennyson* (1962), *Victor Hugo* (1976), *The Life and Letters of John Keats* (1981) and *Baudelaire* (1994).

33

King Roger of Sicily

JOHN JULIUS NORWICH

(May 1970)

John Julius Norwich (son of Duff Cooper, the author of No. 4) is widely known for his writing and broadcasting about medieval and early modern architectural and aesthetic history, particularly that of Italy and Byzantium.

Few kingdoms have had more inauspicious beginnings than the Norman Kingdom of Sicily. By the year 1130 Count Roger II de Hauteville had already reigned in Palermo for a quarter of a century, since his childhood; and after his acquisition, two years before, of the duchies of Apulia and Calabria, he had become one of the richest and mot powerful rulers of Europe. But a royal crown still eluded him; and he knew that without one he would never be able to treat with his fellow-monarchs on equal terms or to weld his three dominions into a single state. Finally, on Christmas Day 1130, he achieved what he had so long desired; but the crown that was laid on his head on that day in Palermo Cathedral was to prove, for most of the next decade, more of a liability than an asset. When he had obtained it from the schismatic anti-Pope Anacletus in return for Sicilian support against the latter's rival Innocent II, it had seemed that this support might prove decisive; all too soon, however – thanks largely to the influence and eloquence of St Bernard of Clairvaux – the rest of Christendom had rallied to Innocent, and Roger had found himself the anti-Pope's sole champion. To change his allegiance was unthinkable; it would have meant disowning the one authority for his Kingship. Thus it was only after Anacletus's death in 1138 and a lucky victory over the papal forces in the following year that Roger was able to wrest from the captive Innocent unwilling confirmation of his royal status. Then, respectable at last, he embarked on a policy of cautious *rapprochement* with the Church of Rome – a policy which, three years later, was to lead to the building of S. Giovanni degli Eremiti, the first and only Latin religious foundation he was ever to allow in Palermo.

S. Giovanni – St John of the Hermits – stands today as little more than an empty shell. Nothing now remains there to suggest that during the halcyon years of the Norman Kingdom it was the richest and most privileged monastery in all Sicily. It was founded in 1142, and by the charter he granted it six years later Roger decreed that its abbot should serve *ex officio* as chaplain and confessor to the King, with the rank of bishop, and should personally celebrate Mass on all feast days in the Palatine Chapel. He further laid down that in its cemetery – which still exists in the open court to the south of the church – should be buried all members of the royal family except the Kings themselves and all the senior officials of the court.[1]

The church itself, now deconsecrated, is surprisingly small. It was built on the site of a much earlier mosque, part of which remains to form an extension of the southern transept. But the inside, despite the traces of tile and mosaic and fresco – and even of the stalactite ceiling of the original mosque – holds little interest for the non-expert. The fascination of S. Giovanni is in its exterior. Of all the Norman churches in Sicily it is the most characteristic and the most striking, its five vermilion domes – each standing on a cylindrical drum to give it greater height – bursting out from the surrounding greenery like gigantic pomegranates, in almost audible testimony of the Arab craftsmen who built them. They are not beautiful; but they burn themselves into the memory and remain there, stark and vivid, long after many true masterpieces are forgotten.

A few yards to the north-west there stands a little open cloister, with gently poised arcading supported on pairs of slender columns, built half a century later than the church and in perfect contrast to it. Sitting there on a hot afternoon, looking up now at the soaring austerity of the royal palace, now at the aggressively baroque campanile of S. Giorgio in Kemonia, yet always aware of those bulbous oriental cupolas half-hidden behind the palm-trees, one is reminded for the hundredth time that in Sicily Islam is never far away. And it is, perhaps, in the church and cloister of what was once the leading Christian monastery of the Kingdom that its presence is most keenly felt.

---

[1] This last decree was never generally observed. Nearly all the royal family were in fact buried in the chapel of St Mary Magdalen next to the old cathedral. When, forty years later, the cathedral was rebuilt and enlarged, the tombs – which included those of Queens Elvira and Beatrice and of four of Roger's sons, Roger, Tancred, Alfonso and Henry – were transferred to another chapel similarly named. This chapel still stands in the courtyard of the *carabinieri* barracks of S. Giacomo. Of the graves themselves, however, there is no longer any trace.

The confrontation at S. Giovanni degli Eremiti between Muslim East and Latin West is so striking that the visitor tends to forget the third essential strand of civilization that made Norman Sicily what it was. In all Palermo there is no longer a single building whose exterior recalls Byzantium. Despite the number of senior Greek officials in the Curia, despite all the Greek scholars and sages whom Roger attracted to the court in the later years of his reign, the capital itself had never boasted an indigenous Greek population of any size. It was, first and foremost, an Arab city, scarcely touched by Byzantine influences in comparison with those regions in which Greek peoples had lived since the days of antiquity – regions such as the Val Demone in eastern Sicily or parts of Calabria, where to this day a Greek dialect is spoken in some of the remote villages.

And yet, from the time of the Arab conquest of Sicily onwards, the Greeks had played a vital part in the building of the new nation. First, they had kept the balance between Christian and Muslim on which the whole future of Norman Sicily depended. Roger's father, the Great Count, had encouraged Latin immigration, both ecclesiastical and secular, as far as he dared; but he could not allow too much too quickly for fear of frightening the Greek and Arab communities and turning them against him. Besides, such immigration brought its own dangers. If it had not been kept under rigid control there would have been nothing to stop swarms of swaggering Norman barons from the mainland pouring into Sicily, demanding to be given fiefs in keeping with their rank and station and gradually reducing the island to that chaos that always seemed to follow in their wake.

Without the Greeks, then, the Christian element during those early days might have been swamped altogether. But they also performed another invaluable function. They neatly counter-balanced the claims of the Latin Church, and provided both Count Roger and his son with a powerful bargaining – if not actually blackmailing – counter in their dealings with Rome. It seems in the highest degree improbable that there was any foundation for the rumours, current at the end of the previous century, that the Great Count was seriously contemplating a conversion to Orthodoxy; but it is a good deal likelier that Roger II, at various moments in his long quarrel with Pope Innocent, may have considered renouncing the pontifical authority altogether in favour of some kind of loose caesaropapism on the Byzantine model. What is certain is that in 1143 the Greek Archimandrite Nilus Doxopatrius of Palermo dedicated to Roger – with the King's full consent – a *Treatise on the Patriarchal Thrones*, arguing that with the transfer of the imperial capital in AD 330 and the recognition of Constantinople as the 'New Rome' by the Council of Chalcedon in 451, the Pope had lost his ecclesiastical primacy, which now properly belonged to the Byzantine Patriarch.

But now, as the twelfth century neared its half-way mark, the situation can be seen to have changed. Sicily, first of all, had grown steadily richer; and as her prosperity increased, so too had her political stability. In contrast to the endemic confusion of the Italian peninsula, the island had become a paragon of just and enlightened government, peaceable and law-abiding, an amalgam of races and languages that seemed to give strength rather than weakness; and, as its reputation grew, more and more churchmen and administrators, scholars and merchants and unashamed adventurers were drawn across the sea from England, France and Italy to settle in what must have seemed to many of them a veritable Eldorado, a kingdom in the sun. Meanwhile, the importance of the Greek minority had begun to decline. It was inevitable that it should. With no comparable immigration from abroad to sustain it, it was increasingly outnumbered by the Latin. In the prevailing atmosphere of religious toleration and easy coexistence, its value as a bulwark against Islam was now negligible. Finally, Roger had now established so firm a control over his Latin Church that he no longer had any need for a counter-balance.

Not that there was any discrimination against the Greeks. In view of the mixed feelings with which the Hautevilles had always regarded the Byzantine Empire – admiration for its institutions and its arts, distrust laced with more than a tinge of jealousy in every other field – they might have been excused for treating as second-class citizens a foreign minority whose political and confessional loyalties were openly divided. But they never did so. Roger and his successors continued to support their Greek subjects whenever their support was necessary; they never lost their concern for the welfare of the Greeks, or of their Church. The great and distinguished line of Greek admirals continued throughout the century; at least until the end of Roger's reign the whole fiscal system of Norman Sicily remained in Greek and Arab hands. It was just that the emphasis had shifted. Though from the outset subordinated to the Latin hierarchy, large numbers of Basilian monasteries had sprung up over the past fifty years, notably S. Maria del Patirion near Rossano in Calabria[2] – founded

---

[2] Visitors to Rossano are usually content to inspect the Byzantine church of S. Marco and the Archbishop's Palace, home of the justly-famed sixth-century purple codex. They would be well advised to make the short detour to S. Maria, lying up in the hills on the way to the neighbouring town of Corigliano. The monastery buildings are in ruins, but the church itself is still there, with a superb mosaic pavement which alone is worth the visit.

by the Regent Adelaide at the beginning of the century – and its daughter-house, the monastery of the Saviour at Messina, established some thirty years later. But the Saviour, soon to be the chief of all the Greek monasteries in Sicily, was also the last. Henceforth the royal favours would be lavished on the new Latin houses – S. Giovanni degli Eremiti and, later, Maniace and Monreale.

Fortunately the way was still wide open for private patronage; and it is fitting that the sublimest legacy of the Greek Church in all Sicily, the only one that still possesses a beauty comparable to that of the Palatine Chapel and the Cathedral of Cefalù, should have been founded, built and endowed by the most brilliant of all the Greeks in the Kingdom's history.

Though the original and rightful name of his church, S. Maria del Ammiraglio, stands as a perpetual monument to its founder, George of Antioch had no need of such memorials to ensure himself a place in history. We first meet him as the gifted young Levantine who, after early service with the Zirid Sultans of Mahdia, transferred his loyalties to Sicily and in 1123 used his perfect Arabic and unrivalled knowledge of the Tunisian coast to score the only victory in Roger's first, ill-fated African expedition. Since then, as commander of the Sicilian navy, he had served his King with distinction on both land and sea, becoming in 1132 the first holder of the proudest title his adopted country had to offer – Emir of Emirs, the high admiral and chief minister of the realm.[3] Despite so distinguished a career, however, his work on the church must not be thought of as the occupation of his declining years, still less of his retirement. In 1143, the year it was endowed, he must have been in his early fifties; within weeks of the endowment he and his fleet were off on another North African adventure, more successful this time; while before he died he was to carry the Sicilian flag to the very banks of the Bosphorus, returning to Palermo with all the secrets – and many of the leading craftsmen – of the Byzantine silk industry.

The Arab traveller, Ibn Jubair, when he visited the church in 1184, prayed that Allah would soon 'honour the building with the sound of the muezzin's call'. Looking at the outside of the Martorana – as it is more usually called today – one almost wishes that his pious supplication had been granted. His co-religionists could hardly have done worse with it than the Christians. The façade itself he would no longer recognize; in

---

[3] It is perhaps worth recalling that the word *admiral* current with minor variations in so many European languages, is derived through Norman Sicily from the Arabic word *emir*; and in particular from its compound *Emir-al-Bahr*, Ruler of the Sea.

sad contrast to that of the adjoining church of S. Cataldo, whose three heavy cupolas unmistakably if somewhat congestedly proclaim it as a Norman building of the mid-twelfth century, this jewel of all Sicilian churches – as opposed to cathedrals or chapels – has been decked out in lugubrious baroque. Only the romanesque belltower, domeless since an earthquake in 1726 but still beautifully proportioned, remains to beckon the traveller within.

There, too, all is not as it was. The eastern extremity is lost, the western bays ought never to have occurred. Miraculously, however, between the two, George's old church has remained, preserving its traditional Byzantine cross-in-square ground-plan and looking still much as it did when it was first consecrated or when, forty-odd years later, it had so alarming an effect on Ibn Jubair:

> The walls within are gilded – or rather, they are made from one great piece of gold. There are slabs of coloured marble, the like of which we have never seen, picked out with golden mosaic and surmounted with, as it were, branches of trees in green mosaic. Great suns of gilded glass ranged along the top blaze with a light that dazzled our eyes and caused us such perturbation of the spirit that we implored Allah to preserve us. We learned that the founder, who gave his name to the Church, devoted many quintals of gold to its building, and that he was vizir to the grandfather of this polytheist King.[4]

Like most of those at Cefalù and the best of those in the Palestine Chapel, the mosaics of the Martorana were all the work of a single team of superb artists and craftsmen imported by Roger II from Constantinople and working in Sicily between 1140 and 1155. Unlike either of the other groups, they contain no later additions. All three show a close interrelation; yet each, unbelievably, has a style of its own. Only the mosaics in the cupola itself strike one as faintly disappointing. Enthroned and depicted at full length, the Pantocrator has lost much of the majesty that he shows in the Palatine Chapel, to say nothing of Cefalù; and the four archangels beneath him have bodies so fantastically distorted as to border on the ridiculous. But drop your eyes now to the supporting walls. Look east to the Annunciation, with Gabriel in a slanting swirl of movement, Mary serene with her spindle as the holy dove

---

[4] Ibn Jubair was writing in the reign of Roger's grandson, William the Good. To devout Muslims all Christians were polytheists. As believers in the Trinity, what else could they be?

flutters towards her. Look west to the Presentation in the Temple, the outstretched arms of the infant Christ on one side and those of St Simeon on the other bridging the entrance to the nave as perfectly as does the great arch they frame. Within its vault, Christ is born and, opposite, the Virgin dies – her soul, like another swaddled child, being carried reverently heavenwards by her Son. Lastly, settle in some comfortable corner and look at everything at once while the dark, glowing gold does its work, irradiating the spirit like a soft and gentle fire.

And now, as you leave the original church, running the gauntlet of those simpering cherubs and marzipan madonnas that mark the real dark ages of European religious art, pause for a moment at the western-facing wall on the north side of the nave near the entrance; and there, in what was probably the narthex of George's building, you will find, glittering wanly in the half-light, his portrait. It is a dedication mosaic, with the Admiral, looking old beyond his years and distinctly oriental, prostrating himself before the Virgin. His body has unfortunately been damaged at some period, and the damage compounded by a clumsy restoration which has given him the appearance of a tortoise; but the head is the original work – presumably done from the life – and almost the entire figure of the Virgin has come down to us unscathed. Her right hand is extended towards him, as if to raise him up; and in her left she holds a scroll on which there is written in Greek:

> Child, holy Word, do thou ever preserve from all adversity George, first among the archons, who has raised this my house from its foundations; and grant him the forgiveness of his sins as thou only, O God, hast power to do.

Across the nave, in the corresponding space on the southern wall, is the Martorana's last and perhaps its greatest treasure – a mosaic portrait of King Roger himself, being symbolically crowned by Christ. There he stands, bending slightly forward, a purely Byzantine figure in his long dalmatic and stole, his crown with jewelled pendants in the manner of Constantinople; even his arms are raised from the elbows in the Greek attitude of prayer. Above his head, great black letters stride across the gold to proclaim him. *ΡΟΓΕΡΙΟΣ ΡΗΞ*, they read, *Rogerios Rex*. This uncompromising use of Greek letters for a Latin word is less curious than it might seem; by Roger's time the normal Greek word for King, *basileus*, was so identified with the Byzantine Emperor that it would have been unthinkable in this context. And yet the simple fact of transliteration makes an impact of its own and – particularly after one has spotted the

Arabic inscription on an adjacent pillar – seems to diffuse the whole spirit of Norman Sicily.

This, too, is a portrait from the life; apart from coins and seals, which are too small to give much information and are anyway largely symbolical, it is the only surviving likeness of the King which we can safely assume to be authentic.[5] Without it we should have nothing to go on but the evidence of Archbishop Romuald of Salerno, a man with a genius for uninformative description. He writes merely that Roger was tall, corpulent, with a leonine face – whatever that may mean – and a voice that was *subrauca*; hoarse, perhaps, or harsh, or just vaguely disagreeable. The mosaic tells us far more. It shows a dark, swarthy man on the brink of middle age, with a full beard and long thick hair flowing to his shoulders. The face itself might be Greek, or it might be Italian; it even has a faintly Semitic cast about it. Anything less like the traditional idea of a Norman knight could scarcely be imagined.

It is always dangerous to read too much of a character into a portrait, particularly when the sitter is already familiar and the portraitist unknown. Dangerous, but irresistible. And even in something so hieratic and formalized as the Martorana mosaic, there are surely certain touches, certain infinitesimal adjustments and gradations of the tesserae, that bring King Roger to life again before us. Here, surely, is the southerner and the oriental, the ruler of subtle mind and limitless flexibility whose life is spent playing one faction off against another; the statesman to whom diplomacy, however tortuous, is a more natural weapon than the sword, and gold, however corrupting, a more effective currency than blood.

King Roger's coronation on Christmas Day, 1130, had inaugurated a decade of storm, when the thunderclouds hung black over the mainland and when Sicily itself, for all its prosperity, was unable altogether to escape their shadow. Afterwards, the sky lightened. It is in the last fourteen years of Roger's reign that the sun really shines on his Kingdom.

---

[5]   The only other certain contemporary portrait to have come down to us is on a curious enamel plaque in the church of St Nicholas at Bari. It depicts Roger's coronation by St Nicholas, and was probably the origin of the church's one-time claim that he was crowned there and not in Palermo. (His reputed crown, an immense circle of iron and copper more suited to a barrel than a human head, is also displayed there with some pride.) The portrait may be from the life, but was more likely copied from another, now lost. The essential physical features appear much the same as on the Martorana mosaic.

And the Kingdom responds. Suddenly the art of Norman Sicily, like some rare subtropical orchid after long seasons of germination, at this moment bursts into glory. So, no less spectacularly, does the court of Palermo. Already, at the time of his coronation, Roger had inherited from his father a civil service, based eclectically on Norman, Greek, Latin and Arab models, which compared favourably with that of any Western nation. When he died, he left his successors a governmental machine that was the wonder and envy of Europe. Under the Emir of Emirs and the Curia, two separate land registries – known as divans[6] after their Fatimid prototypes and staffed almost exclusively by Saracens – supervised the gathering of revenues from customs, monopolies and feudal holdings on Sicily and on the mainland. Another branch of the financial administration, the *camera*, was based on the old *fiscus* of the Roman Empire and administered by Greeks; another followed the model of the Anglo-Norman Exchequer. Provincial government was in the hands of the Chancellors of the Kingdom, the *camerarii*, and below them the local governors – Latin bailiffs, Greek catapans or Saracen *amil*, selected according to the race and language predominant in their district. To avoid corruption or peculation, the very lowest officials had direct access to the Curia or even, on occasion, to the King himself. Wandering justiciars, magistrates condemned to perpetual circuit, had responsibility for administering the criminal law, with the assistance of varying numbers of *boni homines* – good men and true – both Christian and Muslim, often sitting together in what was in effect the forerunner of the modern jury. They too had the right to refer appeals to the King when necessary.

The King: always, everywhere, his people were reminded of his presence, his power, his paradoxical combination of accessibility and remoteness. Himself halfway to heaven, there was no abuse, no miscarriage of justice too insignificant for his attention, if it could not be settled by those empowered to act in his name.

Emirs, seneschals, archons, logothetes, *protonotorii*, *protonobilissimi* – even the titles of the high palace dignitaries seemed to add to the pervading splendour. Yet it takes more than civil servants, whatever their disguise, to give brilliance to a court; and Roger's court at Palermo was easily the most brilliant of twelfth-century Europe. The King himself was famous for his insatiable intellectual curiosity and his passion for facts. (In 1140 when, returning from Ariano, he had made his formal entry into Naples, he had astounded the Neopolitans by informing them of the exact length of their land walls – 2,363 paces, a

---

[6] From which comes the Italian word *dogana* and, through it, the French *douane*.

figure of which, not surprisingly, none of them was aware.) With this curiosity went a profound respect for learning, unique among his fellow-princes.[7] By the 1140s he had given a permanent home in Palermo to many of the foremost scholars and scientists, doctors and philosophers, geographers and mathematicians of Europe and the Arab world; and as the years went by he would spend more and more of his time in their company. Outside his immediate family – and he had been many years a widower – it was with them above all that he was able to cast off some of his regality; we are told that whenever any scholar entered the royal presence, Roger would rise from his chair and move forward to meet him, then take him by the hand and sit him down at his side. During the learned discussions that followed, whether in French, Latin, Greek or Arabic, he seems to have been well able to hold his own.

> In mathematics, as in the political sphere, the extent of his learning cannot be described. Nor is there any limit to his knowledge of the sciences, so deeply and wisely has he studied them in every particular. He is responsible for singular innovations and for marvellous inventions, such as no prince has ever before realized.

Those words were written by Abu Abdullah Mohammed al-Edrisi, Roger's close friend and, of all the palace scholars, the one whom he most admired. Edrisi had arrived in Palermo in 1139; he was to remain there during much of his life, for fifteen years heading a commission set up by order of the King to gather geographical information from all quarters, correlate it, record it in orderly form, and so ultimately to produce one compendious work which would contain the sum total of all contemporary knowledge of the physical world. The results of this work, which was completed in January 1154, barely a month before the King's death, were twofold. The first was a huge planisphere of purest silver, weighing no less than four hundred and fifty Roman pounds, on which was engraved 'the configuration of the seven climates with that of the regions, countries, sea-coasts both near and distant, gulfs, seas and water-courses; the location of deserts and of cultivated lands, and their respective distances by normal routes in miles or other known measures;

---

[7] Henry I of England was admittedly well-educated by the standards of the time – a fact which was considered remarkable enough to earn him the nickname of Beauclerc. But Henry made no effort to form a cultivated court around him, as Roger did.

and the designation of ports.' One would give much for this magnificent object to have been preserved; alas, it was destroyed during the riots of the following reign, within a few years of its completion.

But the second, and perhaps ultimately the more valuable fruit of Edrisi's labours has come down to us in its entirety. It is a book, properly entitled *The Avocation of a Man Desirous of a Full Knowledge of the Different Countries of the World* but more generally known as *The Book of Roger*; and it is the greatest geographical work of the middle ages. On the very first page we read the words:

> The earth is round like a sphere, and the waters adhere to it and are maintained on it through natural equilibrium which suffers no variation.

As might be expected, *The Book of Roger* emerges as a combination of hard topographical facts – many of them astonishingly accurate for a work produced three and a half centuries before Columbus – and travellers' tales; but even the latter suggest that they have been subjected to stern critical appraisal. This is, after all, a scientific work, and we are never allowed to forget it; there is no room for tall stories unless they have at least some claim to veracity. But the author, on his side, never loses his sense of wonder, and the book makes fascinating reading.

Though Roger's court circle was by no means entirely composed of Arabs like Edrisi, they probably constituted the largest single group; while among the Europeans there were many who had been attracted to Palermo by very reason of its predominantly Arab flavour. There was nothing new in this. Unlike Christianity, Islam had never drawn a distinction between sacred and profane knowledge. During the dark ages, while the Church of Rome – following the dire example of Gregory the Great – feared and even actively discouraged secular studies, good Muslims remembered how the Prophet himself had enjoined his Faithful to pursue knowledge all their lives, 'even if the quest led them to China,' for 'he who travels in search of learning travels along Allah's path to Paradise'. Muslim civilization had thus for years been recognized in the West as superior to anything that Christian Europe could boast, especially in the field of mathematics and the physical sciences. Arabic had become the international scientific language *par excellence*. Moreover there was a number of classical works of learning, both Greek and Latin, which had been lost to Christendom through the barbarian invasions or the engulfing tide of Islam and survived only in Arabic translation. By the twelfth century, owing largely to the work of the Sephardic Jews of Spain, some of these were beginning to reappear in Western languages; but this did not appreciably diminish the need for any serious student of science to master Arabic for himself.

Yet it was a diabolically difficult language to learn and, in northern Europe at any rate, competent teachers were few. Thus, for half a century and more, men had been travelling to Spain and Sicily, there to unlock, as they hoped, the secrets of the Muslim world – poor clerks, seeking knowledge that would single them out from their fellows and so clear their path to advancement; dreaming alchemists, combing volumes of oriental lore for formulas of the elixir of life or the philosophers' stone; or true scholars like Adelard of Bath, pioneer of Arab studies in England and the greatest name in English science before Robert Grossetete and Roger Bacon, who came to Sicily in the first years of the century and was later to restore Euclid's *Elements*, retranslated by him from the Arabic, to the cultural heritage of Europe.

For certain more specialized fields of enquiry these early Arabists continued to gravitate towards Muslim Spain and in particular to the school of Toledo, which had long been the spearhead of the international scientific renaissance. For others, however, Sicily possessed one overwhelming advantage: while culturally still very much part of the Arab world, it also remained in perpetual contact with the Greek East. In the libraries of Palermo, to say nothing of all the Basilian monasteries in the island and in Calabria, scholars could find the Greek originals of works known in Spain only in extracts, or in translations of doubtful accuracy. Nowadays we tend to forget that, until this twelfth-century revival of interest in ancient learning, Western Europe was virtually ignorant of Greek; and Roger's Sicily now became the foremost centre of Hellenic studies outside Byzantium itself. But in Byzantium Arabic culture was unknown and mistrusted. Only in Sicily could both civilizations be studied at first hand and employed to explain, complement and cross-fertilize each other. Small wonder, then, that seekers after truth should flock in such numbers to Palermo and that the island should have established itself by mid-century as not only the commercial but also the cultural clearing-house of three continents.

Once again, all this activity was centred on the person of the King. Roger has been accused of being himself uncreative, in contrast to his grandson Frederick II for example, or even to Richard Coeur de Lion, a troubadour poet of considerable ability. It is true that he left no literary compositions of his own; it would have been remarkable if he had, since that marvellous flowering of European vernacular literature that had already begun in Provence had not yet spread farther afield. Such poets as flourished in Palermo in his day – and there were many – were nearly all Arabs. Besides, the King's personal preference was for the sciences.

Beauty he loved, but splendour too; and one suspects that he did not find it easy in every case to distinguish one from the other. Anyway, he loved knowledge more.

Yet to say that he was not creative is to ignore the fact that without him the unique cultural phenomenon that is twelfth-century Sicily could never have occurred. So diversified a nation needed a guiding hand to give it purpose, to weld its various elements into one. Intellectually as well as politically, Roger provided that hand. In a very real sense, he *was* Sicily. His was the conception, his the incentive; he and only he could have created the favourable climate that was a precondition of all the rest. Enlightened yet always discriminating, he was the first royal patron, focusing the efforts and energies of those around him, never once losing sight of his eternal objective – the greatness and glory of his Kingdom.

*   *   *

John Julius Norwich (b. 1929), son of Duff and Lady Diana Cooper, was educated at Upper Canada College, Toronto, Eton, the University of Strasbourg and New College, Oxford. In 1952 he joined the Foreign Office, serving at the embassies in Belgrade (1955–7), Beirut (1957–60), and with the British delegation to the Disarmament Conference at Geneva (1960–4). He resigned from the service in 1964 in order to write. His works include *The Normans in the South* (1967), *The Kingdom in the Sun* (1970), *A History of Venice* (1977), and the Byzantium trilogy, *Byzantium: the Early Centuries, Byzantium: The Apogee* and *Byzantium: The Decline and Fall* (1988–95). His most recent publication is *Shakespeare's Kings* (2000). He is a regular broadcaster on history and architecture and is a lecturer on Venice and other subjects. For nearly thirty years Lord Norwich was chairman of the Venice in Peril fund. He is now chairman of the World Monuments Fund in Britain.

34

The Mechanics of Nomad Invasions

BRUCE CHATWIN

(May 1972)

Bruce Chatwin had travelled widely in Africa and Asia at the time this article was written but had yet to produce his first book.

During the spring of AD 376 the Roman garrisons on the Danube frontier learned of a fresh threat. Nomad peoples were on the move. Over the steppe lands that stretched to the east came news that the Gothic kingdom of Ermanarich in the Crimea had fallen to the Huns, an unknown people of mounted archers, bestial in appearance, whose home lay close to the ice-bound ocean. 'No one ever ploughs a field in their country,' wrote the contemporary historian Ammianus Marcellinus, 'or touches a plough handle. They are ignorant of home, law or settled existence, and they keep roaming from places in their waggons. If you ask one of their children where he comes from, he was conceived in one place, born far away and brought up still farther off.' Gothic refugees implored the Roman government for asylum within the imperial frontiers. And, putting themselves under the protection of the Emperor, they were allowed to cross the Danube in their thousands 'like the rain of ashes from an eruption of Etna'. But their hosts failed in the basic obligations of hospitality, and within two years the Goths had revolted and killed the Emperor Valens himself at the Battle of Adrianople. Thereafter the Empire was doomed to further barbarian inroads.

However momentous the fall of the Roman Empire may seem in retrospect, it was merely an episode in a conflict between two incompatible, yet complementary, systems – nomadism and settled agriculture. The arrival of the Huns on their stocky ponies was no new event. The 'unharvested steppe' forms a continuous strip of grazing from Hungary to Manchuria. It was a reservoir of nomad peoples – Cimmerians, Scythians, Sarmatians and later Avars, Magyars, and Mongols – who migrated up and down it and periodically overflowed on to the sown lands of civilization. Ancient Mesopotamia and Egypt faced the same problem from the men of the fringe, whose mercurial shiftings in the encircling deserts and mountains were a source of anxiety in times of national ascendancy, of terror in times of collapse. As the Hungarian historian Andreas Alfoldi wrote, there existed along the Rhine and Danube a 'moral barrier' between the barbarian and civilized worlds. The grandiose Roman fortifications, like the Great Wall of China, were simply 'the secondary consequences and the reflection of that moral isolation'. In a modified form the confrontation continues as the barrier of incomprehension between the revolutionary insurgent and established authority.

The quarrel of nomad and settler is, of course, the same as that of Abel the shepherd and Cain the planter and founder of the first city. As befitted a Bedouin people, the Hebrews sided with Abel. Jehova found his offering of a 'firstling of the flock' more acceptable than Cain's 'fruit of the ground'. Cain's act of fratricide is judged a typical crime of settlement, and as punishment Jehovah sterilizes the soil and forces him to wander on a penitential pilgrimage 'a fugitive and a vagabond'.

True nomads are sons of Ishmael, the wild man, whose 'hand shall be against every man, and every man's hand against him', activated by what Gibbon called 'the spirit of emigration and conquest'. The *Book of Joshua*, for example, is a paean of praise for the ideal of nomadic insurgency. As the nineteenth-century traveller James Morier wrote of the I'lyats, or wandering tribes of Persia, they 'look down on the *Shehrnishins* (or dwellers in cities) as degenerate, applauding the hardihood and simplicity of manners of those who have no other dwelling place than the tent, and reviling those who recur to the luxuries of a house and the protection of a city'.

In turn the citizen reviled the nomad as a savage wrecker of progress. And, since literature itself is the invention of settlers, the nomadic record looks black in writing. Thus an ancient Egyptian official would write of the Bedouin Hebrews, 'Their name reeks more than the stink of bird droppings,' or a Chinese Imperial Secretary of the Eastern Huns '. . . in their breasts beat the hearts of beasts . . . from the most ancient times they have never been regarded as a part of humanity'. Roman authorities treated the citizens of the Empire as men, outsiders as animals, and their historians could calmly compare the annihilation of a Germanic people to a medical cure (*salubria medicamenta*). Elsewhere, nomad invaders, who migrated onto sown lands, were compared to plagues of locusts and swarms of snakes.

Faced with the acceleration of world population growth, some modern biologists have diagnosed that the human species is rapidly approaching the 'swarming stage', thus refining Malthus's 'dismal theorem' that human populations breed up to the level of their food supply, a proliferation that can only lead to global starvation unless checked by mass mortality. Animal species reach the 'swarming stage' when some pressure of natural selection, to which it has been subjected during its evolution, is removed. The result is a population outburst, followed by a neurosis from overcrowding and panic in the face of starvation. Random migrations ensue.

The suicidal march of the Scandinavian lemming to death in the sea is thought by some to shed light on the tragic refugee problems of our day, and a global situation of wandering refugees is predicted. But the apocalyptic idea of total destruction at the hands of migrating hordes is again nothing new. At the time of the Mongol holocaust in the thirteenth century, observers confidently announced the end of the world. The Mongol Khan was Antichrist himself, his armies of mounted nomads the Legions of Gog and Magog. The Mongol military machine generated the same sort of anxiety as the nuclear bomb, and for this reason alone the mechanics of a nomadic invasion are of more than passing interest.

The word nomad derives from the Greek *nomos* – a pasture. A nomad proper is a mobile pastoralist, the owner and breeder of domesticated animals. To call a wandering hunter 'nomadic' is to misunderstand the meaning of the word. Hunting is a technique for killing animals, nomadism for keeping them alive. The psychology of the hunter is as different from the nomad's as the nomad's from that of the planter. Nomadism is born of wide expanses, ground too barren for the farmer to cultivate economically – savannah, steppe, desert and tundra, all of which will support an animal population providing that it moves. For the nomad, movement is morality. Without movement, his animals would die. But the planter is chained to his field; if he leaves, his plants wither.

Nomads never roam aimlessly from place to place, as one dictionary would have it. A nomadic migration is a guided tour of animals around a predictable sequence of pastures. It has the same inflexible character as the migrations of wild game, since the same ecological factors determine it. But domestication blunts an animal's innate sense of time and space. The herdsman replaces this loss with his own acquired skill, plotting his annual orbit to suit the needs of his own particular livestock.

A nomad's territory is the path linking his seasonal pastures. The tent-dweller invests this path with the emotional attachment a settler reserves for his houses and fields. Iranian nomads call the path *Il-Rah*, The Way. The 'way' of one tribe intersects with the 'ways' of others, and ill-timed movements lead to conflicts of interest. Herdsmen claim to own their 'ways' as their inalienable property; but in practice all they ask is the right of passage through a given stretch of territory at a fixed time of the year. The land holds no interest for them once they have moved on. Thus for a nomad, political frontiers are a form of insanity, based as they are on the aggregation of farm-lands.

Today's nomads, whether they be Quashgais in Iran or Masai in Kenya, are facing their ultimate crisis at the hands of settled administrations. Their way of life is considered an anachronism in a modern state. Nomads are resentful of, and resistant to, change. The 'problem of the tribes' is as much an issue to many a modern government as it was to the rulers of an ancient Near-Eastern city-state. For life in the black tents has not significantly changed since Abraham, the Bedouin sheikh, moved his flock on his 'journeys from the south even unto Bethel, where his tent had been at the beginning'. *Genesis* 13.3.

The automatic discipline of pastoralism encourages a high standard of loyalty among close kin. In most nomad cultures the definition of a human being is 'he who goes on migrations'. The word *arab* means a 'dweller in the tents' as opposed to *hazar* a 'house dweller'. Again, the latter is less than human.

Nomads are notoriously irreligious. They show little interest in ceremonial or protestations of faith. For the migration is of itself a ritual performance, a 'religious' catharsis, revolutionary in the strictest sense in that each pitching and breaking of camp represents a new beginning. The great religions – Jewish, Christian, Muslim, Zoroastrian and Buddhist – were preached among settled peoples who *had been* nomads. Their ceremonial is saturated with pastoral metaphor, their processions and pilgrimages perform the activities of a pastoral migration in mime. The *Hadj*, or holy journey to Mecca, is but an artificial migration for settlers to detach them from their profane homes. What then has given the nomad his bad reputation?

The least helpful view suggests that the 'spirit of emigration and conquest' is a genetically inherited behavioural trait, which through the pressures of natural selection, is highly developed in the nomad. In his *Evolution of Man and Society* Professor C.D. Darlington maintained that the instincts of a gipsy, like the palaeolithic hunter, were adjusted to a life of wandering, and seriously suggested that the royal families of Europe, as well as the Mongols, had a genetic adaption to the horse. This had enabled their ancestors to win wars, but on mechanized battlefields had brought them 'headlong to disaster'. But so far the genetic approach to history has been either misleading or malign. The innate superiority of the wandering Nordic *volk* was a fantasy. Nor is it possible to explain Mongol militancy in genetic terms. The Mongols had been a people of hunters who had broken out onto the steppe, learned the arts of equitation and pastoralism, and had left behind their closely related cousins, the Tungus and Samoyed, who were – and are – among the least violent people in the world; 'deformed and diminutive savages', Gibbon called them, 'who tremble at the sound of arms'.

Others have suggested that the piles of skulls that marked the passage of a Genghiz Khan or the fearsome slave-markets of Bokhara were proof of a primary instinct in man to attack, dominate and kill his own kind, an instinct often suppressed by the institutions of civilized life, but encouraged under the more 'natural' conditions of nomadic barbarism. Again this view is unhelpful. Instead, we should perhaps allow human nature an appetitive drive for movement in the widest sense. The act of journeying contributes towards a sense of physical and mental well being, while the monotony of prolonged settlement or regular work weaves patterns in the brain that engender fatigue and a sense of personal inadequacy. Much of what the ethologists have designated 'aggression' is simply an angered response to the frustrations of confinement.

A primary need for movement is borne out by recent studies of human evolution. Professor John Napier has shown that the long-striding walk is an adaption, unique among the primates, for covering distances over open savannahs. The bipedal walk made possible the development of the manufactory hand, and this led to the enlarged brain of our species. Any human baby also demonstrates is instinctive appetite for movement. Babies often scream for the simple reason they cannot bear to lie still. A crying child is a very rare sight on a nomad caravan, and the tenacity with which nomads cling to their way of life, as well as their quick-witted alertness, reflects the satisfaction to be found in perpetual movement. As settlers, we *walk off* our frustrations. The medieval Church instituted pilgrimage *on foot* as a cure for homicidal spleen.

The main springs of nomadic insurgency must be found within the precarious character of nomadism itself. Arnold Toynbee, following the lead of the fourteenth-century Arab historian, Ibn Khaldun, could never be accused of underestimating the importance of nomad invasions on the course of history. But in *A Study of History* he favoured the mechanical agency of climatic change to account for the periodic eruptions of nomads from their customary pastures. Travellers in Central Asia, like Sven Hedin or Sir Aurel Stein, had observed that the cities of the Tarim Basin were flourishing in the tenth and eleventh centuries, but 200 years later lay abandoned after a shift of climate had desiccated the land. This onset of aridity had coincided with the Mongol outburst, and it inspired the American geographer Ellsworth Huntingdon to plot a sequence of climatic oscillations that would account for every nomad eruption. The idea that the nomads had responded to a climatic challenge admirably commended itself to Toynbee's scheme and was further reinforced by the story of Jacob and his sons coming down to Egypt 'when the famine was sore in the land'. But Jacob came as a suppliant, not a conqueror. Whether or not the insurgents would swamp the civilization depended on its political state at the time. For Toynbee the nomads were either 'pushed off' the steppe or desert or 'pulled out' of it as if by suction when internal chaos invited them to raid.

But Toynbee's scheme is too simple. Shortage of grazing and population pressures certainly contributed towards the great exoduses. Livy tells of a Celtic king who resorted to predatory expansion, 'anxious to relieve his realm from the burden of overpopulation'. Futhermore, once pastureland is overgrazed, the grass becomes sour and less nourishing. Overgrazing also bares the topsoil which is then carried away in the wind. Dustbowl conditions ensue and the rains do not come any more. But such shifts in climate as there were do not coincide with the invasions. No climatic change took place in Arabia to account for the outpouring of Bedouin warriors in the service of Islam.

Moreover, it does not require a major shift in climate to ruin a stock-breeder. Few climates lack a lean season, a time of mental and physical anguish, which the religions ritualized as Lent or Ramadan. In the desert this coincides with the hot dry phase (Ramadan comes from the Arabic *ramz* 'to burn') in the north with the last months of winter. At this time the people are weak, the animals are weaker. And if the lean season lasts too long, a rich man may face total ruin. (Sheep farmers in New South Wales used to calculate that a thirty per cent drop in rainfall would carry off eighty per cent of livestock.) But the lean season is also, in Bedouin terminology, 'the time of the beasts'. The story of David and the Lion reminds us of the danger shepherds faced from carnivorous animals, and wolves will increase their numbers in direct ratio to the availability of edible sheep.

The instability of his profession encourages the nomad to increase and guard his flocks with fanatical obsession. He prefers to eat meat at others' expense and to rustle his neighbour's animals whenever he can. Then he looks about for other alternatives – raids, long distance trade, and protection rackets as an insurance against disaster. 'The soul of them,' Doughty wrote of the Arabian Bedouin, 'is greedy first of their proper subsistence, then of their proper increase. Though Israel is scattered among the most polite nations, who has not noticed this humour in them.' Owen Lattimore, whose knowledge of steppe pastoralism is unrivalled, once said 'The pure nomad is the poor nomad', in that he is unburdened by the luxuries of settlement. But in a society where livestock *is* wealth, the pure nomad is the relatively rich nomad. His obsession with increase is dictated by the fact that, once his flocks decline below a certain level, nomadism loses its viability. He and his family are compelled to find employment as agricultural serfs. As Ellsworth Huntington wrote in *The Pulse of Asia*, 'all the nomads I have ever met seemed to be comfortable. When their flocks diminish, they are obliged to seek new homes and to betake themselves to agriculture, leaving only the rich to continue the nomadic life'. Furthermore, live beasts are the standard medium of exchange, and a man rich in animals has purchasing power to 'buy' wives for himself or his sons, to buy grazing concessions, and buy his way out of a blood-feud.

Nomads are unstable within their tribal lands as a direct result of their 'growth ideology'. And it can be seen that the maximum amount of activity on the steppe will coincide with a climate favouring the growth of herds. With more animals to defend, there will be more herdsmen needed, and in turn more disputes over grazing rights and more raids. The cattlemen of Abraham quarrelled with the cattlemen of Lot. Knowing neither could control the wayward temper of their cowboys, Abraham suggested a parting of the ways. 'Is not the whole land before thee. Separate thyself I pray thee, before me: if thou wilt take the left hand, then I will go to the right; or if thou depart to the right hand, then I will go to the left.' *Genesis* 13.9. But once a split-away group trespasses on the pastures of others because of overstocking, old boundaries and agreements are destroyed.

'Sons are the source of wealth' goes a Turkoman proverb. And as we know from the *Gospel of St John*, a good shepherd owns his own sheep, unlike the hireling who runs away at the first sight of a wolf. The increase of healthy animals demands the increase of healthy sons to look after them. Hence the nomad's exhibitionistic attitude to male potency and his preoccupation with the genealogy of the male line. All stock-raisers have this obsession for 'fine blood', and human stud-books litter the Old Testament. As economic principle, nomads make no effort to limit births, and a plentiful supply of milk from domesticated animals enables a nomad mother to conceive again immediately after birth. Her first child is weaned early and to some extent this rupture weakens the bond of attachment between her and her infant. The latter deflects its attachment onto animal 'substitutes', and is encouraged to fondle baby animals, remaining 'animal-fixed' for life. Boys are taught to ride as soon as they can walk, if not before. Père Huc describes this in *Travels in China, Tartary and Thibet.* 'When a mere infant the Mongol is weaned and as soon as he is strong enough he is stuck upon a horse's back behind a man, the animal is put to a gallop, and the juvenile rider, in order not to fall off, has to cling with both hands to his leader's jacket. The Tartars thus become accustomed, from a very early age, to the movements of the horse and by degrees and the force of the habit, they identify themselves, as it were, with the animal.'

Warfare – or, at least, violent competition – is endemic to nomadism. The tribe is a military machine, and from the age of four boys are trained in the art of war and defence. They are deputed to tend a few animals on pain of punishment for letting them stray. As a result, they are brainwashed into believing that the care of livestock continues one of the main purposes of life. This devotion to animals is invariably accompanied by a weakened regard for the value of human life. The Grand Historian of China, Ssu-Ma Chi'en, describes the process in his account of the Hsiung-Nu or Eastern Huns. 'The little boys start out by learning to ride sheep and shoot birds and rats with a bow and arrow, and when they get older they shoot foxes and hares which are used for food. Thus all the young men are able to use a bow and act as armed cavalry in times of war.' Furthermore, equitation engenders a sort of Olympian grandeur. As the Polish explorer Lt-Col Prjewalsky quaintly remarked of the Kalmuck nomad, 'His contempt for pedestrianism is so great that he considers it beneath his dignity to walk even as far as the next *yurta*'. The Huns, we are told, bought, sold, slept, ate, drank, gave judgement, even defecated without dismounting.

The territorial instability of the nomad may be contrasted unfavourably with the greater security enjoyed by the 'primitive' hunter and gatherer. The former sees territory in terms of good or bad grazing, the latter exploits his territory gratefully for his basic needs, and refuses on principle to store food for more than a few days. This he can afford to do, since hunters take active steps to keep their numbers constant. Without milk from domesticated animals and without beasts of burden, the mothers must suckle *and* carry their children on long journeys till the age of three or more. Meanwhile, they cannot bear any more children. The hunters have been accused of 'merry squandering' and certainly enjoy a far lower standard of living. But by budgeting for the minimum they lack all incentive to overstretch their frontiers unless forced out by others. 'There has never been the least attempt', wrote Spencer and Gillen of the Central Australia Aborigines, 'made by one tribe to encroach on the territory of another. Now and again they may have inter-tribal quarrels or fights, but there is no such thing as the acquisition of fresh territory.' The hunter's sole motive for travel outside his hunting ground is to 'marry far' in accordance with the incest taboo. For this reason, isolated groups of hunters are interlinked in a network of reciprocal trading agreements and marriage alliances with their neighbours. Fights flare up when – and only when – the parity of these exchanges is broken. Thus 'primitive' war and nomadic insurgency cannot meaningfully be compared to one another.

In their own feuds nomads preserve something of this 'archaic' notion of equivalence. The nomad world is racked with vendettas, but justice is personal, brisk and effective. All parties to a quarrel try to prevent it getting out of hand. The instability in their nomad society lacks the cohesion needed for conquest on a mass scale. The nomad armies were military machines co-ordinated by powerful autocrats. Their cohesion can only be explained in terms of the nomad's historical interaction with settled civilization.

It used to suit evolution-minded social scientists to believe that pastoralism preceded agriculture. The hunter had learned to tame wild animals. The nomad settled down to grow crops, and the farmer made the inventions on which the first cities depended. Yet nomadism was not a step towards civilization, but a step away from it. Abraham left the city of Ur to become a nomad. The Central Asian Steppe, like the Great Plains of America, had been under cultivation till the horsemen swept the planters aside.

The great transformation from food-gathering to food-producing, known as the Neolithic Revolution in the Old World, first took place on the flanks of the Fertile Crescent, that great arc of mountains from Palestine to South Persia, where, after the recession of the ice-sheets, the wild ancestors of our sheep and goats browsed over stands of wild wheat and barley. The process by which grains and animals became domesticated was gradual and not yet fully revealed. The important point to remember is this: at first, stock-breeding and agriculture were practised by the people of the same settlement.

But the farmers developed irrigation, and agriculture came down the mountain-sides into the rich alluvial valleys with startling increases in yield. Meanwhile, the herdsmen withdrew to the wild places and developed a new order of their own. There they later domesticated the horse to give them greater range. Thus, nomad and farmer are linked to a common past and, to some extent, share common aspirations. If the nomad recovered the mobility of former times, he was also committed to an ideology of growth. Futhermore, the cleavage deprived the farmer of rich sources of animal protein and the nomad of essential grain. Nomad and farmer might hate each other, yet they needed each other. A nomad independent of settled agriculture has probably never existed. Ammianus

Marcellinus, it is true, heard that the Hunnish cavalry survived on the blood of their horses and foraged roots alone, just as the Masai suck the blood of their cattle. Such were the iron rations of the campaign; but normally settler and nomad exchange grains and vegetables for hides, meat and dairy produce. An Iranian nomad cannot get through the winter without grain. The Sahara camel man cannot live without dates. In an ideal situation the two cultures live symbiotically side by side.

But the nomadic insurgent has tactical mobility and is expert in guerilla warfare, the art of 'attack and withdrawal' which, according to Ibn Khaldun, was the practice of the Bedouin nations. 'Raids are our agriculture', goes a Bedouin proverb. The nomad does not take kindly to being ordered about. He looks down on farmers as sub-human rabble and does not feel obliged to treat them as equals. To quote Lattimore, 'when nomad chiefs patronize agriculture it is a subject agriculture that they prefer, exploited under their military protection and practised by imported peasants, between whom and the dominant nomads there is an emphatic social difference'. A character in the *History* of Priscus said this of the Huns, 'being themselves contemptuous of agriculture, they descended on the Gothic food supply and snatched it away like wolves. Eventually the Goths occupied the position of slaves and toiled for the sustenance of the Huns'.

A barbarous taste for 'fire-bright gold' infected the pastoral world. Its incorruptible brilliance relieved the leaden monotony of waste places. 'They had golden earrings because they were Ishmaelites', goes a line from the *Book of Judges*. The Huns 'burned with an insatiable lust for gold' and their Scythian and Sarmatian predecessors had their goldsmiths perfect ornaments in the celebrated 'Animal Style', an art of seething, snapping monsters where man is a stranger. From the frozen tombs of Pazyryk in the Altai Mountains or that of the Hunnish ruler from Noin-Ula in Mongolia, archaeologists have unearthed precious silks and embroideries, pile carpets and lacquers. Byzantine ambassadors to the camp of Attila noticed that the Hunnish dictator himself ate from a wooden trencher. But his followers wore extravagant silks, garlanded themselves with pearls, and drank from golden bowls encrusted with garnets. Such were the effects of contact with the luxuries of settlement.

The nomad ruler could only attract followers if he rewarded them well. An ungenerous lord was a dead lord. Once the supply of luxuries dwindled, he had a clear choice, blackmail or war. Ssu-Ma Ch'ien records that the Hsiung-Nu appointed a Chinese renegade to handle their diplomatic exchanges with the Imperial authorities; he advised the ambassadors to make sure that their tribute of grain and silks was of fine quality and the right quantity; if not, 'when the autumn harvest comes we will take our horses and trample your crops'. Once the settlers hardened their hearts and the subsidies dried up, the nomad ruler had no alternative, but to risk deploying his 'natural' military machine against the glittering metropolises of the plains.

*   *   *

Bruce Chatwin (1940–89) worked for Sotheby's auction house and the *Sunday Times* before launching his short but varied writing career. His books, beginning with *In Patagonia* (1977), challenged the conventions of travel writing, fiction, biography, anthropology and history, and frequently combined all five genres. In 1981 he wrote the introduction to a reprint of *The Road to Oxiana* by the equally iconoclastic Robert Byron. Chatwin's thesis on nomadism, of which this article forms an early part, was brought to conclusion in *The Songlines* (1987).

35

An Ungovernable People

JOHN BREWER

(January 1980)

The history of crime, argued John Brewer, has tended to take the form either of exotic tales of derring-do or of dry legal records. But insights from the social sciences can now enable the historian to dig deeper and explain why (for example) certain actions were regarded as criminal – and under what circumstances a convicted criminal would receive or evade punishment.

The history of crime has two spiritual ancestors: one exotic, the other mundane. The former is the literature of crime, the latter the history of the law. The literature of crime exerts an almost universal fascination. Even the most law-abiding citizen seems to derive pleasure from its tales. Whether this enjoyment stems from a vicarious *frisson* or a feeling of moral superiority, it has kept many an author in pocket and filled many a library shelf. This is not a new phenomenon: fascination with exotic and daring crimes was as prevalent in Stuart and Hanoverian England as it is today. Popular ballads, the broadsheet, 'dying-speeches' of executed felons, compendia of crimes like *The Counters Commonwealth* of 1617 or of thieves' lives such as Alexander Smith's *A History of the Lives and Robberies of the Most Notorious Highwaymen* (1719), together with such low-life novels as Defoe's *Moll Flanders*, catered to a seemingly inexhaustible appetite for tales of crime and roguery.

Much of this literature is heroic or picaresque. It focuses on such dashing figures as Morgan, the eighteenth-century highwayman, 'a flashy blade' and ladies' man, who declared:

> I scorn poor people for to rob,
> I thought it so my duty;
> But when I meet the rich and gay,
> On them I make my booty.

Such tales of 'social banditry' are complemented, both in criminal literature and histories of crime, by accounts of especially gruesome crimes such as that committed by Sarah Malcolm, a London laundress, who in 1733 robbed and strangled two old ladies, after first cutting the throat of their young maid. The romantic and the horrific go cheek and jowl with the spectacular. Eighteenth- and twentieth-century Englishmen can share admiration for criminals like Jack Sheppard who, though only 5ft 4in and of slight build, escaped from Newgate in 1724 by breaking his chains and fetters as well as forcing his way through six iron-barred doors, or for Jonathan Wild, who has the dubious distinction of being the founding father of the protection racket and of organised crime in eighteenth-century London. Their world – usually an urban one – fascinates us with its exotic crimes and criminal language: 'the rattling lay' – theft from moving coaches, which might involve cutting open their leather roofs and seizing goods from the very heads and hands of disconcerted passengers; 'wild rogues' and 'anglers' – thieves who stole wigs and hats with fishing rods and lines from windows and tenements.

Such picaresque anecdotes are a far cry from the scrupulous dealings of legal historians.They treat the law and offenders in an abstract and impersonal manner, examining rules, principles and precepts, and exploring a highly technical body of knowledge, expressed in an arcane vocabulary. The most outré crime, if it falls clearly within the conventional legal boundaries, may be of no interest to the legal historian. But a minor event – the most famous example is the finding of a snail in a bottle of ginger beer, a case which established the modern rules of tort – may be of enormous legal importance. For legal history has traditionally focused on legal principles, judicial processes and procedures, and on legal institutions.

The history of crime, it would appear, has been as engaging and ill-disciplined as legal history has been rigorous and dull. Whatever their past failings the two are today beginning to join in fruitful union. We can best understand why if we consider the weaknesses to which each is prey.

Too much of the history of crime has depended on criminal literature rather than the criminal record. Checked against the business of the assize and quarter sessions courts, especially those outside London, the romantic highwayman and criminal gangs dwindle into insignificance when compared with the numerous petty thefts and assaults that make up the bulk of prosaic criminal record. At the Wiltshire quarter sessions and assize of 1736, for example, the items stolen included 'a piece of old blanket and a piece of coarse sheet', bread, cheese, butter and a knife, a sow pig, 'a shift worth 5/-' (the woman who stole it was publicly whipped and imprisoned for three months), several pails, 'a pair of grey worsted stockings', faggots of wood, eight brace of pond trout, and a bay gelding taken by a young man who paid for the crime with his life. Such stealing speaks more of poverty than of the big-time criminal operator.

The record of personal violence was equally commonplace. Typical of the numerous assaults that came to the Wiltshire courts in 1736 was the attack made by John Watkins, brickmaker, and his servant, Isaac Carter, on Thomas Hopkins, a mason, in that all-too-common venue of riot and assault, the local ale-house. Watkin apparently called Hopkins 'rogue and son of a whore' and 'pulled the said Hopkins by the nose'.

Juxtaposed with the criminal record the literature of crime often seems flamboyant and therefore needs to be treated with caution. It is more likely to tell us about particular crimes than about 'crime' as a whole, and even more likely to throw light on the complex and usually highly ambivalent attitudes that were expressed towards criminals. This is not an argument for the abandonment of such literature, but for the recognition of its limitations. Much seventeenth- and eighteenth-century criminal biography – particularly the *Accounts* of the Ordinary of Newgate, the lives of condemned felons written by the chaplain of Newgate goal – is valuable for its personal detail and information about criminal language and criminal technique. But to carry conviction it needs the corroborative support of the legal record, and has always to be placed in the context of what we know about day-to-day crime.

It is this gap that legal history seeks to fill. Legal historians want to know what law criminals broke, whether they were prosecuted under a particular statute or the common law, what court they were tried in, what procedures were used to effect the prosecution, and how the trial was conducted. But the legal historian has not, in the past, been inclined to ask why certain acts are designated illegal or why certain offences elicited such violent retribution. 'The law' is often taken as a given, and its development largely explained in terms of its own internal logic. This perspective, however, makes the historian uncomfortable, for it implies that the logic of the law is separable from the society in which it operates.

Recent studies of crime have tried to avoid the pitfalls revealed by the older literature and to incorporate its insights. The new interest in crime is part of a growing willingness among historians to draw on the insights of such 'human sciences' as psychology, sociology, anthropology and geography. Alongside studies of the venerable institutions, of the rich, the well-educated, the bloated and the opulent, we now have studies of crime, sex, family life, death and madness, and of the starving and the destitute, those for whom it was a triumph to make ends meet.

The discipline of history has lost much of its insularity and this development goes far to explain the current preoccupation with both crime and legal records. The historian who seeks to construct the lives of the poor and illiterate is hard pressed to find their testimony: these are not the sort who had the time, skill or leisure to write well-turned letters or keep diaries or accounts destined for the family archive. Yet such people are an ubiquitous presence in the legal record; they flicker in and out of view, leaving us with numerous fragments of many men's lives.

These pieces help solve puzzles of social history. Because such a high proportion of murders were perpetrated by kith upon kin, we can learn much about domestic attitudes and living arrangements from the depositions for murder trials and from the evidence of coroners' courts. Trials for theft or infanticide reveal the plight of the domestic servant; proceedings against rioters reveal their grievances. Prosecutions for drunkenness – 'tippling' – or assault, illuminate the dark interior of the seventeenth- and eighteenth-century ale-house. And there is the plethora of records that cover activities that only the misanthrope would call 'criminal'. Court records inform us about the indigent poor and the vagabond, about the state of roads and bridges in need of repair, and of such public nuisances as an alley or lane that a citizen had carelessly blocked, or a street that he had foolishly fouled with manure or 'night soil'. The ambit and scope of the law was such in seventeenth- and eighteenth-century England that it touched most men's lives, not least those of the humble, and for this reason social historians revere its record.

Criminal and legal records are not just an incidental though important source for the historians of domestic and social life. They also provide answers to the important question of the meaning of crime and criminal activity in Stuart and Hanoverian England. Who broke the law? What were their motives? What is the significance of different types of criminality? To tackle such questions successfully, we need to examine not only the criminal, but the law, the law-maker and the law-enforcer.

Such an approach assumes that the law usually serves several important functions – to legitimate the exercise of authority, regulate social conduct, resolve disputes, and protect and perpetuate highly regarded social values. It also assumes that the substance of the law in a state such as England in the seventeenth and eighteenth centuries had social as well as juridical origins, and that the body of English law was a function of who exercised authority. Law-makers as much as law-breakers create crime. To understand the social significance of crime, we therefore need to know why certain acts were made, or considered to be, criminal.

Seventeenth- and eighteenth-century criminal statistics, like most tables of figures, are deceptively reassuring, derived as they are from criminal indictments. These furnish us with abundant information, including the name, residence and occupation of the person charged, together with the nature of his crime. Complete series of indictments do not, of course, always survive, and they are obtainable only county by county – there are no national crime figures before 1805 – yet the figures have delivered a rich harvest of information. There are, nevertheless, serious inaccuracies and inadequacies in this data. The historian who starts out with the expectation of constructing a social profile of offenders, or of recreating the geographical distribution and seasonal pattern of crime risks a rude awakening if he takes the indictments at face value, for they frequently misdescribe the occupation of the accused, his place of residence and the date of his offence.

Nevertheless the offence itself is usually accurately described and it is therefore possible to chart secular trends in *prosecuted* crime. On the basis of these figures two highly tentative conclusions have emerged. First, in both the seventeenth and eighteenth centuries there was often a link between the prices of basic foodstuffs and observable rates of rural crime. Secondly, the rates of indictable urban crimes against property ebbed and flowed in the eighteenth century according to whether or not the nation was at war. Periods after the termination of hostilities were especially notorious for sharp increases in indictable crime; these are usually explained by the sudden influx of demobilised soldiers and sailors on a labour market already dislocated by the economic transition from war to peace. Thus in both rural and urban cases the increases in indictable crimes against property seem to share a common explanation – want – whether caused by unemployment or high prices, or a combination of both.

But what, it must now be asked, is the relationship between prosecuted crime and the 'dark figure' of crime – the volume and rate of un-prosecuted offences? Moreover, is that relationship constant or liable to fluctuate? Might not a sudden upsurge in indictable crime be as much a consequence of a judicial crackdown as of an absolute increase in the number of offences committed? Can we really demonstrate that, in the judicial system of seventeenth- and eighteenth-century England, where there was no modern police, no systematic attempt at criminal detection, and where prosecution for most offences was brought *privately*, that both the rate of detection and the rate of prosecution bore a reasonably constant relationship to the 'dark figure' of crime? It is only in the *context* both of crime and of criminal prosecution that we can understand what the statistics mean.

In the current state of research we do not have a complete picture of the factors affecting crime rates from the accession of James I to the demise of George III. Rather we have to content ourselves with small studies, executed in a highly impressionistic manner, that have focused on three main subjects: changes in the law that created new categories or types of offence; factors, especially the strength and weakness of authority, that affected law enforcement; and the attitudes of the public towards the law.

The aspect of law-making that has attracted most attention in recent years is the enormous proliferation of statute law after 1688. The Glorious Revolution ensured a standing Parliament which busied itself as never before. By the first decade of George III's reign over 200 acts were being passed every year, four times the rate in the last decade of the seventeenth century. Much of the legislation took the form of private bills effecting local 'improvement' – the building of a turnpike or a canal, the erection of a hospital, dock or lighthouse, or the completion of an enclosure – or was concerned with the nation's burgeoning finances. But crime was also high on the legislators' list of priorities. There were three marked trends in this legislation. Between 1688 and 1820 the number of capital offences increased from about 50 to 200; traditional or customary rights – such as the gathering of firewood from hedgerows for the humble hearth – were converted into acts of theft; and the ambit of summary jurisdiction – trial without recourse to a jury – was extended, especially in legislation that dealt with the common labourer and the poor.

Nearly all the new capital statutes passed in the eighteenth century were designed to protect property from theft, forgery or some form of destruction. The largest single group of newly enacted laws covered forgery and fraud and protected the products of what one contemporary called 'the paper revolution': it was a capital offence to forge any of the instruments of public and private credit – bills of exchange, personal or bank notes, bonds and government securities. These laws were rigorously enforced. Even men of rank convicted of forgery found it almost impossible to win reprieve from the gallows. Thus Rev. William Dodd, fashionable preacher and former royal chaplain, was executed in 1777 for forging Lord Chesterfield's signature on a bond, despite the efforts of important friends, including Dr. Johnson, to secure his pardon. Most of the other capital statutes covered robbery and theft or other attacks on property such as arson and destruction – the deliberate firing of houses and the smashing of turnpike gates and toll-booths are two typical instances. Some idea of the scope of this legislation can be obtained from the most notorious capital statute of the eighteenth century, the Black Act of 1723, which created some fifty new capital offences. These included being armed or disguised in a deer park, breaking down the head of a fishpond, maiming cattle, destroying trees, and sending anonymous threatening letters. It was statutes such as these that led one eighteenth-century commentator to the conclusion that the English criminal code 'breathed the spirit of Draco'.

This sanguinary legislation is eloquent testimony to Parliament's sanctification of property, and lack of regard for human life. It is no coincidence that in the seventeenth and eighteenth centuries most crimes against persons were punished far more leniently than crimes against property. The capital statutes are also presumptive evidence of the desire not merely to deter but to overawe and intimidate. The prospect of the road to the gallows, the gibbet, and thence to the surgeon's dissecting rooms, where the bodies of the most heinous offenders were dismembered in the cause of medical science, was intended to intimidate. Legislators wished to be sure that the populace knew of the courts' terrible powers of retribution, and it was for this reason that they required that the Black Act be read at the beginning of every sessions.

This does not mean that the eighteenth-century landscape was transformed into a suitable subject for the pen of Callot or Goya. Though there were more capital statutes than in the seventeenth century, there were fewer actual executions. This is partly explained by the infrequency with which prosecutions under the new capital statutes were undertaken. Only acts concerned with forgery, sheep-stealing and theft from shops and warehouses were assiduously prosecuted. In other prosecutions under the new laws the jury was more likely to return a partial verdict – valuing the stolen goods below the amount that would have meant the death sentence – or to commit 'pious perjury', acquitting the accused against the evidence, rather than seeing him hang. Judges, as well as juries, were reluctant to send to the gallows an offender charged under a statute that had transformed a trivial theft into a capital offence. Conviction was therefore less likely and royal pardon more probable for offenders prosecuted under these acts. The bark of the new law was fiercer than its bite.

We are, therefore, confronted with a paradox. The capital statutes might be and were employed as instruments of terror; but the overall impact of the capital statutes was to inhibit successful prosecution and conviction of thieves. Why, then, did legislators trade the opportunity for judicial efficiency for the chance to exercise judicial terror? It has been argued that the choice can be explained by the role that the law played as a legitimating ideology of the propertied ruling class. The elaborate spectacle of the law – including gruesome executions – awed the populace. The inefficiency of the law and the tenderness shown towards the rights of the accused helped perpetuate the belief that the 'rule of law' ensured fair and equal treatment for citizens of all classes. Above all, the judicial system conferred discretionary powers on prosecutors, judges and juries that could be used to reward the contrite and deferential and to punish the recalcitrant and unrepentant.

This does not, however, provide an adequate explanation of the proliferation of capital statutes. For if the law served these functions in the eighteenth century, it also did so in the seventeenth, before the rash of new legislation. Sensitivity to the rights of property, judicial discretion, retributive terror, and the ideology of the 'rule of law' were as characteristic of Stuart as of Hanovarian justice. The question why so many new capital statutes were introduced is therefore still largely unresolved.

It seems, however, that the new penal laws were part of a broader phenomenon: the increased willingness of local property owners and interest groups to employ parliamentary statute to further their own ends, and the increased willingness of legislators to respond, in a highly interested way, to their pressures. Thus many capital statutes were passed because of a local crisis – the turnpike riots of Herefordshire and the Bristol area, for example, led directly to a statute making the destruction of turnpikes a capital offence in 1735.

The general thrust of capital legislation, and of criminal and private bill legislation as a whole, is clear enough: it served to facilitate the growth of British capitalism, to protect property, to lay down the ground rules for economic growth, and to stack the legal cards heavily in favour of the landlord and the employer in pursuit of efficiency and greater profit. But more needs to be known about the circumstances that led to the passage of particular capital statutes.

It is much easier for a government to enact legislation than to secure its enforcement. A number of characteristics of the seventeenth- and eighteenth-century legal system militated strongly against the methodical and consistent execution of the law. First there was no official salaried bureaucracy, equivalent to our modern police, whose task was to prevent, detect and prosecute crime. The only full-time, salaried employees of the state who acted as 'policemen' were the much-hated revenue officers who enforced the customs and excise laws. Criminal justice was in the hands of local amateurs: parish constables, elected or appointed annually, and justices of the peace who shouldered the burden of both administrative and criminal law. Neither constables nor justices were paid, though justices charged fees and constables could recover their costs and expenses for their year of service. Their offices were not a profession but a civic responsibility.

This amateur system, though thought to be less efficient than the bureaucratic organisation of the absolutist states of continental Europe, was approved by most Englishmen. The participation of the nation's citizens in the workings of justice helped, it was argued, to ensure an equitable system. Citizens in office were legally responsible for their actions and therefore less likely than lackeys of the state to act arbitrarily.

Indeed, amateur officials were a bulwark of freedom for they prevented the formation of a bureaucracy that could be used by the monarch and his court to subjugate the nation. The weak, relatively inefficient and decentralised system, which largely depended on the gratuitous services of local men, was the price Englishmen paid for their much-vaunted rights and liberties.

Such an exchange was hardly conducive to effective law enforcement. During the late seventeenth and eighteenth centuries the situation was exacerbated by the growing volume of judicial and administrative business. Local constables and justices were inundated with work. New duties were added to traditional tasks. Constables were supposed to keep the peace, bring felons to justice, execute warrants, and draw up local jury lists. Justices' duties, apart from the implementation of criminal justice, included regulation of the poor law, and the state of the highways, prices and wages, marketing practices, and weights and measures. Such a workload did not encourage assiduous prosecution of the law.

The absence of salaries also inhibited prosecutions. Constables paid costs out of their own pocket and then sought reimbursement. This could be a protracted affair that put an office-holder's finances in jeopardy. Even state officials suffered. The Mint Solicitor, whose task was to prosecute those who defaced and forged the coin of the realm, was allowed a *fixed sum* for the expenses he incurred as a prosecutor. A zealous official therefore courted financial misfortune. Indeed, Fountaine Cooke, Mint Solicitor between 1748 and 1755, went bankrupt when the Treasury refused to pay his excess balances.

There were, then, good reasons why officials should want to let sleeping dogs lie. These disincentives to prosecution were not, however, alone responsible for official lassitude. Most citizens entertained a highly circumscribed view of the legitimate realm of official legal activity. It is difficult to convey to the modern reader the extraordinary sensitivity of the seventeenth- and eighteenth-century Englishman to any form of official interference. In consequence, the execution of the law was a hazardous undertaking. In 1751, when the parish constable of Sutton in Surrey tried to serve a warrant on a labourer's wife, she seized the document, 'tore it into several pieces, some of which she put into her mouth and chewed them and then spit it out on the ground and immediately struck him . . . several times in the face'. The court records abound with indictments for assault upon magistrates, constables, churchwardens and bailiffs. Officials also had to beware of legal actions taken against them by easily aggrieved citizens. Legal manuals of the period, such as Paul's *Parish Officer*, give detailed accounts of constables' limited powers of apprehension and entry. Great caution had to be exercised if the constable was not to find himself countersuited for assault or trespass.

Passivity, in other words, was built into the system. There was almost no attempt at criminal detection, except in times of crisis or emergency. Crime was brought to the courts; officials did not go out in pursuit of crime. Almost all prosecutions were brought privately: the victim or prosecutor summoned the local constable from his home, or hurried for a warrant to the justice's parlour. Only then did officials intervene, for any earlier action would have been regarded as an unjustifiable intrusion.

A major reason for this languid approach to law enforcement was the limited amount of physical, coercive force available to justices and constables. Lack of numbers, formal training and organisation all militated against legal *force majeure*. Occasionally a justice would muster a *posse* of servants and tenants – William Blaithwaite, a Gloucestershire magistrate assembled just such a body in 1731 to seize men destroying a local turnpike gate – or could turn, *in extremis*, to government troops. But the military were a cumbersome, expensive and unpopular weapon, liable to cause more trouble than they resolved. Instead of recourse to force of arms, law officers were expected to call for aid on the public, who were legally obliged to assist in the apprehension of felons. Such an appeal, however, depended on the authorities' ability to command popular support for their actions. Because of popular antipathy towards officials, assistance might be hard to win and was certainly not automatically forthcoming.

This helps explain the generally conciliatory and restrained response of officials to law-breaking. Most seventeenth- and eighteenth-century communities, even when they quarrelled bitterly, placed high value on social peace and harmony. They expected officials to help preserve these qualities. An officious constable was likely to create divisions in the community and to excite the wrath of his neighbours, making explicit the tension between two important community values – lawfulness and good neighbourliness.

On the whole, officials favoured a peaceful community over a strictly enforced law. Many constables tried to reconcile disputes in order to avoid vexatious litigation. Similar mediation occurred in cases of theft. Thus one seventeenth-century Essex constable who had apprehended a chicken-thief was able to release him after he had interceded with the owner of the birds. Justices of the peace seem to have adopted much the same approach. Henry Purefoy, the local squire, lord of the manor and justice of Shalstone in Buckinghamshire, was often asked by villagers to arbitrate disputes or to act on behalf of the whole community. When, for example, in 1753 Widow Pennell complained that the curate insisted that he had a right of way through her grounds, Purefoy wrote to the cleric on her behalf: 'I can assure you there is no Horse way there & must desire you to desist & not come there, for the woman is about to hayne her ground.' No formal legal action was necessary. Even during a riot the first action taken by the justices was usually conciliatory. They tried to reason with the crowd, perhaps to promise some form of redress, and to urge the folly of taking direct action.

This pragmatic approach to law enforcement helped determine who ended up in court. Villagers were more likely to prosecute strangers than neighbours, and if they took action against a local man it was probably because he was a persistent offender, or was a reputed troublemaker. The same Henry Purefoy who sided with a gamekeeper's widow against the curate was willing to have the Jaycocks family removed from the parish because he thought them a thoroughly bad lot.

The leeway conferred on magistrates and constables is one explanation of the remarkable discrepancies in levels of local law enforcement. Officials in one parish rigorously enforced laws that were flouted with impunity in another. But the effectiveness of law enforcement also depended on the availability or presence of the agents of justice, and this varied enormously from one place to another. There were some areas with little or no policing at all. These 'lawless' areas included forests and wastes which had been settled by cottages and squatters, industrial parishes such as Halifax whose population had grown apace, and parts of the metropolitan area of London. Few resident gentry were to be found in these places and the Church had little influence. The inhabitants of lawless areas were known for their economic independence, their 'licentiousness', their strong sense of community solidarity, and their marked antipathy towards officers of the law. Such places were regarded by the 'respectable' with a mixture of fear and revulsion. Cranborne Chase in Dorsetshire was described as the seat of 'all kinds of profligacy and immorality' while, according to the Mayor of Bristol, the collier inhabitants of Kingswood Forest, just east of the city, were 'a set of ungovernable people violent in their way, and regardless of Consequences'. When in 1739 a sheriff successfully requisitioned the goods of a Kingswood man, local inhabitants were amazed: 'This may be deem'd a great Favour, no Officer having within Memory of the oldest Man Living, been able to effect an Undertaking of this Nature in so peaceable a Manner.'

Normally those in 'lawless' areas showed scant respect for officers of the law. Any bailiff, for example, who ventured within the precincts of 'The Mint', an ancient debtors' sanctuary that also harboured criminals located in Southwark, did so at his peril. Here clubs of so-called Shelterers defended men against arrest and seized and 'tried' suspected bailiffs. Minter summary justice consisted of 'pumping': the bailiff was plunged under every pump in the district, ducked in tubs of urine, covered and daubed with every sort of filth and finally thrown in the kennel, the malodorous open sewer that ran down the street. In 1705 twenty-one constables and four justices of the peace had to fight a pitched battle with 'Shelterers' before they could seize a bankrupt and his wares.

Part of the difficulty of policing these areas stemmed from their populousness. A textile parish such as Halifax, which also housed the largest eighteenth-century coining and counterfeiting operation, had over 8,000 families by the 1760s but *no* acting magistrate. Most of the justices resided in the agricultural area some distance to the east. Anyone who wanted to take legal action or bring an offender before a justice had to be prepared to travel several miles over difficult terrain. Justices were loath to act in Halifax for they feared the workload that they knew they would incur.

Though 'the law' was national and uniform, applying to all Englishmen, the administration of justice was not only localised but personalised – the strict or lax enforcement of the law was often associated with particular individuals. One or two energetic justices could have considerable impact on a particular region or county. On the other hand, constables or magistrates who disliked a new regulation or parliamentary statute could go far to prevent its implementation or nullify its effect in a particular locality. In sum, judicial officials did not share a clear group identity or common outlook.

The right to enforce the law or exercise authority was not the exclusive prerogative of legal officials, but a privilege that, at least in theory, was enjoyed by all Englishmen. Anyone could join the 'hue and cry' in pursuit of a thief, anyone could bring a private prosecution. In this sense authority was not something separate from or exercised upon the citizenry; it was not 'other' but emanated from the people themselves.

This makes it extremely difficult to speak of 'the authorities' not only as a homogeneous group, but as a body with separate identity from the public at large. Amateur office-holders were considered to be of the law and of the community, never above or beyond them. This does not mean that every Englishman exercised authority or had an equal opportunity to do so; the marked discrepancies in wealth and power rendered this virtually impossible. But legal practice bore a sufficiently close resemblance to the ideal of civic involvement to ensure that it was widely believed that one of an Englishman's rights was that of direct participation in the legal process.

This had profound consequences not only on the prosecution of crime but on the operation of the law as a whole. Private initiative was crucial to the workings of the law. This meant that the law was a weapon that could be used in many ways, not solely as a means of class rule, and could on occasion be turned against the government and to restrain those in power. It was, however, a common complaint that special interests, while professing to act for the public good, manipulated the law to their own partial advantage.

This permissive system was easily abused. Individuals and groups were able to use the law as a means of lining their own pockets. I am not here thinking of lawyers (though they excited much popular resentment in the seventeenth and eighteenth centuries and were frequently criticised for fomenting litigation) but of trading justices, thief-takers and bum-bailiffs. These legal profiteers exploited the amateur and voluntarist aspects of the legal system, either taking office for its profits or bringing prosecutions for their financial reward. They exploited both the absence of *salaried* officials and the incentives for private action. Because office-holders were not paid, a number of expedients were devised to make their work remunerative: constables, justices, bailiffs and gaolers had to charge legal fees or for the food and lodging they provided. Equally, in the absence of 'a police', private citizens had to be encouraged to bring prosecutions by a system of compensation and rewards.

Trading justices, who made their living from the perks and fees of their office, set up their 'justice shops' in London and the larger provincial towns. They sold ale-house licences and warrants, apprehended travellers and citizens out at night for the legal fees and the bail-money, mercilessly bullied the poor, and protected bordellos in return for periodic bribes and services. The trading justice thrived on crime; it was in his interest not to suppress but to stimulate infractions of the law. Smollett's Justice Gobble was typical of this venal and profligate breed:

> Instead of protecting the helpless, restraining the hands of violence, preserving the public tranquillity, and acting as the father of the poor . . . you have distressed the widow and the orphan, given a loose to all the insolence of office, embroiled your neighbours by fomenting suits and animosities, and played the tyrant among the indigent and forlorn.

The employment of thief-takers was similar to the pettifogging work of the trading justice. They earned their ill-gotten gains from the reward money and other perquisites offered by the government, local authorities and private individuals for the successful prosecution of criminals. This sordid and despised business could be very profitable. A reward of £50 was, after all, as much if not more than the annual income of the industrious artisan. Moreover thief-takers, like all citizens, could also sell their 'Tyburn tickets', the life-long exemption from public office (such as constable) that was part of the reward for helping to convict a felon. These could fetch as much as ten guineas.

William Payne, a London thief-taker of Bell Yard new Temple Bar, was described in court records as a carpenter. However, his legal activities probably permitted him little time at the work-bench. Between 1768 and 1771, for instance, he was instrumental in no fewer than sixty-nine prosecutions at the London sessions. He prosecuted or was a key witness in cases of theft, assault, riot, keeping a bawdy house, being a popish priest, receiving stolen goods, burglary and holding an unlawful conventicle. Payne would mingle with the London crowd, looking for custom. Thus on Easter Monday, 1769 he seized a pickpocket who had stolen a silk handkerchief from one of the crowd watching the Lord Mayor return from church. A few weeks later he 'pinched' two pickpockets who were cheekily practising their legerdemain in one of the city's courts.

Though profitable, a thief-taker's work was also dangerous. He was hated and despised, living 'by the price of blood'. William Payne was beaten up on several occasions, and twice in 1768 someone tried to set his workshop on fire.

But the most passionately hated legal profiteer was the bum-bailiff. The antipathy towards him was partly a result of his association with the unpopular practice of imprisonment for debt, though he compounded his offence by taking egregious advantage of the financially oppressed. Bailiffs who seized debtors usually held them in so-called sponging houses – small lock-ups which were often no more than a well-barred private house. Here they mulcted their victims, forcing them to pay what were often exorbitant prices for food and lodging. This exploitation of men and women in dire straits, and who were not regarded by the public at large as 'criminals', excited deep hostility. It is notable, for example, that the only trade or calling explicitly excluded from membership in the rules of most eighteenth-century friendly societies was that of bailiff.

Pecuniary gain was not the only motive for the initiation of prosecutions. Many different groups with an axe to grind turned to the law to gain support. Moralists, concerned with 'godliness' and public conduct, set about prosecuting the impious and dissolute. In early seventeenth-century Essex, for example, yeoman villagers initiated prosecutions to stop ale-house tippling and non-attendance at church. Similarly in eighteenth-century England, Societies for the Reformation of Manners, alarmed by the spread of impiety and social insubordination, raised funds to prosecute the crapulous, the lubricious and politically radical. Associations of florists were formed to prosecute those who stole flowers.

Farmers and gentry banded together to finance the pursuit of horse-thieves. By the last quarter of the eighteenth century there was scarcely a market town in the country without its society or association for the prosecution of felons. These sought to deter crime by increasing the likelihood of prosecution, and all were financed by a common fund on which members could draw in order to initiate legal action.

Law enforcement in seventeenth- and eighteenth-century England, whether carried out by the authorities or as a result of private initiative, was never simply a question of prosecuting crime. Today there are criminal courts; in the seventeenth and eighteenth centuries there were much less precise distinctions between types of legal business. The justices of the peace (and this was also true of judges at the assize courts) dealt with numerous offences that could not be regarded as 'criminal' and with an enormous amount of business that was regulative and administrative. Execution of the law certainly included the prosecution of crime, but it involved much more: England was ruled through the courts (including the highest court of the realm, Parliament) and their chief business was *governance*. It was in the court-room, or at least in the parlour of the justice of the peace, that most humble Englishmen were made aware of the powers that were wielded over them. Weak as it may appear to us today, the long arm of the law was the strongest limb of the body politic.

This situation compounds the difficulties of historians who wish to discuss *attitudes* towards crime. Just as there was no institutional distinction between criminal and other legal business, so there was no clear seventeenth- and eighteenth-century definition of crime. How then does the historian reconstruct attitudes towards 'crime'? There seem to be two answers to this conundrum. One approach, though a highly circumscribed one, is to adopt seventeenth- and eighteenth-century ways of looking at the law: to distinguish between felonies (which approximated to what we would call crime) and trespasses or misdemeanours. The other, which is ahistorical, is to define crime much more broadly so as to include offences that were not felonies but which can plausibly be considered as crimes: poaching and prostitution, for instance, would fall into this category. The pitfalls of both can be avoided if we examine attitudes towards particular offences.

There were numerous instances, in seventeenth- and eighteenth-century England, of clashes between the letter of the law and popular notions of what was just or justifiable. Several offences – poaching is the most notorious example – were regarded as legitimate, though illegal. Farmers and agricultural labourers saw no reason why wild game, which was both nutritious and a pest, should not supply the demotic stew-pot as well as the tables of the landed gentry. Pilferage from work – keeping pieces of wood, scrap metal and excess cloth – was seen as part of labour's reward, not as the heinous crime of embezzlement. This divergence between the law and popular attitudes was not a minor dissonance, an inconsequential interruption to social harmony. The law affected the livelihood of the labouring poor. Grievances periodically erupted into violence; direct action opposed the law.

All of this smacks of what has been called 'social protest' or 'social crime'. The interest in such crimes and the attitudes that they express lies in what they teach us about social conflict and attitudes towards those in authority: was popular hostility confined to particular laws or did it extend to the law as a whole? If the nation was governed through the law and its courts, was antipathy towards laws symptomatic of a conflict of values between rulers and ruled? When men and women stole, poached, smuggled and rioted, when they violently opposed new legislation, were they asserting popular values that rejected the culture of the nation's propertied elite? Were they, in fact, challenging the legitimacy of those in authority?

Such questions are not easily answered and certainly they cannot be satisfactorily resolved by indiscriminate use of such ill-defined terms as 'social protest' and 'social crime'. One can, however, distinguish crimes on the basis of public attitudes towards particular offences. The majority of thefts were regarded by members of all classes as serious, anti-social and morally reprehensible acts. Though the labourer and the artisan were less likely to bring a prosecution for theft to court and more likely to employ an extra-legal form of retribution if they were robbed – tossing the malefactor into a kennel, river or duckpond – they accepted the need for laws to protect most forms of property. This does not mean that they were blood-thirsty advocates of hanging and gibbeting, but when the hue and cry was raised, when a neighbour shouted 'Stop Thief!', they did not hesitate to chase after the offender.

Attitudes towards most other 'crimes' were, however, somewhat different. Offences against public order, minor assaults and altercations that stemmed from disagreements, and such 'victimless' crimes as swearing, gambling, prostitution, and 'tippling' were all viewed by the labouring poor – and by many of their social superiors – with the sort of tolerance that most of the public now confer on the speeding motorist. Naturally those who led a licentious life stirred the sanctimonious bile of some of their fellow citizens. Seventeenth-century puritan yeomen and gentry, for example, vented their righteous indignation by prosecuting the moral laxities of the poor. But it was not until the late eighteenth century that the terms gentility and vulgarity clearly distinguished both social classes and their own peculiar moral qualities.

Yet a third category of crimes were those offences whose permissibility provoked contentious and sometimes violent disagreement. Smuggling, poaching, pilferage by employees, coining and counterfeiting all fall into this group. They were all characterised by a sharp discrepancy between popular attitude and the letter of the law, and they all saw vigorous campaigns by those in authority to suppress them.

Finally, there were those offences committed as a direct challenge to particular laws: the tearing down of newly-erected hedgerows around agricultural and common land to thwart enclosure legislation, the smashing of gates and tolls to prevent the implementation of turnpike bills, the destruction of muster rolls to stop conscription under a militia bill, the deliberate use of illegal acts to draw attention to a particular legal grievance. These crimes constituted the most explicit defiance of the law; they flung down the gauntlet before those in authority. There was little attempt, as there was in smuggling and coining, at concealment of the crime; on the contrary magistrates were often informed of the impending offence. In June, 1753, for example, a crowd went to a meeting of turnpike commissioners at Arthington in Yorkshire and announced their intention of destroying the toll-bar at Harewood bridge. The offence was a *public* act, not only intended to prevent the implementation of a particular law, but to draw attention to a particular grievance. The crime in other words had both instrumental and symbolic force.

How we are to interpret this willingness to set one's face against the law? Antipathy towards particular laws does not seem to have *escalated* into a general critique of 'the law'. Equally, criticism of magistrates rarely went so far as to challenge their right to rule. Usually both individual laws and magistrates were judged according to whether or not they matched the principles and expectations of the English 'rule of law'. Justices were censured for their dereliction of duty; legislation was excoriated for its denial of the spirit of 'the law'. Thus, when the Kingswood colliers who had destroyed local turnpikes sent a collective manifesto to the members of the Bristol turnpike trust in 1727, they justified their action as a salutary corrective to the negligence of the magistrates. The imposition of a turnpike, the colliers claimed, was the direct consequence of the justices' failure to fulfil their obligation to keep the roads in good repair; 'by the Omission of your Duty, and your Carelessness and Oversight you have lost y'r Honourable Magistracy, and brought your self under the reproach of a Turnpike'. The rioters' action was therefore remedial rather than rebellious; they were rapping the magistrates over the knuckles. Their letter even suggested that turnpike profits could usefully be invested in catechisms for the justices 'that they may Learn to do their Duty in that State of Life unto which it shall please God to call them'.

In making the claim that they had the right to intervene in the workings of justice, the rioters reveal to us the extent and strength of the belief, embodied in the law itself, that the implementation of justice was the business of every honest citizen, no matter how humble, and that office-holders, be they ever so proud, were publicly accountable.

Attitudes towards crimes in the seventeenth and eighteenth centuries were therefore varied and disparate. If we equate perceptions of theft with views of such offences as the destruction of enclosures and turnpikes we will have failed to make important distinctions that were all too obvious to Stuart and Hanoverian Englishmen. On the other hand, our examination of the heterogeneous attitudes towards crime reveals a more homogeneous view of 'the law'. For it is remarkable how deeply the belief in the 'rule of law' penetrated English culture. It was even to be found amongst the humblest and most aggrieved members of the nation. The workings of the law and its theoretical under-pinnings were largely accepted by Englishmen because, for all its faults and inadequacies, the law as a whole (and the criminal law was only a part of this ubiquitous phenomenon) conferred tangible benefits. English law was more sensitive to subjects' rights than its continental counterparts; there was substance – as well as a good deal of mythology – incorporated in Englishmen's rights and liberties. And so this ideology or belief, nurtured by certain aspects of the legal system, served to limit or constrain antagonisms, even when particular laws epitomised or exacerbated the numerous social conflicts that rent English society.

*   *   *

John Brewer is John and Marion Sullivan University Professor in English and History at the University of Chicago. He was previously Director of the Clark Library and the Centre for Seventeenth- and Eighteenth-Century Studies at the University of California, Los Angeles 1987–91 and Professor in the Department of History and Civilization at the European University Institute, Florence 1993–9. He is the author of several books including *Sinews of Power* (1989) and *The Pleasures of the Imagination: English Culture in the Eighteenth Century* (1997) and co-editor of *Consumption and the World of Goods* (1993), *Early Modern Conceptions of Property* (1995) and *The Consumption of Culture 1600–1800* (1995).

36

A Nazi Travels to Palestine

JACOB BOAS

(January 1980)

During the early years of the Hitler regime, a Nazi official and a representative of German Zionism, each of them preoccupied with the future of German Jewry, travelled together to Palestine. Predictably, this article by Jacob Boas aroused considerable discussion.

In the spring of 1933 four people gathered on a platform of Berlin's railway station ready to board a train for Trieste, where they were to take a ship bound for Palestine. What made this group unusual was the fact that it was composed of two couples, one Jewish, the other Nazi, only two months after Hitler's appointment as Chancellor of the German Reich and his first legislation against non-Aryans. Yet the two couples were travelling with the sanction of both the Nazi (National Socialist German Workers) Party and the Zionist Federation of Germany. They were engaged in a mission whose invisible fellow-traveller was the fate of German Jewry.

The Nazis boarding the train were Baron Leopold Itz von Mildenstein and his wife. Von Mildenstein was a member of both the Nazi party and of Hitler's elite bodyguard, the S.S. His Jewish travelling companions were Kurt Tuchler, an official of the Zionist Federation of Germany, who was also accompanied by his wife. What had brought them together on this journey to Palestine was their common desire, motivated by radically different objectives, to make Germany 'free of Jews', or as the Nazis put it, *Judenrein*. Literally 'Jew-pure' – i.e. cleansed or purified of Jews. Where the National Socialists had not yet worked out a solution to 'the Jewish question', the Zionists, with their ambition to establish a Jewish homeland and their sponsorship of Jewish emigration to Palestine, had an answer. After the boycott of German Jews of April 1st, 1933, and the introduction of the non-Aryan legislation less than a week later, Hitler remained largely aloof from the Jewish question, and up until the Party orchestrated pogrom of November 9th–10th, 1938, there was no specific policy concerning its solution. This left the field of Jewish affairs wide open to officials like von Mildenstein to advance policies they thought might solve the problem of what to do with Germany's half-a-million Jews.

Radical elements in the Party, headed by Julius Streicher, had wanted to eject all Jews from Germany, but this course was not pursued mainly because the economic consequences of eliminating the Jews from Depression-ridden Germany would have been disastrous. Representatives of big business in Hitler's government waived their racial convictions in the face of monetary realities. The presence of von Hindenburg, the Reich President, and the possibility of repercussions on foreign opinion were additional restraining factors. The press was also by and large unenthusiastic about the boycott.

Unhappy with the Party's performance on the Jewish question, the S.S. proceeded to formulate its own Jewish policy – a policy which, based as it was on the promotion of Jewish emigration to Palestine, was remarkably like the Zionist programme. With this initiative the S.S. was able to move ahead of its rivals in determining the direction of Nazi Jewish policy, and although S.S. pre-eminence in this sphere proved short-lived, lasting roughly from the end of 1934 through the spring of 1936, what success it did have it owed almost completely to the efforts of Baron Itz Edler von Mildenstein.

Von Mildenstein was a man of some accomplishment and flair. A qualified engineer with a passion for journalism and travel, avocations which he managed to convert into cash as a correspondent for the *Berliner Boersenzeitung*, he was also a keen student of the Jewish question. Perhaps it was his background – he was born in Prague in 1902 and grew up in the twilight of the Austrian multi-national empire – which predisposed him to viewing the resolution of the Jewish problem along the lines of national self-determination; at any rate, the upshot of his inquiry was a pronounced sympathy for the Zionist cause. He even began attending its congresses, familiarising himself with the issues and making friends among the delegates. Curiously, von Mildenstein became an ardent Zionist.

The Baron's peculiar fascination soon earned him the reputation among his S.S. superiors of being an expert on Zionism and its bearing on the Jewish question. His belief that the Zionist programme was both realistic and practical led his Party comrades to see it as a way out of the confusion that had for a long time prevailed among the busy theorists of Nazi Jewish policy. Not inconsequently, it was assured the co-operation of Germany's Zionists who, following the Nazi victory of January, 1933, had become a force to be reckoned with in Germany's Jewish community, where they had had only limited success before 1933. Indeed, the fortunes of Zionism soared with the coming to power of Hitler, a change reflected in the great increase in sales of the *Juedische Rundschau*, the bi-weekly newspaper of the Zionist Federation of Germany, with circulation climbing from a pre-Hitler average of less than 10,000 to almost 38,500 by the end of 1933.

On the strength of this newly found popularity, Zionism claimed for itself an ever greater share of power in the Jewish community, basing its demand on the reputed failure of German Jewry's erstwhile leaders to prepare Jews for the coming of Hitler. The day after Hitler came to power, the *Juedische Rundschau* wrote that the struggle for Jewish rights could only be waged by those whose commitment to the Jewish People and nationality (*Volkstum*) had always been beyond reproach, to wit the Zionists. On April 7th the paper declared that of all Jewish groups only the Zionists were capable of approaching the Nazis in good faith, as 'honest partners'. Two-and-a-half months later, in a memorandum addressed to the Nazi authorities dated June 21st, 1933, the Zionist Federation of Germany in fact proposed the regulation of the status of German Jewry on a group basis and petitioned for government assistance towards an orderly emigration.

That request went unanswered. But there were Nazis, von Mildenstein among them, who appreciated the unsparing efforts of the Zionists to make Germany *Judenrein*. Well aware of this particular current in Nazi thought, the Zionist Federation of Germany commissioned Kurt Tuchler to seek out Zionist sympathisers in the Nazi Party and enlist their aid in acquainting the German public with the Zionist cause and the progress of Jewish efforts in Palestine. Tuchler therefore contacted von Mildenstein and proposed that he write something positive about Jewish Palestine in an influential Nazi paper. Von Mildenstein agreed on condition that he be permitted to visit Palestine himself. Moreover, he asked Tuchler to come along as his guide. So on September 26th, 1934, there appeared under the name of 'Von Lim' the first instalment of 'Ein Nazi faehrt nach Palestina' in *Der Angriff*, Goebbels' influential newspaper. Promoted heavily for weeks in advance, the twelve-part illustrated series ran through October 9th, though understandably enough, 'Von Lim' made no mention of his Jewish guide, other than that he was travelling in the company of someone who knew the country well.

Von Mildenstein and Tuchler boarded the train on that spring day of 1933 amidst cries of 'Shalom' from the young Jewish pioneers – *Halutzim* – who, likewise en route to Palestine, were saying their goodbyes to friends and relatives. The S.S.-man von Mildenstein sat observing them. The faces of the younger ones were radiant and the 'ghetto look', he noted, no longer dwelt there. Some of the older ones were making a radical break with their past, giving up professional status and money for manual occupations, since in Palestine they planned to enter a *kvutza*, a small collective agricultural settlement. All of them, young and old, he observed, were full of pride, for they were going to *their* land, *Eretz Israel*.

On arrival in Trieste, the Baron, his Jewish companions, and the young pioneers boarded the *Martha Washington*, the ship that was to take them to Palestine. Nicknamed the 'Raging Moses', the *Martha Washington* was an old pre-1914 tub hurriedly pressed into service by the British Lloyd Line to reap the profits to be realised from Jewish emigration to Palestine. The *Martha Washington* had three classes, each with its own 'kosher commissioner' and a different menu; only the third class was strictly kosher, while everything else could be had in the first and second classes. Most of the Jews on board were travelling third class, four to six to a cabin. Also present among the 700 to 800 passengers were a number of Jewish professionals, who, frightened by the advent of Hitler and fearing for their future in Germany, were about to take a look at Palestine. Suspicious of their Zionist credentials, the *Halutzim* aboard scornfully referred to them as 'January Zionists', by which they meant the type of Jew who had discovered his Zionist convictions on the day Hitler came to power.

The S.S.-man admitted to feeling uneasy among all those Jews, remarking that, outside of the crew, he was 'the only Goy aboard'. On the eve of the Jewish Sabbath he made himself conspicuous by writing a letter in the reading room, the only one there. Next morning he drew disapproving stares when he appeared on deck with his typewriter. Later in the day he was approached by a young Jew, who told him:

> You are going to Palestine because you . . . do not believe that we are truly capable of working with our hands. Many Jews today still think like you and your people. But they do not understand the fanatical will of our youth. You see, *Zionism is giving us Jews a goal once more*. It reminds us not only that we are a people, but also that we have a fatherland. When forty years ago our teacher Theodor Herzl wrote his book *The Jewish State* and told us that assimilation would not help us but only the realization on our part that we are one people with our own fatherland, our people laughed at him and said he was crazy. Herzl did not live to see his Jewish state, but we young ones have made it a reality.

How much of a reality von Mildenstein would soon be able to discover for himself.

As the 'Raging Moses' pulled into the harbour of Jaffa, the Nazi discerned a change of mood among the passengers: their restlessness, he surmised, was caused as much by the thrill of seeing the land of their dreams as by the fear of the British immigration authorities. For the British, under Arab pressure, had virtually closed the gate to Palestine, limiting the entry of unskilled and pauper Jews to 5,000 for the first six months of 1933. This quota, however, explained von Mildenstein, did not affect skilled labourers with at least four years' experience in their trade and some savings, or the so-called 'capitalists', i.e. Jews with assets of at least 1,000 British pounds. In addition, tourists were required to limit their stay to three months. To circumvent the prevailing restrictions, £1,000 in notes were being passed from hand to hand, and since the British did not follow the practice of some European countries of requiring tourists to register with the police, Palestine soon harboured a large number of 'forgotten tourists', prompting the Arab complaint that illegal Jewish immigration was at least equal in scale to legal immigration. The British responded by making possession of a return ticket and the payment of a security deposit conditions for entry into Palestine, the latter being subject to forfeiture, should the tourist overstay his three month limit.

Since he was not scheduled to disembark until Haifa, von Mildenstein remained on board after most of the passengers had left the ship. On arrival there, he was further delayed while waiting for his car to be unloaded. Meanwhile, it was very clear to him, even from so limited a vantage point as a ship's deck, that Britain was making great strides in developing its 'gateway to India'. The harbour was being enlarged to accommodate the increased flow and volume of trade expected to result from the expanding road and rail network linking the Mediterranean with the Persian Gulf. At its massive stone pier, Shell tankers lay at anchor, sea-borne extensions of the British pipeline which originated in the Mosul oil-fields and terminated in Haifa. And further down, attesting to the city's booming construction industry, the grey chimneys of Haifa's cement factories jutted into the sky.

Ironically two Arabs took von Mildenstein for a stranded Jew and offered to smuggle him into Palestine for money. Once disembarked, he had planned to drive straight to Tel Aviv, some 200 kilometres away. But by the time his car had been taken off the ship, his passport and travel papers inspected, the fees paid and the *baksheesh* distributed, it was afternoon and he was advised by a petrol pump attendant against travelling after nightfall because of the bad condition of the roads and the danger of robbers. Von Mildenstein decided nevertheless to risk it and late that evening arrived in Tel Aviv.

Tel Aviv was Palestine's Jewish city *par excellence* – a 'city without Goyim', to quote von Mildenstein's allusion to Hugo Bettauer's popular novel of 1922, *City without Jews*. 'Only Jews', wrote the Baron 'live here, only Jews work here, only Jews trade, bathe and dance here.' The language of the city, he noted, was Hebrew, down to the menus in the restaurant. But though the language was ancient, the city itself, with its broad avenues and attractive shops, had a thoroughly modern and indeed Western look to it. Of the 'East' it had nothing, concluded von Mildenstein, certainly not its lethargy and torpor. For Tel Aviv virtually shook with the rumble of cement mixers and steam-rollers as construction struggled to keep pace with the city's population explosion. Building contractors were hard put to it to fill the demand for housing; so dire was the shortage that prospective tenants had been known to pay rents on apartments that had barely reached the blueprint stage; while some occupied the bottom floors of units whose upper floors were still under construction. Conditions were so primitive that many a newly arrived Jew from Germany, used to the comforts of middle-class well-being and the society of non-Jews, took one look at Palestine and headed back home. 'Nothing but Jews here, it's hard to take; and then the primitiveness of existence!' von Mildenstein quoted a member of a well-to-do German-Jewish family as saying. He and his family had come to Tel Aviv with all their possessions, including a hunting dog, fully intending to make a home in Palestine. But after eight days they could stand it no longer and returned to Germany without even bothering to unpack.

That family, however, was not typical. The overwhelming majority of Jews that von Mildenstein encountered in Tel Aviv and elsewhere in Palestine were optimistic, hard-working and idealistic, intent on building the country by the sweat of their brow – the exact opposite of the Jewish stereotype of Nazi anti-Semitic dogma.

Nowhere indeed was the combination of exuberant optimism and earnestness that characterised Jewish life in Palestine more sharply brought in to focus than at Tel Aviv's annual *Purim* carnival. Von Mildenstein was there as the climax approached of the festivities surrounding the celebration of the Jews' deliverance from the murderous designs of the Persian official Haman. The streets were decked with banners, garlands, and *Purim* arches; parties lasted well into the night and there was endless *hora* dancing. The round of activities culminated in a parade which attracted thousands of Jews to the city from the surrounding area.

Von Mildenstein won an unobstructed view of the proceedings from the top of a coachbox. The theme of that year's parade was 'Jewry of the World, Past, Present, and Future', and chronicled the odyssey of the Jews from the time they entered history as a united people, through their dispersion after the destruction of the Second Temple, down to their latter-day reunification in Palestine. Von Mildenstein watched the floats roll by, beginning with ones representing the twelve tribes of Israel, depicting the Jews as sturdy and fearless warriors. Then came those representing the Jews of the present day: persecuted in Poland and Russia; completely assimilated in France where they danced in a bar beneath the sign, 'We are not Jews at all'; rolling in money and deaf to the needs of Palestine in America. Then a green, three-headed dragon, its body stamped with red Swastikas, came lumbering down the street, while a drum kept up a steady beat alongside. On the float's bed were mounted masks shaped like books, each one bearing the title of a work burned by the Nazis in the literary *auto-da-fé* of May 10th, 1933. Von Mildenstein thought that in this depiction of Germany the organisers had not 'used their intelligence to any great extent'.

The 'Future' presented the spectators with a panorama of economic, social, and cultural accomplishments of the Zionists. Von Mildenstein concluded that Jews were properly proud of their achievements, if to a fault, for with that pride, with that 'childish joy' they took in all that they had created, went a relaxation of critical judgement, which led them, for example, to buy products that were both shoddy and expensive. But given the organisational and commercial talents of the Jews, the day might not be far off, he predicted, when the Jews of Palestine would emerge as formidable rivals of Europe for the commerce of the Near East, in much the same way that they were already proving fierce competitors in Europe with their export of oranges.

But 'Von Lim' was not content merely to experience the pageant of Jewish life vicariously as a spectator at a carnival parade. Eager to take a closer look for himself, he embarked on a journey which took him on a trip of several months round the whole of Palestine. During this sojourn he showed a particular interest in Zionist education and colonisation.

That Zionists considered education of paramount importance and that they held rather advanced ideas on the subject was no secret to the Nazi Baron; but what he witnessed at Ben Shemen, a children's colony situated a short distance east of Tel Aviv, must have seemed bizarre indeed to one raised on Teutonic notions of childhood and adolescence. There, several hundred children from all parts of the world, ranging in age from six to seventeen, were encouraged to look after themselves and their peers with a minimum of supervision from their elders. Combining work with study, they went to school in the morning and worked in the fields or in the various workshops – repair, carpentry and dairy – in the afternoon. Their pride and joy was a swimming pool they had built with their own hands. They even had their own court of justice which heard cases and meted out punishments. Von Mildenstein was impressed, but not so impressed that he could resist poking fun at the educational philosophy which taught the children of Ben Shemen self-reliance, remarking that these young folk became so independent that they soon believed themselves to be smarter than the adults.

From Ben Shemen he went on to Givat Brenner, a *kvutza* southeast of Tel Aviv. Here, too, the children received preferential treatment, the largest dwelling having been set aside for them. Specially trained guardians took care of their needs, while the parents worked on the farm, in the repair shops or central kitchen. In the evening, at dinner-time, the parents would come to the children's home to eat and relax for a few hours with them before returning to their own sleeping quarters. Von Mildenstein was told the history of the settlement, a history of striving against overwhelming odds, a veritable *Kampfzeit* (time of struggle), crowned ultimately with success. He learned how a small band of pioneers, sharing their labour and possessions, had pitched their tents on the barren soil and had made it bloom. Such an achievement, the leader of the *kvutza* assured him with pride, would have been unthinkable but for the use of the collective methods that governed the operation of the colony.

Later on the tour von Mildenstein was to visit yet another *kvutza*, one located in the large Plain of Jezreel in the north of Palestine. Where today, Jewish settlements prospered in large numbers, he wrote, less than ten years before malaria-breeding swamps had effectively shut out native and colonist alike. Parts of the Plain of Jezreel were being developed by individual farmers for personal profit, which was known as *moshav*. Having visited both forms, *kvutza* and *moshav*, in a single day, von Mildenstein questioned the leader of the *kvutza* Gewa, a Russian Jew named Gurion, on the relative merits of the two. In the ensuing discussion, the Baron steered the conversation toward money, something never far from his mind when the subject happened to be Jews, and asked Gurion whether many Jews were not tempted to go to the city where they could earn more money. Gurion replied:

> I don't worry about that. I myself have already been here for twelve years. We have persevered and love our land and our communities. . . . We know that we are building our homeland and that it can only be built when everyone is satisfied with little. We don't get our new land on a silver platter. We must work for it.

For von Mildenstein Gurion signalised the birth of a 'new Jew', a Jew at one with the soil. 'The stocky figure of Gurion', he wrote, 'stands before us in the moonlight. He suits the soil. The soil has reformed him and his kind in a decade. This new Jew will be a new people.'

This 'new Jew' was developing the land in a setting rife with tension and conflict. The more the British imposed their authority on the

Mandate territory, the greater grew Arab demands for independence; the greater the numbers of Jews that entered the country, the more the Arabs resented them. Of the Arab-Jewish conflict von Mildenstein saw evidence enough: Moslems pelting refuse at Jews bent in prayer at the Wailing Wall; the burnt-out Jewish quarter of the city of Hebron, a casualty of the anti-Jewish riots of 1929; the need to fly the German pennant from his car in areas where Jews were not welcome; moreover, any stranger out of uniform was automatically taken for a Jew.

Although the Arab-Jewish conflict did not erupt into open violence during von Mildenstein's visit, the Arab-British one did. Towards the end of October, 1933, shortly before von Mildenstein was due to leave Palestine, the Arabs rose in protest against the entrenchment of British power. The occasion was the planned inauguration of Haifa's new harbour facilities which the British had scheduled for October 31st. The rebellion started up a few days beforehand and quickly spread to all major urban centres of Palestine.

Von Mildenstein happened to be in the city of Safad, north of Lake Tiberias, when the news of the disturbances reached him and he was advised to remain there until they had subsided. But the fearless Baron, not wanting to miss the ceremonies, flew his German pennant and made a successful 'breakthrough' to Haifa, only to find that because of the disturbances they were on a very muted scale. Von Mildenstein was disappointed; security was tight, and of promised glitter and pomp there was little or no evidence.

The Arabs' rebellion, coupled with what he had seen and learned of their anti-Jewish feeling, prompted von Mildenstein to offer an assessment of the Palestinian situation which, given the time, was remarkable for its astuteness. Palestine, he wrote, was a 'country of powerful contradictions', inexorably headed for an explosion – unless Arab and Jew found a way to settle their differences and learned to live together in peace. The presence in Palestine of more than a quarter-of-a-million Jews was a reality that could no longer be denied. But the Jews there, he added, did not need to have a separate state of their own, as statehood offered no auto-matic guarantee of the survival and preservation of a Jewish national identity. The possibility of a significant Jewish return existed, despite Palestine's underdeveloped economic base, provided that, von Mildenstein cautioned, Jews 'creat[ed] their own homeland'. From such a return, concluded von Mildenstein in his final article, not just the Jews but the entire world would benefit, in that 'it point[ed] the way to curing a centuries-long wound on the body of the world; the Jewish question'.

Von Mildenstein was no friend of the Jews (he was, after all, a member of the Nazi Party *and* of the S.S.). His sympathy went out only to that segment of Jewry that called itself Zionist. For the so-called assimilated Jew, the Jew who claimed to be a German first and a Jew second, or denied his Jewishness altogether, and for the Jew who eschewed all racial feeling, he held no brief, his view of them being close to the official Party position. The Baron's support of the Zionist cause was not, however, grounded in expediency alone; rather it stemmed from a liberal application of Nazi racial theories. Briefly, according to these theories, a race was the product of a union – a mystical union – between a people and the soil in which it was historically rooted. And because Jews were said to lack this vital relationship to the German soil, Nazis considered them an alien force in their midst, branding them as a rootless, decadent, parasitical and inferior species of mankind.

In Palestine, on the other hand, von Mildenstein encountered a Jew that he liked, a Jew who cultivated his own soil, the 'new Jew' typified by the stocky figure of Gurion. There he saw a Jew who was struggling against great odds to re-establish his roots in the land of his forefathers; a Jew who gave the lie to the Nazi stock-in-trade that the Jew hated to get his hands dirty and was incapable of idealism. Of this Palestinian Jew von Mildenstein painted a highly flattering portrait, in a manner, to be sure, which left no doubt as to his own superior Aryan pedigree; still, the image of the 'new Jew' projected by von Mildenstein must have left the regular *Angriff* reader shaking his head in disbelief. It is doubtful, though, whether the Baron succeeded in changing many minds about Jews, even though *Der Angriff* had a medal struck to commemorate the voyage of a Nazi and a Jew to Palestine, a medal with the Swastika on one side and the Star of David on the other. Where von Mildenstein did succeed, however, was in securing, early in 1934, the approval of and acceptance by his S.S. superiors for his idea that the solution of the Jewish question lay with the mass emigration of Jews to Palestine. Indeed, the articles earned him promotion, and he was assigned, in the summer of 1935, the Jewish desk in Reinhardt Heydrich's Security Service, the intelligence arm of the S.S. Once installed in his new post, von Mildenstein proceeded to give muscle to the policy he had fathered.

The gist of that policy was to assist the expansion of Zionist influence among Germany's Jews who, despite the oppressive conditions under which they lived, still showed no great desire to emigrate to Palestine. By making a distinction between race-minded, emigration-conscious Zionists and 'assimilationists' out to destroy National Socialism, the S.S. strove to strengthen the Zionist position in the Jewish community. Accordingly, S.S. officials were instructed to encourage the activities of Zionists and to discourage those of non-Zionists. Zionists were given privileges denied to other groups. A police decree of March, 1935, for example, ordered officers to favour Zionist youth groups over non-Zionist ones; the former were to be allowed to don uniforms but not the latter. The S.S. also looked with favour on the Zionist vocational and agricultural training centres which groomed young Jews for a life of toil in Palestine, and access to Nazi functionaries generally proved easier for Zionists than for assimilationists. Even the Nuremberg Laws (September 15th, 1935), which deprived Jews of their German citizenship and condemned them to pariah status, contained a special 'Zionist' provision: forbidden to fly the German colours, Jews were given the right to hoist their own flag, i.e. the Zionist emblem, the blue Star of David between stripes, also blue, against a white background.

But the new direction in Jewish policy did not outlast its sponsor's stay in office. After ten months in the Security Service's Jewish Department von Mildenstein resigned, a victim of internal departmental rivalries and jealousies and, more specifically, of the failure of his policy to bear the expected fruit, as emigration to Palestine was decreasing rather than increasing.

With von Mildenstein's departure a new era of S.S. Jewish policy began. From supporting Zionism the S.S. changed to a policy of repression and harassment, occasioned as much by von Mildenstein's reputed failure as by a 1936 pamphlet which raised the spectre of a strong Jewish state in the Middle East. The author of the pamphlet was Adolph Eichmann. Ironically, it was von Mildenstein who had invited Eichmann to work in Section II/112, as the Jewish department was then known. Hence it seems fitting to conclude this story by citing Eichmann's opinion of his former boss's dealings with Jews, all the more since that opinion is both accurate and reasonable. Von Mildenstein was, Eichmann stated at his 1961 Jerusalem trial, 'very fair and mild . . . sincere in his efforts to find a just solution to the Jewish question'. And that, given the Nazi attitude toward Jews, is saying not a little.

*   *   *

Jacob Boas was born in a concentration camp in Holland in 1943 and has spent much of his adult life immersing himself in the study of the Holocaust. He graduated with honours in History and Political Science from McGill University in Montreal, Canada, and received his Ph.D. in Modern European History from the University of California, Riverside in 1977. He is the editor of *We are Witnesses: The Diaries of Five Teenagers Who Died in the Holocaust* (1995) and has spent ten years as the Education and Research Director of the Northern California Holocaust Center.

37

King Christophe's Citadel, Haiti

MICHAEL CROWDER

(June 1981)

Editor of History Today *between 1979 and 1981 and a renowned Africanist, Michael Crowder contributed this article to his regular series on 'Monuments'.*

The architectural legacy of Black Africa is much less impressive than its prolific and varied artistic heritage. The great majority of buildings south of the Sahara were built in materials that could not withstand the ravages of time and those major buildings from precolonial days which have survived to the present are few. The most notable are the stone ruins of Great Zimbabwe and the mud mosques of the Niger Bend.

One of Black Africa's most impressive architectural achievements is to be found outside the continent in northern Haiti: the mighty Citadelle Laferrière, better known as King Christophe's Citadel. This huge fortress, built on the peak of a mountain nearly a thousand metres above the plain from which it rises, stands as a fitting symbol to the independence Black African slaves wrested in 1804 from the French masters of the Caribbean island to which they had been transported.

Although the Haitians, who had first risen in revolt against the French in 1791 under the leadership of Toussaint l'Ouverture, had finally succeeded in expelling Napoleon's huge army of suppression in 1803 – albeit with the assistance of yellow fever – they continued to fear a return of Napoleon's forces. Haiti, once France's richest possession, remained too tempting an economic and strategic prize for the newly independent state to feel secure from further attack. Accordingly the head of the new state, Jean-Jacques Dessalines, who like his adversary took the title of

Emperor, ordered the construction of fortified positions behind the major ports of the country. General Henry Christophe, his second-in-command, was charged with the construction of a defensive position behind Cap Français, the former French capital, now renamed Cap Haitien.

Henry Christophe was in some ways the most remarkable of all the leaders of the Haitian Revolution. He had been born on the British Caribbean island of Grenada, in 1767, and always used the English spelling of his first name. It is said that he was born into a freed slave family and came to Haiti at the age of eight. At the time of Toussaint's revolt he was working at an inn in Cap Français. Once he had joined the rebels, he quickly demonstrated military prowess as well as political skill and emerged from the struggles and compromises of the succeeding twelve years as second-in-command to Dessalines soon after independence was formally declared on January 1st, 1804.

In the first year of Haiti's independence, work was begun on the mighty Citadel that would serve as an impregnable refuge if the French should return. After Dessalines' assassination in 1806 Christophe was appointed provisional head of state by a military council. Like Dessalines he believed that only autocratic rule could solve the problems of the young state. Nevertheless he appointed a constituent assembly in which Alexandre Pétion, the mulatto leader from the south, succeeded in drawing up a constitution that would give Christophe very little power. Christophe, who would not accept a position without real authority, then did battle with Pétion, but was defeated in January, 1807. He fell back on Cap Haitien and established his own state in the northern half of Haiti, controlling the former French capital as well as the important towns of Gonaïves and Saint Marc.

Despite the many other problems that confronted him in consolidating his new state, which he designated a kingdom in 1811, taking the title of King Henry I, Christophe carried on with construction work on the Citadel. It was not completed until 1813, when his daughter inaugurated it, giving it the name Citadelle Henry. Work, however, continued until 1820 when King Henry, half-paralysed by a stroke and threatened by rebellion, shot himself. His Queen had his body carried up to the Citadel where he was buried and where his grave can be seen today.

The Citadel is situated twenty-eight kilometres from Cap Haitien which, during Christophe's reign, was redesignated Cap Henry. It overlooks the fertile plain that gives the port much of its prosperity and which it was supposed to protect. Built on a rock foundation on the summit of Pic Laferrière, it stands some nine hundred metres above the small town of Milot which lies at the foot of the steep and twisting path up which the building materials had to be dragged by the twenty thousand workers it is estimated participated in its construction. Even without a load it is an exhausting two-hour climb on foot or mule-back. It is still a cause for wonder as to how the huge 24 and 36 cm cannon were transported up the single precipitous path giving access to the Citadel. Not for nothing has it been called the Eighth Wonder of the World.

The irony is that it was never attacked, and for all the energy invested in its construction, it was militarily ill-conceived. At best it could serve only as an impregnable retreat, much as Montsegur did. But in the end its defenders could have been starved out in siege by an invading army as easily as the Cathars were by the forces of Louis IX in 1244.

Whatever its military utility, the Citadel is an amazing architectural feat; it covers an area of ten thousand square metres and its highest wall is twenty-seven metres at the spur. The outer walls range from two to four metres in thickness at their base. It housed two thousand troops and in a siege could have contained up to five thousand without difficulty. Water was made available through a series of six cisterns gathering the frequent mountain rain. It was equipped with up to two hundred cannon, many of them bearing Spanish, French and British crests. But neither Cap Haitien nor the coast was within their range of fire – again emphasising the defensive nature of the Citadel as a refuge.

The architect of the Citadel is thought to have been a Haitian engineer called Henry Barre, though nothing is known about his education or background. Certainly Henry Christophe had a great deal to do with the basic planning of the Citadel and provided apartments for his own use there, including a billiards room. Christophe himself did not reside permanently there, but in the exquisite palace of Sans Souci which he built at Milot at the very gates of the road leading up to his Citadel. Inspired no doubt by the example of Versailles, Henry Christophe decided to establish his court outside his capital. Although he was born on a British island and French was not his first language, he spoke it better than most of his fellow revolutionaries and, although he was himself illiterate, he was a remarkably cultured man, a fact that becomes clear even from the ruins of his beautiful palace at Sans Souci. This he made the focal point around which were set a royal chapel, ministries, a royal library and a royal mint. The architect of this charming palace is unknown, and unfortunately the plans for it have never been found.

Under Christophe the kingdom prospered, though a disproportionate amount of its resources were devoted to the militarily irrelevant Citadel. By 1820 his rule had become increasingly unpopular, for like Dessalines he was an autocrat, albeit an enlightened one.

After his suicide his kingdom became part of the Haitian Republic, and both the Citadel and Sans Souci were abandoned. The latter was largely destroyed by the earthquake of 1842 which also did serious damage to the Citadel. For nearly a century these remarkable monuments to Haiti's independence were neglected. In 1934 President Stenio Vincent had the chapel at Sans Souci restored. In 1940 a law concerning the protection of sites and monuments was promulgated by the Haitian government, but little was done to give effect to this until 1952 when partial consolidation of Sans Souci and the Citadel was undertaken. In 1971 a hitherto unknown section of the Citadel complex was discovered. A kilometre south-east of the Marie-Louise battery a fortified residential complex known as the Ramiers site and connected by a narrow rocky path to the Citadel was uncovered from the tropical vegetation that had obscured it for a century and a half.

In 1973 detailed plans for the restoration and preservation of the Citadel, the Ramiers site and the Sans Souci palace were drawn up by the Haitian Government with the assistance of the Organisation of American States. In 1976 President Senghor of Senegal, whose friend and co-protagonist of the philosophy of *négritude*, Aimé Césaire, had written a major play about the life of Christophe, gave $60,000 to establish a fund for their restoration. The following year the Government of Jean-Pierre Duvalier inaugurated an annual budget of $360,000 for rescue operations in connection with the country's monumental heritage. In 1978 the Director-General of UNESCO offered the Haitian Government technical assistance with its programme of restoration and in 1979 an accord was reached between UNESCO and the newly established Haitian *Institut pour la Sauvegarde de la Patrimoine* (ISPAN) which, under its director, Architect Albert Monganès, is responsible for the restoration of the Citadel and Sans Souci. Much has already been done for the Citadel, but urgent work still needs to be carried out at Sans Souci, in particular shoring up walls which are in imminent danger of collapse. Mr Monganès considers that little less than $4 million over and above the funds allocated by the Haitian Government will be necessary to restore and preserve the Citadel and Sans Souci, which can at this stage not be fully restored since the original plans for it have never been found.

Some idea of the magnitude of the task and the funds required can be appreciated from the fact that for every day of work on the Citadel two days have to be allowed for transporting materials, because the last section of the road to the Citadel is even now not accessible to wheeled transport, so steep is it. Thus a bag of cement sold for $4.00 in Cap Haitien costs $9.00 by the time it passes through the gates of the Citadel.

Mr Monganès hopes that the international community will come to the aid of Haiti – one of the world's poorest countries – in its efforts to preserve the Citadel, once described as 'the first monument to the black race at last liberated from slavery'.

* * *

Michael Crowder (1934–88) was educated at Hertford College, Oxford. During his National Service he was seconded to the Nigeria Regiment, later returning to Lagos to become first editor of *Nigeria Magazine*, 1959–62, and then Secretary at the Institute of African Studies at the Institute of Ibadan. In 1964–5 he taught African History at the University of California, Berkeley and in 1965–7 was at the University of Sierra Leone. From 1968–78 he was based in Nigeria again, at the University of Ife, then from 1971 as Professor of History at the Ahmadu Bello University and finally as Research Professor in History at the Centre for Cultural Studies at the University of Lagos, 1975–8. He returned to London in 1979 to edit *History Today* from 1979 to 1981 and remained Consultant Editor until his death. He was joint editor of the *Cambridge Encyclopedia of Africa* (1981), and of the *Historical Atlas of Africa* (1985).

38

Blacks in Britain: the Eighteenth Century

JAMES WALVIN

(September 1981)

James Walvin was among the writers who contributed to an edition of History Today *that gave special prominence to the history of Blacks in Britain.*

WANTED,

A NEGRO LAD

Of the EBO country, from 15 to 17 years old

Who has had the small-pox, and is of a healthy constitution. The proprietor of such a lad may hear of a purchaser, by applying to John Phillips at his shop near the Exchange.

To be sold, a Negro boy age about fourteen years old, warranted free from any distemper, and has had those fatal to that colour; has been used two years to all kinds of household work, and to wait on table; his price is £25, and would not be sold but the person he belongs to is leaving off business. Apply at the bar of George Coffee House in Chancery Lane, over the Gate. [1756]

These and many other slave advertisements were commonly found in English newspapers from the mid-seventeenth century onwards. They provide a wealth of important evidence about the history of England's black society and, of course, about the individual blacks who were bought and sold like other items of trade. Blacks were sold and bartered, especially in the seaports of London, Bristol and Liverpool; they were bequeathed in wills. England's blacks were widely employed as domestic servants throughout the country, a fact confirmed by the abundance of illustrative material – portraits, cartoons and sketches – in which black servants appear with their employer's family.

In the seventeenth and eighteenth centuries there was an enormous expansion of British slave interests. The 'triangular trade' involved the shipping of ever-more Africans from their homelands in order to satisfy the appetite for black labour in the tropical slave colonies of the Americas. As slavery in the New World became a major institution – transforming the demography of the region as surely as it revolutionised the local economies, those English ships trading with Africa and the slave colonies returned home filled with tropical produce – and with the occasional coffle of slaves. Returning sailors, military and government officials retiring to England and of course planters coming home, brought with them black slaves. In the colonies, whites had surrounded themselves with black domestics; in England the number of black servants offered some indication of an ex-colonial's position or wealth. Soon the habit became fashionable in English propertied circles and blacks were imported to satisfy fashionable taste. But in essence the black slaves sold into England were little more than the flotsam and jetsam of England's burgeoning Atlantic empire.

It had been the maritime explorations of West Africa from the fifteenth century onwards which gradually brought Europeans directly into contact with the goods, produce – and the inhabitants – of black Africa. In a significant way Africa had long attracted European intellectual debate and speculation and there was widespread European mythology about Africa. Thus when the first batches of Africans sailed back to Europe – initially to Spain and Portugal – they were the objects of curiosity and bemusement. By the time the emergent English maritime power was engaged in African trade in the sixteenth century, the situation had changed dramatically. The Iberians had already begun to use Africans as slaves in Europe and the American colonies. The English, though latecomers to the scene, soon put themselves at the forefront of the complex slavery system. Initial curiosity gave way to something quite different: a firm conviction, which was supported by law and economic practice, that the African was less than human. Thus Africans became the victims of a predatory slavery interest which removed them (over the centuries in their millions), casting them ashore in the Americas – and Europe.

As the triangular trade developed so too did the black community in England. It is, naturally, impossible to assess the numbers involved. It is likely, however that, throughout much of the seventeenth century, blacks were commented upon because they were exceptional. This undoubtedly changed in the eighteenth century. The success of the slave colonies ensured that more Africans and Afro-Americans would find their way to England. Until British emancipation in 1838 slavery was the major determinant in the lives of blacks in England. Even those born into freedom in England ran the risk, as long as colonial slavery survived, of being returned against their will to the abject status of a slave in the colonies.

In England, however, unlike for instance in Jamaica, freedom, not bondage, was the norm. Working and living side-by-side with free people it was natural that blacks should become unhappy with their lot. In the words of one contemporary writing in the mid-eighteenth century, they 'cease to consider themselves as slaves in this free country nor will they put up with an inequality of treatment'. Thus black slaves were continually running away. It is significant that, by the late eighteenth century newspapers carried more advertisements for runaway slaves than for slave sales. In general they ran away into the poor warrens of the capital, forming their own black ghettoes, and like so many of the London poor they were obliged to live outside the law.

These people were in a dangerous position. They were at the risk of arbitrary seizure and ill-treatment. This began to change from the 1760s thanks to the efforts of Granville Sharp and, later, because of the campaigns on their behalf launched by the Evangelicals. Throughout much of the eighteenth century however the problems facing England's blacks were compounded by legal confusion. Was slavery legal in England? In a series of legal cases judges had to wrestle with the complex problems posed by the importation of slaves into a society which, though priding itself on its freedoms, was nonetheless committed to slavery in its colonies. Legal judgments differed but the blacks found little comfort from English courts in their efforts to safeguard their freedom in England. Even the famous 1772 Somerset Case did not (contrary to popular opinion) secure freedom for blacks in England and there were numerous examples in later years of slaves being bought and sold in England.

After 1783 there was an influx of more slaves – those who had fought on the losing British side in the American War of Independence. They augmented the black population and raised further political and social arguments. Prompted by the planters' lobby, a series of denunciations of the black community began to reach the public. One political response to the growth of the black community was to 'repatriate' – to Sierra Leone – but the ensuing government scheme ended in disaster and merely confirmed the blacks' worst fears about their position in England. In fact it is difficult to say what, if any, was the major white response to the blacks for it ranged from the open hatred from the West India lobby through to acceptance and friendship. The letters of Ignatius Sancho, a black shopkeeper in Westminster, provide a helpful guide. While he had a string of fashionable and famous friends he also recorded incidents of public hostility. Returning home from a family visit to Vauxhall he wrote, 'We went by water – had a coach home – where gazed at etc. etc. – but not much abused'. On another occasion, he recorded, 'they stopped us in town, and most generally abused us'. In despair he once complained 'from Othello to Sancho the big – we are all foolish – or mulish – all – all without exception'. Similarly he remarked on 'the national antipathy and prejudice . . . towards their woolly headed breathen'.

There can be no doubt that animosity was shown to the blacks. But there was also the friendship and help of a small band of Englishmen who, beginning with Sharp, devoted their lives to securing black freedom in England and, ultimately, throughout the slave colonies. Indeed people often overlook the fact that the campaign against the slave trade and slavery had its origins in the attempts to safeguard the rights of blacks in England.

One source of widespread complaint were relations between blacks and white women. Since the very great majority of eighteenth-century English blacks were men, it was only natural that they would turn to white women. Such relationships however were widely disliked, notably by the West India lobby (who conveniently ignored their own philandering with slave women in the colonies). Of course suspicion of black-white sexual relations was of long standing – as *Othello* eloquently showed.

The growth of the late eighteenth-century black community could have left few contemporaries, especially in London, in doubt about the human consequences of the slave system. It was however the massive campaign launched by the abolitionists which focused public attention on the wider problems of slavery. Public pressure – from all social classes – became an important factor in ending the slave trade in 1807. Yet it was the end of the slave trade which began to undermine the black community. Henceforth slaves were too valuable to export from the colonies and the English black population began to decline and to be absorbed into the wider host society. It did not disappear utterly, however. Throughout the nineteenth century blacks were a frequent sight in England, though rarely in such numbers as in the previous century. Visiting Africans and West Indians were common. So too were travelling American blacks, particularly those lecturing against United States slavery in the years before 1860. It was the development of new steamship lines to West Africa and the Caribbean which led to the settlement of newer black communities in the seaports of Cardiff, Liverpool, Bristol, Newcastle and elsewhere.

Black society in England became much more noticeable however in the course of the two twentieth-century World Wars when Africans and West Indians were persuaded to join the armed forces, the merchant marine or to work in war industries. Furthermore the number of blacks was swelled in the Second World War by thousands of black American servicemen in Britain with the United States army. It was the experiences in Britain in that war, and the prospects of a materially-secure future which persuaded many West Indians to stay or to return to Britain with their families. Thus there began the newer phase of black immigration from the late 1940s onwards and the development of the modern black community.

While it would be untrue to say that the history of blacks in England is uniform and has an unbroken thread since the seventeenth century, it is indisputable that blacks have been a feature of English society and history for centuries. It is, in the main, an unhappy story, for throughout much of the period black-white relations were shaped by the experience of slavery and, later, by imperial domination. The political and social legacy of white dominion over black in England no less than in the colonies has been the survival of notions of superiority which, in their turn, have laid the basis for modern racist ideologies.

*   *   *

James Walvin is Professor of History at the University of York. A widely published authority on the history of slavery and race relations, he is the author or editor of over thirty books including *Black Ivory: A History of British Slavery* (1993), *Questioning Slavery* (1996) and *Fruits of the Empire: Exotic Produce and British Taste* (1997). He has also been the co-editor of the journal *Slavery and Abolition* for over a decade.

39

Reading James Clavell's Shōgun

HENRY SMITH

(October 1981)

James Clavell's romantic best-seller about a westerner in 17th century Japan was published in 1975. Henry Smith, expert on Japanese history, reflected on the ways you can (and cannot) learn about the past from creative fiction.

When confronted with an extremely popular modern novel which is based on historical themes the first instinct of the historian, naturally enough, is to ascertain the 'historicity' of the work. The models for the major characters in James Clavell's *Shōgun* are easy to recognise but Clavell has considerably rearranged and refashioned the events and personalities of the time about which he writes.

These changes can be summarised briefly. The model for Blackthorne, the protagonist of *Shōgun*, is Will Adams (1564–1620), the circumstances of whose arrival in Japan in April 1600 as pilot of a Dutch ship correspond closely to those of Blackthorne. Blackthorne's eventual rise to the position of adviser and retainer of Yoshi Toranaga roughly parallels the career of Adams; a key difference is that Clavell telescopes these events into a single summer, whereas in reality the intimacy of Adams and the historical Tokugawa Ieyasu grew over a matter of years. Clavell also inflates the heroic stature of the historical Adams by having Blackthorne actually save Toranaga's life, by having him introduce effective warfare with guns to Japan (something which had been accomplished several decades before), and above all by having him fall in love with the wife of one of the great feudal lords of Japan.

The depiction of the military struggle for national supremacy in *Shōgun* corresponds to historical fact in broad outline, although the intricate subplots of the novel are wholly of Clavell's invention.

Toranaga's scheming rival 'Ishido' is vaguely modelled after the *daimyo* Ishida Mitsunari (1560–1600), who did in fact organise the coalition against Ieyasu that was defeated at the Battle of Sekigahara in October 1600. The historical Ishida however, was not nearly so powerful as his counterpart in *Shōgun*, nor was his execution in 1600 anything like the gruesome punishment meted out to Ishido at the very end of the novel. Similar and even greater liberties have been taken with the other *daimyo* who appear in *Shōgun*, for many of whom it is even difficult to locate a specific model.

The model of Blackthorne's lover, the Lady Toda Mariko, is Hosokawa Gracia (1563–1600), whose husband Tadaoki (1563–1645) was one of the most cultivated men of his time and is done somewhat of a historical disservice by being transformed by Clavell into the boorish 'Buntaro'. The historical Gracia was one of the most famous of all the Christian converts in Japan of her era, and is revered to this day as a saint by Japanese Roman Catholics. While she was indeed versed in both Portuguese and Latin, the historical Gracia never served as an interpreter for Ieyasu. Nor did she even meet Will Adams, and she certainly would never have had a love affair with him or any other European seaman.

It is this transformation of a chaste Catholic heroine of the sixteenth century into a modish Madame Butterfly that has tended to shock and sometimes offend the sticklers for historicity. Edwin Reischauer, the distinguished American historian of Japan, has written indignantly that Clavell 'freely distorts historical fact to fit his tale' when he stoops to having such an 'exemplary Christian wife' as Hosokawa Gracia 'pictured without a shred of plausibility as Blackthorne's great love, Mariko'.

These charges raise some difficult questions. As a novelist, is Clavell not free to transform his characters as he pleases? The author himself has claimed that there were really no exact 'models' for the characters in *Shōgun*, simply 'sources of inspiration' drawn from the pages of history. He did, after all, change the names of virtually all the historical characters (one notable exception being Gracia's maiden name, Akechi). 'I thought, to be honest', Clavell has said, 'that I didn't want to be restricted by historical personality.'

The more serious charge against Clavell is that of historical plausibility: granted that the historical Will Adams never laid eyes on the historical Lady Gracia, was that sort of liaison conceivable in Japan of the year 1600? Here the answer would certainly be that it was not. The *daimyo* ladies of sixteenth-century Japan were strictly sequestered and rarely had the chance to meet any men other than immediate family. Nor can one imagine any Japanese woman of good breeding entering the bath so casually with another man – much less a 'barbarian'. The only sort of woman who would have behaved with the sexual candour of Mariko in that era would probably been a prostitute (such as *Shōgun*'s 'Kiku').

The issue of historical plausibility arises on other occasions in *Shōgun*. A number of these relate to details about Japanese customs. The careful historian might insist, for example, that such a rare imported luxury as soap would not have been used to bathe a captured barbarian, or that traditional Japanese never celebrated birthdays (as Lady Ochiba does late in the novel), or that the Japanese did in fact eat meat from time to time (contrary to Mariko's claim of total avoidance). In these and other small ways, *Shōgun* will strike the historian as a somewhat flawed depiction of Japanese customs in the year 1600.

Rather more of a problem is the question of Japanese psychology and behaviour as represented in *Shōgun*. Were samurai in fact given to beheading commoners on a whim and then hacking the corpse into small pieces? Were all Japanese of that era (or any other era, for that matter) so utterly nonchalant about sex and nudity? Would a peasant really have been summarily executed for taking down a rotting pheasant? Was '*karma*' in fact such an everyday word among the Japanese of the year 1600? Although precise answers to these questions are not always easy, it can certainly be said that in every case Clavell exaggerates and often distorts the historical reality.

But the real problem is to understand *why* James Clavell has depicted the Japanese in ways that occasionally strike the historian as implausible. Most of the errors of detail were surely unintentional, and probably reflect nothing more than the inadequacy of the English-language materials on which Clavell, who reads and speaks no Japanese, was obliged to depend for his information. As a practical matter it must be admitted that such authenticity is probably of little concern to the average Western reader of *Shōgun*, who knows almost nothing about Japan or its history.

But the exaggeration of Japanese behaviour, particularly with respect to attitudes about such matters as love, death, food and bathing, is clearly intentional on the part of Clavell, since in every case he strives to contrast the values of the Japanese with those of Blackthorne and his fellow Europeans. Even more importantly, the final message of the author is that, as the confused Blackthorne comes to realise, 'much of what they believe is so much better than our way that it's tempting to become one of them totally'. Whereas Western man, as symbolised by Blackthorne, is depicted as ridden with shame over sex, obsessed with a fear of death, raised on an unwholesome diet of animal flesh and alcohol, and terrified of bathing, the Japanese are represented as paragons in each particular. They view sex and nudity as wholly 'natural', are able to face death with composure and even eagerness, eat only fish (preferably raw), rice, and pickles, and of course are wholly addicted to the pleasures of the hot bath.

It is precisely this rather didactic contrast that gives *Shōgun* so much of its interest, both for the average reader and for the historian. Clavell is in effect delivering a sermon on the errant ways of the West. More specifically, he is delivering a polemic against the Christian Church for instilling in Western man his (in Clavell's view) distorted attitudes to sex, death, and cleanliness. This anti-Christian tone runs throughout *Shōgun* and manifests itself most clearly in the depiction of the European Jesuits. Although no responsible historian would claim that the Jesuits were without their faults as missionaries in Japan, it is hard to find the priests of *Shōgun* as anything but caricatures. While the Jesuits did indeed for a time rely on the silk trade to finance their mission, they were scarcely the greedy villains of *Shōgun*, ever ready to stoop to crude assassination plots to thwart their rivals.

The preferable religious attitude, *Shōgun* insistently implies, is the meditative and fatalistic posture of the Japanese samurai, as epitomised by the great warrior Toranaga. About halfway through the novel there appears a description of Toranaga in a state of religious reverie; it is an effective summary of the type of mysticism which Clavell seems to advocate:

> Now sleep. *Karma* is *karma*. Be thou of Zen. Remember, in tranquillity, that the Absolute, the Tao, is within thee, that no priest or cult or dogma or book or saying or teaching or teacher stands between Thou and It. Know that Good and Evil are irrelevant, I and Thou irrelevant, Inside and Outside irrelevant as are Life and Death. Enter into the Sphere where there is no fear of death nor hope of afterlife, where thou art free of the impediments of life or the needs of salvation. . . .

While drawing freely on elements of Asian mysticism (*karma*, Zen, Tao), this sermon is a personal statement by James Clavell. A more authentically Japanese Zen Buddhist, for example, would certainly be far more respectful of 'teachers' and the idea of 'salvation'. Yet the Zen spirit is certainly there, and the message is that the West has much to learn from Asian meditational practice – an idea to which many of Clavell's devotees would seem to be hospitable.

In a sense, then, *Shōgun* is a story of a spiritual quest. It is of course skilfully woven in among other stories – that of a tragic love affair and that of a ruthless power struggle – so that the sermon never becomes obtrusive. But it is a very important element in the overall logic of *Shōgun*. Even less apparent to the normal reader is the fact that this 'quest' is closely related to James Clavell's personal experiences with the Japanese.

As a young soldier in the British army, Clavell was captured by the Japanese in Southeast Asia in 1942 and spent the remainder of the war in Changi prison on Singapore. While his experience understandably left him with many hostile feelings about the Japanese, he grew in time to respect his captors, for much the same reasons that Blackthorne does. In short, the story of Blackthorne's progress, from horror over his captors' 'barbarity' to respect for their 'civilised' values as even more 'civilised' than those of the West, is also the story of Clavell himself.

It is in order to dramatise this theme of spiritual quest in *Shōgun* that the author tends in various ways to idealise, over-simplify, and sometimes distort Japanese values and attitudes. And it is here that the historian can perhaps step in to right the balance a little.

One common form of exaggeration in *Shōgun* is the depiction of values which were historically limited to a certain segment of Japanese society as though they were universally 'Japanese'. Take the simple example of eating meat. Mariko tells Blackthorne that the Japanese never eat meat. This was in fact true at the time only of the Buddhist clergy and the Kyoto aristocracy; the samurai class of which Mariko was a member was in fact fond of meat and frequently consumed wild game. One hastens to add that in terms of contrast with the Europeans, Clavell's depiction is still basically valid. Even samurai ate only wild game, and never raised animals or even fowl for consumption; and never did their level of meat consumption even approach that of the highly carnivorous Europeans of all but the lowest classes.

Another type of simplification which the historian is anxious to pick out is anachronism. An appropriate example here might be that of sexual attitudes, a matter of fundamental East-West contrast as depicted in *Shōgun*. Here the problem lies primarily in the characterisation of European seamen as squeamish about sexual matters as Blackthorne is. The depiction of Western sexuality in *Shōgun* conforms instead to the stereotype known as 'Victorian' – although many people now question whether such prudishness was in fact typical of the nineteenth century.

In this process of trying to 'de-idealise' the sharp Europe-Japan contrasts that appear in *Shōgun*, however, the historian soon learns two important lessons. The first is that we still do not really know the answers to many of these questions about the historical evolution of Japanese attitudes to sex, love, death and other such basic human preoccupations. Nor, for example, do we really know what the Japanese of different classes ate in the sixteenth century. Nor indeed can we give a satisfactory explanation of the historical development and psychological workings of the peculiar samurai practice of ritual disembowelment (*seppuku*). The lament of French historian Lucien Febvre in 1941, would certainly still apply to Japan: 'We have no history of Love. We have no history of Death. We have no history of Pity or Cruelty, we have no history of Joy.' We cannot, quite simply, answer the hard historical questions about the stuff of which a popular novel like *Shōgun* is made.

The second realisation provoked by *Shōgun* is that no matter how much the historian seeks to qualify the rather stark contrasts between Japan and the West that run through *Shōgun*, there remains little doubt that in many ways Japan had by the year 1600 evolved customs and attitudes that really do seem to have been at sharp variance with those in the West. One has only to peruse some of the fascinating reports of European visitors to Japan to realise this. As the Italian Jesuit Alessandro Valignano (the model for Father Carlo dell'Aqua in *Shōgun*) wrote in 1583, 'The things which they do are beyond imagining and it may truly be said that Japan is a world the reverse of Europe'. This metaphor of Japan as a 'topsy-turvy' land, where everything is done in precisely opposite manner, is one that has appeared again and again in Western descriptions of Japan ever since.

Western understanding of Japan has, we may hope, reached the point where we can dismiss the 'topsy-turvy' argument as Europocentric nonsense. This is not, however, to deny the reality of general differences between Japan and the West – provided of course that one remains alert to the wide diversity among different classes in Japan and among the many cultures that make up 'the West'. It is precisely the general differences that make Japan such a fruitful and fascinating object of study for the West: by understanding Japan, we come to understand ourselves. It was the genius of James Clavell to mobilise this learning process as a central theme of *Shōgun*. It remains the task of the historian to probe the roots and refine the limits of Blackthorne's lessons.

* * *

Henry Smith (b. 1940) has been Professor of Japanese History at Columbia University since 1988 and his special interests include the history of modern Japanese urban culture and the history of popular prints. He was previously Professor of History at Princeton University, 1969–75 and Professor of Japanese History at the University of California, Santa Barbara, 1976–88. His publications include *Hiroshige, One Hundred Famous Views of Edo* (1986) and *Kiyochika: Artist of Meiji Japan* (1988).

40

Forum: Facts in History

JONATHAN STEINBERG

(May 1983)

Under Juliet Gardiner's editorship, Forum provided invited historians with a platform from which to air their thoughts. Here, Jonathan Steinberg defends the importance of good old-fashioned 'facts'.

Facts are out of fashion. They are boring, soul-destroying and unsophisticated. Ideas, flair, imagination count and the pupil who simply 'gives you facts' gets the dread B++ mark, the mark for the stolid, uninspired recitation of factual material.

Now, as it happens, I have a soft spot for facts. Some of my fondness is that of the hereditary sporting bore. I can still recite the players on the New York Yankees and the Brooklyn Dodgers who played that memorable all-New York baseball world series in 1941. I can do the heavyweight boxing champions, most of the baseball pennant winners up to the early 1950s, when circumstances severed me from my national game, and a fairish share of the players on the more important English first division football teams – that is, I can do Arsenal or Ipswich but lose heart in the Stoke or Sunderland mid-fields.

This kind of tidy accumulation of important facts must be innate, because nobody told me, as a seven year old, to memorise the players or to collect box scores. I just did it. Later the same urge led me to learn American presidents, kings and queens, Roman emperors and the names of streets in foreign cities. It stopped, oddly enough, where it might have become useful socially, as, for example, memorising fine passages of poems. I can still hardly do that. If it's a fact, on the other hand, I engorge it and store it in my memory: capitals of smaller African states, the dates of French presidents, the reigns of Russian tsars and German emperors, the share of the Danish Gross National Product which the budget deficit represents (13 per cent).

I was repeatedly told that I was cluttering my mind, although I was shrewd enough to notice that the clutter got me A's in geography and history. I was told that I could look things up and that was what mattered. Progressive education, which I also suffered and survived (just), insisted that facts were mere rote and might damage my spirit. In retrospect, that was all bosh. I have learned that memory, like every other human organ, grows with exercise. The more you remember, the more you can remember.

It never occurred to me to use my appetite for facts in any practical way; hence I read no history as an undergraduate. Instead I chose economics, a field for which good mathematics is essential, with a view to becoming a man of affairs. I had a vision of myself getting off the plane at Zurich airport and climbing into the long black Mercedes which would sweep me into the next exciting and slightly unspecified business deal. In fact, I spring of a long line of bankrupts and the one moment I might have become rich and famous (I was offered the German desk at a little organisation employing about ten people called the International Monetary Fund), I turned it down.

When I decided, as an unsuccessful Wall Street tycoon, to do graduate work at Cambridge, I had a marvellous ignorance of my chosen field. I knew less history, in the sense of knowing the facts, when I got my PhD than the average A level candidate, and I may hold the record as the most ignorant man ever to become a University Assistant Lecturer in the University of Cambridge.

The job brought me to a crisis. It is a common human delusion that the autumn of some future year will never arrive. It does, and, if you are like me, you are always startled and disagreeably unready. Imagine my sentiments when, in September 1966, I saw that October was bound to follow and that on a given Thursday in that month I was supposed to lecture on the French Revolution, followed by European History to 1914, a total of twenty-four lectures, twenty-four yawning abysses, each of which might swallow me up.

I have no wish to relive that year again, but it taught me to value the dear old fact. For, I said to myself, if I am to lecture on the French Revolution, I ought to know what happened. I reached for a piece of paper and wrote, in pencil, '1786' on the top left-hand margin. Under it, some inch or so below, I wrote '1787' and then '1788' and by moving inch by inch I got to the bottom and went over to the other side. I stopped at '1799'. I am not quite sure why I chose 1786 as the point at which the French Revolution began, but now fifteen years of lecturing and teaching later, I am sure that was a good choice, say, April, when Calonne informs the King that something pretty drastic has to be done to raise more taxes.

Unwittingly I had stumbled onto some important truths about facts and facts-as-history. The very act of making a chronology is a primary act of historical thought. What I had done was to assert that the phenomenon under study had a beginning and an end, both debatable points, but not obvious or easy ones. Secondly, as I read different books, I picked up different dates from different authors and copied them down on my sheet.

Again unwittingly I was actually doing research. Each time I picked out a date and said to myself 'important; into the chronology!' or 'unimportant; let it be!' I was selecting among the almost infinite number of knowable items those that seemed to me important. As the list of dates grew, it became 'my' reading of the French Revolution. I saw too that different authors have different inner timeclocks and focus on periods quite differently. Some devote a paragraph to July 1789, others a chapter, others several or even a whole book. I saw that events have a rhythm. There is a big difference between grain riots in five successive months or on five successive days.

Finally, I saw that the books left out 1790. Whereas my chronology was dense with dates up to October 1789, it was empty for the whole of 1790. Can Frenchmen not have lived 365 days in that year? No, they lived them, all right, but thought, wrongly, that the French Revolution was over. The National Assembly passed over 2,000 decrees and made modern France what it has become but it happened under a regime which all right-thinking historians know was doomed to fail. Since 1790 fits nobody's revolutionary model, historians simply leave it out.

Facts saved me, which is why I am grateful to them. The desperate collection of fact which preceded each lecture taught me that fact and thought are indissolubly linked. A date or an event is simply a more precise and easily seen, reliably verified, aspect of a past which itself has ceased to be but has left us its artefacts. There is no conflict between theory and fact. They inter-act or, as Goethe said (and he knew everything), every fact is a theory. When you come to a new period, make your chronology first. If you collect your dates and facts intelligently, you will never be short of things to say.

* * *

Jonathan Steinberg is Walter H. Annenberg Professor of Modern History at the University of Pennsylvania where he has recently taken up the chair after more than thirty years at Trinity Hall, Cambridge. He is the author of *Why Switzerland?* (1976) and *All or Nothing: The Axis and the Holocaust, 1941–1943* (1990). In 1997 he was appointed by the Deutsche

Bank of Switzerland to the Historical Commission to Examine the History of the Deutsche Bank in the Period of National Socialism. He served as the principal author of the report *The Deutsche Bank and its gold transactions during the Second World War* (1998).

41

Christmas Clerihews

(*December 1983*)

History can be fun. Readers of History Today *were invited to make it more so.*

Clerihews were the 'invention' of Edmund Clerihew Bentley, who was born in London in 1875 and died there in 1956. He was, for more than twenty years, chief leader writer on the *Daily Telegraph* and was also the author of that 'golden age' detective story, *Trent's Last Case* (1912). His first clerihew, written in 1890 when Bentley was sixteen, was:

> Sir Humphry Davy
> Detested gravy.
> He lived in the odium
> Of having discovered sodium.

and as the poet Gavin Ewart says, 'his first clerihew was never bettered by Bentley'.

But what is a clerihew? It is derived, of course, from Bentley's middle name (his mother's maiden name) and although the Shorter Oxford Dictionary glides from Clericity to Clerisy, one dictionary definition is 'a jingle in two short couplets purporting to quintessentialise the life and character of some notable person'. Or try this: 'a mildly witty pseudo-biographical verse of four lines of varying verse rhyming aabb'. A clerihew is learned, inconsequential, satirical, unexpected, whimsical – and usually benign. And it is invariably historical. So, for the readers of *History Today*, who, we feel sure, nurture the qualities of the clerihew in abundance, we offer our **Christmas Competition for 1983**. A prize of a year's subscription to *History Today* will be given for the best – or so we judge it to be – clerihew about an historical personage of note. To provide inspiration we print a small selection of Bentley's own.

Dante Alighieri
Seldom troubled a dairy.
He wrote the *Inferno*
On a bottle of Pernod.

'The moustache of Adolf Hitler
Could hardly be littler,'
Was the thought that kept recurring
To Field Marshal Goering.

Rupert of the Rhine
Thought Cromwell was a swine,
And he felt quite sure
After Marston Moor.

Mr Bernard Shaw
Was just setting out for the war,
When he heard it was a dangerous trade
And demonstrably underpaid.

George the Third
Ought never to have occurred.
One can only wonder
At so grotesque a blunder.

* * *

41a

Clerihew Competition: Results

(March 1984)

They did!

No man could feel
More injured than Peel
When stung by the witticisms
Of Disraeli's criticisms.
Reginald Petty, Shipley

Richard Clerihew Bentley
Introduces history gently.
What could be more terse
Then four lines of verse?
J.G. Morris, Dorchester

Critics of H.H. Asquith
Thought he approached his task with
An ardour less manly
Than he showed towards Venetia Stanley.
John D. Hargreaves, Banchory

At Montaillou the clerisy
Enjoyed their sex and heresy.
What a pity they'd never see
The money they made for Le Roy Ladurie.
Caroline Bingham, London NW5

John Knox
Never suffered the pox
Or any of the diseases
That you get from doing what pleases.
Jill Sheppard, London NW1

It is the simple truth
That Calvin was uncouth,
But Martin Luther
Was uncouther.
James Wallace, Glasgow

Nell Gwynn
Was prone to sin,
But was highly reckoned
By Charles the Second.
J.P. Burgess, Hythe

Nell Gwynn
Didn't intend to live in sin:
She just hadn't reckoned
With Charles II.

Charles II
Beckoned:
Nell
Fell.
Michael Lennard, Bristol

Archimedes
Lost his bona fides
When he shouted 'Eureka!'
And became the first streaker.
M.G. Morris, Dorchester

Old Abe Lincoln
Was much given to thinkin'.
But we'll never know
What he thought of the show.
Valerie Chambers, Milton Keynes

The wife of Julius Caesar
Rebuffed all attempts to please her.
This frosty disposition
Kept her above suspicion.
Richard Stoneman, Beckenham

*   *   *

42

Why did Charles I Fight the Civil War?

CONRAD RUSSELL

(June 1984)

Conrad Russell, evidently impatient at grandiose long-term explanations of the outbreak of civil war, here reinstates Charles I as a prime mover. Charles was subjected to pressures, some of which he exacerbated, that any monarch would have regarded as intolerable – notably that he was expected to achieve religious uniformity while reigning over multiple kingdoms.

Civil wars are like other quarrels: it takes two to make them. It is, then, something of a curiosity that we possess no full analysis of why Charles I chose to fight a Civil War in 1642. Yet the early seventeenth century was in many ways a good period for gentry, and a bad period for kings. If we were to search the period for long-term reasons why the King might have wanted to fight a Civil War, we would find the task far easier than it has ever been to find long-term causes why the gentry might have wanted to fight a Civil War.

Why, then, has the task never been attempted? The trouble, I think, comes from our reliance on the concept of 'revolution.' Revolutions are thought of as things done *to* the head of state and not *by* him. The result is that Charles has been treated as if he were largely passive in the drift to Civil War, as a man who reacted to what others did, rather than doing much to set the pace himself. This picture is definitely incorrect. Whether the notion of an 'English Revolution' is also incorrect is a question I will not discuss here. Anyone who is determined to find an 'English Revolution' should not be looking here, but later on, in the years 1647–1653, and those years are outside the scope of this article. This article is concerned with the outbreak of Civil War, an event in which the King was a very active participant.

If we look carefully at the slow process of escalation by which the political crisis of 1640 was transformed into the Civil War of 1642, it was usually Charles who raised the stakes by introducing threats of force. It was Charles, in August 1642, who raised his standard and legally began a state of war. This fact repeated a pattern which was already visible. In January 1642, it was Charles who left London, and thereby first separated the combatants into two armed camps. The physical division of the political community caused by the rival summonses to rally to York and to Westminster made an enormous contribution to the creation of an atmosphere in which Civil War became a real possibility. Moreover, the week before Charles left London, it was he who brought armed guards to arrest the Five Members, not the Five Members who brought armed guards to Whitehall Palace.

If we trace the cycle of failed deterrents backwards, and ask who first introduced the threat of armed force, the answer is again Charles. The first threat to use armed force to resolve the deadlock at Westminster was the Army Plot of April and May 1641, and this was clearly Charles's plot. The first Parliamentary strivings towards control of the militia begin the week after the Army Plot, and this is a case where chronology is the best guide to causation. If we go farther back still, and ask who first introduced armed force in the British Isles, the answer is Charles, in the misguided attempt to conquer Scotland, the first round of the conflict which was later localised as the English Civil War.

In the light of these facts, it seems hard to deny that Charles made some contribution to the drift to war. It is, then, important to ask, both how big this contribution was, and what motives, short and long term, might have led Charles to make it.

To understand Charles's contribution, it is necessary to understand the aims of his opponents. They were not aiming at Civil War, though from Charles's point of view, their actions were at least as provocative as if they had been. His opponents were following a strategy with precedents going back at least to Simon de Montfort, in which the object was to impersonalise royal authority by putting it into the hands of a Council and great officers, to be nominated in Parliament and answerable to Parliament. As a Parliamentary declaration put it in May 1642, Charles was to be treated as if he were a minor, a captive or insane. Charles's opponents, many of whom were experienced Privy Councillors, believed government was too important to be left to Kings.

This strategy depended for its success, not on skilled party leadership but on keeping the community united. If it succeeded, there would be no civil war. If it failed, the idea was to be able to blame the King, as Simon de Montfort and Thomas of Lancaster had done, in effect for waging war against his own government. It was thus a secondary objective to be able to blame the King if the strategy failed and fighting did result. This impersonalisation of public authority, under the doctrine of the King's Two Bodies, actually went so deep that Parliamentary declarations complained that gathering of forces round the King might lead to a breach of the King's peace, and that the King's forces might start a 'rebellion'.

Every time this strategy had been used in the past (1215, 1258, 1311, 1386), it had produced the same result. Each time, after a delay of two years or more, it had produced a civil war in which the King had been the apparent aggressor. Each time, the delay in the outbreak of fighting had depended on the length of time the King's critics were in power before they built up their own body of enemies, and thereby presented the King with a party. Each time, this baronial strategy had forced the King to play a waiting game, until he could divide his critics enough to raise a force and fight back. The situation was one which forced the King to divide the nation, as it forced his opponents to try to unite it. Thus, some part of the appearance that the King began the war is illusory: it is the result of Parliamentarian tactics which put the pressure to fight, and therefore the blame for doing so, squarely onto the King's shoulders.

Yet, though this appearance is in part illusory, it is also in part genuine. True, Charles was under pressure to fight, but it was a pressure he showed no great determination to resist. Indeed, he nearly threw away his chance by trying to fight too soon. Twice, over the Army Plot and over the attempt on the Five Members, Charles moved before the reaction in his favour had gone far enough, and thereby did his critics the priceless service of reuniting them. Richelieu, before the Army Plot, had wisely advised him to wait until the wheel of fortune turned, but Charles was too impatient to take his advice.

Charles, then, had become eager to fight. In creating this eagerness, he was influenced by short-term indignities he suffered during the Long Parliament, but he was also influenced by long-term frustrations, and the study of those frustrations tells us something important about seventeenth-century government.

Among these frustrations, the issue of money is somewhere near the centre of the stage. All through his reign, he had tried to do, and indeed was expected to do, things for which the money was simply not available. On a number of occasions, notably 1626, his Parliaments had made helpful noises about the shortage of money, but no action had ever followed. By August 1642, Charles was quoting Rudyerd's 1626 offer to make him 'safe at home and feared abroad' as simply a piece of mockery. In 1628, after agreeing to the Petition of Right, Charles had expected a grant to allow him to collect Tonnage and Poundage legally, to be faced instead with a remonstrance for collecting it illegally. In 1629, he had called another session of Parliament largely in the hope of getting a legal grant of Tonnage and Poundage, only to find that the Commons wanted instead to punish those who had obeyed his orders to collect it. In 1640, he had listened to Parliamentary offers to give him a legal grant of Tonnage and Poundage and a new book of rates to assess it by. Instead, by the end of 1641, he had been given a series of grants for a few weeks at a time, no new book of rates and an Act of Parliament saying he could not collect it without Parliamentary assent. Since over 50 per cent of his ordinary revenue was covered by Tonnage and Poundage, it is no wonder that Charles's hope of ever getting a permanent grant had grown slim, and his irritation had grown large in proportion.

It was clear by 1642 that royal revenue had failed to keep up with the previous century's inflation. Some major new source of revenue was needed, and Charles was entitled to his scepticism about whether the House of Commons was ever likely to provide it. The Bill of Tonnage and Poundage has been rightly described as 'the bill the Commons never seemed to have time to pass', and other proposals for revenue reform had made even less progress than Tonnage and Poundage. By contrast, Charles's attempts in the 1630s to increase his revenue without Parliamentary assent had been comparatively successful. If, as appears probable, Charles decided sometime around December 1641 that he would never be solvent until he ceased to rely on Parliaments concerned to ease burdens on their constituents, it is not possible to dismiss his conclusion as against the weight of the evidence.

More specifically, Charles appeared to be facing a situation in which he could not fight when relying on Parliaments. Over the century before the Civil War, the costs of war had inflated more than most other costs, and the growth of firearms, together with the need for standardisation they implied, had increased the proportion of military costs which had to fall on public funds. In 1624–5, Charles believed with some plausibility that he had entered into a war with Spain which a Parliament really wanted him to undertake, only to find, when the war came, that the next Parliament would only vote a paltry supply, and the next none at all unless they could impeach his chief minister. Yet in 1626, even the sums the Commons had offered to vote if they could impeach Buckingham were less than half what the King needed. What was the point of making his peace with Parliaments, at great political cost, if they did not then give him enough to avoid arbitrary taxes likely to lead to another crisis? No king during the Thirty Years' War could accept a situation in which he could never fight. If Charles, as appeared likely, could never fight with parliaments, he might have to make himself able to fight without them.

It was also Charles's misfortune to rule at about the time when the Augsburg principle of *cuius regio, eius religio* became out of date. With each generation since the Reformation, confessional loyalties became more established, and therefore harder to change with a change of monarch. When Charles looked back at the history of the Church of England, he could see that Henry VIII, Edward VI, Mary, Elizabeth, and to an extent James had all been able to make it in their own image. In trying to introduce Laud's brand of ceremonial Arminianism, Charles was only trying to do what they had done. Moreover, this commitment seems to have been, for Charles, something which was not negotiable. Even in January 1641, when he went farther in exploring possible concessions than at any time before or after, he still hoped the Arminian William Juxon could succeed Laud as Archbishop. If he hoped, as he appears to have done, that he could have Juxon as Archbishop at the same time as he had Bedford as Lord Treasurer and Pym as Chancellor of the Exchequer, he was living in cloud cuckoo land. He simply did not see that what had been perfectly possible for Edward VI and Mary was not possible for him. If he believed, as he appears to have done, that a situation in which he could not enforce his own religion was one in which he would have lost a substantial part of his authority, we must allow that he was probably right. Since both Charles and his critics took it for granted that religious unity must be enforced, if Charles could not enforce his religion on the country, he would have to let the country enforce theirs on him. One may understand why he found such a notion a threat to his authority.

The belief that it was the duty of a ruler to enforce uniformity in the true religion was one which caused difficulties for other authorities, as well as Charles I. A century after the Reformation, religious choice was too established a fact to be very easily denied, and rulers who believed that it was their duty to enforce one form of religion were increasingly obviously setting themselves an impossible task. Philip II in the Netherlands failed in this task for reasons not altogether different from those of Charles I. Both felt themselves obliged to fight rather than give up the struggle.

Other rulers in Europe also found it difficult to achieve harmony between multiple kingdoms, but Charles was the only one who faced the problem of religious unity blended with the problems of multiple kingdoms. For him, then, the problem of religious unity was one of unity between kingdoms, even more than of unity within one kingdom. On this point, Charles's Scottish opponents agreed with him. They too thought that unless there was unity of religion and church government between England and Scotland, there would be permanent instability. Just as Charles was prepared to fight to enforce English religion on Scotland, so the Scots were prepared to fight (and remained so through the Civil War), to enforce Scottish religion on England. Charles, moreover, did not only have a King of England's resistance to Scottish notions of Presbyterianising England: he also had to view such a proposal through the eyes of the King of Ireland. A religious settlement in which it would have been a key point that no papists were to be tolerated would hardly have led to stability in Ireland, and any responsible King of Ireland had to resist such a proposal, by force if need be. Of all the participants in the crisis of 1640–42, Charles was the only one whose position forced him to a genuinely British perspective, which did a lot to restrict his freedom of manoeuvre. It was also his British perspective which led him, back in 1639, to start the war against the Scots from which all the later troubles followed. In thinking of his supposed duty to achieve religious unity between all the parts of the British Isles, Charles could well have repeated Laud's words on his appointment to Canterbury: 'there is more expected of me than the craziness of these times will give me leave to do'.

Indeed, if one were to write a job description of the British monarchy in the early seventeenth century, it would not be an attractive one. The King was expected to cut a major European figure on an income which bore no comparison with those of his European colleagues, and to do so without raising illegal taxes. He was expected, in religion, to enforce both unity and truth, while anyone who did not believe that what he was enforcing was the truth could exclaim: 'we ought to obey God rather than man'. He was expected to solve the problem of multiple kingdoms, in a context in which religious differences merged with the various nationalisms of his kingdoms. The tasks conventional contemporary opinion assigned to Charles I were ones no ordinary political skills could have discharged, and if he finally tried to cut the Gordian knot, we should, perhaps, not be too surprised. It is certainly easier to understand why sheer frustration might have driven Charles to fight than it has ever been to understand why the English gentry might have wanted to make a revolution against him.

* * *

Conrad Russell (b. 1937) was educated at Eton and Merton College, Oxford and has taught at Bedford College, London, and Yale University. Since 1990 he has been Professor of British History at King's College,

London. An expert on seventeenth-century political and parliamentary history, his principal publications include *Parliaments and English Politics 1621–1629* (1979); *The Causes of the English Civil War* (1990); *The Fall of the British Monarchies, 1637–1642* (1991) and *Judicial Independence in the Early Seventeenth Century* (1997). Lord Russell (whose father was Bertrand Russell) is the Liberal Party spokesman on social security in the House of Lords.

43

All Change

DAVID STARKEY

(May 1985)

In this opinion piece, David Starkey, just then producing his first book (on Henry VIII), already displayed the provocative capacity to link past and present for which he would later become famous.

'Change is not made without inconvenience, even from worse to better!' –
Richard Hooker

Recently I noticed that two professors of Government, who, like Bobbies in Brixton, go in pairs for safety, had attacked the upper civil service for its conservatism (with a very small 'c') and hostility to change. Not only didn't the mandarins like what Margaret Thatcher was trying to do; they were even sceptical of the possibility of change as such. Which, our professors felt, was quite deplorable and showed that they should be sent on long courses in business management in country house hotels.

Now I would be the last man to come between our administrators and their iron rations of computers and caviare. But it is the professors who are wrong and the civil servants who are right. Governmental reform is difficult and messy. And that is not only the counsel of worldly wisdom; it is also the lesson of almost all historical experience.

Professors of Government are usually historians too, albeit closet ones. The trouble is that they are historians of only the last hundred years or so. And in that period governmental change has been relatively painless because government has been continually expanding. Any fool can set up a new organisation and many have. The difficulty comes when you try to change an existing organisation within a constant or even contracting budget.

The dilemmas of change on a shoestring are new to us; they were bitterly familiar to almost all pre-Victorian governments. Often, like our

342

civil servants, they shrugged lightly stooped shoulders and gave up; but sometimes necessity drove them to strikingly effective action – as in fifteenth-century England. This was the age of the Wars of the Roses, when 'the Barons . . . made a stupendous effort to revive the old Feudal amenities of Sackage, Carnage and Wreckage and so stave off the Tudors for a time'. In fact the 'Wars', often not much worse than a miners' picket line, involved issues of principle just as much as dynasticism or crude power politics. Richard, Duke of York put himself at the head of the party of reform. York held power only fleetingly, but when his son came to the throne as Edward IV he did that rarest of things and carried out in government the policy his father had espoused in opposition.

The policy had two prongs. First, the revenue basis of government was changed. The crown lands were vastly expanded and supplied a larger proportion of the King's income than they had done for hundreds of years, larger perhaps indeed than ever before. Second, financial administration was reformed. Traditionally the finances were handled by the Exchequer. The Exchequer building was sited in Westminster, a hundred yards or so from the present Treasury. And its inhabitants (is it the fetid Thames-side air?) were much the same as now. They wore black coats (though not, admittedly, pin-striped hose) and were bureaucrats through and through. That is to say they were good at carrying out rules but hopeless at commercial calculation. But commercial flair is what you need to manage a landed estate, royal or otherwise. So as land became more and more important in the royal finances, the Exchequer was driven further and further into the margin. Special auditors and surveyors screwed up the yield of the crown lands, and the money raised was handed over, not to the Exchequer, but to the treasurer of the King's Chamber. The results were gratifying. Royal revenues from land, which stood at only about £5,000 in 1450, had risen to £40,000 by 1500.

Mrs Thatcher would be wild with delight if any of her administrative policies had been similarly successful. So what did Edward IV have that she doesn't? First is direct, unyielding commitment. Mrs Thatcher has shown this with Galtieri and Scargill but not with the civil service. But Edward did. Most unusually he announced his determination to reform publicly in parliament, and then stuck to it. The Exchequer fought tooth and nail to retain its control of finance, but the King sat on it as only the King could. The second difference is that the King had a household and the Prime Minister does not. Edward's body servants were sworn to him and owed everything to him. Some were sent out as the field army of surveyors and auditors to run the royal estates on the spot; others – like the treasurer of the Chamber – remained as the headquarters staff at the centre to collect the money in. Mrs Thatcher, bereft of a politically appointed

Prime Minister's department, finds herself like Archimedes, wishing to move the world, but without either a fulcrum or a lever to do it.

So Thatcher's failure seems certain. The triumph of Edward and his successors should not be exaggerated either. Even with all the authority of kings they made little attempt either to reform or suppress the Exchequer itself. Instead they merely by-passed it with a new, shoe-string organisation. And once royal determination weakened, the Exchequer made the usual noises about sound government on traditional lines and resumed control. I doubt very much if the Gulags of Chewton Glen or the Berias of the London Business School will prevent a similar outcome for the Thatcher revolution.

* * *

David Starkey (b. 1945) is a historian and broadcaster, and Fellow of Fitzwilliam College, Cambridge. In 1998 he presented a Channel 4 TV series on *Henry VIII; Elizabeth* followed in 2000. An expert on constitutional and monarchical history, he has written and/or edited several books on the Tudor period including the *Reign of Henry VIII: Personalities and Politics* (1985, 1991), *Revolution Reassessed: Revisions in the History of Tudor Government and Administration* (1986), *The English Court from the Wars of the Roses to the Civil War* (1987), *Henry VIII: a European Court in England* (1991) and (joint editor) *The Inventory of Henry VIII* (1998). He is a member of the academic advisory board of *History Today*.

44

Women's History Forum

ANNA DAVIN

(June 1985)

What is Women's History? It was a question much in the air in the '70s and '80s, and a number of women historians were invited to suggest their answers, among them Anna Davin.

Women's history and feminist history overlap but they are not identical. Women's history is defined by its subject matter – women. Feminist history is defined by its conscious standpoint – feminism. Feminist historians often, though not necessarily, do women's history, but they can also bring their political understanding to the historical analysis of the male world.

All historians have a set of beliefs and experiences which influence the questions they ask in their research and the answers they find, but not all are aware of their standpoint and its effects. Most conventional history (even when written by women) is marred by an unconscious male bias, in the definition of what is historically interesting and in the reading of the sources. 'Men's histories have been presented as universally human. The frameworks, concepts and priorities of these "universal" histories reflect male interests, concerns and experiences' (Jill Matthews, *Good and Mad Women: the historical construction of femininity in twentieth-century Australia*, Allen & Unwin, 1985). Such work, partial in content and biased in standpoint, would more accurately be called 'men's history' or 'masculinist history'. Feminist historians start consciously with the experience and recognition of women's oppression in their own society, and the desire to end it, though they may differ in their analysis of that oppression and in their favoured mode of attacking it.

Over many generations women who have questioned the restrictions placed on their sex have turned to the past for ammunition or for understanding. Mary Wollstonecraft fuelled her indignation by 'considering the historic page', and concluded that 'the civilisation which has hitherto taken place in the world has been very partial'. Margaret Fuller, in New York in 1845 (*Woman in the Nineteenth Century*), challenged women's alleged inferiority both in contemporary ideology and in historical convention by cataloguing examples of strong and noble women from classical times onwards, and contended that despite 'great disparity betwixt the nations as between individuals . . . yet the idea of Woman has always cast some rays and has often been forcibly represented'. Similarly, suffrage tableaux and pageants presented 'women warriors, artists, scholars, monarchs and saints' to show 'the physical intellectual, creative and ethical strengths of women' as Julie Holledge points out in her book on the Edwardian theatre (*Innocent Flowers*, Virago, 1981). And in rather the same spirit some women search the historical record for goddesses and matriarchs. History can supply evidence of long injustice, or examples to disprove stereotypes and assertions of inevitable destiny, or inspirational figures from a golden past. Its uses are obvious; their weaknesses equally so.

My preference is for a more exploratory approach, seeking to understand the present through the past, asking 'why is it like this now?', 'has it always been this way?', 'what are the processes of change and can we control them?' Thus Olive Schreiner, in *Woman and Labour* (1911), compared primitive and modern societies (with a touch of 'goldenage-ism', it is true) and traced connections between accumulation of wealth and the subjugated 'parasitism' of women; while Alice Clark's book (*The Working Life of Women in the Seventeenth Century*, 1919) explored the lives of seventeenth-century women in meticulously researched detail so as to examine the influence of capitalism on women's productive capacity and their position in society. Clark also justified her enterprise in historio-graphical terms. She pointed out that historians had 'paid little attention to the circumstances of women's lives' because they had mistakenly regarded women as unchanging, 'a static factor in social developments'; further, since men and women were indissolubly linked, the study of both was indispensable for full understanding of society. This insight continued to be ignored by mainstream historians. Women's history remained a tenuous and little regarded minority tradition, largely conducted by women, and rarely integrated into teaching.

Today the appetite for women's history is widespread, though satisfied largely outside the academic world. Evening classes proliferate, along with tape-slide shows and videos, exhibitions, novels (cf. Zoe Fairbairns' *Stand We at Last* and Meredith Tax's *Rivington Street*), plays, schoolbooks (Carol Adams' *Ordinary Lives*), which recall the earlier efforts of Rhoda and Eileen Power, do-it-yourself guides (Deirdre Beddoe's *Discovering Women's History*) and other publications. The success of Virago's reprints of classic fiction, as well as of historical work like Sheila Rowbotham's, testifies to women's eager interest in their past. Nor is the demand only from the counter-culture of the women's movement: women (and men) of a wider political and cultural range are also involved. The popularity of 'people's history' pamphlets and of History Workshop is part of the same development: response and stimulus to the attempt to democratise history.

Feminist historians are stimulated by the interest in their work, but the row they hoe is a long one. It is easier than it was ten years ago to convince authority of the validity of studying women. But informed and helpful supervision is in short supply and disparagement or incomprehension not uncommon. Source material is likely to be scattered and difficult, and there is little secondary work to provide short cuts or signposts.

The academically marginal position of women's history, like its pioneering difficulties, is beneficial as well as irksome. Links with beleaguered feminists in other disciplines, such as anthropology and psychology, have produced exciting cross-fertilisation. Feminist historians work in museums, libraries and archives, in theatre and radio, TV and film, in community history projects, schools, and above all adult education. Such employment expands methodological horizons; it forces consideration of how historical work is best presented; and it allows an immediacy of response rarely produced by academic monographs. Feminist resistance to authoritarian and competitive practices makes for lively meetings, constructive discussion and much mutual support – none of them guaranteed in more formal circles. There are local working groups in a number of cities: the London Feminist History Group (set up in 1972 to provide a supportive forum) has published a book (1983) and some of its members are organising an international conference for July 1985. Autonomous resource centres such as the Feminist Library (previously the Women's Research and Resources Centre) in London, the Feminist Archive, and the Lesbian Archive have grown up partly to compensate for shortcomings in conventional collections. Involvement in practical politics is producing new historical questions about racism, for instance, or sexual violence, or the role of the state.

There is a creative tension in feminist history between the historian and the feminist. The feminist's political commitment makes some findings and analyses more palatable than others. She is also aware of an urgent demand for her work. The historian, on the other hand, wants to be sure of her facts and her conclusions even if people are kept waiting. Historical truth is elusive – probably indeed unobtainable – but political ends are best served by getting as close to it as possible. That is why it will not be enough simply to add women's history on to the existing men's history. We have to work towards a more complete understanding of the past, encompassing the complementary and sometimes conflictual diversities of both.

*   *   *

Anna Davin is a Research Associate and part-time lecturer at the University of Middlesex with a special interest in women's history and the history of childhood. Her book, *Growing Up Poor – School, Home and Street in London 1870–1914* was published in 1996 and was a runner-up in the Longman/*History Today* Book of the Year Award 1996. She is an editor of *History Workshop Journal.*

45

Islam and the West

FRANCIS ROBINSON

(May 1986)

Westerners have long regarded the Muslim world through a mixture of prejudices. But how have Islamic scholars regarded the West? A timely explanation by Francis Robinaon.

For more than a millennium few relationships have exhibited greater lack of understanding than that between the Christian and the post-Christian civilisation of the West and that of Islam which reaches from West Africa through West, Central and South Asia to the island archipelago of south-east Asia. The 'WORLD'S DEBATE' which Gibbon found in the Crusades has long remained a dialogue of the distinctly hard of hearing.

For much of the period Westerners have regarded Muslims as a menace, a threat both to Christian revelation and to western security. Since Westerners have come to dominate the world, which is a relatively recent event, they have also come to regard them as a foil against which western identity might be explored and as a yardstick against which western superiority might be measured. Rarely, if ever, have Westerners valued Muslims for themselves.

Up to the eighteenth century Muslims were no less cocooned within their own world-view. God had told them that they were the best community raised up for mankind, and over one thousand years of expansion and success had followed this revelation through Muhammad. Certain that history was on their side, they showed little interest in the West, indeed, it seems that not one Muslim scholar ever bothered to learn a western European language.

We all have some inkling of western prejudices regarding the followers of the Prophet. Among them, and echoing the old medieval polemic against Islam, there would be some focus on the Muslim's supposed uninhibited enjoyment of sex and sensuality; the Prophet did, after all, have twelve wives, and the founder of modern Saudi Arabia over three hundred. There would probably be a tirade against a religious system which, by contemporary western standards, oppresses women. Reference would be made both to the arbitrary violence which Islam seems to encourage and to the brutal punishments imposed by holy law, lapidation for adultery and hands lopped off for theft. Something undoubtedly would be said about fanaticism, the suicide car-bombers who hope to go straight to paradise, the soldiers barely in their teens who seek martyrdom on the field of battle. Indeed, we would expect to hear the disdain of post-Enlightenment culture for a world which seems in such large part still to be moved by the irrational forces of religion.

On the other hand, we probably have a much less clear idea of Muslim prejudices regarding the West, and so these require rather more attention. One problem should be aired straightaway; Muslim attitudes are less harmonious than those of Westerners. They range from those of a western-educated élite whose hearts and minds have been stolen by the West, to those of a proud Islamic resistance which is determined to thrust back every advance of western culture, values and power in their world. But, in spite of this battle of the cultures which is being fought within all Islamic societies, most will share to some degree in the following attitudes.

Elements of the medieval feeling that Westerners are dirty may still linger. 'You shall see none more filthy than they,' al-Qazwini complained of the Franks in the thirteenth century, 'they do not cleanse or bathe themselves more than once or twice a year, and then in cold water, and they do not wash their garments from the time they put them on until they fall to pieces'. Today such feelings might focus on neglect of finger nails, failure to shave pubic hair, and the keeping of dogs.

A mixture of fascination and horror at the freedom, dress and behaviour of western women will be prominent. When Muslims first came across Frankish women in the Middle Ages their jaws dropped and their eyes widened. 'They brought the beautiful maidens of the city,' wrote one shocked Ottoman visitor to Nice, 'and they cavorted around them like cocks. In their customs, the women do not cover themselves decently, but on the contrary are proud to kiss and embrace. If they grow tired of their games and need to rest, they sit on the knees of strange men.'

Jaws drop and eyes widen no less today whether it be those of the liberal, who embraces freedoms in the West that he would not tolerate at home, or of the conservative, who complains to a leading Arab newspaper that 'on the street, in the bus, at work, everywhere we encounter immodestly attired women who arouse turmoil in men's souls', or of the fundamentalist like Maududi of Pakistan, who finds in the liberty of western women both a major source of moral corruption and a major threat to Islamic society. At a more general level the accusation will often be made that the West is a man-centred and not a God-centred civilisation, that great material progress has been made at the too high price of spiritual death. 'The Westerners have lost the vision of heaven,' declares the poet Iqbal, 'they go hunting for the pure spirit in the belly'. Both capitalism and communism make the same mistake, 'both of them know not God, and deceive mankind', both are 'bodily burnished and utterly dark of heart'.

There may also be a sense of outrage at the ignorant presumption of many Westerners, at their belief that their form of civilisation is the only universal form, at their certainty that they are right to try to impose on others their own ideas and practices, at their conviction that their perspective is *the* perspective over human history. 'You never ceased proclaiming that Islam was spread by the sword,' a poet told the British at the beginning of this century, but 'you have not deigned to tell us what it is the gun has spread'.

Similarly, a contemporary Muslim intellectual assails A.J.P. Taylor's *Observer* review of the *Hutchinson History of the World*, by J.M. Roberts, in which Taylor congratulates the author for being 'unbelievably accurate' in his facts and 'almost incontestable' in his judgements, for 'holding the balance fairly between the different civilizations', and for 'devoting most attention to the European civilization he knows best and to which he belongs'. This is not history proper, the Muslim asserts, but a western view of history, which devalues the thousand years of Muslim dominance to emphasise the hundred years or so of western dominance. His outrage at western arrogance is echoed widely throughout the non-western world.

For a millennium such conflicting attitudes and prejudices barely mattered because Muslims and Westerners came rarely into contact. For the past one hundred years or so they have mattered little more because the West has dominated and most Muslim élites have wished to fashion their societies after its pattern. But over the past twenty years things have begun to change. The Muslim world-view has come to be asserted with increasing force and confidence. In some societies, for instance Turkey or Egypt, westernised leaders have been forced to take increasing note of Islamic preferences; in others, for instance Iran or Pakistan, men have come to power who insist on a wholly Islamic way forward for their societies.

Throughout the Islamic world men look to a more Muslim future for their peoples, and the likelihood is that this process will continue to be consolidated, and on occasion be so in the extreme forms of Muslim fundamentalism. In consequence the regard of Muslims and Westerners for each other matters as never before. Unless there is a softening of prejudice on both sides, which seems unlikely, we are offered the prospect of an increasingly abrasive discourse over the coming decades.

*   *   *

Francis Robinson is Professor of the History of South Asia and Vice-President at Royal Holloway, University of London. His books include *Separatism among Indian Muslims: The Politics of the United Province's Muslims, 1860–1923* (1974) and *Atlas of the Islamic World Since 1500* (1982). His latest book is *Islam and Muslim History in South Asia* (2000).

46

Katharine Hepburn

SUSAN WARE

(April 1990)

Katharine Hepburn mère, *argued Susan Ware, was almost as celebrated –
and just as strong-minded – as her film star daughter was to become.* History
Today *has frequently treated the cinema as a significant factor in social
history. Here, Susan Ware examines the significance of a feminist screen idol.*

Her stationery is proudly emblazoned 'Katharine Houghton Hepburn',
the name she shares with her mother. She uses the same distinctive dating
nomenclature (XII.13 for December 13th) that her mother employed.
Recently she gave her support to Planned Parenthood for a major
fundraising drive called the Katharine Houghton Hepburn Fund.

Both mother and daughter figure prominently in twentieth-century
women's history: Mother Hepburn as a suffragist and birth-control activist
under Margaret Sanger, and daughter as one of the century's most
prominent film and stage actresses, a symbol of women's autonomy and
independence.

In many ways, Katharine Hepburn is very much her mother's daughter.
Hepburn proudly identifies her mother as a pioneer of women's
liberation, and she has continued her mother's outspoken support for
reproductive rights. But despite her mother's example – she raised six
children in the midst of an active career as a volunteer and reformer – the
actress questions whether women can successfully combine marriage and
career. 'It just never occurred to me that I could have a career and a
family', she told an interviewer in 1984. 'You cannot have it all'. And she
rejects a feminist interpretation of her life: 'When you come right down
to it, I haven't lived life as a woman after all. I've lived life like a man. Like
a selfish man'.

Such statements seem out of character with the liberated persona that
Hepburn projects both on screen and off. But Katharine Hepburn is,

ahove all, a woman of her times, reflecting attitudes and experiences that shaped the history of women in early twentieth-century America.

Coming of age in the 1920s, she inherited an incomplete feminist agenda from her mother's generation. Told she was the equal of any man, she was encouraged to forge her way in the male realm, and she did so with perseverance and style. But she never saw herself as typical, or even as a role model for other women. Instead, she sought to make her way as an *exception* to the traditional women's role of wife and mother, a role she did not presume to challenge.

Such a philosophy of individualism helps to explain the success of exceptional women like the 'next' Katharine Hepburn. But while a personal credo of independence and autonomy enabled a highly motivated and talented minority to overcome conventional limitations on women's place, it did little to change conditions for women as a whole. Until the revival of feminism in the 1960s and 1970s, only these 'glorious exceptions' could aspire to success in what remained, for most, a man's world.

Had she not mothered one of America's most famous actresses, Katharine Houghton Hepburn (1878–1951) would be remembered as typical of the early twentieth-century college-educated matrons who tackled social issues in the Progressive era and continued to fight for reform in the 1920s and the 1930s. These women were motivated not just by a desire to help the less fortunate but also by a principled determination to demonstrate what intelligent, educated women could contribute to public life.

A member of the family that founded the Corning Glass Works, Katharine Houghton grew up outside Buffalo, New York. Her father committed suicide when she was fourteen, and her mother died soon after at the age of thirty-six. Katharine and two sisters were placed under the care of an uncle, and they had to fight to carry out their mother's deathbed wish that they attend the recently opened Bryn Mawr College outside Philadelphia. Katharine received her B.A. in 1899, and stayed on for a masters degree in 1900. On graduation she announced her intention 'to raise Hell with established customs', a trait nurtured at Bryn Mawr by her women professors and the college's charismatic president, M. Carey Thomas.

It was not so easy, in 1900, for a female college graduate to find her way in the world, even if she subscribed to Carey Thomas' 'You Can Do It' philosophy. For several years Katharine Houghton travelled and taught at schools while she tried to 'find herself'. One thing she did find was a husband, although husband-hunting was hardly her objective. He was Thomas Norval Hepburn, a red-haired Virginian studying at the Johns Hopkins Medical School, where her sister, Edith Houghton Hooker, was also enrolled. The Hepburns were married in 1904 and moved to Hartford, Connecticut, their home for the rest of their lives. They eventually had six children, born between 1905 and 1918; Katharine was the second, and the eldest daughter.

Katharine Houghton Hepburn was not cut out for life as a society matron attending teas and pushing prams. Never timid about speaking her mind (a trait her eldest daughter inherited), she actively embraced woman suffrage and the crusade against prostitution and vice in Hartford with the full support of her broad-minded husband. When she asked him whether her activism might hurt his career prospects, he replied, 'Of course it will, but do it anyway. If you don't stand for the things you believe in, life is no good. If I can't succeed anyway, then let's fail'.

Hepburn later credited a 1909 speech by British suffrage militant, Emmeline Pankhurst, with opening her eyes to the importance of the suffrage cause. Determined to revitalise the moribund state suffrage organisation, Hepburn served as president of the Connecticut Woman Suffrage Association from 1910–11 and from 1913–17. In 1917, however, she publicly renounced the policies of the mainstream suffrage movement as 'hopeless', 'futile', 'academic', and 'out of date'. Instead, Hepburn declared her support for the younger, more militant Woman's Party led by Alice Paul. She even travelled to Washington to join the suffrage picket lines outside the White House, but could not risk arrest because she was pregnant with her sixth child.

Women finally won the vote in 1920, but the suffrage victory did not signal an end to Katharine Houghton Hepburn's political activity. She was, however, less visible in the 1920s than either the preceding or following decade. For one thing, she was coping with the demands of an active, growing family; her last child, Margaret (Peggy), was born in 1918 when Hepburn was forty. The family also coped with personal tragedy; the death, in 1921, of the eldest Hepburn child, sixteen-year-old Tom. He was found hanging by a rope, a circumstance which the family interpreted as a prank gone awry rather than as suicide.

In the decade of the 1920s, Katharine Houghton Hepburn volunteered for a variety of causes, but increasingly she gravitated towards birth control, the cause with which her name is most closely associated. In 1929, when her family responsibilities were diminishing, Hepburn accepted Margaret Sanger's offer to become the legislative chairwoman of the newly formed National Committee on Federal Legislation for Birth Control in Washington.

Until 1937, Katharine Houghton Hepburn devoted her considerable energy and talents to the committee, emerging as one of Sanger's main lieutenants. When Sanger took a leave of absence in 1935, Hepburn became acting president. Through their collaboration, these two women went quickly from 'Mrs Sanger' and 'Mrs Hepburn' to 'my sweet and charming creature' and 'Beloved Kate'.

Hepburn's work drew on the organisational skills she had been honing since suffrage days. Contacts developed through her husband helped build support for birth control in the often conservative medical community. And her stature as the mother of a budding actress (Katharine Hepburn won her first Oscar for *Morning Glory* in 1933) enhanced her visibility. 'Hepburn's Ma Begs OK of Birth Control' ran one 1934 headline. Many of her speeches could be published verbatim by Planned Parenthood today.

As the mother of six children, Hepburn was a perfect foil for those who claimed that birth control allowed women to avoid their responsibilities as mothers. 'The terror of race suicide is nonsense, for women want children', Hepburn emphasised, 'but they want children that they can properly take care of, children that they can afford, both physically and economically'. At the House Judiciary hearings in 1934, one Congressman proudly bragged that he had six children and had never allowed a contraceptive in his home. Hepburn smiled sweetly and said, 'I also have six children'.

It was through the courts, not Congress, that the breakthrough finally came. In the 1936 case of *United States v One Package of Japanese Pessaries*, the United States Court of Appeals struck down federal laws dating back to the 1873 Comstock Act that classified birth control information as obscene. The next year the American Medical Association recognised contraception as a valid area for medical attention. These victories put Hepburn and the Federal Committee out of a job, much to their satisfaction.

In 1937, Katharine Houghton Hepburn was almost sixty years old and had given more than a decade to the cause. She approached retirement as the birth-control movement experienced subtle changes. No longer a reform movement headed and staffed by women volunteers like Sanger and Hepburn, it was increasingly becoming a professionally-oriented organisation, staffed by social workers and dominated by doctors, most of whom were men. By the time Planned Parenthood was founded in 1942, Sanger had lost control of the movement, and Katharine Houghton Hepburn's prototype – the volunteer reform woman – was on the way out.

Katharine Houghton Hepburn lived until 1951, lending her name to various feminist causes, including the Equal Rights Amendment. But she never again participated so actively in a movement as she had during those years in Washington under Margaret Sanger. Instead, she devoted more time to following the successful acting career of her eldest daughter. On the day she died, mother and daughter spent the morning going over the reviews of Katharine's latest play, *As You Like It*.

Had Katharine Houghton Hepburn reflected on the changes in women's status over her lifetime, she would have been justifiably proud. Women had broken out of their total identification with the domestic realm and won access to higher education, the professions, even politics. With many of the artificial barriers impeding women's progress removed, Katharine Houghton Hepburn's generation of pioneers felt that women had at last broken into the human race. Now it was up to individual women – their daughters – to take advantage of the new opportunities.

The contours of Katharine Hepburn's life are more familiar than those of her suffragist mother. Born in 1907, she had by all accounts an exceptional childhood. 'The single most important thing anyone needs to know about me', she once said, 'is that I am totally, completely the product of two damn fascinating individuals who happened to be my parents'.

The Hepburn household nurtured independence and self-esteem. 'My mother always brought me up to believe that women were never to be underdogs', Kate recalled, 'and she taught me from a very early age that we are not necessarily the weaker sex'. As a child, she marched in suffrage parades and met such prominent feminists as Charlotte Perkins Gilman, Margaret Sanger, and Emmeline Pankhurst. 'I knew so many fascinating women when I was growing up, women who had real daring, who did all the legwork for the stuff that's being done now', she later observed. 'All this talk about women always strikes me as funny because it never occurred to me that they were in any way inferior to men'.

Following her mother's example, she enrolled at Bryn Mawr, graduating in 1928. By the 1920s, higher education for women no longer represented as daring a statement of women's emancipation as it once had. The younger Hepburn was hardly an intellectual. Contrasting herself with her 'brilliant' mother, a member of the class of 1899, Hepburn considered herself 'just mediocre', relieved to have got through 'by the skin of my teeth'. But Bryn Mawr taught her to work hard and persevere, a lesson she found of 'tremendous help' when she was fired from nearly every job she undertook in the early part of her acting career.

On graduation, she decided not to follow her father into medicine and turned instead to the stage. Dr Hepburn was initially appalled at his daughter's choice: 'Your mother's work was in the public interest. This is nothing but your own vanity'. Eventually he relented; her mother had been supportive from the start, delighted with her daughter 'for being sort of a free soul'.

The choice of an acting career shaped Katharine Hepburn's ideas about feminism and women's equality in subtle ways. Had she pursued a career in medicine, she would have faced blatant sex discrimination: in the 1950s, for example, most hospitals refused to permit women medical graduates to serve as interns, the gateway to prestigious medical careers. The theatre and Hollywood, on the other hand, seemed to provide unlimited opportunities for both sexes. 'In the theatre there is complete equality between men and women', Hepburn observed in 1942. 'If that has worked well for the theatre, why not for all walks of life?' Despite the ups and downs of her career, Katharine Hepburn always claimed that she was never held back by her sex.

Katharine Hepburn's main priority in the 1930s was her burgeoning acting career, but she publicly supported Franklin Roosevelt and the New Deal. And she did not hesitate to take potentially controversial stands supporting the Equal Rights Amendment and the birth-control movement. When Mrs Hepburn testified before Congress in 1934, her daughter told reporters that she stood behind everything her mother and Margaret Sanger said on the subject. As her mother wrote to Sanger afterwards, she never doubted that Kate would do the right thing, even if her studio protested. 'I'd have spanked her if she hadn't!'

In the 1930s, Katharine Hepburn made a conscious decision to forego motherhood, and (after a short, unsuccessful stint at being married) matrimony as well. Temperamentally self-centred and intent on her acting career, she felt she would have made a terrible parent. As she remarked in 1976, 'It was a matter of becoming the best actress I could be or becoming a mother. But not both; I don't think I could do justice to both'. Rather than make a husband and children victims of her career, she would simply avoid the conflict entirely. And with no regrets. 'I also chose not to make a career of medicine. And I don't regret that either'.

Katharine Hepburn often praised motherhood as a worthy career, but such a route never held much appeal for this free-spirited daughter. 'Being a housewife and a mother is the biggest job in the world', she told an interviewer in 1976, 'but if it doesn't interest you, don't do it. It didn't interest me, so I didn't do it'. The two younger Hepburn daughters, however, followed their mother's pattern more closely by pursuing extensive volunteer activities while raising large families.

Hepburn's choices seem to have been influenced not only by her personality and the demands of the acting profession, but by selective and romanticised memories of her childhood. 'Maybe I'm old fashioned, but I had the most wonderful childhood, and I would not bring up a family in any atmosphere except the one I was brought up in'. Her strongest memory was of her mother, no matter how busy with her various good causes, always sitting by the fireplace when her children came home from school. She drew this somewhat curious lesson from her mother's combination of activism and family life: 'I learned early on that you can't be both'.

In many ways, Katharine Hepburn was correct that it would have been difficult, if not impossible, to succeed in Hollywood in the 1930s while maintaining family life on the model of her parents. Her inability to imagine a world where women could combine careers and marriage stemmed not just from the rigours of the acting profession, but from the incomplete feminist revolution that she inherited from her mother's generation. Once again, history helps us understand her options and choices.

The message to young women in the 1920s and 1930s was to be independent and autonomous, to forge their own way in the previously male-dominated public realm. Now that the vote had been won, it was up to individual women to strive and succeed. If they failed, they blamed themselves, not society, for their disappointments or setbacks. Given the flush of optimism following passage of the Nineteenth Amendment (votes for women), the aspirations of this generation were neither as naive nor as unrealistic as they have later been portrayed. These women had seen an enormous expansion in opportunities since their mothers' and grandmothers' times, and in the context of their recent enfranchisement it was not really all that surprising that such women felt liberated, free, and men's equals. Self-styled modern women may even have breathed a sigh of relief that they could now be taken seriously as human beings, not just as the second sex.

This credo of personal liberation was exhilarating, but it had significant limitations. As the historian Nancy Cott has observed, individualism offered no way to achieve the goal of equality other than to act as if it had already been achieved. And this credo of individual success left little room for women who also wanted a personal life that included more than work. As long as women retained primary responsibility for domestic and child-rearing duties, they would be disadvantaged as they tried to compete in the male realm. The need for a more systematic restructuring of gender roles was something that turn-of-the-century feminists like Katharine Hepburn's mother failed to anticipate. In reality, the supposed equality of the 1920s was far from complete.

Katharine Hepburn saw this trap more clearly than most: 'It's ridiculous to compete in a man's world on a man's terms', she noted at the height of the women's movement in the 1970s. Instead, Katharine Hepburn made personal choices that served as her own slightly idiosyncratic alternative to traditional gender roles. When she says, 'I put on pants so many years ago and declared a sort of middle road', she is talking both literally and symbolically. This androgynous message also comes through in many of Hepburn's films, especially from the 1930s. As a commentator once observed, it is almost a case of being female without the inconvenience.

Hepburn admits that many people, especially women, find this image highly appealing: 'They think it's free and that I've done it all. But it hasn't been for free, and I really don't have it all. They don't understand, for example, that maybe they had five children, and I don't have any'. Her theme begs the question, must women live like men to be free? 'That's what we're going to find out, isn't it?' she replied recently. Some, like Katharine Hepburn, revel in this individualistic approach: 'I had a lot of energy and looked as if I was (and I was) hard to get – wasn't mad about the male sex – perfectly independent, never had any intention of getting married, wanted to paddle my own canoe, didn't want anyone to pay my way.' Her privileged background and supportive family allowed her to make choices free of such concerns as earning a living or fear of being alone. But not all women want to or are able to live their lives as 'glorious exceptions'; being Katharine Hepburn is not an option for most.

Both in her way of life and credo, Katharine Hepburn stands as a transitional figure in twentieth-century women's history. She lived by the philosophy of personal autonomy and independence that emerged in the 1920s as an important breakthrough for women. But she did not challenge, nor did many others until the 1960s, the underlying social structures that continued to define women predominantly in terms of home and family. For Katharine Hepburn, politics in the post-war world meant liberalism, not feminism or women's issues. She tempted the wrath of the House Un-American Activities Committee in the late 1940s by her public anti-censorship stance, for example, and added her support to the civil rights movement through movies such as *Guess Who's Coming To Dinner* (1967). But only on the issue of birth control, her mother's cause, did Hepburn consistently support the agenda of the modern women's movement.

Hepburn's pronouncements about putting on pants and living like a man, so jarring to modern-day feminists, must therefore be considered in their historical context. What we may be hearing is the voice of a woman who, despite her supportive family background and her own feminist sympathies, was raised in a period of American history when there was no broadly-based feminist movement to support women's aspirations. The only way for these women to think of themselves, and to act, was as exceptions. In the end, Katharine Hepburn's views on women's roles and feminism may be less important than the enduring hold she, and other highly visible and independent women like Amelia Earhart and Eleanor Roosevelt, have on the popular imagination. In a period without an active feminist movement (that is, between 1920 and the mid-1960s), the heroines of popular culture took on especially large symbolic roles. The examples they set – that women can be autonomous human beings, can live life on their own terms, and can overcome conventional social barriers – resonated through the culture. This model of female independence and autonomy may in turn have served as a substitute for a more overtly political feminist vision.

Katharine Hepburn's life, as portrayed in the press and in her films, has conveyed this spirit of liberation and autonomy over many decades. Her mother's path-breaking contributions to public life live on through her daughter's impact on popular culture. From the perspective of the 1980s, we may not necessarily call these messages feminism, but if we deny them that context, we may miss the real story.

*   *   *

Susan Ware is a historian affiliated with the Radcliffe Institute for Advanced Learning, Harvard University. She specialises in twentieth-century American women's history and biography and is the author of *Beyond Suffrage: Women in the New Deal* (1981); *Still Missing: Amelia Earhart and the Search for Modern Feminism* (1994); and *Letter to the World: Seven Women Who Shaped the American Century* (1998).

47

Les Invalides

DOUGLAS JOHNSON

(February 1991)

Douglas Johnson, for many years virtually History Today's *official historian of modern France, describes one of the great monuments of Paris.*

Louis XIV should not be associated exclusively with Versailles. He was responsible for one of the finest buildings in Paris, Les Invalides, or, as one should say, l'Hôtel des Invalides. Not only is it a magnificent creation. It was one of his acts that has always been received with enthusiasm. Montesquieu, writing in the eighteenth century, said: 'There is no institution more worthy of respect than the Hôtel des Invalides. If I were a prince I would rather have founded this institution than have won three battles'.

The distinction of the Invalides was that it was a response to a particular problem. Before it existed Paris was filled with old soldiers. They were mutilated, destitute and miserable, and in their claims for a special charity that would save them from their deplorable circumstances and reward them for their devotion to duty, they could be both obstreperous and dangerous. For centuries there had been confusion about what could be done for these veterans apart from quartering them on the many abbeys and priories of the church, where their presence was unwelcome and where they were often neglected and maltreated. Several attempts to create a special community for them where they would be looked after came to nothing. But in 1670, at a time when Paris was inundated with veterans who had been reduced to the last extremity, a royal edict ordered the construction of an Hôtel des Invalides which would serve as a refuge for these victims of the wars. Within six years the first inmates were installed. Eventually their numbers rose to some 6,000.

It was Libéral Bruant who was the architect responsible for the great façade, with its 200 metres of symmetry and its 133 windows. The

362

entrance takes the form of a triumphal arch, with an arcade that is decorated by the royal emblem, the sun. Beyond this lies a vast but somewhat austere courtyard. Amongst the relatively small number of decorations is one which shows a sense of humour. It was the Minister for War, Louvois, who was most determined that this building should be finished rapidly and who most closely supervised all the details. One of the lucarnes (on the left as one enters) shows the head and the paws of a wolf (in French, 'loup voit'; the wolf is watching).

It was not because of this joke (but rather because of his ill-health) that Louvois took the work away from Bruant and asked Mansart to complete the building. It was he who created the great church of the Invalides, with its magnificent dome, surmounted by a campanile in golden copper and a cross, the whole standing well over 100 metres high. This ensemble still dominates the vast esplanade of the Invalides which extends northwards to the Seine.

A number of legends are associated with Louis XIV and the Invalides. Some of them may be true. Once when he visited it he came in a carriage drawn by eight white horses and accompanied by numerous grand escorts. But when he entered the courtyard the old soldiers who were there would not let the escorts proceed. They claimed that they had protected their king on the battlefield and that they could defend him when he visited them. The king supposedly agreed, and ever afterwards when he came to the Invalides the royal guards had to wait outside. On another occasion, when Madame de Maintenon was accompanying the king, it was said that an old soldier hobbled towards her and offered her a piece of the regulation bread that was served in the establishment. The court ladies found it disgusting and the order was given that bread of higher quality should be supplied. Such stories concerning the Sun King are rare, but Louis XIV was certainly deeply attached to the Invalides and in his will he commended the establishment to the particular care of his successor.

Louis XV placed a dominating equestrian statue of Louis XIV in front of the entrance, and it was this as well as many altars and religious objects that were destroyed by the revolutionaries after 1789 (most of them were subsequently restored). But the Constituent Assembly, and later the Convention, voted for the special protection of the Invalides and asked that the pensioners and their families should be well treated.

It was Napoleon, whether as first consul or as emperor, who showed the greatest enthusiasm for the Invalides. He held special celebrations there. It was in that church that he founded the Legion of Honour. He rescued the remains of the great general Turenne, who had died of wounds in 1675, and installed them with ceremony in the Invalides, which, he said, should become the resting place of France's military heroes.

It was therefore natural that when, in 1840, the government of Louis-Philippe decided to bring back the remains of Napoleon from Saint Helena, they should be interred in a crypt in the Invalides. It was on a freezing day in December that a million people witnessed Napoleon's last journey. For some, the spectacle was ludicrous. All the more so because the route was lined with enormous plaster statues, supposedly representing Justice and Eloquence. Victor Hugo, who was present, refused to believe that the coffin that was paraded before him actually contained the body of the emperor. Others believed that the ceremony symbolised the end of the Napoleonic legend. A largely indifferent crowd had witnessed his effective burial. But the future proved otherwise. Within a decade a Bonaparte was in power. And for a century and more, when people, whether French or not, visit the Invalides, it is in order to see the circular crypt where Napoleon is buried.

He lies immediately beneath the dome. His crypt took some twenty years to design and build, and the huge sarcophagus, which contains several coffins the last of which encloses the uniformed body of the emperor, is composed of reddish brown porphyry marble which the Tsar Nicholas had sent especially from Finland. The legend meets the gaze of the visitor. 'I desire that my ashes shall repose by the banks of the Seine. in the midst of the French nation, which I have so dearly loved'. The anecdote that one hears is different: as Napoleon was a man of small stature he wanted to be placed where everyone would look down on him in death, as they had done in life. In so doing, they would recall his true greatness.

The Invalides has always been the centre of myth, and perhaps that became its real function. It was said that when Louis XIV visited there in 1674 the first two soldiers to be presented to him had served at the battles of Arques and Ivry, eighty-five and eighty-six years earlier. Towards the end of the nineteenth century it was widely believed that more than one of the inmates had been present at the battle of Waterloo and curious Parisians would seek them out in order to ask them what Napoleon looked like. Many stories were told too about a Madame Brulon who, disguised as a man, had fought in many campaigns with great valour. She died in 1848 but the idea that a woman lurked amongst these old soldiers persisted.

The ceremonial guns which are placed on the esplanade side of the Invalides are made up of many which were captured from various enemies. It is said that when the Germans occupied Paris in 1940 they immediately removed those pieces that were Prussian. But they were returned after 1945, to the immense satisfaction of Parisians who were conscious of the symbolism of these acts.

The Invalides has become many things. It is now a military museum, as well as the residence of the Military Governor of Paris. But it still remains a hospital and a refuge for old soldiers. At the present moment it houses some of those who were wounded in the Indo-Chinese and Algerian wars. It also remains a memorial for distinguished soldiers. The tombs of Marshals Lyautey and Foch decorate the chapels. A railway station, a metro station and an air terminal are nearby and bear the name 'Invalides'

One night, shortly before 1848, Chateaubriand contemplated the dome. On one side was the waning moon; on the other the rising sun. Light from each illuminated each side of the cross. Chateaubriand saw this as a symbol of his own life, standing between the old regime of the past and the new regime of revolutions. The Invalides is this. But it is also much more. It is a gesture to the past, and it is a brooding magnificence for the present.

*   *   *

Douglas Johnson (b. 1925), for many years Professor of French History at University College, London, received part of his education at the Ecole Normale Supérieure, Paris. Johnson is a member of the Franco-British Council, the British representative on the Council for the Fondation Charles de Gaulle in Paris and a member of the Commission Nationale pour la Publication des Oeuvres d'Alexis de Tocqueville. His published works include *France and the Dreyfus Affair* (1966) and *A Concise History of France* (1971). An interest in old Breton buildings is but one more facet of his fascination for French history, politics and literature. He has been a member of *History Today*'s academic advisory board since the 1980s.

48

Columbus: Hero or Villain?

FELIPE FERNÁNDEZ-ARMESTO

(May 1992)

The 500th anniversary of Columbus' first transatlantic voyage produced heated controversy over the 'Discovery', or 'Encounter' (or 'Genocide') being commemorated. Felipe Fernández-Armesto summed up the case for and against the man of the hour.

This year, his statue in Barcelona exchanged symbolic rings with the Statue of Liberty in New York; meanwhile, the descendants of slaves and peons will burn his effigy. In a dream-painting by Salvador Dalí, Columbus takes a great step for mankind, toga-clad and cross-bearing – while a sail in the middle distance drips with blood. The Columbus of tradition shares a single canvas with the Columbus of fashion, the culture-hero of the western world with the bogey who exploited his fellow man and despoiled his environment. Both versions are false and, if historians had their way, the quincentennial celebrations ought to stimulate enough educational work and research to destroy them, Instead, the polemical atmosphere seems to be reinforcing *à parti pris* positions.

It is commonly said that the traditional Columbus myth – which awards him personal credit for anything good that ever came out of America since 1492 – originated in the War of Independence, when the founding fathers, in search of an American hero, pitched on the Genoese weaver as the improbable progenitor of all-American virtues. Joel Barlow's poem, *The Vision of Columbus*, appeared in 1787. Columbus remained a model for nineteenth-century Americans, engaged in a project for taming their own wilderness. Washington Irving's perniciously influential *History of the Life and Voyages of Christopher Columbus* of 1828 – which spread a lot of nonsense including the ever-popular folly that Columbus was derided for claiming that the world was round – appealed unashamedly to Americans' self-image as promoters of civilisation.

Yet aspects of the myth are much older – traceable to Columbus' own times and, to a large extent, to his own efforts. He was a loquacious and indefatigable self-publicist, who bored adversaries into submission and acquired a proverbial reputation for using more paper than Ptolemy. The image he projected was that of a providential agent, the divinely-elected 'messenger of a new heaven', chosen to bear the light of the gospel to un-evangelised recesses of the earth – the parts which other explorers could not reach. His plan for an Atlantic crossing 'God revealed to me by His manifest hand'. Playing on his Christian name, he called himself 'Christo ferens' and compiled a book of what he said were biblical prophecies of his own discoveries. Enough contemporaries were convinced by his gigantic self-esteem for him to become literally a legend in his own lifetime. To a leading astrological guru at the court of Spain, he was 'like a new apostle'. To a humanist from Italy who taught the would-be Renaissance men of Castile, he was 'the sort of whom the ancients made gods'.

From his last years, his reputation dipped: writers were obliged to belittle him in the service of monarchs who were locked in legal conflict with Columbus' family over the level of reward he had earned. Yet his own self-perception was passed on to posterity by influential early books. Bartolomé de Las Casas – Columbus' editor and historian – professed a major role for himself in the apostolate of the New World and heartily endorsed Columbus' self-evaluation as an agent of God's purpose. Almost as important was the *Historie dell'Ammiraglio*, which claimed to be a work of filial piety and therefore presented Columbus as an unblemished hero, with an imputed pedigree to match his noble soul.

Claims to having access to a divine hot-line are by their nature unveri-fiable. Demonstrably false was the second element in Columbus' self-made myth: his image of tenacity in adversity – a sort of *Mein Kampf* version of his life, in which he waged a long, lone and unremitting struggle against the ignorance and derision of contemporaries. This theme has echoed through the historical tradition. That 'they all laughed at Christopher Columbus' has been confirmed by modern doggerel. Vast books have been wasted in an attempt to explain his mythical perseverance by ascrib-ing to him 'secret' foreknowledge of the existence of America. Yet almost all the evidence which underlies it comes straight out of Columbus' own propaganda, according to which he was isolated, ignored, victimised and persecuted, usually for the numinous span of 'seven' years; then, after fulfilling his destiny, to the great profit of his detractors, he was returned to a wilderness of contumely and neglect, unrewarded by the standard of his deserts, in a renewed trial of faith.

These passages of autobiography cannot be confirmed by the facts. The documented length of his quest for patronage was less than five years.

Throughout that time he built up a powerful lobby of moral supporters at the Castilian court and financial backers in the business community of Seville. His own protestations of loneliness are usually qualified by an admission that he was unsupported 'save for' one or two individuals. When added together, these form an impressive cohort, which includes at least two archbishops, one court astrologer, two royal confessors, one royal treasurer and the queen herself. In his second supposed period of persecution, he was an honoured figure, loaded with titles, received at court, consulted by the crown and – despite his woe-begone protestations of poverty – amply moneyed.

The explanation of the image of Columbus-as-victim must be sought in his character, not in his career. He was what would now be called a whinger, who relished his own misfortunes as good copy and good theatre. When he apppeared at court in chains, or in a friar's habit, he was playing the role of victim for all it was worth. His written lamentations – which cover many folios of memoranda, supplications and personal letters – are thick with allusions to Jeremiah and Job. The notions of patience under suffering and of persecution for righteousness' sake fitted the hagiographical model on which much of his self-promotional writing was based: a flash of divine enlightenment; a life transformed; consecration to a cause; unwavering fidelity in adversity.

The most successful promotional literature is believed by its own propagators. To judge from his consistency, Columbus believed in his own image of himself. It is not surprising that most readers of his works, from Las Casas onwards, have been equally convinced. Columbus seems to have been predisposed to self-persuasion by saturation in the right literary models: saints, prophets and heroes of romance. Despite his astonishing record of achievement, and his impressive accumulation of earthly rewards, he had an implacable temperament which could never be satisfied, and an unremitting ambition which could never be assuaged. Such men always think themselves hard done by. His extraordinary powers of persuasion – his communicator's skills which won backing for an impossible project in his lifetime – have continued to win followers of his legend ever since his death.

Like Columbus-the-hero, Columbus-the-villain is also an old character in a long literary tradition. Most of the denunciations of him written in his day have not survived but we can judge their tenor from surviving scraps. The usual complaints against servants of the Castilian crown in the period are made: he acted arbitrarily in the administration of justice; he exceeded his powers in enforcing his authority; he usurped royal rights by denying appeal to condemned rebels; he alienated crown property without authorisation; he deprived privileged colonists of offices or perquisites; he favoured his own family or friends; he lined his pockets at public expense. In the course of what seems to have been a general campaign against Genoese employees of the crown in the late 1490s, he was 'blamed as a foreigner' and accused of 'plotting to give the island of Hispaniola to the Genoese'.

Other allegations attacked his competence rather than his good faith, generally with justice. It was true, for instance, that he had selected an unhealthy and inconvenient site for the settlement of Hispaniola; that he had disastrously misjudged the natives' intentions in supposing them to be peaceful; and that his proceedings had so far alienated so many colonists that by the time of his removal in 1500 it was a missionary's opinion that the colony would never be at peace if he were allowed back. All these complaints reflect the priorities of Spaniards and the interests of the colonists and of the crown. There were, however, some charges against Columbus which anticipated the objections of modern detractors, who scrutinise his record from the natives' point of view, or who look at it from the perspective of fashionably ecological priorities.

First, there was the issue of Columbus' activities as a slaver. Coming from a Genoese background, Columbus never understood Spanish scruples about slavery, which had been characterised as an unnatural estate in the most influential medieval Spanish law-code, and which the monarchs distrusted as a form of intermediate lordship that reserved subjects from royal jurisdiction. Castilian practice was, perhaps, the most fastidious in Christendom. The propriety of slavery was acknowledged in the cases of captives of just war and offenders against natural law; but such cases were reviewed with rigour and in the royal courts, at least, decision-making tended to be biased in favour of the alleged slaves.

Shortly before the discovery of the New World, large numbers of Canary Islanders, enslaved by a conquistador on the pretext that they were 'rebels against their natural lord' had been pronounced free by a judicial inquiry commissioned by the crown, and liberated, in cases contested by their 'owners', in a series of trials. This does not seem, however, to have alerted Columbus to the risks of slap-happy slaving.

Although the ferocious Caribs of the Lesser Antilles were generally deemed to be lawful victims of enslavement (since the cannibalism imputed to them seemed an obvious offence against natural law) Columbus' trade was chiefly in Arawaks, who, by his own account, were rendered exempt by their amenability to evangelisation. By denying that the Arawaks were idolatrous, Columbus exonerated them of the one possible charge which might, in the terms of the time, be considered an 'unnatural' offence. Even when the monarchs reproved him and freed the Arawaks he sold, Columbus was astonishingly slow on the uptake. In a colony where the yield of other profitable products was disappointing, he traded slaves to allay the colony's grievous problems of supply. 'And although at present they die on shipment,' he continued, 'this will not always be the case, for the Negroes and Canary Islanders reacted in the same way at first.' In one respect, contemporary criticisms of the traffic differed from those made today. The friars and bureaucrats who denounced Columbus for it did so not because it was immoral, but because it was unlawful.

Slavery was only one among many ills which Columbus was said to have inflicted on the natives. The current myth incriminates him with 'genocide'. In the opinion of one *soi-disant* Native American spokesman, 'he makes Hitler look like a juvenile delinquent'. This sort of hype is doubly unhelpful: demonstrably false, it makes the horrors of the holocaust seem precedented and gives comfort to Nazi apologists by making 'genocide' an unshocking commonplace. Though he was often callous and usually incompetent in formulating indigenist policy, the destruction of the natives was as far removed from Columbus' thoughts as from his interests. The Indians, he acknowledged, were 'the wealth of this land'. Their conservation was an inescapable part of any rational policy for their exploitation. Without them the colony would have no labour resources. At a deeper level of Columbus' personal concerns, they were the great glory of his discovery: their evangelisation justified it and demonstrated its place in God's plans for the world, even if the material yield was disappointing to his patrons and backers. And Columbus had enough sense to realise that a large and contented native population was, as the monarchs said, their 'chief desire' for his colony. 'The principal thing which you must do,' he wrote to his first deputy, 'is to take much care of the Indians, that no ill nor harm may be done them, nor anything taken from them against their will, but rather that they be honoured and feel secure and so should have no cause to rebel.'

Though no contemporary was so foolish as to accuse Columbus of wilfully exterminating Indians, it was widely realised that his injunctions were often honoured in the breach and that his own administrative regulations sometimes caused the natives harm. The missionaries almost unanimously regarded him as an obstacle to their work, though the only specific crime against the natives to survive among their memoranda – that 'he took their women and all their property' – is otherwise undocumented. The imposition of forced labour and of unrealistic levels of tribute were disastrous policies, which diverted manpower from food-growing and intensified the 'culture-shock' under which indigenous society reeled and tottered, though Columbus claimed they were expedients to which he was driven by economic necessity.

Some contemporaries also condemned the sanguinary excesses of his and his brother's punitive campaigns in the interior of Hispaniola in

1495–96. It should be said in Columbus' defence, however, that he claimed to see his own part as an almost bloodless pacification and that the 50,000 deaths ascribed to these campaigns in the earliest surviving account were caused, according to the same source, chiefly by the Indians' scorched-earth strategy. The outcome was horrible enough, but Columbus' treatment of the Indians inflicted catastrophe on them rather by mistakes than by crimes. In general, he was reluctant to chastise them – refusing, for instance, to take punitive measures over the massacre of the first garrison of Hispaniola; and he tried to take seriously the monarch's rather impractical command to 'win them by love'.

It would be absurd to look for environmental sensitivity of a late twentieth-century kind in Columbus' earliest critics. Yet the accusation of over-exploitation of the New World environment, which is at the heart of the current, ecologically-conscious anti-Columbus mood, was also made before the fifteenth century was quite over. According to the first missionaries, members of Columbus' family were 'robbing and destroying the land' in their greed for gold. Though he declined to accept personal responsibility, Columbus detected a similar problem when he denounced his fellow-colonists' exploitative attitude: unmarried men, with no stake in the success of the colony and no intention of permanent residence, should be excluded, he thought. They merely mulcted the island for what they could get before rushing home to Castile.

The danger of deforestation from the demand for dyestuffs, building materials and fuel was quickly recognised. The diversion of labour from agriculture to gold-panning aroused friars' moral indignation. The usefulness of many products of the indigenous agronomy was praised by Columbus and documented by the earliest students of the pharmacopoeia and florilegium of the New World. The assumption that there was an ecological 'balance' to be disturbed at hazard was, of course, impossible. On the contrary, everyone who arrived from the Old World assumed that the natural resources had to be supplemented with imported products to provide a balanced diet, a civilised environment and resources for trade. The modifications made by Columbus and his successors were intended, from their point of view, to improve, not to destroy. They introduced sources of protein – like livestock; comforts of home – like wheat really disastrous is hard to judge dispassionately. The loss of population in the early colonial period was probably due to other causes. In the long run, colonial Hispaniola proved able to maintain a large population and a spectacular material culture.

Since it was first broached in Columbus' day, the debate about the morality of the colonisation of the New World has had three intense periods: in the sixteenth century, when the issues of the justice of the

Spanish presence and the iniquity of maltreatment of the natives were raised by religious critics and foreign opportunists; in the late eighteenth century, when Rousseau and Dr Johnson agreed in preferring the uncorrupted wilderness which was thought to have preceded colonisation; and in our own day. Until recently, Columbus managed largely to avoid implication in the sins of his successors. Las Casas revered him, and pitied, rather than censured, the imperfections of his attitude to the natives. Eighteenth-century sentimentalists regretted the colonial experience as a whole, generally without blaming Columbus for it. This was fair enough. Columbus' own model of colonial society seems to have derived from Genoese precedents: the trading factory, merchant quarter and family firm. The idea of a 'total' colony, with a population and environment revolutionised by the impact and image of the metropolis, seems to have been imposed on him by his Castilian masters. In making him personally responsible for everything which followed – *post hunc ergo propter hunc* – his modern critics have followed a convention inaugurated by admirers, who credited Columbus with much that was nothing to do with him – including, most absurdly of all – the culture of the present United States. Columbus never touched what was to become US territory except in Puerto Rico and the Virgin Islands. The values which define the 'American ideal' – personal liberty, individualism, freedom of conscience, equality of opportunity and representative democracy – would have meant nothing to him.

Columbus deserves the credit or blame only for what he actually did: which was to discover a route that permanently linked the shores of the Atlantic and to contribute – more signally, perhaps, than any other individual – to the long process by which once sundered peoples of the world were brought together in a single network of communications, which exposed them to the perils and benefits of mutual contagion and exchange. Whether or not one regards this as meritorious achievement, there was a genuine touch of heroism in it – both in the scale of its effects and in the boldness which inspired it. There had been many attempts to cross the Atlantic in central latitudes, but all, as far as we know – failed because the explorers clung to the zone of westerly winds in an attempt to secure a passage home. Columbus was the first to succeed precisely because he had the courage to sail with the wind at his back.

Historians, it is often said, have no business making moral judgements at all. The philosophy of the nursery-school assembly, in which role-models and culprits are paraded for praise or reproof, seems nowadays to belong to a hopelessly antiquated sort of history, for which the reality of the past mattered less than the lessons for the present and the future. A great part of the historian's art is now held to consist in what the examiners call 'empathy' – the ability to see the past with the eyes, and to re-construct the feelings, of those who took part in it. If value judgements are made at all, they ought at least to be controlled by certain essential disciplines. First, they must be consistent with the facts: it is unhelpful to accuse of 'genocide', for instance, a colonial administrator who was anxious for the preservation of the native labour force. Secondly, they should be made in the context of the value-system of the society scrutinised, at the time concerned. It would be impertinent to expect Columbus to regard slavery as immoral, or to uphold the equality of all peoples. Conquistadors and colonists are as entitled to be judged from the perspective of moral relativism as are the cannibals and human-sacrificers of the indigenous past. Thirdly, moral judgements should be expressed in language tempered by respect for the proper meanings of words. Loose talk of 'genocide' twists a spiral to verbal hype. Useful distinctions are obliterated; our awareness of the real cases, when they occur, is dulled.

Finally, when we presume to judge someone from a long time ago, we should take into account the practical constraints under which they had to operate, and the limited mental horizons by which they were enclosed. Columbus was in some ways a man of extraordinary vision with a defiant attitude to the art of the possible. Yet he could not anticipate the consequences of his discovery or of the colonial enterprise confided to him. Five hundred years further on, with all our advantages of hindsight, we can only boast a handful of 'successful' colonial experiments – in the United States, Siberia, Australia and New Zealand – in all of which the indigenous populations have been exterminated or swamped. The Spanish empire founded by Columbus was strictly unprecedented and, in crucial respects, has never been paralleled. The problems of regulating such vast dominions, with so many inhabitants, so far away, and with so few resources, were unforeseeable and proved unmanageable. Never had so many people been conquered by culture-shock or their immune-systems invaded by irresistible disease. Never before had such a challenging environment been so suddenly transformed in an alien image. In these circumstances, it would be unreasonable to expect Columbus' creation to work well. Like Dr Johnson's dog, it deserves some applause for having performed at all.

So which was Columbus: hero or villain? The answer is that he *was* neither but has *become* both. The real Columbus was a mixture of virtues and vices like the rest of us, not conspicuously good or just, but generally well-intentioned, who grappled creditably with intractable problems. Heroism and villainy are not, however, objective qualities. They exist only in the eye of the beholder. In images of Columbus, they are now firmly impressed on the retinas of the upholders of rival legends and will never be expunged. Myths are versions of the past which people believe in for irrational motives – usually because they feel good or find their prejudices confirmed. To liberal or ecologically-conscious intellectuals, for instance, who treasure their feelings of superiority over their predecessors, moral indignation with Columbus is too precious to discard. Kinship with a culture-hero is too profound a part of many Americans' sense of identity to be easily excised.

Thus Columbus-the-hero and Columbus-the-villain live on, mutually sustained by the passion which continuing controversy imparts to their supporters. No argument can dispel them, however convincing; no evidence, however compelling. They have eclipsed the real Columbus and, judged by their effects, have outstripped him in importance. For one of the sad lessons historians learn is that history is influenced less by the facts as they happen than by the falsehoods men believe.

*　　*　　*

Felipe Fernández-Armesto is the award-winning author of ten books to date, including *Columbus* (1991), *Millennium: A History of Our Last Thousand Years* (1995) and *Truth: A History* (1997). He has been a member of the Faculty of Modern History at Oxford University since 1983, was a Fellow of the Netherlands Institute for Advanced Study in 1999–2000 and in 2000–1 Union Pacific Visiting Professor at the University of Minnesota. Honours won for his work on maritime and colonial history include the Caird Medal of the National Maritime Museum in 1997 and the John Carter Brown Medal in 1999. He contributed to a regular column, Time and Tide, in *History Today* in the mid-1990s.

49

Mediawatch: Nietzsche's Sister

HUGH DAVID

(August 1992)

Hugh David kept an eye and ear on the media, occasionally alighting upon gems of historical improbability – such as the story of Nietzsche's sister.

It was unfortunate that the first part of *The Story of Elisabeth Nietzsche* went out on April Fools' Day. Already unnerved by a spoof on that morning's *Today* programme that one's sense of humour is genetically-based, for a good twenty minutes I wondered whether I should be laughing.

The programme sounded so preposterous with its account of how the hitherto little-known sister of the philosopher, Friedrich Nietzsche, had set up an Aryan homeland in Paraguay decades before the Third Reich was even thought of. There were copious amounts of Wagner on the sound-track and plenty of jungle scenes intercut with archive footage of marching Nazis. There were interviews with blond-haired, blue-eyed Aryans – in German, with sub-titles – and lots of voice-over readings. I kept thinking of that *Panorama* spaghetti-harvest spoof.

Soon, however, fact proved once again that it can be far stranger and more awful than fiction. *Timewatch* (BBC2) had an important tale to tell; and as usual told it supremely well, spreading over two programmes to do so.

Elisabeth Nietzsche was only too real. I have subsequently been able to see Ben Macintyre's new book about her, *Forgotten Fatherland* (Macmillan) on which the *Timewatch* programmes were based. Like her brother, she was one of the 'Wagner set' and a hanger-on at Bayreuth. Unlike Friedrich, however, she was an uncomplicated, anti-Semitic racist; and her views were further narrowed when she came under the influence of, and later married, Bernhard Förster (or Foerster). Much to her brother's dismay, it was Förster who inspired her to establish the 'Nueva Germania' settlement in Paraguay.

The interviews with the *schnitzel*-eating descendants of the Germans Elisabeth had persuaded to travel to Paraguay, more than a hundred years ago, were notably fair-minded. (Not unexpectedly, there being no Jews in the compound, the comments they made about the 'inade-quacies' of the native Paraguayans were particularly revealing.) But, extraordinary as it seems, even such a rich seam as this was only the start – just as 'Nueva Germania' was only the start of Elisabeth Nietzsche's proto-fascist career.

With forensic precision, the *Timewatch* team went on to chart the remainder of Elisabeth's life. In many ways this was the most interesting part of the two programmes, for if the interviews with survivors of 'Nueva Germania' made good television, the legacy of Elisabeth's vision can be said to have changed the face of twentieth-century Europe.

Back in Germany – having effectively left her new Germanians to their fate in the jungle – she set about reforming the country itself. She tirelessly promoted Wagner (and all the wrong aspects of *his* vision) and ruthlessly doctored the works of her brother, by then dead of syphilis. It was a relentless and blatantly dishonest campaign . . . and it succeeded. Hitler was taken in – he was ever-solicitous to this 'mother of the Reich' – and so too were a couple of generations of philosophers. At university in the mid-seventies, I well recall the contempt which had been heaped on the works of Friedrich Nietzsche for the previous thirty years.

God is dead! Übermenschen! No one took him seriously. But at that time no one knew how grievously his thoughts had been distorted by his sister's tireless and sometimes downright criminal attempts to prove that God was not dead – that indeed he was alive and well and living at the Chancellery in Berlin.

*   *   *

Hugh David (b. 1954) is a journalist, playwright and author whose regular contributions on history in the media appeared in *History Today* between 1987 and 1993. His books include *The Fitzrovians*, *Stephen Spender: A Portrait with Background* and *On Queer Street*.

50

Soane's Museum

RICHARD CAVENDISH

(February 1994)

This was the first in a new series in which Richard Cavendish, a regular contributor on the highways and byways of British historical life, investigated some of Britain's smaller museums.

A museum is a respectable articulation of collecting mania. In one direction lie lunatic accumulations of old newspapers, used light bulbs and obsolete mousetraps. In the other looms all the majesty of the British Museum. The collection on view in Sir John Soane's Museum, displayed as he organised it in the rooms he himself designed, lies somewhere between the cabinet of curiosities and the museum proper.

Soane was an odd fish, said to have looked like a picture on the back of a spoon. Born in 1753, the son of a country bricklayer, he made his way by his own talents to the top of the tree as an architect. Marrying Elizabeth Smith, a rich builder's heiress, he rebuilt three houses on the north side of Lincoln's Inn Fields as his family home and office, and to display his treasures. Always conscious of his humble origins (his elder brother remained a bricklayer all his life), Soane was vulnerable and demanding, irritable and easily upset. Architect to the Bank of England for many years, he was knighted in 1831 and died in 1837 aged 83.

His accumulations of half a century are housed in a warren of rooms and passages where Soane indulged his delight in spatial surprises and effects of light. His artful use of mirrors, skylights and interior windows and openings creates an illusion of far more space than is actually there. The most famous items are the two great Hogarth *Rake's Progress* and *Election* series. Soane commissioned canvases from leading painters of the day and paid handsomely for them, but the pictures are only the grace notes to the vast array of objects of different types, sizes, shapes and periods all jammed together, crowded on the walls, perched on shelves and brackets or fighting for a toehold on the floor.

Soane collected an enormous quantity of classical and Renaissance statues, busts and casts, from a replica of the Apollo Belvedere to stray bits of feet and toes. He bought up Greek and Roman marbles, bronzes and terracottas, altars and urns, antique gems, stray medieval objects and fragments from demolished London buildings. He acquired Indian ivory furniture and Napoleonic medals, engraved seals, Peruvian pottery and Chinese ceramics. He had cork models of Greek temples and Etruscan tombs, books and manuscripts, architectural drawings by Wren, Piranesi, Robert Adam and others (running to thousands of items). He also had numerous models and casts of statues by Flaxman, who was a valued friend.

When the British Museum could not afford it, Soane bought the sarcophagus of Pharaoh Seti I and installed it in a place of honour in his sepulchral catacombs. If not haunted, the museum ought to be, and at least one watchman has left in terror after a single night alone in the place.

Soane also delighted in a Roman table leg, a scold's bridle, fossil ammonites, the tooth of a Burmese elephant, two mummified cats and a mummified rat, and a large fungus from Sumatra. He had a sense of humour and liked surprises. You look out of a window to see a moping monkish cloister, mournfully appointed, with a tomb startlingly inscribed, 'Alas Poor Fanny'. Fanny turns out to have been Mrs Soane's much-loved pet dog.

Poor Mrs Soane found it increasingly difficult to live among her husband's constantly rearranged rooms and treasures, while trying to keep the peace with the couple's spoiled sons, who failed to live up to their father's expectations of diligence and duty. She looks miserable in the Flaxman drawing in the house. Eventually she gave up and died, in 1815, when Soane was sixty-two. In 1833, to the fury of his ne'er-do-well, treacherous son George, Soane obtained a private Act of Parliament which preserved his house and collection as a museum for 'amateurs and students' (not any passing Tom Noddy), stipulating that it should all be kept 'as nearly as possible in the state in which Sir John Soane shall leave it'.

The stipulation has been honourably adhered to by successive curators, including one who rejoiced in the wonderful name of Wyatt Angelicus Van Sandow Papworth (and soon died, perhaps of excessive nomenclature).

Instead of a small number of objects in a large space, with captions which take a week to read, there is a multitude of objects crammed together, with few captions or none (the excellent guidebook shepherds you through). There's not a sound effect to be heard, not a simulated smell, and nothing lights up when you press a button. The effect is powerfully atmospheric and thoroughly engaging, and pressures to bring the museum spuriously up to date should be sternly resisted.

*   *   *

Richard Cavendish was educated at Christ's Hospital, Horsham and Brasenose College, Oxford. He worked in insurance for a time and subsequently in publishing, and spent eight years in the United States. He made his reputation as a historian of magic and the occult, with books including *The Black Arts* (1967) and the *History of Magic* (1977). He was the editor of the partwork encyclopedia *Man, Myth and Magic* and the *Encyclopedia of the Unexplained* (1974). He later edited *Out of Time* magazine and has written extensively on places to visit and things to see in Britain. He is General Editor of the Automobile Association's 1995 gazetteer *Road Book of Britain* and is a regular contributor to *History Today.*

51

Contemporary History

PETER HENNESSY

(March 1994)

*Peter Hennessy's lecture, which inaugurated the first Longman/*History
Today *awards for new historical writing, suggested another level of meaning
in the magazine's name.*

Historians are not supposed to have heroes. To do so is often detected as
evidence that detachment and cool reason have fled. But two men who
matter to me have delivered verdicts on my adopted craft that genuinely
give me pause.

The first is the finest constitutional analyst my old profession –
journalism – has ever produced, Walter Bagehot. In his 1856 essay on
Gibbon, Bagehot declared that history:

> may generally be defined as a view of one age taken by another; a
> picture of a series of men and women painted by one of another
> series. Of course, this description seems to exclude contemporary
> history; but if we look into the matter carefully, is there such a thing?
> What are all the best and most noted works that claim the title –
> memoirs, scraps, materials – composed by men of like passions with
> the people they speak of, involved it may be in the same events
> describing them with the partiality and narrowness of eager actors;
> or even worse, by men far apart in monkish solitude, familiar with
> the lettuces of the convent-garden, but hearing only faint dim
> rumours of the great transactions which they slowly jot down in the
> barren chronicle. These are not to be named in the same short
> breath, or included in the same narrow word, with the equable,
> poised philosophic narrative of the retrospective historian.

The second put-down to my branch of the historical profession is even
more painful to recall as it was delivered to me in person within a few

weeks of my being appointed Professor of Contemporary History at Queen Mary and Westfield College, University of London. In my 'Establishment'-watching way, I was about to lunch with Sir Douglas Hague at the Athenaeum, when, in the bar, Eric Hobsbawm crossed the room to tell me how pleased he was to hear I was joining academic life. Professor Hobsbawm paused to tell his guest, Sir Isaiah Berlin, of the news of my appointment.

'Good, good', said Sir Isaiah, 'contemporary history is the *most* interesting thing. In my time it used to be called *journalism, journalism*'.

To be raised up only to be cast down in the space of a couple of sentences from one such as he was an experience as anguish-laden as it was unforgettable. And if a journalist like Bagehot took much the same line, who am I to cavil? But cavil I do, for several reasons.

First, top flight journalism – 'the deeper end of the current affairs market', as the television producer, author and former MP, Phillip Whitehead, once put it – should not be that different in rigour and approach from the historians' craft. It is the use of evidence and the application of analysis that are the keys to both. And was not Philip Graham right to describe high quality journalism as the 'first rough draft of history?'

Secondly, is Bagehot right about either the meagreness of 'materials' or the similarity of 'passions' between the writers and the written about? Let us consider the 'materials' point first.

If you sat, as I have sat, last week and today in the Public Record Office at Kew sifting the newly released files for 1963, 'shortage' is not the word you would apply to the archive. It is not just that the volume of record-keeping grew with the growth of the twentieth-century British state: the amount is even greater this year thanks to the Major Administration's open government policy, especially its archives dimension known as the 'Waldegrave Initiative', after the minister responsible for openness.

For example, but for the recent changes on intelligence-related material, I am sure we would not have available at Kew today a file on the Profumo Affair from the No. 10 archive which contains a scatter of MI5 matter. Similarly, but for the public avowal of the 'Central Intelligence Machinery' last summer, I do not believe the Cabinet Committee Book for 1963 (the first of its kind to be released in full) would be accessible in the PRO from this morning, complete with its references to the membership and remits of the Joint Intelligence Committee and its offshoots: or that strange hybrid committee of Whitehall figures and broadcasters, which would have, in effect, taken over the British media during the transition to World War III and what remained of it after Broadcasting House and Television Centre lay in irradiated ruins.

Bagehot's 'materials' point remains relevant, however, to the period between yesterday and the biting of the Thirty Year Norm, but no earlier than that, at least in terms of the British state archives. Though there are, of course, exceptions and not just in the deeper intelligence world. For example, in an area of special fascination for Bagehot, the operations of the royal prerogative, the files remain very sparse, especially since 1952 when the present monarch succeeded her father. There are occasionally revealing snippets on other files, but the core archive covering what one senior crown servant recently called the 'very special . . . relationship between the prime minister and the sovereign' will remain closed for the foreseeable future. Though we have some for the Attlee-George VI relationship, there is no intention of declassifying the so-called 'Audience Notes' of the present Queen and her nine premiers (so far) at least until her demise.

What about Bagehot's 'men of like passions' argument? It is a danger, of course. For me, politicians rarely come close to any 'hero' category, however generously defined. Very occasionally, however, they do. In preparing my volume on early post-war British History, *Never Again*, I had to take care not to be over-generous in my treatment of that tersely admirable diminutive, Clement Attlee.

But let us take the recent PRO material once more to put Bagehot's strictures in a realistic, contemporary perspective. The party labels may be the same, but the political ecology of early 1960s Britain is very different from the political climate of the early 1990s. Take an archival rarity that was declassified in January 1993 – an unprecedented verbatim transcript of a prime minister's opening remarks at a Cabinet meeting.

It is Harold Macmillan on the aftermath of the single most famous post-war Liberal by-election triumph (he was acutely concerned by what he called 'the middle classes' – the Orpingtonians brooding on the need for an incomes policy to supplement the work of that 'delicate plant', the National Economic Development Council).

Preoccupied by the need 'to retain full employment; to secure if we can stable prices; to have a strong pound which means a favourable balance of payments both on current and capital accounts, and to gain growth and expansion in the economy', he speaks of the need to ease class antagonisms and to increase 'Government expenditure on the things we know are necessary – the housing, the slums, the universities, the schools . . .' at a time when 'I don't think anybody seriously suggests the conscious creating of unemployment'.

It *was* a different country. Even Conservative Ministers did things differently then. Those thought patterns are almost as remote from today's, certainly, as Attlee's if not Lloyd George's.

Enough of Bagehot. Let me move for a moment out of his long shadow to explain the special pleasure of writing contemporary history which, for me, is so constant and so potent as to override the pains and the pitfalls. It is the special impulse, not just to get behind the scenes of events one remembers oneself (like that extraordinary Profumo summer of 1963 when, at my sensible, down-to-earth grammar school in Gloucestershire we talked of ministers and tarts, pimps and spies in between sitting our O Levels), but to make sense of one's own times, too, in a more general sense.

In a way, men and women of my generation are the living artefacts of the post-war settlement, those babies into whom 'putting milk', according to Churchill, was the finest investment any community could make. As the broadcaster and critic, Gillian Reynolds, has expressed it, 'The 1944 Education Act taught me to read and think. The National Health Service has given me nice teeth and the BBC gave me Shakespeare and Beethoven'. (She was, of course, referring to that great 1946 invention, the BBC Third Programme.)

The danger in all this, of course, is lack of detachment. I still suffer emotional spasms (disturbingly conflicting ones) when the word 'Suez' is mentioned. And there is a constant danger of seemingly prime and glowing material being snatched away from one's pages by surviving participants who say, 'It simply wasn't like that' – a problem to which our colleagues with earlier specialities are, mercifully, strangers.

Let me give an example from the writing of *Never Again*. Shortly before the proofs went to the publishers, I ran across Lord Sherfield, the former Sir Roger Makins, a titan of the post-war Foreign Office. I told him that I was going to display in technicolor his oft quoted one-liner dismissing both the Schuman Plan and its author Jean Monnet, in the Hyde Park Hotel on May 16th, 1950, with the words, 'We are not ready; and you will not succeed', as recalled by Monnet's assistant, Etienne Hirsch. Lord Sherfield could not remember saying that and thought it most unlikely he would have used such language. In so doing, he snatched away the quote cherished as the encapsulation of the British 'official mind' in the spring of 1950 by so many who teach the strained relationship between Britain and an integrating Europe in the post-war period.

It is, however, of enormous value to enjoy the company of the Lord Sherfields of this world when new material is declassified at the PRO, especially when several surviving practitioners ponder the material together, with tape-recorders running, at the 'witness seminars' run jointly by the Institute of Contemporary British History and the Institute of Historical Research.

But the final defence of contemporary history is not that much cited notion of 'the bottom line' (though there plainly exists a rich and numerous market for it among other children of the Attleean Settlement now in the prime of their professional lives who can afford a £20 hardback without undue stress). It is a test of which Bagehot would have approved – utility.

How else, but with the help of a good grounding in the recent past, can one explain Britain's continuing emotional deficit with Europe, our clinging to that elusive 'special relationship' with the United States, our desire to remain 'punching heavier than our weight' in international counsels (to adapt a phrase favoured by the Foreign Secretary, Douglas Hurd)? All of these *current* phenomena reflect the hand history has 'dealt' the UK, which no government is going to 'cast away' lightly, as Sir Percy Cradock, former chairman of the Joint Intelligence Committee, puts it.

And on the vexing terrain covered by my own current research – the constitutional aspects of the premiership – wasn't it Bagehot himself in the opening paragraph of his immortal *The English Constitution*, who said of his mercurial subject, 'an observer who looks at the living reality will wonder at the contrast to the paper description'?

In a political system which relies on what Philip Ziegler has called 'instantly invented precedents', where the royal prerogative is a living, daily reality and where, as one of its guardians confessed to me, 'If you have an unwritten constitution you make it up as you go along', the only reliable way to reconstruct what that system is at any given moment, is to trace it through the CAB and the PREM files at the PRO. For the British Constitution is now, as it has always been, an accretion of the past, both deep and recent, accumulating generation on generation like coral.

If historians do not claim and retain this very Bagehotian reef of national life, those model-building political scientists, who are strangers to the PRO, will do so. And then where should we be?

Walter Bagehot, I am sure, would understand. And so, I hope, do you.

* * *

Peter Hennessy, Professor of History at Queen Mary and Westfield College, University of London, is a former journalist and an expert on contemporary British government and politics. A frequent broadcaster, his books include *Cabinet* (1986), *Whitehall* (1989), *Never Again: Britain 1945–51* (1992) and *The Hidden Wiring* (1995). His most recent book is *The Prime Minister* (2000), a study of the job and those who have held it since 1945.

52

American Democracy through Ancient Greek Eyes

BARRY STRAUSS

(April 1994)

The Founding Fathers revered classical Greece and Rome. Modern America is of course a vastly different political entity from ancient Athens – yet Barry Strauss identifies certain striking similarities.

Two thousand five hundred years after the founding of democracy in Athens, the United States of America is a larger, wealthier, and more powerful democracy than any Athenian could have imagined. But would an Athenian indeed consider America to be a democracy? If he could be restored to life and brought to Washington DC, would an Athenian visitor feel at home, even among the marble columns and the neo-classical façades? Would he judge the American government to embody 'the power of the people', as did Athens' *demokratia* (a compound of *demos*, 'people', and *kratos*, 'power')?

America a democracy? It is not merely the vast difference in size of territory and population between Athens and America that might make an ancient democrat reject the idea. At a size of about 1000 square miles, the American state of Rhode Island is no larger than Attica (as the territory of ancient Athens was called), but no Athenian would be any more the willing to consider Rhode Island a democracy. Nor would either the equality of women or the abolition of slavery or the ethnic and racial diversity of America be the crux of the problem for an Athenian. In early nineteenth-century America women could neither vote nor hold office, African slavery was widespread, and most free citizens traced their ancestry from within the British Isles. Americans nonetheless considered their country a democracy, as did such European observers as Alexis de

Tocqueville, whose visit to the States in 1831–32 furnished the material for his classic analysis, *De la démocratie en Amérique* (*Democracy in America*). An Athenian, however, might well have been unconvinced.

For him, the chief stumbling block would have been the American notion of representative democracy, which he would have considered an oxymoron, if not an impossibility. In Athens the people ruled not through representatives but directly. Their power was embodied in a popular assembly, a legislative and deliberative body open to all adult male citizens, as well as in jury courts, magistracies, and a council that served as a sort of executive committee. Each of these institutions was large, thereby offering every one of Athens' adult male citizens (a number that fluctuated between *c.* 25,000 and 50,000 in the two centuries of Athens' democratic regime) a chance to play at least a small part in self-government. Athenian ideology, moreover, emphasised participation and alternation in office. Take Athenian juries. Never composed of fewer than 201 men, they offered plenty of opportunity for participation to the pool of 6,000 jurors chosen at random each year. Seven hundred magistrates served annual terms in Attica (an additional number, varying in different eras, served abroad), most were chosen by lottery, thereby equalising opportunity between rich and poor. The 500 members of the Council, who also served annual terms, were selected by a combination of election and lottery.

Athenian insistence on direct democracy was not merely a constitutional detail. Direct popular participation in the government, rather, *was* democracy. The alternative, government by an élite, was considered to be not democracy but oligarchy, literally, 'rule by the few'. No matter how free the people were otherwise, Athenians did not consider them to be fully free unless they could govern themselves. Nor were the people deemed to enjoy full equality unless all adult male citizens had an equal opportunity to govern. Without such an opportunity, the Athenians believed, the government would be run not only by an élite but in the interests of an élite. Since the élite would generally be wealthier than ordinary people, the economic dimension was a key constituent of democracy.

Aristotle understood this well. As he put it, democracy is not only majority rule, but a regime run by poor and ordinary people in their own interests. Oligarchy is a regime run by an élite of wealthy people in their own interests.

The workings of American democracy have little in common with Athenian direct democracy. Legislation is carried out by the representatives of the people rather than by the people themselves. Magistrates are chosen by election or appointment, not lottery. Ordinary citizens may consider it their duty to be informed about public affairs and to vote, although a very large number of adult Americans rarely, if ever, vote. Even those who do vote feel no responsibility to hold public office, as Athenians did: in America politics is a profession, the province of a few, just like law, engineering, or acting. Indeed, the American press usually judges whether a foreign government is truly a democracy by the presence or absence of free elections. Only the American jury system emphasises the direct empowerment of poor and ordinary people, who, as in Athens, sit in judgement on the élite. Only a small percentage of Americans actually do jury duty, however. Unlike Athenian courts, moreover, American courts are supervised by professionals, judges and lawyers, who are usually members of the élite; in Athenian courts, amateurs dominated the proceedings.

In constitutional terms, then, American government places power in the hands of far fewer people than Athenian government. Hence an Athenian might be less likely to judge America a democracy than an oligarchy.

The American Founding Fathers, moreover, would be neither surprised nor disturbed by that conclusion. The Founders tended, of course, to be admirers of Greek and Roman antiquity, but they were selective in their admiration. Having rebelled against the British crown, the revolutionary leaders of the thirteen British colonies of North America looked outside English history for models of behaviour. Ancient history, which loomed large in eighteenth-century American education, proved a rich source. The Founders looked to the republics of antiquity for models of martial ardour, public virtue, self-sacrifice, political pluralism, balanced and stable confederations, agrarian hardiness, and above all, love of liberty. They found Sparta a more appealing paragon than Athens, however, and the Roman Republic preferable to either. In fact, they evinced little love for Athenian democracy, which they considered to be unstable, prone to faction, and prey to demagogues. John Adams, for instance, thought its history of factional strife rendered Athenian democracy a system of government contrary to 'all human and divine benevolence'. Alexander Hamilton confessed to 'feeling sensations of horror and disgust' at the continual agitation and revolutions of 'the petty republics of Greece and Italy'. Thomas Jefferson praised America's 'introduction of this new principle of representative democracy', arguing that it 'renders useless' almost all earlier political writings, including perhaps even Aristotle.

Pride in America's novelty and purity balanced the Founders' love of antiquity. The attitude resulted in part from the colonies' Puritan heritage of belief in special election as a chosen people doing the Lord's work, and in part from the sense of novelty and freshness of a frontier society. Hence, Samuel Adams of Massachusetts said that while America should be like Sparta, it should he a Christian Sparta. John Taylor of

Virginia went a step further, emphasising the radical difference between the new American republic and its Greco-Roman antecedents; in America, he wrote, 'human character has undergone a moral change'.

It was not difficult, therefore, for the American Founders to reject Athens. They considered direct democracy as repugnant as the Athenians considered it essential, and for several reasons. First, having experienced what they considered to be tyranny under British colonial rule, the Founders had a considerable scepticism of direct governance of any kind. Hence their insistence on creating a federal government of checks and balances, where competition would limit the power of any one person or institution. The two chambers of the federal legislature, for example, the Senate and the House of Representatives, would each balance the other, while the legislative branch as a whole would act as a counterweight to the executive branch, led by the president. Judicial review, provided by the courts, would enforce the constitution against encroachments by the legislative or the executive. The power of the individual states, moreover, would balance the power of the federal government.

Second, having effected a revolution against an ancient institution, the British crown, the Founders had a strong sense of the fragility of regimes. They worried intensely about the corrosive effect of factionalism. The corrective, they felt, would be a written constitution, difficult to amend, hence a factor for stability. Then too, they believed that a system of checks and balances would, in addition to other virtues, prevent faction – although America's subsequent history of vigorous party politics belies their hope.

Third, while some were considerably more egalitarian than others, none of the Founders was willing to entrust governmental power to poor people. Some looked to government by the rich, others idealised the virtues of yeoman farmers, but none believed that political excellence was obtainable without a minimum of wealth and education. None was willing to allow the landless, the destitute, or the urban poor to vote, let alone to hold public office. Left to their own devices, ordinary people were too ignorant and excitable to offer good government: so the Founders believed. Prey to clever and unscrupulous demagogues, ordinary people needed the guidance and protection of 'some temperate and respectable body of citizens', as James Madison, at the time of the debate over the United States Constitution, described his proposed Senate. Until a constitutional amendment of the twentieth century, American Senators were chosen by state legislatures, not by popular election, rendering the Senate highly élitist – precisely a virtue that would greatly have aided democratic Athens, Madison thought. 'What bitter anguish would not the people of Athens have often escaped', he writes:

if their government had contained so provident a safeguard [i.e., a Senate] against the tyranny of their own passions? Popular liberty might then have escaped the indelible reproach of decreeing to the same citizens the hemlock on one day and statues on the next.

No ancient Greek oligarch could have decried better the alleged flaws of democracy.

The ink had hardly dried on the Constitution, however, when 'popular liberty' began to break the bonds that Madison had tried to impose upon it. Over the past two centuries, America has grown far more democratic than the Framers would ever have wanted. As it currently exists, democracy in America lacks many of its original Madisonian checks on popular passions. The citizen body has expanded to include people whom the Framers might have considered dubious material for the fashioning of republican virtue: women, freed slaves and their descendants, immigrants from the four corners of the earth. Living in a largely rural country, Jefferson and many of his contemporaries praised agrarian virtues. What would they make of today's American electorate, which is overwhelmingly urban or suburban? Nor are there any property requirements for voting: standard in Madison's America, they were overthrown early in the nineteenth century. Suffrage is universal, office-holders are heterogeneous. Both women and the descendants of slaves serve as mayors of big cities, as state governors, US senators, and as justices of the US Supreme Court; only the presidency continues to elude them.

The barriers to the direct expression of American popular will have fallen considerably since the 1790s. Although the American president is chosen by a slate of electors from each state, the so-called electoral college has become a mere technicality, as each state's electors are bound to support the candidate who wins a plurality of the popular vote in that state. On the state and local level, many judges are chosen by election rather than appointment. Sophisticated polling of public opinion makes it difficult for an elected official to ignore the voice of the people, not if he or she wants to be re-elected. Not that checks and balances have been entirely removed from the American federal political system: indeed, compared to a parliamentary democracy, their continued importance is striking. Unlike a prime minister, the American president does not necessarily command a working majority in the legislature, as the results of congressional elections are independent of those of the presidential election. It is not unusual for one party to control the presidency and another to control the Congress. Each chamber of the legislature, moreover, is quite independent, meaning that a president has to find support in both the House of Representatives and the Senate in order to have a bill become law. Recent years, moreover, have seen a weakening of the ties of party loyalty. The end of the Cold War and its sense of emergency have brought a certain diminution in the prestige of the presidency. Hence, although Bill Clinton's Democratic party has majorities in both House and Senate, it is no easy matter for him to have a legislative programme enacted. Nor can legislators in one chamber of Congress easily enact their programme without obtaining the support of the president; and without the support of the other chamber of Congress, they can enact nothing at all. Popular liberty, therefore, is indeed held in check, just as Madison would have wished.

Yet having written off America as an oligarchy, an Athenian might well have second thoughts. The closer he looked at America, particularly if he left the confines of Washington, the more similarities he might have detected between ancient *demokratia* and modern democracy. Like Athens, the United States prides itself on freedom. Each society's ideologists grounded that freedom in an act of armed rebellion against foreign (or at least what was perceived as foreign) domination. America's national holiday is July 4th, celebrating the official declaration of the War of Independence against Britain (a nation now, ironically, both revered as the fountainhead of American culture and respected as America's closest ally). Athenian tradition celebrated both the failed aristocratic revolt of *c.* 515 BC against the tyranny that ruled Athens and the successful popular revolt against Sparta in 508/7 BC. The celebration of martial virtue as the guardian of freedom is to be found in both Athens and America. In Athens, military service was all-but universal, while America guarantees every citizen the right to bear arms – even, in recent years, in the face of unprecedented and at times anarchic violence. The notion of the independent American, armed against the threat of tyranny, runs deep in the national consciousness.

In large part because of its frontier legacy, America is a more violent society than was Athens. Yet Athens, no less than America, promoted an ideology according to which the ideal citizen would be active, not passive: enterprising, patriotic, vigorous, even, when need be, a busybody. Both Athenians and Americans have acquired a reputation for litigiousness. Neither society has shown much patience for strict libel laws or the protection of a politician's privacy.

Both Athens and America imagined themselves as open societies, offering asylum for refugees and economic opportunity for enterprising immigrants. Athenian immigrants, it is true, had virtually no chance of ever becoming citizens – a striking contrast to the universal citizenship of modern America. By the mid fifth-century BC, the Athenian democratic citizen body was largely a closed group. Athenian resident aliens or metics, as they were known, nonetheless attained great prosperity and a substantial amount of both individual and political freedom. Metics wrote speeches delivered by citizens in court and in the assembly. During the civil war of 404–405 BC metics fought and died for the democrats.

Like America, Athens was considered to be a highly cosmopolitan society, a babel of foreign voices, to the delight of democrats and disgust of conservatives. The philosopher, Plato, no admirer of democracy, satirised Athens as resembling a multi-coloured coat, because of its diversity. Even worse, for him and like-minded thinkers, Athens was a society that prized equality.

Oligarchic Greeks looked down on Athenians for their easy-going and egalitarian manners. The benches of the Athenian assembly, critical sources state, were filled with boorish farmers and uneducated artisans and tradesmen. Athenians, one source reports, had the bad taste to let slaves walk the streets dressed like masters! America too has a strong egalitarian strain. Of many indices, consider only the scandal to refined opinion when, on the occasion of his inauguration as US president in 1829, Andrew Jackson opened the White House to ordinary citizens, never before admitted to such a celebration. 'Country men, farmers, gentlemen, mounted and dismounted, boys, women and children, black and white', entered the White House, as a contemporary reports, leaving china, crystal, and silk upholstery ruined in their wake.

Both societies particularly prize freedom of speech. Athenians focused on the right of every citizen to address the assembly. They recognised a more general freedom of speech, but they had nothing like the protection of the American Bill of Rights of 1791 (comprising the first ten amendments to the Constitution), which prohibits any federal legislation restricting the people's freedom of speech. The Bill of Rights goes further, moreover, by also guaranteeing the people's right to assemble peaceably and to petition and lobby their representatives in Congress. It prohibits the creation of an established religion, while protecting the people's freedom of religion more generally. Hence, freedom of speech is established more firmly and interpreted more broadly in the United States than in Athens.

None of this is to deny the enormous differences between Athenian and American democracy; indeed, the American freedom of religion merely highlights those differences. Modern Western liberalism emerged from the terrible wars of religion of the sixteenth and seventeenth centuries. Hence it places great emphasis on individual religious freedom, and on the separation of public and private more generally. An Athenian, by contrast, tended to turn to the polis, not the individual conscience, for ideological guidance. Athenian religion, with its gods and festivals, was civic religion. There was no separation of church and state. Public and private were considered to be distinct, but the distinction was weaker than in modern democracy. Athenians were far more willing to intervene in private affairs than are contemporary democrats. Consider an extreme but revealing case, the trial of Socrates, who was executed in 399 BC for the crimes of not recognising the gods the city recognised, of having invented new gods and of having corrupted the youth. An American court would throw such charges out.

On the other hand, an Athenian court would dismiss the host of suits heard in American courts over the last generation, suits based on a seemingly open-ended notion of rights. The Athenian notion of 'rights' was attenuated in the first place, 'privilege' and 'duty' being far more important concepts in its political lexicon. In the second place, Athens had little room for the rectification of alleged discrimination against ethnic and racial minority groups, women, the handicapped, religious sects, the allergic, and now, even animals – whose demands for justice loom increasingly large in American justice and politics.

Perhaps the most striking difference between ancient and modern is capitalism. To be sure, certain similarities do exist between the ancient and modern economies. Athens, no more than America, practised communism. Athenians evinced great respect for private property. Like Americans, they expected their government to provide a minimum of prosperity, especially for the poor. The poor looked to the Athenian state for employment in the navy and in such public works as building projects and the dockyards, as well as for reimbursement for jury duty, service in public office, and even for attending the theatre (in what was a kind of primitive welfare system). Yet Athens lacked the ideology as well as the technology for promoting modern economic growth. Athenians were relatively unacquisitive, and owned relatively few possessions. Unlike Americans, Athenians did not consider it the purpose of the polis to promote an ever-improving standard of living for its citizens. They might have been surprised to learn that 'the state of the economy' is generally considered the single most important issue in any American election.

The differences are indeed enormous. Yet one must not forget the thread of similarity that runs from ancient to modern democracy. Both Athens and America are societies that emphasise an ideology of equality and freedom, and the right of every citizen to have a say in the running of the country. An Athenian might dismiss America as an oligarchy. He would be astounded by the size and wealth of the United States and by the abolition of slavery. He would be distrustful of the freedom accorded women, and dismissive of the ever-greater number of 'rights' claimed by an ever larger number of people. And yet, when he encountered a group of American citizens openly criticising the government and organising a lobbying campaign to do something about it by fighting for their rights, the Athenian would probably nod in recognition and join right in.

*   *   *

Barry Strauss is Director of the Peace Studies Program and a professor of history and classics at Cornell University. A member of the American School of Classical Studies, he is author of several books including *The Anatomy of Error: The Lessons of Ancient Military Disasters for Modern Strategists* (1990) and *Rowing against the Current: On Learning to Scull at 40* (1999). He is writing a new book, *A Family Made by War: One Family's Twentieth Century*, which follows the thread of military experience through three generations in his family from Poland to America to Israel.

53

Downfall or Liberation?

EBERHARD JÄCKEL

(May 1995)

On the 50th anniversary of peace in Europe, History Today *teamed up with* Rodina *and* Damals, *its counterpart magazines in post-Communist Russia and united, democratic Germany. In a remarkable East-meets-West edition, Eberhard Jäckel examined the complex reactions of ordinary German people in 1945 as they began to come to terms with the Nazi past.*

Ten years ago, delivering his now famous speech on the fortieth anniversary of the end of the Second World War, Richard von Weizsäcker, President of the Federal Republic of Germany, spoke emphatically. 'May 8th was a day of liberation. It freed us all from the inhumane system of National Socialist rule'. Accurate as this remark was, in 1945 most Germans by no means greeted the end of the war as a liberation. Aside from persecuted groups and prisoners in concentration camps, almost no one felt liberated. They did not even feel relieved that hostilities and air raids had ceased. Germans unanimously called the event a downfall, meaning not only the fall of the state, but the collapse as well of their hopes and desires.

Otherwise every German experienced the war's end in his or her own particular way. Most of the country was already occupied by foreign troops by the time capitulation was announced. For the majority, the decisive transition came in the moment when the town where they lived changed occupying forces, or when they had to flee.

1918 had been completely different. When the First World War ended, all Germans were living more or less under identical conditions: under-nourished in the fifth winter of war, plagued by an influenza epidemic, but still seriously hoping for a favourable conclusion. And then news of armistice and defeat broke upon them. They all received it simul-taneously, whether they lived in Lörrach or Interburg, in Flensburg or

Munich, or stood at the Front. This was also how 1945 was experienced in most other countries.

In Germany, however, the end of the Second World War came in fits and starts, differing greatly from place to place. Soviet troops had already entered East Prussia in October 1944, triggering the flight of millions of refugees. But in May 1945, the Frische Nehrung peninsula on the Gulf of Danzig was still in German hands. Even as Dresden was being destroyed by an air attack in February 1945, residents of Aachen, insofar as they had remained there, had already lived under American occupation for four months. In March, when the Americans and British crossed the Rhine, people in rural areas of Bavaria and Schleswig-Holstein still lived almost as though at peace.

The occupation arrived everywhere in a different fashion, in some places only after heavy fighting, in others suddenly and without resistance. Germans in each place experienced it differently. It is understandable that they did not feel liberated. Soldiers, when they survived, were taken prisoner. The civilian population saw itself subjected to the measures of the occupying powers. These were mostly brutal in the east, more lenient in the west. And yet what Germans felt as the war ended was everywhere much the same.

We are rather well informed about this. Of course, there were no opinion polls at the time, but the Nazi government had always been interested in finding out what people thought, what their mood was. Numerous agencies, most importantly the SD (Sicherheitsdienst) – the security arm of the party – kept written records of everything they heard. Such reports were gathered locally, then collected for larger areas, and finally summarised for the entire Reich. Thousands of reports have survived and have been published in many volumes. Reading them conveys precise impressions of what the average German thought and felt, hoped and dreaded, and how the changing situation was judged.

Unlike 1914 Germans had not been enthusiastic when the war began in 1939. But they had desired that their country did not again suffer defeat. The victories in the first three years of the war filled them with optimism. The elation first began ebbing in 1942. Uncertainty about when the war would end, mounting difficulties with food supply, and, most importantly, bombings of German cities brought on pessimism, which turned into resignation after the defeat at Stalingrad and finally evolved into a somehow still-hopeful fatalism. When would it all end, and how?

On May 4th, 1944, one SD report summarised dispatches about public opinion as follows: 'The population is currently most concerned about the air war. It affects all emotions and creates the greatest doubt in faith that the situation can be reversed'. Otherwise it was the so-called 'invasion'; a landing of American and British forces in Western Europe, which was most anticipated:

> The belief that a decisive turnaround in the progress of the war to our favour must come soon encourages most of our people to view an invasion with great hope. It is considered the last chance to turn the tide. Fear of invasion can hardly be detected. Instead, a terrible defeat for the enemy is expected.

This presumption was in keeping with the propaganda and coincided with the leadership's own assessments. Hitler also looked forward to the landing with optimism, believing it could be repelled. Most German troops could then be pulled out of the west and thrown to the Eastern Front. The population also assigned great significance to the leadership's announced intention to answer a landing with new weapons, so-called 'weapons of retribution'. The mood was appropriately sanguine when the landing actually began on June 6th, 1944. 'News that the invasion had started was received partly with great enthusiasm'. That 'air attacks on the Reich have ceased since the invasion began' contributed to such feelings. The majority curiously saw this as evidence of weakness; almost no one drew the conclusion that the Allies needed their air forces for the landing in Normandy.

The public mood was still rising on June 16th when the daily Wehrmacht report laconically announced: 'Southern England and the city of London were bombed with new warheads last night and early this morning'. Someone was reported as telling an acquaintance, 'I have wonderful news for you, the retribution has begun'. The report of June 19th, summarised: 'Jubilation which immediately followed even greater than at beginning of invasion. End to war seen coming soon'.

But already by the end of June, dejection had returned. The report of June 28th, listed four reasons for this. The new 'V-1' weapon (the pilot-less flying bomb, nicknamed the Doodlebug, used by Hitler in the closing days of the war) was not producing the desired effect. The landing in France had not been turned back. Instead, on the Eastern Front, a Soviet offensive began on June 22nd, and was moving very rapidly forward. And bombings had resumed. 'The elation of the first days after the start of the invasion and the retribution is very quickly and generally deflating', commented a report one day later. And, on July 14th: 'Spirits are continuing to fall'. This was the setting for the failed assassination attempt on Hitler on July 20th, 1944. Remarkably, no further worsening of the general mood resulted, according to the reports. On the contrary:

The population is greatly relieved that the Führer did not fall victim to the attack. Connection to the Führer has been thoroughly deepened, and faith reinforced in the leadership, who proved to be in command of the situation.

In fact, even a 'general rise in fighting spirit and the will to hold fast at all costs are evident'.

But once again the upturn did not last long. The report of August 10th, recorded:

The unfavourable news from all fronts and also in the political arena is greatly damaging the public mood. The will to resistance is very well present in most districts, but there is no small doubt about whether this can really help very much anymore.

Indeed, the Anglo-Americans had successfully broken through in France, bombardments increased, the Soviet troops marched nearly to the East Prussian frontier. 'The situation on the Eastern Front constitutes the main reason for the current powerful depression'.

One week later, on August 17th: 'In the midst of this depression, desire is growing for an end to the war soon, and with it the illusion "that the end won't be as terrible as everyone has always been told"'. Within the rural population opinions were 'now and then' encountered 'that there is no point anymore in sweating and straining, it is all for nothing anyway, and besides, not much can happen to farmers because everyone needs them'.

For the first time feelings that the war was lost became widespread, and thoughts turned to the time after the 'downfall'. There are barely any SD public opinion reports from the months that followed. The popular depression was irritating the leadership, so much so that Martin Bormann, head of the party chancery, prohibited reports altogether. But we can imagine the rest of the story: a last flaring of hopes during the Ardennes offensive in December and then, as it too failed, adjustment to the inevitable. We have a last report from March, 1945. It is thoroughly characteristic, systematically summarising the following 'fundamental facts':

1. No one wants to lose the war. Everyone had heartily desired that we would win it.
2. No one believes any more that we will win. The spark of hope preserved until now is being extinguished.
3. If we lose the war, the general feeling is that we are at fault, meaning not the common man, but the leadership.
4. The people no longer trust the leadership. They harshly criticise the Party, particular leading figures, and the propaganda.

5. For millions the Führer remains the last hold and hope, but the Führer is also day by day being mentioned more prominently in criticism and the issue of trust.
6. Doubts about the sense in continued fighting are undermining engagement and the faith of our people in themselves and in each other.

This report probably describes the mood in Germany in spring 1945 fairly well. Certainly there were some people, opponents of the Nazis, especially in the concentration camps, who desired the fastest possible defeat because it would bring their own liberation. Others so longed for an end to war that they were completely indifferent to who would win. But the majority still hoped 'that we will win it'. Perhaps that is all too understandable. After all, who desires the defeat of their own country?

The overwhelming difference in the way Germans think today is thus all the more remarkable. Nowadays the vast majority feel that May 8th, as the president said ten years ago, was a 'day of liberation'. For those who know history, such a change in opinion is not particularly unusual. The assessment of a situation by contemporaries ('the perception', as historians call it) often does not reflect reality. People experience the present, and it is quite real to them, but they fail to see through it because they lack information. Only much later do they recognise that their original judgements, and thus also their feelings at the time, were false. The German transformation is primarily due to greater knowledge. It must unfortunately be admitted that National Socialism, and above all Hitler, had enjoyed broad popularity. Certainly almost no one had wanted a war. In 1939, the last war was barely twenty years past. All adults still had their own memories of it, and anyone with a modicum of political understanding knew that Germany could not win a war against the Western Allies, who had all the resources of the world at their disposal.

Nonetheless, almost no one knew at the time that Hitler had started the war consciously and recklessly. To Germans in 1939, it seemed as though a conflict with Poland had arisen, in which the Western powers intervened with their entry into the war. Nazi propaganda was constantly trying to persuade Germans that war had been forced upon them. In every war, solidarity with one's own government and army arises. Even in 1941, when Hitler fell upon the Soviet Union with truly no justification this time, many believed his fabricated claim that he was only pre-empting a threat. They did not know that Hitler himself did not believe what he was saying, that he in no way felt threatened and instead wanted to conquer the so-called 'Lebensraum'; and, at least to begin with, they did not know what terrible crimes he would commit in the process.

With time they began to suspect. When German troops discovered mass graves of Polish officers in Katyn near Smolensk in 1943 and German propaganda loudly denounced this crime of Stalin, SD public opinion dispatches reported 'a large part of the population' found this 'curious' or 'hypocritical' and explained, 'we have no right to get excited about such Soviet measures because Poles and Jews were eliminated in much greater numbers on the German side'.

Also characteristic is a joke that was making the rounds in 1945: If only we hadn't started this war that was forced upon us! More than a few thus seem to have had an inkling that not everything had been right and proper. But only a very few were prepared to draw the conclusion that the country had to be liberated from its criminal government. Most importantly, the people were not ready to see Hitler as the main perpetrator. While the Party's image got increasingly worse, Hitler remained exempted from all criticism. Many even deluded themselves that he was not informed of the true situation. 'If only the Führer knew this' was another widespread saying.

Only after the war did it become obvious that the Führer had indeed known everything, that he had consciously and intentionally led the country into a hopeless war and in the process ordered crimes on a scale that had never been seen before. Even then it still took a long time before this certainty settled into the minds of the majority. Older people especially did not want to part with their earlier beliefs and feelings, and many people lacking insight actively encouraged them. Perhaps even that is all too understandable. After undergoing great suffering, and certainly many Germans also suffered during the war, it is not easy to recognise and admit it was all for nothing, that all sacrifice had been for an evil cause.

It is, after all, difficult to deliver a negative verdict on an entire epoch of one's own history. In 1945, everyone was certainly forced to recognise it had ended badly. But had everything therefore been bad from the very beginning? Even long after the war, opinion polls revealed that many still believed National Socialism had been a good idea, and only badly executed. And among those prepared to admit German crimes, excuses were still sought in whatever crimes were said to have been committed on the other side.

A lively confrontation with the past began, and it became ever stronger, so that some finally claimed it was enough, a line had to be drawn somewhere. But this proved impossible. Ever more facts came to light, and the most indisputable evidence was in the writings of the perpetrators themselves. Nonetheless some people are still incapable of learning, and deny crimes against humanity and especially the worst crime of all, the murder of the European Jews in the Second World War, or try to find other justifications for the Nazi regime. But while many thought this way in 1945, there are only a few left today. This is a remarkable transformation, and it resulted in the conviction that the downfall was in truth a liberation.

*   *   *

Eberhard Jäckel (b. 1929) is Professor Emeritus of Modern and Contemporary History at the University of Stuttgart. His academic career has taken him all over the world, to the universities of Florida, Paris, Oxford, Tel Aviv and the Punjab University in Chandigarh, India. An expert on Germany and the Holocaust, Jäckel's books include *Hitler's World View* (1981) and *Das deutsche Jahrhundert* (1996). He has been an advisor to several television films on the subject of the Holocaust, and is a member of the advisory committee of *Damals*, the German history magazine.

54

India's Divided Loyalties

PETER HEEHS

(July 1995)

Subhas Chandra Bose, the Indian leader who sided with Japan in World War II, is widely regarded as a traitor. Peter Heehs argued that, for all his faults, Bose thought of himself as a patriot to whom the war offered an opportunity to bring closer the dream of Indian independence.

The fall of Singapore was one of the greatest disasters ever suffered by the British armed forces. Left unprotected by the destruction of the American fleet in Pearl Harbor and the sinking of the warships *Prince of Wales* and *Repulse*, the garrison waited helplessly as the Japanese army swept down the Malay peninsula. The siege began on February 8th, 1942, and was over a week later. 85,000 men, what was left of the British, British-Indian, and Australian forces, surrendered to the invader.

Not all the defeated soldiers had to spend the next three years in Japanese prison camps. Of the 60,000 Indians who surrendered, 25,000 chose to go over to the enemy. They became the core of the Indian National Army (INA), which two years later took part in the Japanese invasion of India. In that campaign INA soldiers faced their own countrymen, members of General William Slim's mostly Indian 14th Army, which crushed them and the Japanese army they served, greatly hastening the end of the war. In May 1945 Rangoon was retaken by an Indian division; the same month the ragtag remains of the INA laid down their arms.

Soldiers are sworn to serve their country in peace and war. But to what country did the Indians who surrendered in Singapore owe their loyalty? To Imperial Britain, or to an India that was engaged in a struggle for independence? After the war, arrested members of the Indian National Army were classed as 'white', 'black', or 'grey' according to the perceived innocence or culpability of their motives. Most were considered grey.

However much wartime publicists, and even some historians, view complex issues in monochromatic terms, little in warfare is really black-and-white.

Indian soldiers had helped Britain conquer India and Indian soldiers helped them retain it. During the First World War nearly a million Indian troops fought for the Empire in Europe and Mesopotamia. Up to this time all higher officers of the Indian army were British; after the war belated efforts were made to 'Indianise' the officer corps. This was in line with Britain's recently announced aim of progressively conceding self-government to India – a grudging response to a nationalist movement that, under the leadership of Mahatma Gandhi, was beginning to mobilise the masses.

During the 1930s the Indian war budget was reduced and the army's strength fell to less than 200,000 men. Few thought that a European conflict might have repercussions in India. When Britain declared war on Germany in September 1939, the viceroy announced that India also was at war. Provincial governments resigned in protest, but thousands of young Indians flocked to the recruiting stations. Most were turned away. Military experts did not feel that India and Burma, which until 1937 formed part of the Indian empire, were in danger. As late as August 1941 the Chiefs of Staff Committee considered 'the invasion of Burmese territory' a 'distant threat'. When the viceroy asked whether the Japanese, who had occupied French bases in Indochina, might attack Burma through neutral Thailand, he was told that with the American fleet in Pearl Harbor, they would never try it.

On December 11th, 1941, three days after the start of the Malayan campaign, the Japanese 15th Army moved across Thailand into Burma. Advancing against ineffective opposition, they reached Rangoon by March. Once Burma's capital and main port had fallen, the loss of the rest of the country was a foregone conclusion. Sweeping north, practically annihilating the Chinese forces defending Toungoo, the imperial army reached Lashio, the southern terminus of the Burma Road. Achieving their main objective in Burma by closing the only supply route to Chungking, the Japanese pursued the Chinese across the border into Yunnan, and forced Indian and British troops to withdraw, demoralised and in disarray, into Assam in north-east India. In just five months a relatively small Japanese army had conquered most of South-East Asia.

After the start of the monsoon the Japanese established a firm defensive line along the Chindwin River, not far from the Indian border. Apart from a few air raids on Calcutta and other ports, they made no move against India. But the north-eastern part of the country was vulnerable to attack, and the British soon turned this region, and much of the rest of India as well, into a huge military camp. More than 200 airfields were built, some of which became points of origin for supply flights to China across 'the hump' of the Himalayas. Voluntary enlistment to the Indian Army was stepped up, and by the end of the war it numbered 2 million combatant and a half-million non-combatant troops – the largest volunteer army in the history of the world.

The loss of Malaya and Burma was due largely to British unpreparedness; the Japanese owed much of their success to detailed planning. Part of their strategy was to mobilise anti-British elements in Malaya, Burma and India. Since before the First World War, Indian nationalists had tried to enlist the aid of foreign powers in their struggle. Much hope was placed in Japan, which after its defeat of Russia in 1905 had appeared to many to be the torchbearer of renascent Asia. A number of activists had taken refuge in various countries of Asia, Europe and North America, establishing organisations such as the Indian Independence League (IIL), with branches in Tokyo, Bangkok and other capitals.

In October 1941 Imperial General Headquarters sent Major Fujiwara Iwaichi to Bangkok to make contact with Indians, Malays and Chinese who might help in the Japanese invasion of Malaya. Fujiwara got in touch with members of the Bangkok IIL, signing an agreement of mutual assistance with one of them, a Sikh named Pritam Singh. During the invasion Fujiwara and Pritam Singh approached captured Indians and offered them freedom if they went over to the Japanese side. Their biggest catch was Mohan Singh, a colonel in the 1/14 Punjab Regiment. Resentful of discrimination in the Indian army, and influenced by nationalist ideas, Singh agreed to work with Fujiwara to win over Indian prisoners of war. Two days after the fall of Singapore, the two men addressed a huge assembly of Indians in a city park. Fujiwara told them: 'The independence of India is essential for the independence of Asia and the peace of the world. . . . Japan is willing to give all-out aid and assistance to Indians in East Asia to achieve their aspirations.'

Singh announced that he was forming, with Japanese help, the *Azad Hind Fauj* or Indian National Army, and asked for volunteers. The initial reaction to his proposal was mixed, but before long thousands of Indian soldiers and civilians had agreed to join the INA.

Why did more than a third of the captured Indian troops agree to go over to the enemy? Indian soldiers traditionally were loyal even in the face of racial discrimination (which, however, many found increasingly upsetting), and relatively untouched by the national movement. Philip Mason, wartime secretary to the Indian war department, placed the 25,000 defectors in four classes 'in proportions about which one can hardly be precise'. He felt that only a small number were ardent nationalists; another small number were 'frankly opportunist'; a few honestly planned to escape and return to their own lines; but the majority 'were puzzled, misinformed, misled, and on the whole believed that the course they took was the most honourable open to them'. Mason spoke of one battalion that was approached by a former officer: 'He told them that the war was over and that they had the choice between digging latrines for the Japanese and once more becoming soldiers – but this time in the service of an independent India. They chose to be soldiers.'

Despite the effectiveness of such blandishments, most of the captured soldiers stood firm, and paid the price. Some officers who refused to co-operate with the Japanese were tortured or otherwise mistreated, for example by being confined in underground cages or latrines. About one-fifth of the 35,000 Indian troops who remained loyal did not survive to the end of the war.

During 1942 the Indian National Army and the Indian Independence League had a brief flowering. Meetings of the IIL were held in Tokyo in March and Bangkok in June. These were presided over by Rashbehari Bose, a Bengali revolutionary who had fled to Japan after masterminding a bomb-attack on the viceroy Lord Hardinge in 1915. Bose was able to remain in the country with help from friends in the Black Dragon Society, a group opposing the British presence in India as part of its pan-Asiatic ideology. The events of 1941–42 gave the almost forgotten Bose and the IIL an importance they had never before enjoyed.

At Bangkok the IIL resolved to take steps to bring about 'the complete independence of India free from any foreign control'; but before much could be done Mohan Singh began to quarrel both with Rashbehari Bose and with the Japanese. The Punjabi soldier grew suspicious about Japan's intentions in India, and came to think that Bose was a puppet of Tokyo. He wanted the INA to be a fighting force and was dismayed when he learned that the Japanese planned to use it only for preserving law and order in occupied territories. In December Singh decided to disband the INA. Later the same month he was placed under arrest.

If the Japanese were to profit from the INA and the League, they needed someone other than Mohan Singh or the ageing Rashbehari Bose to lead them. For more than a year they had had their eye on a man who was ideally suited for the job, and who wanted to have it as much as they wanted to give it to him. But this man, Subhas Chandra Bose (no relation to Rashbehari), was in Germany.

During the 1930s Subhas Bose had been one of the most important leaders of the Indian National Congress, his influence exceeded only by Gandhi's and perhaps Nehru's. Elected president of the party in 1938, he

had challenged Gandhi's candidate the next year and won an unprecedented second term. The members of the Congress Working Committee
refused to co-operate with him, however, and he was forced to resign. As
leader of the left-wing Forward Bloc, Bose took a strong anti-government
stance, and in July 1940 he was jailed. Escaping from house-arrest in
January 1941, he journeyed to Berlin by way of Kabul and Moscow.

Between 1933 and 1936 Bose had lived in Europe, spending much of
his time in Italy and Germany. These countries, along with Spain and
Russia, provided him with models for the sort of government he wanted
for India: not 'democracy in the mid-Victorian sense of the term', but
'government by a strong party bound together by military discipline'.
When he returned to Berlin in 1941 he found such a system in full flower,
and did not altogether like what he saw. Nevertheless he met Nazi
leaders, including eventually Hitler, and asked for German support. He
obtained little but vague promises. A trip to Rome brought similar
results. Like the Germans, the Italians did not know what to make of
Bose. 'The value of this upstart is not clear,' wrote Foreign Minister
Count Ciano after a brief meeting.

Bose was thrilled by the Japanese victories in South-East Asia, and
realised at once that he could do more to further his aims there than in
Europe. The Japanese made no secret of the fact that they would be glad
to have him. After consulting with Rashbehari Bose, who said he would
step down in Subhas Bose's favour, they arranged with the Berlin government to have Bose transferred to the East. On February 8th, 1943, he left
Kiel on board a German U-boat. Three months later he was transferred
to a Japanese submarine, which took him to an island off Sumatra. From
here he flew to Tokyo, arriving on May 16th. A month later he was
received by the Japanese Premier Tojo Hidecki. The two men hit it off at
once. On June 16th, Bose was invited to attend a session of the Diet,
where Tojo announced: 'We firmly resolve that Japan will do everything
possible to help Indian independence'.

Tojo had made similar statements even before the fall of Singapore.
Early in 1942 he had invited India to 'rid herself of the ruthless
despotism of Britain and participate in the construction of the Greater
East Asia Co-prosperity Sphere'. Calling on the Indian people not to miss
this opportunity for political and economic rebirth, he assured them that
Japan entertained 'not the slightest thought of antagonising them'. Later,
at a public meeting with Bose in attendance, Tojo reaffirmed that Japan
had no territorial, military or economic ambitions in India.

Bose could not but be happy that Tojo had given him immediately what
Hitler had always refused to consider: a clear statement of support and
promise of non-interference. In his speeches he gratefully acknowledged

Japan's assistance, but was independent enough to stress that he had accepted it to fulfil his own aims. Addressing his former friends in America, he said: 'Japan is offering us help and we have reason to trust her sincerity. That is why we have plunged into the struggle alongside of her. It is not Japan that we are helping by waging war on you and our mortal enemy – England. We are helping ourselves – we are helping Asia.'

It is hard to say how uncritically Bose took Tojo's assurances that Japan had no military ambitions in India. He was not unaware that the puppet governments of Manchukuo and other places occupied by Japan did little to check Japanese oppression of local populations. But he was confident in his own strength. He insisted that the Japanese recognise him as the leader of the Provisional Government of Free India and grant him the rights and privileges of a head of state. The Japanese seemed to respect him for this.

In July Bose arrived in Singapore, where he was given an enthusiastic welcome by the Indian community. He told them that he was: '. . . going to organise a fighting force which will be powerful enough to attack the British Army in India. When we do so a revolution will break out not only among the civil population at home, but also among the Indian Army which is now standing under the British flag.'

The Indian National Army was reborn. Over the next year, while three divisions were organised and trained, Bose travelled throughout South-East Asia, delivering speeches and meeting heads of state on equal terms. Aides let it be known that he wanted to be called 'Netaji' (Respected Leader). When someone pointed out the resemblance between this title and that of Germany's dictator, his secretary answered: 'The role of India's Führer is just what Subhas Chandra Bose will fill'.

Many British and American histories of the war do not mention the INA, or else relegate it to a footnote. This is not surprising. Bose's dream that the men of the Indian Army would join the INA as soon as his men shouted some slogans was never fulfilled. INA propaganda did contribute to the surrender of three or four small bodies of Indian soldiers, and in one case this gave the Japanese momentary advantage in battle. But as a rule the Indian Army treated the INA with special contempt. Many Indian and Gurkha soldiers were unwilling to let the turncoats surrender, and Slim was forced to issue orders 'to give them a kinder welcome'.

During the monsoon of 1944 the Japanese and INA regrouped while the Allies prepared for an all-out offensive the following year. In December the Indian Army swept through the Arakan, and began moving eastwards from the Chindwin towards the Irrawaddy. During February 1945 the mile-wide river was crossed in several places. At Pagan the initial attempt failed due to enemy fire. Then soldiers of the 7th Division saw a boat flying a white flag moving towards them. It carried two INA men, who said that the Japanese had withdrawn, and that they wanted to surrender. The 7th soon was safely across the river. This incident may be taken as representative of the contributions of the Indian army and the INA in the Burma campaign. Indian divisions of the 14th Army were always in the forefront, helping to take Mandalay, to reopen the Burma Road, to push south towards Rangoon. INA soldiers surrendered and deserted in droves, to such a degree that Bose issued orders that any INA officer or soldier who suspected another of treason could arrest and if necessary shoot him.

Bose had little knowledge of what was going on at the front line until late in the campaign, when he moved to a forward position. He wished to die fighting; but as Indian and British forces approached, his men pleaded with him to withdraw. He agreed, and during his retreat showed the finer side of his character, refusing to cross rivers until INA men and women had gone before him. But now the end was near. On May 1st Indian paratroopers were dropped near the port of Rangoon. The next day the 26th Indian Division captured the city. Mopping up operations continued through the next few months, but the surrender of Shah Nawaz Khan's second division on May 13th marked the end of the military career of the Indian National Army.

Ironically, the INA's real contribution to the Indian freedom movement had just begun. As the British-Indian Army liberated South-East Asia, it gathered up 25,000 INA personnel, all of whom were sent to India for trial. Technically each captured soldier could have been shot for mutiny and desertion, but capital punishment on such a scale was unthinkable. The government decided to divide the men into three groups. Some 4,000 whose plea that they intended to escape from the Japanese seemed plausible, were considered 'white' and restored to their former privileges. The 14,000 'greys' were adjudged to have been misled, and were released. But 6,000, the ringleaders and those who had committed atrocities, were considered 'black' and held for trial. Three officers whose crimes seemed clear were selected as the first to appear before the courts martial.

The trial was held in the Red Fort in Old Delhi, the very place Bose had said would be the site of the INA's victory parade. Many in India were sympathetic to the 'freedom fighters' and both Congress and the Muslim League chose to come out in their favour. The case was not as open-and-shut as the prosecution had hoped, and as the trial progressed there were demonstrations, often violent, in many parts of the country. The three defendants were found guilty and cashiered but not otherwise punished.

Defending this leniency, India's commander-in-chief, General Claude Auchinleck, wrote: 'It is quite wrong to adopt the attitude that because these men had taken service in a British-controlled Indian army that, therefore, their loyalties must be the same as British soldiers.'

Public demonstrations in favour of the INA continued. Discontent spread even to the ratings of the Royal Indian Navy, who mutinied in February 1946. The INA, ineffective on the battlefield, had become what Bose always had wished, an inspiring force in India's struggle for freedom. As it became clear that India soon would be granted independence, the government decided not to hold further trials.

Independent India gives little thought to the men of the wartime Indian Army, who fought against Italians, Germans and Japanese in Africa, Europe and Asia, and without whom, as Auchinleck said, 'the war could not have been won'. On the other hand India remembers the soldiers of the Indian National Army as heroes and martyrs in the independence movement, and has transformed the life of Subhas Chandra Bose into legend. Killed in a plane crash on August 17th, 1945, Bose was believed by millions to be alive well into the 1970s. For a time sightings of him were almost as common as sightings of Elvis are today. In schoolbooks and magazine articles his many faults are glossed over and his military genius celebrated – this in spite of the fact that even a friend like Fujiwara had to admit that 'the standard of his operational tactics was, it must be said with regret, low'. His political acumen is more difficult to evaluate. He managed to gain the respect of many highly placed men in Tokyo, but was never taken seriously by the Japanese field commanders he had to work with. According to M. Koirang Singh, later Chief Minister of the Indian state of Manipur, the Japanese army did not plan to honour Tojo's promise that Bose would assume administrative control over parts of India occupied after the fall of Imphal and 'certainly intended to control India as effectively as they controlled Burma'. Bose knew from first-hand observation in Rangoon what this would be like. He told sceptics that the British had never been able to take advantage of him and the Japanese would not succeed if they tried. With his great confidence in himself and in the Indian people, he seems to have felt that he could handle the Japanese once he was in his own country as its designated leader. This may not have been a realistic attitude, but it could hardly be called cowardly.

Western writers are inclined to dismiss Bose as a Fascist collaborator. He certainly consorted with dangerous Fascists and made statements that today read very badly, for example that the *Azad Hind Dal* (Free India Party) would 'be organised on the lines of the SS Party in Germany, or the Communist Party in Russia'. But Bose was not the only Oxbridge-educated intellectual to be swayed by Fascism or Communism during the 1930s (though his dream of a 'synthesis of National Socialism and Communism' may have been unique). His arrogance, intolerance of opposition, and love of militarism seem part and parcel of the Fascist mind-set, but his dynamism, inspiring leadership, and patriotism have also to be taken into account. It is probably best to agree with those who hold that 'Netaji' was basically a nationalist, even if misled.

*   *   *

Peter Heehs is a member of the Sri Aurobindo Ashram. Since the early 1970s he has worked as an editor at the Ashram's Archives and Research library and has prepared editions of many of Sri Aurobindo's works, including the first transcriptions of his yogic journal, *Record of Yoga*. He has undertaken biographical and historical research on three continents and has contributed papers to a number of academic journals. He is the editor of *The Essential Writings of Sri Aurobindo* (1998) and author of *Night and Dawn* (1974), *Image of Adoration: Section of a Cycle* (1977), *India's Freedom Struggle, 1857–1947: A Short History* (1988), *Sri Aurobindo, a Brief Biography* (1989) and *The Bomb in Bengal: The Rise of Revolutionary Terrorism in India* (1993).

55

Could the Jacobites Have Won?

JEREMY BLACK

(July 1995)

The 1990s saw a spate of counter-factual 'what if?' history. 250 years after the outbreak of the Jacobite revolt, Jeremy Black wondered how close Bonnie Prince Charlie came to restoring the Stuart monarchy.

On July 23rd, 1745, Charles Edward Stuart, Bonnie Prince Charlie, and the 'Seven Men of Moidart' reached Eriksay in the Western Isles of Scotland. On the afternoon of December 4th, 1745, en route for l.ondon, the now victorious prince entered Derby at the head of an army. Two days later, this force began its retreat to Scotland and on April 16th, 1746, it was crushed by the Duke of Cumberland on Culloden Moor. It was unclear to contemporaries whether the prince could have taken London had he pressed on from Derby or indeed had he followed a different strategy in 1715. This can be regarded as one of the great might-have-beens of history.

A Jacobite Britain would probably have been a very different state internally. In addition, restored with French support, the Stuarts would have been unlikely to challenge the Bourbons for global maritime hegemony, and the history of both North America and India would have been very different.

It is easy to suggest that the '45 was doomed. It failed after all, and the basic precondition of Jacobite plans over the previous fourteen years – the landing of a supporting French army in southern England – was not achieved. The British navy did not lose its superiority in home waters. Within England few rose for the prince and his Scottish supporters were demoralised as a result. At the Jacobite Council meeting at Exeter House, Derby, on 'Black Friday', December 5th, 1745, Lord George Murray pressed, in the absence of English and French support, for retreat. Under pressure, the prince was forced to admit that he had no promises of support from the English Jacobites and no idea of when the French would invade. The situation seemed even worse when the council was told by Dudley Bradstreet, an English spy, that a larger army of 9,000 blocked the route to London at Northampton, a deliberately misleading report. The decision was taken to retreat.

Leaving aside government disinformation, the factors mentioned at Derby were pertinent. The lack of English support ensured that the Jacobite army had received few reinforcements in its march south. The French had not landed and thus divided the government forces. Aside from these points, the eventual failure of the Highland charge at Culloden in the face of the disciplined firepower of Cumberland's army suggested that Jacobite tactics were anachronistic.

Against this must be set Jacobite success prior to Derby and the strategic situation at that juncture. A Highland charge at Prestonpans on September 21st had crushed Sir John Cope's force, the sole royal army in Scotland. Cope's army had not simply been defeated; it had been shattered and the government had to move troops back from the war with France in the Low Countries to confront the Jacobites. An army under Field Marshal Wade assembled at Newcastle, but on November 5th, the Jacobites, about 5,500 strong, crossed the Esk into England. By striking to the west of the Pennines they gained the initiative. Carlisle castle, with its weak defences and small garrison, surrendered on November 15th, and the Jacobites pressed south. Wade's attempt to relieve the castle had been thwarted by the weather and his own sloth.

After Carlisle the Jacobites encountered no resistance on the march south. Penrith fell on November 18th, to be followed by Kendal, Lancaster, Preston and Manchester. The fragility of the Hanoverian state was brutally exposed. The speed of the Jacobite advance thwarted governmental plans to have their troops in southern Lancashire first, while the local resistance was derisory. The Lancashire militia was disbanded and the magistrates at Lancaster wisely abandoned their plan to defend the castle. The Earl of Cholmondeley, Lord Lieutenant of Cheshire and Governor of Chester Castle, felt that it would be impracticable to raise the county militia and was pessimistic about his chances of holding the castle. Until the Jacobites turned back, the situation was comparable to the Bosworth campaign of 1485 with most of the political nation inactive; whatever their intentions, they were in effect sitting on the sidelines and awaiting the outcome of a trial by battle between the two claimants. The stability of the political culture established by the first two Georges and by Walpole had collapsed with the first serious challenge.

The defence of the Hanoverian regime had to rely on regulars, but Wade moved south through Yorkshire only slowly: he did not leave

Newcastle until November 26th, and had only reached Wetherby by December 6th. The crucial force was therefore Cumberland's army, which marched from Lichfield on November 28th. Cumberland was, however, misled by deliberately circulated reports that the Jacobites intended to advance on Chester and North Wales, and responded to the feint by a Jacobite detachment to Congleton, leaving the road to Derby clear.

Thus the campaign hitherto had revealed that the Jacobites could expect little resistance except from regulars and that these could be outmanoeuvred. The sole battle, Prestonpans, had suggested that the firepower of the regulars was of little value unless the Jacobites fought on their terms, as they were to do at Culloden.

When the Jacobites entered Derby they held the strategic initiative. Cumberland's army was exhausted by its marches in the West Midlands. The 2nd Duke of Richmond, commander of the cavalry, claimed 'these dreadful fatiguing marches will make them [the troops] incapable of fighting'. On December 4th, Cumberland wrote to explain his failure to try to intercept the Jacobites at Derby after he had discovered their feint: 'troops that had scarcely halted six hours these seven days, had been without victuals for twenty-four hours, and had been exposed to one of the coldest nights I have ever felt without any shelter . . . were not able to march without a halt and provisions, so we immediately came to a resolution of intercepting them at Northampton'. It is by no means clear that he could have done so and he might have exposed his army, strung out on the march, to attack. The duke was more realistic when he assured Wade that he would be able to get to Finchley 'with the cavalry'. On Finchley Common the government was trying to assemble a new army to protect London. This force of about 4,000 men was, however, far smaller than Cumberland's army, which contained most of the good units. The Black Watch, one of the units ordered to Finchley, was of questionable reliability. Signs of pro-Hanoverian enthusiasm in London were of limited military value. The London weavers offered 1,000 men but the experience of the campaign hitherto did not encourage the use of poorly-trained volunteers.

London itself would have been a formidable task for the Jacobite army. On November 28th, Lieutenant-General Sir John Ligonier emphasised the problems that the Jacobites would have encountered had they attacked Chester: 'Is it possible for them to fly over the walls? . . . Three pounders neither can make a breach in a thousand years, or make a garrison uneasy behind their walls, who on the contrary can slaughter everything that approaches from behind their sand bags'.

Lacking heavy artillery, the Jacobites might have made as little impact on the Tower of London as they did on Edinburgh Castle. Yet the fall of the towns of Carlisle and Edinburgh was scarcely an encouraging omen for the defenders of London. Furthermore, the War of the Austrian Succession on the Continent revealed the possibility of a successful storming of even a well-fortified and defended position, as with the Franco-Bavarian-Saxon capture of Prague in 1741 and the French capture of Bergen-op-Zoom in 1747.

What if London had fallen? During the War of the Spanish Succession Philip V lost Madrid to the British-supported claimant 'Charles III', but he was able to fight on, supported by the troops and the proximity of his grandfather, Louis XIV. Frederick the Great lost Berlin temporarily during the Seven Years' War, but fought on successfully. Would Britain have been different? Some of George II's supporters would have probably fought on, especially in Ireland where there were both troops and concern about the maintenance of the Protestant ascendancy. It is unclear whether George II would have been prepared to lead his troops into battle as he had done only recently on the Continent in the Dettingen campaign of 1743, nor whether he and the rest of the Royal Family would have bolted back to Hanover if the Jacobites had seriously menaced London. Certainly George II lacked popularity in 1745, not least because of the strident criticisms made in 1744 that he was devoting British resources to Hanoverian ends.

It is difficult to envisage Cumberland accepting Jacobite success without a battle. However, without London, the logistical and financial infrastructure of the military establishment would have collapsed. Pay and supplies would have become a serious problem for Cumberland, probably encouraging desertion among his soldiers and helping to dictate his strategy. It could be argued that there would have been a measure of activity from the English Jacobites once London had fallen. Possibly some of the Tories would have revealed their hands as Jacobite activists, thus repeating the pattern of Whig activity in 1688 once William of Orange's invasion appeared successful. Even without that, a weakened regular army might not have been able to obtain victory had there been a battle. The Jacobite success at the battle of Falkirk on January 17th, 1746, revealed the vulnerability of Hanoverian cavalry to Highland infantry.

The fall of London would also probably have affected the British fleet, disrupting its supplies and influencing the determination of some officers. This might have lessened the chances of a successful resistance to a French invasion. On October 3rd, the French council decided to send 6,000 men to invade England as soon as seemed propitious. On November 5th, the naval minister, Maurepas, ordered his protégé, the Jacobite shipowner, Antoine Walsh, to assemble the ships for the crossing. On December 2nd, the Irish Brigade began to move towards Dunkirk, and the embarkation of cannon and supplies there began on December 12th. Admiral Vernon, the commander of the British fleet in the Downs, considered his force small and outnumbered, and feared that the French invasion would be covered by a squadron from Brest, the scheme the French had attempted in 1744. *That* year the French had planned to send the Brest fleet to cruise off the Isle of Wight in order to prevent the British from leaving Spithead or, if they did, to engage them in the western Channel. Five of the Brest ships were to sail to Dunkirk to escort the invasion force under Maurice of Saxe to the mouth of the Thames. The plan was, however, thwarted by delay and storms.

That did not mean that French naval power was not a threat. On December 16th, 1745, the ever-complaining Vernon wrote from the Downs: '. . . with a southerly wind it was very practicable for them to get by unobserved by our ships to the westward, and, if the others were ready to sail with them when they had slipped by, and they too strong for me, they might execute their descent before their lordships [of the Admiralty] could have time to provide a preventive remedy against it . . . My particular province . . . is to watch the coasts of Kent and Sussex, and therefore, if with a southerly wind we should put to sea, without certain advice of the enemy being at sea, and which way they were gone, if it comes to overblow for one night southerly we must be driven to the northward by it, and of course, leave the coasts of Sussex and Kent exposed to the enemy's attempts, which their constant spies the smugglers would not fail to give them advice of'.

Unlike the next invasion attempt, in 1759, which was to be smashed by Hawke's victory at Quiberon Bay, there was no close blockade of Brest, while Forbin's success in taking an invasion squadron from Dunkirk to the Firth of Forth in 1708 indicated the problems of blockading that port successfully.

On December 17th, 1745, the Marshal-Duke of Richelieu, the commander of the invasion force, reached Dunkirk and considered an embarkation that day: the winds were favourable but he decided that not enough cannon had yet arrived. The British government was very concerned about the danger of an invasion. Had Richelieu's force embarked on the 17th they could probably have reached England. Amphibious operations in this period were far from easy, but, like William III's successful landing in Torbay in 1688, this would have been an unopposed landing. Richelieu was to be successful with his next amphibious operation, the invasion of British-ruled Minorca in 1756.

Had the French landed in 1745–46 they would have been able to defeat whatever irregular forces the local authorities had raised and they would have outnumbered the regular troops in and around London. The speed of the French advance would have been affected by their ability to obtain horses, on their choice of route, on the weather and on whether they decided to march straight on London or to seize local ports in order to open communications with France. In 1745 they planned to transport horses, once Dover or Dungeness had been seized.

The threat to the Hanoverian regime was therefore serious. Separately, both a Jacobite advance from Derby and a French invasion in the south were serious challenges. In combination they could each contribute to the threat posed by the other. Jacobite forces in the London area could have handicapped any attempt to mount coherent opposition to a French advance. The French could offer the Jacobites what they lacked: siege artillery, regular infantry able to stand up to British regulars in a firefight, and a secure logistical base.

Speculation on this theme can be, and has been, dismissed as pointless hypotheses or the revisionist obscurantism and nostalgia that interest in Jacobitism has been held to display; but such arguments are of value only if the options facing individuals in the past are ignored and it is assumed not only that the path of history is pre-ordained and obvious but that the past belongs to the victors.

A Jacobite or Franco-Jacobite victory would have been a major triumph for one important tendency of the early 1740s: the attempt to reverse the European order that had stemmed from the developments of the 1680s. That decade had led to a shift in relative power away from France and towards Austria and Britain. In Eastern Europe the period from the 1680s until 1721 had seen the defeat of Sweden and the Turks and a collapse in Polish strength, cause and consequence of the rise of Austrian and Russian power.

The success of the 'Glorious Revolution' in Britain was thus an important aspect of a new European order that had been contested unsuccessfully by Louis XIV, his allies, including the Jacobites, and a number of other powers. The 1740s saw a renewed struggle. War broke out between Sweden and Russia in 1741, France and her German allies sought to overthrow Habsburg power from 1741, and from 1744 France provided support for the Jacobites. To contemporaries, it was far from clear who would triumph, and the eventual limited territorial and political outcome of the War of Austrian Succession seemed far from likely earlier in the struggle.

A full range of hypothetical phrases is called for when discussing what would have happened in Britain. It is unclear how far the restored Stuarts would have respected the position of the Church of England and the constitutional changes since 1688. Their impact on the situation in Scotland and Ireland is open to discussion. The degree of their unpopularity is unclear. Jacobitism represented an attempt to challenge developed and strengthening patterns of control: of Ireland by England, of Scotland by England, of northern Scotland by the Presbyterians of the Central Lowlands, of northern England by the south; and indeed of the whole of Britain by its most populous, wealthy and 'advanced' region: south-east England.

Jacobitism thus represented an attempt to reverse the spatial process of state formation that had characterised recent (as well as earlier) British history. Proximity to centres of power, such as London, the Ile de France, and the Scottish Central Lowlands, brought a greater awareness of the political reality of 'England', 'France' and 'Scotland' than life in many regions that were far from being economically and politically marginal. Such proximity was crucial to processes of state formation and resource mobilisation.

At one level Jacobitism sought to resist this process in Britain. It was the expression of the desire for Highland and Irish autonomy. Culloden ensured that the new British state created by the parliamentary union of 1707 would continue to be one whose political tone and agenda were set in London and southern England. This was the basis of British consciousness, a development that did not so much alter the views of the English political élite, for whom Britain was essentially an extension of England, but, rather, that reflected the determination of the Scottish and Irish Protestant élites to link their fate with that of the British state.

William III's defeat of Jacobitism in Ireland in 1690–91 ensured that the Catholic challenge to this process was defeated in Ireland, and this result was sustained by Culloden. In strategic and geopolitical terms this was of tremendous importance: an autonomous or independent Ireland would probably have looked to the major maritime Catholic powers, France and Spain, rather than Austria, and this challenge to English power within the British Isles would have made it difficult to devote sufficient resources to the maritime and colonial struggle with the Bourbons.

Jacobitism was also, particularly in England and at the court of the exiled Stuarts, an attempt not to dismember Britain or to alter the spatial relations within the British Isles, but rather to restore the male line of the Stuarts. The degree of their unpopularity is unclear. Most of the evidence commonly cited for anti-Stuart feeling in 1745 relates to the period after the retreat from Derby and offers little guide to the likely response to a successful invasion. In England neither side appears to have enjoyed the enthusiastic support of the bulk of the population; and certainly not to the extent of action. Possibly we need to rethink views of political culture in this period to take note of this quiescence, and to appreciate that the political structure of Britain was based on the successful use of force.

*   *   *

Jeremy Black is Professor of History at Exeter, specialising in the history of war and the early modern world. After graduating with a starred first from Cambridge, he undertook research at Oxford before joining the staff at Durham University, where he eventually became Professor of History. Editor of *Archives* and a Council member of the Royal Historical Association, the British Records Association and the Army Records Society, Jeremy Black has lectured widely around the world, and has held visiting chairs in the USA. He has written over thirty books including *War for America* (1991), *Maps and Politics* (1996), *A History of the British Isles* (1996), *Maps and History* (1997), *War and the World 1450–2000* (1998) and *Why Wars Happen* (1998).

56

Late Medieval Crusading

NIGEL SAUL

(June 1997)

Why did the Crusades come to an end? Nigel Saul shows that the really surprising thing was that crusading lasted as long as it did.

In 1395 the crusading propagandist Philippe de Mézières sent an eloquent plea for an Anglo-French crusade to Richard II of England. 'Remember', he wrote:

> ... that the Holy Catholic Faith for which so many of your ancestors, the blessed kings of England, suffered martyrdom, today in Jerusalem and Syria, Egypt and Turkey, and throughout the East, is trodden under foot, dishonoured, deserted and abandoned ... and the divine sacrifice and Office forgotten and held in abomination. . . God grant that you two kings (Richard and Charles VI of France) may do all that remains to be done, to the consolation of all good people.

De Mézières wanted the two kings to bury their differences and set out on crusade for the East together. He said that he had the perfect military instrument to offer them:

> This simple medicine . . . is none other than the blessed new Order of Passion of Jesus Christ, conceived forty years ago under God's inspiration, and now to be submitted to the devotion of your Majesties.

De Mézières, an ex-chancellor of King Peter of Cyprus now living in retirement in Paris, had made the launching of a new crusade the driving ambition of his life. From the mid-1360s he had penned one passionate plea after another for action against the Infidel; and around 1368 he had launched his own crusading Order. By the early 1390s the political circumstances of Europe seemed to favour the realisation of his ambition. Hostilities between England and France had been ended by a truce, and Richard and Charles seemed disposed to join forces. By May 1395, Charles' kinsmen, the dukes of Orleans and Burgundy, were seeking financial support and negotiating for allies. Difficulties had been caused a year earlier by the outbreak of a rebellion against John of Gaunt's rule in Aquitaine which largely put paid to English participation. Nonetheless, in April 1396 a force of 10,000 or more, under Philip of Burgundy's son John, set out. Its main aim was to strike deep into Turkish territory in the Balkans.

Successful assaults were made on the Turkish fortresses of Vidin and Rhova, and in September the key Danubian fortress of Nicopolis was invested. But by now a relieving force under the Sultan Bayezid was on its way. South of Nicopolis, on September 25th, the decisive engagement between the two sides was fought. Details of the fighting are obscure, but it seems that the French and Burgundian knights recklessly charged forward, much as their forbears had at Crecy. The predictable massacre followed, and the Western army was destroyed.

The disaster at Nicopolis brought to an end nearly a generation of intense crusading activity. The immediate spur to it had been the rapid Infidel advance into Europe. By 1348, the Ottoman Turks had established a bridgehead into Europe at Gallipoli, and by the 1350s they were pouring into the Balkans. Edirne fell to them in 1361, Plovdiv in 1363, and in 1371 a victory at Maritsa gave them control of most of Macedonia. By 1389, when they extinguished the Serbian kingdom at Kossovo, the whole of Central and Eastern Europe lay open to their advance. The response on the Christian side was a series of initiatives by the papacy and 'front-line' leaders. In 1344 Pope Clement VI organised an anti-Turkish coalition in the East which succeeded in taking the port of Smyrna. In 1361 the swashbuckling Peter of Cyprus captured Antalya and four years later briefly took possession of Alexandria. Later in the 1360s, Count Amadeus of Savoy led an expedition which succeeded in recovering some Black Sea cities for the Byzantines.

Underlying this often frenetic activity against the Turks lay a much deeper enthusiasm for the crusade. In the minds of many late-medieval faithful there remained a powerful commitment to the Holy Land. This manifested itself in a variety of ways. Prayers were often said by guildsmen in England for the Holy Land. In a fraternity at Wiggenhall, Norfolk, meetings began with prayers 'for the Holy Land and the Holy Cross . . . that God might bring it out of heathen power and into the rule of Holy

Church'. In many upper-class households relics of crusading were still cherished: in 1376, for example, Mary, Countess of Pembroke possessed a 'cross with a foot of gold' which her long-deceased father-in-law had brought back from the Holy Land. At the same time, pilgrimages to Jerusalem were still very popular. Among Englishmen who visited the Holy City were Henry Bolingbroke (the future Henry IV), Thomas, Lord Clifford and the Earl of Warwick. Among less exalted pilgrims was the Gloucestershire knight Sir John de la Rivière who in 1346 combined a pilgrimage with spying on the Turks.

If crusading drew on a deep well of popular enthusiasm, it nevertheless appealed in particular to the military élite. Participation in crusading brought a nobleman renown; in Maurice Keen's words, 'it carried a special, sovereign honour'. There was often a link between crusading and the secular Orders of chivalry which flourished in the later Middle Ages. For example, Peter of Cyprus' Order of the Sword had its origins in the king's crusading plans, and it lived on after his death as an association of nobles visiting Cyprus who committed themselves to fighting the Turk. Equally, the regulations for Louis of Taranto's Company of the Knot (1352) and Charles of Durazzo's Order of the Ship (1381) both contained rules obliging members to take part in a crusade to recover Jerusalem, to which Louis and Charles both had claims.

However, it was less in the military Orders than in the careers of individual knights that the aspirations of the age found most obvious fulfilment. Dozens, even hundreds, of knights from England, France and elsewhere can be shown to have gone East. A neat illustration is provided by the inscription on the brass of Sir Hugh Johnys (*c.* 1500) at Swansea, which records that Hugh not only fought for five years in the wars against the Turks but had actually been knighted at the Holy Sepulchre at Jerusalem. Hugh's experience was not particularly unusual. Sir Richard Waldegrave, who was to be Speaker of the Commons in 1381, had fought against the Infidel in Prussia, had assisted in the taking of Antalya and had been present at the storming of Alexandria. A contemporary, Nicholas Sabraham, on his own admission 'had been armed in Prussia, Hungary, at Constantinople, at the Bras de St Jorge, and at Messembrid'. Quite possibly, someone like Waldegrave or Sabraham provided the model for the crusading Knight of Chaucer's *Canterbury Tales*. A century later a Buckinghamshire knight, Sir John Cheyne, was noted on his brass as having combated the Turks, slain a giant and visited the Holy Sepulchre.

Although the widespread crusading activity of the late Middle Ages is well documented, historians have often underestimated its appeal because there were no general *passagia* (crusades) in the period. Grand set-piece passagia to the East largely died out in the thirteenth century. The crusades of the late Middle Ages were smaller and more limited in objective; however, they were staged more frequently, and in more varied locations. In the 1340s, for example, there was a flurry of crusading activity in Spain following a major Muslim advance from North Africa; in 1342 knights from Germany, England and France were present when Alfonso of Castile took Algeciras. Again in the fourteenth century there was regular campaigning in the Baltic against the heathen Lithuanians. John 'the Blind', King of Bohemia, Henry Duke of Lancaster, and the future Henry IV again, were among the Western notables who joined the Teutonic Knights in their raids into the (until 1385) heathen wastelands further east.

However, late medieval crusades were not only preached against the Infidel. To the disapproval of critics like Bartholomew of Neocastro, they were also preached against fellow Christians. Crusading against Christians was not new; indeed, it was inherent in the very definition of crusading. A crusade, according to the most widely accepted definition, was a holy war preached against Christendom's enemies by the pope, in which the participants gained the benefits of an indulgence. As repeated challenges to the Church's authority had made clear, Christendom's enemies could be internal, as well as external. In the thirteenth century crusades were preached against popular heterodox groups, such as the Cathars in southern France, and political enemies of the papacy, like the Emperor Frederick II, while in the mid-fourteenth century the weapon had been used against the *routier* companies threatening Avignon.

In the years of the Great Schism from 1378 to 1417, however, crusading against fellow Christians became more controversial. This was partly because some blatantly political crusades were preached – the most notorious being the bishop of Norwich's crusade against the pro-French cities in Flanders. But it was also because heterodox groups were becoming more common. In England, for example, the Lollards, the followers of John Wyclif, became an active force from the 1380s and, in the following century, the Hussites took over the state of Bohemia. Both Lollards and Hussites were highly critical of crusading. Hus denounced it as testimony to the Church's internal corruption.

It has sometimes been argued that political manipulation of crusading by the papacy contributed to its decline in the fifteenth century and later, but it is doubtful if this was the case. A number of fourteenth-century knights can be shown to have enlisted in crusades against Christians as well as more orthodox crusades. John Holland, Earl of Huntingdon, Richard II's half-brother, for example, fought in John of Gaunt's 'crusade' in Spain from 1386 and negotiated with Boniface IX for an anti-Avignon crusade in 1397. The signs are that service in a crusade against fellow Christians was assimilated into the general chivalric culture of the age.

So why, in that case, did crusading eventually wither and decay? Part of the reason is that, with the passage of time, the goal of recovering Jerusalem receded further and further towards the horizon. After the extinction of the Crusader Kingdom in 1291, in the wake of the fall of Acre, taking Jerusalem was no longer a practical military proposition. As a result, something of the drive, something of the enthusiasm and passion which had driven twelfth century crusading ebbed away. It is true that there were plenty of other crusading destinations. An obvious one was Egypt: as St Louis had recognised, if Egypt fell, Palestine would probably fall later; and in the fourteenth century, as we have seen, there were many other eastern Mediterranean destinations. But the very vitality, the rich pluralism, of crusading was a source of weakness. For the more diverse it became, the more incoherent it became too – and ultimately the less successful. The key element of direction was lacking.

However, there was another, and perhaps a more important, reason for the decline of crusading. Gradually, crusading was rendered impractical by adverse developments in Europe's political, military and financial structures. Although crusading as an ideal survived, at least up to a point, the institution itself perished. A number of factors can be identified as contributing to this. Growing distrust of papal leadership was one. In the fourteenth century, when it was based at Avignon, the papacy was widely perceived, particularly in England, as being sympathetic to the French. Secondly, the levying of public taxation to pay for a crusade became more difficult once such taxation came to be sanctioned, as it generally was in England and France by the fourteenth century, only for national defence. Finally, the long and bitter wars of the later Middle Ages, most notably the Hundred Years' War between England and France, made collaboration between rulers ever more difficult. It is no coincidence that the last general passagia took place in a period of relative peace – the thirteenth century.

Yet the remarkable feature of crusading in the late Middle Ages is not so much that eventually it declined, as that it flourished for so long. Even in the fifteenth century, when the tradition of passagia to the East had virtually ceased, crusading remained part of the body of ideals which the chivalric élites, and even hard-headed kings and princes, took for granted. The court which appears to have been most strongly influenced by crusading ideas was the Burgundian. The Valois dukes had, of course, long been associated with crusading. Philip the Bold, the first duke of his line, had taken the Cross in 1363 and had regularly subsidised crusading in Prussia. John of Nevers, Philip's son, had been the commander of the force that had been defeated at Nicopolis. But John's son, Philip the Good, was the dynasty's greatest enthusiast. At a celebrated feast – the Feast of the Pheasant – at Lille in February 1454 Duke Philip had a live pheasant brought into the hall and swore on it that he would undertake a crusade provided that at least one other ruler also took the field. At a later stage the duke went further, swearing to take on the Grand Sultan in single combat. Perhaps surprisingly, a practical proposal emerged from this prodigious showmanship: in 1456 a report was drawn up showing how an actual crusade could be organised. Old age, however, prevented the duke from putting any of its recommendations into practice.

A ruler like Philip the Good realised that involvement in crusading could bring a dynasty fame and prestige. More than that: he probably realised that it could bring these benefits regardless of outcome. It is a curious paradox that in 1396, when John of Nevers returned from Nicopolis, he was fêted as a hero even though he had been defeated and had suffered imprisonment. Failure did not matter. John had won renown for himself, and his experiences in the East were instrumental in winning legitimacy for his dynasty.

Yet, for all the importance of *la gloire*, there was a less wordly aspect to the appeal of crusading. Late medieval princes were deeply conscious of their status as *personae mixtae*: in other words, the fact that they were both priest and layman. To realise the spiritual aspect of their *persona* they increasingly manifested an interest in matters of piety and public religion. For example, they encouraged the moral reformation of their households; they made lavish religious benefactions and mass-endowments. And, more relevant here, they maintained a personal commitment to the crusade. A clear illustration of this is provided by the policy of England's Henry VII. Henry demonstrated his crusading interest from almost the beginning of his reign. In late 1485 he ordered prayers to be said throughout England for the success of Ferdinand and Isabella's offensive against the Moors of Granada. Later he promised the Spaniards an English contingent, and by May 1486 a force under the command of Sir Edward Woodville, the queen's uncle, was distinguishing itself in the capture of Loja in Granada.

In the final years of his reign Henry developed an interest in the crusade to the East. In 1502 he sent the Emperor Maximilian £10,000 to help fight the Turks, and two years later he handed to the pope at least £4,000 from the 1502 crusade tax. In the light of all this, it is hardly surprising to find that Henry was regarded as something of a crusade enthusiast: in 1506 he was made 'protector of the Order of St John of Jerusalem at Rhodes', a hitherto unique privilege; while in 1508 Wolsey reported that the imperial negotiators had called Henry 'the most suitable instrument of Christ to defeat the enemies of the Christian religion'.

The point that emerges from all this is that crusading became associated in kingly minds with Christian renewal. The connection had been manifested in English kingship as early as Henry V's reign. Henry, a royal *dévot*, had sponsored a policy of religious renewal at home, repressing heresy and encouraging deeper spirituality; and at the same time, according to Monstrelet, he had died proclaiming his intention to rebuild the walls of Jerusalem. In Henry's mind, there was a connection between Christian renewal and crusading; both, in their different ways, bore witness to the ideal of a united Christendom and the ruler's responsibility to promote that ideal.

The appreciation that rulers had of the Christian responsibilities of their office was a factor in the long afterlife of crusading. Along with such other factors as the continued Muslim advance into Europe, it helped to ensure that princes like Charles V and Philip II were active in fighting the Infidel well into the sixteenth century. However – and here was the difficulty – the connection between crusading and public religion was simultaneously a factor in the decline of the movement. Crusading, to its disadvantage, became associated with a particular form of religion – Catholic religion: a connection reinforced by the pope's responsibility for authorising it. Once, as in Northern Europe, religion and spirituality began to run in different channels, crusading lost its appeal; indeed, from this time in the North it was condemned as an evil. English involvement in promoting crusade ended in the reign of Henry VIII. English experience of being a target of crusade began in his daughter's.

*   *   *

Nigel Saul was educated at Hertford College, Oxford, and was appointed a lecturer at Royal Holloway College, University of London in 1978. He became Professor of Medieval History in 1997. His first book, published in 1981, was a pioneering study of the English medieval gentry. More recently he has published a major biography, *Richard II* (1997), and a general study, *The Oxford Illustrated History of Medieval England* (1997). Saul's interests also extend to medieval church monuments and brasses, and his next book will be a study of a magnate family, the Cobhams, and their magnificent tombs at Cobham (Kent) and Lingfield (Surrey). He is a member of the *History Today* academic advisory board.

57

Chinese Immigrants to Australia

JANIS WILTON

(November 1997)

Immigration restriction – effectively a 'White Australia' policy – was enacted at the outset of federation in 1901 and was to last until the 1960s. But Australia already contained some non-white immigrant communities. Janis Wilton used the techniques of oral history to piece together testimony to provide this portrait of one of them.

Australia's past and present is dotted and, at times, swamped by the expression of racist sentiments and by an ethnocentric fear of cultural difference. In the mid-1990s it surfaced in the bigoted and ignorant statements of a small number of right-wing politicians whose foremost spokesperson was Pauline Hanson, who in early 1996 became the newly elected federal parliament member for the seat of Oxley. (She was dubbed 'the Oxley moron' by one local newspaper.) Their words plug in to a long tradition of racism in this country, one which the media delights in focusing on. It is also a tradition which historians over the past two to three decades have spent time and intellectual effort to dissect, analyse and explain.

More recently, there have been attempts to move beyond racism to examine the histories and contributions of Australia's indigenous people and ethnic communities. This has entailed moving away from traditional documentary sources, government archives and newspapers to work from within indigenous and ethnic communities, with their participation, using recorded memories, family photographs and memorabilia, personal and business papers. In the light of this work, different perspectives and emphases are emerging that proclaim positive aspects of cultural diversity.

The history of the Chinese contribution to Australia provides a case study. First lured to the country to work as shepherds, cooks and farm labourers in the early part of the nineteenth century, the number of Chinese expanded rapidly with the discovery of gold from the 1850s. Their presence and success frightened other Australians. They were vilified for their work practices, living conditions, leisure pursuits and their potential for destroying the 'purity' of white Australia. As one parochial newspaper editorial declared in 1857:

> Without dwelling upon the injuries the Chinese do to a gold field – the peculiar vices they introduce to the country – the dreaded, withering leprosy that in instances has accompanied their path – I would protest against the introduction of them from their being a race having low mental and bodily powers and half-savage habits, utterly unfit for assimilating with a nation of such a boasted degree of civilisation as our own. And I would ask, will the idolmongers promote our Christianity? Will the almond-eyed yellow-skins improve our race? Will the habits and viciousness of the Celestial empire advance Australia? Not very likely . . .

Such racist attitudes were sufficiently powerful to provide the basis for a bevy of later nineteenth-century colonial legislation directed at controlling the flow of Chinese into the country. This legislation found its ultimate expression in what became colloquially known as the 'White Australia Policy'. Its cornerstone was the Immigration Restriction Act which was passed in 1901 as one of the first enactments of the newly-federated nation. The intention of the Act was to limit, as much as possible, the immigration and settlement of non-Europeans in Australia. The device used was the arbitrary imposition on intending immigrants of a dictation test in any European language.

The result of the legislation combined with the drying up of gold and tin deposits and with the intention of many Chinese immigrants that they should ultimately return home, witnessed a dramatic fall in their number in Australia. Despite the pressures, some Chinese continued to settle, bringing with them customs and networks which shaped their lifestyles and their ability to negotiate the hostile legislation and attitudes which frequently confronted them. They also put down roots, had families and made significant contributions to the economic development of Australian localities and regions.

The recounted experiences of a small group of Chinese-Australians who, from around the end of the nineteenth century, settled in a particular area in northern New South Wales, confirm the vital role of an oral and local history approach in evaluating the Chinese contribution, beyond that afforded by conventional sources.

The area of interest is a part of the northern tablelands of New South Wales and, in terms of the history of the Chinese in Australia, is defined by the discovery of gold in the 1850s and especially the discovery of tin in the 1870s and 1880s. These events saw an explosion in the number of Chinese in the district. According to the 1891 census, for example, the area contained one of the highest concentrations of Chinese (over 11 per cent of the recorded population in a particular district) in New South Wales at the time. Once the tin was mined, many of the Chinese moved to other areas or returned to China, and the 1901 Immigration Restriction Act discouraged new immigration and settlement. The number of Chinese born in the district dropped from the 1891 figure of around 1,300 to 593 in 1901, 169 in 1921 and forty-seven in 1947. This decrease, however, did not mean a cessation of new arrivals. Many Chinese living in the district regarded the opportunities sufficiently rewarding for them to sponsor relatives and fellow villagers to migrate to Australia. The methods and networks involved emerge through the stories passed on about the immigration of fathers and uncles.

One such story relates to the efforts and acumen of Percy Young, the founder of an Australian branch of the Kwan clan. Percy was born in about 1865 in the village of Wing Ho, Shekki, Chungshan. When he was about twenty years old he emigrated to Australia where, through Chinese (most likely Chungshan) networks, he spent the next ten years working in a number of different Chinese stores, largely in rural New South Wales. He also spent some time in China, although he saw his future in Australia as he sought naturalisation in 1883. In the late 1890s the network led him to a Chinese store, Kwong Sing War, which had been established in Glen Innes, northern New South Wales, in 1889. By 1907 he had become a partner in the business and by 1912 was a major shareholder and manager of the store. Percy's children were born in Australia and he sponsored his nephews, one by one, to come to Glen Innes to work in his shop. They then branched out and established their own stores, married and had families of their own.

This sponsorship, expansion and settlement all took place after the imposition of the Immigration Restriction Act of 1901. Percy Young, and other storekeepers in the northern tablelands, took advantage of exemption clauses in the Act to sponsor relatives, and to seek regularly and successfully to extend their stay in the country. The exemption clauses were a recognition by the legislators that, by the turn of the century, some Chinese had already settled in Australia, and that among those still in the country were a number who were providing a boost to the economy through owning and running profitable small businesses, especially shops. Store owners were permitted to bring in Chinese-born assistants and family members provided they stayed for limited periods, and that the businesses in which they were employed had a minimum turnover and were engaged in a certain amount of export trade with Hong Kong or China. As Daisy Yee, Percy Young's daughter, explained:

> Dad brought out all the nephews one after the other. He had to take out a bond of £100 for each member, and he had to import/export a certain amount of goods for each member. I can remember apples. He brought the nephews out gradually. They had to be at least sixteen to come out.

Elaine Jang whose parents, John and Mary Hong, owned the Hop Sing store in the town of Tenterfield, recalled the networks and strategies used to make the legislation work for the benefit of relatives and fellow villagers in Australia and China. It was a network which they utilised until 1950:

> I think . . . my father knew the people in Sydney who had business [in assisting with immigration papers] and he'd write to them to give them names of people who could want somebody from China as an assistant of a shop. That way the law said you can be brought out to help. . . . That's one of the ways he brought people out. There were other ways as well, but this was the main one.

The legislation requirement that a shop could only employ a certain number of Chinese-born assistants provided a stimulus for business expansion which went beyond concerns for profit. The more stores that were established, the more relatives could be sponsored to come to Australia. This was particularly apparent in the branches and businesses which stemmed from another of the Chinese stores on the northern tablelands. The Hong Yuen store in the town of Inverell had been established in 1899. By 1915 its manager and major shareholder was Harry Fay, an Australian-born Chinese who had spent a good part of his childhood and adolescence in his ancestral village of Dau Tau, Shekki, Chungshan. By the late 1930s, the Hong Yuen store had become the centre of a network of businesses which included three other small shops in Inverell itself, three Hong Yuen branch stores and two cash-and-carry shops in nearby towns.

These businesses, and the other twenty to thirty Chinese stores on the northern tablelands, were located in small communities. The largest town boasted a population of around 5,000. Consequently, the Chinese did stand out as different and were subjected to, at times, what could only be described as racist and discriminatory jibes and practices. Yet the businesses prospered. They provided a much-needed service offering the jumble of goods familiar to Australian country stores of the time, while, increasingly, assistants serving in the stores were local non-Chinese residents or Australian-born Chinese. Descriptions offered through oral history interviews evoke this past era of country stores. Beatrice Winmill who joined the staff of the Hong Yuen store in Inverell in about 1915 recalled the store's layout and the goods offered:

> The drapery section was a big long counter with everything on it, even shoes, all the men's mercery (trousers and cardigans), haberdashery, dress materials. At the bottom [end] of the counter there was a showroom with corsets and dresses. And we had lots of hats then. You don't have so many hats now. There were big shelves behind the counter for stockings and things like that. The cash box was in the middle of the shop. And the counter on the other side was for all the groceries and veggies and fruit. We also had a bit of furniture – you went through a door to the furniture. And an ironmongery.

Ken Gett provided the following recollection of the inside of his parents' store, Yow Sing and Company, which was opened in the old tin mining town of Emmaville in the early 1930s:

> As a child I remember going into the store. It had two big doors and when you entered the first thing that you saw was all the products hanging off the ceiling. You know those country stores. We had bicycles and tubs hanging off the ceiling. . . . We sold a tremendous range of things. We sold guns, we had things like horseshoes and horseshoe nails. We had drapery, a haberdashery section, grocery section. We had a produce section – chaff, bran, all those things – kitchen ware.

Bessie Chiu, whose father, Ernest Sue Fong, also had a store in Emmaville particularly remembered a different atmosphere and different tasks compared to stores of the late twentieth century:

> In the olden days you had a lot of people's loyalty, people would speak to you. We used to have a couple of chairs and they'd come and have a talk. Now there's nothing like that. In those days we used to weigh everything – sugar, dates, sultanas – everything was bulk.

What was clearly different were the activities and lifestyles of the Chinese storekeepers and their Chinese staff. Behind the scenes, store owners worked through their network of associates which stretched through Sydney and Hong Kong to home villages in Chungshan to negotiate the immigration of family members, and to further their business interests. It was here that the cultural and social needs of Chinese employees were looked after. It was here that the mainly young men brought out from China contemplated the strangeness of their new environment and sought to put down foundations for some sort of life.

Recollections of the routines involved in working in the stores provide a sense of the specifically Chinese community and traditions which under-pinned business and employment practices. Overseas and Australian-born, young Chinese men were provided with jobs, accommodation and food, and worked in an atmosphere permeated by paternalism and a Chinese work ethic. Ernest Sue Fong who joined the staff of the Hong Yuen store in Inverell in the early 1930s recalled his early years at the store:

> I worked at Hong Yuen for 25 bob [shillings] and keep. I lived in the shack with about seven other Chinese boys from all over. Another five lived upstairs [above the shop].
>
> Now the way it worked: at 7.30 in the morning the cook would ring the bell, and everyone would go down to the kitchen . . . and we'd have a Chinese breakfast with rice and Chinese food. Then into the shop until the shop opened and we'd cut up bacon, fill the shelves, jobs like that. At lunchtime, the bell would ring again and all the staff [Chinese and non-Chinese] would go for lunch. It would always be English meals. . . . Then back to work.
>
> At 6 pm supper was served. Chinese food this time. . . . Some nights, say two or three a week, we'd go back to the store to, for example, bag up sugar, depending on what was needed. We'd work until 9 pm.

In the Kwong Sing store in Glen Innes, manager and owner Percy Young framed and hung on the wall some Chinese proverbs (in Chinese characters) demonstrating the values he honoured which he, presumably, exhorted his Chinese employees to follow. They included, for example:

> When men are born they all want to be wealthy, but you have to learn to be satisfied with what you have in your daily life.
> If you are poor it is because you are lazy.
> Work hard at your business and never complain of hardships.

Harvey Young evoked what took place out of sight of the customers of the Kwong Sing store in Glen Innes in the late 1930s and early 1940s. Among the boiling water used for melting honey, the sheds, the stables, and the loading bays for chaff, wheat, super phosphate and rock salt, he could remember:

> . . . growing vegetables round the back of the shop. There was quite a bit of land there. Chooks and ducks. They used to kill those quite regularly.
> Then there were the cooks. They used to make noodles out the back of the shop. Fresh noodles. And the old method then was on a table with a bamboo pole which was tied at one side and a person with one leg over it jumping up and down on this thing to make fresh noodles.

Harvey Young's sisters, Valmai Au and Olma Gan, recalled the accommodation and facilities available for the Chinese cooks and other staff. They remembered specific employees and where they stayed:

> There was George Woo and Jimmy Sheah. . . . They were in the bedrooms upstairs, on the side facing Tattersalls Hotel. And I think the cook lived there too. Though not Kum Jew [one of the cooks] . . . he lived in a room close to the kitchen.
> There was another cottage, separate cottage, at the back of the shop which has now been pulled down. The kitchen was there. . . . And then there was the dining room where the staff used to eat . . .

Leona Tong, another sister, also remembered the Kwong Sing cooks whose presence figured in her childhood:

> I can remember three or four different cooks in my time. When I was little there was big fat Long Go. He was bald and big like a giant. He ate a great bowl of rice. Then there was George Lay. He had long finger nails. I can remember him stirring the rice at night with a big stick.

The presence of Chinese cooks, staff, food, language and other cultural practices were a constant reminder of the roots and links which extended well beyond the relatively isolated Australian rural towns they serviced. These links were reinforced by regular visits to China by family members. Visiting relatives, pursuing business interests, returning to share material goods and wealth acquired while overseas, honouring ancestors, revering the ancestral village, providing children with a Chinese education,

431

contemplating a permanent return to the home village: these were the motives behind such visits.

The experiences they entailed were not always the happy homecomings anticipated, however. After all, these Chinese had lived for some time in a foreign country and many of the children were born overseas. They had become strangers in their ancestral land. Recorded recollections capture a sense of this dislocation. Members of the Fay family from the Hong Yuen store in Inverell visited Hong Kong and China in the early 1930s. Joyce Sue Fong (nee Fay) recalled her visit to the family's ancestral village:

> Well [Dau Tau] was strange at first. All little Chinese children running around with no shoes on and just playclothes. And when we first went there, they all followed us and called us – you know, how we call people 'Ching Chong Chinaman' here.
>
> They called us the opposite when we went over there. Because we looked different. . . . We had English clothes on and they had Chinese clothes on, pants and that.

Joyce Sue Fong's sister, Eileen Cum, added:

> I can also remember the Chinese kids used to throw stones at us and call us 'white girl' – Ton Yang.

Not all differences and experiences were seen as negative or disconcerting. There are recollections of a comfortable life and a feeling of being 'at home' which strengthened bonds to China or which at least emphasised that some differences were due to a wealth and cosmopolitanism unfamiliar to the lifestyles available in northern New South Wales. Eileen Cum, for example, was stunned by the vibrant nature of 1930s Shanghai:

> It was like the Paris of the East. One part was American, one part was French. There were beautiful buildings and lovely things. Lots of American things. It was under the Nationalists then. There were also lots of friends who'd been in Australia and had gone back to China.

The pull of China remained. However, the Sino-Japanese War of the 1930s followed by the Second World War and then, in the late 1940s, the Communist revolution closed the door to China. Visits ceased. Emigration ceased. Chinese in Australia had little option but to view their new country as the site of their and their families' immediate futures.

The stores had provided a base. Then, as Australian-born children acquired Australian education, and careers, other occupations became possible. Many of the children and grandchildren moved to metropolitan centres like Sydney and Brisbane and away from the rural towns in northern New South Wales. Some pursued careers in business; others joined the ranks of the professions.

At the same time the climate of tolerance in Australia was slowly undergoing a change. By the late 1950s, it was becoming clear that the attitudes and practices associated with the White Australia policy were becoming untenable. Over the next three decades the official climate moved from racism through assimilation to multiculturalism. Chinese-Australians born before the Second World War lived through these changes. In the eras of officially-sanctioned racism and assimilation they had learnt to remain silent about their Chinese heritages. In the era of multiculturalism they were encouraged to claim or perhaps reclaim those heritages. As May Lun and her daughter-in-law, Rosalie Lun, observed:

May Lun: In the old days, when we were quite small, people hated you because you were Chinese. They were not only not friendly, they really had a hate for you. I used to be frightened to walk home by myself in case they bashed me up . . . for nothing at all. . . .

Rosalie Lun: Years ago it wasn't good to speak another language . . . outside. You just wouldn't. But nowadays, tradition, culture, it's changed and is becoming more broadminded, so you wish you had that second language.

It was partly this sense of a changing climate, a more tolerant Australia, which made it possible for historians and others to document and present histories of Australia's ethnic communities from the perspectives of the communities themselves. Multicultural Australia fostered a pride in cultural diversity and recognised the depth of the contributions which immigrant Australians from non-English-speaking backgrounds have made to the development, tone and texture of the country despite its racist policies and discriminatory practices.

The concern now is whether the tolerant Australia of the past three decades can stand its ground and fight off the attempts to reinvent the White Australia Policy with all its racist and discriminatory trappings. Will the second and third generation Chinese-Australians, whose Australian origins were anchored to a series of Chinese stores which served isolated rural towns in northern New South Wales, continue to feel free to explore and present the diversity of their heritages and experiences? Will the voices of intolerance pause long enough to accept that looking beyond racism means appreciating the varied contributions made by Australians from different cultural backgrounds? Will we as historians continue to upend approaches to the history of immigration by seeking perspectives which document the lives and contributions of ethnic communities rather than just focusing on official policies and attitudes, statistics and conventional documentation?

*   *   *

Janis Wilton has a PhD from the University of New England, Australia, where she lectures in Australian history. Her historical passion is for the discoveries that can be made through oral history, ethnic community history and museums. Wilton is Vice President of the International Oral History Association and a Trustee of the Historic Houses Trust of New South Wales. She is the co-author of *Old Worlds and New Australia: The Post-war Migrant Experience* (1984) and *'Outside the Gum Tree': The Visual Arts in Multicultural Australia* (1992).

58

Reading is Bad for your Health

ROY PORTER

(March 1998)

*Few historians have written (or read) as much as Roy Porter. Perhaps his witty and erudite Longman/*History Today *lecture, delivered to a hall full of professional colleagues, was a plea from the heart (or retina, or vertebrae or nether regions . . .).*

'A good book is the precious life blood of a master spirit', writes John Milton, proleptically puffing the Everyman series. Or listen to Doris Lessing on learning to read: 'The delicious excitement of it all. . . the discoveries. . . the surprises. . . I was intoxicated a good part of the time'. Or Sue Townsend: 'Reading became a secret obsession. . . I went nowhere without a book – the lavatory, a bus journey, walking to school'.

The propaganda is endless. Ignore it! *Caveat lector*, I say – and don't pretend you weren't warned, 'Much learning doth make thee mad', cautions the *Acts of the Apostles* a long time back, while the Greeks well knew the dangers. Plato's *Phaedrus*, you will recall, recounts an Egyptian myth concerning the invention of writing. Thoth offers the gift of writing to King Thamus, claiming it will 'make the people of Egypt wiser and improve their memories'. The real effect, counters Thamus, will be the opposite: writing 'will implant forgetfulness in their souls [and] they will cease to exercise memory because they rely on that which is written'. Knowledge may thus wax, but wisdom will wane. Writing, moreover, is a deceiver; as the reading habit grows, love of the real atrophies.

And since Antiquity there have been countless cautions against the pride of the pen. Foolish beyond belief 'are those who strive to win eternal fame by issuing books', declared Erasmus in the *Praise of Folly*:

. . . watch how pleased they are with themselves when they are praised by the ordinary reader, when someone points them out in a crowd with *'There is that remarkable man'*, when they are advertised in front of the booksellers' shops.

Such *exposés* accompanied post-Gutenberg misgivings about the perils of print. 'How poor is the proficiency that is merely bookish!', declared Montaigne. The Moderns in the *Battle of the Books* proclaimed truth was to be found in Nature, through observation and experiment. So poring over books was pointless.

In short, an honourable dissenting tradition has fired off books against books, and such fusillades have been echoed by others of different ideological stripes, fearful of books sapping virtue and piety – hence the setting up in 1559 of the Index Librorum Prohibitorum. The salutary idea that people are better off illiterate has had its political champions too. 'Reading, writing and arithmetic are. . . very pernicious to the poor', argued the Dutch-born satirist Bernard Mandeville, since they would get uppity. Indeed, positively criminal, according to the nineteenth-century French psychiatrist Lauvergue, who observed 'the most unreformable criminals are all educated'. His compatriot Hippolyte Taine similarly drew attention to the fact that the Anglo-Saxons were the sole people in Europe among whom criminality was declining. Why was that? It was because the British education system was so bad.

If book learning were dangerous in general, it was doubly so for the weaker vessel. The seventeenth-century poet, Alessandro Tassoni, cautioned:

> There is no doubt, but that study is an occasion of exciting lust, and of giving rise to many obscene actions. . . Hence, as I suppose it is, that we find, in Euripides and Juvenal; that the learned women of antiquity were accused of immodesty.

Of course, all such wholesome reasonings have now been hopelessly compromised by today's politically correct nostrums of human right, democracy and feminism. That is why it is so important for me to get across the true dangers: the *medical* ones. Reading is, quite literally, disastrous for your health. Now that T-bone steaks have been banned in Britain, I look to government action. So let me explain. Every occupation has its maladies: housewife's knee, athelete's foot. Authors too have their predilections. One of course is writer's block. Joseph Conrad despaired:

> I sit down religiously every morning, I sit down for eight hours every day. . . . In the course of that working day of eight hours I write three

sentences which I erase before leaving the table in despair. . . . It takes all my resolution and power of self-control to refrain from butting my head against the wall. I want to howl and foam at the mouth but I daren't do it for fear of waking the baby and alarming the wife.

The diametrically opposite disorder is writer's itch. 'Scribble, scribble, scribble, Mr Gibbon', George III (or, some say, his brother, the Duke of Gloucester) famously buttonholed the historian of the *Decline and Fall of the Roman Empire*. Linked to the *libido sciendi*, this *cacoethes scribendi* had already reached epidemic proportions by the Renaissance. Robert Burton confirms in his *Anatomy of Melancholy* (1621):

'Tis most true, *there is no end of writing of books*, as the Wise-man found of old, in this scribbling age especially, wherein *the number of books is without number*, (as a worthy man saith) *presses be oppressed.*

Overall, however, the perils of writing were judged but a fleabite compared with those of reading. Having had our nose in a book, as any Renaissance doctor would inform you, was bad for the humours. 'Students', thought Burton, are commonly troubled with

. . . gouts, catarrhs, rheums, wasting, indigestion, bad eyes, stone, and colick, crudites, oppilations, *vertigo*, winds, consumptions and all such diseases as come by overmuch sitting.

'The Scholar', he concluded, 'is not a happy man'.
Poring over books moreover ruined the posture. That risk was poetically expressed by William Wordsworth:

Up! Up! my friend, and quit your books!
Or surely you'll grow double.
Up! Up! my friend and close your books
Why all this toil and trouble?

To forestall such physical troubles, the nineteenth-century German doctor and pedagogue Moritz Schreber developed a variety of orthopaedic devices to force children to sit straight and keep their chins up. Take his 'straightener' (*Geradehalter*), a device that prevented its wearer from bending forward while writing, which he claimed had done the trick with his own offspring. Or the 'head-holder', meant to promote proper posture by pulling the wearer's hair as soon as the head began to droop.

The evils of enforced book-learning had long been stressed. Samuel Johnson's friend, Mrs Thrale, told the tale of a fourteen-year old who had been bashed over the head by his Master with a dictionary.

> . . . which so affected his health that his powers of Study were straingely impaired, his Memory lost, and a perpetual pain pressing the part. . . Physicians of course were called in, who blistered, bled and vomited him; but the Complaint continuing obstinate he was actually *Trepanned.*

Only the sublimely witless would escape unscathed. One such was Gargantua. In Book One of the *History of Gargantua and Pantagruel,* Rabelais related how

> . . . they appointed as Gargantua's tutor a great doctor and sophist named Thubal Holofernes, who taught him his letters so well that he said them by heart backwards; and he took five years and three months to do that. Then the sophist read to him Donatus, Facetus, Theodolus, and Alanus *in Parabolis,* which took thirteen years six months and a fortnight. . . [and so forth] by the reading of which he became as wise as any man baked in an oven.

But our Gargantua was proof against all these malign influences!

> He studied for a miserable half-hour, his eyes fixed on his book, but – as the comic poet says – his soul was in the kitchen.

Gargantua was fortunate, because *clever* pupils had their wits warped by the nonsense the pedants dinned into them, as his own son Pantagruel was to discover from his fellow students:

> 'So you come from Paris', said Pantagruel. 'And how do you spend your time, you gentlemen students at this same Paris'?
> 'We transfretate the Sequana at the dilucule and crepuscule; we deambulate through the compites and quadrives of the urb; we despumate the Latin verbocination and, as verisimile amorabunds, we captate the benevolence of the omnijugal, omniform, and omnigenous feminine sex. . .
> At which Pantagruel exclaimed: 'What devilish language is this? By God, you must be a heretic'.

That other Rabelaisian hero, Panurge, was to note a further hazard of reading hard matter: constipation.

I happened to read a chapter of the stuff once, at Poitiers, at the Scotch Decretalipotent doctor's, and devil take me if I wasn't constipated for more than four, indeed for five days afterwards. I only shat one little turd.

The rectum was thus at risk, but that was not the only vulnerable part of the anatomy. 'On Tuesday last', reported the *Glasgow Journal* on June 21st, 1742, 'as an Old Man was lying in the Green reading a Book, he was attack'd by the Town Bull, who tore two of his Ribs from the Back Bone, and broke his Back Bone. His Life is despair'd of'. The price of learning can be high indeed.

Above all, reading, as everyone knows, was murder on the eyes – Milton blamed it for his blindness, and Samuel Pepys too thought he was going the same way. '19 March 1668: So parted and I to bed, my eyes being very bad – and I know not how in the world to abstain from reading', he lamented to his soon-to-be-discontinued diary.

Alongside the physical damage, psychiatrists have long urged upon us the harm reading could also do to your mind. For one thing, it encouraged hypochondria. In his *Treatise of the Hypochondriack and Hysterick Diseases* (1730), the aforementioned Bernard Mandeville laid bare the psychopathology of print through a dialogue between a physician, Philopirio, and his patient, Misomedon.

Misomedon relates his sad history. A well-bred gentleman, he ruined his constitution by 'good living'. He then consulted a gaggle of learned physicians but none of their treatments worked. Convinced he was sinking from every sickness known to scholars, he developed 'a mind to study Physick' himself – but his studies merely made bad worse, until finally he persuaded himself that he had the pox – 'when I grew better, I found that all this had been occasion'd by reading the *Lues*, when I began to be ill; which has made me resolve since never to look in any Book of Physick again, but when my head is in very good order'.

If not hypochondria, too much reading would certainly induce exhaustion or what would today be called ME or Chronic Fatigue Syndrome – a condition versified by that eminent Victorian, Matthew Arnold:

> But so many books thou readest
> But so many schemes thou breedest
> But so many wishes feedst
> That thy poor head almost turns.

Reading addled the brain, a situation exacerbated as books multiplied. Anxious about that 'horrible mass of books which keeps on growing',

Leibniz called for a moratorium back in 1680. To no avail. According to the late eighteenth-century Bristol physician, Thomas Beddoes, his era was suffering from chronic information overload – all those pamphlets and periodicals, novels and newspapers befuddling the brain! *Did you see the papers today? Have you read the new play – the new poem – the new pamphlet – the last novel?'*, was all you heard: 'You cannot creditably frequent intelligent company, without being prepared to answer these questions, and the progeny that springs from them'. The consequences?

> You must needs hang your heavy head, and roll your bloodshot eyes over thousands of pages weekly. Of their contents at the week's end, you will know about as much as of a district through which you have been whirled night and day in the mail-coach.

The inevitable result was that you blew a fuse. 'He might be a very clever man by nature for aught I know', wrote Robert Hall of the compiler of encyclopaedias, Dr Andrew Kippis, 'but he laid so many books upon his head that his brains could not move'. Bookishness was recognised as addictive, psychopathological, as the Manchester physician John Ferriar versified in his *Bibliomania*:

> What wild desires, what restless torments seize
> The hapless man, who feels the book-disease.

'Beware of the *bibliomanie*', Lord Chesterfield counselled his son. He might also have had Walter Shandy in mind. But the classic fictional case-history of reading precipitating madness is, of course, *Don Quixote*. Cervantes explains how his hero got into tilting at windmills:

> The reader must know, then, that this gentleman, in the times when he had nothing to do – as was the case for most of the year – gave himself up to the reading of books of knight errantry; which he loved and enjoyed so much that he almost forgot his hunting, and even the care of his estate.

Thus Cervantes unfolds,

> . . . he so buried himself in his books that he spent the nights reading from twilight till daybreak and the days from dawn till dark; and so from little sleep and much reading, his brain dried up and he lost his wits.

Small wonder, then, that mad-houses had their bibliomaniacs, surrounded by books, reading obsessively. On visiting Bethlem in 1786, the German novelist Sophie von la Roche found an unnamed man, doubtless a historian, 'in the lowest cells, with books all around him'. She also met Margaret Nicholson, George III's would-be assassin, sitting reading Shakespeare.

Visiting Ticehurst asylum in Sussex in 1839, Mr and Mrs Epps came across a certain Joshua Mantell, seated in a large, comfortable room, by a good fire, encircled by books and papers. They had a long talk concerning a book Joshua said he was about to publish. Only later were the Eppses informed that he was suffering from delusions of authorship.

Such cases abound. At the Gloucester asylum, one Sarah Oakey, a Cheltenham laundress, was admitted in 1826 suffering from melancholia, 'supposed to be brought on by reading novels'. At the Nottingham asylum, John Daft – *nomen est omen* – 'was brought in by the Overseer . . . his father reports that he has been sober and industrious and ascribes his morbid mind to the reading of Carlisle's [*sic*] works'. Or take the Reverend William Thomson, admitted in 1817 to the Glasgow Royal. 'For ten months previous to his illness', states his record, 'he had been engaged in publishing a book'.

Sometimes it worked the other way round: the mad took to reading. In 1872, Dr William Chester Minor, a Connecticut surgeon, was sent to Broadmoor. While there he became a collaborator in compiling the *Oxford English Dictionary*. Permitted to turn his rooms into a library, with a writing desk and floor-to-ceiling teak bookshelves, he was even able to buy books from London antiquarian dealers, which were briefly brought to him by the woman whose husband he had murdered.

The pathology of print became all too familiar. Novel-reading among fashionable young ladies was said to lead to hysteria or the vapours. 'If women who spent their energies on their brains married', warned the Victorian psychiatrist Thomas Clouston, 'they seldom had more than one or two children', and 'only puny creatures at that, whom they cannot nurse, and who either die in youth or grow up to be feeble-minded folks'. 'Beware, oh beware!', mocked Frances Power Cobbe, the feminist, 'Science pronounces that the woman who – *studies* – is lost!'

All were agreed that, of all the harmful trash, 'NOVELS undoubtedly are the sort most injurious'. Romances, Beddoes noted, 'increase indolence, the imaginary world indisposing those who inhabit it in thought to go abroad into the real'. Above all, they provoked vicarious sexual arousal. Hence 'a variety of prevalent indispositions. . . may be caught from the furniture of a circulating library'.

So what was to be done? Beddoes was convinced that what was needed was good healthy activity – 'Botany and gardening abroad, and the use of a lathe, or the study of experimental chemistry at home'. Stressing how self-abuse 'often ends in a lunatic asylum', Lord Baden-Powell later advocated scouting for boys. But the favoured remedy for nervous prostration was the rest cure, pioneered by Dr Silas Weir Mitchell in the US. This involved total bed rest and a complete ban on all stimulus. His most famous patient was Charlotte Perkins Gilman, later author of *The Yellow Wallpaper*. In 1887, suffering from chronic acute depression, she had consulted Mitchell, who enforced the rest cure for a month and then discharged her, commanding her to lead a domestic life, to cut her reading to two hours a day, and to give up writing altogether. 'I went home', she related, 'and obeyed these directions for some three months, and came so near the borderline of utter mental ruin'.

The same treatment was also prescribed for the young Virginia Woolf by the psychiatrist Sir George Henry Savage. Forced to stay bookless in Cambridge with an aunt, she rebelled:

London means my own home, and books, and pictures, and music, from all of which I have been parted since February now – and I have never spent such a wretched eight months in my life. And yet that tyrannical, and as I think shortsighted Savage insists upon another two. . . . I long for a large room to myself, with books and nothing else, where I can shut myself up, and see no one, and read myself into peace. This would be possible at Gordon Sq: and nowhere else. I wonder why Savage doesn't see this.

The reason is plain. Savage judged reading one of the key causes of female derangement.

Books indeed can kill. The saddest story is related by Dr James Currie of Liverpool around 1800. It concerns a mental patient whose mind gave way after he indulged in visionary speculations on the perfectibility of man. To put him right, the kindly Currie explained Malthus' principle of population. His response, however, was to produce 'a scheme for enlarging the surface of the globe, and a project for an act of parliament for this purpose, in a letter addressed to Mr Pitt'. To show that even this fantastic measure could not provide a way out of the Malthusian trap, Currie actually handed the young man Malthus' Essay. This he read twice, aloud the second time, not omitting a single word, and then, after a few distressing days, he quietly lay down and died. 'At the moment that I write this', Currie concluded, 'his copy of Malthus is in my sight; and I cannot look at it but with extreme emotion'.

So Disraeli was right. In his early novel *Lothair*, one of his characters exclaims:

> Books are fatal; they are the curse of the human race. . . The greatest misfortune that ever befell man was the invention of printing.

Yet I must not end on a negative note. Occasionally at least the printed page has been positively therapeutic. Many suffering from the toothache, Rabelais recorded,

> . . . after expending all their substance on doctors without any result, have found no readier remedy than to put the said *Chronicles* between two fine linen sheets, well warmed, and apply them to the seat of the pain, dusting them first with a little dry-dung powder.

Sterne offers his variant in *Tristram Shandy*. When Phutatorius' *membrum virile* is frazzled by a roast chestnut which plops off his plate down into his breeches, cure is effected by application of a leaf from a new book, still damp and inky from the press. 'No furniture so charming as books', quipped Sydney Smith, while Grub Street writers reflected that sheets from unread books at least achieved some utility as pastry cases or paper bags.

That might, however, be sacrilege, if the work in question were theological. One of Rabelais' clerics observes that when a holy book was used as wrapping paper, 'I renounce the devil if everything that was wrapped up in them did not immediately become spoiled'. The most sacrilegious use of such spare sheets was as bum fodder – and naturally this had the direst repercussions:

> 'One day', said Friar John, 'when I was at Seuilly, I wiped my bum with a page of one of these wretched *Clementines* that John Guimard, our bursar, had thrown out into the cloister meadow, and may all the devils take me if I wasn't seized with such horrible cracks and piles that the poor door to my back passage was quite unhinged'.

The secular Lord Chesterfield, however, had no hesitations about treating literature as bumf. Urging time-discipline upon his recalcitrant son, he told a little tale:

> I knew a gentleman, who was so good a manager of his time, that he would not even lose that small portion of it, which the calls of nature obliged him to pass in the necessary-house; but gradually went

through all the Latin poets, in those moments. He bought, for example, a common edition of Horace, of which he tore off gradually a couple of pages, carried them with him to that necessary place, read them first and then sent them down as a sacrifice to Cloacina: this was so much time fairly gained; and I recommend you to follow his example. It is better than only doing what you cannot help doing at those moments, and it will make any book, which you shall read in that manner, very present in your mind.

Try that perhaps, but, above all, don't get hooked on books. Heed the immortal words of the superintendent in Joe Orton's *Loot*: 'Reading isn't an occupation we encourage among police officers. We try to keep the paper work down to a minimum'.

*   *   *

Roy Porter is Professor of the Social History of Medicine at the Wellcome Institute for the History of Medicine. His interests in eighteenth-century medicine and the history of psychiatry and of quackery are amply reflected in his 15 publications since 1977. These include *Mind Forg'd Manacles: Madness and Psychiatry in England from Restoration to Regency* (1987) and *'The Greatest Benefit to Mankind': A Medical History of Humanity* (1997). Porter's interests extend to other areas as well: *Edward Gibbon: Making History* (1988), *London: A Social History* (1994) and *Enlightenment: Britain and the Creation of the Modern World* (2000) take his bibliography beyond medical matters. His interests also lie beyond the subject of history: Porter is taking early retirement in 2001 to take up the saxophone.

59

Point of Departure: Roots and Rituals

RONALD HUTTON

(December 1998)

History Today*'s editor, Peter Furtado, invited selected historians to reveal what led them to become interested in the past. Here are the radically different points of departure recalled in successive issues of* History Today *by Ronald Hutton and Pamela Tudor-Craig.*

When I discovered the family photograph album, I must have been about five or six years old – in that intermediate period when individual memories are sharp and lasting, yet before a child has acquired any real sense of the sequence of events, so that one year melts into another.

The album was a large, imposing, leather-bound volume, somewhat tattered by time and travel; the faded and yellowing quality of many of the black and white prints lending it an additional air of age and authority. The real power of the contents, however, consisted of their subject matter. Most of the more recent photos portrayed scenes in the India of the British Raj, with a backdrop of forested mountains, towering temples, and the neat lawns and villas of colonial grandees. My mother appeared as a girl, playing with a pet leopard, as a young woman arrayed in ball gowns and jewels with patient turbaned servants in attendance, and as a new wife, watching an elephant going about his work of clearing timber on the estate. My father featured less frequently, but was none the less imposing, a lean young man in the kilted uniform of the Argyle and Sutherland Highlanders, and then fishing in Himalayan lakes, sailing upon the Arabian sea, and (repeatedly) dancing the night away in white tie, beneath the chandeliers of vice-regal society.

Tucked into another part of the volume were older photographs from my mother's side of the family, displaying proud and confident people in the dress uniforms and white lace gowns of Tsarist Russia.

What was so devastating in the impact of these pictures was their complete dissonance with the world in which my mother and I actually lived, centred upon a small and decaying council flat in a poverty-stricken estate recently built at the furthest extremity of the East London suburbs. My father had died of typhoid in India before I had any memory of him, and my mother had left the country soon after, unwilling to bring up a young child there by herself, in the potentially unstable political conditions following the end of British rule. She moved to an England she hardly knew, with her own health broken by tropical illnesses, to live off a small pension amid a totally alien society. She never did adapt, and isolation and depression compounded her physical frailty, hastening her, too, to an early grave – before I was old enough to earn the money which could have rescued her.

Without the photograph album I could barely have made sense of the situation in which I passed my childhood. My mother did not talk much about her former life, and although there were a few relics tucked into boxes – a leopardskin cape from India, a wolfskin one from Russia – they might just as well have been bought in an antique shop, had it not been for the pictures which revealed how they once had fitted. They made sense of my mother's inability to blend into the rather brutal and tribal working-class neighbourhood that surrounded us; outsiders, saddled with accents which attracted the derision of local children. The album showed me that we had a tribe, a lineage, of our own. We were not completely alone in time and space; our true place of belonging existed in another dimension – in the past.

As I grew old enough to explore the area round about, I became aware that there were physical remains within it which, like myself, were products of that other dimension. The old Essex forest on the outskirts covered prehistoric earth-works and encircled villages which still had medieval churches and Georgian mansions. There was even a Tudor hunting lodge. The forest glades were sometimes overgrown with exotic shrubs, gone wild from the grounds of long-vanished stately homes. Even the suburbs which ran up to its southern fringe had parks which had once been laid out by gentry and still incorporated their follies and statues, while solitary medieval and Early Modern buildings could be found hidden in the vast wasteland of brick beyond, flowing westwards towards London.

All these structures were now as much out of place as my mother and I, but just as the album had given me a context for us, so I found that reading into works of history provided these monuments with a setting, an explanation and a certain grandeur. In a sense we belonged together, to a past which I now discovered was filled with people and events a good deal more glamorous than any in my daily life, and which became in some ways more real to me.

In this fashion I became a historian before I left childhood. But all this does not explain why I became the sort I am; one with an abnormally wide range of interests spanning topics from the Old Stone Age to the present, but focused on the British Isles. Had I actually followed the path suggested by the album, I would have become an expert in nineteenth-century India or Russia. I did not, because I wanted to succeed where my mother had failed, and to adapt to the islands in which we had settled. By studying the whole palimpsest of cultures which had created their present societies, I could understand them better and find my own place within them. In mediating between past and present, I hoped I could find a place in the latter.

At the age of ten, therefore, I became interested in Britain's prehistoric monuments: both the loneliness of their settings, like the Iron Age forts in my woods, and the mystery surrounding their use, allowed me to make a more personal relationship with them than later structures. By twelve I persuaded my mother to join the local archaeological group with me, and she helped me between the ages of thirteen and fifteen as I wrote a guide to chambered tombs. At fourteen I discovered Sir James Frazer's classic work on ancient religion, *The Golden Bough*. This seemed to me to raise the veil over the religious practices of prehistory, and I formed the idea of writing an equivalent work for Britain, using every scrap of evidence to reconstruct the history of its ancient seasonal festivals. By sixteen I had collected a lot of material for this.

Then at thirteen I read a popular work on Prince Rupert from the public library. This led to a school project on the Civil War. I was enthralled by a period in which English society had for once become genuinely dysfunctional, and so many possible futures were glimpsed. My sympathies were royalist purely because of my instinctive distaste for Puritans, and by the time I was fifteen I had determined to write a book about the Cavaliers or, if I did not get to university, a series of novels about them along the lines of Dennis Wheatley's books set in the Napoleonic Wars.

The rest of my working life has followed neatly from that. Once I had worked my way through the state system to a first degree, I wrote my book on the Cavaliers as my doctoral thesis, then three more on the Stuart period. Then I felt driven to tackle all the unfinished business of my early teens. In 1991 I published a book on ancient religion in the British Isles which included my earlier work on prehistoric monuments. I was now free to write the work on seasonal festivals in Britain which I had drafted when I was fourteen. The result was a pair of books (1994 and 1996) which raised questions about the way in which the British view their past and enabled me to confront at last my own relationship with it.

I never did quite learn how to fit in to British society, but I have found instead that the British will honour oddity if they find it interesting enough. The photograph album is still in my possession; and now my five-year-old daughter pores over it. Dangerous books come in many different forms.

*   *   *

Ronald Hutton was born in India in 1953 and educated at Cambridge and Oxford Universities. He is now Professor of History at Bristol University. Hutton's bibliography reveals the diversity of his interests. Author of a number of books on the Stuart period, the most recent being *The British Republic, 1649–1660* (2000), he has also published works on the British ritual year, including *Stations of the Sun* (1996), and *The Triumph of the Moon* (1999), a history of the development of modern pagan witchcraft. Hutton is frequently asked to broadcast about aspects of British neo-paganism.

59a

Point of Departure: Blunt Speaking

PAMELA TUDOR-CRAIG

(January 1999)

In the second year of our degree course at the Courtauld Institute of Art in 1948, we were introduced to the heady experience of tutorials with the senior staff. A small group of us would assemble regularly at 20, Portman Square, in the palatial study of the Institute's new and relatively young Director, Professor Anthony Blunt. Van Gogh's self-portrait with the bandage over his freshly amputated ear hung just inside the door.

I was the only one in my year to have come to university straight from school. All the others had several years of wartime work behind them, constituting a lifetime of greater maturity. At our first session the Director asked each of us whether we had yet chosen our period for special study. First to be asked was a petite, dark haired lady with an air of enviable sophistication. She declared that she was thinking of becoming a medievalist.

'I cannot encourage that idea', Blunt replied. 'Hardly any serious work has been done on the Middle Ages, and there are no jobs'. At that time, posts in the British Museum, for instance, or in other senior museums, were given to those with degrees in the Classics. (Art History had no place in the school or art school curriculum and there were no departments devoted to the discipline at any of the English universities outside the Courtauld Institute itself.)

'But', he added vigorously shuffling a heap of photographs of Poussin's 'Inspiration of the Poet' on his desk, 'there is everything to be discovered in the seventeenth century. The richness of iconographic reference, the literary sources, the classicism. A whole field is opening up, work to do . . .'

My companion responded to Professor Blunt's advice with enthusiasm, agreeing to take up the seventeenth century as her chosen field. He then turned to me, and I diffidently confessed that I, too, had intended to study the Middle Ages, but after what he had said . . .

'But of course', he interrupted, making a note on his piece of paper, and moving swiftly on to the young man interested in the nineteenth century.

I looked at the lady wearing her new seventeenth-century mantle and she glanced at me. What was happening? We neither of us ever asked Anthony Blunt, but when, many many years later, his life was shattered I wrote and thanked him for the decision apparently of a split instant that had decided my professional career.

Those were the heroic days of the early *Warburg Journal*, of the close collaboration between the staff of the Warburg Institute, under the much loved and revered Fritz Saxl, and the young Courtauld Institute itself, earning its spurs as the exponent of a discipline of largely German origin. We were treated on a regular basis to lectures by the Warburg scholars, who had come over *en bloc* in flight from Nazi Germany. In almost impenetrable English, they introduced us to inaccessible mountain peaks of learning. We sat awestruck at the feet of men whose names, Panofsky, Wittkower, Buchthal, Gombrich, continue to resound wherever Art History is considered. I wish I could say that I learned a great deal of the subject from them, but I fear I was too ignorant to do so. What I did learn was to admire the humility of the truly great. These professors were prepared to write out their lectures in their own tongues, to translate them with the help of their wives, and then to read them or deliver them by heart. Of course this stage did not last beyond my time at college: total fluency in English was quickly mastered by such minds.

I only recall one more conversation of consequence on a medieval topic that I shared as a student with Anthony Blunt. He was showing me photographs of the interior of Hagia Sophia. 'I look forward to the day,' he said, 'when all cathedrals are museums'. 'And I shall be prepared to give whatever I may have,' I boldly replied, 'to prevent that from happening.' As I went on to serve for fifteen years on the Cathedrals Advisory Commission, nineteen on the Architectural Advisory Panel for Westminster Abbey, and spells of various lengths on the Fabric Committees of Wells, Exeter, Lincoln, Peterborough and Southwell cathedrals I suppose I have done my best to fulfil my part of that exchange.

But why was I one of the first in England to study Art History for my degree and perhaps the first to go to it straight from school? That takes us into the field of not only what, but who you know, and the value of parents. My father was one of the musicians to be encouraged by the legendary Samuel Courtauld, so he and my mother were among those who before the Second World War had dined in that wonderful Robert Adam house in Portman Square. They were aware of how it had come to be bequeathed as the first home in England devoted to Art History, together with the unrivalled Courtauld collection of largely French paintings. These were not hung in a separate gallery, but adorned the walls of the rooms, so that when we moved into the study of Professor Johannes Wilde, who guided us for a whole term through the first ten working years of Michelangelo, he did so with Cézanne's 'Card Players' puffing away beside him.

To reach eighteen in 1946 carried special problems. My generation came to higher education at the same moment as those in the Forces who had endured five or six years of deferred education. Their chance to now enter college was viewed as an honourable priority, theirs by well-earned right. In that bottle-neck year my mother sped to the Courtauld and laid my case before the Registrar, Charles Clare. My mother was very charming, and as luck should have it, he did have, or he could contrive to find, just one space for a school-leaver.

It only remains to consider why, on that fateful autumn day, I admitted to Anthony Blunt my preference for the Middle Ages, and why his quick agreement might have been based on more than intuition. My parents were not religious people in the formal sense, but they did realise during the war that their children might wake up to find themselves orphans. After all, our house in Kensington had been destroyed by a landmine only hours after they had changed their minds and gone to Dorking for the night instead of sleeping there. They felt that a religious framework might be a help to us in the event of bereavement. So we were sent to a French Convent School that was evacuated to Godalming. And what an education it was for a potential medievalist! The post-Tridentine, pre-Vatican 2 Mass is as familiar to me as the Magnificat. The Monastic Offices, that I have tried to explain to generations of students to whom they are as strange as the burial customs of penguins, lie along my pulse; all of it was not just taught to us but believed and lived (in Latin, too). Some of the Sisters who taught us are still among our most treasured friends. I do not see myself as a 'good' medievalist, but I do see the Middle Ages from a basically medieval standpoint.

How did the visual aspect enter the equation? Certainly not through our school history book, with a smudgy postage stamp, second-hand illustration of that mysterious portrait of Henry V with a droopy, dopey lower lip and no apparent back to his head. During the wartime school holidays Mother frequently took me and my sister to one of the few places that remained (partially) open to the public: Hampton Court

Palace. There were only a few rooms to be seen, and these were sparsely furnished. Nevertheless they found it difficult to get me around, as I would stare bemused at one picture, Lorenzo Lotto's 'The Collector', for instance – I still find it compelling.

There came a day when the Schools Inspector was going to attend our history class. Our teacher pinned up two photographs, something she had never done before. In he came, and she asked me to describe the difference between them. One was the interior of the chapel of St John in the Tower of London; the other was the interior of Henry VII's chapel in Westminster Abbey. I plunged in with all the enthusiasm of total ignorance. It seems he passed the school with flying colours. The photographs came down, the smudgy books were re-opened, and medieval architecture went back into storage until some three years later when Dr Margaret Whinney projected a black and white slide of the interior nave of Amiens Cathedral onto the screen. It came to me in the same moment that within a building of that kind I would feel at home. I still do.

*   *   *

Pamela Tudor-Craig, Lady Wedgwood (b. 1928), was educated at a French convent school (evacuated to Godalming during the war), and the Courtauld Institute, University of London, where she received her PhD in 1952. She was Professor of Art History to the University of Evansville at Harlaxton College and served for fifteen years on the Cathedrals Advisory Commission and nineteen on the Architectural Advisory Panel for Westminster Abbey. She has also spent time on the Fabric Committees of Wells, Exeter, Lincoln, Peterborough and Southwell cathedrals. A frequent broadcaster, she is the author of several publications including *The Secret Life of Paintings* with Richard Foster (1986).

60

Review of Cannadine Books

MAX BELOFF

(February 1999)

In his review of David Cannadine's two new books, the elderly Lord Beloff tried to be as fair as he could to a younger writer he clearly disapproved of. Coincidentally, while Beloff was writing his text, Cannadine himself was drafting this lecture on the art, craft and psychology of the book review.

In an article published in 1992, David Cannadine declared that what was needed in order to understand the 'status-conscious nature of British society' was 'a comprehensive study of social structure and social attitudes for Britain as a whole'. It was a daunting task. 'Who, if anyone,' he asked, 'is willing to try?' Now some six years later, the newly established Director of the Institute of Historical Research has not only reprinted the article in his sparkling new collection of essays and reviews but has also answered his own question by offering us a whole book on this topic. What is one to make of it?

Two main themes occupy the book, both, as one would expect, very thoroughly documented. In all three centuries between Elizabeth I and Elizabeth II, Cannadine traces a basic continuity in assessments of the social scene both by contemporaries and by historians following in their footsteps. The dominant interpretation has been of a continuous social fabric within which individuals and new groupings resulting from technological change could find their place, that is hierarchy. The second way of looking at things was in terms of a tripartite division – upper, middle and lower classes with variant qualities distinguishing them. It was the interpretation most favoured by the middle class, since it enabled them to claim the most virtuous and constructive role. The final approach, only found in periods of particular tension, was a simple division into two conflicting strata – the bosses and the workers, the washed and the unwashed, us and them.

The second theme of the book is the danger of separating social history from the political context – in particular after the development of party politics and the parties' command of the instruments of persuasion. What politicians have been engaged in was trying to get the electorate to accept that version of the social scene that was most likely to persuade it to endorse their particular policies. One major task of politicians 'from Wilkes to Major' has been 'to change people's sense of identity'.

While these subjective elements are clearly important, attention to them should surely not obscure changes in the objective situation. Can we be certain that there has not been in the last half century a major departure from the social developments of the previous 250 years? As the creation of a 'Social Exclusion Unit' indicates, we have now a situation in which the majority of people pay tax, but in which a minority in certain specific areas are wholly dependent upon the proceeds of those taxes and play no part in wealth creation or the management of their own lives. A household in which for three generations there has been no breadwinner is surely a novelty worth trying to encompass in any analysis of social structure.

As the mention of Major indicates, one feature of Cannadine's writing has been an interest in the present political and social scene almost equal to his interest in the past. A number of the essays in *History of Our Time* show that as a commentator Cannadine has much to commend him. But this interest in the here and now is not necessarily a benefit to the historian. Cannadine is well aware that successive generations have always interpreted the past in different ways, seeing the same events in a different light from those who lived through them. But he seems to assume that we can in our own day already pronounce judgements that will stand up to future scrutiny. Lady Thatcher did many remarkable things and some of these are set out in Cannadine's essay, written as long ago as 1989 when she was still in office. Yet can one already be sure that, as he says in the book on Class, 'she went a long way to achieving her ambition of banishing the language of class from public discussion and political debate about the structure and nature of British society'? Equally dubious is the remark in the preface about the 'bracing advent of New Labour'. Eighteen months after the election of 1997 that already sounds odd – who is braced and for what?

It must be appreciated that Cannadine is more than a mere commentator on the British scene. He has an agenda of his own. He would clearly like to get rid of all the ways in which any aspect of hierarchy is maintained – a monarchy of pomp and circumstance, hereditary titles, decorations, modes of address. He turns out to be a follower of Paine rather than Burke. It is sad that an eminent scholar should be in the same camp as the ignorant young men who pullulate in 'Demos', 'Charter 88' and the other 'think-tanks' of the current Left. Although one may find their views repellent, Cannadine is obviously entitled to share them. But a weakness of Cannadine's stance is that he is convinced that Britain is unique in the developed world in its attention to class and its symbols. Only the British and particularly the English seem, to Cannadine, to have class on the brain. I would think that if one chose to look at French or German society in the same way, allowing for some difference in symbols, one could come to the same conclusion about both of them.

Cannadine's attention is not in fact directed towards our neighbours but across the Atlantic. After a decade in the United States he has returned full of enthusiasm for remodelling British institutions and British behaviour on American lines. Americans think of themselves as overwhelmingly middle-class and therefore as living in a society without fissures – or, if fissures exist, only those of race. What worries one here is that, while there is some truth in this picture, it is based on a view of American history which bears little relation to the facts. It is not true that the democratic assumptions of some (not all) of the Founding Fathers were transmitted unblemished to subsequent generations. On the contrary we see in American history a succession of attempts to fortify American society by incorporating a measure of hierarchy without which no society can achieve stability.

For a couple of generations the old ruling class of the pre-Revolutionary era held onto power. After that it was the turn of the Boston Brahmins. Since the Jacksonian revolution we have seen a succession of newly enriched entrepreneurs and their heirs moving into positions of power and providing institutions, social registers, exclusive clubs and accepted codes of behaviour to exact the respect they thought was their due. The most recent new such aristocracy has been composed of the moguls of Hollywood, who have been the powerhouse behind President Clinton. Did David Cannadine ever think of a home in Beverly Hills or a little vacation spot at Martha's Vineyard?

One final point of substance is worth making. Cannadine takes the view that the existence of an important sector of private education is a mark of the class-orientated nature of English society. But it has always been true in the United States that the educational pattern has fortified hierarchy, and that with the state system in both countries suffering from the application of theories first adumbrated in the United States, Americans who can afford it are more and more moving towards private provision for their children. What Cannadine does, in brief, is to juxtapose a highly realistic version of British history with a wholly romantic – not to say sentimental – version of American history. Will distance enable him to correct it?

*   *   *

Max Beloff (1913–99) was educated at St Paul's School, London and Corpus Christi College, Oxford, graduating with a First in History in 1935. He held a number of Research Fellowships at Oxford before moving to Manchester University in 1939. After the war, he returned to Oxford as Nuffield Reader in the Comparative Study of Institutions and was a Fellow of Nuffield College from 1947 to 1957. In 1957, he became Gladstone Professor of Government and Public Administration, and Fellow of All Souls College, Oxford. He retained this chair until 1974 when he became the first Principal of the privately-funded University at Buckingham which he helped to found. Beloff, once an active Liberal but in later life a Conservative life peer, remained a prolific writer and reviewer after his retirement and was a regular columnist in *The Times* until his death. His first article in *History Today* was in its second-ever issue; the review reprinted here was published shortly before Lord Beloff's death.

60a

On Reviewing and Being Reviewed

DAVID CANNADINE

(March 1999)

As anyone knows who has tried their hand sufficiently at both activities, it is a great deal easier to review books on history that it is to write them. Even the most turgid and mediocre volume about the past is likely to show traces of expertise, curiosity, stamina, empathy and creativity – qualities that are sometimes conspicuously lacking in reviews and reviewers. But since reviews are quick, short and cheap whereas books are by comparison slow, long and expensive, they are often thought to exert an influence out of all proportion to their length and merit. Such, at least, are the opinions of literary editors, publishers and authors – and of many reviewers themselves. Of course, they would say that, wouldn't they? But whether they are right or wrong, it cannot be denied that, for the best part of 200 years, since the launching of the *Edinburgh Review* in 1802, history reviews have been an integral part of the public and academic culture of Britain. Whether we know or like it or not, those of us who turn our hands to this task are scribbling in a line of succession which, however uncertainly and intermittently, reaches back to the young Macaulay, who first made his public reputation as a coruscating writer in the 1820s.

Of course, Macaulay was a genius. As a poet, reviewer, essayist, parliamentary orator, conversationalist, letter-writer and author of state papers, he was never less than a scintillating stylist and consummate rhetorician. He was also prodigiously learned, across a far wider spectrum of human knowledge than is possible for any professional historian today. The result was that he fashioned and projected an inimitable authorial voice – by turns jaunty, authoritative, vigorous, ebullient, highly-coloured and warm-hearted – which can still captivate the reader today. No one since

Macaulay has ever written historical reviews quite like he did, and no one could, or should, try to do so now. But when I was learning about history in the 1960s and 1970s, scholars such as J.H. Plumb, Lawrence Stone, A.J.P. Taylor and Hugh Trevor-Roper were at the peak of their powers and productivity, and they were regularly reviewing in newspapers and periodicals on both sides of the Atlantic. They, too, were accomplished and confident stylists, with distinctive and opinionated voices, who reached a broad public audience, and as such they were Macaulay's direct and legitimate descendants.

I am not sure that the same can be said of the later generation of historians to which I myself belong, let alone of those younger scholars coming up fast behind us. Although there are now more professional historians in this country than ever before, they impinge less on the public and cultural life of the nation than their forebears did a quarter of a century ago, and one indication of this is the decline in serious histori-cal reviewing in the Saturday and Sunday papers. There are many explanations for this. One is that, as historical knowledge becomes more specialised, it becomes increasingly difficult to write confidently across a range of subjects sufficiently broad to establish an identity as a regular and distinctive reviewer. Another is that the university Research Assess-ment Exercise takes no note of such brief, ephemeral and unfootnoted activities, which means there is a strong disincentive for hard-pressed historians to undertake them. And as even the broadsheet newspapers 'dumb down' their pages, there is less scope for serious historical reviewing. Yet there remain many opportunities: in the ever-proliferating number of scholarly journals; in the 'literary' periodicals on both sides of the Atlantic; and (albeit diminishingly) in the 'quality' press.

This inevitably means that reviews come in a wide variety of shapes and sizes, lengths and weights. Short notices, between 5–800 words, are usually little more than a (very inadequate) precis of the book; 1,000 to 1,500 words allow more scope for discussion and debate; and in a review-essay of 2,000 words or more, there is opportunity to venture into a more general treatment of the subject, in the way that Macaulay pioneered and perfected. But this is not the only way in which historical reviews vary, for they are also aimed at readers who are themselves very diverse. Those produced for scholarly journals can take for granted an expert, pro-fessional audience; those appearing in the 'literary' periodicals can assume most readers are academics or intellectuals, but not necessarily experts; those written for the 'quality' press are intended for the 'intelligent general reader', which in the 1990s usually means university graduates in any subject. Writing for each of these audiences requires its own expositional strategy.

There are, notwithstanding, two aspects of historical reviewing which remain constant, and should be constantly borne in mind. Neither should need spelling out, but there are occasions when it is helpful and necessary to state the obvious. The first is that the prime purpose of any review should be to discuss the book, the author and the subject. Even if the reviewer is more famous than the author, the historical work that is being discussed is the thing that matters most. The review is parasitic on the book, and so is the reviewer, and this should never be forgotten. The second is that, regardless of the precise number of words required, or the particular nature of the audience, there are four essential tasks that any serious reviewer must always conscientiously seek to discharge: read the book; place the book; describe the book; judge the book. It is worth examining each of these activities in more detail.

It may seem absurd to insist that any book to be reviewed must first be read by the reviewer. Surely, this is self-evident? No serious work of history can be completed in under two years, and some take more than a decade: out of common decency, any author who has laboured thus hard and long is entitled to a full reading and a fair hearing. No conscientious reviewer should venture into print without having read and pondered the book not just once, but preferably twice. Yet many reviews are less thorough than they ought to be. Sometimes this arises from the pressure of tight deadlines, as in the case of the first volume of Margaret Thatcher's memoirs (*The Downing Street Years*, 1993). The book was embargoed before publication, but most newspapers carried reviews within forty-eight hours, which means that none of them could have been based on a thorough reading. But all too often lapses occur for the simple reason that the reviewer has merely dipped into the book or idly skimmed it. Most experienced authors can identify such cursory and unprofessional reviews of their books, because the telltale signs are obvious: excessive concentration on the introduction, conclusion and a few particular chapters, and confusion or ignorance about the general argument.

Only when the book has been read, pondered and understood, should the review of it be begun, and this must be done in such a way as to catch the reader's attention. It can be with a memorable and arresting anecdote; but when the word-count is limited, there is often insufficient space. It is usually better to open with an outline of the broader historical and contemporary issues with which the book engages, and with some remarks about who the author is, and how the subject is being approached. When publishing in the professional historical journals, some of this scene-setting can be dispensed with; but the closer towards the 'general reader' the review is directed, the more important it becomes. For one of the prime purposes of such reviewing is to bring outstanding works of scholarly history to the notice of the non-academic public, and the only way to do this is to begin by explaining why the subject, the book and the author matter. A classic instance of this is G.M. Trevelyan's review of Lewis Namier's *England in the Age of the American Revolution*, which he published in *The Nation* in 1930. Trevelyan wanted to draw attention to the novelty of Namier's approach, and the importance of his findings, in the hope that this might encourage a British university to give him a much-needed academic job. Soon after, Manchester did just that.

Having read and placed it, the next thing to do is to give some clear sense of what the book is about. Here, again, there are snares and pitfalls aplenty. Many reviewers simply fail to discharge this responsibility: having neglected to read the book, they sound off on the subject which they believe it to be about, venting their feelings and parading their prejudices, but with virtually no reference to the book itself. The result is not so much a review as an intellectual or (more usually) emotional spasm. But even for the conscientious reviewer, the summary is no simple task. It is virtually impossible to describe any book of many thousand words in a mere few hundred: with the best will in the world, the argument will be simplified and abridged to (or beyond) the point of caricature. And if the book is an edited collection such as a *Festschrift*, it is difficult to avoid a laundry-list enumeration – author by author, subject by subject – in a remorseless catalogue which may please the contributors, since none will feel slighted by having been left out, but which usually sends the reader in search of more exciting fare elsewhere. Dullness in reviews is unforgivable, but describing books in ways that are not dull can tax the expositional resources of the most experienced and accomplished reviewer.

All that remains is to give some verdict – an activity which provides the greatest scope for fun and irresponsibility and for causing offence. The desire to trash a book can sometimes be very strong, because the reviewer dislikes the book or the author or both. On the whole, this desire should be resisted – partly because few books are completely contemptible (and if they are, why bother to review them?); and partly because it is better to be generous than to be negative, since in reviewing, as in life, one should do unto others as one would wish to be done by oneself. Of course, there should be some criticism and disagreement: the work of history that is without fault or flaw has yet to be written, and reviews that are unrelievedly hyperbolic rarely carry conviction. Above all, it is essential to 'engage' with the book – to argue with it, agree with it, dissent from it – and thereby to convey the flavour of the book, and of what the author is trying to do: in short, to take it seriously. And in doing this, it is no less essential to engage with the book 'as written': to see how far the author has accomplished what he (or she) set out to do, rather than chastise him (or her) for not having written a different sort of book.

These, it bears repeating, are the elementary rules for good reviewing, which any responsible reviewer should seek to observe. It might be protested that they are absurdly naive: they might be what reviewing 'ought' to be about, but they are not what reviewing is actually about. In practice, it might be argued, reviewing is really about showing off, or about furthering one's own career at the price of someone else's, or about demonstrating that the author of the review is so much cleverer than the author of the book, or about the pursuit of deeply-felt and long-running scholarly vendettas, or about the waging of party-political battles by other means (as in the *Edinburgh* and the *Quarterly* early in the nineteenth century). The lengthy conflict between Geoffrey Elton (a Tory empiricist) and Lawrence Stone (a Whig generalist) certainly came within both of these last two categories, and it provided gladiatorial entertainment of a high order. But while these personal, polemical and political temptations can be difficult (sometimes impossible) to resist, they should ideally be kept within bounds and firmly subordinated to the serious business of placing, describing and judging the book.

The fact that they are so often unresisted may explain why many authors fear and hate being reviewed. Of course, there are many authors who fear and hate *not* being reviewed: no one enjoys having laboured long and hard to produce a book which they believe to be of major importance, only to discover that this view is not widely shared by literary editors. But being reviewed can be an even worse ordeal than not being reviewed. Even when a book is well received, being subjected to the caprice of the critics remains for many authors a nerve-racking experience. Few books receive (or deserve) unalloyed praise; many are routinely trashed, not just in one review, but again and again. It may be true that there is no such thing as bad publicity, that it is better to be loathed than ignored. But few authors enjoy reading hostile things about themselves in print, and they rarely forgive or forget what they regard as wicked reviews. And reviews can be very hostile indeed: scornful, dis-missive, vituperative, mendacious, dishonest, misleading. Even for the most thick-skinned writer (and most writers are obliged to develop thick skins), this is no fun. If, like Virginia Woolf, you don't have a thick skin, it can be a nightmare.

Here is a more recent example. In the middle of 1998, Victoria Glendinning, who is by any reasonable yardstick an accomplished and successful writer (and, incidentally, reviewer), took a whole column of

The Spectator to describe how badly she felt she had been treated by Terry Eagleton's critical review of her biography of Swift in *The Sunday Times*. She was clearly very upset, and it was difficult not to feel some sympathy with her. But it was also difficult not to feel that, in parading her pain, she had made a big mistake. For while there are many rules about how to review, there is only one rule about how to respond to being reviewed. And that is, quite simply, never reply. Well, as W.S. Gilbert would have said, hardly ever. There is nothing wrong in thanking someone for a generous or thoughtful review, provided the letter is not too sycophantic in tone. Alternatively, if a review is libellous and defamatory, then there are traditional recourses: the courts or a horsewhip. But litigation is usually best avoided, while physical retribution is a very high-risk strategy. And if the review is critical, hostile or antagonistic but not actionable, it is much more prudent and seemly to suffer it in silence.

But many authors are incapable of maintaining such a dignified and taciturn front, and are easily provoked into responding. The obvious way to do this is to write to the journal in which the offending review appeared. This is an unwise strategy because the editors often simply refuse to publish such letters, which merely serves to intensify authorial outrage still further because the obvious conclusion is that the editor is on the side of the reviewer, not the author. And such rebuttal is even more galling because the leading literary periodicals thrive on their correspondence columns, and academic journals are also increasingly allowing authors the right of reply. These exchanges – often displaying petulance, wounded pride, bad temper and bloody-mindedness in equal quantities on both sides – can be great fun to read. But no self-respecting author should ever resort to such misguided epistolary combat. However unfair, inaccurate or distorting the offending review may have been, letters of protest invariably sound peevish and whinging. And since the rules of engagement in the correspondence columns usually allow the reviewer the last word, it is almost inconceivable that any author will get the better of the exchange.

An alternative mode of redress is for the author to write a private letter of protest or remonstrance to the reviewer. This avoids the unseemly spectacle of publicly parading one's hurt or outrage, but it is again an unwise and unedifying stratagem. To the recipient, it always seems a cheap form of rejoinder: the reviewer upsets the author, so the author responds in kind by trying to upset the reviewer. I once found myself on the receiving end of such ill-judged retaliation after reviewing Geoffrey Elton's study of Maitland. I do not think that his most ardent admirers would regard it as his best book, and in pointing this out in my review I disregarded several of the precepts I have outlined above. 'Elton's

Maitland', I rightly but intemperately concluded, 'bears a remarkable resemblance to Elton's Elton.' 'And', I added, scaling new heights of tactlessness, 'we have already had rather a lot of that.' A scorching letter arrived by return, denouncing and ridiculing the review, and inquiring whether Lawrence Stone had paid me to write it. I replied proposing it would be a good idea for us to have a drink together, to which Elton retorted that it would be insufferably effronterous for him to presume to take refreshment with someone who had recently told the world we had had enough of Elton.

On this absurdly petulant note, the correspondence ended. I later learned that Elton was notorious for writing such hectoring letters: although exceptionally brave and bold when berating other historians for not doing the subject his way, he became astonishingly touchy and tender when anyone dared to try to mete out the same treatment to him. This was not – and is not – a sensible or grown-up way to respond to being critically reviewed. Even worse is the lengthily-delayed private letter, which is ostensibly about something else, but which is really a long-pondered, and long-postponed protest. Thus: 'I'm sorry, I cannot attend your meeting next week and, by the way, while I am writing, I ought to add that I hope when next you review a book of mine, you will be less gratuitously hostile than you were last time.' Such letters, whose laboured afterthoughts are in fact their real purpose, deceive no one except the sender. And, far from upsetting them, they invariably give the recipients exquisite pleasure: for there are few things that make a reviewer happier than knowing a critical notice has hit home, and that it has rankled and festered with the author for months thereafter. No self-respecting writer should ever give a reviewer such satisfaction.

With very rare exceptions, therefore, authorial silence is the best policy in the face of disobliging reviews. Whatever the provocation, and however unfairly treated the author may feel, it accomplishes nothing useful to parade one's outrage, hurt, annoyance and insecurity: far better to take mute consolation in Prokofiev's remark that 'No statue was ever put up to a critic'. For, as this observation reminds us, it is much more important to be an author than a reviewer. Good reviews should cheer up an author for half an hour; bad reviews should depress an author for a morning: but in the end, it is the book the author has written that matters. Moreover, as many publishers privately recognise, books sell, or do not sell, more on the basis of word of mouth than they do on the basis of good or bad reviews in the press or the periodicals. This means that, when a book is launched into the public domain, the author is powerless to influence how the public will react to it, and there is no point in trying to do so. It will inevitably take on a life of its own, and people will respond to it as they will, and these things have to be recognised and accepted.

When done well, reviewing can be a worthwhile activity: it offers a way of ensuring important books get known and read by a wider public than they might otherwise reach; a way of summarising scholarly trends and historiographical debates, and of suggesting new developments and approaches; and, under really inspired editorship, a way for promising young writers to learn to put sentences together in a more vivid and vigorous way than is usually encouraged in doctoral dissertations. But at its worst, reviewing is a carping, mean-spirited, axe-grinding exercise in academic envy and scholarly resentment, as narrow-minded, uncreative historians set out to disparage the achievements of those of greater gifts and accomplishments than themselves. When writing my biography of G.M. Trevelyan, I compiled an extensive anthology of the reviews his many books had received. Most of them were critical, negative and sometimes downright hostile, written by second-rate figures who had seized their chance to belittle a historian of incomparably greater abilities than they, before returning to the mediocre obscurity from which they should never have emerged. Trevelyan ignored these scholarly snipers: and he was right to do so.

Even at its best, reviewing is an ephemeral activity, and this helps explain why no major historian (not even Macaulay) has ever made a life-long reputation primarily, let alone exclusively, as a reviewer. It looked for a time as though Jack Hexter might be the exception who would prove the rule, since he fashioned almost an entire literary career from reviewing other people who, unlike him, were themselves writing real history. But although he wrote with an engaging combination of wit and style, humour and savagery, these pieces remain ultimately confined, earthbound and dependent on the greater and more imaginative works of scholarship that they discuss, dissect, and sometimes dismiss. And that is just as it should be: for the real business of our profession is not to write reviews of each other's work (which is easy), but to produce what Trevelyan called real books of enduring value (which is much more difficult). At the end of the day, creativity is much more important than criticism, which means that books rightly matter much more than reviews. These are things which no historian – and no reviewer – should ever forget.

*   *   *

David Cannadine was born in Birmingham in 1950, and educated at the universities of Cambridge, Oxford and Princeton. From 1975 to 1988, he was a Fellow of Christ's College, Cambridge and University Lecturer in History and he has also taught at Columbia University, New York. He is now Director at the Institute of Historical Research, University of London. He is the editor and author of several books, including the *Decline and Fall of the British Aristocracy* (1992), *Aspects of Aristocracy* (1994); *G. M. Trevelyan* (1997); *The Pleasures of the Past* (1989); *History in Our Time* (1998), *Class in Britain* (1998) and *Ornamentalism* (2001). He writes regularly for newspapers and reviews in London and New York, and is a well-known broadcaster.

61

Asa Briggs

DANIEL SNOWMAN

(October 1999)

This was one of a regular series by Daniel Snowman, starting in October 1998, on the work of contemporary historians. Others whose oeuvre was considered included David Cannadine, Eric Hobsbawm, Peter Burke, Theodore Zeldin, John Keegan, Eric Foner, Geoffrey Hosking, Antonia Fraser, David Starkey and Ian Kershaw. Asa Briggs has been an academic advisor to History Today *since its foundation.*

Thought, work and progress: the key words of mid-Victorian England according to Asa Briggs. And they might stand as the personal motto of Lord Briggs of Lewes, a man whose monumental productivity as scholar, author and doer of good public works would have won him the plaudits of a Prince Albert or a Gladstone. But if the burghers of Leeds or Lewes ever decide to erect a statue of Asa Briggs, I hope they don't make it look too earnest, for he is the most engaging of men, utterly without pretension. 'I suppose I am a bit of a Victorian,' he acknowledges, but with an almost schoolboyish grin which instantly offsets any suggestion of stuffiness.

The author of *The Age of Improvement* was born in Keighley in 1921 and rose through sheer ability, and an unquenchable thirst for hard work, to become Professor of History at Leeds, co-founder and Vice-Chancellor of the University of Sussex, Provost of Worcester College, Oxford, Chancellor of the Open University, Chairman or President of a score of learned and historical societies and author of countless articles and books great and small. You can read Briggs on Victorian cities, people and things, on steam and transportation, public health and education, science and technology, music and literature, food and drink, sport and public entertainment, print and publishing, Chartism and the Channel Islands and, in five mighty tomes, on the history of British broadcasting.

Chronologically he ranges from prehistory (in the opening chapter of his *Social History of England*) to the present and future (in *Fins de Siècle*), while his core writings about Victorian England are peppered with comparative material from or about Sydney and Melbourne, New York and Chicago, Dublin, Lyons, Tokyo and Berlin.

Samuel Smiles, apostle of self-help, would have approved. Grandfather Briggs, an engineer (like Asa's father), heard Smiles's lecture and told his grandson about them years later. 'My grandfather got me interested in history,' Briggs recalls. 'He took me to every abbey and castle and small town in Yorkshire when I was a boy.' It was through his grandfather, too, that Asa developed a lifelong interest in science and technology. His mother's family farmed land in nearby Oxenhope where the cashier in the mill was a Mr Butterfield – whose son Herbert was also to become one of England's best-known historians.

A scholarship to Keighley Grammar School led Briggs, under the influence of a forceful and encouraging headmaster, to Sidney Sussex College, Cambridge. Here he famously obtained not only a Double First in History but also – concurrently (and in secret from his college) – a First in Economics as an external student at the LSE, which was evacuated to Cambridge during the war. Thus, Briggs was able to feast at the table of Postan and Saltmarsh, Oakeshott and Ernest Barker, Hayek, Laski and Eileen Power. He revelled in the richesse, devouring lectures, consuming books and pouring out weekly essays for both sets of masters on such diverse subjects as medieval and constitutional history, political philosophy and economic theory.

His versatility was soon to be stretched yet further. After a brief stint teaching at his old school, Briggs was called up into the Royal Corps of Signals where he learned Morse and was trained in fast interception. Then he received a call: he was to go on a cryptographic course – and thence to Bletchley where he spent three years as part of the top-secret team that broke the Enigma code.

While still at Bletchley, Briggs was wooed by both Oxford and Cambridge, finally accepting a Fellowship at Worcester College, Oxford, where he obtained a Readership and stayed for ten years. He was wooed by Churchill, too, who had asked Bill Deakin to recruit bright young historians (Alan Bullock was another) to help check the text of his forthcoming *History of the English-Speaking Peoples*. Apparently the curmudgeonly old aristocrat was graciously receptive to the strictures of the Keighley scholarship boy, even when Briggs accused him of having been – of all things – too Marxist in his interpretation of the American Constitution. But the most substantial products of Briggs's Oxford years were his history of Birmingham (a work of 'total history', not to mention urban and social history, well before such things became commonplace) and a bustling volume of essays on mid-Victorian 'persons and themes' which he entitled *Victorian People*.

In October 1955, Asa Briggs, recently married and still only thirty-four, became Professor of Modern History at Leeds University. Here, this natural bridge-builder brought the history of social and scientific thought into the syllabus, introduced an experimental series of History 'general' subjects and discovered a taste for spotting and hiring new talent. He also developed a profound distaste for academic territoriality and departmentalism. At Leeds, Briggs was already 'redrawing the map of learning', something he was soon invited to do on a far wider scale.

The University of Sussex was to Asa Briggs what the Great Exhibition had been to Prince Albert or the BBC to Reith: a visionary undertaking for the betterment of the nation. Sussex was the first of seven 'New Universities' planned for the 1960s, all placed near coasts and cathedrals in deliberate contrast to the urban 'redbrick' of Leeds, Manchester and the rest. Briggs was there from the start, appointed to take overall charge of academic affairs.

Briggs at Sussex was a torrent, a dynamo, an engine. Buildings were designed and assigned, deans and dons appointed (I was lucky enough to be one of them), new concepts coined. Students would major in the 'core subject' of their choice (somewhat in the American style) while also studying a series of 'contextual' subjects in the 'Schools of Study' to which they were assigned. Quality control was guaranteed by an Oxbridge-style tutorial system. Buzz words in this academic terra nova were 'interdisciplinary' and 'cross-cultural'. There were taboo words, too; what 'sex' was to the Victorians, 'departments' were to Sussex.

Throughout this surge of social engineering, Briggs remained an active historian. He had already embarked upon what must have seemed the commission of (and doubtless for!) a lifetime: a multi-volume history of British broadcasting. The first instalment appeared in 1961: four hundred packed pages chronicling the birth of the British Broadcasting Company and its transformation into a Corporation. Briggs had research help throughout the broadcasting project. If the outcome sometimes reflects the official sources on which it is largely based, it is worth remembering that there was little 'media' or 'cultural' history when Briggs began, and it is perhaps unfair to criticise a pioneer for not having adopted an approach that his own work helped stimulate. One of the by-products of Briggs' work, incidentally, was that he was able to persuade the BBC to set up a properly catalogued written archive at Caversham.

He also found time during the early years at Sussex to write *Victorian Cities*, a richly allusive set of essays on the pattern of *Victorian People* which brought together years of accumulated research and personal experience of Birmingham and Leeds, Manchester, Melbourne and Middlesbrough, and that great 'world' city, London.

Briggs became Vice-Chancellor in 1967 and soon found himself having to pilot Sussex through the choppy waters of student protest. But not even the most disaffected student could accuse the VC – self-evidently a conscientious academic who wrote books, gave lectures and talked to students – of being a grey administrator. As a result, Sussex was a pretty happy ship, experiencing nothing like the disruption that afflicted (for example) the University of Essex or the LSE. Briggs remained at the helm for a decade, finally leaving Sussex in 1976. That year he was given a life peerage. Before accepting, he made it clear to prime minister Callaghan that he would not accept a party whip in the Lords, and would not have time to attend very often. Apart from everything else, he had a new job.

As Provost of Worcester College, Oxford, Lord Briggs was, in a sense, going home. This was where he had done his earliest historical research and penned his first books. To many great men of action, the headship of an Oxbridge college is a final reward for a life of service, grassland for a warhorse no longer required for serious battle. Retired cabinet ministers, ambassadors and even professors have learned to enjoy the unrelenting round of drinks and homage that come with the territory, and who can complain if their presence brings the college added lustre? Briggs is not averse to such pastimes and good company, but he went to Worcester for more than that. For fifteen years (until 1991 when he was seventy) he moved and shook with the mightiest of them. But he also tried, as he had at Sussex, to break down the barriers between teachers and taught, artists and scientists, town and gown. One of Briggs's proudest achievements as Provost was to make the house (previously the abode of the formidable Oliver Franks) more accessible to undergraduates.

Meanwhile, the great broadcasting juggernaut pushed its way through to the war years and beyond, while in 1983 Briggs published the most important longitudinal study of English social history since Trevelyan, a book bursting with typically Briggsian detail about coins and medals, ballads and baubles, cities and seasides – plus much of the politics which Trevelyan had proclaimed inappropriate to social history. A couple of years later Briggs' collected essays began to appear in volume form.

My own favourite among Briggs's books, and I suspect it may be his, is *Victorian Things*, a companion piece to its predecessors on People and Cities, which appeared in 1988. The Victorians filled their lives and packed their homes with objects: hats and bonnets, stamps and matches, pots and pans, tongs and coal scuttles, photos, phones and phonographs. *Victorian Things* makes no claim to be comprehensive, nor does Briggs squeeze arcane symbolism from his multifarious bits and bobs as a French semiologist might have done. But, in its undemonstrative way, the book breaks new ground as Briggs gives pride of place to the objects themselves. Things, more than documents, are the new emissaries from the past.

Here, as so often, it is Briggs' insatiable curiosity about the past that drives his history. If he tends to give less prominence than some historians to analysis and explanation it is because he objects to 'premature generalisation' and the sterile academic debates this can lead to. Rather, he attempts to communicate the direct experience of the past to his readers via the detail, backed up by an army of apposite quotations. Briggs typically dazzles with detail – especially, perhaps, in the Victorian trilogy where an overall picture emerges of a sensible, bourgeois world populated by energetic people genuinely dedicated to the idea of ameliorating their lot and that of their progeny. An age of improvement, indeed.

At seventy-eight, Asa Briggs, looking and sounding like a man ten years younger, remains as industrious as ever. Projects and presidencies come and go. The Workers' Educational Association and the Open University, the University Grants Committee, the Labour and Social History Societies, the Commonwealth of Learning, the Booker Committee and Glyndebourne Trust, the Brontë Society, Ephemera Society, Victorian Society and the editorial boards of journals and magazines (including this one) – Briggs has sat on them all and chaired most. With homes in Lewes and Scotland, an office in London and a hideaway in Portugal, he still rushes to and from trains and planes. Deadlines loom. New projects are accepted while previous ones lie unfinished. Recent books include collaborations with Patricia Clavin on a volume on European History since 1789, Roy Porter on Bethlem and myself on *Fins de Siècle*, plus a short history of Chartism (for a series of pocket histories of which he is general editor). Next off the assembly line are a book about Michael Young and a history of the Royal College of Physicians, while awaiting completion are a history of Longman, a book with Peter Burke on the history of communications and a project about forms of work during the Second World War. As for the BBC, Briggs was furious when the Corporation closed its broadcasting history unit and is determined to do a volume, entirely under his own steam, to include the John Birt years.

What has driven the engine so ferociously for so long? Why does Briggs still work so hard, travel so extensively? Has he written too much? Briggs knows all the jibes about 'Lord Briggs of Heathrow' and laughs them off without quite denying their truth. 'I love writing,' he says, 'and am never completely happy unless I have a book on the go.' There is a moral dimension, too. 'I always feel there are certain questions that I ought to look at,' says Briggs, evidently inspired by the sense of service that also motivated the Victorians. His critics say that no one man can master the range of topics Briggs writes about and point to phrases, quotations and examples that recur in Briggs's writings. Some of his writings are indeed partly reworkings of earlier material. Also, the style and subject matter are highly discreet in a rather old-fashioned way; if you want to find out about Disraeli's sex life or Rowntree's drinking, don't go looking in Briggs. This is doubtless because Briggs abhors the modern obsession with prurience. But some readers also sense a busy writer skating along the public surface of a topic and missing some of the more suggestive crevasses beneath.

As this chronicler, beneficiary and product of Victorian idealism looks back over our own times he perceives what he believes to be the rise and decline of many of our great institutions of public improvement – the BBC, the Arts Council and the National Health Service, for example. It is deeply ironic that this apostle of all that was best in Victorian values should have seen them evoked, erroneously in his view, by a prime minister, Margaret Thatcher, who aspired to tear down so much that genuine Victorian values had helped to erect.

There is a further reason why we are losing touch with the qualities bequeathed by our Victorian ancestors, of course, and that is the sheer passage of time. The Victorians, so well remembered (and in some cases encountered) when Briggs was a lad, have long since passed away, and the Victorian era itself will shortly become 'the century before last'. The revival of interest in the Victorian era, which Briggs (with John Betjeman) did so much to pioneer and spearhead, is ebbing away as younger scholars gravitate towards more recent periods.

Perhaps each generation is attracted to the era just outside its own collective memory. That is healthy enough, and Briggs holds no special brief for the primacy of Victorian studies. But he worries that our political leaders encourage very little sense of history (and fulminates about the lack of history in the Dome – an exhibition presumably mounted to mark a calendrical watershed). To Asa Briggs, nobody can expect to plan the future who does not also understand the forces which have created the present. But this preternatural optimist is not given to cursing the darkness. Briggs's instincts, rather, are to light a candle by which to get on with the next job. Whichever of the many on his plate that might be . . .

*   *   *

Daniel Snowman (b. 1938) has a Double First in History from Cambridge and an MA in Politics from Cornell. At twenty-four a Lecturer at the

University of Sussex (1963–7), he spent much of his professional life (until 1995) at the BBC where he became Chief Producer, Features (Radio), specialising in historical and cultural projects. His books include a history of twentieth century America, a comparative study of British and US values and a volume, with Asa Briggs, on previous ends of centuries (plus critical portraits of the Amadeus Quartet and Placido Domingo). Snowman is a frequent contributor to *History Today* and other journals. His next book (2002) will assess the impact of the 'Hitler émigrés' on British cultural history.

62

Monstrous Acts

ERICA FUDGE

(August 2000)

Not the sort of article Hodge and Quennell would have commissioned or published, Erica Fudge's scholarly and entertaining piece about bestiality in early modern England was followed, in the September issue, by an illustrated feature on some of the pornographic art in the British Museum's collections. One wonders what we will be including in History Today's *centenary anthology!*

In 1670 Thomas Rigg of Hadmore in the North Riding of Yorkshire appeared before a Justice of the Peace. His deposition reads:

Upon Sunday last being the 22nd day of May betwixt nine and ten of the clock in the morning, as he and Elizabeth his wife were going through Gillimore town field . . . they espied one Christopher Sunley of Gillimore aforesaid being upon a mare with his arms clasped about her loins, and jumping at her with his body, in beastly and unseemly manner for the time they were going about twenty yards. And saith that when he came off her he looked down betwixt his legs, then looking about him he espied this informant and his wife, whereupon he went to the other side of the mare, and laid him down.

The Riggs were not the only people to find their walks interrupted in the seventeenth century. In June 1656, for example, John Sweedale of Easby had a similar experience. He stated that:

On Saturday last as he was going to look at some horses belonging to the Lord Eure that pastured in my lands around Easby for fear they should get into the corn, he saw William Clarke of the same town,

labourer, about the hour of ten of the clock at night standing very
near a mare, and coming near unto him perceived him (to the best
of his judgment) committing buggery with the said mare, being
William Ripley's. He saith the mare is of a chestnut colour, and that
this fact was committed in a place called Burrow Green, belonging to
the Lord Eure. When this informant came first up to and spoke with
this said William Clarke and asked him what he was doing for he had
a wife of his own, the said William Clarke prayed him for God's sake,
to keep his counsel, and he would not stay two days in England.

When Clarke himself was questioned – he obviously had not left the
country – he stated that he was, as Sweedale had deposed, in Burrow
Green, but that he was

> . . . looking at the thighs of a mare behind, to see whether the ox
> had hipped or gored her behind or not, for as his master's draught
> was going down a hill that same day in the afternoon he saw one of
> the oxen hip at the said mare which was then in the draught, but
> denies that he committed buggery with the said mare.

Clarke's denial of the accusation made against him was not surprising.
Since 1533 bestiality had been a felony without benefit of clergy, and
anyone convicted of the offence would 'suffer such pains of death and
losses and penalties of their goods, chattels, debtors, lands, tenements,
hereditaments'. The 1533 statute presented the offence as 'that detestable and abominable vice', and used the term 'buggery' to describe it. A
later statute of 1548 added an additional clause advising that:

> No person be received for witness or to lay or give evidence against
> the said offendor [. . . who] should take any profit or commodity by
> the death of the said offendor if he were attained or convicted of the
> said crime and offence.

This addition can only be regarded as a protection against wilful accusations made for gain. Buggery was too serious an issue to be threatened
lightly.

The particular danger of an accusation of bestiality was not only the
threat of execution, however. In legal documents the terms vice, crime
and sin were all used to describe the offence, and the slippage in the
language hints at the variety of ways in which people living in England in
the sixteenth and seventeenth centuries understood bestiality. There is
more to this than just committing an illegal act. For Edward Coke, the
seventeenth-century systematiser of the common law, bestiality was 'a

detestable and abominable sin, amongst Christians not to be named.' It was beyond words; outside of the propriety of godly conversation. Going even further than this, Michael Dalton wrote, in his advice manual on the common law, *The Countrey Justice* (1618), that bestiality was 'a sin against God, Nature and the Law'. That is, in committing the crime, the offenders did not merely break the law of the land, they also broke the law of God, and of the natural order.

Bestiality had not always been regarded as the serious offence it became in the sixteenth century. In the second century AD, for example, in *On the Characteristics of Animals* Aelian recorded a number of human-animal relationships: 'at Soli in Cilicia a dog loved a boy of the name of Xenophon; at Sparta another boy in the prime of life by reason of his beauty caused a jackdaw to fall sick of love'. He tells a similar tale of the 'groom who fell in love with a young mare, the finest of the herd, as it might have been with a beautiful girl, the loveliest of all thereabouts'. There is no moral concern here about these cross-species relationships, rather it is a celebration of humanity's place in the natural order. In her book *The Beast Within* (1994), Joyce E. Salisbury argues that in Aelian we can trace the ancient idea that 'animals were not very different from people. They suffered the same emotions of love, anger and jealousy'. In the second century, this is something that was not regarded as a threat to humanity.

Early Christians abandoned Aelian's celebration of human-animal relationships and turned instead to the biblical injunctions against bestiality, such as that found in Leviticus 18.23: 'Neither shalt thou lie with any beast to defile thyself therein'. However, in the earliest penitential manuals, wherein priests found listed appropriate penalties for a variety of sins, punishment for bestiality was remarkably light. In the seventh-century Irish Penitential of Columban, for example, is written: 'If anyone practices masturbation or sins with a beast, he shall do penance for two years'. The Penitential returns to the subject later, and the sin, again, holds an interesting place:

> If a layman commits fornication with a beast, he shall do penance for a year if he has a wife; but if he has not, for half a year. So also shall he do penance who, having a wife, practices masturbation.

Less sinful for a single man than a married one, and no more dangerous than onanism, bestiality is hardly to be perceived as having the dangerous status it was to come to hold in 1533. So why was there a change in attitude to bestiality?

The sixteenth and seventeenth centuries were a time when many of the previously held assumptions about humanity were coming under threat. Colonialists were bringing back stories of monstrous races which appeared to confirm medieval ideas, and which upset many of the established perceptions about the final work of the Creation. The Reformation had caused a new interrogation of the self, and a new emphasis on what it was that made a human human, while the New Science saw bodies investigated in a way that compromised the distinction between human and animal. In the light of changes such as these to the category of the human, animals were moving ever closer; gone was Aelian's sense of the wonder of nature, instead beasts became a threat.

The tales of the 'animalisation' of humans that can be traced in the early modern period come in a variety of forms. For Robert Gray, in a sermon given before members of the Virginia Company in 1610, the New World natives 'wander up and down like beasts, and in manners and conditions differ very little from beasts'. These humans were portrayed as hardly human, and this was a reason offered by colonialists for their colonial practices: the natives could not own the land because they were not fully human. In the Reformed religious ideas of William Perkins an animal was a creature that lacked a conscience, but how to prove that humans had consciences remained a problem. On a more popular level, were cases like the 'pig-faced' woman from Holland who was put on display in early seventeenth-century London. Her 'head like a swine' was said by one ballad to be due to her over-indulgence in bacon. Here, eating animals does not cement the boundary between the species but actually undoes it: the woman has become the thing she eats. There are several other similar stories, but the status of humanity was coming under threat in a variety of ways, and it was because of this that bestiality came to be perceived as a danger, and one that must be severely dealt with.

Central to this reaction was the belief that bestiality caused a pollution of the species. This pollution was not merely due to illicit sexual contact, but rested on the belief in the possibility of reproduction across species boundaries. Animal cross-breeding was already a clearly recognised occurence: the mule, a cross between a donkey and a horse, had been around for thousands of years. But the similarities between the horse and the donkey meant that this particular blend did not seem outside of nature. However, more extraordinary crosses were also said to have taken place. In his 1569 work, *Certaine Secrete Wonders of Nature*, a translation of the French text by Pierre Boaistuau, Edward Fenton records a dog whose parents were a bear and a mastiff. He writes that this cross-breed came from the Bear Garden, London's baiting arena:

> where the dogs and the bears do lie in little cabinets or vaults of wood, one fast by an other: and being in their heats, those that do govern

them, will not stick oftentimes to put a bear and a dog in one house together, when being pricked with their natural impressions, they convert their cruelty into love: of which conjunctions are engendered oftentimes creatures like unto this, although very seldom.

Fenton also notes Aristotle's belief that 'the Indian dogs be engendered of a dog and a tiger'. With such a belief in the possibility of reproducing across the boundaries of individual animal species, it is not a great leap to assume the possibility of human-animal cross-breeds. This view of the possible outcome of bestiality was not a new one. In the second century AD Aelian recorded the 'strange union' of a human groom and a mare that produced a foal, and in the thirteenth century William of Auvergne wrote of the possibility of women reproducing with bears. The threat of bestiality which can be traced in sixteenth- and seventeenth-century writings, therefore, does not present new evidence. Rather, at the heart of these discussions of bestiality – in legal depositions, popular and 'scientific' writings – is a new fear about the status of humanity. As Salisbury has said of the penitential manuals, 'When there was no threat of blurring the lines between species, there was no need to regulate strictly the distinctions.' By implication, where there was a perceived threat regulation became more strict. The statute of 1533, in this sense, represents a change in the perception of the boundary which existed between humans and animals. By the early sixteenth century a new understanding had emerged.

This is exactly what Fenton recognises. He tells the story of

. . . a child who was conceived and engendered between a woman and a dog, having from the navel upwards, the form and shape of the mother, so well accomplished, that nature had not forgotten anything unperformed, and from the navel downwards, it had the form and figure of the beast who was the father, who (as Volateranus writeth) was sent to the Pope which reigned at that time there, to the end it might be purified and purged.

Ambroise Paré tells the same story in *Of Monsters and Prodigies* (1573) which he says took place in 1493, and the tale appears again in William Turner's *Compleat History of the Most Remarkable Providences* (1697), where it is dated to 1556. Whatever the origin or date of the story it is significant that it is reproduced across a century. From Fenton's discussion of numerous natural eccentricities, through Paré's medical text to Turner's book of wonders, the human-animal cross-breed has a wide-ranging appeal. It is scientific, as Paré would have understood the term, and it is also a wonder.

The way in which these writers depicted the product of a bestial relation-ship places these creatures within the wider cultural understanding of prodigies: that is, of things that exceed nature. The important difference between the prodigious monster and the product of a bestial relationship was that the monster could only be explained by recourse to the super-natural. A bestial relationship, on the other hand, was, paradoxically, wholly natural. But the representation of prodigious monsters reminds us of the anxieties about the natural world that were particularly prevalent during the early modern period.

Monstrous births were recorded in ballads, broadsides, religious tracts and medical treatises, and held both popular and learned attention. Often presented with lurid illustrations, works detailing these aberrations of nature offered meaning where there seemed to be no explanation, and in many the meaning was clearly supernatural: the monster was a warning from God who was presented as the author of the oddities. Fenton argued that:

> It is most certain that these monstrous creatures, for the most part, do proceed of the judgment, justice, chastisement and curse of God, which suffereth that the fathers and mothers bring forth these abominations, as a horror of their sin.

In 1562, for example, the birth of a monstrous pig near Charing Cross is reported in a broadsheet. After a lengthy description and illustration the author notes:

> These strange sights, the Almighty God sendeth unto us that we should not be forgetful of his mighty power: nor unthankful for his so great mercies. The which he showeth specially by giving unto us his holy word wherby our lives ought to be guided and also his wonderful tokens whereby we are most gently warned.

This paragraph is reproduced almost verbatim in another broadsheet of the same year describing another monstrous pig, this time born in Hampstead.

It was not only animals, however, which could be meaningful when thinking about the disturbance of nature. In 1595 at Oteringham in Holderness, for example, a mother gave birth to a healthy daughter, and then two days later to a monster:

> The head whereof was like a cony [rabbit]: The hands was like a mole: The body, legs, and feet like a woman, having also the privities like a woman.

This extraordinary event was regarded as 'a thing . . . sent of God to fore-warn us of our wickedness'. The local gentleman who recorded the event in a letter added a further moral explanation for the birth:

> Let no man think that such things do come by chance or fortune, but that they are appointed to be messengers of ensuing plagues which are like to fall upon us, except with repenting hearts we turn unto our God and forsake our wicked ways.

The monster represents humanity's fall away from purity and truth into corruption and sin. Where the first Fall saw Adam exiled from Eden, this one sees humanity lose its superior human status altogether. This monster can only be described as a human-animal.

The readings of these, and other prodigies are supernatural. In the words of Paré, these monsters embodied God's attempt to display 'his immense power . . . to those which are ignorant of it'. The appearance of what was unnatural was impossible for nature to produce, and could only be explained with recourse to God. He alone could create the new, the unique, which, in turn, symbolised His power which was displayed for a reason: monstrosities show how He 'may either punish men's wickedness, or show signs of punishment at hand'. The appearance of a deformed creature, in this interpretation, was a warning to humans from the Almighty. But this was not the only explanation available to sixteenth- and seventeenth-century writers, and both Paré and Fenton noted that a monster could also be produced through 'the confusion and mingling together of the seed': through the mixing of the species. Explanation for these latter creatures did not require recourse to God, only to nature itself. Instead of merely contemplating the power of the Almighty and His creation, humans were asked to look closely at themselves, and at some of their assumptions about their own place in the created order.

But the two types of monster – the supernatural, and the dangerously natural product of a bestial relationship – were not always wholly distinct. The monstrous product of a bestial relationship could, like the prodigious birth, hold moral meaning. William Turner records such a case occurring in *c.* 1674:

> At Birdham near Chichester in Sussex, about 23 years ago, there was a monster found upon the common, having the form and figure of a man in the fore-part, having two arms and hands, and a human visage, with only one eye in the middle of his forehead: the hinder part was like a lamb. A young man of the neighbourhood was supposed to have generated this monster by a bestial copulation, and

that the rather, because he was afterwards found in the like beastly act with a mare; upon discovery whereof, he fled out of the country. This young monster was nailed up in the church porch of the said parish, and exposed to public view a long time, as a monument of divine judgment.

The young man may have escaped the punishment of his neighbours for his heinous crime, but his offence did not go unrecorded. The product of his bestial relationship was sent by God to express the horror of the act. The body of the half-human-half-sheep monster is natural, but it holds a more abstract meaning. It is the product of a sexual relationship, like all other animals (including humans), but it is also a 'monument' of God's anger at such an abuse of nature. Its display in the church porch reminds the congregation of God's ever-present justice, but it also reminds them of the fragility of their own status. Nothing in life, it would seem – not even the human – should be taken for granted.

It is for this reason that legal depositions have a constant interest in the details of the sexual act. One recurring issue in the testimonies in bestiality cases is whether the accuser can be absolutely sure that penetration took place. Without this no crime was deemed to have been committed: as Edward Coke wrote, 'there must be *penetratio*'. The possibility of cross-breeding hinges on this.

In 1647 William Bayly of Bingley said that he 'stood still a long time' watching John Walton commit buggery with a mare, so that 'he might the more and fairly depose the truth therein'. The implication is that Bayly waited to observe actual penetration. This observant citizenship was not always, however, the case, and other accusers were clearly asked by the attendant Justice of the Peace if they had seen actual penetration. In 1642, for example, Nathaniel Clegge of Netherton in the West Riding of Yorkshire was called to a cowshed by Richard Broadbent where Edward Wilton, the cow-keeper, 'stood very suspiciously to commit buggery' with a cow. Having told this story, however, Clegge goes on to add that 'the said Wilton [was] standing then with his back toward him' and that he therefore 'could not discern whether he did actually commit buggery with the said kine'. In another case from 1664 Matthew Ward of Eskwick in the East Riding of Yorkshire deposed that he saw 'a grey mare standing within the middle ditch of Brigg-close and William Milner standing astride the ditch behind the mare with her tail in his hand'. His deposition goes on: 'being asked whether he saw the privy member of the said William Milner out or no he saith he did not'. Ten years later in Grindleton William Bowne declared that he saw John Cromlinton 'to have gotten the said mare into a deep ditch and had put a slip upon her head, and himself standing upon the bank of the said ditch with his yard drawn, and making several attempts to enter her body with his said yard, but doth not certainly know whether or not he entered her body'. Execution could hinge on this fact.

Ironically, the significance of proving penetration was something which seemed to work in the favour of John Swallow of Hoyland in 1678. He confessed that he had 'thought to have buggered' his master's grey mare, 'but God gave him grace that he did it not.' His desire, he argues, is innocent, it is the act itself which is the crime. The reason for Swallow's distinction is that the act, as opposed to the wish for the act, will produce that which threatens the human. It is the act which will uproot, as Michael Dalton put it, 'God, Nature and the Law': all things which create the status of humanity. This is where Swallow sees the real crime being committed.

Bestiality, then, is not only to be regarded as a mainly rural crime which involved only individual humans and animals, its significance in early modern England must be understood as being far more wide-ranging. A bestial relationship had the potential to upset the very fragile order of nature which placed humans at the top of the chain. Sixteenth- and seventeenth-century writers presented cross-breeding as a supernatural warning but also as a natural possibility. Where prodigious monsters – such as the deformed pig of Hampstead – warn of human sinfulness and corruption, the appearance of the monster in Birdham questions not only human purity, but human status as well. If it is so easy to pollute the species with cross-breeds, where does the stability of the species lie? From this perspective it is no surprise that bestiality was so heavily punished in the early modern period. It was an act against God, nature and the law which revealed the fragility of humanity itself.

*   *   *

Erica Fudge is lecturer in the School of Humanities and Cultural Studies at Middlesex University. She is the author of *Perceiving Animals: Humans and Beasts in Early Modern English Culture.*